REA's Test Prep Books

(a sample of the <u>hundreds of letters</u> REA receives each year)

" I did well because of your wonderful prep books... I just wanted to thank you for helping me prepare for these tests. "

Student, San Diego, CA

" My students report your chapters of review as the most valuable single resource they used for review and preparation. "

Teacher, American Fork, UT

" Your book was such a better value and was so much more complete than anything your competition has produced—and I have them all! "

Teacher, Virginia Beach, VA

" Compared to the other books that my fellow students had, your book was the most helpful in helping me get a great score. "

Student, North Hollywood, CA

" Your book was responsible for my success on the exam, which helped me get into the college of my choice... I will look for REA the next time I need help. "

Student, Chesterfield, MO

" Just a short note to say thanks for the great support your book gave me in helping me pass the test... I'm on my way to a B.S. degree because of you! "

Student, Orlando, FL

The Best Test Preparation for the

GRE®

Biochemistry, Cell and Molecular Biology Test

 **With REA's TESTware® on CD-ROM**

Thomas E. Smith, Ph.D.
Department of Biochemistry and Molecular Biology
College of Medicine, Howard University
Washington, D.C.

Marguerite Wilton Coomes, Ph.D.
Department of Biochemistry and Molecular Biology
College of Medicine, Howard University
Washington, D.C.

 Research & Education Association
Visit our website at
www.rea.com

Research & Education Association
61 Ethel Road West
Piscataway, New Jersey 08854
E-mail: info@rea.com

The Best Test Preparation for the GRE Biochemistry, Cell and Molecular Biology Test With TEST*ware*® on CD-ROM

Printed in the United States of America

Library of Congress Control Number 2007937188

ISBN-13: 978-0-7386-0422-0
ISBN-10: 0-7386-0422-4

Windows® is a registered trademark of Microsoft Corporation.

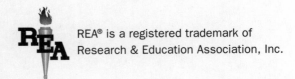
L07-0101

About the Authors

Thomas E. Smith, Ph.D., is a professor in the Department of Biochemistry and Molecular Biology, College of Medicine, Howard University in Washington, D.C. He is also professor of ophthalmology at Howard University Hospital.

He began his career at Benedict College in S.C., where he received a B.S. in chemistry/biology in 1953. In 1959 he received an M.S., and in 1962 a Ph.D., in biochemistry at George Washington University in Washington, D.C., and a post-doctoral in 1963 at Washington University in St. Louis, Mo.

Dr. Smith's professional experience spans five decades, from his work as a chemist with the National Heart Institute in 1953 to his work 50 years later with the National Science Foundation. In various roles under the umbrella of biochemistry and chemistry, his expertise has been exercised at Melpar, Inc.; the Lawrence Livermore Laboratory at the University of California; National Urban League (Black Executive Exchange Program); E.I. du Pont de Nemours and Company; University of Texas Health Science Center; United Negro College Fund; College of Medicine at Howard University, and others.

Among his many activities, Dr. Smith was on the editorial board of the Archives of Biochemistry and Biophysics from 1976-1994, was a leading member of the Association of Medical and Graduate Departments of Biochemistry from 1980-1999. Over the years he has also been active in various important roles with Massachusetts Institute of Technology, Washington Academy of Sciences, the American Association of Medical Colleges, the American Society of Biochemistry and Molecular Biology, the National Board of Medical Examiners, the National Institutes of Health, National Caucus of Basic Biomedical Sciences (one of the founding members), American Cancer Society (grant review committee), National Science Foundation (grant review committee), and the Committee on Research Infastructure in Minority Institutions, University of the District of Columbia.

Dr. Smith is the recipient of a number of research and teaching awards, a member of many professional societies, and is a published contributing author.

Marguerite Wilton Coomes, Ph.D., is associate professor in the Department of Biochemistry and Molecular Biology, College of Medicine, Howard University in Washington, D.C., where she has been since 1983. In 1994, she received the Kaiser-Permanente Award for Teaching from Howard University College of Medicine. In the same year, she received the Howard University Health Science Teaching Award.

A sometime GRE question writer in cell and molecular biology, Dr. Coomes received her Ph.D. in Biochemistry in 1980 from The University of Texas Health Science Center, Dallas, Texas. She received her M.S. in 1975 and B.S. (summa cum laude) in 1973, both from North Texas State University in Denton, Texas.

From 1980 to 1982, she was Staff Fellow at the Laboratory of Pharmacology, National Institute of Environmental Health Sciences in N.C., and prior to that she was a teaching assistant, Department of Biological Sciences, North State University in Denton, Texas.

Dr. Coomes has applied her professional expertise to review activities with the Minority Biomedical Research Support (MBRS) Program, National Institute of General Medical Sciences, as well as manuscripts submitted to the Archives of Biochemistry and Biophysics, various biochemistry and medical journals, the Journal of the National Medical Association, and others.

Her other credentials include: Various projects and workshops with the American Association for the Advancement of Science; subcommittees with American Association for Biochemistry and Molecular Biology; 10 years as Chief Proctor of the United States Medical Licensure Examination for Howard University College of Medicine; and has served on the review panel for graduate and postdoctoral awards for the Howard Hughes Foundation and the Ford Foundation. She is also a published author and contributing author of scientific books and papers.

Acknowledgments

In addition to our authors, we would like to thank Larry B. Kling, Vice President, Editorial, for supervising development; Pam Weston, Vice President, Publishing, for setting the quality standards for production integrity and managing the publication to completion; John Cording, Vice President, Technology, for coordinating the design and development of REA's TEST*ware*®; Molly Solanki, Associate Editor, for project management and preflight editorial review; Diane Goldschmidt, Senior Editor, for post-production quality assurance; Heena Patel, Technology Project Manager, for her design contributions and software testing efforts; Christine Saul, Senior Grapic Designer, for cover design; Caragraphics for typesetting; and Jeff LoBalbo, Senior Graphic Designer, for post-production file mapping and typesetting revisions.

About Research & Education Association

Founded in 1959, Research & Education Association is dedicated to publishing the finest and most effective educational materials—including software, study guides, and test preps—for students in middle school, high school, college, graduate school, and beyond.

REA's Test Preparation series includes books and software for all academic levels in almost all disciplines. Research & Education Association publishes test preps for students who have not yet entered high school, as well as high school students preparing to enter college. Students from countries around the world seeking to attend college in the United States will find the assistance they need in REA's publications. For college students seeking advanced degrees, REA publishes test preps for many major graduate school admission examinations in a wide variety of disciplines, including engineering, law, and medicine. Students at every level, in every field, with every ambition can find what they are looking for among REA's publications.

REA's practice tests are always based upon the most recently administered exams, and include every type of question that you can expect on the actual exams.

REA's publications and educational materials are highly regarded and continually receive an unprecedented amount of praise from professionals, instructors, librarians, parents, and students. Our authors are as diverse as the fields represented in the books we publish. They are well-known in their respective disciplines and serve on the faculties of prestigious high schools, colleges, and universities throughout the United States and Canada.

Today REA's wide-ranging catalog is a leading resource for teachers, students, and professionals.

We invite you to visit us at *www.rea.com* to find out how "REA is making the world smarter."

Contents

Introduction xv
    About This Book and TEST*ware®* xv
    About REA's Test Experts xv
    About the Test xv
    Format of the GRE Biochemistry, Cell and Molecular Biology Test xvi
    Scoring the Test xvii
    Score Conversion Chart xvii
    Test-Taking Strategies xviii
    The Day of the Test xviii
    During the Test xix
    Study Schedule xx

PART 1

BIOCHEMISTRY

Introduction 3
Chemical Bonds and Energy Conservation 3
    Thermodynamics and Energy Conservation 4
        Potential Energy Curve 7
        Redox States 8
    Water, pH, Acid-Base Reactions, and Buffers 10
    Structure of Water 10
        Acid-Base Reactions 11
            Concept of Acids and Bases in Relationship to pH 11
            Buffers 12

Biomolecular Structures 13
    Amino Acids and Proteins 13
    Structure of Proteins 14
    Primary Structure 14
        Secondary Structure 16
            α-Helix 16
            β-Pleated sheets 16
            β-Turns 16
        Tertiary Structure 18
        Quaternary Structure 18

Chemical and Enzymatic Reaction Mechanisms 20
    Chemical Reaction Mechanisms 20

CONTENTS

First-Order Reactions 20
Second-Order Reactions 20
   Some Factors That Influence Reaction Rates 21
   Enzymatic Reaction Mechanisms 22
How Does an Enzyme Help Lower the Energy/Heat of Activation of a Reaction 22
   Proximity and Orientation 22
   Covalent Catalysis 22
   Strain and Distortion 24
   Acid-Base Catalysis 24
   Selected List of Coenzymes and Their Roles in Catalysis 25
Classification of Enzymes by the Types of Reactions They Catalyze 25
     Oxidoreductases 26
     Transferases 27
     Hydrolases 27
     Lyases 27
     Isomerases 28
     Ligases 29

Enzyme Kinetics 30
Practical Aspect of Initial Velocity Measurement 33
Lineweaver-Burk Plots 34
Diagnostic Value of Lineweaver-Burk Plots: Enzyme Inhibition 34
   Classification of the Types of Enzyme Inhibitors 34
     Mechanism-Based Inhibitors 37

Two-Substrate Reactions 37
Sequential Reactions May Be Either Random or Ordered 37
Ping-Pong or Double-Displacement Reactions 38
Antibodies as Catalysts 38

Regulation of Enzymatic Activity 40
Summary of Regulatory Mechanisms 40
Kinetic Models for Allosteric Regulation 41
Kinetic Description of Allosteric Interactions: The Concerted Model 44
Significance of the Hill Coefficient 45

Metabolism 45
Forms of Conserved Energy in Metabolism 46
Glycolysis 47
Reaction That Commits Glucose Metabolism to Glycolysis 49
Aldolase Catalyzes the Production of Two 3-Carbon
 Compounds from Fru 1,6-P_2 50
   Triose Phosphate Isomerase 50
   Glyceraldehyde 3-Phosphate Dehydrogenase (GAPDH) Reaction 51
   Phosphoglycerate Kinase Reaction 51
   Phosphoglycerate Mutase Reaction 51
   Enolase Catalyzes the Second "High-Energy" Compound in Glycolysis 51
   Pyruvate Kinase Generates the Second ATP Molecule in Glycolysis 52
   Summary of Glycolysis 54

Pyruvate Metabolism: Formation of Acetylcoenzyme A 56

The Tricarboxyclic Acid Cycle (TCA Cycle) 57
Regulation of the TCA cycle 61
Anaplerotic Reactions for the TCA Cycle 61
Oxidative Phosphorylation 62

Pentose Phosphate Pathway 66
Oxidative Phase of the Pentose Phosphate Pathway...67
Nonoxidative Phase of the Pentose Phosphate Pathway....................................67

Glucuronic Acid Oxidative Pathway 68

Gluconeogenesis and Glycogenesis 68
Summary of Entry Points in the TCA Cycle
and Glycolysis That Can Lead to Gluconeogenesis 70

Glycogen Metabolism..72
Glycogenesis 72
Glycogenolysis..72
Regulation of Glycogen Metabolism 73

Photosynthesis..75
Photochemical Consideration of Light Absorption and Energy Generation...........77
Light Independent Reactions of Photosynthesis: The Calvin Cycle......................82
Adaptive Photosynthetic Mechanisms...86

Nitrogen Metabolism 87
Nitrogen Fixation 87
Chemical Reactions of Pyridoxyl Phosphate Relative to Amino Acid Metabolism 88
Biosynthesis of Amino Acids..89
Amino Acids Derived from Oxaloacetate/Aspartate 91
Amino Acids Derived from 3-Phosphoglycerate 96
Cysteine...96
Serine..97
Glycine...97
Amino Acids Derived from Pyruvate...98
Amino Acids Derived from α-Ketoglutarate.................................98
Amino Acids Derived from Phosphoenolpyruvate and Erythrose-4-phosphate......98
Histidine...102
Degradation of Amino Acids 102
Methionine 102

The Urea Cycle 104

Nucleotide Structure and Metabolism 109
Synthesis of Purines 110
Summary of Key Points About Purine Biosynthesis 114
Degradation of Purines 116
Synthesis of Pyrimidines...116
Synthesis of Deoxyribonucleotides...119
Regulation of Ribonucleotide Reductase Activity 120
Thymine Biosynthesis 123
Degradation of Pyrimidines 123

Heme Metabolism..123
Heme and Chlorophyll Biosynthesis..123
Heme and Chlorophyll Degradation 126

Lipid Metabolism 127
Fatty Acid Biosynthesis...127
Elongation of Palmitic Acid 128
Formation of Unsaturated Fatty Acids..129
Nomenclature and Other Positions Where Desaturases Function 130

CONTENTS

Arachiodonic Acid and Signaling/Regulatory Molecules 131
Cholesterol and Steroid Hormones Are Derived from Acetate 131
Fatty Acids Are Stored as Triglycerides 133
Sphingolipids 134
Fatty Acid Oxidation 135
Special Cases to Consider for b-Oxidation of Fatty Acids 136

Methods 139
  Methods for Cell Disruption 139
    Mechanical Methods 139
    Nonmechanical Methods of Cell Disruption 141
    Separation of Cellular Components by Centrifugation 141
    Centrifugal Force Required to Pellet Selected Cellular Components 142
  Purification of Soluble Proteins 142
    Chromatography 144
      Ion Exchange Chromatography 145
      Hydrophobic Interaction Chromatography 145
      Gel Filtration Chromatography 145
      Affinity Chromatography 145
      High Performance Liquid Chromatography (HPLC) 146
  Isotopes Used to Study Biological Systems 146
    Radioactive Isotopes 146
    Stable Isotopes 147
  Relationship of Solute Concentration to Its Absorbance of Light 148
    Absorbance of Light and the Lambert-Beer Law 148
  Sample Analyses by Electrophoresis 150
    Polyacrylamide Gel Electrophoresis (PAGE) 150
      Two-Dimensional Gel Electrophoresis 150
      Determination of Molecular Mass Using SDS Denaturing Gels 151
      Western Blot Analysis 152

PART 2

CELL BIOLOGY

Cellular Compartments of Prokaryotes and Eukaryotes 153
  Organization, Dynamics, and Functions 153
    Microscopy 153
    General Introduction to Prokaryotes and Eukaryotes 154
    Prokaryotes 155
    Eukaryotes 156
    Cell Death 156
      Apoptosis 156
      Necrosis 156
  Cellular Membrane Systems (Structure and Transport) 156
    Prokaryotic Cells, Plasma Membrane, and Cell Wall 156
    Eukaryotic Plasma Membranes and Cell Walls 158
    Membrane Biogenesis 158
    Membrane Transport 159
      Inactive Transport 159
      Active Transport 160
      Exo- and Endocytosis 162

Nucleus (Envelope and Matrix) and Chromosomes...163
   Prokaryotic Cells—Chromosome 163
   Eukaryotic Cells—Chromosomes and Nucleus 164
Other Intracellular Structures, Including Mitochondria and Chloroplasts 165
   Prokaryotes 165
   Eukaryotes 165
   Specialized Structures and Other Characteristics...168
   Cell Dynamics 169

Cell Surface and Cell Communication **169**
   Extracellular Matrix...169
      The Extracellular Matrix of Connective Tissue 169
         Connective Tissue 169
         The Proteins of Connective Tissue 170
      The Extracellular Matrix of Endothelial Tissue.......................................171
      Cell–Cell Interaction 171
         Binding of Cells to the Extracellular Matrix 171
         Communication between Extracellular Matrix and Cytoskeleton 171
         Cell Adhesion and Junctions: Cell–Cell Communication..................172
   Signal Transduction and Receptor Function 173
      Cell Membrane Receptors 173
      Second Messenger Systems 173
         The cAMP Pathway 174
         The Phosphatidylinositol Pathway 175
         G-Protein-Associated Ion Channels...176
         Receptors That Are Enzymes...176
         Steroid and Thyroid Hormones 176
   Excitable Membrane Systems 176

Cytoskeleton, Motility, and Shape..**178**
   Actin Filaments 179
      Actin in Muscle Contraction 179
   Microtubules 179
   Intermediate Filaments 181
   Organization of the Cytoskeleton 182
   Cell Surface Structures of Prokaryotes 182

Protein Synthesis and Processing...**182**

Cell Division, Differentiation, and Development **182**
   Bacterial Cell Division 182
   Eukaryotic Cell Cycle 183
   Mitosis and Cytokinesis...184
      Cytokinesis 184
      Growth Factors...185
   Meiosis and Gametogenesis...186
   Fertilization and Early Embryonic Development 188
      Fertilization 190
      Embryogenesis...191
      Early Mammalian Development...191
      From Gastrula to Fully Developed Organism...192
      Positional Information 193
      Nuclear/Cytoplasmic Interactions...194
      Tissue-Specific Expression...194

CONTENTS

MOLECULAR BIOLOGY

Mendelian and Non-Mendelian Inheritance 195

Punnett Square Diagrams 196

Transformation, Transduction, and Conjugation 198

Recombination and Complementation 199

Mutational Analysis 200

Genetic Mapping and Linkage Analysis 201

Chromatin and Chromosomes 202
Karyotypes 202
Translocations, Inversions, Deletions, and Duplications 202
Aneuploidy and Polyploidy 203
Structure 203

Genomics 205
Genome Structure 205
Repeated DNA and Gene Families 205
Centromeres and Telomeres 206
Gene Identification 207
Transposable Elements 207

Gene Maintenance 208
DNA Replication 208
The Challenges of DNA Replication 209
DNA Damage and Repair 211
DNA Modification 214
DNA Recombination and Gene Conversion 214
Branch Migration 215
Gene Conversion 215
The Genetic Code 216
Transcription 218

Gene Regulation in Prokaryotes 227
Positive and Negative Control of the Operon 227

Gene Regulation in Eukaryotes 230
Cis- and Trans-Acting Regulatory Elements 230
Gene Rearrangements and Amplification 230

Bacteriophages and Animal and Plant Viruses 231
Genome Replication and Regulation 231
Virus-Host Interactions 232

Methodology 233
Restriction Maps 233
DNA Cloning in Prokaryotes and Eukaryotes 235
Other Uses of Restriction Endonucleases 238
Nucleic Acid Blotting and Hybridization 239
PCR 241
Sequencing and Analysis 243

Protein-Nucleic Acid Interaction 244
Site-Directed Mutagenesis 245
Answer to Mapping Problem 245

Practice Exams **247**
Answer Sheet: Practice Exam 1 249
Practice Exam 1 251
Answer Key 275
Detailed Explanations of Answers 277
Answer Sheet: Practice Exam 2 293
Practice Exam 2 295
Answer Key 319
Detailed Explanations of Answers 321

Index **338**
Installing REA's TEST*ware*® **348**

Introduction

ABOUT THIS BOOK & TEST*ware*®

This book, along with REA's exclusive TEST*ware*® software, provides you with an accurate and complete representation of the GRE Biochemistry, Cell and Molecular Biology Subject Test. REA's two full-length practice tests are based on the latest editions of the exam. Our topical reviews are designed to prepare you for the very kind of material you are most likely to encounter when taking the actual test. Our sample tests have been carefully calibrated to match the GRE Biochemistry, Cell and Molecular Biology Subject Test's level of difficulty, its format, and, of course, the type and proportional representation of its content. Following each practice test you will find an answer key along with detailed step-by-step explanations designed to help you master the relevant material and score high.

The practice tests in this book and software package are included in two formats: in printed form in the book and in TEST*ware*® format on the enclosed CD. We recommend that you begin your preparation by first taking the practice exams on your computer. The software provides timed conditions, and instantaneous, accurate scoring that makes it easier to pinpoint your strengths and weaknesses.

ABOUT REA'S TEST EXPERTS

To aid us in meeting our objective of providing you with the best possible study guide for the GRE Biochemistry, Cell and Molecular Biology Test, REA's test experts have carefully prepared our topical reviews and practice exams. Our authors come armed with specific knowledge of the GRE Biochemistry, Cell and Molecular Biology Test. They have thoroughly examined and researched the mechanics of the GRE Biochemistry, Cell and Molecular Biology Test to ensure that our model tests accurately depict the exam and appropriately chal-

lenge the student. Our experts are highly regarded in the educational community. They have taught and conducted scientific research at competitive institutions. They have an in-depth knowledge of the subjects presented in the book and provide accurate questions that will put you in a position to do your very best on the exam.

ABOUT THE TEST

The GRE Biochemistry, Cell and Molecular Biology Test is taken by students applying to graduate programs in biochemistry. Most programs require that applicants submit scores for both the GRE General Test and the GRE Biochemistry, Cell and Molecular Biology Test; together with other undergraduate records, they are part of the highly competitive admission process to graduate school. Both tests are offered by Educational Testing Service (ETS) and administered throughout the United States and abroad. You can obtain a test registration booklet from your college or by contacting ETS directly. To determine if you should take the GRE Biochemistry, Cell and Molecular Biology Test, contact the universities you are applying to for admission. For questions pertaining to GRE Biochemistry, Cell and Molecular Biology policies, contact:

Graduate Record Examinations
Educational Testing Service
P.O. Box 6000
Princeton, NJ 08541-6000
Phone: (866) 473-4373
Fax: 1-610-290-8975
Website: *www.gre.org*

THE GRE BIOCHEMISTRY, CELL AND MOLECULAR BIOLOGY SUBJECT TEST AT A GLANCE

Subject	Percent
Biochemistry:	36%
Chemical and Physical Foundations	
Biomolecules: Structure, Assembly, Organization, and Dynamics	
Catalysis and Binding	
Major Metabolic Pathways	
Bioenergetics (Including Respiration and Photosynthesis)	
Regulation and Integration of Metabolism	
Methodology	
Cell Biology:	28%
Cellular Compartments of Prokaryotes and Eukaryotes: Organization, Dynamics, and Functions	
Cell Surface and Communication	
Cytoskeleton, Motility, and Shape Actin-Based Systems (Including Muscle Contraction)	
Protein Synthesis and Processing	
Cell Division, Differentiation, and Development	
Molecular Biology and Genetics:	36%
Genetic Foundations	
Chromatin and Chromosomes	
Genomics	
Genome Maintenance	
Gene Expression	
Gene Regulation in Prokaryotes	
Gene Regulation in Eukaryotes	
Bacteriophages and Animal and Plant Viruses	
Methodology	

SSD ACCOMMODATIONS FOR STUDENTS WITH DISABILITIES

Many students qualify for extra time to take the GRE Biochemistry, Cell and Molecular Biology Test. For information on how ETS meets disability needs, contact:

ETS Disability Services
Educational Testing Service
P.O. Box 6054
Princeton, NJ 08541–6054
Phone: 1-866-387-8602 (toll free)
Monday–Friday 8:30 a.m. to 5:00 p.m. Eastern Time (New York)
TTY: 1-609-771-7714
Fax: 1-973-735-1892
E-mail: stassd@ets.org

FORMAT OF THE GRE BIOCHEMISTRY, CELL AND MOLECULAR BIOLOGY TEST

The test is usually given three times a year and contains approximately 180 multiple-choice questions, which you must answer in 2 hours and 50 minutes. Each of the 180 questions is worth one point. There is a penalty for wrong answers, which serves to correct for "guessing." For each wrong answer, one-quarter of a point is deducted from your score. Unanswered questions don't count for or against you.

ABOUT THE REVIEW

REA's targeted subject review concisely and systematically summarizes the main areas tested on the GRE Biochemistry, Cell and Molecular Biology Test. We have prepared it to help you better grasp concepts that your textbook explores in far greater detail.

By studying our review, your chances of scoring well on the actual exam will be greatly increased. It affords you a kind of master checklist for everything you need to know. After thoroughly studying the material presented in the review, you should go on to take the practice tests. Used in combination, the review and practice tests will enhance your test-taking skills and give you the confidence needed to obtain a high score.

HOW TO PREPARE FOR THE GRE BIOCHEMISTRY, CELL AND MOLECULAR BIOLOGY TEST

"Don't worry." Easier said than done, but rest assured that this book will help you assess yourself as well as the test. As with other GRE subject tests, the GRE Biochemistry, Cell and Molecular Biology Test gauges knowledge that you have gained throughout your academic career. Most of what's tested on the GRE Biochemistry, Cell and Molecular Biology Test will require you to make use of information you learned in your General Biochemistry courses in college.

We at REA believe the best way to prep for the GRE Biochemistry, Cell and Molecular Biology Test is to replicate the complete GRE test-taking experience. Toward that end, we provide two full-length exams that accurately reflect this subject test in terms of format, content, and degree of difficulty. Our practice exams mirror the latest GRE Biochemistry, Cell and Molecular Biology Test forms and include every type of question that you can expect to encounter when you take the exam. Following each of our practice exams is an answer key complete with detailed explanations and solutions. Designed specifically to clarify the material for the student, the explanations not only provide the correct answers, but also explain why the answer to a particular question is indeed the best choice. By completing both practice exams and studying the explanations that follow, you will isolate your strengths and weaknesses. This, in turn, will enable you to concentrate on attacking the sections of the exam you find to be toughest.

Participate in Study Groups

As a final word on how to study for this test, you may want to study with others. This will allow you to share knowledge and obtain feedback from other members of your study group. Study groups may make preparing for the exam more enjoyable.

SCORING THE TEST

Each correct response on both our practice tests and the actual exam earn you one "raw score" point, while each incorrect answer results in a 1/4-point deduction; omitted responses are not counted. Here is a formula for calculating your raw score:

$$\underbrace{\rule{2cm}{0.4pt}}_{\substack{\text{\# of questions}\\\text{correct}}} - (\underbrace{\rule{2cm}{0.4pt}}_{\substack{\text{\# of questions}\\\text{incorrect}}} \times 1/4) = \underline{\rule{2cm}{0.4pt}}$$

Now use the Conversion Chart on the next page to determine your scaled score range.

Scoring Worksheet

	Raw Score	Scaled Score
Practice Exam 1	_____	_____
Practice Exam 2	_____	_____

YOUR PRACTICE TEST SCORE CONVERSION CHART

ETS administers three different editions of the GRE Biochemistry, Cell and Molecular Biology Test; therefore, a range of raw scores is associated with your scaled score.

Raw Score	Scaled Score
162–180	800–860
131–161	700–790
101–130	600–690
70–100	500–590
39-69	400–490

REA's practice tests emulate every content and formatting aspect of the actual test. Your performance on our practice tests will, of course, only approximate your score on the actual GRE Biochemistry, Cell and Molecular Biology Test, because ETS uses a computerized statistical formula to weight performance.

TEST-TAKING STRATEGIES

Although you will probably have to take both the GRE General Test and the GRE Biochemistry, Cell and Molecular Biology Subject Test, try to avoid taking them on the same day. Taking any test is stressful, and after sitting for one extremely long standardized test, you will hardly be at your best for a second.

Be sure to register for testing dates several months before the due date to ensure that the graduate schools you designate will receive your scores by the application deadlines. Most schools will not consider an incomplete application.

Because the test is not divided into sections, you are completely responsible for budgeting your own time. All the questions are worth the same number of points, so you should not spend too much time on any one item. The GRE Biochemistry, Cell and Molecular Biology Test attempts to cover a broad range of topics. It is unlikely that you will have complete knowledge of all of them. It is important that you do not spend too much time on questions you find difficult at the expense of working on those that are easier for you.

The time constraints are such that, on average, a little less than a minute is allotted for each question. Thus, it is unlikely that you will have time to answer all 180 questions; however, you can still receive an excellent score without answering all of them. Because the questions are in no particular order, we recommend making a complete sweep through all the questions on the test. Answer the ones that are immediately easy for you and mark those that you want to revisit. Once you have answered all of the easier questions, you can use the remaining time to go back through the test and work on the harder questions, which require a greater amount of your time. In this way, you will ensure that you have the chance to answer all the questions you are likely to get correct, instead of spending valuable time on difficult questions near the beginning of the test and leaving easy questions at the end of the test unanswered.

The penalty for wrong answers should not deter you completely from guessing. If you have no clue what the answer might be, by all means press on. However, if you can eliminate one or two of the five choices, it is to your advantage to make an educated guess. Statistically, guessing randomly among the five choices would give you the possibility of guessing correctly 1/5 of the time. (This is what the quarter-point deduction for wrong answers is designed to balance.) Being able to eliminate three of the choices as wrong answers means that guessing between the two remaining choices would give you a far better chance of being correct.

THE DAY OF THE TEST

On the day of the test, you should wake up early (after a decent night's rest, we hope) and enjoy a good breakfast. Make sure you dress comfortably—in layers—so that you are not distracted by being too hot or too cold while taking the exam. You should plan on arriving at the test center early. Doing so will spare you the needless anxiety that comes from racing the clock. It will also allow you to collect your thoughts, focus, and actually relax before taking the exam.

Before you leave for the test center, make sure that you have **two** forms of identification. You will not be admitted to the test center without proper identification. Acceptable forms of identification include a driver's license, Social Security card, birth certificate, passport, and green card.

Make sure you bring at least two sharpened No. 2 pencils, with erasers, to the exam. You may want to wear a watch to the test center; however, only ordinary watches will be permitted. Watches with alarms, calculator functions, flashing lights, beeping sounds, etc., will not be allowed. In addition, neither food nor calculators will be allowed into the examination room.

DURING THE TEST

When you arrive at the test center, try to sit in a seat where you feel you will be comfortable. No breaks are given during the exam. If you need to use the rest room, or if you become ill, you may leave the examination room, but you will not be allowed to make up any lost time.

Once you enter the test center, follow all of the rules and instructions given by the test supervisor. If you do not, you risk being dismissed from the examination or having your GRE Biochemistry, Cell and Molecular Biology scores voided, meaning that they will not be scored.

When all of the test materials have been distributed, the test instructor will give you directions for filling out your answer sheet. You must complete this sheet carefully since the information on it will be printed on your score report. Write your name exactly as it appears on your identification documents and admission ticket, unless otherwise instructed.

Make sure you do not write in your test booklet or on your answer sheet, except to fill in the oval corresponding to the answer you choose. Scratch paper will be provided. You will be marking your answers on side two of your answer sheet. Each numbered row will contain five ovals corresponding to each answer choice for that question. Fill in the oval corresponding to your answer darkly, completely, and neatly. You can change your answer, but remember to completely erase your old answer. Only one answer should be marked. This is very important, as your answer sheet will be machine-scored, and stray lines or unnecessary marks may cause the machine to score your answers incorrectly.

Work only on the test section on which the test instructor has instructed you to proceed. You should begin only when instructed to do so, and stop immediately when instructed to stop. Do not turn to the next section of the test until you are told to do so. When all of the sections have been completed, you should remain seated until all of the test materials have been collected.

Good luck on the GRE Biochemistry, Cell and Molecular Biology Subject Test!

Study Schedule

This study schedule allows for thorough preparation for the GRE Biochemistry, Cell and Molecular Biology Test. Although it is designed for eight weeks, it can be condensed into four weeks by combining each two-week period into one. Whichever study schedule you choose, remember that the more time you spend studying, the more prepared and relaxed you will feel on the day of the exam.

Week	Activity
1–2	Read and study the review.
3	Take TEST*ware*® Practice Test 1 to determine your strengths and weaknesses. Any area in which you score low will require that you thoroughly review the relevant review sections.
4–5	Locate and review any notes you might have from previous biochemistry classes. Be sure to spend extra time on material you haven't looked at lately.
6	Take and score TEST*ware*® Practice Test 2 to determine your strengths and weaknesses. (Be sure to record your scores on the Scoring Worksheet to track your progress.) Any area in which you score low will require that you thoroughly review the relevant review sections.
7–8	Once again read through our review section to familiarize yourself with any information you may still be having difficulty grasping. Further your studies by cracking open old Biochemistry textbooks for a more comprehensive presentation of the subject matter. For additional practice you may retake Practice Tests 1 and 2 either in printed form, or using our TEST*ware*®. This will help strengthen the areas where your performance is still lagging and build your confidence.

Parts 1–3

REVIEW

Biochemistry

1. INTRODUCTION

Biochemistry as a discipline seeks to define at the molecular level chemical mechanisms that explain how living organisms assemble nutrients from environmental sources and affect processes of growth, reproduction, adaptation, and metabolism within the confines and complexity of cellular environments. On a broad scale, biochemists ask and seek answers to questions such as the following: (1) By what *chemical* mechanisms are nutrients used for the growth of cells? (2) By what *chemical* mechanisms do cells reproduce? (3) What are the *chemical* mechanisms used by cells that allow them to adapt to their environments? (4) What are the *chemical* mechanisms used by cells to metabolize nutrients for the extraction of energy and the formation/assimilation of the building blocks that are necessary to make them the unique entities that they are? If these questions are kept in mind as readers peruse this book, connections between various topics discussed here will be facilitated, and remembering important facts will be easier.

A fundamental understanding of some basic chemical principles is necessary to accomplish this task. Basic principles that govern these processes are those of general chemistry, organic chemistry, and physical chemistry—**thermodynamics** and **kinetics**. Each of the fundamental questions asked above relates in some way to the making and/or breaking of chemical bonds of some form. A covalent chemical bond is an attraction between atoms brought about by the sharing of electrons between two atoms or a complete transfer of electrons. There are other types of chemical interactions, but the first part of this discussion will be concerned with covalent bonds only.

2. CHEMICAL BONDS AND ENERGY CONSERVATION

In general, energy is required to make bonds, and energy is given off when bonds are broken. Of course, there are exceptions. But it is appropriate to state that there is potential energy in every chemical bond and that the process of metabolism, for example, is one of breaking those bonds in a controlled manner (**catabolism**) to obtain or store energy or making bonds in a controlled manner (**anabolism**) using some of that stored energy for synthetic purposes. So, one among many questions that must be addressed is, What are the types of chemical bonds that are more prevalent in biochemistry? The following table (Table 1-1) lists some of the most common types of bonds that are made or broken in biochemical reactions and the energies of these bonds.

Table 1-1.
Common Types of Bonds

Bond type	Average bond energies	
	kcal/mole	kJ/mole
C—H	98	410
C—C	80	335
C—O	78	326
C—N	65	272
H—H	103	431
H—O	110	460
O=O	116[a]	485
C=O	187[b]	782
C=C	145[c]	607

[a](2×58), [b](2×93.5), and [c](2×72.5)

Note: 1.0 kcal = 4.184 kJ. For the most part, calories or kilocalories (kcal) will be used throughout this text.

When any chemical bond is broken, as much energy is released as it took to make the bond. Thus, it has to be kept in mind that chemical activities of cells are such that bonds are broken in a conservative and efficient manner: as much of the energy as possible can be captured for use in the many synthetic processes and other anabolic processes that keep the cell alive and help it to grow.

The decomposition of a simple but important molecule like water, H_2O (in fact, the decomposition of two molecules of water) requires +118 kcal.

$$2H_2O \longrightarrow 2H_2 + O_2$$

This is because the bond energy for H—H is 103 kcal, for O=O 116 kcal, and the decomposition of two molecules of water requires breaking 4 H—O bonds with an input of 440 kcal. Products of the reaction, however, are the formation of two moles of hydrogen and one molecule of oxygen. The formation of the two molecules of hydrogen requires 206 kcal, and the formation of one mole of oxygen requires 116 kcal. Thus, the net energy consumed in its decomposition is 118 kcal (440 – [206 + 116]). Consistent with the statement made above, that as much energy is released in breaking a chemical bond as is consumed in making it, the reverse reaction of making water from two molecules of hydrogen and one of oxygen would result in the release of –118 kcal of energy ([206 + 116] – 440).

2.1. Thermodynamics and Energy Conservation

The water example given above may be used as a simple statement of the **first law of thermodynamics**, namely, that *the total energy of a system and its surroundings is constant*. The above example, however, does not mention anything about the surroundings in which the reaction occurs. If the decomposition of water were to occur in an open environment at one atmosphere of pressure, the approximately 36 mL of water (approximately 2 moles) would have produced 44.8 liters of hydrogen and 22.4 liters of oxygen. Thus, the volume of gas released affects the surroundings, but the energy involved does not change. Similarly, if the process were carried out at constant volume, the pressure would increase. For the reverse reaction, the same amount of energy is involved, but much of it is released as heat. The net effect of energy change is 118 kcal—positive in one direction for the reaction, and negative in the other direction. The "free" energy involved is the same, but its effect on the surroundings is different.

What the above example illustrates is that the total energy involved in a chemical reaction (considering all of its components) is the same but may be expressed to the observer in different ways, one of which is heat, and another of which is a change in the order of other components within the surrounding area. In summary, and as stated previously, chemical bonds have constant amounts of energy. When a chemical reaction occurs, the energy from those bonds may be broken and may form other bonds with different amounts of energy, but the total amount of energy of the system remains the same. Some of that energy may result in the production of heat; some may result in increases in volume or pressure affecting the surroundings in which the reaction takes place.

At this point, it may be appropriate to introduce another thermodynamic term, **enthalpy** (H), and define it as the sum of the internal energy plus the product of pressure (p) and volume (v).

$$H = E + (p \times v).$$

If enthalpy (*H*) is the sum of the internal energy, and if, as has been shown above, a certain amount of that energy is free to do work and to effect changes in the surrounding environment, then enthalpy must also be composed of those components as "state functions" and can be defined as follows:

$$H = G + TS$$

For sake of simplicity, consider that reactions of interest are being conducted at constant temperature (*T*). Energy released for work, or Gibbs free energy (*G*), is also a component of this term called *enthalpy* (*H*). The other term introduced in this equation is **entropy** (*S*), which may be defined as the state of order or disorder of a system (the reaction and its environment). In the water example given above, the decomposition of water to hydrogen and oxygen requires a net input of 118 kcal and makes the components of the molecule less ordered—namely, a hydrogen-bonded liquid becomes two different molecules of gaseous material capable of free diffusion. In the reverse reaction, 118 kcal of energy are released, but the molecule produced is more ordered (i.e., a decrease in the state of randomness), which correlates to decreased entropy (*S*).

Two factors involved in the determination of spontaneity of reactions are exothermicity, or the release of heat (118 kcal in the case of water), and the tendency to introduce randomness into the system. The relationship that reflects the balance between these two forces is the following:

$$G = H - TS$$

where *G* is defined as Gibbs free energy. Components of that equation are expressed in terms of the state of a system and are not measured in absolute values but rather as changes in values. They are therefore expressed as follows:

$$\Delta G = \Delta H - \Delta(TS)$$

In most cases, constant temperature is assumed, and the equation is written as follows:

$$\Delta G = \Delta H - T\Delta S$$

A reaction is considered to be spontaneous when the value of ΔG is negative, and that value is negative if ΔH is negative or if the numerical value of $T\Delta S$ is larger than ΔH. The change of free energy of a system can be determined under any set of conditions, but it is important to have absolute standards under which many reactions can be compared. Standard-state conditions are used and defined as the state in which the reactions are conducted when all components are at 1 atmosphere of pressure, an important consideration since many thermodynamic quantities were derived considering behavior of ideal gases. Further, in chemical reactions like the water example given above, there can be both pressure and volume changes; if one or the other of these is kept constant, heat has to be considered a factor, and enthalpy can be expressed as follows:

$$\Delta H = \Delta E + \Delta(pv)$$

where *p* and *v* represent pressure and volume, respectively. Thus, if there is contraction or expansion of a system under constant pressure, ΔH can either increase or decrease.

An important consideration is that systems tend to approach equilibrium. This tendency can depend on the effect the reactions have on ΔH or ΔS at constant temperature, conditions under which most biochemical reactions take place.

$$\Delta G° = \Delta H° - T\Delta S°$$

When a system is not at equilibrium, ΔG can be almost any value; but at equilibrium, $\Delta G = \Delta G°$.

Up to this point, Gibbs free energy has been defined and so have the conditions under which a reaction is considered to occur spontaneously. The **second law of thermodynamics** has also been described but not stated explicitly. It states that *the total entropy of a system and its surroundings always increases for a spontaneous reaction and/or process*. This law may be expressed somewhat differently elsewhere, but the meaning is the same: namely, systems (the universe) naturally tend toward a state of randomness, and ΔS increases for spontaneous reactions.

Consider what has been said above about the components of ΔH and ΔS, and accept without derivation the following:

$$\Delta G = \Delta G^0 + RT \ln K_{eq}.$$

where R is the gas constant and is equal to 8.314 Joules $\times$ moles^{-1} $\times$ degrees Kelvin^{-1} (or 1.987 cal $\times$ mol^{-1} $\times$ K^{-1}), and T is the temperature in degrees Kelvin (K). ($RT = 592.14$ cal $\times$ mol^{-1} at 25°C.)

Now consider the following reaction defined by the equilibrium constant K:

$$A + B \xrightarrow{\quad K \quad} C + D$$

Equilibrium can be approached from either direction, and at equilibrium, $k_f[A][B] = k_r[C][D]$. Thus, the value of ΔG can have many values, either positive or negative at any place along the dotted line in the following diagram (Figure 1-1). At equilibrium, $\Delta G = 0$ since the *rate* of the back reaction is equal to the *rate* of the forward reaction and $\ln(\text{rate}_r/\text{rate}_f) = 0$. At equilibrium, no work (defined here as Q) is being done. This may be visualized diagrammatically as follows:

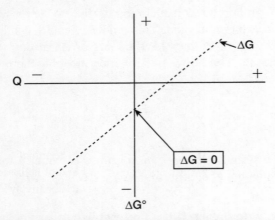

Figure 1-1. Diagrammatic representation of the relationship between ΔG^0, ΔG, and work.

In the above diagram, Q is defined as the ability to do work, and Q and ΔG are related to each other and to the following expression.

$$\ln\left(\frac{k_r[C][D]}{k_f[A][B]}\right)$$

This expression becomes 0 at equilibrium since the rates of the forward and reverse reactions are equal and the ratio of the two is 1.0, the natural log of which is zero. In this example, the value of ΔG^0 (actually $\Delta G^{0\prime}$, a state function) is represented by the point where the dotted line crosses the ΔG^0 axis. This is shown here as a linear relationship for simplicity, but that does not necessarily follow in actuality. At this point, however, the equation above, $\Delta G = \Delta G^0 + RT \ln K_{eq}$, becomes $0 = \Delta G^0 + RT \ln K_{eq}$ and $\Delta G^0 = -RT \ln K_{eq}$. If values for R and T (see above) are substituted into this equation and it is converted to log10, the following equation is obtained.

$$\Delta G^0 = -2.303 RT \log_{10} K_{eq} \text{ or } \Delta G^{0\prime} = -1.36 \text{kcal} K_{eq}.$$

This equation can be used to calculate ΔG^0 from known values of K_{eq} or K_{eq} from known values of ΔG^0. Another point to consider in relation to ΔG and the work function Q is that the **law of mass action** dictates that reactions may be driven in either direction by increasing the concentration of reactants or products. This is an important chemical principle that is exercised in cellular metabolic reactions.

If a system is already at equilibrium, **Le Châtelier's principle** holds, which states that whenever a system at equilibrium is subjected to a perturbation (change in concentration of one or more of its components), then the equilibrium will shift in a direction so as to relieve that perturbation. So, even though the concentrations of reactants and products will change, K_{eq} will remain the same in most biochemical reactions; but K_{eq} may change if the perturbation causes changes in volume, pressure, or temperature. The different K_{eq} will then reflect the new *physical* changes under which the reaction is measured, and the law of mass action for those conditions (i.e., changes in concentrations of reactants or products) still holds. A technique called *temperature jump experiments*, which is used to study rapid reaction kinetics for determining enzyme mechanisms, takes advantage of this principle.

This section has summarized some of the important principles of thermodynamics that aid in the understanding of the operation of many biochemical reactions, particularly those related to metabolic processes where covalent bonds are broken and made. Other types of chemical bonds are also important, many of which are involved in the secondary and tertiary structures of proteins and in other types of specific interactions involving ligand binding to different types of biological molecules.

A table summarizing the major types of bond interactions is shown below (Table 1-2), including an estimation of the relative strengths of those interactions and bond distances. It is not necessary to remember numbers, but relative strength of these bonds is important. Some of the letters in the last column under "Example" represent the 1-letter code for amino acids (see Figure 1-11 on page 15). The dipolar nature of the helix is important in controlling the flow of ions through some types of membrane ion channels, particularly ions like Cl^-.

2.1.1. Potential Energy Curve

Various conditions must be met for the various types of interactions to occur between molecules. Particularly in covalent bonds, but in others as well, there is a certain amount of vibrational and rotational motion. The nuclei are not a fixed distance apart but oscillate about a mean distance, r_o. If the nuclei are closer together than r_o, there is repulsion; if they are further apart than r_o but within a certain range, there is attraction. If sufficient energy is put into the molecule to overcome this attraction, the two atoms dissociate and/or the forces that hold them together dissipate. These facts may be represented by means of a potential energy curve such as that shown on the next page (see Figure 1-2).

Morse developed a useful equation that gives the potential energy (V) of a diatomic molecule as a function of internuclear distance (r):

$$V = D'[e^{-2a(r-r_o)} - 2e^{-a(r-r_o)}]$$

where D' is the energy of dissociation plus the zero-point energy and a is a complex parameter that takes into account several factors including vibration frequency and dissociation energy—parameters that determine the width of the potential well. The important thing to

Table 1-2.
Summary of the Types of Chemical Bonds

Interactions	Nature	Length (Å)	Strength (kcal/mol)	Free energy (kcal/mol)	Example
Atomic bond	Covalent	1.0–1.6	50		Peptide bond
Ion pair	Electrostatic	1.8–10.0*	1–6	0.1–6**	R, K, H, D, E
Hydrogen	-H—:R-	2.6–3.5	2–10	0.5–2.0	-HN⋯H⋯O—R-
Hydrophobic	Entropy		2–3	0–2.5	Amino acid R groups
van der Waals		2.8–4.0	<1		All atoms
Partial charges	Electrostatic				δ+ and δ−
Helix dipole	Electrostatic		10	0.5	N-terminal end of helix to negatively charged group
Aromatic-Aromatic	Hydrogen	4.5–7.0	1–2	0.6–1.3	F, W, Y
Amino-Aromatic	Hydrogen	2.9–3.6	2.7–4.9		H—N(sp2) donor to side chain F, W, Y

Note: Proteins in solution would involve all of the above types of interactions.

*Opposite charges have bond lengths of up to 4.0 Å, and those of like charges would be 3.5 – 10.0 Å.

**Those exposed to solvent have stabilization/free energy of 0.1–0.5 kcal mol^{-1}, and those buried within proteins have energy levels of 3–6 kcal mol^{-1}.

remember, however, is that atoms/molecules must be close enough for attraction to occur and that repulsion will occur if they get too close together.

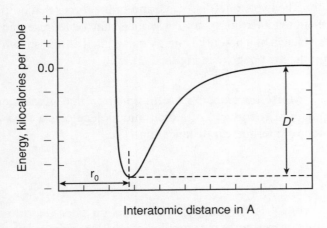

Figure 1-2. Morse potential energy curve of a molecule as a function of internuclear distance
(Adapted from Daniels, F. and Alberty, R. S., *Physical Chemistry*. John Wiley & Sons, Inc., New York, 1955, p. 563.)

2.1.2. Redox States.

There is a connection between Volta's discovery of the battery in 1796 and modern-day chemistry, namely, that there is an electrical interaction between two different metals submerged near each other in an acidic solution. This is the result of the chemical interactions of the acid and the two metals. This led eventually to production of the first chemical device that produced and stored electric current: the battery. Physical chemistry became a branch of chemistry in the late 1880s, and the importance of electrical interactions among neutral molecules (organic molecules) was realized in the 1920s. This final realization led to an appreciation that many organic chemical reactions involve the removal or addition of electrons as an important aspect of organic chemical mechanisms and that it is intimately involved in the processes of extracting and storing energy from covalent bonds. This energy can subsequently be used for biosynthetic reactions. Conceptually, it is important to realize that reactions of metabolic pathways and the storage of energy through processes such as oxidative phosphorylation occur in a small, stepwise fashion where, in general, only one or two electrons are removed from a compound at a time. These reactions occur in pairs, where one molecule is oxidized and another is reduced. The removal of electrons is **oxidation**, and the

addition of electrons is **reduction**. For example, the following reaction represents oxidation:

$$Fe^{++} - e^- \rightarrow Fe^{+++}$$

A generic example of this reaction is $X^- \rightarrow X$. Reduction may be represented as follows:

$$Fe^{+++} + e^- \rightarrow Fe^{++}$$

A generic example of this reaction is $X \rightarrow X^-$.

The process of electrolysis is probably familiar to most students of science. In an electrolysis solution where several different ions are competing for the transfer of an electron, the transfer will occur from the one with the greatest potential to give up an electron.

Electromotive forces are measured in a device similar to the one shown in the diagram below (Figure 1-3). Note that only electrons flow from one chamber to the other, not the reactants (A/A⁻ or B/B⁻).

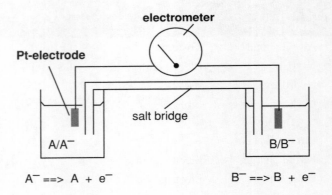

Figure 1-3. Example of an electrochemical cell.
(This diagram was adapted from *http://www.life.uiuc.edu/crofts/bioph354/redox.html*, which was still accessible on 09/25/2006)

First, consider the fact that redox reactions are also thermodynamic reactions, and the devices used to measure redox potential, namely, electrochemical cells, measure free energy changes (work potential) of redox reactions directly. The device shown in the diagram can be considered as two half cells. One half cell contains the electron donor pair, and the other half cell contains the electron receptor pair. The device is set up such that there is no flux of chemical material from one half cell to the other, meaning that the flux of chemical material is maintained at zero. This is done by use of a potentiometer that applies voltage to the cells to maintain the flux of material at zero. The amount of voltage required to maintain that flux is a direct measure of the potential differences between each half cell. For general chemical reactions, the **zero potential**, or reference electrode (half cell), consists of 1.0 M of H^+ under 1.0 atmosphere of H_2. The other electrode (half cell) consists of the other pair of components whose redox potential is to be measured. For biochemical reactions, the reference electrode contains hydrogen ions at a concentration of 1×10^{-7} M or pH 7.0. In practical cases, another more convenient type of electrode that has been standardized against the zero potential electrodes mentioned above is used, and corrections made accordingly. Generally, a calomel or Ag/AgCl electrode is used.

If the reduced form of a compound has a lower affinity for electrons than does H_2, it has a negative reduction potential. If it has a higher affinity for electrons than does H_2, it has a positive reduction potential. Thus, electrons

flow in the direction of greater reduction potential, just as spontaneous chemical reactions proceed faster in the direction of equilibrium. The relationship between free energy and reduction potential may be defined as follows:

$$\Delta G^{\circ\prime} = -nF\Delta E^{\prime}_0$$

where $\Delta G^{\circ\prime}$ refers to ΔG° at the standard conditions of pH 7.0, and $\Delta E^{\prime}_0$ refers to standard reduction potential at pH 7.0. F is Faraday's constant (96.48 kJ/mol/V or 23.06 kcal/mol/V) and n is the number of electrons.

The table below (Table 1-3) gives standard reduction potentials of some reactions of biochemical importance. Thus, an analogy can be drawn between a chemical reaction being spontaneous when ΔG is negative and the flow of electrons down an electromotive or electrochemical gradient. Keep in mind, however, that the flow of electrons is from the more negative to the more positive. If a compound has a negative reduction potential, its reduced form has a much lower ability to accept electrons.

Table 1-3.
Standard Reduction Potentials of Some Biochemical Reactions

Oxidant	Reductant	n	$E_0{'}$ (V)
Succinate + CO_2	α-Ketoglutarate	2	−0.67
Acetate	Acetaldehyde	2	−0.60
Ferredoxin (oxidized)	Ferredoxin (reduced)	1	−0.43
2 H^+	H_2	2	−0.42
NAD^+	NADH + H^+	2	−0.32
$NADP^+$	NADPH + H^+	2	−0.32
Lipoate (oxidized)	Lipoate (reduced)	2	−0.29
Glutathione (oxidized)	Glutathione (reduced)	2	−0.23
FAD	$FADH_2$	2	−0.22
Acetaldehyde	Ethanol	2	−0.20
Pyruvate	Lactate	2	−0.19
Fumarate	Succinate	2	0.03
Cytochrome b (+3)	Cytochrome b (+2)	1	0.07
Dehydroascorbate	Ascorbate	2	0.08
Ubiquinone (oxidized)	Ubiquinone (reduced)	2	0.10
Cytochrome c (+3)	Cytochrome c (+2)	1	0.22
Fe^{+3}	Fe^{+2}	1	0.77
½O_2 + 2 H^+	H_2O	2	0.82

2.2. Water, pH, Acid-Base Reactions, and Buffers

2.2.1. Structure of Water

Life as we know it could not exist without water. Though it is sometimes referred to incorrectly as the universal solvent, that is not an accurate statement because not all molecules will dissolve in water. Those that do dissolve generally have the ability to form hydrogen bonds and/or to be hydrated by water molecules. Those molecules that do dissolve in water are called **hydrophilic**. There are other molecules that do not have the ability to exercise either of the above properties and will not dissolve in water; they are referred to as being **hydrophobic**. There are also hybrid-type molecules in which portions of the molecule have the ability to interact with water while other portions of the same molecule do not have that ability. Thus, these molecules have some of both properties and are referred to as being **amphiphilic**. Some examples of various types of molecules of biochemical importance that form hydrogen bonds are listed in Table 1-2, some of which are acceptors and some of which are donors. Some of the properties of water that facilitate these interactions are given below.

It was pointed out earlier that the strength of a hydrogen-oxygen bond is 110 kcal. Other important aspects of the water molecule are not just the strength of the H—O—H bonds, but also their arrangement. The arrangement permits an enormous number of intermolecular hydrogen bonds, which imposes on water other important physical properties. A diagrammatic example of a water molecule is shown below (Figure 1-4).

This picture shows not only the angle between oxygen and the hydrogen atoms, but also the van der Waals envelopes of the various components as well as bond distances.

Hydrogen bonding occurs, and some of the constraints for those interactions may become apparent from the following diagram. In the diagram in Figure 1-5, which consists of two molecules of water, the one on the left is the donor, and the one on the right is the acceptor.

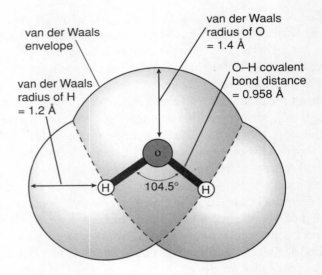

Figure 1-4. Diagram of a water molecule.
(Adapted from Voet, D, and Voet, J.G., *Biochemistry*, John Wiley & Sons, New York, 1990 p. 30)

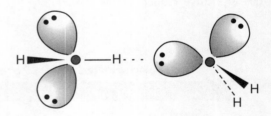

Figure 1-5. Hydrogen bonding of water molecules.
(Adapted from Voet, D, and Voet, J.G., *Biochemistry*, John Wiley & Sons, New York, 1990 p. 30)

The structure of water is far more complex than this, as the following diagram (Figure 1-6) of ice crystals shows. The extensiveness to which hydrogen bonding occurs in water is evident. This highly organized structure contributes to many of the physical properties of water, including its high boiling point (100°C). Compare the boiling point of water with that of methane (−20°C); both are close to the same mass, 18 for water 16 for mehane, but methane does not have the ability to form the type of intermolecular interactions as does water. This important property of water plays an important role in solvating hydrophilic molecules.

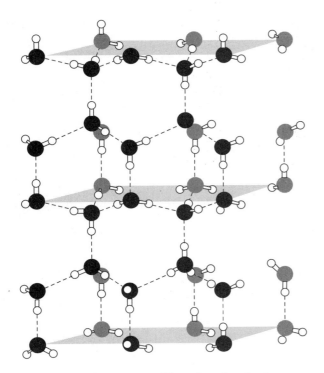

Figure 1-6. Structure of ice showing hydrogen bonding of water molecules.
(Adapted from Voet, D, and Voet, J.G., *Biochemistry*, John Wiley & Sons, New York, 1990 p. 31.)

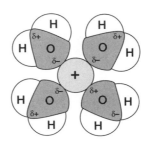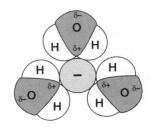

Figure 1-7. Orientation of water molecules in the solvation of ions.
(Adapted from Voet, D, and Voet, J.G., *Biochemistry*, John Wiley & Sons, New York, 1990 p. 32)

Even when a molecule is not soluble in water but dispersed in it as in emulsion formation, the structural orientation of water molecules is disturbed such that it becomes less ordered thermodynamically (i.e., there is a change in entropy of the system).

2.2.2. Acid-Base Reactions

There are several definitions used in biochemistry for acids and bases. The first relates to compounds capable of donating protons for acids and forming hydroxyl ions for bases. A more general and accepted definition for an acid is a compound capable of donating a proton, and a base is one that is capable of accepting a proton. For other types of reactions, especially those catalyzed by enzymes, an acid may be characterized as a compound that is capable of accepting a pair of electrons, and a base as a compound that is capable of giving up a pair of electrons.

2.2.2.1. Concept of Acids and Bases in Relationship to pH

Water itself may be considered an acid, and it dissociates in accordance with the following equation:

$$H_2O \leftrightarrow H^+ + OH^-$$

In reality, H^+ would exist as an hydronium ion H_3O^+, but the above equation is sufficient for this discussion.

The K_{eq} for the dissociation of water is as follows:

$$K_{eq} = \frac{[H^+][OH^{-1}]}{[H_2O]}$$

Like the ice structure shown above, liquid water is also highly interactive through hydrogen bond formation. When molecules dissolve in water, the structural orientation of the water molecules changes to accommodate solvation of the solute. In the case of ions, hydration occurs, resulting in structures similar to the following (see Figure 1-7). These structures also reflect the fact that a water molecule is dipolar. The negative part of the structure is involved in solvating the positive ions, and the negative part of the molecule is involved in solvating the positive ions. The **dipole moment** of water (in simple terms, the direction and strength of its degree of polarization) is 1.85 debye units. The dipole moment is not a major determining factor in the ability of water to form the intermolecular interactions shown above. The dipole moment of methanol under similar conditions is 1.70 debye units. However, the interaction of a hydrogen atom of one molecule of water with oxygen of another molecule of water is significant, a condition that does not exist with methanol.

Since, however, there is very little dissociation of H_2O, the concentration of water is approximately constant at 55.5 M. So the above equation may be simplified to

$$K_w = [H^+][OH^-]$$

in which K_w is the product of the concentrations of $[H^+]$ and $[OH^-]$ ions. At 25°C, this value is 1×10^{-14} M. It should be obvious that there is a reciprocal relationship between the concentration of H^+ ions and OH^- ions; if one is 10^{-4} M, the other is 10^{-10} M such that the product is always equal to 1×10^{-14} M.

One of the definitions of an acid is that it is a proton donor; conversely, a base is a proton acceptor. There are basically two types of acids and bases: strong and weak. Strong acids and bases are essentially always completely or nearly completely ionized and serve little to no function as buffers. So this section will concentrate on weak acids and bases. Classic examples of the latter two are acetic acid and ammonium hydroxide, as shown below.

$$CH_3COOH \leftrightarrow H^+ + CH_3COO^-$$

and

$$NH_4OH \leftrightarrow NH_4^+ + OH^-$$

A general equation representing the ionization of a weak acid in water is

$$HA + H_2O \leftrightarrow H_3O^+ + A^-.$$

The equilibrium constant for that reaction is

$$K_{eq} = \frac{[H_3O^+][A^-]}{[HA][H_2O]}.$$

But, as in previous cases where the concentration of water is relatively constant, the above equation may be written as

$$K_a = K[H_2O] = \frac{[H^+][A^-]}{[HA]}$$

and the above equation, in terms of $[H^+]$, may be rewritten as

$$[H^+] = K_a \left(\frac{[HA]}{[A^-]} \right).$$

This equation may be written in logarithmic form as

$$\log[H^+] = \log K_a + \log([HA]/[A^-]).$$

Multiplying both sides of the equation by -1, and defining pH as $-\log[H^+]$, changes the equation to

$$pH = -\log K_a - \log([HA]/[A^-]).$$

Similarly, if pK_a is defined as $-\log K_a$, the equation becomes

$$pH = pK_a + \log([A^-]/[HA])$$

which is the Henderson-Hasselbalch equation and defines the relationship of acid to base at various pH values of known K_a or pK_a values for the weak acids of interest. Note that $[HA]$ is the concentration of the conjugate acid, and $[A^-]$ is the concentration of the conjugate base. Also, when $[HA] = [A^-]$, the value of the ratio is 1.0, and pH = pK_a.

2.2.2.2. Buffers

Weak acids serve as good buffers, especially in the vicinity of their pKa values. The addition of acid or base to a buffer solution at its pKa value when the concentrations of its conjugate base and acid are approximately equal will cause very little change in pH of the solution. This is demonstrated in a simulated titration curve for acetic acid (see Figure 1-8).

The pK_a of acetic acid is 4.8, and, as shown in Figure 1-8, this is the point where the concentrations of the conjugate acid and base are equal. As shown from the dashed lines at approximately 0.37 and 0.63 equivalents of base above and below the pK_a, there is very little change in pH, as evident from projections of the positions of the dashed lines onto the abscissa.

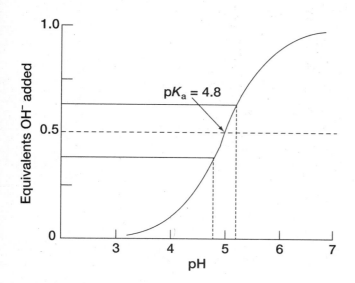

Figure 1-8. Titration curve of a weak acid.
(Adapted from Berg, J.M., Tymoczko, J.L., and Stryer, L., *Biochemistry*, Fifth Edition, W. H. Freeman and Company, New York, 2002, p. 74.)

$$+NH_3\text{—}\overset{\overset{H}{|}}{\underset{\underset{R}{|}}{C}}\text{—COOH} \qquad +NH_3\text{—}\overset{\overset{H}{|}}{\underset{\underset{R}{|}}{C}}\text{—COO}^- \qquad NH_2\text{—}\overset{\overset{H}{|}}{\underset{\underset{R}{|}}{C}}\text{—COO}^-$$

Acidic pH   Isoelectric pH   Basic pH

All amino acids, except proline, have this same basic structure. The amino group is on the α-carbon atom, and in proteins, amino acids are generally all of the same stereochemical (chiral) configuration, the **L configuration**. The other configuration of atoms around this asymmetric center is the **D configuration**. All of the amino acids are optically active and have at least one asymmetric center, except for glycine, where the R group is another H atom (Look at its structure in the Figure 1-11).

The origin of the D and L nomenclature, now more frequently referred to as **R** and **S**, originated from consideration of the absolute configuration of glyceraldehydes. The nomenclature defines the orientation of substituents around the asymmetric carbon as shown below.

$$\overset{OH}{\underset{H}{HOCH_2\text{—}\boxed{}\text{—CHO}}} \qquad \overset{OH}{\underset{H}{HCO\text{—}\boxed{}\text{—CH_2OH}}}$$

(*R*)-Glyceraldehyde   (*S*)-Glyceraldehyde

3. BIOMOLECULAR STRUCTURES

3.1. Amino Acids and Proteins

The building blocks of proteins are amino acids. There are 20 for which there are genetic codes. There is a 21st amino acid in proteins, selenocysteine, for which there is a genetic code. The process of utilization of the code for selenocysteine is not straightforward and will not be discussed further. Focus will be on the first 20 amino acids. As the name implies, amino acids have an amino functional group and an acid (carboxyl) group. The general structure for an amino acid is

$$NH_3\text{—}\overset{\overset{H}{|}}{\underset{\underset{R}{|}}{C}}\text{—COOH}$$

where R is the side-chain structure and is different for each amino acid as shown in the table of amino acid structures shown in Figure 1-11. In solution, amino acids may have one of three forms, depending on pH.

The R, S system of designating chirality, or the stereochemistry of substitutions on an asymmetric carbon atom (generally the sp^3 carbon—tetrahedral—with 4 substituents), follow the Cahn-Ingold-Prelog priority rules for compounds in organic chemistry. The first thing that must be done is to identify the chiral/asymmetric center containing the four different substituents. Next, a priority must be assigned to each group (high to low, for example, 1–4, respectively) based on atomic number of the atom *attached* to the chiral center—the higher the atomic number, the higher the priority. Position the lowest priority group away from you. Determine the direction of high to low priority (1 to 3) for the other three groups. If the direction is clockwise, then the chiral or asymmetric center is R (Latin: *rectus* = right); if the direction is counterclockwise, then it is S (Latin: *sinister* = left). If two atoms attached to the chiral center have the same

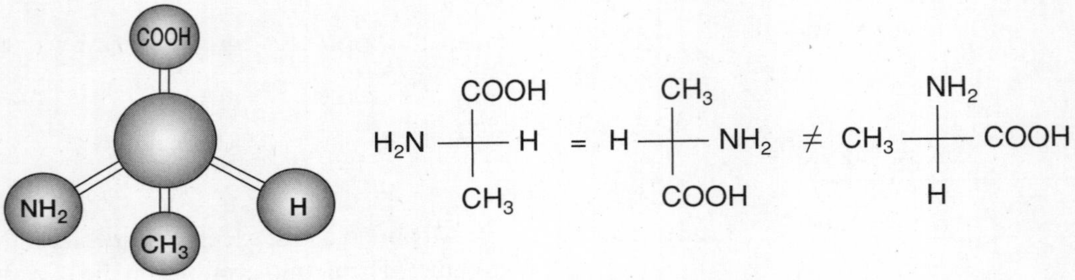

Figure 1-9. Structure of L-alanine.

atomic number, then the sum of the atomic numbers of the atoms one bond further from the chiral center is totaled, and so on, progressing out from the chiral center until one branch or the other originating at the chiral center is found to have higher priority. (If no such difference is found, then the carbon in question is not, indeed, a site of chirality.) [*http://www.chem. ucalgary.ca/courses/351/Carey5th/Ch07/ch7-6.html*] [*http://encyclopedia.thefreedictionary.com/Cahn% 20Ingold%20Prelog%20priority%20rules*]

L amino acids are of the S configuration. Note the structure of alanine shown above (Figure 1-9).

Structures of the 20 amino acids found in proteins are shown on the next page (Figure 1-11) along with their three- and one-letter symbols, respectively. This number of amino acids is sufficiently large enough to make all of the proteins necessary for all known functions in biology. Consider that random assembly of proteins each containing 100 amino acids (a protein of approximately 12,000 daltons total mass) would result in 20^{100} unique combinations of amino acids and hence proteins. Genetic selectivity through coding has prevented this and results in a biologically manageable number of proteins and functions. The role of the genetic code will be discussed later.

3.2. Structure of Proteins

There are four levels of protein structure: primary, secondary, tertiary, and quaternary.

3.2.1. Primary Structure

The primary sequence is the linear arrangement of amino acids in a protein as coded for by the gene for that specific protein. Each amino acid is linked by a peptide bond formed between the carboxyl group of one amino acid and the amino group of another. By tradition, two amino acids linked in this manner are referred to as a dipeptide even though there is but one peptide bond, and three amino acids linked in this manner are referred to as a tripeptide, and so forth. An example of a peptide bond and its resonance structure appears in Figure 1-10.

Figure 1-10. Resonance structures of a peptide bond.

(Adapted from Berg, J.M., Tymoczko, J.L., and Stryer, L., *Biochemistry*, Fifth Edition, W. H. Freeman and Company, New York, 2002, p. 54.)

Formation of each peptide bond results in the loss of one molecule of water. Note that peptides, like proteins, have a carboxyl terminal end and an amino terminal end. References made to peptides usually refer to a relatively small number of amino acids linked together.

Six atoms of the *trans* conformation of a peptide bond lie within the same plane: the two *alpha* carbons, the carboxyl carbon and its attached oxygen, and the nitrogen and its attached hydrogen atom. This is the pri-

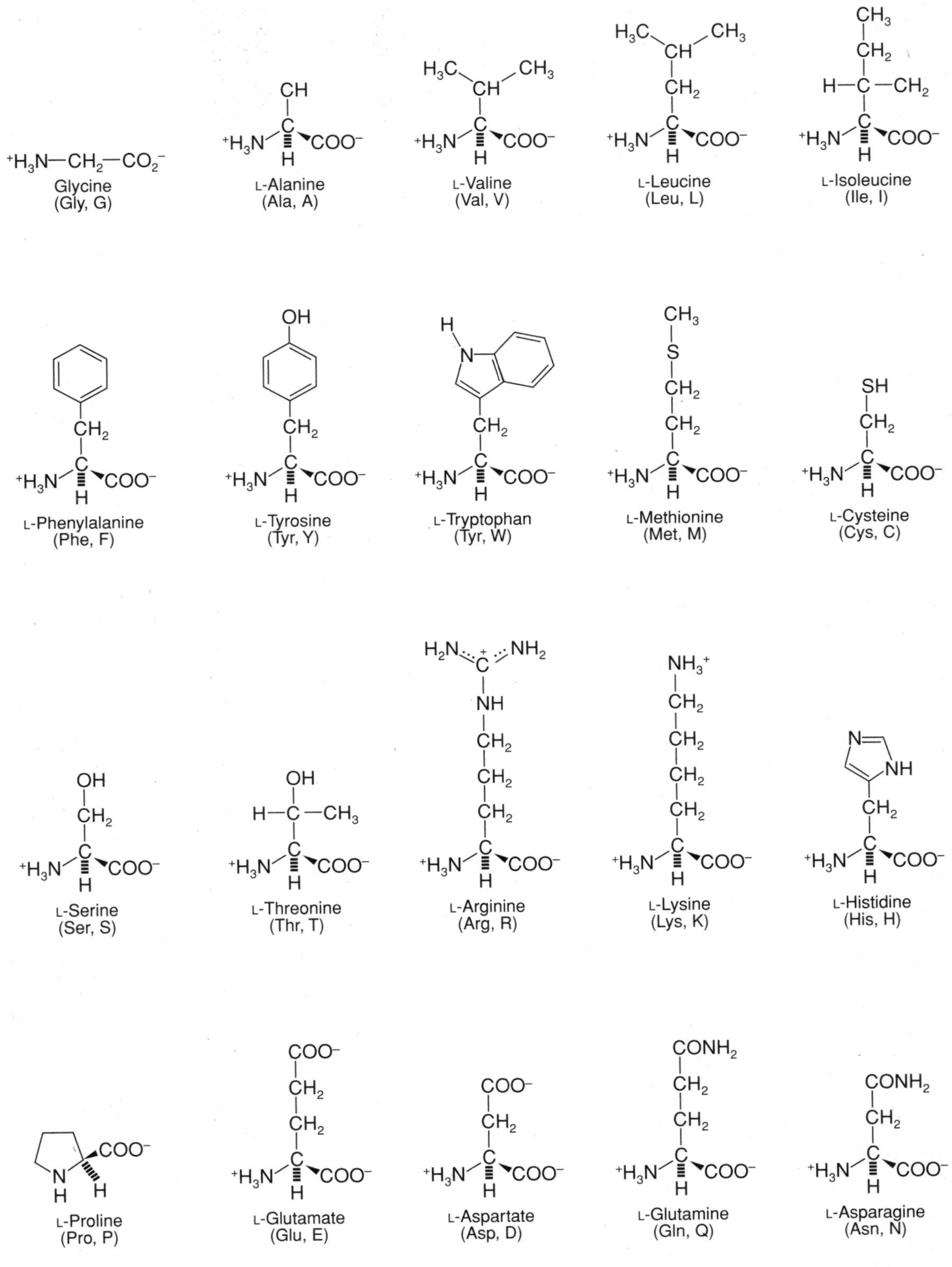

Figure 1-11. Structures and names of amino acids in proteins.
(Adapted from the inside cover of Abeles, R. A., Frey, P. A., and Jencks, W. P., *Biochemistry*, Jones and Bartlett Publishers, Boston, 1992.)

mary conformation of peptide bonds found in proteins (see Figure 1-12).

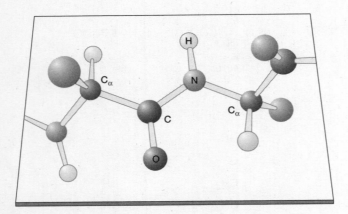

Figure 1-12. Planar arrangement of atoms in a peptide bond.
(Adapted from Berg, J.M., Tymoczko, J.L., and Stryer, L., *Biochemistry*, Fifth Edition, W. H. Freeman and Company, New York, 2002, p. 54.)

3.2.2. Secondary Structure

The secondary structure of proteins refers to the folding pattern of the polypeptide backbone structure (i.e., helices, pleated sheets, and turns). The folding pattern is influenced by the sequence of amino acids of the polypeptide, specifically the R groups of the amino acid residues.

Consider that in an aqueous environment, polar R groups of amino acids would tend to interact with water molecules, and nonpolar R groups would have a greater tendency to be shielded from such interactions (see Figure 1-13).

Other factors include sizes of the R groups. Steric hindrance in folding would be minimized or excluded.

3.2.2.1. α-Helix

The α-helix is one of the major secondary structures found in proteins. For L-α-amino acids, the helical structure is right-handed; if held in the right hand with fingers pointing in the direction of the turns, the pitch (as in the turn of a screw) of the helix would be in the direction of the thumb. There are 3.6 amino acid

Figure 1-13. Arrangement of water molecules around nonpolar molecules.
Nonpolar molecules tend to associate with each other.
(Adapted from Abeles, R. A., Frey, P. A., and Jencks, W. P., *Biochemistry*, Jones and Bartlett Publishers, Boston, 1992, p. 221.)

residues per turn, and the pitch of the helix (linear distance between turns) is 5.4 Å. Hydrogen bonding occurs within the helix such that the C=O of the nth residue forms a hydrogen bond with the (n + 4)th residue. This optimizes the N—O distance (2.8 Å) and permits tight packing that also optimizes van der Waals interactions. R groups are to the outside and point in a somewhat downward direction. The diagram in Figure 1-14 depicts left-handed (A) and right-handed (B) α-helical forms of a polypeptide chain.

3.2.2.2. β-Pleated Sheets

This is another type of secondary structure found in proteins, and it exists in two forms: parallel and antiparallel. In parallel β-pleated sheets, the backbone of the polypeptide chains that H-bond with each other run in the same direction (both C → N), whereas in the antiparallel β-pleated sheets, each runs in opposite directions (one C → N, and the other of the hydrogen-bonded pair runs in the N → C direction). This causes a different orientation of the side-chain residues. Note the positions of the R groups shown within the circles of each structure (see Figure 1-15).

3.2.2.3. β-Turns

There are segments of the polypeptide chain that must form loops in globular proteins in order to form β-sheets and in some cases to change directions of the chain between helices. Four amino acid residues gener-

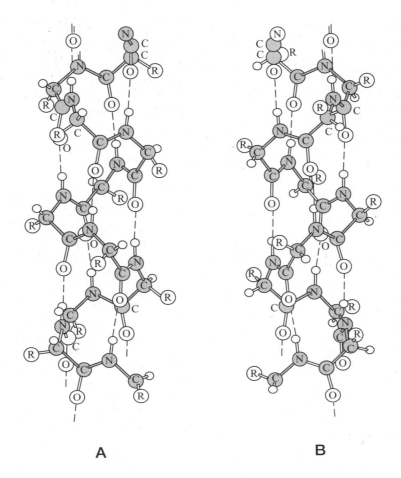

A

B

Figure 1-14. Diagram of a left-handed (A) and a right-handed (B) α-helix.
(Adapted from Abeles, R. A., Frey, P. A., and Jencks, W. P., *Biochemistry*, Jones and Bartlett Publishers, Boston, 1992, p. 201.)

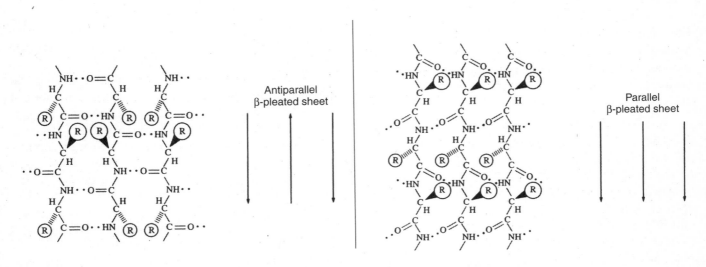

Antiparallel
β-pleated sheet

Parallel
β-pleated sheet

Figure 1-15. β-Pleated sheet structures in proteins.
(Adapted from Abeles, R. A., Frey, P. A., and Jencks, W. P., *Biochemistry*, Jones and Bartlett Publishers, Boston, 1992, p. 202.)

ally make up this turn and consist of glycine residues, proline residues, an imino acid, and one or more hydrophilic amino acid residues that would permit interaction with the aqueous environment at the surfaces and/or those capable of posttranslational modification such as asparagine, serine, and residues with formal positive or negative charges. The following is a diagrammatic representation of a β-turn (Figure 1-16).

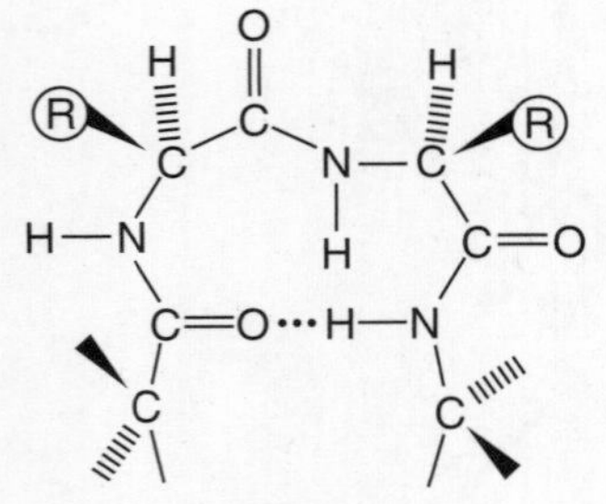

β-Turn

Figure 1-16. Diagram representing β-turn structures in proteins.
(Altered from Abeles, R. A., Frey, P. A., and Jencks, W. P., *Biochemistry*, Jones and Bartlett Publishers, Boston, 1992. p. 203)

3.2.3. Tertiary Structure

Tertiary structure refers to the three-dimensional arrangement of the complete polypeptide chain where its helices, pleated sheets, and disulfide bridges (2–Cys—SH → –Cys—S—S—Cys–) in which two cysteine residues from different parts of the polypeptide chain are linked together, all come together to form the three-dimensional structure of the protein. This is the functional protein, and important reactive groups are brought into close proximity to form appropriate active centers.

The dark line with its numbered circles (Figure 1-18) represents the primary backbone structure of the enzyme carbonate dehydratase. This enzyme contains zinc, and the α-carbons of its ligand are in squares. β-Structures are in the center of the diagram and hydrogen bonds involved in those structures are indicated by the straight lines. Curved lines indicate positions of amino acids involved in α-helices. The other lighter straight lines show some of the H-bonds

and indicate residues that are close to each other in the tertiary structure.

The tertiary structure of the enzyme assumes the following shape.

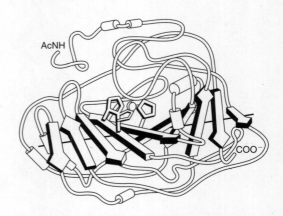

Figure 1-17. Tertiary structure of carbonate dehydratase shown in Figure 1-18
(Adapted from Dixon, M. and Webb, E.C. *Enzymes*, Third Edition, Academic Press, New York, 1979, p. 537)

In this diagram (Figure 1-17), the broad arrows represent β-pleated sheets, cylinders represent α-helices, and the dark filled circle in the middle represents zinc surrounded by its coordinating amino acid residues.

3.2.4. Quaternary Structure

The quaternary structure of a protein is defined by the interaction and arrangement of subunits of a protein. A subunit is the individual tertiary arrangement of an individual peptide chain as shown above for carbonate dehydratase (Figure 1-17). Many other proteins, such as lactic dehydrogenase and glyceraldehyde 3-phosphate dehydrogenase, consist of a discrete number of subunits held together by noncovalent bonds. The individual subunits that constitute the quaternary structure may be polypeptides that are identical, as in glyceraldehyde 3-phosphate dehydrogenase, or nonidentical, as in lactate dehydrogenase. The simplest quaternary structure would be that of a dimer (see Figure 1-19). Most allosteric (regulatory) enzymes are multi-subunit structures. An example of quaternary structure of an allosteric enzyme is that of aspartate transcarbamoylase. This protein consists of different size subunits that also have different functions.

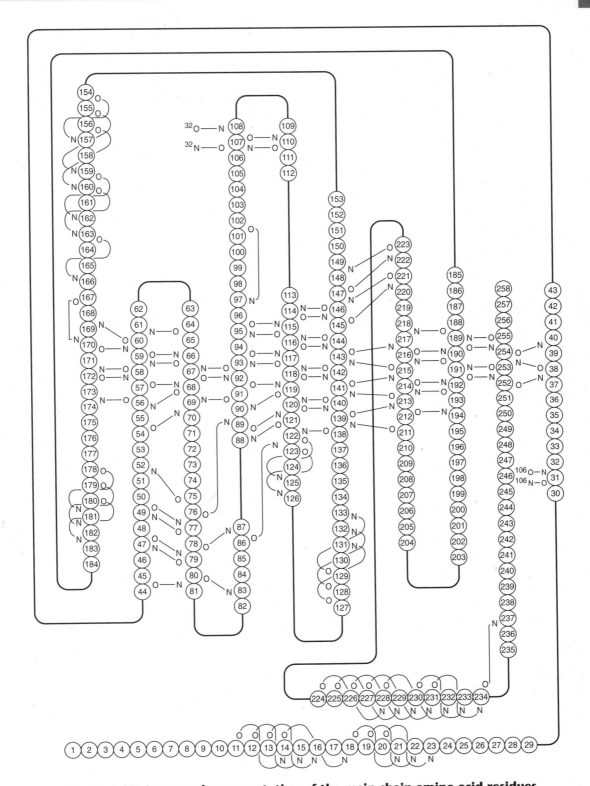

**Figure 1-18. Structural representation of the main chain amino acid residues
of carbonate dehydratase (carbonate hydrolyase, EC 4.2.1.1).**
(Adapted from Dixon, M. and Webb, E.C., *Enzymes*, Third Edition, Academic Press, New York, 1979, p. 536.)

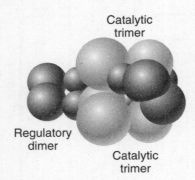

Catalytic trimer

Regulatory dimer

Catalytic trimer

Figure 1-19.
(Adapted from Berg, J.M., Tymoczko, J.L., and Stryer, L., *Biochemistry*, Fifth Edition, W. H. Freeman and Company, New York, 2002, Fig. 10.5(B), p.264.)

4. CHEMICAL AND ENZYMATIC REACTION MECHANISMS

Enzymes are specialized macromolecules that function to accelerate rates of chemical reactions. Many reactions that are required to maintain the normal biological activity of cells could not occur fast enough at the normal pH and temperatures if it were not for the existence of these specialized macromolecules. Essentially all enzymes involved in cellular metabolism are proteins, but another class of enzymes derived from ribonucleic acids exists—namely, ribozymes. These are RNA molecules that are capable of catalyzing specific reactions, mostly reactions involved in some aspect of RNA processing.

The term that defines the speed of a chemical reaction is rate or velocity. **Reaction rate** is defined as the change in amount of material or substrate altered chemically per unit of time. In theory, chemical reactions could occur and they would approach equilibrium whether catalyzed or uncatalyzed. Enzymes are catalysts and increase the rate at which equilibrium is reached. Some of the mechanisms by which enzymes accomplish these tasks will be discussed later. Enzymes fit the true definition of catalyst and may be recovered in their initial form after the reaction is competed.

Consider the reaction A ↔ B in the absence of a catalysis and the same reaction in the presence of an enzyme. Both must go through a transition state, but in the presence of an enzyme as catalyst, the transition state energy is lower. The enzyme facilitates the reac-

tion by altering the mechanism and/or the processes by which S is transformed to P.

4.1. Chemical Reaction Mechanisms

4.1.1. First-Order Reactions

The velocity for the reaction $A \xrightarrow{k} B$ may be written as $v = k[A]$, which means that the velocity of the reaction is directly proportional to the concentration of the reactant, A. This may be defined mathematically as

$$\frac{d[A]}{dt} = k[A]_0 \ .$$

Integrating the above equation between the limits of time leads to

$$\ln[A] = -kt + \ln[A]_0.$$

which can be converted to log form, base 10

$$k = \frac{2.303}{t} \log \frac{[A]_0}{[A]} \ .$$

The dimension of k for a first-order rate constant is expressed in units of reciprocal time, t^{-1}. A convenient method for determining k is to plot data according to the following equation.

$$\log[A] = -kt/2.303 + \log[A]_0.$$

4.1.2. Second-Order Reactions

The rate equation for a second-order reaction may be derived in a similar manner, giving an equation that looks like

$$k = \frac{2.303}{t([A]_0 - [B]_0)} \log \frac{[B]_0([A]_0 - [A])}{[A]_0([B]_0 - [B])} \ .$$

The dimension of k for a second-order reaction is expressed in units of reciprocal concentration times reciprocal time or $M^{-1}t^{-1}$.

Units for first-order and second-order reactions are important to have an understanding of the meaning and

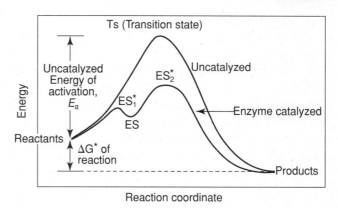

Figure 1-20. Energy diagrams for noncatalyzed and enzyme catalyzed reactions.
(Adapted from Devlin, T. M., Editor, *Textbook of Biochemistry with Clinical Correlations*, Fourth Edition, Wiley-Liss, New York, 1997, p. 159.)

use of enzyme kinetic constants. Their significance will become more obvious during discussions of Michaelis-Menten kinetics.

4.1.3. Some Factors That Influence Reaction Rates

For a reaction to occur between two molecules, they must collide with each other, and each must have sufficient energy and orientation to affect the reaction. Arrhenius made the assumption that the fraction of molecules possessing energy (E) greater than a certain amount to effect reaction is approximately proportional to $e^{-E/RT}$, and thus

$$k = A \, e^{-E/RT}.$$

Expressing this equation in logarithmic form, where k is rate, gives

$$\log k = \log A - \frac{E}{2.303RT}.$$

This expression states that the frequency factor, A, for the reaction and the energy of activation could be obtained by plotting the log k versus $-1/T$. This equation derived by Arrhenius is an empirical expression that allows estimation of the energy of activation for a chemical reaction.

It was shown earlier that at equilibrium, $\Delta G° = -RT\ln K_{eq}$ and $\Delta G° = \Delta H° - T\Delta S°0$. Thus, it follows that the forward and the reverse reactions (k_1/k_{-1}) would proceed through the same transition state; a term containing both would be more closely related to the transition state energy for the reaction. Combining the Arrhenius and the thermodynamic equations given above results in the following:

$$-RT\ln K_{eq} = \Delta H° - T\Delta S°$$

and

$$K_{eq} = e^{\Delta S°/R} e^{-\Delta H°RT}.$$

This latter equation takes into account the forward and reverse reactions since it includes K_{eq}, The log of this

equation is similar in form to the empirical Arrhenius equation. Thus, a plot of $\ln K_{eq}$ versus $1/T$ will give a straight line, the slope of which is $-\Delta H°/R$ and allows calculation of the heat of activation. The heat of activation differs from the energy of activation since $\Delta H = \Delta E + \Delta(pv)$. More detailed thermodynamic analysis provides proof that the Arrhenius equation is related to the heat of activation, but in a more stringent manner than that shown above. It is important to recognize that the frequency factor in the Arrhenius equation is dimensionless and has the same units as those for first-order reactions, $time^{-1}$. The overall rate of the reaction depends on the concentration of molecules in the activated state, and there is equilibrium between those in the activated state and those that are not. The introduction of the term K_{eq} above and its relationship to ΔH and $T\Delta S$ is to show that this relationship is real, namely

$$K_a = c_{activated}/c_{reactant}.$$

A more complete equation derived by Eyring in his theory of absolute reaction rates is

$$k = (RT / Nh)e^{\Delta S_a/R}e^{-\Delta H_a/RT}$$

where N is Avogadro's constant and h is Planck's constant, 6.624×10^{-27} erg sec molecule^{-1}. The term RT/Nh is about 5×10^{13}, the same as vibration periods of atoms within molecules. So, even though some biochemical reactions such as catalase and possibly triose phosphate isomerase may be diffusion limited (i.e., the rate of catalysis is faster than the rate of diffusion of product from the enzyme), the reaction probably has occurred within the confines of Eyring's theory of absolute reaction rates. As implied, other factors related to binding interactions and release of products would have considerable control of the reaction rates observed for other enzyme catalyzed reactions also.

The important point, however, is that molecules must have sufficient energy to react and that they must have enough to reach the transition state. In uncatalyzed reactions, rates depend on the frequency of all reacting molecules reaching the transition states and whether they collide with each other in the proper orientation at those precise moments. The situation differs with enzyme-catalyzed reactions since enzymes will bind molecules (their substrates) for a significantly long period of time and assist in bringing them to the transition states through specific bonding type interactions. The concept that enzymes "stabilize the transition state" must be taken in context with the speed at which these reactions can occur. Stabilization of a million-fold may take only microseconds. Figure 1-20 illustrates that the energy required to reach the transition state will be lowered by the inclusion of an enzyme in the reaction, but the K_{eq} for the reaction will not be altered by the enzyme and, thus, neither will $\Delta G°$. Remember, $\Delta G° = -RT\ln K_{eq}$.

4.2. Enzymatic Reaction Mechanisms

4.2.1. How Does an Enzyme Help Lower the Energy/Heat of Activation of a Reaction?

Most textbooks will state that enzymes lower activation energy by one or more of or a combination of four mechanisms: (1) proximity and orientation, (2) covalent catalysis, (3) strain and distortion, and (4) acid-base catalysis. While all of these are correct, it must be remembered that it is not one or the other of these mechanisms, it is much more often a combination of these mechanisms that effect catalysis.

4.2.2. Proximity and Orientation

A good example of proximity and orientation is apparent in the enzyme glyceraldehyde 3-phosphate dehydrogenase. This enzyme catalyzes the conversion of glyceraldehyde 3-phosphate to 1,3-bisphosphoglycerate in the presence of the coenzyme NAD^+. In order for the aldehyde to be oxidized to the acid form, it must be bound to the enzyme in close proximity to the oxidant, NAD^+. This, however, is not only a case of proximity, but it is also a case of covalent catalysis since the first reaction of the glyceraldehyde 3-phosphate is to form a thiohemiacetal with a specific cysteine of the enzyme molecule. This may be seen in Figure 1-21.

4.2.3. Covalent Catalysis

The previous section is primarily to emphasize approximation, but it also shows a necessity for covalent catalysis. A more general example of covalent catalysis found in most textbooks is that of proteolysis—for example, the action of chymotrypsin.

Kinetics of the reaction catalyzed by chymotrypsin using a synthetic substrate is shown below (see Figure 1-22). The product measured spectrophotometrically is the *p*-nitrophenylate ion.

Each curve represents product formation under conditions when substrate is added to different concentrations of enzyme. The kinetic pattern is that observed from reactions that typically show "burst" kinetics. The initial phase of the reaction shows a rapid release of one product the amount of which is equivalent to the amount of enzyme present followed by a slower rate of release of the second product – a rate that is also proportional to the amount of enzyme present. This type of kinetic pattern is typical of reactions where a covalent intermediate is formed rapidly upon substrate interaction, followed by a subsequently slower rate characterized by the release of product from the enzyme. In the case of chymotrypsin as well as other "serine-type" proteases, the reaction mechanism would be a two-step reaction of the following kind:

p-Nitrophenylacetate + Enz →
p-Nitrophenolate + acetyl-Enz

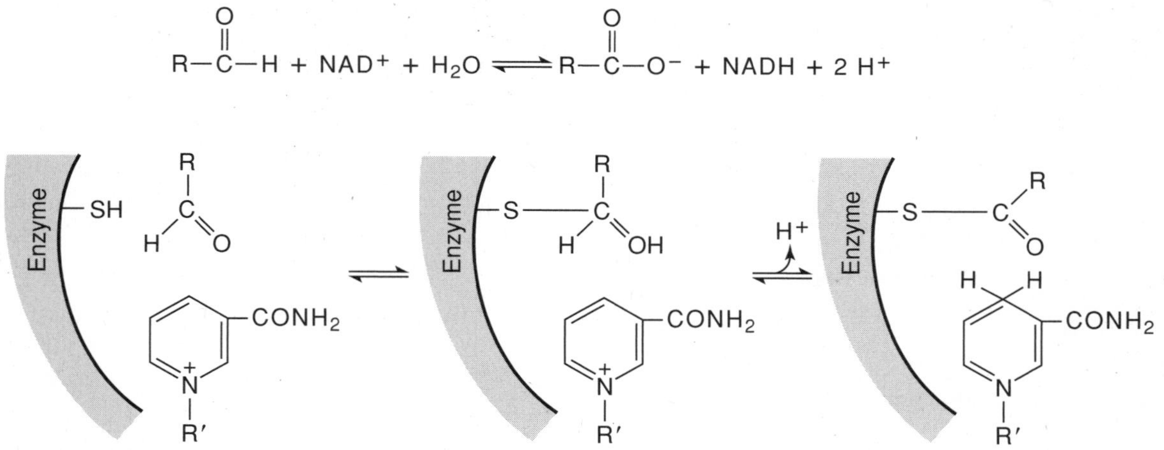

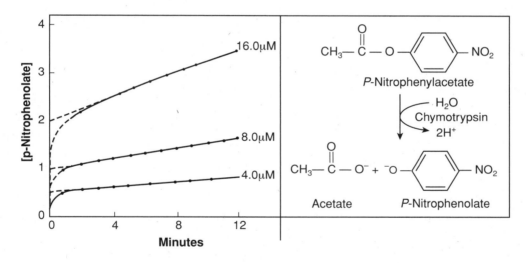

Figure 1-21. Formation of a thiohemiacetal as an initial step in the glyceraldehyde 3-phosphate dehydrogenase reaction.
(Adapted from Stryer, L., *Biochemistry,* Third Edition, W. H. Freeman and Company, New York, 1998, p. 367.)

Figure 1-22. Kinetics of hydrolysis of p-nitrophenylacetate by chymotrypsin.

The *p*-nitrophenolate ion released at the beginning of the reaction is in direct proportion to the amount of enzyme present. The second slower phase reflects the fact that the rate-limiting step is hydrolysis of the acetyl group from the enzyme.

$$\text{Acetyl-Enz} + H_2O \rightarrow H^+ + \text{Acetate} + \text{Enz}$$

It follows that further product (the chromophore) cannot be formed until there is free enzyme with which the substrate can react. The second phase of this reaction is the rate-limiting step. Thus, enzymes of this type facilitate reactions by altering the pathway and using some of its acidic and basic groups to catalyze release of the acyl group from the enzyme. Clearly, covalent catalysis in this case is also accompanied by acid-base catalysis. In all serine proteases, there is a specific serine within the protein structure that has a specific affinity for ester bond formation. For chymotrypsin, it is serine-195. Its hydroxyl group, as in others, is made more chemically active through interaction with a "catalytic triad" consisting (almost exclusively) of aspartate, histidine, and serine.

A selected list of serine proteases is given in the following table (see Table 1-4).

Table 1-4.
Selected List of Serine Proteases

Protease	Function	Possible side effects of defective action
Factor IXa	Blood coagulation	Various types
Factor VIIa	Blood coagulation	of clotting
Factor Xa	Blood coagulation	disorders.
Factor Xia	Blood coagulation	
Factor XIIa	Blood coagulation	
Plasma kallikrein	Blood coagulation	
Protein C (activated)	Blood coagulation	
Thrombin	Blood coagulation	
Trypsin	Digestion	Pancreatitis
Enteropeptidase	Digestion	
Elastase	Digestion	
Chymotrypsin	Digestion	
Acrosin	Fertilization	Infertility
Cathepsin G	Extracellular	
Granulocyte elastase	protein and peptide	
Mast cell chymases	degradation.	

4.2.4. Strain and Distortion

This mechanism refers to a distortion of the substrate to make it more nearly like the transition state. Strain is brought about by binding forces that hold the substrate in place at the active site of the enzyme. A good example of this is the enzyme lysozyme and its substrate.

This diagram (Figure 1-23) is a near linear representation of a substrate for lysozyme. Lysozyme cleaves polysaccharides of cell walls of some bacteria. Six of the polysaccharide groups fit across the active site cleft of lysozyme and it cleaves this polysaccharide between the D- and E-ring groups.

4.2.5. Acid-Base Catalysis

Acid-base catalysis was initially referred to as a separate mechanism for enzyme rate enhancement and, more specifically, with reference to hydrolytic type of reactions. As more detailed information becomes available on structure and mechanism of enzyme action, it also becomes clearer that acid-base catalysis exists in many different types of reactions and that it may be more appropriate to define acid-base catalysis as a more general mechanism by which many chemical reactions are facilitated. Many of these reactions will be discussed in other places in this book. Remember that acid-base catalysis in most biochemical reactions is effected by specific groups that exist as part of the structure of enzymes as conjugate acids of weak bases or groups that can function as acceptors of electrons. Some biologically

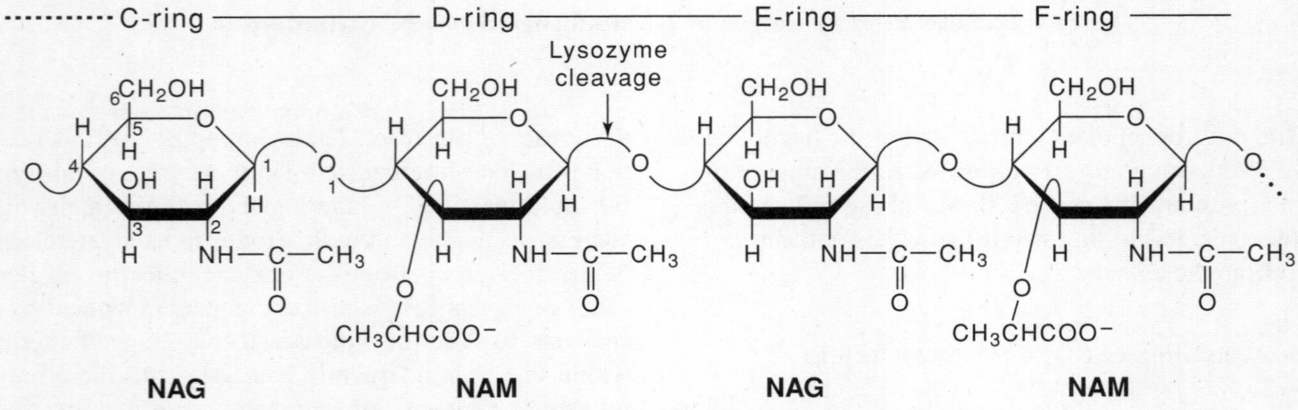

Figure 1-23. A representative structure of a substrate for lysozyme.
NAG is N-acetylglucosamine; NAM is N-acetylmuramic acid.
(Adapted from Voet, D., Voet, J. D., and Pratt, C. W., *Biochemistry*, 2nd Edition, John Wiley & Sons, Inc., New York, 2006, p. 331.)

important nucleophilic groups and electrophiles are shown in Figure 1-24.

When these groups exist within the active sites of enzymes, they may play important roles in the overall catalytic process of acid-base catalysis. The active site or catalytic sites of enzymes are discrete regions formed within the tertiary structure of the protein due to its unique folding. This structure is dictated by the amino acid sequence, although other proteins called heat shock proteins and/or chaperones often assist in ensuring effective and proper folding.

4.3. Selected List of Coenzymes and Their Roles in Catalysis

The number of active groups necessary to catalyze all of the functions necessary in cellular metabolism does not always reside in the side-chain structures of the protein. Other groups are often necessary to effect some of the chemistry and to stabilize the transition state and/or maintain other reactants in a proper redox state. These other molecules are referred to as **coenzymes** or **cofactors**.

Coenzymes generally are nonprotein compounds that aid and/or participate in the reaction. They may

be vitamins, metal ions, or other molecules like ATP. Depending on their ease of binding and dissociation from the enzyme during the course of the reaction, they may function either as cosubstrates, if they dissociates from the enzyme during the course of the reaction and can participate in other reactions, or as prosthetic groups, if they are tightly bound to the enzyme and undergo the complete reaction cycle without dissociating from the enzyme. In the latter case, the active protein in combination with its coenzyme is referred to as the **holoenzyme**. Most water-soluble vitamins fit one or the other of these categories, but so does vitamin K, a "fat-soluble" vitamin. A list of some of the major types and functions of vitamins is shown below (Table 1-5). Examples of some of these, especially as they relate to acid-base chemistry and specific types of reactions that occur in biochemistry will also be demonstrated.

4.3.1. Classification of Enzymes by the Types of Reactions They Catalyze

In 1961, the *Report of the Commission on Enzymes of the International Union of Biochemistry* was published. The report contained recommendations for a standard nomenclature for enzymes, how their reactions are presented, and units of measurement. Although the list appears more complicated because of subdivisions of

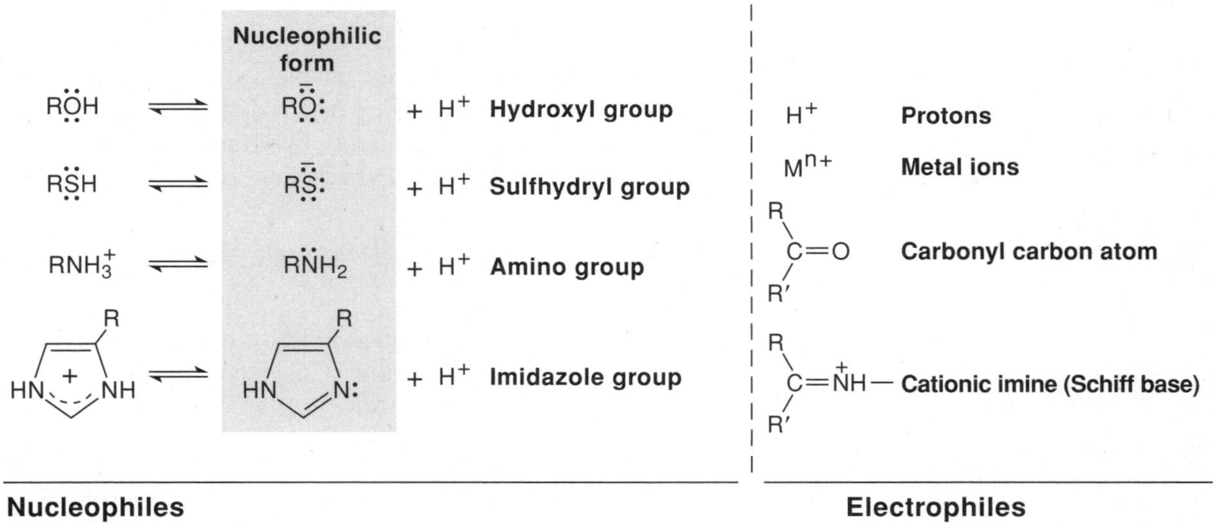

Figure 1-24. Nucleophilic and electrophilic groups in proteins.
(Adapted from Voet, D., Voet, J. D., and Pratt, C. W., Fundamentals of *Biochemistry: Life at the Molecular Level.* John Wiley & Sons, New York, 2006, p. 326.)

Table 1-5.
Vitamins and Their Coenzyme Forms

Type	Coenzyme or active form	Function promoted
Water-soluble		
Thiamin	Thiamin Pyrophosphate (TPP)	Aldehyde group transfer
Riboflavin	Flavin mononucleotide (FMN)	Hydrogen-atom (electron transfer)
	Flavin adenine dinucleotide (FAD)	Hydrogen-atom (electron transfer)
Nicotinic acid	Nicotinamide adenine dinucleotide (NAD)	Hydrogen-atom (electron transfer)
	Nicotinamide adenine dinucleotide (NADP)	Hydrogen-atom (electron transfer)
Pantothenic acid	Coenzyme A (CoA)	Acyl-group transfer
Pyridoxine	Pyridoxal phosphate	Amino-group transfer
Biotin	Biocytin	Carboxyl group transfer
Folic acid	Tetrahydrofolic acid	One-carbon-group transfer
Vitamin B12	Coenzyme B12 (Cobalamin)	1, 2 shift of hydrogen atoms
Lipoic acid	Lipoyllysine	Hydrogen-atom & acyl-group transfer
Ascorbic acid	Dihydroascorbic acid	Cofactor in hydroxylation
Fat-soluble		
Vitamin A	11-cis-Retinal	Phototransduction (visual cycle)
Vitamin D	1,25-Dihydroxychole-calciferol	Calcium and phosphate metabolism
Vitamin E		Antioxidant
Vitamin K	Dihydroquinone (reduced)	Protein (glutamyl) carboxylation

reactions, there are only six classes of enzymes that affect these reactions. The enzymes are (1) oxidoreductases, (2) transferases, (3) hydrolases, (4) lyases, (5) isomerases, and (6) ligases (synthetases). Each enzyme that catalyzes one of these reactions is assigned a number that begins with the number of the class in the order listed above. There are, however, many subclasses, also assigned numbers, for each category that defines the enzyme uniquely. For example, an oxidoreductase acting on a –CH-OH group would have the first three numbers 1.1.1 when NAD^+ or $NADP^+$ are reductants. When a cytochrome is the reductant, the number would be 1.1.2. With O_2 as the acceptor, the number would be 1.1.3. A fourth number would define the enzyme more specifically.

Do not confuse lyases with ligases. **Lyases** are enzymes that remove groups from their substrates (not by hydrolysis), leaving double bonds, or that conversely add groups to double bonds. **Ligases**, also known as **synthetases**, are enzymes that catalyze the joining together of two molecules coupled with the breakdown of a pyrophosphate bond in ATP or a similar "high energy" triphosphate compound.

Examples of reactions catalyzed by specific classes of enzymes and their coenzyme requirements are discussed below.

4.3.1.1. Oxidoreductases.
A typical 1.1-type oxidoreductase is the oxidation of an alcohol, like ethanol, to an aldehyde. The second "1" after the period means that it belongs to the subclass of enzymes that uses a pyridine nucleotide as an oxidant or a reductant. The reaction

$$CH_3CH_2OH + NAD^+ \leftrightarrow CH_3CHO + NADH + H^+$$

may be represented in terms of a chemical mechanism, as shown in Figure 1-25.

Three important points are emphasized about this reaction: it is acid-base catalyzed (note that *B:* abstracts a proton from the H—O— group of the alcohol), the reaction occurs in a stereospecific manner, and the H— of the —C—H bond ends up on the 4-position of the pyridine ring of NADH.

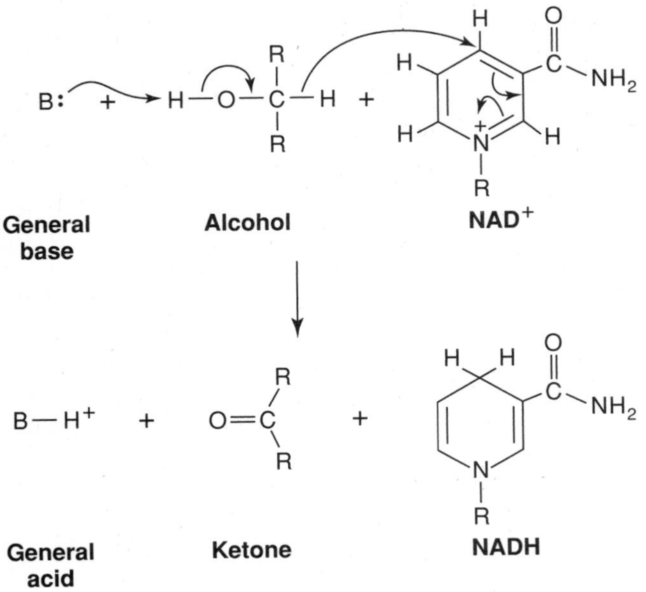

General base — Alcohol — NAD⁺

General acid — Ketone — NADH

Figure 1-25. Example of an oxidoreductase catalyzed reaction.
(Adapted from Voet, D. and Voet, J. D., *Biochemistry*, John Wiley & Sons, New York, 1990, p. 400.)

The two hydrogen atoms at position 4 in NADH were originally designated as H_A (now known as ***pro*-R**) and H_B (now known **as *pro*-S**), and the two sides of the nicotinamide ring as **A** and **B** (see Figure 1-26). Alcohol dehydrogenase, for example, always removes the H_A (*pro*-R) hydrogen, and 3-phosphoglyceraldehyde dehydrogenase removes the H_B (*pro*-S) hydrogen from NADH.

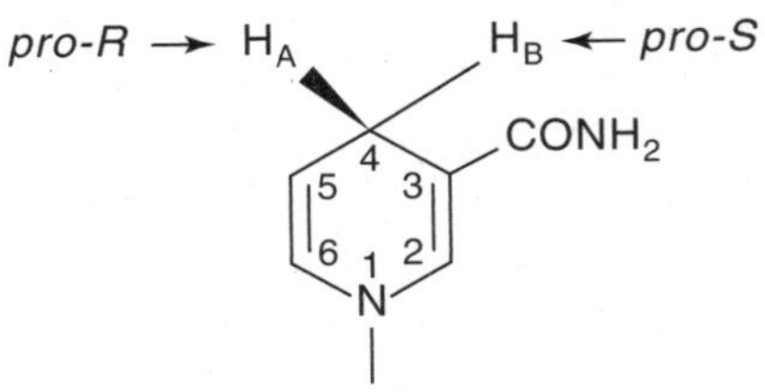

Figure 1-26. Structure of NADH showing orientation of the pro-chiral hydrogens.

4.3.1.2. Transferases.

A typical transferase reaction is the transfer of the terminal (γ) phosphate of ATP. The following example (Figure 1-27) is that of hexokinase.

The chemistry of this reaction is that of a Sn2-type reaction. The transfer results in a conversion of configuration of the original phosphate upon transfer to the glucose molecule.

4.3.1.3. Hydrolases.

Examples of hydrolases have already been discussed (i.e., chymotrypsin and lysozyme, both of which catalyze acid-base reactions in addition to carrying out covalent catalysis and strain and distortion, respectively).

4.3.1.4. Lyases.

A carbon-oxygen lyase identified as 4.2.1.2, L-malate hydro-lyase or fumarase catalyzes the following reaction:

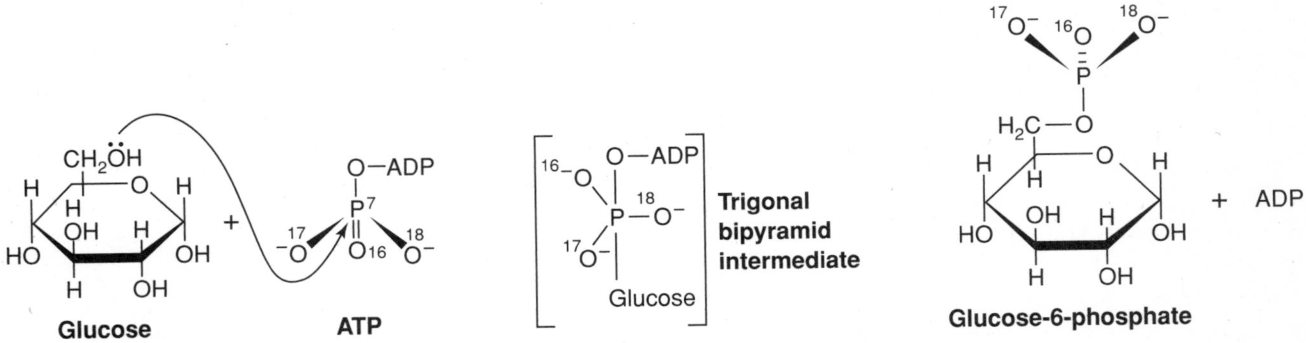

Figure 1-27. Example of a transferase catalyzed reaction.
(Adapted from Voet, D. and Voet, J. D., *Biochemistry*, John Wiley & Sons, New York, 1990, p. 400.)

$$^-OOC—CHOHCH_2COO^- \leftrightarrow {}^-OOC—CH=CH—COO^- + H_2O$$

This reaction also requires base catalysis. Experiments suggest that the mechanism by which the substrate L-malate sits in the active site is as shown below (Figure 1-28), where *B:* represents a base involved in the catalytic process.

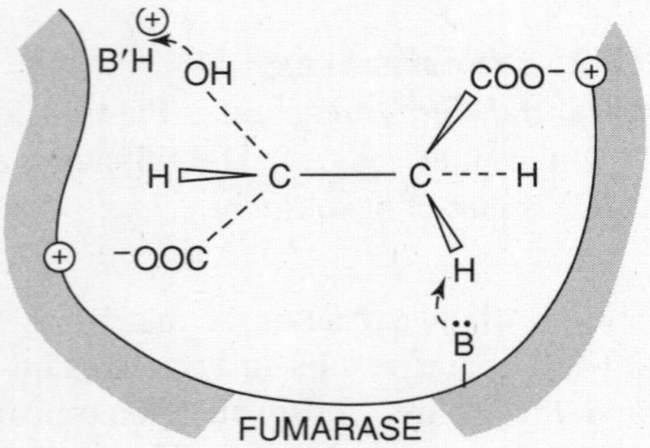

Figure 1-28. Example of a lyase catalyzed reaction.
(Adapted from Dixon, M and Webb, E. C.,
Enzymes, Third Edition, p. 318.)

4.3.1.5. Isomerases.

Isomerases catalyze a wide variety of reactions, such as conversion of a keto- to an aldo- form of a hexose, inversion of asymmetric groups such as L to D forms of amino acids, and other types of reactions where the mass and empirical formula of the compound is unchanged but the arrangement (or position) of atoms in the compound is changed.

This reaction (see Figure 1-29) also shows the general use of a nucleophile on the enzyme to abstract a proton from the substrate to effect the chemical conversion.

Another type of isomerization reaction that involves a free radical mechanism and is particularly important in the oxidation of odd chain fatty acids and in catabolism of some branch-chain amino acids is conversion of methymalonyl coenzyme A to succinyl coenzyme A. This conversion is shown in Figure 1-30, along with the structure of vitamin B12 (cobalamin).

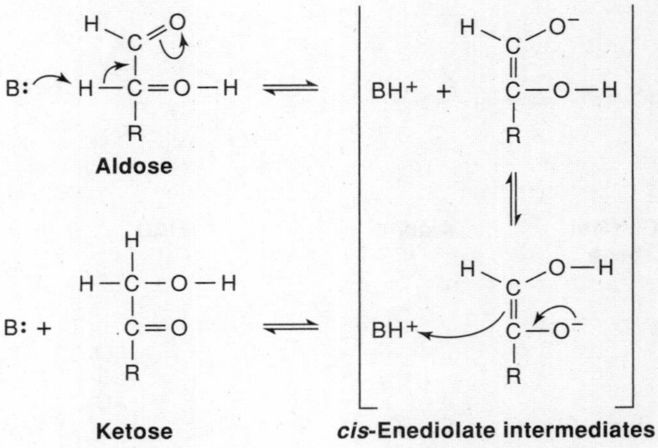

Figure 1-29. Example of an isomerase catalyzed reaction.
(Adapted from Voet, D. and Voet, J. D., *Biochemistry*, John Wiley & Sons, New York, 1990, p.401.)

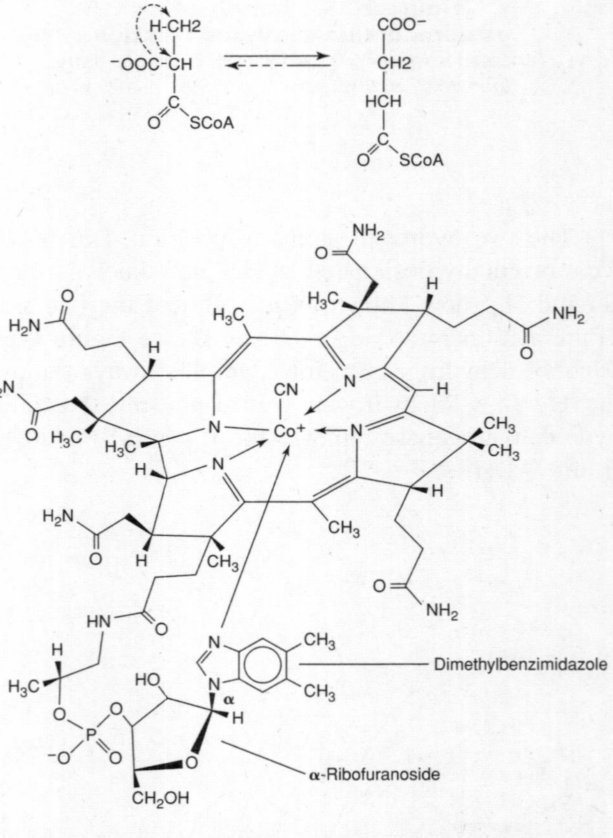

Figure 1-30. Example of a mutase catalyzed reaction—a subclass of the isomerase classification of enzymes. This reaction also shows the involvement of vitamin B12 (cobalamin) in catalysis.

4.3.1.6. Ligases.

This class of enzymes catalyzes the linking of two molecules, coupled with the utilization of energy obtained from the breaking of "high energy" bonds such as in ATP and/or its equivalent. Many enzymes in this class are referred to as *synthetases*. This term is used exclusively for enzymes that perform ligase reactions requiring the input of energy from pyrophosphate-like bond cleavage. Other enzymes that join two molecules without the requirement for "high energy" phosphate bond cleavage are referred to as *synthases*.

An enzyme of this class that also uses a vitamin as a cofactor is pyruvate carboxylase (EC 6.4.1.1, Pyruvate: CO_2 ligase(ADP)). The vitamin is biotin, which is attached to the enzyme by a peptide linkage involving the carboxyl group of biotin and an ε-amino group of a lysine residue of the enzyme (see Figure 1-31). Biotin is a prosthetic group of this enzyme.

Concepts emphasized in this section have included the relationships between thermodynamics and biochemical reactions, the importance of the transition state in both chemical and enzymatic reactions, general mech-

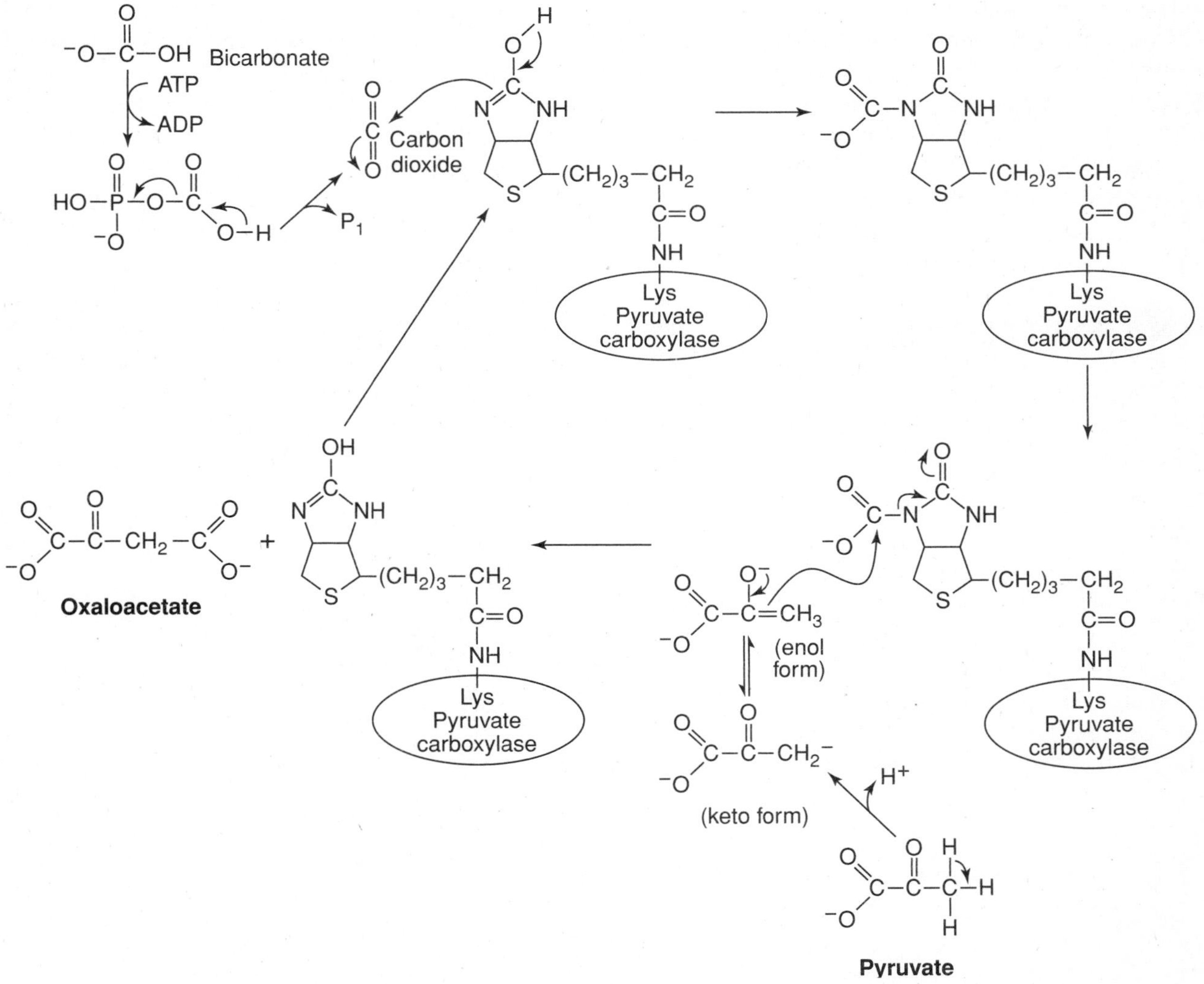

Figure 1-31. Pyruvate carboxylase is an example of a ligase catalyzed reaction.
(Adapted from Figure 1-15-13, p. 466: Lehninger, A. L., Nelson, D. L., and Cox, M. M.,
Principles of Biochemistry, Second Edition, Worth Publishers, Inc., New York, 1993.)

anisms of enzyme catalysis and how they facilitate attainment of the transition state, and how a selected group of vitamins participate in effecting catalysis. Many of these points may be emphasized again in other sections.

Another vitamin whose mechanism of action is worthy of consideration as a coenzyme is that of the fat-soluble vitamin, vitamin K. It catalyzes a carboxylation reaction, but since that reaction does not require the use of energy from a compound like ATP, it does not fit the ligase category of enzyme action. Vitamin K is an essential coenzyme/cofactor in the carboxylation of glutamyl residues in specific classes of proteins. The carboxylation occurs at the γ-position. It is presumed to function as a very strong base and to abstract the pro-S H atom (proton) as part of the mechanism of its action. The overall process is complex, but the following diagram (Figure 1-32) shows some of the essential elements. The product is the dicarboxylic acid residue called *Gla* for γ-carboxyglutamyl residue.

5. ENZYME KINETICS

An analysis of enzyme kinetics historically can be traced back to several investigators. Considering modern-day usage, it appears necessary to emphasize

for this review only Briggs and Haldane's analysis (G. E. Briggs and J.B.S. Haldane, 1925, *Biochem. J.* 19, 338–339), Michaelis and Menten (L. Michaelis and M. L. Menten, 1913, *Biochem. Z.* 49, 333–369), and Lineweaver and Burk (H. Lineweaver and D. Burk, 1934, *J. Amer. Chem. Soc.* 56, 658–666). This discussion will be general, but those more interested in historical development may wish to start by checking the references listed.

Michaelis and Menten treated the first step of an enzymatic reaction as an equilibrium reaction between substrate and enzyme. Briggs and Haldane introduced the theory of steady-state treatment for enzymatic reactions, and Lineweaver and Burk rearranged the Michaelis-Menten equation such that information about the values of the important constants that defined the shapes of Michaelis-Menten curves could be calculated, although *estimated* would be a more accurate term. Currently, computational methods can be used to estimate the values of these kinetic constants with the same degree of accuracy as measurements of the independent ($[S]$) and dependent (v_i) variables. Graphical presentations as introduced by Lineweaver and Burk and others, however, make interpretation of perturbations from normal behavior easier and are of general use. This discussion will begin with the Michaelis-Menten equation.

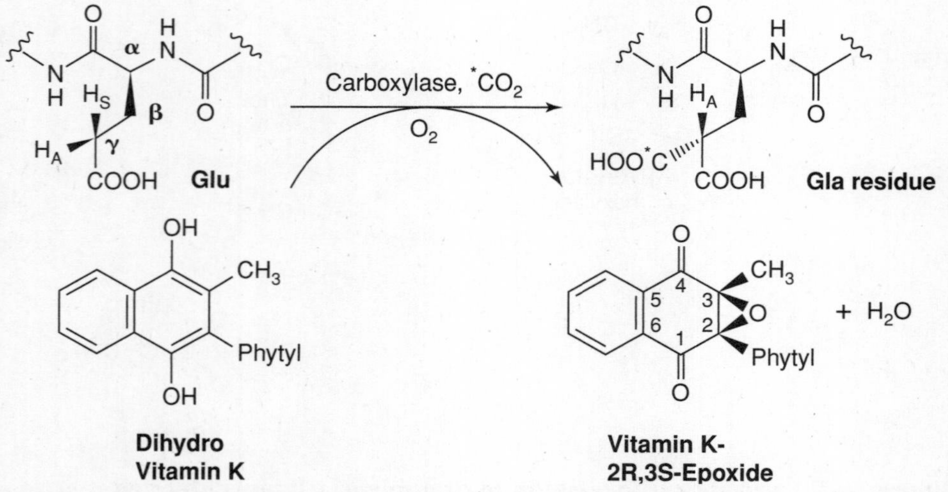

Figure 1-32. Coenzyme role of vitamin K in carboxylation of glutamyl residues in proteins.
(Adapted from Kuliopulus, A., Hubbard, B. R., Lam, Z., Koski, I. J., Furie, B., Furie, B. C., and Walsh, C. T., Dioxygen transfer during vitamin K-dependent carboxylase catalysis. *Biochemistry* 31:7722, 1992.)

The major assumption is that when a substrate reacts with an enzyme, an enzyme-substrate complex is formed, and it is that complex that leads to formation of product and free enzyme. That is the cycle that is repeated during the course of an enzyme catalyzed reaction. This series of reactions may be written as follows:

$$E + S \underset{k_2}{\overset{k_1}{\rightleftarrows}} ES \xrightarrow{k_3} E + P$$

where reaction velocity depends on the concentration of the ES complex. Thus,

$$v_i = k_3[ES]$$

There is special significance placed on the value v_i, which means initial velocity. That is the only time when the measured velocity of the reaction most closely approximates that expected for the substrate concentration used in the reaction.

The course of the reaction shown above with enzyme and substrate suggests that at any constant enzyme concentration and increasing concentration of substrate, the rate of the reaction approaches a maximum. This is consistent with the theory of mass action in that as [S] increases, so would the concentration of ES until essentially all of E is in the ES complex. Thus, a plot of v_i versus [S] is a hyperbolic curve (see Figure 1-33).

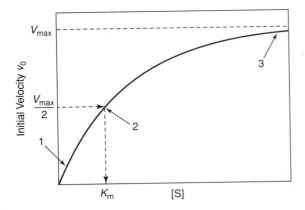

Figure 1-33. Plot of initial velocity versus substrate concentration.
(Adapted from Devlin, T. M, Editor, *Textbook of Biochemistry with Clinical Correlations*, Fourth Edition, Wiley-Liss, New York, 1997, p. 138.)

This curve is defined by the Michaelis-Menten equation, which is

$$v_i = \frac{V_{max}[S]}{K_m + [S]}$$

V_{max} is defined as the product of $k_3[ES]$ when all E is in the ES complex and can thus be written as $V_{max} = k_3[E]_T$. This occurs at the point marked 3 in the diagram (Figure 1-33). K_m is defined as the concentration of S that gives half-maximum velocity. The point marked 2 in the diagram represents this. The third significant region in that diagram is marked 1 and is best understood after an analysis of major assumptions made in deriving this equation.

The rate of an enzymatic reaction depends on the concentration of the ES complex. There is not a generally easy way to measure the ES concentration directly, so its concentration must be determined using components of the reaction mixture that can be measured. Those are [S], v_i, and sometimes [E]. It is not necessary to measure [E] directly, but it is necessary to maintain it at a constant concentration during analyses of K_m and V_{max}. So, for all practical purposes, the only things easily measurable are [S] and v_i. Thus, the objective is to determine indirectly how the rate depends on [ES]. An important assumption is that the process as shown in the equation above represents a series of steady-state reactions, namely, that initial rate measurements are made when the rate of change of [ES] = 0 (a Briggs and Haldane contribution). This can be represented mathematically as

$$d[ES]/dt = 0$$

which means that the rate of formation of [ES] is equal to its rate of disappearance. Included in this equation are the rate of formation and the rates of disappearance of [ES], it thus becomes

$$k_1[E]_{free}[S]_{free} = k_2[ES] + k_3[ES]$$

because there is one reaction that leads to formation of [ES] and two that lead to the disappearance of [ES].

Formation: $d[ES]/dt = k_1[E]_{free}[S]_{free}$

Disappearance: $d[ES]/dt = -k_2[ES] - k_3[ES]$

Thus, when the rate of formation of *ES* equals the rate of disappearance of *ES*, these two rates are equal to each other. Note also that the rate of formation of *ES* is defined by a second-order rate constant, and the rates of *ES* disappearance are defined by first-order rate constants. This is an important consideration (as mentioned above) in defining the units of K_m. The concentration of *S* is also generally much larger than the concentration of *E*, but the affinity of binding of *S* to *E* is such that stoichiometric binding of *E* to *S* does not occur when $[E] = [S]$.

It follows, therefore, that if $[S]$ is always much larger than $[E]$, it will also be much larger than $[ES]$, such that $[S]_{free} \approx [S]$. The one condition where that is most nearly true is at the very beginning of the reaction, and that is why only measurements of initial velocities are valid for use in the Michaelis-Menten equation.

It is not correct to make the same assumption for $[E]_{free}$, so the concentration of *ES* must be considered, and the expression for $[E]_{free}$ becomes ($E_{total} - ES$). The steady-state equation thus becomes

$$k_1([E]_T - [ES])[S] - k_2[ES] - k_3[ES] = 0 .$$

or in its expanded form, where $[E]_T = [E]_{total}$

$$k_1[E]_T[S] = [ES](k_1[S] + k_2 + k_3) .$$

[ES] can now be expressed in terms of measurable quantities as follows:

$$[ES] = \frac{k_1[E]_T[S]}{k_1[S] + k_2 + k_3} .$$

Since the velocity of the overall reaction is expressed as $v = k_3[ES]$, the equation for reaction velocity becomes

$$v = k_3\left(\frac{k_1[E]_T[S]}{k_1[S] + k_2 + k_3}\right) .$$

Multiplying by k_3 and dividing numerator and denominator by k_1 gives

$$v = \frac{k_3[E]_T[S]}{[S] + \frac{k_2 + k_3}{k_1}} .$$

This may be written as

$$v = \frac{V_{max}[S]}{[S] + K_m} ,$$

which is the Michaelis-Menten equation. Implicit in the Michaelis Menten equation are two definitions: the first is that $V_{max} = k_3[E]_T$, and the other is that $K_m = (k_2 + k_3)/k_1$.

The dimension or unit of k_3 is that of a first-order rate constant, time^{-1} (t^{-1}), and V_{max} is directly dependent on the concentration of total enzyme. Its units are M/t. Initial velocity also fits the same category and shows a first-order dependence on enzyme concentration.

The dimensions or units of K_m are concentration (i.e., molar concentrations). It can be seen from the equation representing the reaction pathway that k_2 and k_3 are first-order rate constants, and k_1 is a second-order rate constant with units of $M^{-1}t^{-1}$. Thus, the ratio of the constants that make up the K_m is $t^{-1} \div M^{-1}t^{-1}$ and is equal to M.

In reference to Figure 1-34, it was stated earlier that the region labeled 1 also has significance. In that region of the Michaelis-Menten plot, the reaction essentially follows first-order kinetics. In that region, $[S]$ is significantly less than K_m, and the Michaelis-Menten equation reduces to

$$v = \frac{V_{max}[S]}{K_m}$$

and is equivalent to

$$v = \left(\frac{V_{max}}{K_m}\right)[S] .$$

V_{max}/K_m has the unit t^{-1} and therefore approximates that of a first-order rate constant. This fact is taken advantage of in the use of enzymes to determine concentrations of specific enzyme substrates in complex mixtures such as occur in many clinical laboratory situations. For example, the first-order-rate equation shown above may be written

$$\ln[S] = -\left(\frac{V_{max}}{K_m}\right)(t) + \ln[S]_0.$$

where the ratio of V_{max}/K_m is equivalent to k. Thus, a plot of $\ln[S]$ versus time (t) allows a calculation of the value of $[S]_0$, the starting concentration of $[S]$, since the Y-intercept = $\ln[S]_0$.

Similar manipulations of the relative values of K_m to $[S]$ will provide proof of the validity of the other two points of emphasis in Figure 1-33 (i.e., when $K_m = [S]$ and when $[S] \gg K_m$).

5.1. Practical Aspect of Initial Velocity Measurement

The following diagram (Figure 1-34) shows that for a particular set of conditions, $[ES]$ is low and remains relatively constant over a short period of time. During that time period, the rates of product $[P]$ formation and substrate $[S]$ disappearance remain relatively constant. It is during this time period that a measure of velocity of the reaction is considered to be a measure of the initial velocity, v_i. It is the velocity measured during those time periods that is plotted versus $[S]$ in Michaelis-Menten kinetics and that allows construction of the substrate saturation curve, which has been discussed. The second of the two diagrams presented (Figure 1-35) is essentially the same as the first, but uses different concentrations of substrate. It should be clear from the tangents of the lines near the ordinate that the period of time when $d[ES]/dt \approx 0$ will vary. So, initial velocity measurements must be made within the correct time interval. Note also that the reaction pathway used as a model for the derivation of the Michaelis-Menten equation did not consider the overall reverse reaction, namely, $E + P \rightarrow EP \leftrightarrow ES$ ... There is only one point in time when $[S]$ is known, and that is at the very beginning of the reaction. Thus, it is important to measure velocity as early as is practical after the ES complex is formed.

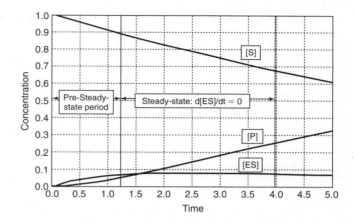

Figure 1-34. Diagrammatic representation of substrate disappearance and product formation during pre-steady-state and steady-state periods of an enzyme-catalyzed reaction.

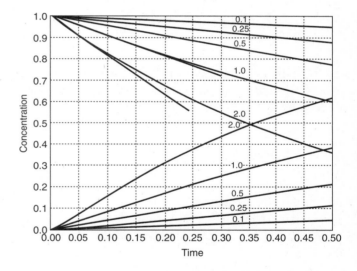

Figure 1-35. Simulation of initial velocity measurements as a function of substrate concentration. Lines at the top of the graph represent substrate disappearance at different initial values of $[S]$. Straight lines drawn from the initial time periods represent initial velocity and would be the periods where $d[ES]/dt = 0$. The bottom part of the graph is a mirror image of the top and represents product formation. Numbers on the lines simulates different values of $[S]$ for each set of curves.

It is assumed that formation of that complex is rapid. There is a pre-steady-state phase that can be analyzed using specialized equipment.

The line labeled [ES] at the bottom of the graph shows that the concentration of [ES] is small and does not change significantly during the steady-state period.

During that period, straight lines are obtained for substrate concentration rate changes and can be used to generate the Michaelis-Menten curve as shown above.

5.2. Lineweaver-Burk Plots

Lineweaver and Burk made the observation that the reciprocal of the Michaelis-Menten equation is the equation for a straight line

$$\frac{1}{v_i} = \frac{K_m}{V_{max}[S]} + \frac{1}{V_{max}}$$

where the slope of the line is represented by the ratio K_m/V_{max} and the intercept on the y-axis is equal to $1/V_{max}$.

V_{max} is the reciprocal of the y-intercept, and K_m can be estimated either by calculation, namely, slope divided by the intercept on the y-axis,

$$\frac{K_m}{V_{max}} \div \frac{1}{V_{max}} = \frac{K_m}{V_{max}} x \frac{V_{max}}{1} = K_m$$

or graphically because it is the limit of the plot of $1/v_i$ versus $1/[S]$ when $1/v_i = 0$, as shown by the arrow in the lower left quadrant of the above Figure 1-36.

$$0 = \frac{K_m}{V_{max}}\left(\frac{1}{[S]}\right) + \frac{1}{V_{max}}$$

or rearrange the equation to give

$$-\frac{K_m}{V_{max}}\left(\frac{1}{[S]}\right) = \frac{1}{V_{max}}.$$

Divide both sides of the equation by K_m/V_{max} gives $-1/[S] = 1/K_m$.

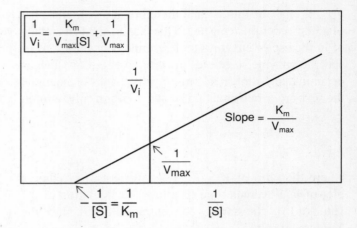

Figure 1-36. Lineweaver-Burk plot of initial velocity versus substrate concentration.

5.3. Diagnostic Value of Lineweaver-Burk Plots: Enzyme Inhibition

5.3.1. Classification of the Types of Enzyme Inhibitors

Enzymes show specificity for specific substrates or for specific classes of substrates as may be surmised from the classification schemes given above. Compounds that interact with them in specific ways may also inhibit them. The following table (Table 1-6) lists some of the types of inhibitors normally encountered.

There are basically two types of enzyme inhibitors: reversible and irreversible. A reversible inhibitor is characterized by a dissociation constant (K_i), which is defined by the ratio of the rate of dissociation of the EI complex over the rate of formation of the EI complex, k_{-1}/k_{+1}. Since the units of k_{+1} are $M^{-1}t^{-1}$ and the units of k_{-1} are t^{-1}, units of the dissociation constant, K_i, are M^{-1}. The expression defining K_i is

$$K_i = \frac{k_{-1}}{k_{+1}} = \frac{[E][I]}{[EI]}.$$

The reaction defined by K_i is $E + I \xleftrightarrow{K_i} EI$. This equation is for a reversible competitive inhibitor. The

Table 1-6.
Classification of Enzyme Inhibitors

1.	**Reversible: Measure K_i (Dissociation constant)**
	a. Competitive
	b. Non-competitive
	c. Un-cmpetitive
2.	**Irreversible: Measure k_i (rate constant)**
	Effect of [S] on k_i(apparent)

	a. Competitive	decrease
	b. Non-competitive	none
	c. Un-competitive	increase

3.	**Examples of reversible & irreversible inhibitors:**
	a. Malonate & SDH (reversible)
	b. Iodoacetate & GA3PD (irreversible)
4.	**Special cases of inhibitor types:**
	a. Active site directed
	b. Transition-state analogs
	c. Mechanism-based (suicide)

SDH = succinate dehydrogenase; GA3PD = glyceraldehyde 3-phosphate dehydrogenase

format is the same for noncompetitive and uncompetitive inhibitors, but the forms of enzyme and/or enzyme complexes with which the inhibitor interacts will differ.

For a simple noncompetitive reversible inhibitor where the K_i is the same for inhibitor interaction with either free E or the ES complex, K_i for interaction with the free enzyme would be the same as written above. For inhibitor interaction with the ES complex, the numerical value of K_i would be the same, but it would also define the reactions $E + I \xleftrightarrow{K_i} EI$ and $ES + I \xleftrightarrow{K_i} ESI$ and would be represented by

$$K_i = \frac{[E][I]}{[EI]} + \frac{[ES][I]}{[ESI]}.$$

In the case of uncompetitive inhibition, the inhibitor interacts only with an intermediate in the reaction, and K_i would be represented by the expression

$$K_i = \frac{[ES][I]}{[ESI]}.$$

Discussions of the effects of inhibitors on Michaelis-Menten kinetics will involve those in class 1 where K_i values can be determined. Those would include competitive, noncompetitive, and uncompetitive. Malonate (under 3) is competitive, and so are active site directed and transition-state analogs. Mechanism-based (suicide) inhibitors are also competitive with substrate, but they result in irreversible inhibition of enzymes in a manner similar (so far as final results are concerned) to other competitive-type irreversible inhibitors. They are represented by the reaction shown with the rate constant, k_i.

A composite summary of the action of reversible inhibitors with enzymes is shown in the following diagram (Figure 1-37).

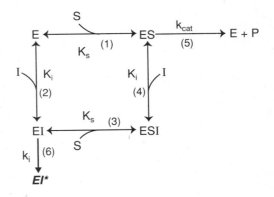

Figure 1-37. Graphic summary of the reactions between enzymes, substrates and various types of inhibitors.

Reactions 1 and 5 represent the normal course of reaction and would give a straight line in the Lineweaver-Burk plot as discussed. Reactions 1, 2, and 5 would represent the case for a competitive inhibitor. Reactions 1, 2, 3, 4, and 5 represent the reactions for a noncompetitive inhibitor. Reactions 1, 4, and 5 are those for an uncompetitive inhibitor; and reactions 1, 2, 5, and 6 for a mechanism-based (suicide) inhibitor or an active site directed irreversible inhibitor. In this idealized scheme, complexes containing inhibitor, EI and ESI, do not lead to product formation. It can be rec-

$$\frac{1}{v} = \left(\frac{K_m}{V_{max}}\right)\left(1+\frac{[I]}{Ki}\right)\frac{1}{[S]}+\left(\frac{1}{V_{max}}\right)$$

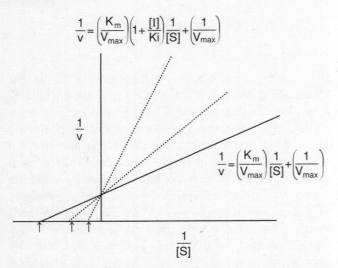

$$\frac{1}{v} = \left(\frac{K_m}{V_{max}}\right)\frac{1}{[S]}+\left(\frac{1}{V_{max}}\right)$$

Figure 1-38. Lineweaver-Burk plot for a competitive inhibitor. Note that V_{max} does not change for the competitive inhibitor. This means that the intercept on the y-axis remains the same, but the slope changes and hence the "apparent" K_m. The apparent K_m differs from the actual K_m by the factor $(1 + ([I]/K_i))$ as shown above. Arrows on the intercept on the abscissa show that the apparent K_m increases with increasing [I]. Remember that those are inverse values, and the closer the intercept is to zero, the larger the number.

$$\frac{1}{v} = \left(\frac{K_m}{V_{max}}\right)\left(1+\frac{[I]}{Ki}\right)\frac{1}{[S]}+\left(\frac{1}{V_{max}}\right)\left(1+\frac{[I]}{Ki}\right)$$

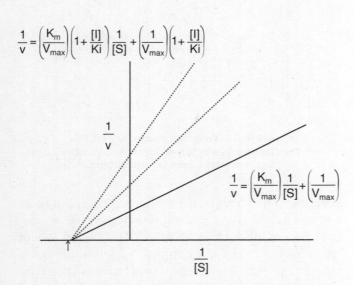

$$\frac{1}{v} = \left(\frac{K_m}{V_{max}}\right)\frac{1}{[S]}+\left(\frac{1}{V_{max}}\right)$$

Figure 1-39. Lineweaver-Burk plot for a noncompetitive inhibitor. In this case, both the slope and the intercept on the y-axis change, but the intercept on the x-axis does not change. A noncompetitive inhibitor does not change the K_m for the enzyme but simply reduces the amount of enzyme available to participate in the normal reaction.

$$\frac{1}{v} = \left(\frac{K_m}{V_{max}}\right)\frac{1}{[S]}+\left(\frac{1}{V_{max}}\right)\left(1+\frac{[I]}{Ki}\right)$$

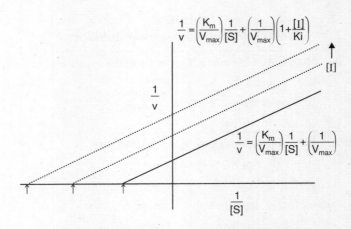

$$\frac{1}{v} = \left(\frac{K_m}{V_{max}}\right)\frac{1}{[S]}+\left(\frac{1}{V_{max}}\right)$$

Figure 1-40. Lineweaver-Burk plot for an uncompetitive inhibitor. For an uncompetitive inhibitor, the slope remains the same, but the intercept on the y-axis and the x-axis both change. Thus, the "apparent" K_m and the V_{max} also change. The arrows on the abscissa show that the apparent K_m for an uncompetitive inhibitor decreases with increasing inhibitor concentrations as indicated by the arrows being farther away from the zero point on the abscissa.

ognized from this scheme that competitive inhibitors react only with free enzyme, the same as substrate. Noncompetitive inhibitors react with any form of the enzyme because they bind at a site different from the substrate, and uncompetitive inhibitors react only with an intermediate (*ES* in the above scheme) of the reaction. These are summarized by Lineweaver-Burk plots and equations in figures (Figure 1-38, Figure 1-39, and Figure 1-40).

One fact that should have been noticed by now is that it does not matter whether it is the slope or the intercept that changes. The factor that causes the change is the same, namely,

$$\left(1+\frac{[I]}{K_i}\right).$$

Thus, for a competitive inhibitor, for example, the apparent K_m ($K_m{}^{app}$) contains the terms for the true K_m and the factor by which it is changed, as follows:

$$K_m^{app} = K_m\left(1+\frac{[I]}{K_i}\right)$$

where

$$K_i = \left(\frac{[I]}{\left(K_m^{app} / K_m \right) - 1} \right).$$

5.3.1.1. Mechanism-Based Inhibitors.

Mechanism-based inhibitors are like substrates and undergo partial reaction with the enzyme. They contain a potentially chemically active group that only becomes highly reactive during the course of the reaction, and it binds irreversibly with the enzyme and does not dissociate from it. Thus, the active site is blocked, and additional substrate can no longer interact with the enzyme. An example is the inhibition of GABA transaminase with the drug Vergabatrin®. See Figure 1-41.

Active site directed inhibitors have a chemically reactive group already attached. The molecule is attracted to the active site because it resembles substrate, but it is not active as a substrate. When it binds to the active site, the chemically reactive group binds, generally by covalent interaction, with a complementary reactive group within the active site and inhibits the enzyme.

6. TWO-SUBSTRATE REACTIONS

Most biochemical reactions require two or more substrates. Kinetic information can be obtained about their behavior also. It is necessary, however, to vary the concentration of only one substrate at a time. It is also possible to determine the order of binding of substrates and the release of products. Initial velocity measurements are still made varying the concentration of each substrate separately and also using products of the reaction (individually) as inhibitors of the forward reaction. Studies of this type show that there are basically two types of mechanisms for two-substrate reactions: sequential and double displacement or ping-pong type reactions. Amino transferases (pyridoxal phosphate requiring enzymes) generally fit the latter category. The following diagram (Figure 1-42) summarizes these reactions.

6.1. Sequential Reactions May Be Either Random or Ordered

The one thing that is common among sequential mechanisms is that reaction only occurs from a ternary complex. For random sequential reactions, it does not matter which substrate binds first or which product leaves

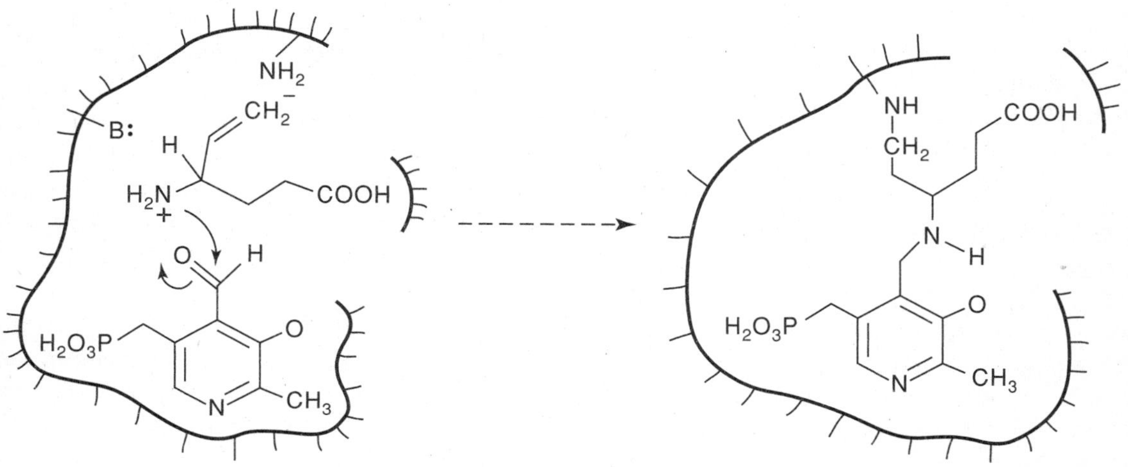

Figure 1-41. Mechanism-based inhibition of GABA transaminase by Vergabatrin®.

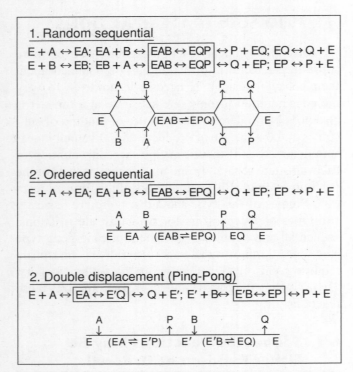

Figure 1-42. Mechanisms for two-substrate reactions. Each mechanism is shown as linear equations and as Cleland-type diagrams immediately below each set of equations.

first. There is a definite order of binding of substrates and a definite order of release of products for ordered sequential mechanisms. There are several diagnostic patterns of product inhibition for these type reactions. From the schemes above, it can be deduced that each product would be competitive with each substrate in the random sequential scheme, but only the product released last would be competitive with the first product binding the enzyme in an ordered sequential mechanism. What is the reason for this? Both bind to free enzyme.

6.2. Ping-Pong or Double-Displacement Reactions

Aminotransferases are enzymes that fit this category, but there are also many others. In all cases of this type, one substrate binds the enzyme and undergoes a chemical reaction in which it is transformed to product, but some component of the substrate remains attached to the enzyme, altering it in some way. For aminotransferases, the altered enzyme contains an amino group from the

substrate attached to its prosthetic group. The first product dissociates from the enzyme, and the second substrate binds to the altered enzyme. The altered enzyme transfers the bound group (amino group in aminotransferases) to the new substrate, and another product dissociates from the enzyme. During the last reaction, the original enzyme will have been regenerated.

6.3. Antibodies as Catalysts

Throughout this discussion, the importance of the transition state in catalysis has been emphasized directly or implied. It has also been emphasized that enzymes stabilize transition states during the course of their reactions. Primarily through the work of researchers such as Lerner, Schultz, and Benkovic, it has become apparent that antibodies could be raised against transition state analogs for various types of organic chemical reactions, and that some of those antibodies would have catalytic activity. The fact that some catalysis could occur in the presence of antibodies was in fact observed maybe as long as a century ago, but it remained an enigma. Possibly, this technology could not be exploited because of the lack of knowledge about enzyme mechanisms and how cells produced antibodies, and the inability to raise monoclonal antibodies.

Antibodies have among the highest binding affinities of any proteins for "foreign" objects. Thus, they became very attractive agents for transition-state stabilization. Most antibodies are raised naturally against other proteins and/or large foreign objects. To raise antibodies effectively against small molecules such as transition-state analogs for chemical catalysts, the analog is chemically attached to a highly antigenic molecule and injected, usually into mice. Monoclonal antibodies are isolated, some of which will most likely have the ability to bind the pure analog specifically and to facilitate catalysis using the appropriate substrate of the original reaction, provided also that they contained appropriate amino acid residues within the binding region to effect the necessary chemistry for the reaction to occur. A few classical organic chemical reactions that have been catalyzed by antibodies are shown in Figure 1-43. Antibodies were raised against the analogs shown beneath the brackets between substrates and products. The compounds shown within the brackets are the proposed/theoretical transition states for the reactions. In

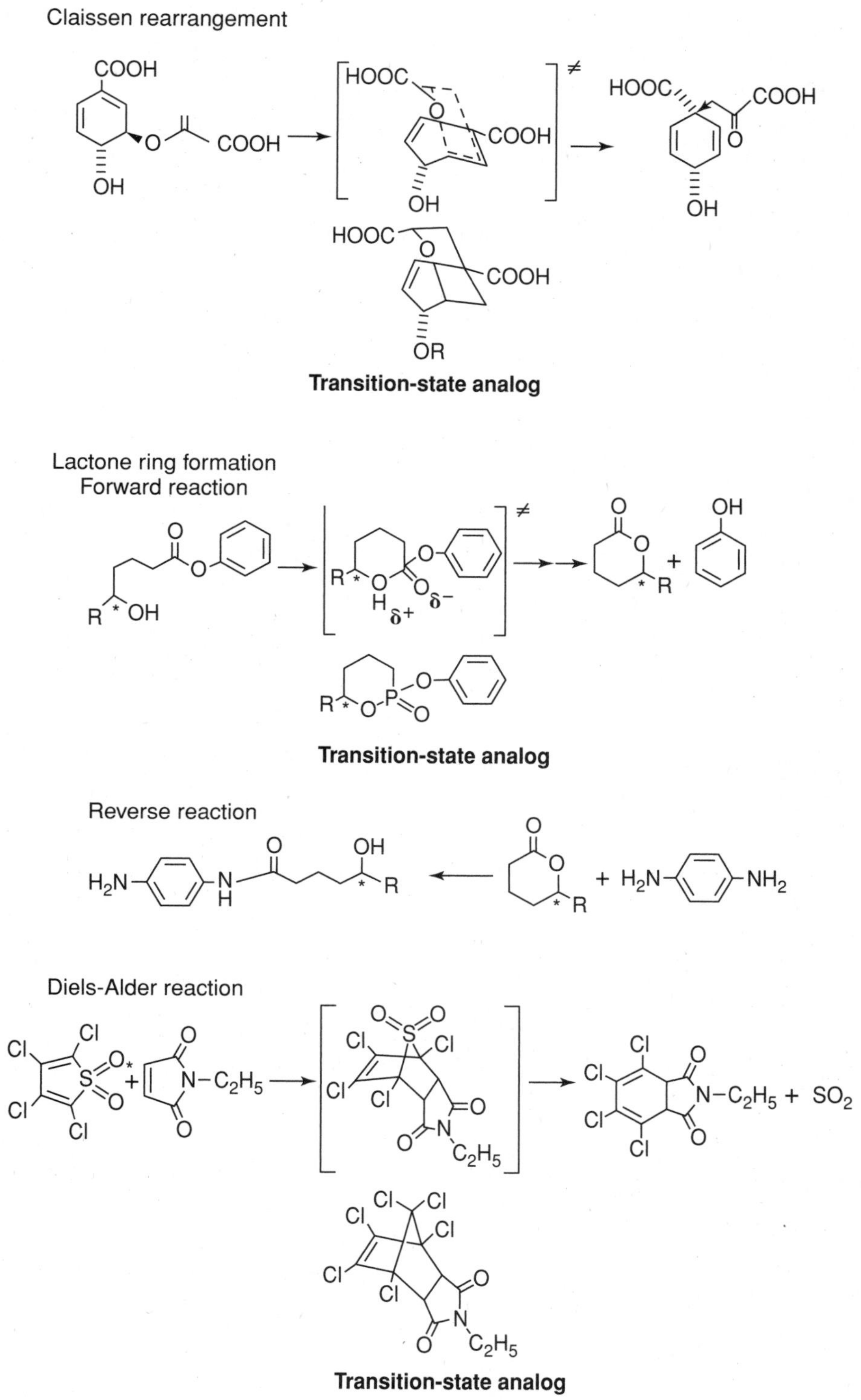

Claissen rearrangement

Transition-state analog

Lactone ring formation
Forward reaction

Transition-state analog

Reverse reaction

Diels-Alder reaction

Transition-state analog

Figure 1-43. Examples of transition-state analogs used to make catalytic antibodies for specific types of reactions.
(Adapted from the research of Lerner, R. A., Benkovic, S. J., and Schultz, P. G. (1991) "At the crossroads of chemistry and immunology: Catalytic antibodies", *Science* 252:659-667.)

theory, catalytic antibodies can be made for any reaction in which an appropriate transition-state analog can be made. **Catalytic antibodies** are frequently referred to as **abzymes**. The reaction scheme for abzymes is exactly the same as for Michaelis-Menten type kinetics and has been represented in the literature as follows, where k_{-1} is equivalent to k_2, and k_{cat} is equivalent to k_3.

$$A + S \underset{k_{-1}}{\overset{k_1}{\rightleftharpoons}} A \cdot S \overset{k_{cat}}{\longrightarrow} A + P$$

$$V = \frac{k_{cat}[A_T][S]}{K_M + [S]} \qquad K_M = \frac{k_{cat} + k_{-1}}{k_{-1}}$$

The same type of Michaelis-Menten saturation curves and Lineweaver-Burk plots would apply to abzyme-catalyzed reactions. Transition-state analogs would be among the best, if not *the* best, inhibitors for these reactions.

7. REGULATION OF ENZYMATIC ACTIVITY

Thousands of enzymatic reactions take place in a cell in order to keep it alive and viable. In order for the cell to utilize metabolites efficiently, methods exist to regulate the activity of certain enzymes in key positions of various metabolic pathways such that excessive intermediary metabolites will not be made in a wasteful manner.

7.1. Summary of Regulatory Mechanisms

Types of regulatory mechanisms that exist in cells may be summarized as follows.

A. Compartmentation: the transport of enzymes after synthesis directs them to specific subcellular compartments. The enzymes may follow normal Michaelis-Menten kinetics, but the environment in which they act places limits on their catalysis. For example, many hydrolyases exist in lysosomes where the environment is more acidic and favorable

to the reactions that they catalyze. Other enzymes may exist only in mitochondria, nuclei, and so forth.

B. Coarse control mechanisms: This involves the synthesis and degradation of enzymes. This type of regulation generally occurs at the genetic level where synthesis of enzymes may be required to metabolize specific compounds introduced by some means into the cell. Once that function is completed, the enzyme may be degraded.

C. Fine control mechanisms: This involves direct effects on the enzyme itself and may occur quickly. There are basically three types of fine control mechanisms that are functional in the regulation of metabolic pathways:

1. Protein-protein interaction

2. Covalent modification of amino acid residues of the protein

3. Allosteric regulation

An example of regulation of activity by protein-protein interaction is the enzyme cyclic-AMP (cAMP) protein kinase. This enzyme consists of four subunits, two of which are catalytic and two regulatory. The regulatory subunits block the catalytic sites, and the enzyme cannot function. cAMP binds to the regulatory subunits and causes a conformation change resulting in their dissociation from the catalytic subunits. The catalytic subunits are now active and free to function. This is represented in the diagram of Figure 1-44.

The most common amino acid residues modified by this enzyme are serine, threonine, or tyrosine residues within specific locations in protein molecules. In some cases, covalent modification by phosphorylation facilitates other changes in the enzyme that affects its ability to be regulated in an allosteric manner (Figure 1-45).

This example, actual and theoretical, is one of protein-protein interaction (protein kinase A activation and phosphorylation), covalent modification, and allosteric regulation. Other examples of protein-protein interactions that control enzyme activity are found in blood coagulation, where some of the hydrolyases are active only after combining with pro-

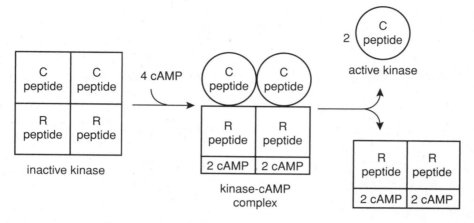

Figure 1-44. Model representation of the structure and regulation of cAMP-dependent protein kinase.

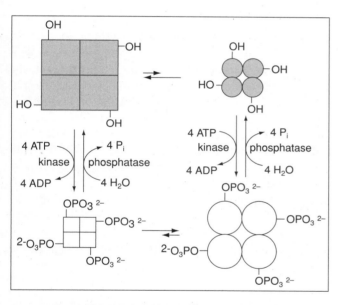

Figure 1-45. Model representation of an allosteric enzyme that is also regulated by covalent modification.

tein cofactors to form catalytically active complexes. Those complexes activate other enzymes by cleavage of specific peptide bonds within those proteins—covalent modification.

Allosteric regulation is a type of regulation very commonly encountered in the control of metabolic pathways. The term *allosteric* was initially coined by Monod, Wyman, and Changeux to explain competi-

tive inhibition of enzymes by compounds that did not resemble substrates. Normally, competitive inhibitors are isosteric to substrate, but these compounds were not and, hence, referred to as allosteric. It was also proposed that these inhibitors acted at sites on the enzyme different from substrates and caused a conformation change in the protein that influenced activity. It was also observed that enzymes subjected to this type of inhibition often showed sigmoidial kinetics, curves similar to those observed in oxygen binding to hemoglobin. Characteristics of substrate saturation curves for these enzymes resemble those shown in the following figure (Figure 1-46). Substrate saturation curves may be sigmoidial in the absence of any other type of ligand. If an activator is added, the curve shifts to the left, approaching the shape of a Michaelis-Menten curve. The amount of substrate required to give half-maximum velocity decreases. If an inhibitor is added, the curve shifts to the right, and more substrate is required to give half-maximum velocity. Maximum velocity could also be obtained by the addition of a sufficient amount of substrate.

7.2. Kinetic Models for Allosteric Regulation

Several models have defined this type of kinetic pattern. The two models most referred to and most consistent with experimental observations are the *concerted model* of Monod, Wyman, and Changeux and the *sequential model* of Koshland, Nemethy, and Filmer. Essential postulates of the concerted model are:

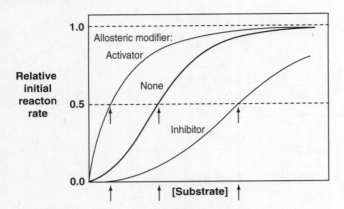

Figure 1-46. Kinetic pattern of an allosteric enzyme that shows positive cooperativity.

1. Allosteric proteins are composed of more than one subunit that are associated with each other in such a way that they posses at least one axis of symmetry.

2. Each subunit contains a specific binding site for each ligand. If the protein contains subunits of different types, the minimum functional unit is defined as a protomer consisting of one of each of the different subunits.

3. Binding sites within each molecule for each ligand that it binds are equivalent.

4. There is cooperativity of interaction among the subunits such that the conformation of each subunit will be the same in each molecule. If one subunit changes conformation, all will change to the same conformation.

5. The protein exists in two different conformational states that are in equilibrium with each other, and each of the conformational states has a different binding affinity for ligands.

Major differences between the concerted and sequential models are that the sequential model assumes that individual subunits only change conformation upon binding to a ligand and that the conformation change that each subunit undergoes affects the conformation of subunits adjacent to it such that binding of additional ligands may be made easier or harder (i.e., binding with increased affinity or with decreased affinity). In both models, there is cooperativity between subunits, but in the sequential model, negative cooperativity is

more easily explained. Further, the sequential model is kinetically more complex because how adjacent subunits are influenced depends on the overall structural arrangement of the free protein, whether it is in a tetrahedral, square, or linear conformation. It is important to remember postulates of the concerted model: that the sequential model differs from it primarily in that each individual subunit undergoes a conformation change upon binding ligand; and that in the sequential model, the conformational change undergone by one subunit upon binding ligand can influence binding of ligand to other subunits in a positive or a negative manner. Shown in Figure 1-47 is an abbreviated example of the two models. The example shown for the sequential model is for the square arrangement of subunits in the free enzyme.

In the concerted model, there is strong cooperativity between subunits such that the oligomeric protein subunits will always have the same conformation, the more active or the less active form. In the sequential model, each subunit changes conformation upon binding a ligand, and that change in conformation influences the conformation of its adjacent subunits such that they can bind additional ligand either more easily or with more difficulty. If binding is facilitated, there is positive cooperativity. If binding is made more difficult, there is negative cooperativity. The types of effectors may also fit into one of two classes: *homotropic*, which is usually substrate and will only activate the enzyme, and *heterotropic*, which is structurally different from substrate and may either activate or inhibit activity of the enzyme.

In the substrate saturation curve shown in Figure 1-46 for an allosteric enzyme, the curve labeled "none" (for no modifier being present) represents homotropic activation. V_{max} can be obtained by increasing concentrations of substrate alone. Those curves labeled "positive" and "negative" represent curves typical of those seen with heterotropic modifiers. Aspartate transcarbamoylase may be used as an example to illustrate some of these points. This enzyme is the first committed step in the synthesis of pyrimidine nucleotides. It is regulated in part by feedback inhibition by the end product of that pathway, cytidine triphosphate, as shown on the next page (Figure 1-48).

Thus, CTP is a *negative* modifier and shifts the saturation curve to the right. Not shown is the fact that

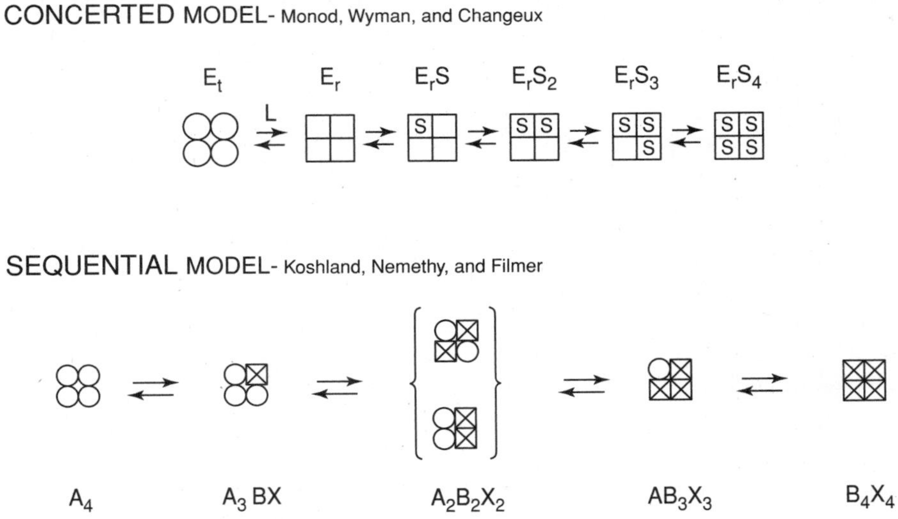

CONCERTED MODEL- Monod, Wyman, and Changeux

$E_t \quad E_r \quad E_rS \quad E_rS_2 \quad E_rS_3 \quad E_rS_4$

SEQUENTIAL MODEL- Koshland, Nemethy, and Filmer

$A_4 \qquad A_3BX \qquad A_2B_2X_2 \qquad AB_3X_3 \qquad B_4X_4$

Figure 1-47. Comparative representation of concerted and sequential models for allosteric enzymes.
(Adapted from Cornish-Bowden, A., *Principles of Enzyme Kinetics*, Butterworths Publishers, Inc., Boston, 1976, pp. 116-141;
Concerted model: Monod, J., Wyman, J., and Changeux, J.-P. (1965) *J. Mol. Biol.* 12, 88-118;
Sequential model: Koshland, D. E. Jr., Nemethy, S., and Filmer, D. (1966) *Biochemistry* 5, 365-385.)

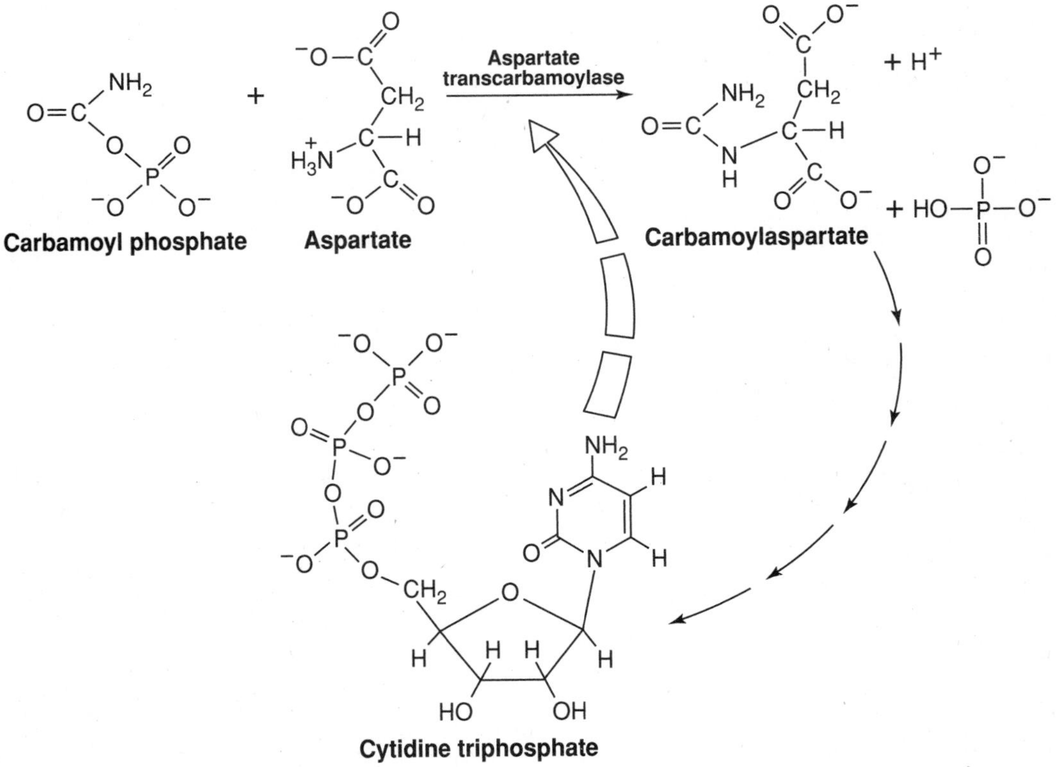

Figure 1-48. Feedback inhibition of aspartate transcarbamoylase by CTP.
(Adapted from Zubay, G., *Biochemistry*, Addison-Wesley Publishing Company, Reading, MA, 1983, p. 187 (Fig. 5-6)).

ATP is a *positive* modifier, and it shifts the curve to the left. The major point is that both CTP and ATP are heterotropic modifiers.

This enzyme's regulatory pattern follows the concerted model of Monod, Wyman, and Changeux in that it is either in the *R* (relaxed) conformation or the *T* (taut or tense) conformation. The enzyme differs structurally from many allosteric enzymes in that it also has specific regulatory subunits that bind modifiers that cause conformation changes. From structural analyses, the following models represent structural changes that accompany activation and inhibition of this enzyme by modifiers (Figure 1-49).

T state
(less active)

R state
(more active)

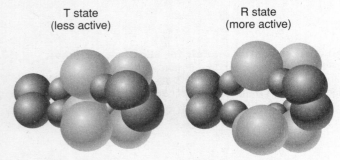

Favored by CTP binding

Favored by substrate binding

Figure 1-49. Models of the T state and the R state of aspartate transcarbamoylase. CTP has higher affinity for binding to the T state and substrate (or the allosteric activator, ATP) has higher affinity for binding to the R state. (Adapted from Berg, J. M., Tymoczko, J. L., and Stryer, L., *Biochemistry*, Fifth Edition, W. H. Freeman and Company, New York, 2002, p. 266.)

7.3. Kinetic Description of Allosteric Interactions: The Concerted Model

This model is defined by three equilibrium constants: *L* defines the equilibrium between the two forms of the enzyme, with or without bound ligand; K_R defines the binding of substrate (ligand) to any one of the R-forms of the enzyme; and K_T defines the binding of substrate (ligand) to any one of the T-forms of the enzyme. These interactions are summarized as follows (Figure 1-50).

A mathematical expression of the saturation function for *S*, substrate (ligand) binding, can be described that takes into account all of the interactions shown in the following scheme:

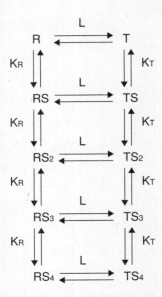

Figure 1-50. Diagrammatic representation of the equilibra between enzyme forms for the concerted model of allosteric interactions. (Adapted representation of the model of Monod, J., Wyman, J., and Changeux, J.-P. (1965) *J. Mol. Biol.* 12, 88-118). Redrawn by author.)

$$\bar{Y} = \frac{\alpha(1+\alpha)^{n-1} + Lc\alpha(1+c\alpha)^{n-1}}{(1+\alpha)^n + L(1+c\alpha)^n}$$

where $\alpha = S/K_R$, $c = K_R/K_T$, and thus $c\alpha = S/K_T$. In the special case where *L* approaches zero, the saturation binding equation becomes similar to the Michaelis-Menten equation.

$$\bar{Y}_s = \frac{\alpha(1+\alpha)^{n-1}}{(1+\alpha)^n} = \frac{\alpha}{1+\alpha} = \frac{1}{1+\frac{K_R}{S}} = \frac{1 \times S}{S+K_R}$$

Remember that $\bar{Y}_s$ refers to fractional saturation. So at maximum saturation, its value is 1.0 and equivalent to V_{max} in the Michaelis-Menten equation.

The sigmoidal substrate saturation curve for an allosteric enzyme is similar to the hemoglobin-oxygen saturation curve and may be defined also by an equation similar to the Hill equation. The Hill equation is

$$\log\left(\frac{Y}{1-Y}\right) = n\log[S] - \log K_{eq}$$

where Y is defined as fractional saturation, and 1.0 defines complete saturation. A similar equation may be written for an enzymatic reaction where V_{max} represents the rate value when the enzyme is completely saturated with substrate, and v the value at some fractional saturation point. Thus, the Hill equation for an enzymatic reaction takes on the form

$$\log\left(\frac{v}{V_{max} - v}\right) = n\log[S] - \log K_{eq}$$

A plot of $\log(v/(V_{max} - v))$ versus $\log[S]$ would give a straight line, the slope of which is n and is the Hill coefficient. The appropriate data (generally between 20% and 80% saturation) must be plotted since at very low and very high saturation, the slope of the curve approaches 1.0 regardless of the actual degree of cooperativity.

7.4. Significance of the Hill Coefficient

The significance of the Hill coefficient is that it is an indication of the degree of cooperativity in allosteric enzymes. If there is no cooperativity as in Michaelis-Menten kinetics, $n = 1.0$. If there is negative cooperativity, $n < 1.0$. If there is positive cooperativity, n is > 1.0. Examples of the importance of this phenomenon in metabolic regulation will be discussed later. It is interesting to note that if the Hill coefficient were 0.5, it would take a 6,561-fold change in cellular substrate concentration to change the rate of an enzyme reaction from 10 percent to 90 percent activity. If the Hill coefficient were 1.0, as in normal Michaelis-Menten kinetics, an 81-fold change in concentration would be required. But if the Hill coefficient were 4, only a 3-fold change in cellular substrate concentration would be required to effect the same 10 percent to 90 percent change in reaction rate. The latter value is well within the physiological range for substrate concentration changes.

8. METABOLISM

It was stated earlier that a cell contains thousands of proteins, many of which are enzymes. These enzymes catalyze only six major types of reactions, but there are many variations of those six reaction types. All of the reactions that take place in a cell cannot be demonstrated in a readable format on a single chart. Several general observations can be made, however, and some are obvious from the chart shown below (Figure 1-51).

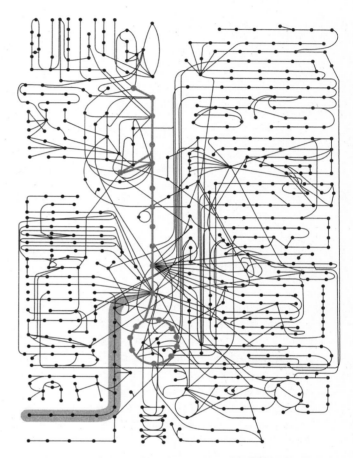

Figure 1-51. Cartoon view of a metabolic chart.
(Adapted from Alberts, B., Bray, D., Lewis, J., Raff, M., Roberts, K., and Watson, J. D., *Molecular Biology of the Cell,* Garland Publishing, Inc., New York, 1983, p. 83)

There are many interlinking and overlapping lines representing many different types of reactions. Substrates of one set of reactions are products of another. Reaction rates of some of these are strictly dependent on the concentrations of substrates for the enzymes that catalyze them in a Michaelis-Menten manner, and others are regulated by various means and maintain an orderly flow of metabolites from one pathway to another in a manner as efficient as possible. Precursor to product relationships maintain adequate and possibly constant concentrations of key metabolites throughout the life

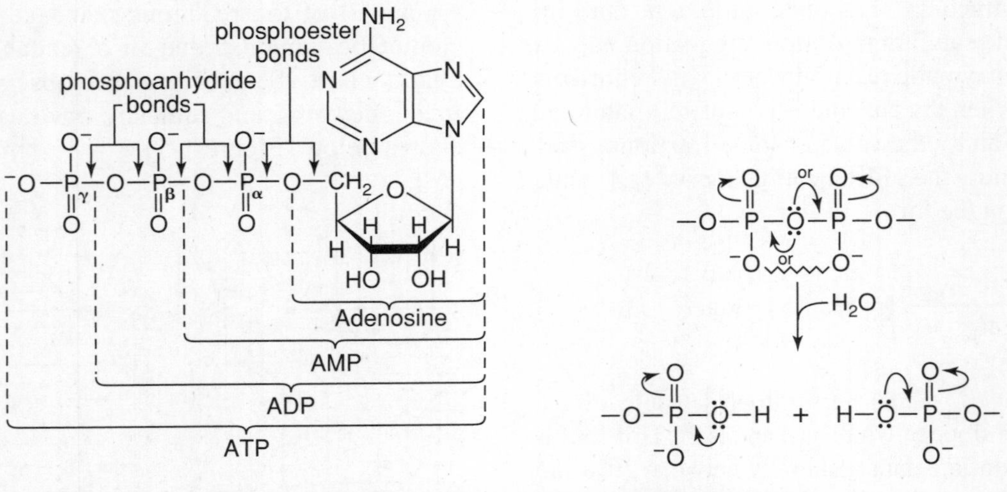

Figure 1-52. High energy bonds of ATP and ADP.
(Adapted from Figures 15-18 and 15-20, pp. 409 and 411, respectively, of Voet, D. and Vote, J. D., *Biochemistry*, John Wiley & Sons, Inc., New York, 1990)

cycle of the cell. Imbalance in this relationship generally leads to some disease and/or growth abnormality.

Another major observation from the chart above is the fact that there is a central pathway of metabolism, as indicated by the larger dark circles, from which most metabolites are derived or to which most contribute. The linear portion of that pathway represents glycolysis (Embenden-Myerhof pathway), and the circular portion represents the tricarboxycyclic acid cycle (TCA/citric acid /Krebs cycle). Those two pathways represent major sources of carbon for the generation of metabolites that are necessary for generation of energy and for synthesis of other intermediary metabolites that eventually find their way into cellular components. Knowledge of the purposes, reactions, and control mechanisms of these pathways is important because it provides a foundation for understanding their operation.

8.1. Forms of Conserved Energy in Metabolism

Energy is conserved in the forms of ATP and $NADH + H^+$. Under oxidative conditions, $NADH/H^+$ is oxidized to NAD^+ in mitochondria through the electron transport chain. Under anaerobic conditions, the end product of glycolysis is lactate. The formation of lactate from pyruvate is important because it regenerates NAD^+ that is necessary for continuous operation of one

of the enzymes of the glycolytic pathway. This reaction will be emphasized again later.

ATP is classified as a "high-energy" compound because the terminal phosphate groups (of ATP and ADP) contain negatively charged oxygen atoms on the phosphate groups that contribute to electrostatic repulsion and increased destabilization (Figure 1-52). Hydrolysis of the terminal (γ) phosphate gives inorganic phosphate, which has an increased number of resonance forms and is more stable. The difference in energy between the two forms of that phosphate group is approximately −7.3 kcal/mole. The terminal (β) phosphate on ADP fits essentially the same category and also releases approximately −7.3 kcal/ mole upon hydrolysis. This type of electrostatic repulsion does not exist for the terminal phosphate of AMP, and the thermodynamic drive for its hydrolysis is considerable less and it does not qualify as a "high-energy" compound. This "excess" energy in the terminal phosphate groups of ATP and ADP coupled with other reactions is useful for driving reactions in directions that make them more favorable and helps direct the flow of metabolites through metabolic pathways. The following is a diagrammatic representation (Figure 1-53) showing the direction to which the flow of energy from higher- to lower-energy compounds may occur.

Note that the transfer of "high-energy" phosphate generally goes from compounds with more negative

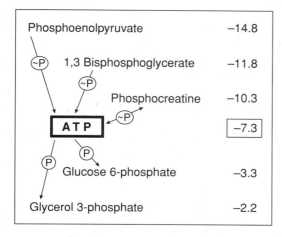

Figure 1-53. Energy levels of various compounds compared with ATP.

$\Delta G°$ values to compounds with less negative $\Delta G°$ values. Phosphocreatine serves as a buffer or reservoir for ATP. The difference in $\Delta G°$ value between ATP and phosphocreatine is small enough that this reaction is easily reversible under physiological conditions. A major driving force for reactions under cellular conditions is the relative concentrations of reactants (ΔG). The reader can calculate the K_{eq} for this reaction from information discussed previously. Observe that the difference in $\Delta G°$ **numerically** is 3.0. What is K_{eq} and in which direction would the reaction be favored? At what value of ΔG would the concentrations of ATP and phosphocreatine be approximately equal?

8.2. Glycolysis

Starting with glucose, there are ten reactions in the glycolytic scheme. These do not include the fact that reactions starting at step 5 are repeated twice in order to completely convert glucose to two molecules of pyruvate. The net reaction for glycolysis is

$$Glucose + 2ADP + 2P_i + 2NAD^+ \rightarrow 2Pyruvate + 2ATP + 2NADH/H^+ + 2H_2O.$$

At pH 7.0, 25°C, and 0.25 M ionic strength, the $\Delta G° = -80.6\,kJ\,mol^{-1}$ or $-19.3\,kcal\,mol^{-1}$ for the overall process. (From Alberty, R. A., *Thermodynamics of Biochemical Reactions,* Wiley Interscience, New York, 2003, p. 82) These data suggest overall favorable spontaneity. But

the $\Delta G°$ value for each reaction is not favorable, so a more important driving force is ΔG and the value of Q (see above), where concentrations of reacting components become a more important driving force.

The overall scheme for glycolysis is shown in Figure 1-54. One of the functions of glycolysis is to produce energy under nonoxidative conditions. When glycolysis operates under nonoxidative conditions, the end product is lactate instead of pyruvate because NAD^+ must be regenerated for glyceraldehyde 3-phosphate dehydrogenase in order for glycolysis to continue. NAD^+ is regenerated by action of lactate dehydrogenase which uses $NADH/H^+$ to reduce pyruvate to lactate. Thus, the net reaction under anaerobic conditions would be

$$Glucose + 2\,ADP + 2\,P_i \rightarrow 2\,Lactate + 2\,ATP + 2\,H_2O.$$

The overall yield for energy production is relatively small. Two molecules of ATP are required for reactions of glycolysis to proceed, and the net output is two molecules of ATP. Six of the ten reactions of glycolysis involve chemical transformations in which the position of a phosphate group is changed. Two reactions for each of the three carbon substrates derived from glucose involve transformation to "high-energy" phosphate compounds. These are the reactions that lead to ATP generation at the level of substrate, hence the term *substrate-level phosphorylation.*

The first step for glucose metabolism is phosphorylation to produce glucose 6-phosphate. This reaction is catalyzed by hexokinase, a relatively nonspecific enzyme that catalyzes the phosphorylation of several hexoses using ATP in the presence of Mg^{2+}. There is another enzyme in the liver of mammalian species that also catalyzes the phosphorylation of glucose (specifically) to glucose 6-phosphate. These enzymes are different and have different physiological functions in cells. Hexokinase has a very low K_m for glucose, in the range of 0.1 mM, whereas glucokinase has a K_m of approximately 5 mM, approximately the same as that of glucose 6-phophatase (3 mM). Together these two enzymes help maintain blood glucose levels approximately constant within the 5 mM range. Activity of hexokinase is inhibited by glucose 6-phosphate, but glucokinase activity is not. Under the same conditions given above for the overall $\Delta G°$ value for glycolysis, the $\Delta G°$

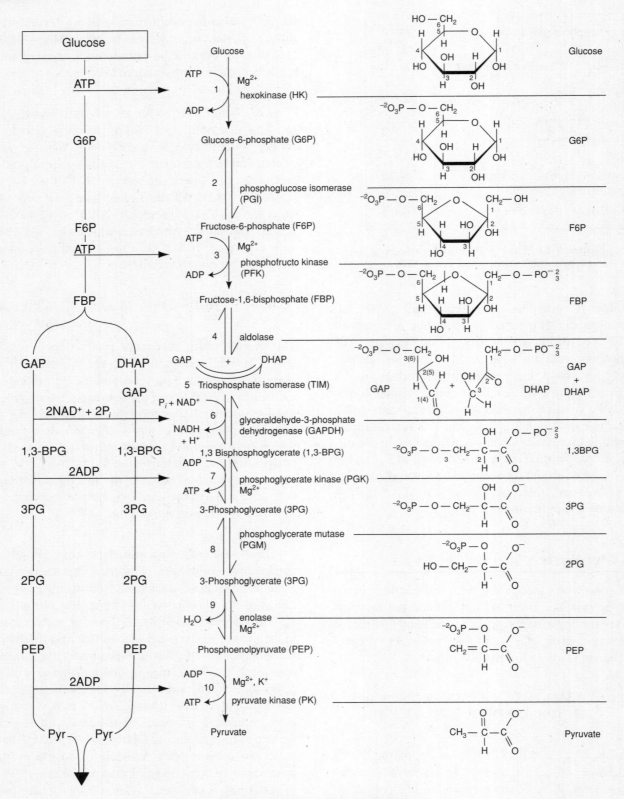

Figure 1-54. Glycolytic pathway.
(Adapted from Voet, D. and Voet, J. D., *Biochemistry*, John Wiley & Sons, New York, 1990, p. 428.)

value for the hexokinase reaction is −24.42 kJ mol^{-1} or −5.78 kcal mol^{-1}.

Glucose 6-phosphate can participate in several different pathways as a result of various types of reactions catalyzed primarily by transferases (kinases) and isomerases. The next step in glycolysis is the conversion of G6P to fructose 6-phosphate (F6P). This reaction is catalyzed by phosphoglucose isomerase, which has a $\Delta G°$ at pH 7 of 0.76 kcal mol^{-1} and means that it can proceed in either direction at cellular concentrations with relative ease.

8.3. Reaction That Commits Glucose Metabolism to Glycolysis

The transformation that commits metabolism of glucose to glycolysis is the conversion of fructose 6-phosphate to fructose 1,6-bisphosphate (FBP, Reaction 3) by the enzyme phosphofructokinase (PFK1). The $\Delta G°$ value for this reaction is −5.56 kcal mol^{-1}. It is the first irreversible step along this pathway, and its activity in many species is under allosteric and/or hormonal control. Its activity is increased by AMP and inhibited by ATP and citrate. Considering that one of the functions of glycolysis is rapid production of energy from glucose, regulation by those metabolites is easily rationalized. If there is excess energy or increased concentration of the initial substrate of the TCA cycle for aerobic metabolism for concomitant energy production, the rate of glycolysis can be decreased. If there is a demonstrated need for energy as evident by a high concentration of AMP, the necessity for glycolysis is increased. The diagram in Figure 1-55 is an example of allosteric regulation of PFK1 by high concentration of AMP. (Refer back to the earlier discussion of allosteric regulation of enzyme activity.) Within the physiological range of AMP concentrations, there can be dramatic increases in the activity of PFK1. Another important allosteric regulator of PFK1 is fructose 2,6-bisphosphate, which is not a normal intermediary metabolite. In livers of some species, glycolysis would not be able to occur in an efficient manner without the coregulation

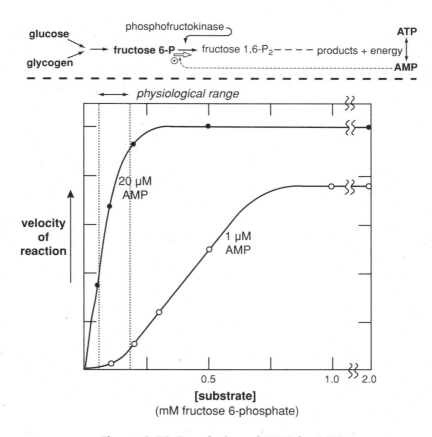

Figure 1-55. Regulation of PFK1 by AMP.

of PFK1 and fructose 1,6-bisphosphatase by fructose 2,6-bisphosphate (Fru 2,6-P_2), because dephosphorylation of Fru 1,6-P_2 by fructose 1,6-bisphosphatase would occur too fast and insufficient Fru 1,6-P_2 would be present to support glycolysis. Fru 2,6-P_2, in those species where it is an important regulator, is an allosteric activator of PFK1, as is AMP. Fru 2,6-P_2 is synthesized and degraded by PFK2 (Figure 1-56). PFK2 is a bifunctional enzyme whose activity is hormonally controlled through a second messenger mechanism involving its phosphorylation and dephosphorylation by protein kinase A and phosphoprotein phosphatase, respectively. It is a kinase in its dephosphorylated form and a phosphatase in its phosphorylated form. Make note of the fact that PFK1 is directly involved in glycolysis and PFK2 is in allosteric regulation.

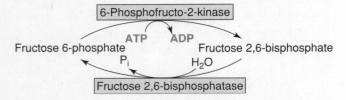

Figure 1-56. Synthesis and degradation of Fru 2,6-P_2 by its hormonally controlled bifunctional enzyme. (Adapted from Devlin, T. M., Editor, *Textbook of Biochemistry with Clinical Correlations*, Fourth Edition, Wiley-Liss, New York, p. 293.)

From this point, reactions involving phosphate eventually lead to their transformation into "high-energy" compounds and production of ATP. Some of these compounds may also be siphoned off to other pathways to produce other metabolites necessary for cellular growth and maintenance, but this must not distract attention from the importance of glycolysis in the production of energy as ATP. Glycolysis is a major source of ATP production in many species under anaerobic conditions. Under anaerobic conditions, the end product is lactate; under aerobic conditions, the major product is pyruvate and NAD_{red}. It is very important to produce lactate under anaerobic conditions, as will be discussed later, because that is the only mechanism within the scheme to reoxidize NADH + H^+ to NAD^+ that is required for reaction 6 (glyceraldehyde 3-phosphate dehydrogenase) of the pathway. In yeast, however, pyruvate can be decarboxylated to yield acetaldehyde and carbon dioxide. When yeast is used in cooking (baking), carbon diox-

ide is a leavening agent. Under other circumstances where anaerobiosis is retained, NAD^+ can be regenerated by reduction of acetaldehyde to ethanol. Ethanol is an important ingredient of wine and other "spirit" beverages.

8.3.1. Aldolase Catalyzes the Production of Two 3-Carbon Compounds from Fru 1,6-P_2.

This reaction results in the formation of one molecule each of dihydroxyacetone phosphate (DHAP) and glyceraldehyde-3-phosphate (GAP). This reaction is the reverse of an aldol condensation reaction in which the $\Delta G°$ is approximately +5.5. Thus, it would appear to be as unfavorable as the formation of ATP from FBP. Because, however, the reactions are driven in the forward direction by ΔG where concentrations of reactants are important (refer to the definition of Q, the potential to do work, mentioned above) and the coupling of reactions where product of one reaction is the substrate for another, glycolysis continues in the correct direction in an efficient manner. All other reactions of glycolysis involve transformations of GAP. Complete conversion of glucose to pyruvate/lactate through this scheme does occur, however, because of the extremely efficient transformation of DHAP to GAP by the enzyme triose phosphate isomerase.

8.3.2. Triose Phosphate Isomerase (TIM).

This enzyme catalyzes the interconversion of DHAP and GAP. DHAP is derived from the first three carbons of FBP and GAP from the last three carbons. This reaction like other enzyme-catalyzed reactions is stereospecific. Other points worthy of note about this enzyme include the following: (1) The enzyme is essentially a perfect catalyst. That is, the interconversion of these two compounds occurs faster than the diffusion rate of product from the active site. (2) The carbon atom in position 1 of FBP is carbon 3 of DHAP, and the carbon atom in position 6 of FBP is also carbon 3 of GAP. This means that carbons 4 and 5 of FBP are carbon atoms 1 of each product, respectively.

8.3.3. Glyceraldehyde 3-Phosphate Dehydrogenase (GAPDH) Reaction.

This enzyme catalyzes synthesis of the first "high-energy" compound in glycolysis. Earlier in this section, there was a brief discussion of this enzyme relative to mechanisms by which enzymes enhance reaction rates. It was pointed out that a covalent intermediate is formed between the substrate GAP and the enzyme, a thiolhemiacetyl, and that this occurred with a cysteine residue close to the binding site for NAD^+. Thus, the enzyme reaction involves proximity or orientation effects as well as oxidation-reduction. This cysteine residue is critical for reaction of this enzyme. It is subject to irreversible inhibition by sulfhydryl reacting agents such as iodoacetic acid (ICH_2COO^-). The overall reaction catalyzed by GADPH is as follows.

Glyceraldehyde-3-phosphate (GAP)   **1,3-Bisphoglycerate (1,3-BPG)**

Although 1,3-bisphosphoglycerate is a "high-energy" compound, the reaction is easily reversible. Under the standard conditions referred to throughout this section, pH 7.0, $\Delta G^\circ = 1.12$ kJ mol^{-1} or 0.27 kcal mol^{-1}.

Because this is such an intriguing enzyme, and because of its historical importance in determining mechanisms of enzyme actions, many textbooks give a mechanism for this reaction in one of two possible forms relative to when NAD^+ and NADH exchange occurs on the enzyme. Some textbooks show the exchange occurring prior to phosphorolysis, and some show it occurring after phosphorolysis that produces the 1,3-bisphosphoglycerate. It is important to be aware that the correct mechanism of action for this enzyme, as given here, is consistent with other dehydrogenases in which NAD^+ binds first and leaves last. In fact, in mammalian species (rabbit muscle, for example) the enzyme crystallizes with NAD^+. NAD^+ is not a prosthetic group since it exchanges rapidly with free NAD^+ and with some analogs of NAD^+ in the absence of substrate. The K_D for NAD^+ is very low. Thus, it has high affinity for

this enzyme and an almost stoichiometric amount of it remains attached to the enzyme during purification. The appropriate mechanism for the reaction shown in Figure 1-57, is based in part on direct observation of the fluorescent properties of the ternary *versus* binary complexes and the inability of free NAD^+ to displace NADH of the ternary complex.

8.3.4. Phosphoglycerate Kinase Reaction.

This enzyme catalyzes formation of the first molecule of ATP in glycolysis. ΔG° for this reaction is -8.22 kJ mol^{-1} or approximately -2 kcal mole^{-1}. The reaction catalyzed by this enzyme is diagrammed in Figure 1-58.

8.3.5. Phosphoglycerate Mutase Reaction.

This enzyme is in the isomerase category and catalyzes the mutation of the phosphate group from position 3 of phosphoglycerate to position 2. It is called a *mutase* because it catalyzes the transfer of a functional group from one position in the molecule to another. It is not a simple reaction, and the chemical mechanism is interesting since it involves a enzyme that contains phosphohistidine.

An intermediate in the reaction is 2,3-bisphosphoglycerate (2,3-BPG), a compound that is an allosteric modifier of hemoglobin in its oxygen-binding reaction. Although Figure 1-59 shows that 2,3-BPG can dissociate from this enzyme, this is not the mechanism of its formation in erythrocytes.

8.3.6. Enolase Catalyzes the Second "High-Energy" Compound in Glycolysis.

This enzyme fits the general category of lyases since it catalyzes the removal of a molecule of water and produces a product with a double bond. In this case, because of the relationship of the double bond to the phosphate group and the resonance structure created, the product, phosphoenolpyruvate, is a "high-energy" compound. A proposed mechanism for this reaction is diagrammed in Figure 1-60.

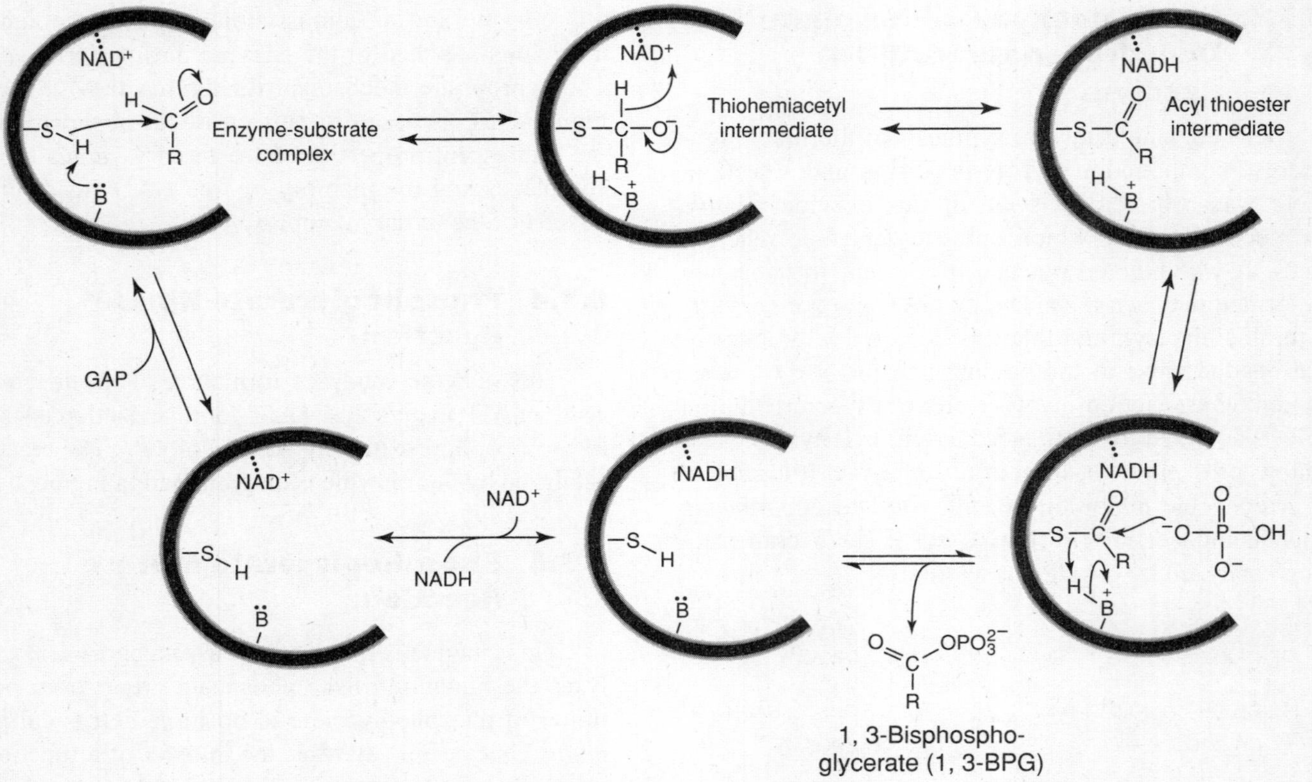

Figure 1-57. Mechanism of action of glyceraldehyde 3-phosphate dehydrogenase.
(Adapted from Voet, D. and Voet, J. D., *Biochemistry*, John Wiley & Sons, New York, 1990, p. 438. Modification based on data from Smith, T. E., Biochemistry 5, 2919, 1966.)

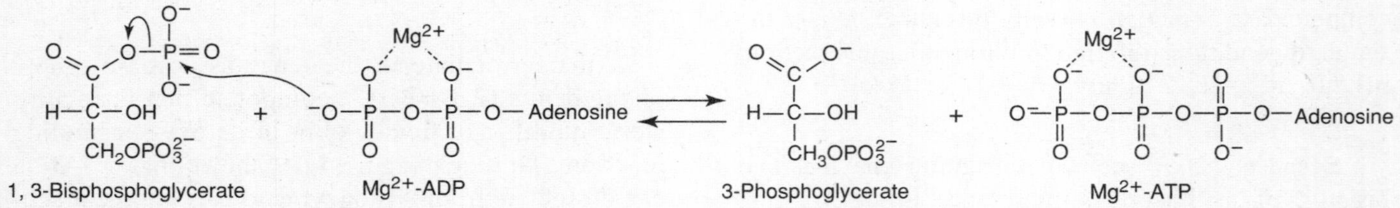

1, 3-Bisphosphoglycerate   Mg²⁺-ADP   3-Phosphoglycerate   Mg²⁺-ATP

Figure 1-58. Mechanism of action of phosphoglycerate kinase.
(Adapted from Voet, D. and Voet, J. D., *Biochemistry*, John Wiley & Sons, New York, 1990, p. 439)

8.3.7. Pyruvate Kinase Generates the Second ATP Molecule in Glycolysis.

This enzyme transfers the phosphate group from PEP to ATP. It was shown in an earlier diagram that ΔG° values for PEP and ATP are −14.2 and −7.3, respectively. Thus, it is quite a favorable reaction and essentially irreversible under all physiological and practical conditions. The mechanism for the reaction is shown in Figure 1-61.

In some species, pyruvate kinase activity is allosterically regulated. It is activated by FBP and inhibited by ATP. Also, the enzyme may be phosphorylated by protein kinase to give a phosphoprotein (covalent modification) that is inactive. These regulatory steps are easily rationalized when it is recognized that one of the major functions of this metabolic scheme is energy production.

This is the final step in glycolysis under aerobic conditions. Under anaerobic conditions, however, NAD⁺ must be regenerated to keep the pathway opera-

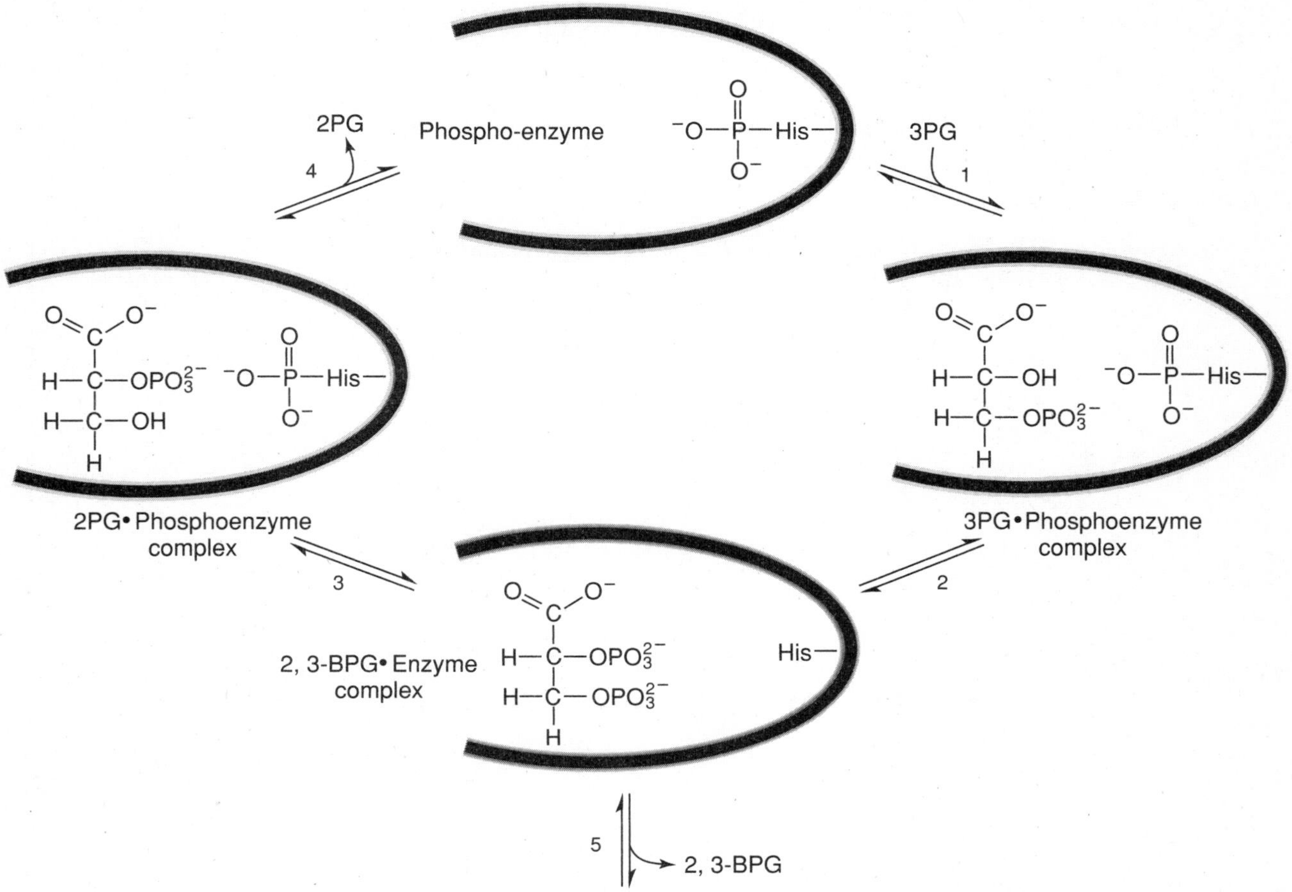

Figure 1-59. Mechanism of action of phosphoglycerate mutase.
(Adapted from Voet, D. and Voet, J. D., *Biochemistry*, John Wiley & Sons, New York, 1990, p. 441.)

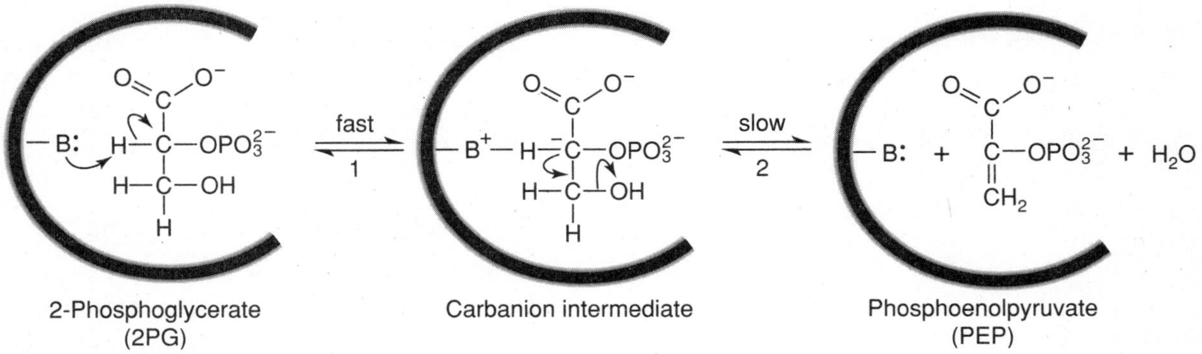

Figure 1-60. Mechanism of action of enolase.
(Adapted from Voet, D. and Voet, J. D., *Biochemistry*, John Wiley & Sons, New York, 1990, p. 442.)

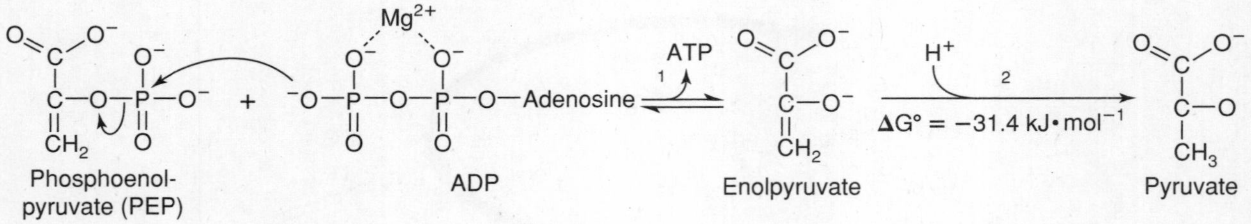

Figure 1-61. Pyruvate kinase reaction.
(Adapted from Voet, D. and Voet, J. D., *Biochemistry*, John Wiley & Sons, New York, 1990, p. 443.)

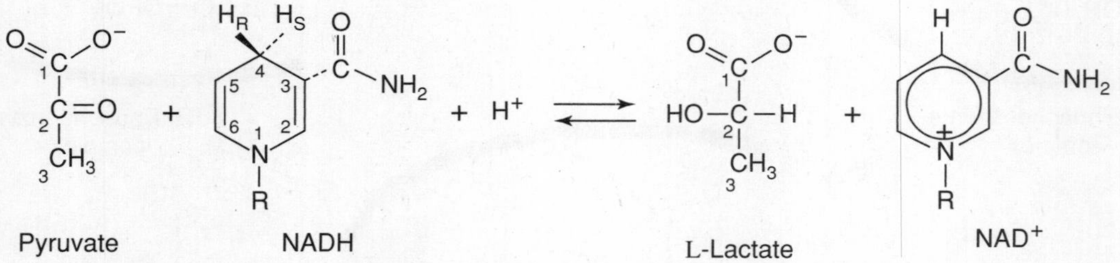

Figure 1-62. Lactate dehydrogenase catalyzed reaction.
(Adapted from Voet, D. and Voet, J. D., *Biochemistry*, John Wiley & Sons, New York, 1990, p. 444)

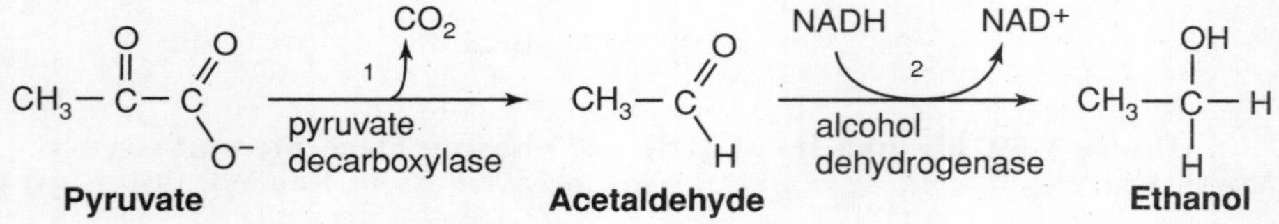

Figure 1-63. Metabolism of pyruvate to ethanol.
(Adapted from Voet, D. and Voet, J. D., *Biochemistry*, John Wiley & Sons, New York, 1990, p. 446.)

tional. Glyceraldehyde 3-phosphate dehydrogenase requires NAD^+ as an essential component of its reaction, and if it were not regenerated, the reactions would stop. Regeneration of NAD^+ is accomplished in many species by the reduction of pyruvate to lactate by the enzyme lactate dehydrogenase (LDH), as shown in Figure 1-62.

LDH shows stereospecificity in the transfer of a hydrogen atom from NADH to lactate. It is the pro H_R hydrogen that is transferred.

In some species where fermentation is important, NADH is regenerated by decarboxylation of pyruvate to acetaldehyde and its subsequent reduction to ethanol (Figure 1-63).

8.3.8. Summary of Glycolysis.

The reactions described represent metabolism of only one of the three carbon fragments generated from glucose. Triose phosphate isomerase converts DHAP, which is also formed from the action of aldolase, to GAP, and all of the subsequent reactions from step 6 of the scheme are repeated. Two molecules of ATP are utilized in the activation process (i.e., from glucose to glucose 6-phosphate and from fructose 6-phosphate to fructose 1,6-bisphosphate). Two molecules of ATP are formed from metabolism of each half of the hexose—a total of four for a complete glucose molecule. Thus, net synthesis of ATP from glycolysis is two molecules of ATP. Refer to the overall formula for glycolysis given above.

The first "high energy" compound generated in glycolysis is 1,3-bisphosphoglycerate ($\Delta G°$ of approximately -11.8 kcal/mol), a product of the glyceraldehyde 3-phosphate dehydrogenase reaction. Substrate level phosphorylation (i.e., generation of ATP), occurs at the pyruvate kinase reaction where

Phosphoenolpyruvate + ADP $\rightarrow$ Pyruvate + ATP.

The $\Delta G°$ for phosphoenolpyruvate is approximately -14.8 kcal/mol, and that for ATP is approximately -7.3 kcal/mol.

ATP regulates the activity of hexokinase by inhibiting its activity. The product of hexokinase, glucose 6-phosphate, has other metabolic routes such as being directed toward the pentose phosphate pathway as well as glycogen synthesis. Also, glucose in some species is specifically required for transport into other tissues where it can be utilized in other metabolic pathways. Thus, regulation of the activity of hexokinase ensures that all of the glucose and inorganic phosphate are not consumed in this one reaction and are available for other needs.

Within the glycolytic pathway, the two major steps of regulation involve phosphofructokinase (PFK1) and pyruvate kinase (PK). PFK1 is activated by AMP and fructose 2,6-bisphosphate (Fru-2,6-P$_2$), which is synthesized by PFK2. PFK2 is a bifunctional enzyme that controls the cellular concentration of Fru-2,6-P$_2$ in several species, and in mammals the enzyme itself is under the control of hormones. The mechanism of this control will be demonstrated later. Figure 1-64 summarizes where some of the regulatory control points are in glycolysis. Metabolites with arrows pointing to circles with "−" signs indicate that those metabolites

inhibit enzymes for the targeted reactions, and those pointing to circles with "+" signs indicate activation of the targeted enzymes.

Fru-2,6-P$_2$, for example, activates PFK1 and inhibits Fru-1,6-bisphosphatase. PFK1 is inhibited by ATP, citrate, and H$^+$, suggestive of higher concentrations of NADH + H$^+$ or organic acids as occur in the TCA cycle and active oxidative phosphorylation. Remember that a major role of glycolysis is rapid generation of energy from glucose metabolism. If sufficient ATP is present, the necessity for operation of glycolysis is diminished. Similarly, if citrate is present in sufficient concentrations for operation of the TCA cycle and H$^+$ concentration is high, possibly indicative of active oxidative phosphorylation, the rate of glycolysis decreases.

Pyruvate kinase is activated allosterically in a "feedforward" manner by Fru-1,6-P$_2$ and is inhibited by ATP and alanine. High alanine concentration indicates a greater necessity for gluconeogenesis and that the more

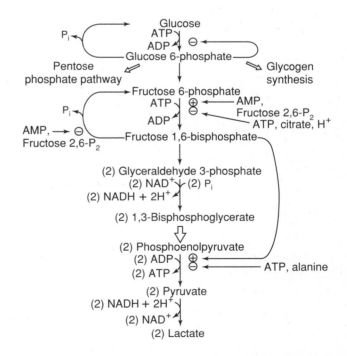

Figure 1-64. Some reactions that regulate glycolysis. (Adapted from Devlin, T. M., Editor, *Textbook of Biochemistry with Clinical Correlations*, Sixth Edition, Wiley-Liss, Hoboken, NJ, 2006, p. 596.)

efficient use of PEP would be in the phosphoenolpyruvate carboxykinase reaction for gluconeogenesis rather than continued production of more ATP, a topic that will be discussed in a later section. Not shown in the diagram is the fact that under some conditions, synthesis of pyruvate kinase is induced.

Several of the types of mechanisms by which enzyme activity can be controlled are evident in glycolysis: (1) allosteric effectors (feedback and feed-forward), (2) covalent modification, (3) protein-protein interaction (activation of protein kinase by cAMP), and (4) protein synthesis are among those discussed here.

Hormonal control of PFK2 activity operates through second messenger mechanisms in which hormones bind to receptors on the cell surface, activate adenylate cyclase, which catalyzes formation of cAMP. cAMP activates protein kinase, which phosphorylates the bifunctional PFK2 (also known as 6-phosphofructo-2-kinase/fructose-2,6-bisphosphatase to reflect its dual activities). The phosphorylated enzyme favors phosphatase activity. Thus, the cellular concentration of Fru-2,6-P_2 decreases and so does the flux of glucose through the glycolytic pathway. An example of glucagon (a hormone) effect and the structure of cAMP are shown in Figure 1-65.

9. PYRUVATE METABOLISM: FORMATION OF ACETYLCOENZYME A

Under aerobic conditions, much of the pyruvate produced during glycolysis is oxidized to acetylcoenzyme A, CO_2, and $NADH + H^+$. The overall reaction for this step is

$$Pyruvate + CoA + NAD^+ + H_2O \rightarrow CO_2 + NADH + H^+ + AcetylCoA$$

The approximate $\Delta G°$ for this reaction is -30.5 kJ mol^{-1} or -7.3 kcal mol^{-1}. This is not a simple reaction and requires the participation of four coenzymes, derived from vitamins, to facilitate the chemistry involved. Another vitamin, pantothenic acid, participates in the reaction as part of a co-substrate. The other four coenzymes are thiamin pyrophosphate (TPP), lipoyllysine (lipoic acid as a prosthetic group), FAD, and NAD^+. In general and as shown in the scheme below, three

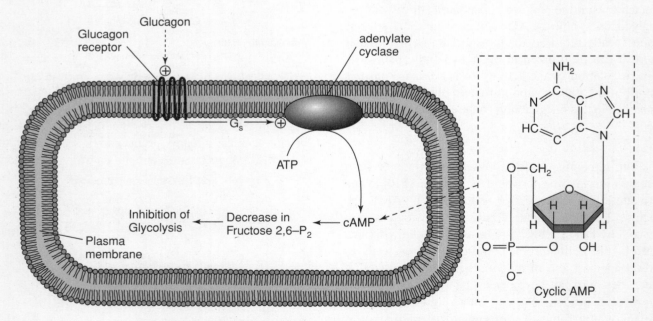

Figure 1-65. Mechanism of glucagon action on hepatic glycolysis.
(Adapted from Devlin, T. M., Editor, *Textbook of Biochemistry with Clinical Correlations*, Sixth Edition, Wiley-Liss, Hoboken, NJ, 2006, Figs. 15.19 & 15.20, p. 603.)

enzymes are involved: pyruvate dehydrogenase (E_1), dihydrolipoyl transacetylase (E_2), and dihydrolipoyl dehydrogenase (E_3). An intermediate in the reaction is TPP—CHOH—CH_3, which refers to α-hydroxyethyl-thyamin pyrophosphate.

In some mammalian species, the reaction is even more complex because its regulation involves the participation of a specific protein kinase and a specific protein phosphatase.

For subsequent metabolic and energy producing reactions, the main products are CH_3CO—S—CoA and NADH + H^+ (see Figure 1-66). This reaction is not part of the Tricarboxylic Acid Cycle, but the NADH + H^+ produced can be reoxidized by the electron transport chain.

The structure of TPP and its most reactive group are shown in Figure 1-67. An interesting note about the chemistry of TPP is that the carbon atom between

the N and S of the thiazole ring can form a carbanion ion spontaneously under some conditions. It is one of few compounds where hydrogen of a —C—H bond can undergo exchange reaction with hydrogen atoms of water.

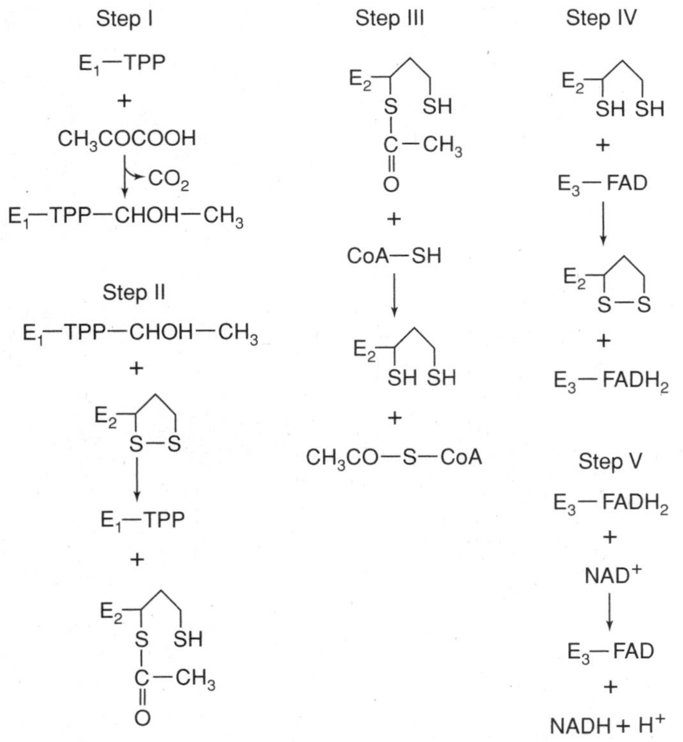

10. THE TRICARBOXYCLIC ACID CYCLE (TCA CYCLE)

The TCA cycle was first referred to as the citric acid cycle. Sir Hans Krebs first postulated its existence, but many others contributed to final definitive proof of its operation. The cumulative $\Delta G°$ value for the nine reactions of the TCA cycle is -53.17 kJ mol^{-1} or -12.71 kcal mol^{-1}. The least favored of the reactions is the conversion of malate to oxaloacetate where $\Delta G°$ is -28.84 kJ mol^{-1} (6.9 kcal mol^{-1}) and favors malate formation. It is important to remember that reactions in metabolic pathways are driven by the overall ΔG for the pathway. Also, reactions are coupled to other reactions where the product of one reaction is the substrate for another and the sum of ΔG for the couple is favorable. Reactions are also driven by mass action (concentration of reactants), which will also push reactions in a desirable direction. Review the section on thermodynamics.

The major functions of the TCA cycle are to provide energy for most reactions that occur in cells and to provide intermediary metabolites that can be transformed into other necessary cellular components. Thus carbon flows into the cycle to be transformed into energy, and carbon flows out of the cycle in other forms to make metabolites that are required for making other compounds for maintenance of cellular integrity or that can be stored for future use. The TCA cycle is a catabolic pathway that requires oxygen. Thus, it functions in an aerobic manner. Enzymes for its operation are located in the mitochondrial matrix, except for succinate dehydrogenase, which is located in the inner membrane of the mitochondria. A diagrammatic representation of mitochondrial organizational structure is shown in Figure 1-68.

The outer membrane of mitochondria is less complex than the inner membrane and also less discriminating relative to the transport of molecules. Particles and/or molecules of up to approximately 10 kDa can

Figure 1-66. Pyruvate dehydrogenase reaction.
(Adapted from Leninger, A. L., *Principles of Biochemistry*, Worth Publishers, Inc., New York, 1982, Fig 16.4, p. 439)

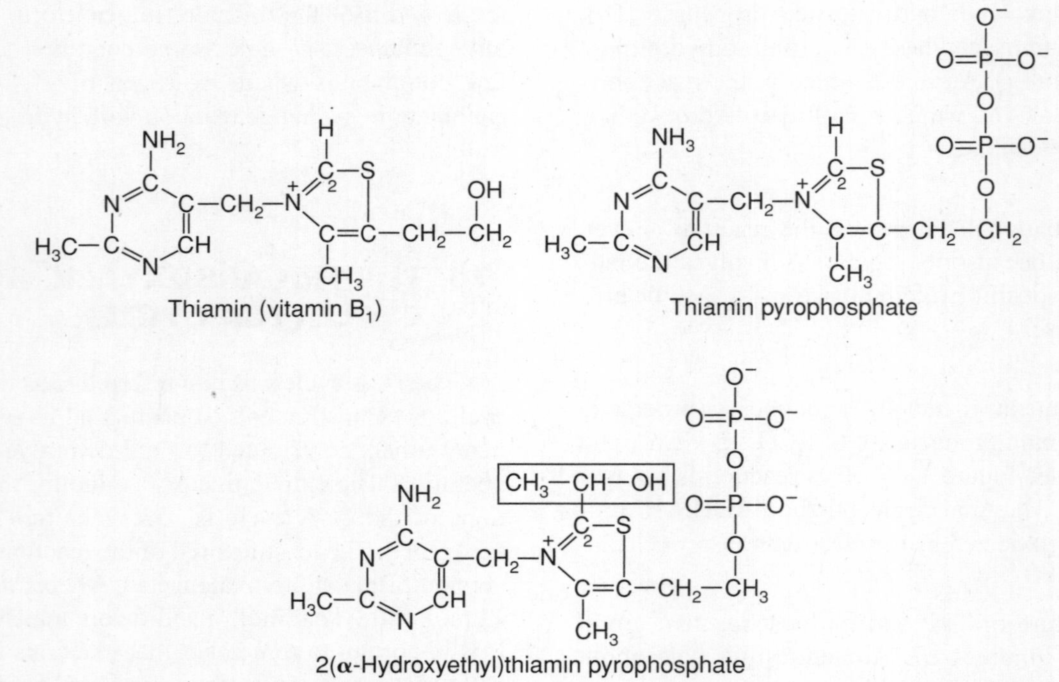

Figure 1-67. Structures of thiamin and some of its functional derivatives.
(Adapted from Leninger, A. L., *Biochemistry*, Second Edition, Worth Publishing, Inc., New York, 1975, (Fig 13-1), p. 338.)

pass through it with relative ease, whereas transport mechanisms are necessary for many molecules to cross the inner mitochondrial membrane. The electron transport system is located within this membrane. TCA cycle enzymes, except succinate dehydrogenase, are located within the matrix enclosed by the inner membrane. Some of the enzymes of the urea cycle, fatty acid oxidation, transcription, and protein synthesis are also located within the mitochondrial matrix, as well as DNA and RNA. Primary emphasis in this section is on operation of the TCA cycle and oxidative phosphorylation.

The primary initiating metabolite for entry into the TCA cycle is acetate in the form of acetyl CoA, and its first reaction is condensation of acetyl CoA with oxaloacetate to form citrate, a reaction catalyzed by citrate synthase. Other enzymes of the cycle are: aconitase, isocitrate dehydrogenase, α-ketoglutarate dehydrogenase, succinyl CoA synthetase, succinate dehydrogenase, fumarase, and malate dehydrogenase. Two molecules of carbon are released as CO_2 during its operation. Thus, it accomplishes the complete oxidation of the equivalent of one molecule of acetate for each turn of the cycle. The overall reaction for the TCA cycle is as follows:

$$\text{Acetyl CoA} + 3\,\text{NAD}_{ox} + \text{FAD}enz_{ox} + \text{GDP} + P_i + 4H_2O \rightarrow 2CO_2 + 3\text{NAD}_{red} + \text{FAD}enz_{red} + \text{GTP} + \text{CoASH}$$

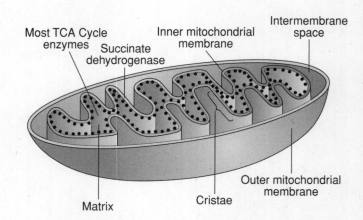

Figure 1-68. Diagrammatic representation of mitochondrial compartments. Location of TCA cycle enzymes and of succinate dehydrogenase are also shown.
(Adapted from Devlin, T. M., Editor, *Textbook of Biochemistry with Clinical Correlations*, Sixth Edition, Wiley-Liss, Hoboken, NJ, 2006, Fig. 14.28, p. 551.)

A diagram of the overall reactions of the TCA cycle is shown in Figure 1-69.

There is one reaction that catalyzes substrate-level phosphorylation, namely, the one catalyzed by succinyl-CoA synthetase. Energy conserved by formation of GTP in this reaction is equivalent to that of one molecule of ATP, and it is counted as such in balancing the overall energy yield from the cycle. Also, the boxes in the diagram containing 2H atoms represent reactions that yield NADH + H$^+$ or *FADH$_2$. NADH/H$^+$ and FADH$_2$ are reoxidized by the electron transport chain with con-comitant production of ATP. Points of entry of electrons into the electron transport chain from NADH/H$^+$ and FADH$_2$ are different and so are the number of mole equivalents of ATP produced: 2.5-3.0 from NADH/H$^+$ and 1.5-2.0 from FADH$_2$. Note also that the carbon atoms in the two molecules of CO$_2$ released from the cycle are not the same atoms of carbon that entered the cycle from acetyl-CoA. This is shown better in Figure 1-70.

During the first turn of the cycle, neither of the original carbons of acetyl-CoA is lost as CO$_2$. Instead, both

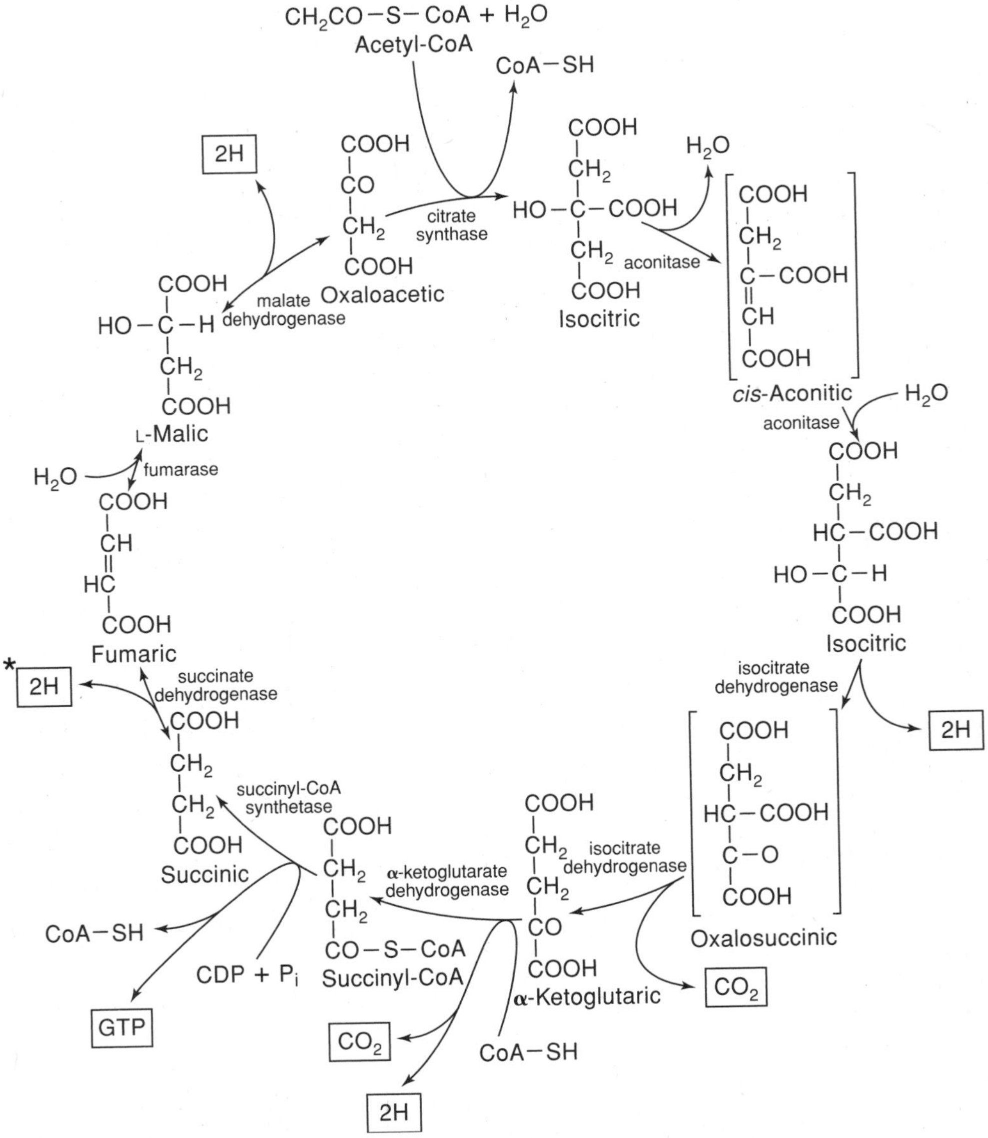

Figure 1-69. Tricarboxylic acid (TCA) cycle.
(Adapted from Lehninger, A. L., *Biochemistry*, Second Edition, Worth Publishing, Inc., New York, 1975, (Fig. 17-2) p. 446.)

molecules of CO_2 come from the original oxaloacetate: one is lost upon decarboxylation of isocitrate, and the other upon decarboxylation of α-ketoglutarate. Two of the subsequent dicarboxyclic acid molecules in the cycle, succinate and fumarate, are symmetrical compounds, and the positions of the labels become indistinguishable to the enzymes that produce malate and oxaloacetate. Thus, the second turn of the cycle results in the lost of approximately one-half of the label from the original acetyl-CoA. Follow the carbon atoms with the "*" and "°" beside them. All of the enzymes catalyze reactions in a stereospecific manner. The degree of stereospecificity can be visualized also by following the distribution of H atoms shown in the circles, squares, and triangles. This is also consistent with the previous statement that reactions catalyzed by dehydrogenases that use NAD^+/$NADP^+$ systems show specificity for the hydrogen atoms removed from and/or added to their substrates.

Some of the reactions shown in Figure 1-70 occur only in some species and under special conditions.

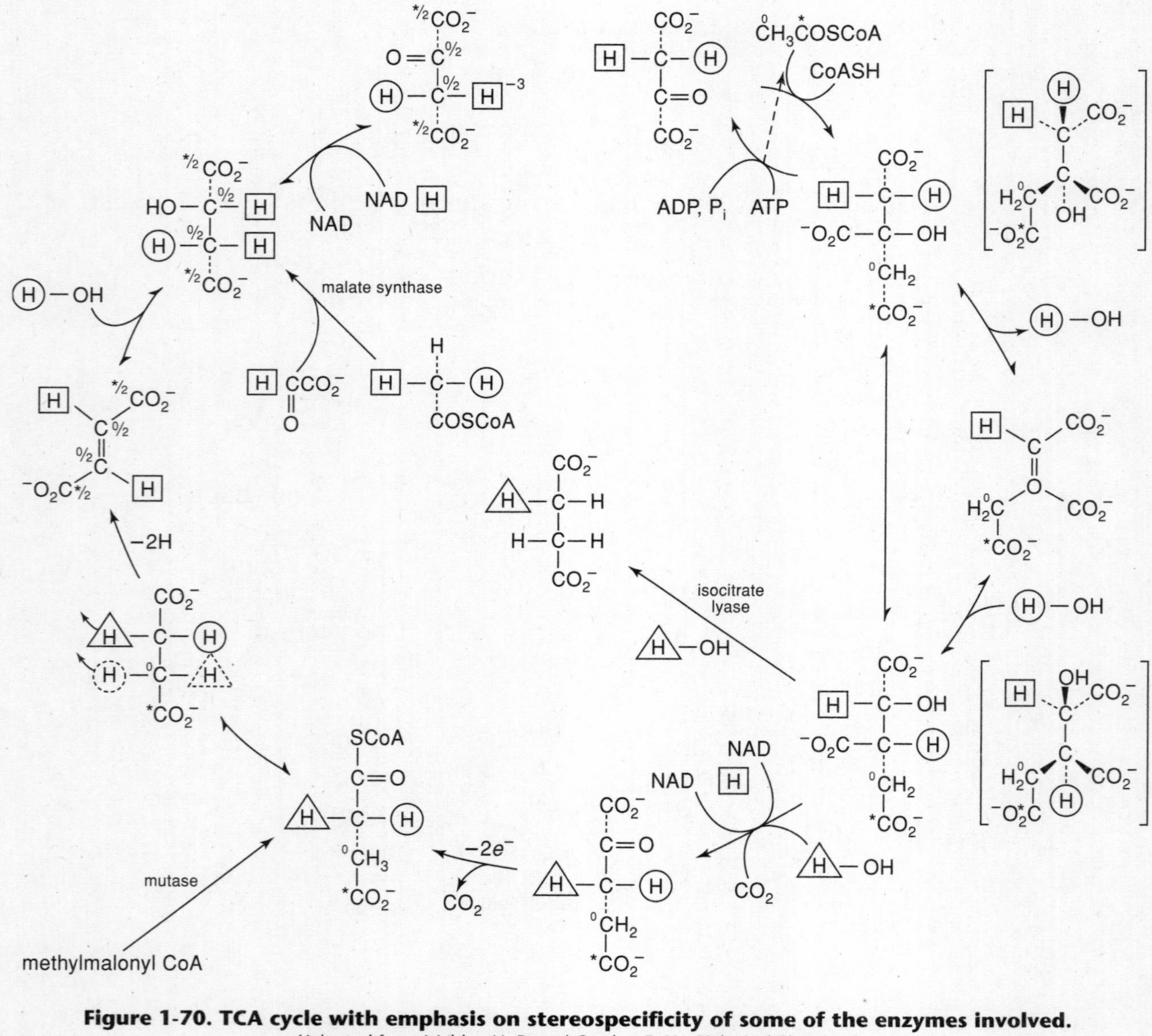

Figure 1-70. TCA cycle with emphasis on stereospecificity of some of the enzymes involved.
(Adapted from Mahler, H. R. and Cordes, E. H., *Biological Chemistry*)

For example, isocitrate lyase occurs in some germinating seeds and some microorganisms where growth on 2-carbon (producing) compounds is necessary. Together with malate synthase, C-4 compounds leading to glucose formation can occur. These enzymes are absent in higher organisms. On the other hand, fatty acids can be made from citrate in animals. Citrate is transported out of the mitochondria and into the cytosol where it is cleaved by citrate lyase to yield acetyl CoA and oxaloacetate. Acetyl CoA can be used for fatty acid synthesis and oxaloacetate can be reduced to malate, converted by malic enzyme to pyruvate and NADPH/H$^+$. This is another source of NADPH/H$^+$ for synthetic reactions.

10.1. Regulation of the TCA Cycle

Metabolites that regulate the TCA cycle are those expected consistent with its overall function, supplying energy and metabolites for other processes. The following figure (Figure 1-71) shows points of regulation of the TCA cycle and of pyruvate dehydrogenase.

Each of the major enzymes indicated as a point of regulation of the TCA cycle diagramed in Figure 1-71 catalyzes an irreversible reaction, and the inhibi-

tors and activators are consistent with operation of the cycle in an efficient manner. Places where NADH/H$^+$ and FADH$_2$ are formed are also places where reductants enter the electron transport chain. The one place in the cycle where substrate-level phosphorylation occurs is the conversion of succinyl CoA to succinate.

Some of the effectors of pyruvate dehydrogenase are shown. Pyruvate dehydrogenase is an enzyme complex composed of five different activities, and it uses an equivalent number of cofactors. In eukaryotes, its activity is also controlled by a pyruvate dehydrogenase kinase, which inactivates it upon phosphorylation, and a phosphatase, which activates it by removing the phosphate group.

10.2. Anaplerotic Reactions for the TCA Cycle

A second major function of the TCA cycle is to supply intermediates for synthesis of other intermediary metabolites necessary for cell survival and maintenance. Since intermediates of the cycle are drained off for these purposes, it is essential that mechanisms exist for replacing cycle intermediates in order to keep

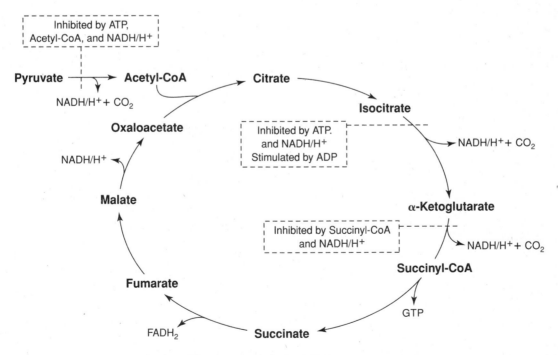

Figure 1-71. Regulators of the TCA cycle.
Drawn by author

it operating. Reactions that perform this function are called *anaplerotic reactions* since they replenish intermediates of the cycle. The following figure (Figure 1-72) shows some of the reactions that have been classified as fitting this category.

The more important of these anaplerotic reactions in eukaryotes is pyruvate carboxylase, and in prokaryotes, phosphoenolpyruvate carboxylase, both of which produce oxaloacetate by reactions that are irreversible under normal physiological conditions.

10.2.1. Oxidative Phosphorylation

An abbreviated sketch of sources of acetate for entry into the TCA cycle at the level of citrate is shown in Figure 1-73. Also shown are positions where oxidation occurs and where reducing equivalents enter the electron chain for ultimate reduction of O_2 to H_2O and concomitant generation of high-energy phosphates in the form of ATP.

Figure 1-73 shows diagrammatically each of the complexes involved in the flow of electrons down the electro-potential gradient. The chart at the top shows

the standard reduction potentials of the initial and final products of the chain. The reduction potential of the $NAD^+/NADH_2$ couple is –32V, and that of the $\frac{1}{2}O_2/H_2O$ is +0.82. From the relationship (see above section on thermodynamics)

$$\Delta G^{0'} = -nf\Delta E_0'$$

where n is the number of electrons being transferred, f is the Faraday constant (96.48 kJV^{-1}), and E_0' is the electron potential, $\Delta G^{\circ'} = -219$ $kJmol^{-1}$ or 51.6 kcal/mol^{-1}, more than enough energy that is contained in three high-energy bonds of ATP. This energy, however, is not used directly for that purpose. It is used to provide the means for generating an electrochemical gradient across the inner mitochondrial membrane and possibly for controlling the "switches" that shuttle H^+ into the intermembrane space (see Figure 1-75)—a mechanism that must involve protonation/deprotonation of specific carriers since the movement cannot be through open channels. The net effect is that $NADH/H^+$ and $FADH_2$ are oxidized by components on the matrix side of the inner mitochondrial membrane, electrons move down their electro-potential gradient, and the energy generated from that process facilitates movement of H^+ from

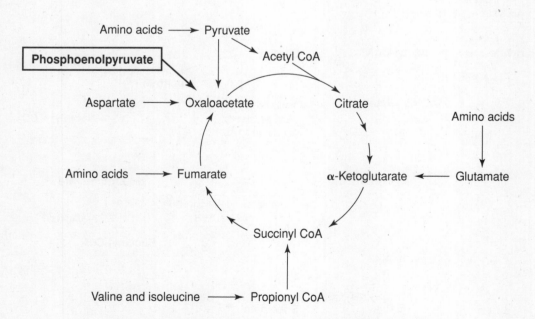

Figure 1-72. Anaplerotic reactions for the TCA cycle.
(Adapted from Devlin, T. M., Editor, *Textbook of Biochemistry with Clinical Correlations*, Sixth Edition, Wiley-Liss, Hoboken, NJ, 2006, p. 551, Fig. 14.24.)

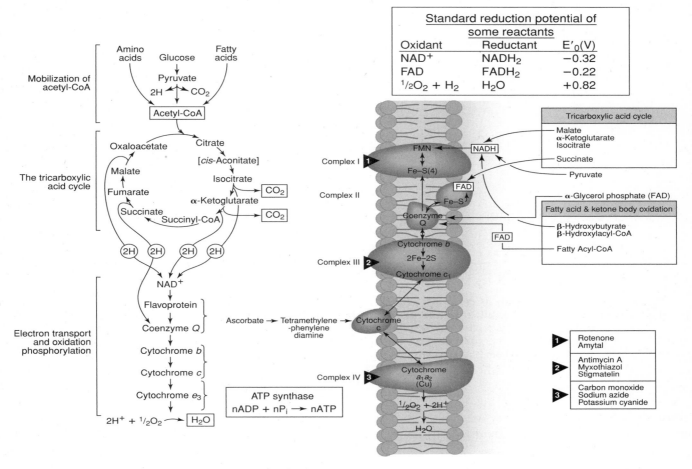

Standard reduction potential of some reactants		
Oxidant	Reductant	$E'_0(V)$
NAD^+	$NADH_2$	-0.32
FAD	$FADH_2$	-0.22
$^1/_2O_2 + H_2$	H_2O	$+0.82$

Figure 1-73. Sources of acetyl CoA for the TCA cycle and schematic of components of the electron transport chain indicating binding sites for specific inhibitors.
(Adapted composite figure from: Leninger, A. L., *Biochemistry*, Second Edition, Worth Publishing, Inc., New York, 1975, Fig. 17.1, p. 445 and Devlin, T. M., Editor, *Textbook of Biochemistry with Clinical Correlations*, Sixth Edition, Wiley-Liss, Hoboken, NJ, 2006, Fig. 14.44, p. 563.)

inside to outside, increasing the positive character of the membrane. The energy generated by the flow of H^+ through the ATP synthase complex (from the inner membrane space to the matrix) provides the energy necessary to effect the reaction of $ADP + P_i \rightarrow ATP$.

The mechanism for oxidative phosphorylation is the chemiosmotic mechanism as introduced by Peter Mitchell in 1961. It states "…the free energy of electron transport is conserved by pumping H^+ from the mitochondrial matrix to the intermembrane space to create an electrochemical H^+ gradient across the inner mitochondrial membrane. The electrochemical potential of this gradient is harnessed to synthesize ATP…" [Copied from Voet, Voet, and Pratt, *Fundamentals of Biochemistry*, 2nd Ed., Wiley, 2006, p 568.]

This theory imposes specific requirements on the inner mitochondrial membrane: (1) it must be intact and (2) it must be impermeable to ions such as OH^-, K^+, and H^+ that would interfere with the establishment or stability of a proton gradient.

The following Figure 1-74 shows that electron flow is coupled to oxidative phosphorylation. The figure

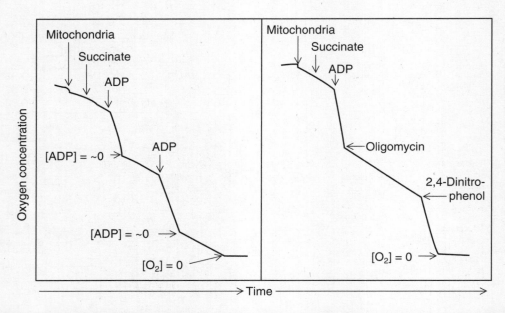

Figure 1-74. Demonstration of coupling of electron transport to phosphorylation and oxygen utilization (diagram on the left); and inhibition and uncoupling of oxidative phosphorylation (diagram on the right). Oligomycin inhibits proton flow through F_0 of ATP synthase and 2,4-dinitrophenol dissipates the proton gradient and permits electron flow and oxygen utilization without phosphorylation of ADP. (Adapted from Figures 14.46 and 14.47, pp. 564 and 565, Devlin, T. M., Editor, *Textbook of Biochemistry with Clinical Correlations*, Sixth Edition, Wiley-Liss, Hoboken, NJ, 2006.)

illustrates oxygen consumption (y-axis) in a closed system as a substrate, succinate, is oxidized.

The diagram on the left shows that even in the presence of succinate, there is no increase in oxygen consumption above background level unless ADP is present. This means that the flow of electrons through the electron transport chain to reduce oxygen to water cannot continue unless the mechanism for dispersing the electro-chemical gradient is operational. That mechanism is the flow of protons back into the matrix through ATP synthase (F_0F_1 complex) with concomitant production of ATP. As the concentration of ADP approaches zero, the rate of oxygen consumption decreases. Addition of more ADP result in another increase in the rate of oxygen consumption, which means that the potential energy of the chemi-osmotic gradient can again be used for synthesis of ATP, i.e., the gradient is dispersed as H^+ flows back into the matrix from the intermitochondrial space.

The right side of Figure 1-74 shows that inhibition of ATP synthase by oligomycin also inhibits the flow of

electrons down the electron transport chain. On the other hand, if the membrane is made permeable to protons by the addition of a compound like 2,4-dinitrophenol, electron transport is uncoupled from oxidative phosphorylation and oxygen consumption, i.e., substrate oxidation with concomitant reduction of oxygen to water, proceeds unimpeded. A proton gradient and membrane potential does not develop in the presence of 2,4-dinitrophenol.

There are other chemicals that inhibit the electron transport chain by blocking electron transport through specific carriers, chemicals that could cause cell death. For example, Rotenone binds to complex I and prevents reduction of coenzyme Q. Antimycin A inhibits electron transport through complex III. Carbon monoxide, azide, and cyanide inhibit complex IV by binding to either Fe^{+3} (the latter two) or, in the case of carbon monoxide, Fe^{+2}.

The electron transport chain consists of four protein complexes that exist in close proximity to each other within the inner mitochondrial membrane. Each complex has a greater affinity for electrons than the preceding one. Electrons can flow from one to the other even if they are not touching each other, but the rate of flow decreases as the distance between them increases. Electron carrier groups in the electron transport chain are flavins, iron-sulfur clusters, quinones, heme, and copper ions. If these groups are separated from each other by ~15 Å beyond their van der Waals contact distance, the rate of electron transfer is ~ $10^4 \, s^{-1}$ (about 0.1 sec) and is facilitated by the protein in some manner, possibly using some of the energy from the electro-potential gradient.

Another use of energy from the electro-potential gradient is to provide energy for some of the mechanisms that eject protons from the matrix to the inter-mitochondrial space. For each pair of electrons that passes through Complex I and III, 4 H^+ are transported from the matrix and 2 are transported at Complex IV. There are basically two mechanisms for H^+ transport from the matrix: one is being pumped out by complexes I, III, and IV, and the other involves operation of the "Q-cycle" – ubiquinone – "*ubique* or *ubiquitas*" from the Latin meaning it is everywhere. These protons help establish the proton gradient.

Complex I is a very large and complex protein consisting of about 34 subunits. The mechanism it uses to pump protons across the membrane is not completely understood.

Complex III also pumps 4 H^+ from the matrix to the intermitochondrial space. It makes use of coenzyme Q (the Q-cycle). Coenzyme Q (ubiquinone) accepts one electron at a time and becomes reduced to dihydroquinone, obtaining protons from the matrix. It interacts with an iron-sulfur cluster that facilitates its ability to give up 2 H^+ to the intermembrane space. The Q cycle turns twice per pair of electrons and transports a total of 4 H^+ to the intermembrane space—two per turn.

Electrons from the iron-sulfur cluster are transferred to cytochrome c that transfers them to complex IV that pumps two protons into the intermembrane space. Complex IV is also responsible for reduction of O_2 to H_2O. Protons are apparently passed along a "proton wire" that involves protonation-deprotonation of a series of specific amino acid residues in its protein

moiety. There cannot be open channels because, if there were, oxidative phosphorylation would be uncoupled since a H^+ gradient could not be established.

The protons that have been ejected from the matrix would have created an H^+ gradient and also a membrane potential that is "+" on the intermembrane space side and "–" on the matrix side. After the gradient, chemical and electrical, builds up to a certain point, it is dissipated by H^+ flow back into the matrix through ATP synthase, a transmembrane protein denoted F_1F_0 synthase. F_0 portion of this complex protein transects the membrane and contains the controlled pore through which protons flow. F_1 portion is on the matrix side and synthesizes ATP as the chemiosmotic gradient is dispersed. If the ΔpH across the membrane is 1.4 units, $\log_{10}(c_2/c_1)$ is also 1.4. If $\Delta E°'$ is 0.14 and Z = 1.0 for H^+, the number of kcal mol^{-1} for each proton transported can be calculated.

$$\Delta G = RT \ln\left(\frac{c_2}{c_1}\right) + ZF\Delta V^{0'} =$$

$$2.303RT \log_{10}\left(\frac{c_2}{c_1}\right) + ZF\Delta V^{0'}$$

This value is 5.2 kcal mol^{-1} for each proton transported.

ATP gets out of the mitochondrial matrix through the adenine nucleotide translocase, an ADP-ATP carrier protein. It operates through an antiporter mechanism where ADP is carried into the matrix as ATP is carried out of the matrix.

This is a relatively brief and simplified overview of the process of oxidative phosphorylation. There has been no attempt to account for all reactions, all components, nor to balance all equations. It will become obvious later that the process of oxidative phosphorylation is similar to the process of ATP formation during photosynthesis, but the gradient formation is in the opposite direction.

Part A of Figure 1-75 shows the general structure of mitochondria and its membrane structures, the orienta-

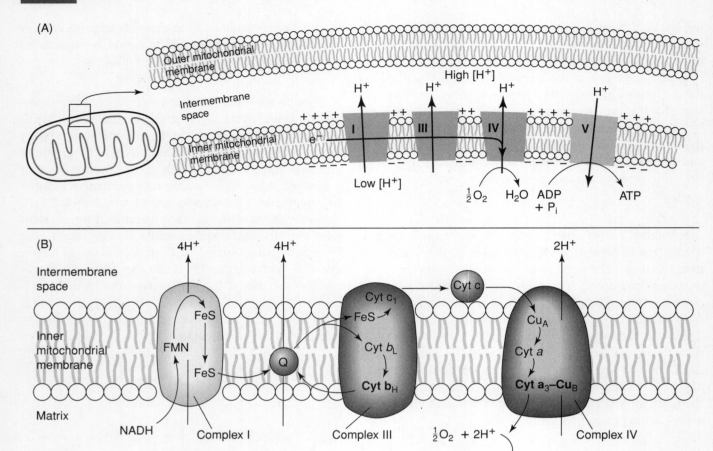

Figure 1-75. (A) Diagrammatic representation of coupling of ATP synthesis to electron transport concomitant with generation of a proton gradient. (B) Diagrammatic representation of components of the electron transport chain.
(Adapted from Voet, D., Voet, J.D., and Pratt, C. W., *Fundamentals of Biochemistry: Life at the Molecular Level*, Second Edition, John Wiley & Sons, New York, 2006, (Figs. 17-20 & 17-8) pp. 568 & 553.)

tion of polarization of the inner membrane, the direction of flow of protons during electron transport, and the direction of flow that dissipates the gradient and powers production of ATP. Part B shows some of the complexes involved during electron flow.

On average, 2.5–3.0 molecules of phosphate are fixed in a high-energy bond for each atom of oxygen reduced to H_2O when NADH/H^+ is the reductant. Thus, the P/O ratio for NADH oxidation down the electron chain is 2.5–3.0, while that for $FADH_2$ is 1.5–2.0. Current data suggest that the lower numbers for P/O ratios are more nearly accurate than the numbers on the higher end of the range cited here.

11. PENTOSE PHOSPHATE PATHWAY

Another major metabolic route for glucose 6-phosphate is the pentose phosphate pathway. Three major functions of this pathway include the following: (1) production of NADPH + H^+ for many biosynthetic reactions in cellular metabolism; (2) production of ribose 5-phosphate for synthesis of nucleotides and as a precursor metabolite for purine, pyrimidine, and histidine biosynthesis (among others); and (3) interconversion of sugar molecules, one of which is erythrose 4-phosphate, which is needed for synthesis of aromatic amino acids. Other metabolic intermediates of the pentose phosphate pathway can be metabolized through the glycolytic scheme to provide energy or metabolites for other metabolic pathways. The pentose phosphate pathway is divided into two phases: an oxidative phase where $NADPH/H^+$ is formed and a nonoxidative phase where the interconversion of various sugar molecules take place.

11.1. Oxidative Phase of the Pentose Phosphate Pathway

$NADPH + H^+$ production occurs during this phase. These reactions are shown in the diagram below (Figure 1-76).

The first step is the oxidation of glucose 6-phosphate by glucose 6-phosphate dehydrogenase (enzyme 1) using $NADP^+$ as an oxidant to produce one molecule of 6-phosphoglucono-δ-lactone, which is hydrolyzed by 6-phosphoglucolactonase (enzyme 2) to 6-phosphogluconate. The second $NADPH/H^+$ is produced by reductive decarboxylation of 6-phosphogluconate by 6-phospho-

gluconate dehydrogenase (enzyme 3) to give ribulose-5-phosphate. Ribose 5-phosphate isomerase (enzyme 4) converts ribulose 5-phosphate to ribose 5-phosphate.

Cells capable of photosynthesis can convert ribulose 5-phosphate to ribulose 1,5-bisphosphate, which is a substrate for ribulose 1,5-bisphosphate carboxylase (RubisCO). Ribulose 1,5-bisphosphate is a necessary substrate for CO_2 fixation in the Calvin cycle.

11.2. Nonoxidative Phase of the Pentose Phosphate Pathway

The nonoxidative phase of the pentose phosphate pathway begins with ribulose 5-phosphate and involves primarily two classes of enzymes: isomerases and transferases. Phosphopentose isomerase (EC 5.3.1.6) and phosphopentose epimerase (EC 5.1.3.1) are enzymes in the isomerase classification, and transaldolase (EC 2.2.1.2) and transketolase (EC 2.2.1.1) are among the transferase

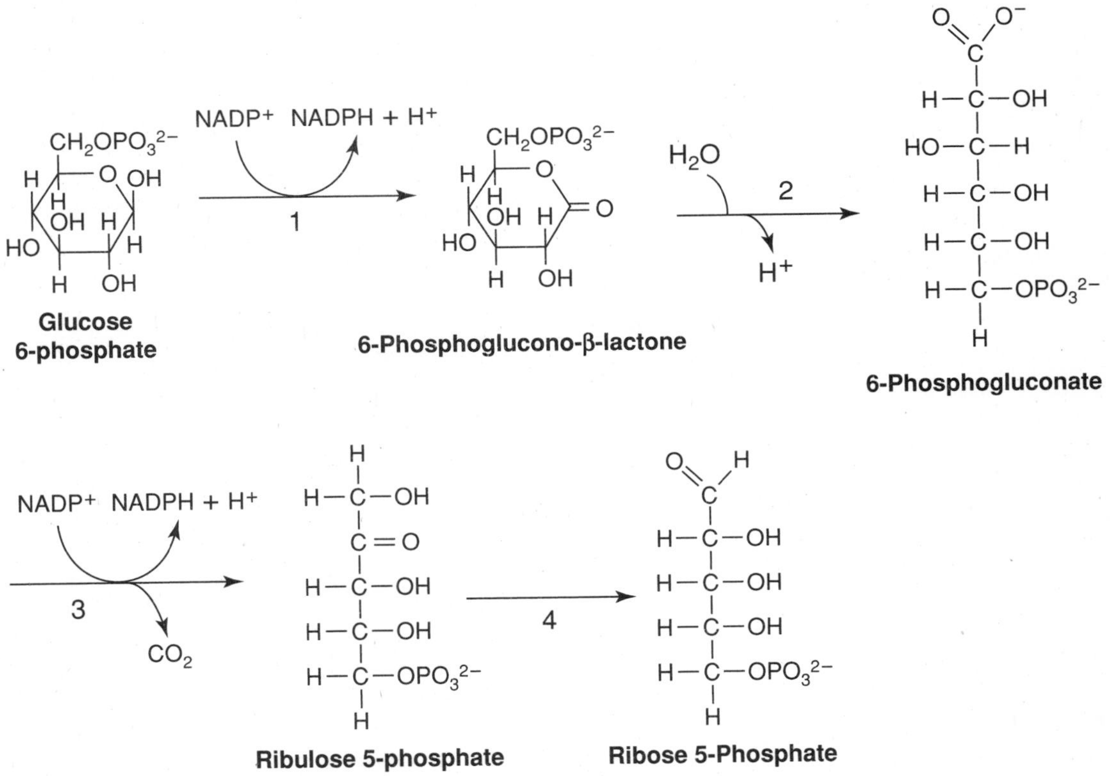

Figure 1-76. Oxidative phase of the pentose phosphate pathway.
(Adapted from Devlin, T. M., Editor, *Textbook of Biochemistry with Clinical Correlations*, Sixth Edition, Wiley-Liss, Hoboken, NJ, 2006, Fig. 16.1, p. 639.)

classification of enzymes. The transformations that take place in this phase of the pentose phosphate pathway are shown in the next diagram (Figure 1-77).

12. GLUCURONIC ACID OXIDATIVE PATHWAY

One other pathway of glucose utilization must be considered, namely, that involving glucuronic acid. Glucuronic acid is important in several metabolic reactions including those involved in xenobiotic metabolism where modification and excretion of foreign substances must occur.

Glucuronic acid is formed by oxidation of UDP-glucose by a NAD^+-dependent UDP-glucose dehydrogenase. UDP-glucuronic acid may form conjugates with certain hydrophobic metabolites increasing their water solubility and facilitating their excretion. The enzyme UDP-glucuronyltransferase catalyzes formation of glucuronyl-conjugates. Free glucuronic acid is metabolized to L-xylulose where it can be converted through a series of reactions to D-xylulose, phosphorylated by xylulose kinase to xylulose 5-phosphate, and further metabolized by the pentose phosphate pathway and eventually back to glucose. Myoinositol can be oxidized to glucuronic acid and be metabolized further along a similar pathway.

L-Gluconate can be converted to l-gulonolactone. In some species, this can be converted to 2-keto-L-gulonlactone and then to L-ascorbic acid. Humans and guinea pigs do not have the enzyme that oxidizes l-gulonolactone to 2-keto-L-gulonlactone and, therefore, they cannot make ascorbic acid. Since ascorbate is a vital reactant in certain metabolic transformations in these species, it must be supplied in their diets. It is a vitamin for them. Its metabolism follows the pathway shown on the right-hand side of Figure 1-78 and enters the glucuronic acid metabolic pathway upon conversion of L-xylose to L-xylulose.

13. GLUCONEOGENESIS AND GLYCOLYSIS

In some tissues, glucose is the major, if not the only, source of energy. Regardless of its importance for

energy in some cells, it is also an important constituent of various cellular structures. Thus, a mechanism must exist for its de novo synthesis, namely, gluconeogenesis. Figure 1-79 is a diagram contrasting the steps in glycolysis and gluconeogenesis.

Three reactions in glycolysis are irreversible, namely, hexokinase, phosphofructokinase (PFK), and pyruvate kinase. In order to form glucose, other enzymatic steps are necessary to get around those reactions.

Pyruvate as the starting source of carbons must first be converted to oxaloacetate. This uses the biotin-dependent enzyme, pyruvate carboxylase, ATP, and bicarbonate. Acetyl-CoA is an activator of pyruvate carboxylase and presumably signals the necessity for increased concentrations of oxaloacetic acid, which could stimulate activity of the TCA cycle or provide a concentration of oxaloacetate sufficiently high enough for increased activity of phosphoenol-pyruvate (PEP) carboxykinase and thus favor gluconeogenesis. Since PEP carboxykinase requires GTP as a substrate, the "energy charge" (high ATP/(ADP + AMP) ratio) of the cell would be high, and gluconeogenesis favored. Products of this reaction are PEP, GDP, and bicarbonate. It is a reversible reaction under physiological conditions. This step bypasses the third irreversible step in glycolysis and constitutes the first step on the pathway to glucose synthesis.

All of the other steps in glycolysis are reversible up to the one catalyzed by phosphofructokinase. Fructose 1,6-bisphosphate is a substrate for fructose 1,6-bisphosphatase, an enzyme whose activity is also controlled by fructose 2,6-bisphosphate. During glycolysis, fructose 2,6-bisphosphate activates PFK1 and inhibits fructose 1,6-bisphosphatase. In the liver of animals, hormones (glucagon for example) stimulate the activity of adenylate cyclase, which produces cAMP. cAMP activates protein kinase, which in the presence of ATP phosphorylates PFK2, changing its activity from that of a kinase to that of a phosphatase (see Figure 1-79). This leads to a reduction in the cellular concentration of fructose 2,6-bisphosphate and decreases both the stimulation of glycolysis and the inhibition of fructose 1,6-bisphosphatase, thus favor-

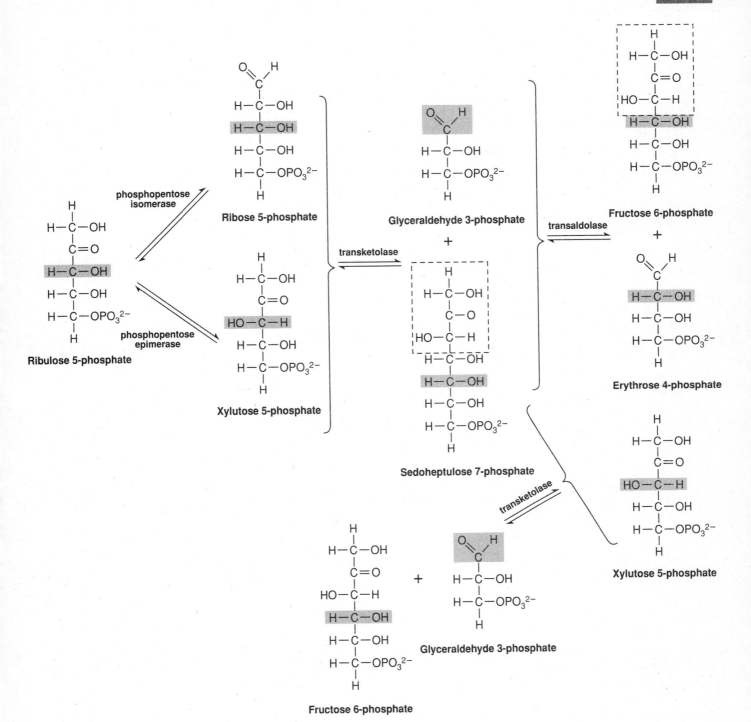

Figure 1-77.
(Adapted from Devlin, T. M., Editor, *Textbook of Biochemistry with Clinical Correlations,*
Sixth Edition, Wiley-Liss, Hoboken, NJ, 2006, Fig. 16.1, p. 639. Fig. 16.2. p. 641.)

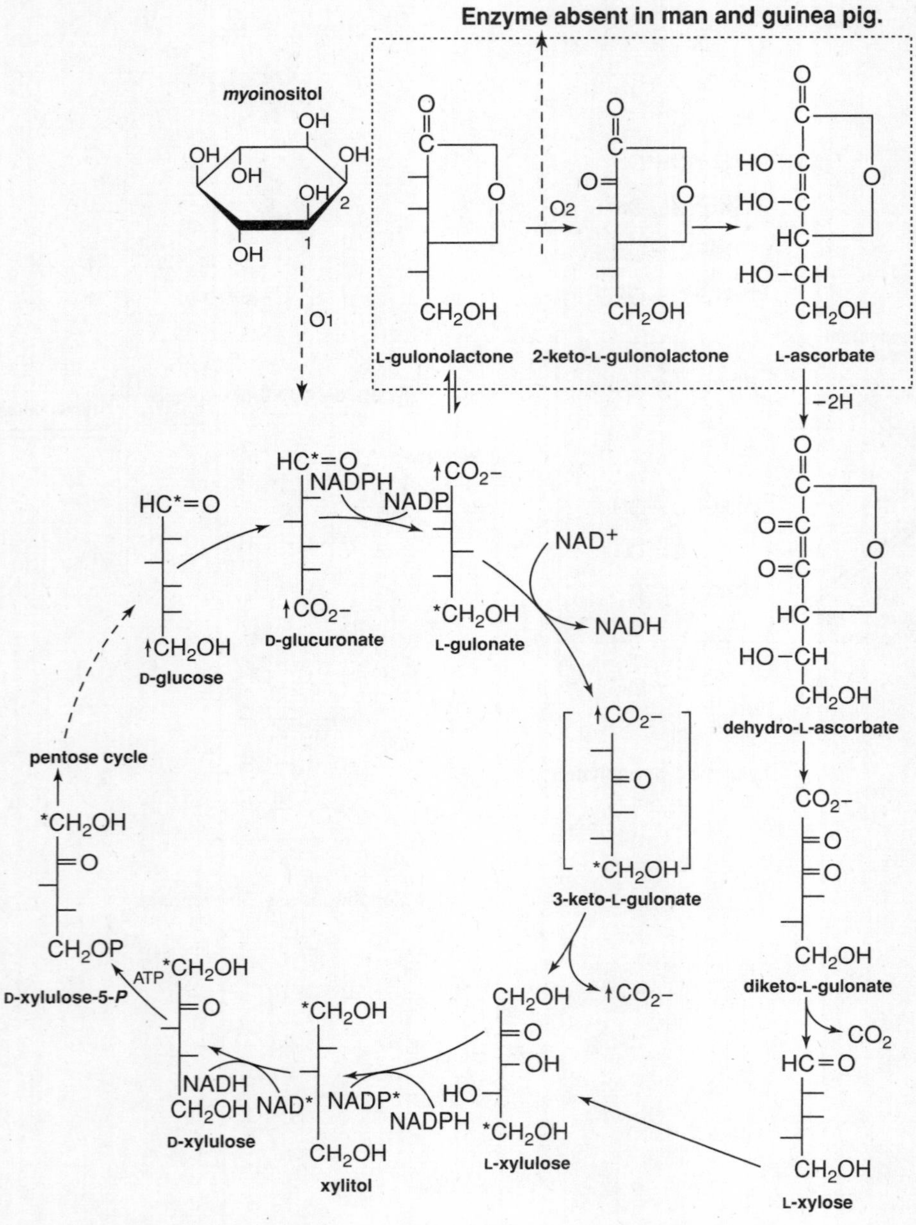

Enzyme absent in man and guinea pig.

Figure 1-78. Non-oxidative phase of the pentose phosphate pathway.
(Adapted from Mahler, H. R. and Cordes, E. H., *Biological Chemistry*, Harper & Row Publishers, New York, 1971, Figure 11-10, p. 540.)

ing gluconeogenesis. This bypasses the second irreversible step in glycolysis.

Phosphoglucoisomerase catalyzes the conversion of fructose-6-phosphate to glucose-6-phosphate, and the final enzyme, glucose-6-phosphatase, hydrolyzes glucose-6-phosphate to give glucose. Thus, gluconeogenesis will have been achieved.

13.1. Summary of Entry Points in the TCA Cycle and Glycolysis That Can Lead to Gluconeogenesis.

There are five major intermediates in the TCA cycle and glycolysis that are on the degradation pathways of amino acids and one type of fatty acid (odd chain) that can be directed toward biosynthesis of glucose.

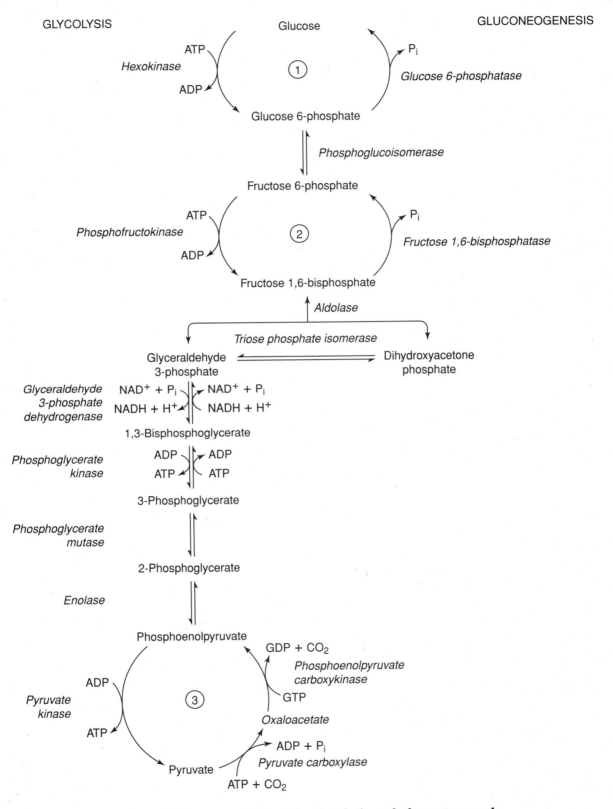

Figure 1-79. Enzymes involved in glycolysis and gluconeogenesis.
(Adapted from B. D. Hames et al. *Instant Notes in Biochemistry*, Bios Scientific Publishers, Leeds, UK. p. 240.)

Those compounds are α-ketoglutarate, succinyl-CoA, fumarate, oxaloacetate, and pyruvate. α-Ketoglutarate, succinyl-CoA, and fumarate can be transformed to oxaloacetate by enzymes of the TCA cycle.

14. GLYCOGEN METABOLISM

14.1. Glycogenesis

Excess glucose may be stored in animals as glycogen. It is a quick source of energy in muscle and a quick source of glucose in liver. Glycogen is a highly branched molecule with the general structure shown in Figure 1-80; each dot represents a glucose molecule. The area encircled by the dashed line in the center of the molecule represents glycogenin, an initiator protein for glycogen synthesis.

Glycogenin is a small protein that functions as a dimer. It, like glycogen synthase, requires UDP-glucose as the activated source of glucose units.

Glycogenin also requires Mn^{2+}, and the muscle form attaches glucose units to a tyrosine residue (Tyr194) in each subunit. Approximately ten units of glucose are added before glycogen synthase takes over and builds up a highly branched structure similar to that shown in the diagram in Figure 1-80.

Three enzymes are required for glycogen synthesis: (1) UDP-glucose pyrophosphorylase, (2) glycogen synthase, and (3) branching enzyme [amylo-(1-4→1-6) transglycoslase]. The reaction catalyzed by the first enzyme is shown in Figure 1-81.

Glycogen synthase adds glucose units to preexisting polymers of glycogen, either partially degraded from structures similar to the one shown above or to initial units starting with glycogenin-glucose$_{(n\sim10)}$ as mentioned above. The reaction catalyzed by glycogen synthase is shown in Figure 1-82.

Each addition adds a glucose residue to the 4-position of the preexisting molecule. The chains of glucose molecules in glycogen always end with the 4-position

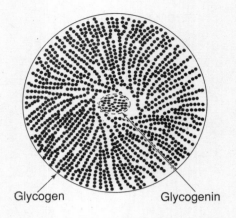

Glycogen   Glycogenin

Figure 1-80. Diagrammatic structure of a glycogen molecule.
(Adapted from: Antonio Zamora, Copyright 2005. *http://www. scientificpsychi.com/fitness/carbohydrates1.html*)

(nonreducing end) free. The bonds formed by glycogen synthase are α-1-4 bonds.

After the chain has grown to approximately ten units, branching enzyme will cleave about seven units and transfer them to the 6-position of another chain at about five glucosyl residues from the end, creating a branch point with an α-1-6-linkage (see Figure 1-83).

14.2. Glycogenolysis

Glycogen breakdown is initiated by the enzyme glycogen phosphorylase. The reaction catalyzed by this enzyme is as follows:

$$^{[Glycogen]}Glucose_{(n)} + P_i \rightarrow$$
$$^{[Glycogen]}Glycogen_{(n-1)} + Glucose\text{-}1\text{-}P$$

Glucose can then be metabolized to glucose-6-phosphate and to free glucose by the enzymes phosphoglucomutase and glucose-6-phosphatase, respectively:

$$Glucose\text{-}1\text{-}P \rightarrow Glucose\text{-}6\text{-}P \rightarrow Glucose + P_i$$

Phosphorylase action ceases when it comes to within four glucose residues of a branch point. Another enzyme, debranching enzyme, is required for further degradation.

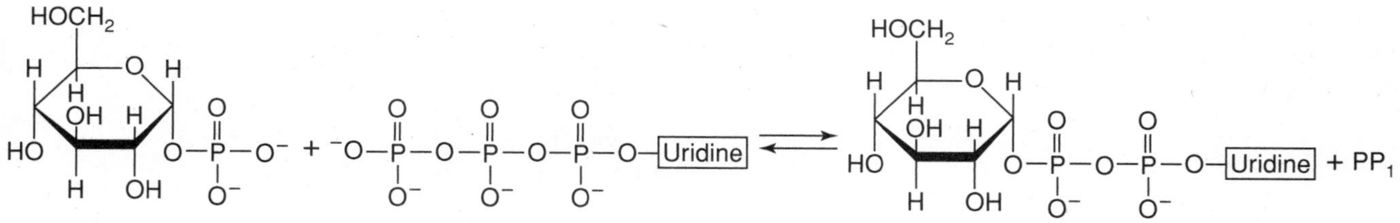

Figure 1-81. Formation of UDP-glucose.
(Adapted from B. D. Hames et al., *Instant Notes in Biochemistry*, Bios Scientific Publishers, Leeds, UK. p. 252.)

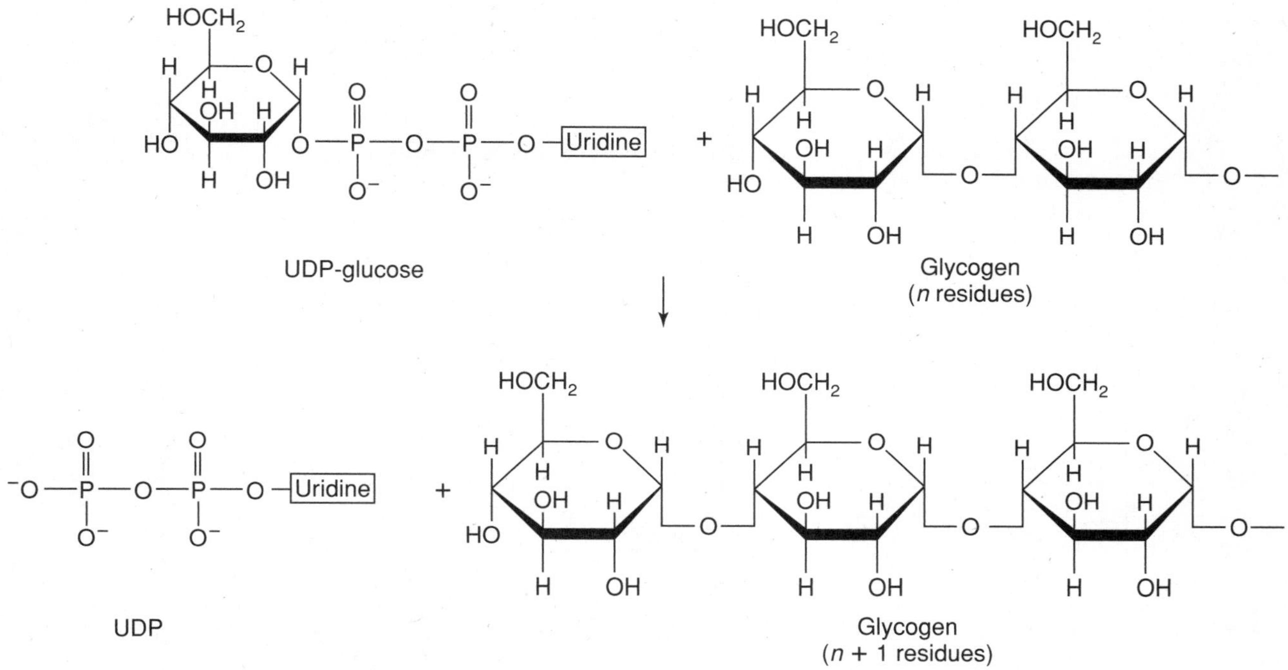

Figure 1-82. Glycogen synthase reaction.
(Adapted from B. D. Hames et al., *Instant Notes in Biochemistry*, Bios Scientific Publishers, Leeds, UK. p. 252.)

Debranching enzyme has two activities. The first is 4-α-D-glucanotransferase, which transfers a strand of three glucose units from a branch containing four glucosyl units to the free 4-OH end of an adjacent branch, making a longer unit with three additional α-1,4-glucosyl units. The single unit that is attached by an α-1,6-bond is hydrolyzed by the amylo-α-1,6-glucosidase activity using H_2O to give one molecule of free glucose and a longer chain subject to phosphorylase action. These activities are demonstrated in Figure 1-84.

14.3. Regulation of Glycogen Metabolism

Regulation of glycogen metabolism can be rather complex and can differ to some extent depending on the tissue and organism in question, much of which is under hormonal control. An indisputable fact, however, is that both glycogen synthase and glycogen phosphorylase cannot both be active at the same time. The net result of such action would be a futile cycle resulting only in the hydro-

73

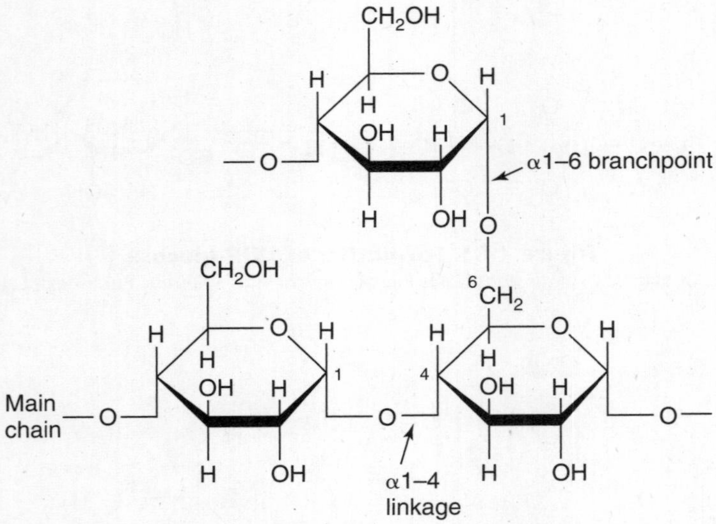

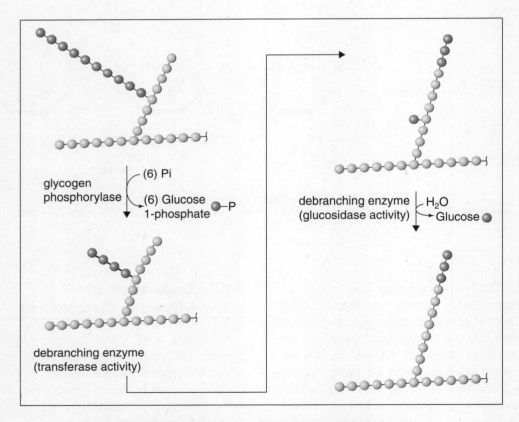

Figure 1-83. Linkage formed by glycogen branching enzyme.
(Adapted from B. D. Hames et al., *Instant Notes in Biochemistry*, Bios Scientific Publishers, Leeds, UK. p. 226.)

Figure 1-84. Reaction of glycogen branching enzyme.
(Adapted from Devlin, T. M., Editor, *Textbook of Biochemistry with Clinical Correlations*, Sixth Edition, Wiley-Liss, Hoboken, NJ, 2006, Fig. 15.52, p. 622.)

lysis of GTP. One regulatory mechanism that prevents this from happening involves covalent modification of glycogen synthase and phosphorylase. This mechanism is demonstrated in the diagram below (Figure 1-85).

This figure shows that glycogen synthase (scheme B) is active in its dephosphorylated form, while glycogen phosphorylase (scheme A) is inactive. Conversely, glycogen synthase is inactive in its phosphorylated form, while glycogen phosphorylase is active. The phosphorylation-dephosphorylation activities are under hormonal control, but there are also other allosteric effectors that interact with these enzymes.

15. PHOTOSYNTHESIS

Photosynthesis is a complex series of chemical reactions initiated by the absorption of sunlight by special organelles and proceeds to completion without the requirement of light. The first phase of photosynthesis is referred to as **light reactions** and the latter phase is referred to as **dark reactions**. The overall process, including light and dark reactions, may be represented as follows:

$$CO_2 + 2H_2A \xrightarrow{h\nu} (CH_2O) + H_2O + 2A$$

where H_2A is a substrate that can be oxidized to a product, A. In plants, the substrate is H_2O, and the product is

O_2. In some bacteria, the substrate may be H_2S in which case the product is elemental sulfur, S.

The dark reactions of photosynthesis result in the synthesis of carbohydrates and the concomitant storage of energy in chemical bonds of these carbohydrates. The overall reaction of this phase, represented here with a hexose as the end product, is as follows:

$$6CO_2 + 12H_2O \rightarrow C_6H_{12}O_6 + 6H_2O$$

This overall reaction, by some accounts, involves the use of 24 electrons that reduce six molecules of carbon dioxide to form one molecule of a hexose. The overall reactions of photosynthesis that result in formation of this hexose molecule occur at an overall $\Delta G°$ of approximately +690 (+686) kcal/mol, which is approximately equivalent to the energy produced by 30 electrons being pushed by photons through a potential difference of 1 volt. This is not inconsistent with the initial statement of this paragraph since there is not a requirement that each electron involved in the process must be pushed through a potential difference of only 1 volt.

The combination of these two phases of photosynthesis, namely, light and dark reactions, accomplishes essentially three tasks:

1. Photolysis (oxidation) of water to produce oxygen and reducing equivalents in the form of NADPH +

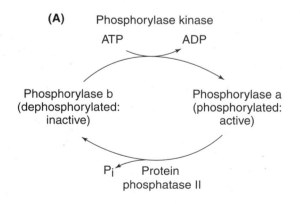

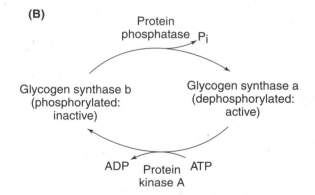

Figure 1-85. Regulation of glycogen synthesis.
(Adapted from Figures 15.56 and 15.57, pp. 625 and 627, Devlin, T. M., Editor,
Textbook of Biochemistry with Clinical Correlations, Sixth Edition, Wiley-Liss, Hoboken, NJ, 2006.)

H^+, which is necessary for some of the metabolic transformations that effect the third task.

2. Generation of high energy phosphates, ATP, through a process of photophosphorylation, which is also necessary for some of the metabolic reactions that occur during the third task.

3. Conversion (reduction) of carbon dioxide into stable, usable compounds (carbohydrates) that serve as sources of energy and as metabolites for growth and cell maintenance.

Photons of light are the source of energy used to effect these processes. Only light energy that is absorbed can effect chemical changes. The major light absorbing pigments that effect photosynthesis are chlorophylls. Plants and some other photosynthesizing organisms such as algae and cyanobacteria may also contain other accessory pigments such as carotenoids, neoxanthins,

and phycoerythrins that absorb specific wavelengths of light and transfer energy that they absorb to chlorophyll molecules. Structures of some of these ancillary pigments are shown in Figure 1-86).

These ancillary pigments absorb light primarily within the 450 nm to 650 nm range, where chlorophylls have the least amount of absorbance (see Figure 1-87). There is considerable spectral overlap among them that facilitates the transfer of energy to chlorophylls by various physicochemical mechanisms.

Light energy is directed to active pairs of chlorophylls located within two photosystem complexes, photosystem I and photosystem II, where selective electrons are knocked out of orbits and absorbed by specific compounds to effect the initial reductive transformations (i.e., loss of electrons). Subsequent chemical reactions complete the photosynthetic process.

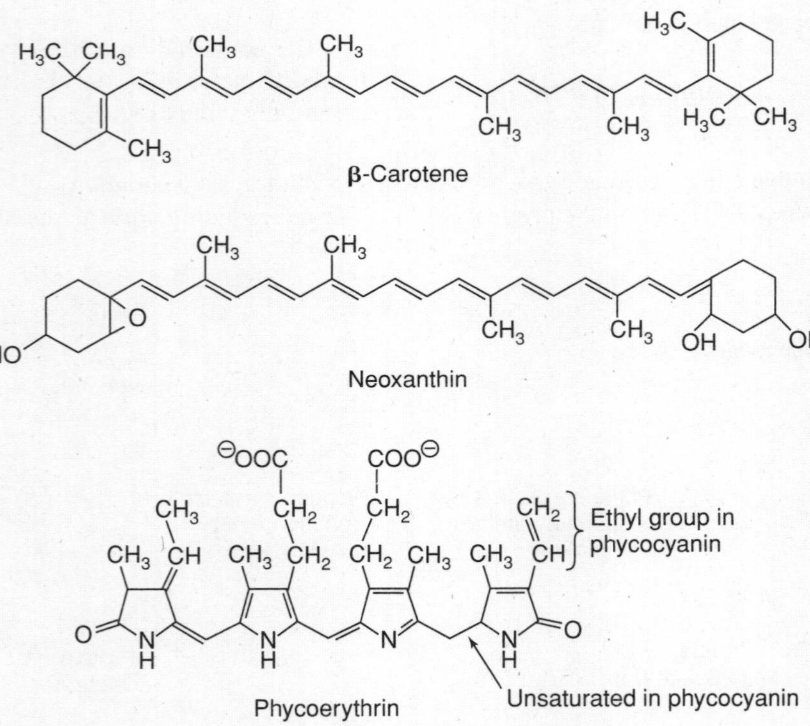

β-Carotene

Neoxanthin

Phycoerythrin

Figure 1-86. Structures of some ancillary pigments found in plants.
(Adapted from Figure 19.4, p. 19.5, Moran, L. A., Scrimgeour, K. G., Horton, H. R., Ochs, R. S., and Rawn, J. D., *Biochemistry*, Second Edition, Neil Patterson Publishers/Prentice Hall, Englewood Cliffs, New Jersey, 1994.)

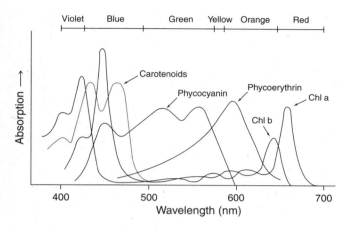

Figure 1-87. Absorption spectra of light sensitive plant pigments.
(Adapted from Figure 1-19.5, p. 19.5, Moran, L. A., Scrimgeour, K. G., Horton, H. R., Ochs, R. S., and Rawn, J. D., *Biochemistry*, Second Edition, Neil Patterson Publishers/Prentice Hall, Englewood Cliffs, New Jersey, 1994.)

15.1. Photochemical Consideration of Light Absorption and Energy Generation

Einstein's law of photochemistry states that *in the primary photochemical process each molecule is activated by the absorption of one photon or quantum of light* (Daniels and Alberty, *Physical Chemistry*, John Wiley & Sons, 1956, pp. 580–581). There is not a 100 percent degree of efficiency of absorption of light, so every photon of light that reaches an absorbing species does not effect a chemical reaction. There are 6.023×10^{23} molecules per mole. Thus, the absorption of 6.023×10^{23} electrons or quanta is defined as the absorption of one "einstein" of photons.

The energy in one quantum is defined by the equation

$$\epsilon = h\nu$$

where h is Plank's constant (6.624×10^{-27} erg sec) and ν is the frequency (wavelength, λ) of the light in reciprocal seconds ($\nu = c/\lambda$). The velocity at which light travels, c, is 3×10^{10} cm sec^{-1}. The energy per einstein is the energy per quantum times Avogadro's number or

$$N\epsilon = Nh\nu = (6.023 \times 1023 \text{ molecules mole}{-1})$$
$$(6.624 \times 10{-27} \text{ erg sec})\nu.$$

In photochemistry, an energy unit is referred to as an electron volt (ev) and defined as the energy acquired by an electron falling through a potential difference of 1 volt. The charge of an electron is 1.602×10^{-19} joule electron^{-1}. Thus 1 electron volt is

$$ev = \frac{(1.602 \times 10^{-19} \text{ joule} \times \text{electron}^{-1})(6.023 \times 10^{23} \text{ electrons} \times \text{mole}^{-1})}{(4.184 \text{ joule} \times \text{cal}^{-1})}$$

$$= 23{,}060 \text{ cal} \times \text{mole}^{-1}$$

The reducing potential of 1 ev, therefore, is approximately equivalent to the amount of energy necessary to produce 3 high-energy phosphate bonds of ATP (3×7.3 kcal = 21.9 kcal).

There is some "reverse" similarity between energy production in mitochondria of higher organisms through oxidative metabolism of carbon containing compounds where NAD$^+$ is reduced to NADH. NADH is reoxidized by electron transport down an electrochemical gradient to reduce oxygen to water with conservation of some of that energy through production of ATP. In photosynthesis, the reductive photochemical reactions at specific centers within chloroplasts lead to oxidation of water to produce oxygen, and the conservation reactions lead to production of NADPH and ATP, with long-term storage of energy in the bonds of carbohydrates. The anabolic reactions of photosynthesis that produce carbon compounds for growth of organisms higher up in the food chain obtain their energy from the sun, and those processes take place in chloroplasts. The catabolic reactions that utilize that energy in higher organisms obtain their energy from breaking the bonds made in photosynthetic reactions, and most of the energy conservation reactions of these organisms take place in mitochondria and/or through other oxidative or substrate-level phosphorylation mechanisms.

Chloroplasts have three membrane structures: (1) outer membrane, (2) inner membrane, and (3) thylakoid membrane (see Figure 1-88). The outer membrane is permeable to small molecules and ions. The inner membrane and the thylakoid membranes are impermeable to most molecules and ions. The thylakoid membrane encloses stacks of disks, called *grana*, which resemble stacks of pancakes or disks in the rods and cones of eyes in mammals.

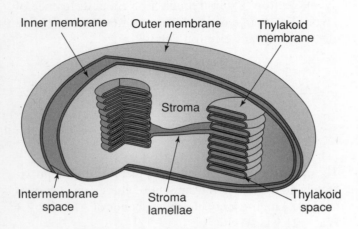

Figure 1-88. Chloroplast diagram.
(Adapted from Berg, J.M., Tymoczko, J.L., and Stryer, L., *Biochemistry*, Sixth Edition, W. H. Freeman and Company, New York, 2007, Figure19.3, p. 543.)

Chloroplasts also contain three different spaces: (1) the intermediate space between the outer and inner membrane, (2) the stroma is the space between the inner membrane and the thylakoid membrane, and (3) the thylakoid space (lumen)—the space within each disk-like structure. Grana are connected to each other by stroma lamellae, which are intermittent extensions of the thylakoid membrane. In green plants, it is within the thylakoid membrane that the photosensitive structures lie and where the light-dependent reactions take place (see Figure 1-89). It is within the stroma that the dark reactions (light-independent biochemical reactions) take place.

Grana contain high concentrations of basically two types of chlorophyll that are efficient traps for specific wavelengths of light energy. They are chlorophyll *a* and chlorophyll *b*, the structures of which are shown below (Figure 1-90).

Both contain a porphyrin ring structure with a magnesium ion held in its center through coordinate bonds formed from nitrogen atoms of the pyrrole ring moieties.

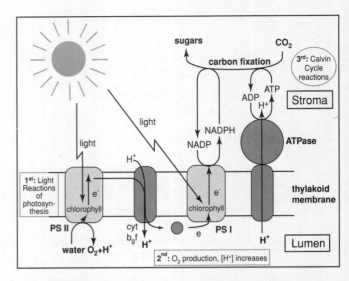

Figure 1-89. Schematic overview of photosynthesis and arrangement of photosynthetic elements.
(Modification of a diagram by Wim Vermaas, "An Introduction to Photosynthesis and Its Application", Arizona State University, *http://photoscience.la.asu.edu/photosyn/education/photointro.html*.)

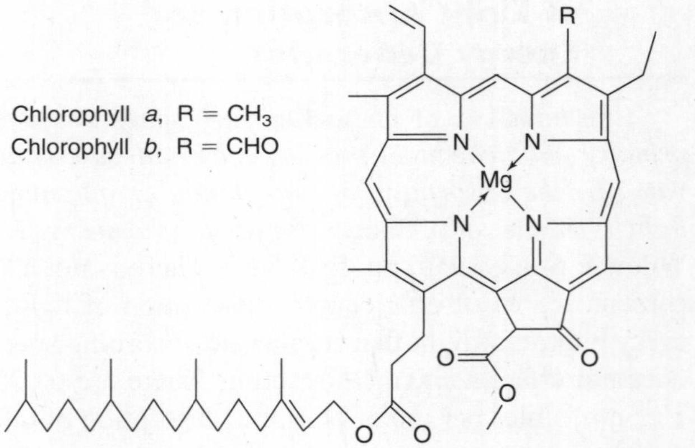

Chlorophyll *a*, R = CH$_3$
Chlorophyll *b*, R = CHO

Figure 1-90. Structure of chlorophyll a and b.
(Adapted from a Web page posting entitled "Chlorophyll" by Paul May, School of Chemistry, University of Bristol. *http://www.bris.ac.uk/Depts/Chemistry/taff/pwm.htm*.)

Chlorophyll *a* differs from chlorophyll *b* in that the R group in chlorophyll *a* is CH$_3$, and in chlorophyll b, it is CHO. These groups and the environment in which they reside give them different absorption spectra, as shown below (Figure 1-91). These two types of chlorophyll molecules complement each other in absorbing light between 400 and 500 nm and between 600 and 700 nm. They do not have significant light absorption between 500 nm and 600 nm.

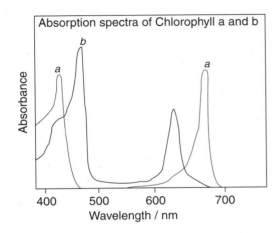

Figure 1-91. Absorption spectra of chlorophyll a and chlorophyll b.
(Adapted from a Web page posting entitled "Chlorophyll" by Paul May, School of Chemistry, University of Bristol. *http://www.bris.ac.uk/Depts/Chemistry/taff/pwm.htm*.)

Each of these types of chlorophyll reside in one of two different complex transmembrane structures called **photosystem I (PSI)** and **photosystem II (PSII)**. The products resulting from the light transduction process that occurs in each of these systems differ, but they are functionally connected through specific electron transport carriers (cytochrome *bf* and others) to effect the light reactions of O_2 production, CO_2 reduction, and energy production and conservation in the forms of NADPH + H^+ and ATP (see Figure 1-92).

The wavelength of maximum absorbance of light by PSI is approximately 700 nm, and that of PSII is approximately 680 nm. Even though both are exposed to light and absorb it simultaneously, the flow of electrons that normally initiates the phototransduction process is initiated by PSII.

PSII is a complex protein that consists of two 32 kDa subunits that span the thylakoid membrane. It contains a large number of chlorophyll molecules that serve as photoactivation centers or light traps. The extinction coefficient of chlorophyll *a* is approximately 10^5 M^{-1}cm^{-1}, almost 20-times higher than that of NADPH at

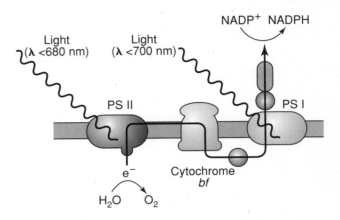

Figure 1-92. Cytochrome *bf* is a major component of the electron transport system that connects photosystem II and photosystem I.
(Adapted from Berg, J.M., Tymoczko, J.L., and Stryer, L., *Biochemistry*, Fifth Edition, W. H. Freeman and Company, New York, 2002, Figure 19.11.)

340 nm—an indication of its efficiency to absorb light at its peak wavelength of about 680 nm.

There is a special pair of chlorophyll molecules located at approximately the center of this molecular complex that function to effect charge separation (i.e., loss of an electron upon light activation). Structures of these molecules, as determined from a bacterial reaction center, are shown in Figure 1-93.

Note that bacteriopheophytin does not contain a magnesium ion as does chlorophyll *b*. Instead, it has two protons attached to nitrogen atoms of two of the four pyrrole ring moieties.

There is a manganese center (cluster) consisting of 4 manganese ions on the lumen side of PSII in the thylakoid membrane. Manganese in this cluster can exist in multiple oxidation states. A calcium ion, chloride ion, and a protein tyrosine residue (that is presumed to be able to form a free radical), are also associated with this cluster. Importantly, H_2O molecules are associated with this center, and it is here that the oxidation of H_2O to produce H^+ and O_2 occurs. Associated with this complex and the thylakoid membrane is cytochrome *bf*, which provides an electron transfer pathway to PSI. Plastoquinone (Q) is also associated with PSII. Plasto-

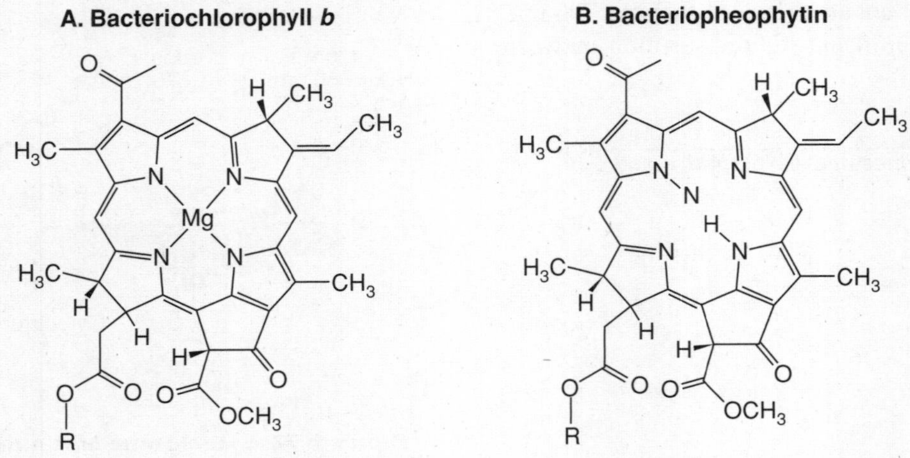

A. Bacteriochlorophyll b

B. Bacteriopheophytin

Figure 1-93. Structures of the "special pair" of chlorophyll molecules of PSII and PSI as obtained from bacteria.
(Adapted from Berg, J.M., Tymoczko, J.L., and Stryer, L., *Biochemistry*, Fifth Edition, W. H. Freeman and Company, New York, text Figures, p. 532)

quinone exists in two pools: one exchangeable (Q_B) and one fixed (Q_A).

The overall reaction of the initial step in plant photosynthesis is the extraction of electrons (oxidation) from water to produce oxygen, a reaction in which manganese ions participate. This reaction also involves the reduction of plastoquinone. The net reaction is as follows:

$$2H_2O + 2Q \xrightarrow{h\nu} 2QH_2 + O_2$$

The process followed by PSII to effect those reactions is as follows:

1. Many chlorophyll molecules in PSII are activated (electrons are knocked into a higher energy state) by absorption of light at 680 nm.

2. This energy is transmitted to the special pair of chlorophyll molecules near the center of the protein structure. This pair is often referred to as P680.

3. P680 rapidly (~10 nanoseconds) transfers an electron to pheophytin, the chlorophyll with the $2H^+$ at its center instead of Mg^{2+}.

4. The electron is then transferred to a tightly bound plastoquinone at site Q_A and then to the exchangeable pool of plastoquinone (Q_B).

5. The arrival of a second electron at this quinone results in the transfer of two protons from the stroma side of the membrane, (see below) to quinone yielding reduced plastoquinone (QH_2) and a positive charge on $P680^+$ (the special pair).

6. The manganese cluster serves as a very strong oxidant and extracts electrons from H_2O. A molecule of O_2 is formed for every $2H_2O$ that reacts in this system.

7. Each time a photon "kicks" an electron out of the P680 system, the $P680^+$ extracts an electron from the manganese center. The net result is the reaction shown above with production of O_2 from H_2O. Manganese is a transition-state metal with good oxidizing potential and reacts effectively in this system. These reactions occur on the lumen side of the thylakoid membrane, and $4H^+$ ions are produced for each molecule of O_2 formed. These protons are one of the sources that contribute to formation of the proton gradient.

There are two pools of plastoquinone: one fixed and one exchangeable. The fixed pool is next to pheophytin (the chlorophyll without Mg) and functions to convert pheophytin back to its reduced state using protons obtained from the exchangeable plastoquinone. The exchangeable reduced plastoquinone (QH_2) obtains its protons from water from the stroma, thus, contributing also to increasing the strength of the proton-motive force across the membrane.

Even though the electrons that replace those in pheophytin (as a result of the light reaction) come from manganese (Mn^{n+}) in plants, the protons come from plastoquinol (QH_2). Plastoquinol extracts its protons from water of the stroma. For the process to continue, plastoquinol must be reoxidized to the quinone form. This is accomplished by an electron transport system involving the cytochrome *bf* complex and a copper-containing protein, plastocyanin. This electron transport chain crosses the thylakoid membrane diagonally and links PSII to PSI—figuratively referred to as the Z-system in photosynthesis (see Figure 1-94).

Cytochrome *bf* complex, which contains a Fe-S complex, abstracts electrons from plastoquinol and transfers them to plastocyanin, and protons from plastoquinol that were obtained from the stroma side of the thylakoid membrane are released into the lumen of the thylakoid, further increasing the strength of the proton gradient.

The net result up to this point is the production of O_2 down one leg of the Z-system, reduction/reoxidation of reactants for the next cycle of events, and creation of a proton gradient from lumen to stroma of the thylakoid membrane.

PSI is a one-electron oxidation-reduction system. It consists of a protein complex composed of two subunits of slightly different sizes that are both larger than similar subunits of the PSII system, but there are functionally homologous regions. PSI contains two special chlorophyll molecules that absorb light maximally at 700 nm, and hence, by analogy with PSII, it is referred to as P700. A photon of light with an energy level of approximately 41 kcal mol^{-1} kicks an electron out of this center, leaving it with a positive charge ($P700^+$). The positive charge is neutralized by accepting an electron from plastocyanin, the terminal component in the connecting pathway between PSII and PSI. The 700 nm photon-induced release of an electron from P700 is driven through an electron chain consisting of chlorophyll (A_0), quinone (A_1), through an iron-sulfur (4Fe-4S) complex to ferredoxin (Fd) with reduction

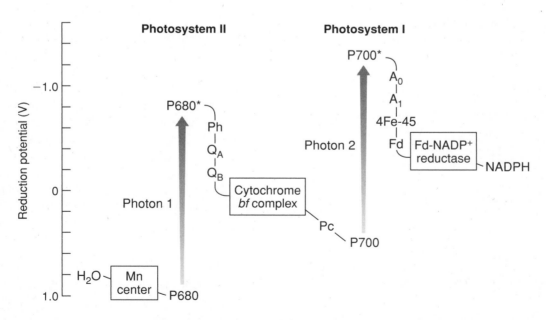

Figure 1-94. Diagrammatic representation of the Z-system of photosynthesis.
(Adapted from Berg, J. M., Tymoczko, J. L., and Stryer, L., *Biochemistry*, Fifth Edition,
W. H. Freeman and Company, New York, 2002, Figure 1-19.22, p. 538.)

potential of approximately –45 V. The 41 kcal mol^{-1} energy level of the photo-induced reaction at P700 is more than sufficient to drive the oxidation of reduced plastocyanin from PSII by oxidizing ferredoxin, which requires ~19 kcal mol^{-1}. Thus, the net reaction is the following:

$$Pc(Cu^+) + Fd_{ox} \xrightarrow{h\nu} Pc(Cu^{2+}) + Fd_{red}$$

There is a ferredoxin-NADP$^+$ reductase, a flavoprotein that uses reduced ferredoxin to reduce oxidized NADP$^+$ to NADPH. NADP$^+$ requires two electrons for reduction. Upon receipt of the second electron, it abstracts a hydride ion from water on the stroma side of the thylakoid membrane to produce NADPH in the stroma. This process also increases the strength of the proton gradient across the membrane. The net effect of the reactions of PSI is the light-driven production of NADPH in the stroma and a concomitant increase in the proton gradient across the membrane i.e., higher [H$^+$], or lower pH in the lumen of the thylakoid membrane than in the stroma.

The thylakoid membrane contains an ATP synthase (chloroplast ATP synthase) that is structurally and functionally similar to mitochondrial ATP synthase; CF$_1$-CF$_0$ ATP synthase is comparable to the F$_1$-F$_0$ mitochondrial complex.

CF$_1$-CF$_0$ ATP synthase is a transmembrane protein oriented such that the CF$_1$ site where ATP synthesis occurs is on the stromal side of the membrane. The proton gradient (approximately 10,000-fold difference in [H$^+$]; that is, pH is approximately 8 on the stromal side and approximately 4 in the lumen) is dissipated by the passage of H$^+$ through the center of the CF$_1$-CF$_0$ complex and provides energy for the reaction:

$$ADP + P_i \rightarrow ATP + H_2O$$

Thus, both NADPH and ATP are formed in the stroma where the light-independent (dark) reactions of photosynthesis occur—the Calvin cycle.

PSI is capable of catalyzing cyclic phosphorylation (Figure 1-95). In the absence of sufficient NADP$^+$,

electrons of reduced ferredoxin can be transferred to the cytochrome bf complex (dashed line). These electrons will then be used to reduce plastocyanin (PC), which will be reoxidized by P700$^+$. The net result is pumping protons into the lumen of the thylakoid membrane, regeneration of a gradient that drives ATP synthesis.

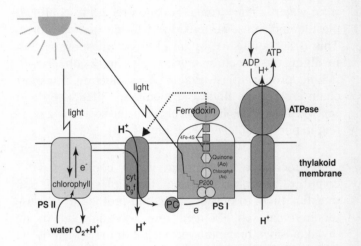

Figure 1-95. Cyclic phosphorylation catalyzed by PSI. (Modification of Figure 1-93 above to show electron flow in the absence of sufficient NADP+. Original diagram by Wim Vermaas, "An Introduction to Photosynthesis and Its Application", Arizona State University, *http://photoscience.la.asu.edu/ photosyn/education/photointro.html.*)

Chlorophylls form the major reaction centers for photosynthesis. Other molecules such as carotenoids, phycocyanins, and phycoerythrins absorb light and, in their excited states, can transfer energy through resonance transfer mechanisms to reaction centers and enhance efficiency of the photosynthesis process. For them to be effective in this process, they must be in appropriate physical arrangements, and the energy transfer must be from a higher to a lower energy state. The absorption spectra of these compounds (Figure 1-87) are in the 400 nm to 500 nm ranges and of higher energy than the active center chlorophylls that are in the 600 nm to the 700 nm range.

15.2. Light Independent Reactions of Photosynthesis: The Calvin Cycle

The next phase of photosynthesis (phase 3 as listed at the beginning of this section) is the conversion of carbon dioxide into stable, usable compounds (carbohydrates) that serve as sources of energy and as metabolites for growth and cell maintenance. These reactions occur in the stroma of plant cells, the same compartment of the cell where NADPH and ATP have been generated as a result of the light-dependent reactions. The initial aspects of this process occurs in basically three stages: (1) the fixation of CO_2 into an organic linkage with a suitable acceptor, (2) a series of reduction reactions that lead to formation of usable sugars and/or starches, and (3) regeneration of the CO_2 acceptor molecule. These three stages are summarized schematically in the following diagram (Figure 1-96).

The acceptor molecule is ribulose-1,5-bisphosphate. This reaction is catalyzed by ribulose-1,5-bisphosphate carboxylase (RubisCO) by the mechanism shown in Figure 1-97.

In this mechanism, CO_2 is added to the 2 position of ribulose-1,5-bisphosphate (Ru-1,5-P_2) to produce on the enzyme the intermediate, 2'-carboxy-3-keto-D-arabinitol-1,5-bisphosphate, which is hydrated and cleaved to produce two molecules of 3-phosphoglycerate. In summary, the net result of this reaction is the formation of two molecules of 3-phosphoglycerate from the five-carbon Ru-1,5-P_2 and CO_2.

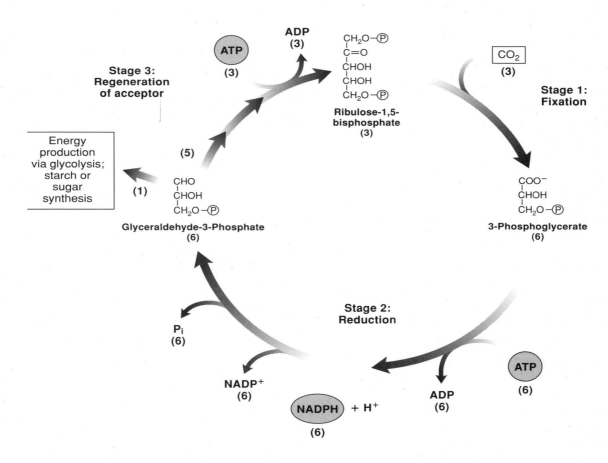

Figure 1-96. Summary of the three stages of the Calvin cycle.
(Adapted from Lehinger, A. L., Nelson, D. L., and Cox, M. M., *Principles of Biochemistry*, Second Edition, Worth Publishers, New York, 1993, (Fig. 19-19) p. 619.

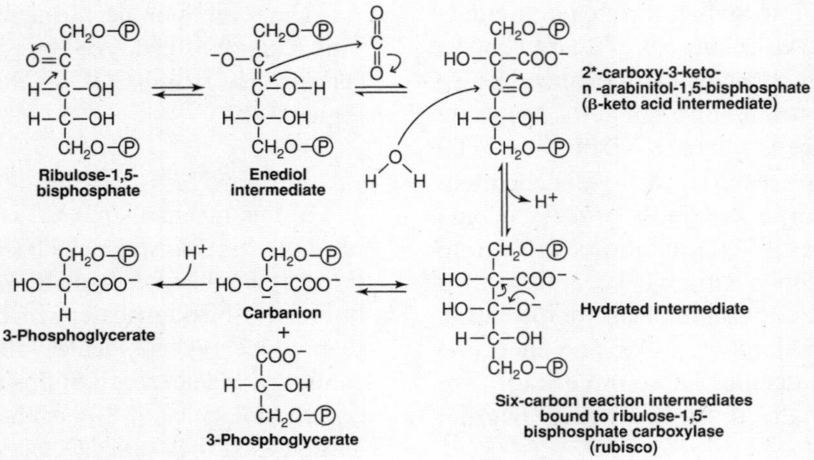

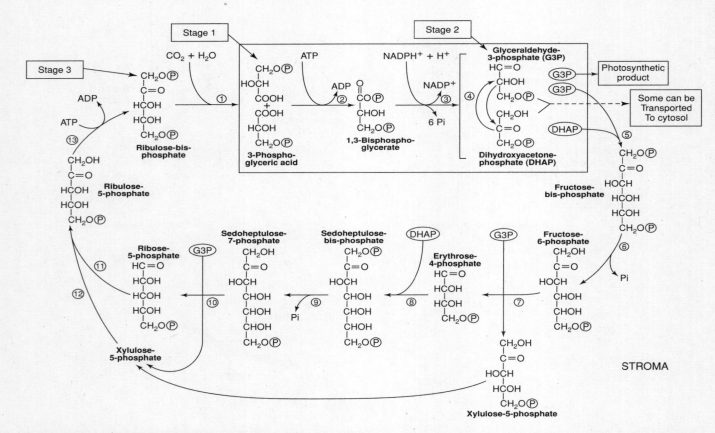

Figure 1-97. RubisCO reaction.
(Adapted from Lehinger, A. L., Nelson, D. L., and Cox, M. M., *Principles of Biochemistry*, Second Edition, Worth Publishers, New York, 1993, (Fig. 19-20) p. 620.)

Figure 1-98. Details of the second phase of the Calvin cycle. Numbers in the circles next to the arrows in the figure refer to the enzymes responsible for the corresponding transformation: (1) RubisCO, (2) phosphoglycerate kinase, (3) NADP-G3P dehydrogenase, (4) triose-phosphate isomerase, (5) aldolase, (6) fructose bisphosphatase, (7) transketolase, (8) aldolase, (9) sedoheptulose-1,7-bisphosphatase, (10) transketolase, (11) ribose-5-phosphate isomerase, (12) ribulose-5-phosphate epimerase, and (13) phosphoribulokinase.
(Adapted from Conn, E. E., Stumpf, P. K., Bruening, G., and Doi, R. H., *Outlines of Biochemistry*, Fifth Edition, John Wiley & Sons, New York, 1987, (Fig. 15.4), p. 491.)

The second stage of the Calvin cycle involves the reductive formation of glyceraldehyde-3-phosphate. This series of reactions requires use of ATP and NADPH that were formed during the light-requiring phase of photosynthesis. These reactions occur within the stroma of plant cells—the same compartment where ATP and NADPH were formed. Formation of the starting product for CO_2 fixation also occurs in the stroma. These reactions are also shown in Figure 1-98. Note that some of these reactions mimic those of the reductive phase of the pentose phosphate pathway.

Even though other storage forms of sugars can be formed in the stroma, the more common place for their formation is the cytosol. A major starting metabolite for their formation is triosephosphate. Plants have a transport system for moving triosephosphates from the stroma to the cytosol.

This process involves, in a reaction requiring ATP, the conversion of 3-phosphoglycerate to 1,3-bisphosphoglycerate, which is then converted to glyceraldehydes-3-phosphate. This reaction is similar to the reverse of that which occurs in glycolysis, but the reductant is NADPH instead of NADH. Glyceraldehyde-3-phosphate, in a freely reversible reaction catalyzed by triose phosphate isomerase, is converted to dihydroxyacetone phosphate. Dihydroxyacetone phosphate, through an antiport mechanism, is transported to the cytosol and inorganic phosphate is transported into the stroma. DHAP can then enter into carbohydrate metabolizing pathways through the glycolytic scheme or into other necessary metabolic pathways. Glyceraldehyde-3-phosphate from the cytosol, however, can be transported into the stroma through a similar antiport mechanism where inorganic phosphate is transported from the stoma into the cytosol. These transport mechanisms are shown schematically in Figure 1-99.

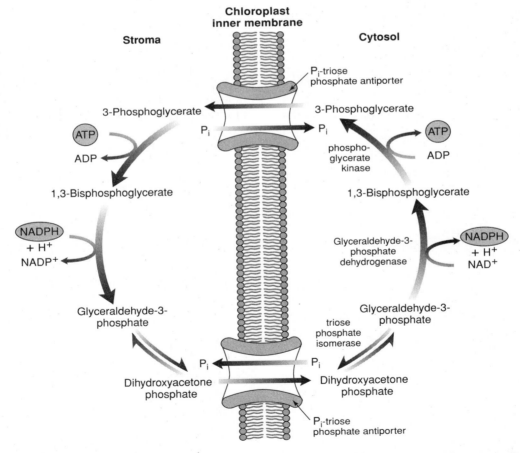

Figure 1-99. Transport system in plants for moving triosephosphates from the stroma to the cytosol.
(Adapted from Lehinger, A. L., Nelson, D. L., and Cox, M. M., *Principles of Biochemistry*, Second Edition, Worth Publishers, New York, 1993, (Fig. 19-29) p. 628.)

PART 1

BIOCHEMISTRY

15.3 Adaptive Photosynthetic Mechanisms

There are fundamentally three types of "adaptive" photosynthetic mechanisms. A brief description of each follows.

1. The more common C-3 photosynthetic mechanism where CO_2 is incorporated directly into C-3 compounds through direct use of the RubisCO system: This system is more efficient than the other two, especially in cool, moist conditions. It takes place throughout the leaf and requires no special anatomical features of plant cells. The stomata of plant leaves are open during the day. Stomata are tiny pores, usually on the underside of leaves, that allow the exchange of CO_2 and O_2 and are also the main routes of transpiration (water loss).

2. C-4 photosynthetic mechanism involves the initial incorporation of CO_2 into C-4 compounds in one type of plant cell and transport of the C-4 compound to another type of cell within the plant where RubisCO resides. There, it is metabolized back to CO_2 and a three-carbon compound. Thus, in effect, it delivers CO_2 directly into an environment where it can be used effi-

ciently by RubisCO in the same manner as indicated for C-3 plants. Plants that use the C-4 mechanism require a special type of anatomy called Kranz (the German word for *wreath*) anatomy, which is illustrated in the Figure 1-100. In this diagram, bundle sheath cells are surrounded by a layer of mesophyll cells in a wreathlike configuration. The bundle sheath cells contain large amounts of chlorophyll, RubisCO, and organelles. CO_2 is fixed in the mesophyll cells by the enzyme phosphoenolpyruvate carboxylase, which forms oxaloacetic acid. The oxaloacetic acid is quickly converted to malate where it is transported to the bundle sheath cells and reconverted to CO_2, generally by an NADP-dependent malic dehydrogenase. This process was described by M. D. Hatch and C. R. Slack and is sometimes referred to as the Hatch-Slack cycle for C-4 carbon fixation. The reactions and the anatomical configuration in plant cells required for C-4 type photosynthesis are summarized in Figure 1-100.

C-4 photosynthesis occurs effectively under high light intensity and higher temperatures. The CO_2 is delivered directly to inner leaf cells that contain RubisCO. This reduces the chances of RubisCO participating in photorespiration because this mechanism produces a higher CO_2/O_2 environment. Also, because

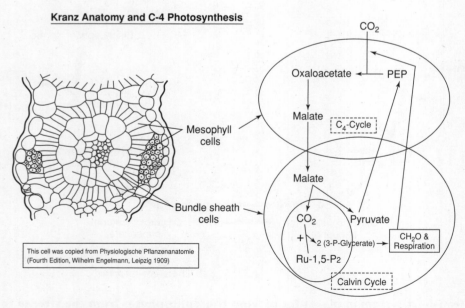

Kranz Anatomy and C-4 Photosynthesis

This cell was copied from Physiologische Pflanzenanatomie (Fourth Edition, Wilhelm Engelmann, Leipzig 1909)

Figure 1-100. Kranz anatomy and C-4 photosynthesis.
Ru-1,5-P2 is ribulose-1,5-bisphosphate and PEP is phosphoenolpyruvate.

the stomata do not have to be left open as long at higher temperatures, less water is lost by transpiration.

3. CAM photosynthesis occurs in plants of the *Crassulaceae* family—succulents such as cactuses where conditions relative to sunlight and water may be extreme. CAM stands for **C**rassulacean **A**cid **M**etabolism. The photosynthetic mechanism is of the C-4 type in these plants, but they are distinguished by the fact that they conserve water by opening the stomata at night and storing CO_2 in C-4 acids. During the day, CO_2 is released to RubisCO, where photosynthesis can take place. Under extremely arid conditions, CAM plants can leave the stomata closed during both day and night for an extended time period. They use the O_2 generated during photosynthesis for respiration and can, thus, survive relatively long dry periods (CAM-idling). After a rain, they can cease their "waiting to exhale" period and revert to their normal photosynthetic mode.

16. NITROGEN METABOLISM

This section will be divided into six parts: (1) nitrogen fixation, (2) chemical reactions of pyridoxal phosphate relative to amino acid metabolism, (3) biosynthesis of amino acids, (4) degradation of amino acids, (5) purine and pyrimidine metabolism, and (6) heme metabolism. Each section will be brief and as independent as possible so that the reader can concentrate only on sections of most interest. None will contain detailed chemical mechanisms, but only that sufficient to provide a reasoned understanding of the reactions involved.

16.1. Nitrogen Fixation

The original source of nitrogen for the amino group in amino acids, as well as other bio-organic compounds, is atmospheric nitrogen, N_2. In order to make it available for use by biological systems, it must first be converted to NH_3. The bond energy in N_2 is approximately 225 kcal mol^{-1} and, thus, strong reducing power is necessary to effect this process. The overall reaction is

$$N_2 + 3H_2 \rightarrow 2NH_3.$$

This reaction is effected by a process called "nitrogen fixation," a process that is generally carried out by some bacteria and archaea. The enzyme system responsible for effecting nitrogen fixation is the nitrogenase complex (EC1.18.6.1). The overall reaction catalyzed is

$$N_2 + 8H^+ + 8e^- + 16ATP + 16H_2O \rightarrow$$
$$2NH_3 + H_2 + 16ADP + 16\,P_i$$

The nitrogenase complex consists of two components: a reductase and the nitrogenase component. Both are Fe-S proteins, the latter of which also contains molybdenum, Mo. The reductase serves to provide reducing equivalents to the nitrogenase to effect reduction of molecular nitrogen to ammonia. Reducing equivalents are obtained from ferridoxin produced either from reactions of photosynthesis or oxidative electron transport. These reactions are represented schematically in the following diagram (Figure 1-101).

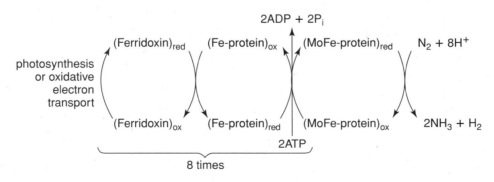

Figure 1-101. Summary of reactions of the nitrogenase complex.
(Adapted from: www.tau.ac.il/~ecology/virtau/2-tali/The%20Nitrogenase%20complex.htm)

Prebiotic NH_3 probably came from electrical charges, lightning, in the atmosphere and possibly also ultraviolet light. Even though that process may still occur, it is not a major source of ammonia formation for biological purposes. Some nitrogen fixation occurs in the roots of leguminous plants through symbiotic relationship with *Rhizobium* bacteria, thus, supplying a usable form of nitrogen for both bacteria and plants. Nitrogen fixation is an energy intense process, and in leguminous plants, a high amount of oxygen is required to support metabolic processes that lead to production of sufficient reducing equivalents to support nitrogen fixation. Leguminous plants contain a special, high affinity oxygen-binding monomeric protein called leghemoglobin that serves the function of collecting, storing, and supplying oxygen for metabolic processes that produce those equivalents.

The useful biological form of ammonia is the ammonium ion, which is obtained by solution of ammonia in water:

$$NH_3 + H_2O \leftrightarrow NH_4^+ + OH^-.$$

The first step of nitrogen incorporation into amino acids involves the formation of Glutamate from NH_4^+ and α-ketoglutarate, which comes from the TCA cycle. The enzyme responsible for effecting this reaction is glutamate dehydrogenase.

$$NH_4^+ + \alpha\text{-ketoglutarate} + NADPH + H^+$$
$$\leftrightarrow glutamate + NADP^+ + H_2O$$

This reaction proceeds through, first, formation of a protonated Schiff base resulting from the reaction of ammonium ion with α-ketoglutarate. The next step is reduction of the protonated Schiff base using NADPH $+ H^+$. Note that this is an anabolic reaction and not a catabolic one. Thus, it uses $NADP^+$ rather than NAD^+. The catabolic reaction occurs primarily in the reverse direction, and NAD^+ is the oxidant.

A second ammonium ion may be incorporated into glutamate using glutamine synthetase to form glutamine. An obligatory intermediate in this reaction is γ-glutamyl phosphate.

$$Glutamate + NH_4^+ + ATP \rightarrow$$
$$Glutamine + ADP + P_i + H^+$$

Glutamate and glutamine are the initial sources of nitrogen for synthesis of all of the amino acids and, through various transformations, other nitrogenous compounds of biological importance.

16.2 Chemical Reactions of Pyridoxyl Phosphate Relative to Amino Acid Metabolism

Pyridoxal phosphate is involved in one or more phases of the metabolism of every amino acid—anabolism and catabolism. Thus, a review of the chemical reactions of pyridoxal phosphate containing enzymes is appropriate.

Pyridoxal phosphate is derived from vitamin B6, pyridoxol, the alcohol form (see Figure 1-102). In the organism, it is phosphorylated and oxidized to the aldehyde to produce the active coenzyme, pyridoxal phosphate (PLP). PLP is bound to enzymes through a protonated Schiff base with the ε-amino group of a specific lysine residue. It is also bound to the enzyme by other types of bonding interactions, including charge-charge interactions, and it does not dissociate from the protein during the course of reactions in which it participates. Thus, it functions as a prosthetic group.

Among the more important reactions in which it is involved relative to amino acid metabolism are the following: (1) transamination, (2) racemization, (3) decarboxylation, (4) β-elimination and replacement, (5) deamination, and (6) aldol condensation. This is a rather broad and diverse group of reactions, but there is a common mechanistic theme among them. PLP forms a Schiff base (an external aldimine) with the substrate amino acid. What the substrate is and which type of reaction will occur is dictated by the protein (enzyme) to which the PLP is attached. In all cases, PLP and its

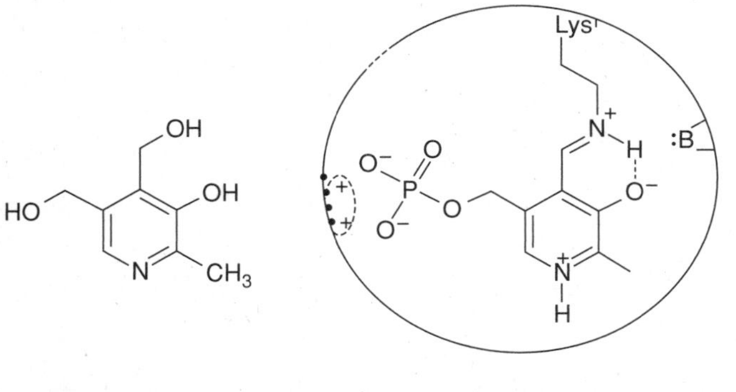

A. Pyridoxol (Vitamin B6)   B. Pyridoxal phosphate-Enzyme

Figure 1-102. Pyridoxol and diagram of an enzyme containing a pyridoxal phosphate prosthetic group.

sition state to produce a carbanion at that position. The carbanion is stabilized by charge delocalization throughout the *pi* bonds of the ring system. Thus, it serves as an electron sink through the formation of a quinonoid intermediate, as illustrated in the following diagram (Figure 1-103).

Structures of various enzymes in which PLP participates facilitate removal of the C_α-proton, a reaction that would otherwise require a pKa of ~30, a condition that could not otherwise be achieved under physiological conditions. Examples of reactions of PLP-enzymes are shown below (Figure 1-104). Specificity of the reactions catalyzed is dictated by the structures of the proteins to which PLP is attached.

altered form, pyridoxamine, remains attached to the protein throughout the entire course of the reaction. In enzymes such as aminotransferase, kinetic analyses show a mechanism consistent with double displacement or ping-pong.

The scope of reactions catalyzed by PLP-dependent enzymes is broad. The general unifying mechanistic principle of its involvement in catalysis, however, follows a unifying theme. A first step in reactions of PLP involves displacement of the protein lysine amino group with the substrate amino group to produce a Schiff base (an aldimine). This is followed by removal of a hydride ion from the α-carbon during the tran-

The above series of reactions may be used as a reference to PLP reactions for the remainder of discussions on amino acid synthesis and degradation. With a few exceptions, the biosynthesis of amino acids will be presented in groups categorized by the major origin of the carbon atoms that make up their skeletons.

16.3. Biosynthesis of Amino Acids

Structures of the 20 common amino acids found in proteins are shown in Figure 1-11. Generally, plants and bacteria can synthesize all 20 of them, but mammals can synthesized only half, or 10. The others are dietary essentials for mammals since mammals do not

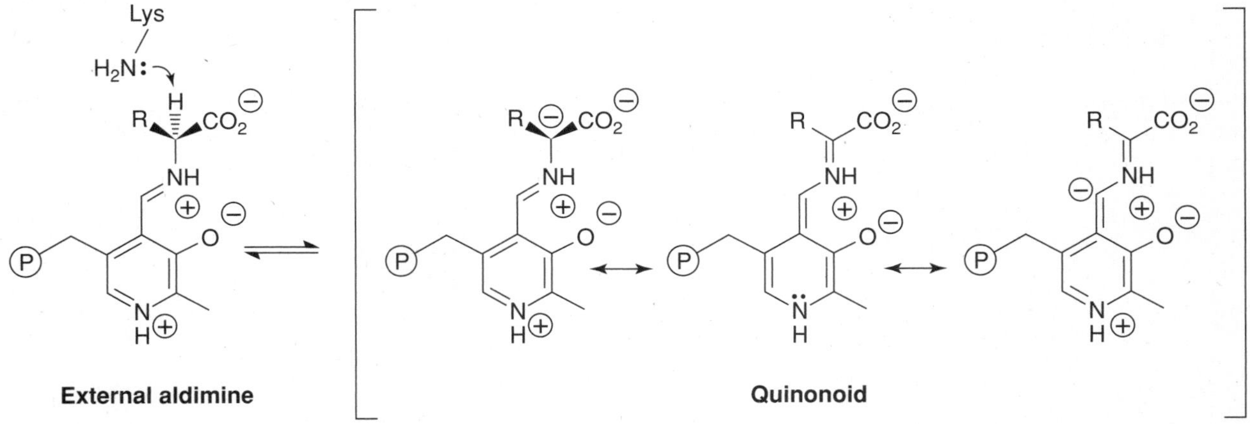

External aldimine   **Quinonoid**

Figure 1-103. Functional role of pyridoxal phosphate (PLP) in transition-state stabilization
(Adapted from: Eliot, A. C. and Kirsch, J. F. (2004) Annu. Rev. Biochem. 73:383–415.)

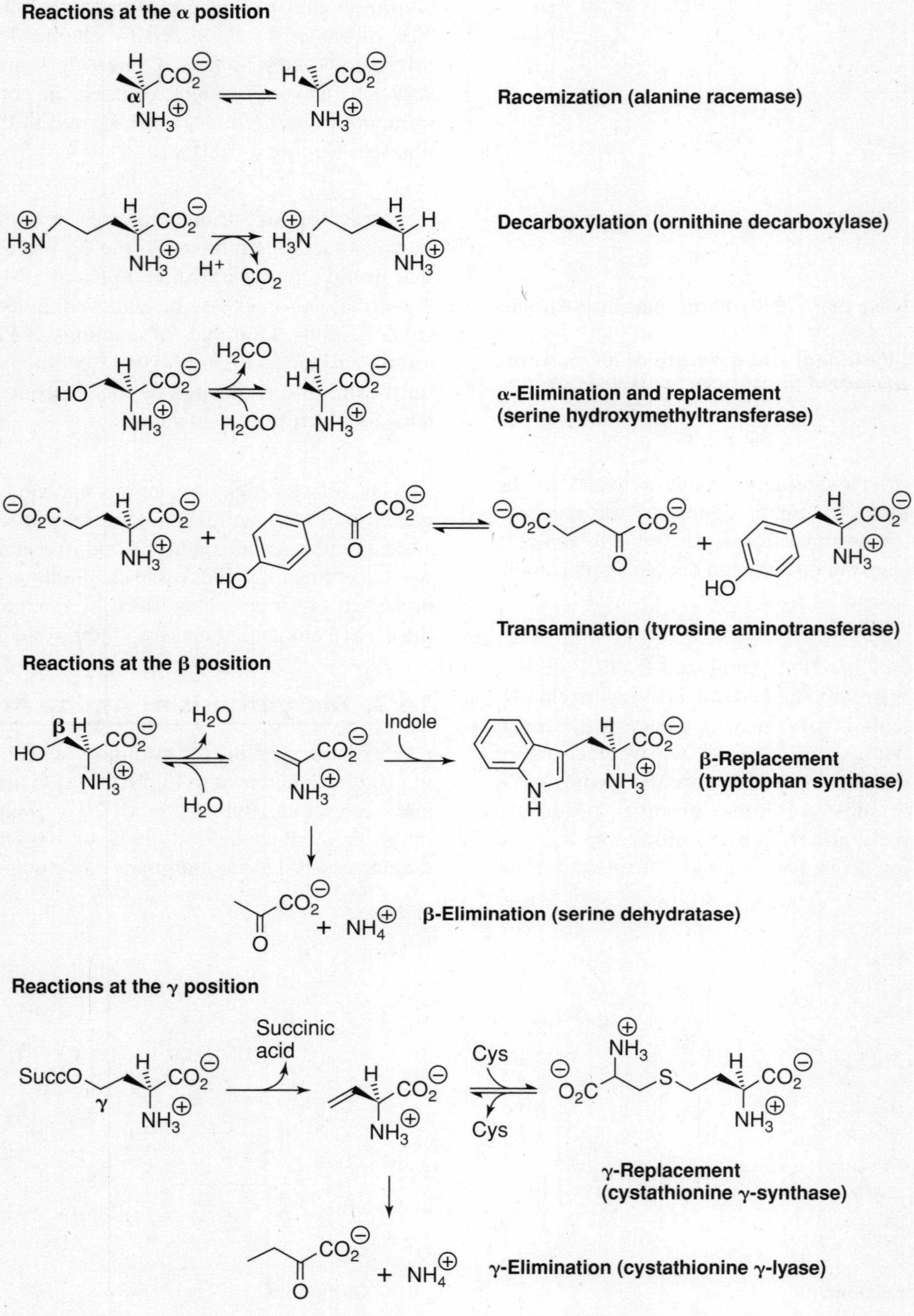
Reactions at the α position
Racemization (alanine racemase)
Decarboxylation (ornithine decarboxylase)
α-Elimination and replacement
(serine hydroxymethyltransferase)
Transamination (tyrosine aminotransferase)
Reactions at the β position
Indole
β-Replacement
(tryptophan synthase)
β-Elimination (serine dehydratase)
Reactions at the γ position
Succinic
acid
Cys
Cys
γ-Replacement
(cystathionine γ-synthase)
γ-Elimination (cystathionine γ-lyase)

Figure 1-104. Examples of reactions of PLP-enzymes.
(Adapted from: Eliot, A. C. and Kirsch, J. F. (2004) *Annu. Rev. Biochem.* 73:383–415.)

contain the necessary enzymes for biosynthesis of the carbon skeletons of essential amino acids. A list of the essential and nonessential amino acids is shown in the following table (Table 1-7). Arginine* is listed as an essential amino acid; however, adults are generally able to obtain sufficient quantities of this amino acid from the urea cycle whereas growing infants and children cannot.

The carbon skeletons of all of the amino acids are derived from intermediates of other major metabolic pathways of carbohydrate (glucose) metabolism (see Figure 1-105).

Two amino acids are derived directly by aminotransferase reactions involving glutamate as the source of the amino group. These are alanine and aspartate. A generic summary of the aminotransferase reaction is shown by the equation of Figure 1-106.

The α-keto acid for alanine biosynthesis is pyruvate, and that for aspartate is oxaloacetate. The aminotransferase reaction is freely reversible, and most of the amino acids can serve as the amino donor for the formation of glutamate from α-ketoglutarate. Thus glutamate is a third amino acid that can be formed directly from an intermediary metabolite of the TCA cycle. An important point to remember is that glutamate is always one of the participants in aminotransferase reactions. Also remember that glutamate can be formed directly from ammonium ion and α-ketoglutarate in a reaction catalyzed by glutamate dehydrogenase.

Other compounds formed directly from carbohydrate metabolism that contribute sources of carbon skeletons for amino acid synthesis are 3-phosphoglycerate, phosphoenolpyruvate, erythrose-4-phosphate, and ribose-5-phosphate. Table 1-8 contains the same information as Figure 1-105. It is an outline of the amino acids (second column) whose biosynthesis require direct utilization of carbohydrate intermediates shown in the first column. This is followed in the third column by amino acids that are derived by metabolic transformations of the primary amino acids and/or their carbon atoms. The last column contains only cysteine, which can be synthesized from cystathionine, an intermediate in methionine biosynthesis.

Table 1-7.
Essential and Nonessential Amino Acids

Essential	Nonessential
Arginine*	Alanine
Histidine	Aspartate
Isoleucine	Asparagine
Leucine	Cysteine
Lysine	Glutamate
Methionine	Glutamine
Phenylalanine	Glycine
Threonine	Proline
Tryptophan	Serine
Valine	Tyrosine

Carbons that eventually end up as the cysteine moiety of cystathionine can be formed by two pathways, but the sulfur atom still comes from methionine.

Amino acids in bold letters are essential amino acids. Those with symbols (*, #) beside their names need further explanation. Arginine*, as stated above, can be synthesized in mammals but by reactions that are involved in the urea cycle from ornithine in a cyclic manner, which does not generate a sufficient net excess to support growth—only enough to support maintenance as required by mature animals. Thus, it is essential only in growing mammals. This is primarily a "salvage" pathway for #cysteine biosynthesis and also a mechanism for conservation of sulfur.

16.3.1. Amino Acids Derived from Oxaloacetate/Aspartate

Amino acids derived from the oxaloacetate/aspartate precursors are asparagine, methionine, threonine, and lysine, the latter three of which are essential amino acids.

Further metabolism of aspartate for the biosynthesis of other amino acids in this group requires energy from ATP, which forms active intermediates at the β-carboxyl group of aspartate. For the synthesis of asparagine, an AMP derivative is formed with release of inorganic pyrophosphate. For synthesis of the other amino acids

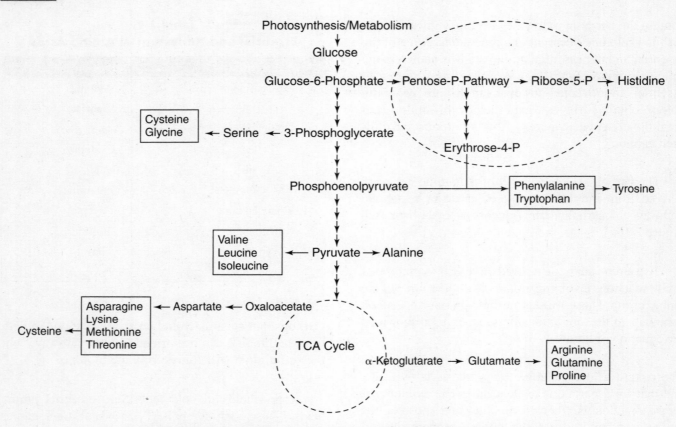

Figure 1-105. Metabolic sources of carbon for all of the amino acids.

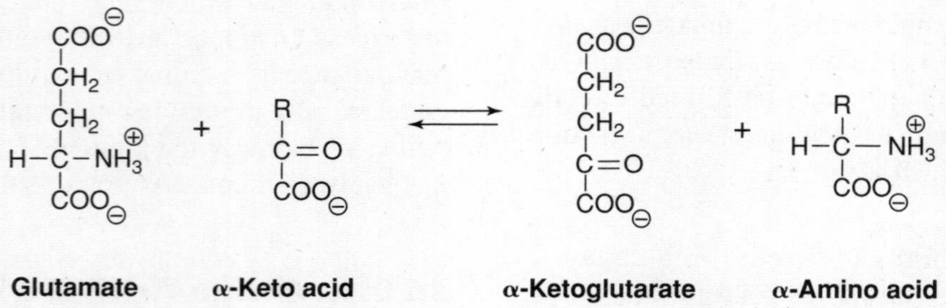

Figure 1-106. Summary of the aminotransferase reaction.
(Adapted from: *http://web.indstate.edu/thcme/mwking/nitrogen-metabolism.html#gs*)

in this group, activation results in formation of an acyl-phosphate at the β-carboxyl position of aspartate. These reactions are illustrated in Figure 1-107.

Asparagine is formed directly by transfer of the amide group of glutamine to aspartyl β-AMP accompanied by release of AMP.

The pathway for *lysine* biosynthesis is the more complex of the group and begins with condensation of pyruvate with aspartate semialdehyde to form 2-amino-4-hydroxy-6-ketopimelate. The series of reactions that eventually leads to formation of lysine is shown in Figure 1-108. Note that the ε-amino group of lysine is added by a transaminase (PLP-dependent) reaction involving glutamate and N-suc-

Table 1-8.
Metabolic Origin of Carbon Skeletons for Various Groups of Amino Acids

Intermediary metabolite	Primary amino acid formed	Secondary amino acid formed	Tertiary amino acid formed
Oxaloacetate	Aspartate	Asparagine **Methionine** **Threonine** **Lysine**	— Cysteine# — —
Pyruvate	Alanine	**Isoleucine** **Valine** **Leucine**	— — —
α-Ketoglutarate	Glutamate	Glutamine Proline Arginine*	— — —
P-Enolpyruvate + Erythrose-4-P	**Phenylalanine** **Tryptophan**	Tyrosine —	— —
Ribose-5-P	**Histidine**	—	—
3-P-Glycerate	Serine	Cysteine Glycine	— —

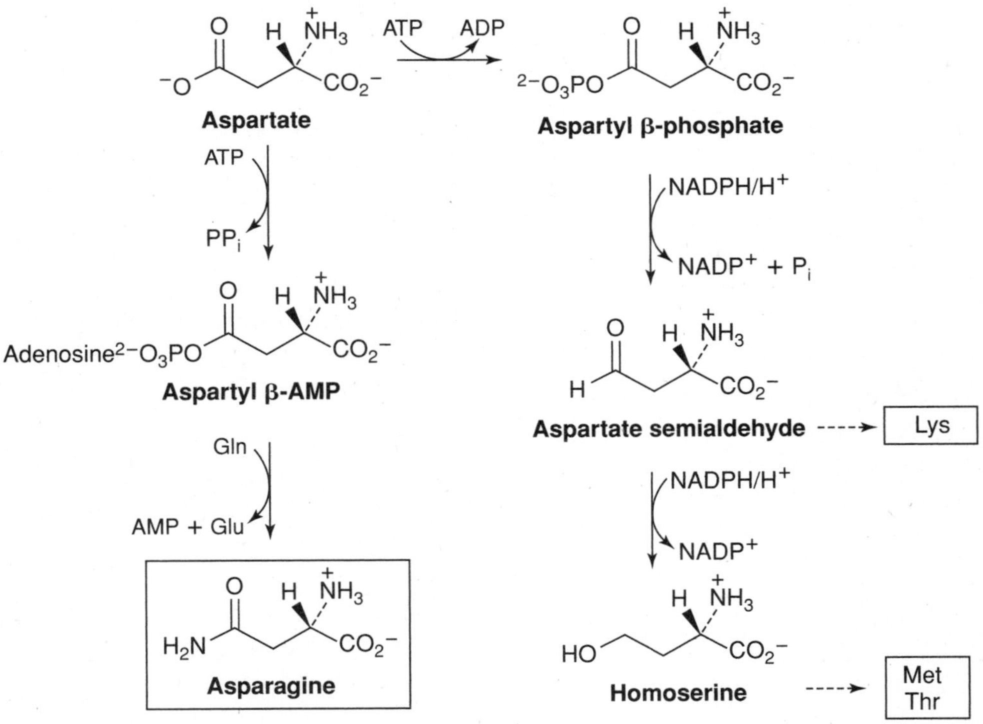

Figure 1-107. Formation of asparagine and homoserine from aspartate requires ATP.
(Adapted from McMurray, J. and Begley, T., *The Organic Chemistry of Biological Pathways*,
Roberts and Company Publishers, Englewood, Colorado, 2005, pp. 273-274.)

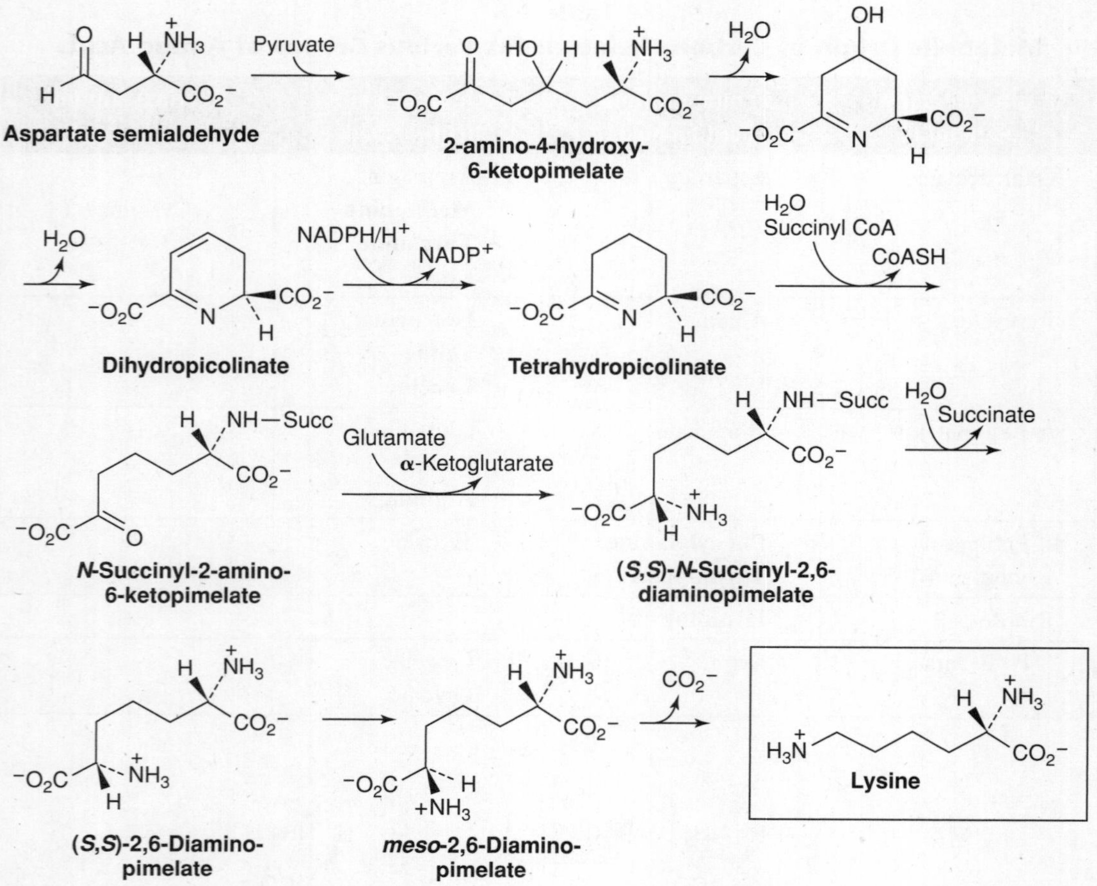

Figure 1-108. Lysine biosynthesis from aspartate semialdehyde.
(Adapted from McMurry and Begley, T., *The Organic Chemistry of Biological Pathways*, Roberts and Company Publishers, Englewood, Colorado, 2005, Figure 1-5.33, p. 277.)

cinyl-2-amino-6-ketopimelate. The product of this reaction, (S,S)-N-succinyl-2,6-diaminopimelate, is converted in three additional steps to lysine.

Aspartate semialdehyde can be reduced to homoserine in a NADPH + H$^+$ requiring reaction. This is the branch point for methionine and threonine biosynthesis. The reactions for *methionine* biosynthesis are as shown in Figure 1-109. The sulfur atom comes from cysteine, but none of the carbon atoms. Mammals lack the ability to synthesize the carbon chain (homocysteine) of methionine; hence it is an essential amino acid.

The methyl group of methionine is introduced from N-methyl-tetrahydrofolate (N-methyl-THF) in a reaction that also requires vitamin B12, specifically, its

coenzyme form, methylcobalamine. The methyl group is first transferred from N-methyl-THF to cobalamine to give methylcobalamine where it is then transferred to homocysteine to give methionine (Figure 1-110).

The branch point for *threonine* biosynthesis is also homoserine. Its synthesis occurs in two steps (see Figure 1-111). The first is a kinase reaction that produces phosphohomoserine. The next step involves a PLP-dependent enzyme whose mechanism of action includes a proton abstraction from the β-position giving an enamine intermediate followed by elimination of the phosphate group and the eventual creation of an intermediate with a double bond between carbons 2 and 3. H$_2$O is added across the double bond prior to its release from the enzyme-PLP complex as threonine.

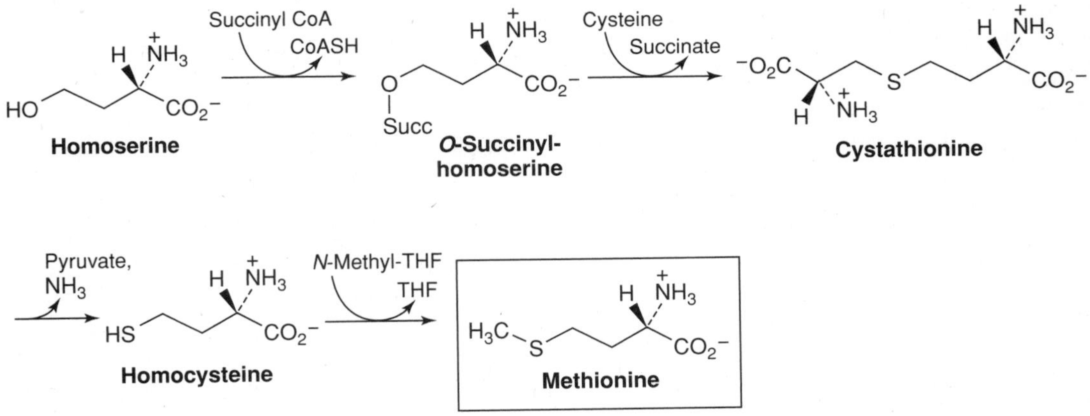

Figure 1-109. Methionine biosynthesis from homoserine.
(Adapted from McMurry and Begley, T., *The Organic Chemistry of Biological Pathways*, Roberts and Company Publishers, Englewood, Colorado, 2005, Figure 1-5.35, p. 280.)

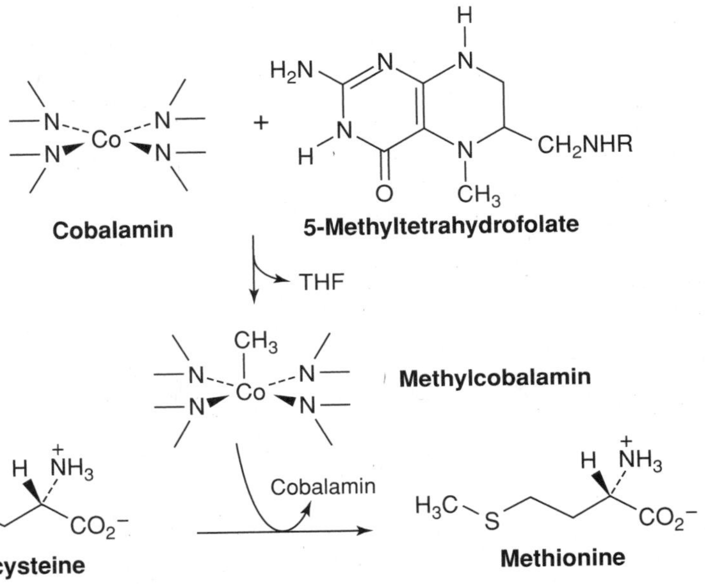

Figure 1-110. Cobalamin (vitamin B12) and tetrahydrofolate are required to add the methyl group to homocysteine to form methionine.
(Adapted from McMurry and Begley, T., *The Organic Chemistry of Biological Pathways*, Roberts and Company Publishers, Englewood, Colorado, 2005, Figure 5.37, p. 282.)

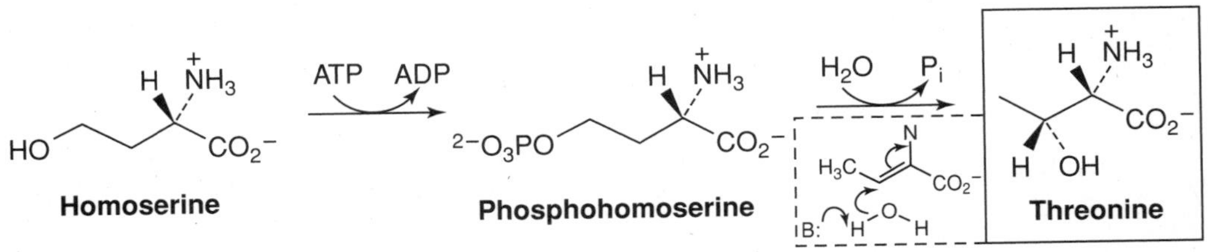

Figure 1-111. Threonine formation from homoserine.
(Adapted from McMurry and Begley, T., *The Organic Chemistry of Biological Pathways*, Roberts and Company Publishers, Englewood, Colorado, 2005, p. 283.)

Cysteine can also be formed from methionine as part of a "salvage" pathway. Cysteine formation using the "salvage" pathway is the result of action of the enzyme cystathionase on cystathionine. It is a PLP-dependent enzyme that catalyzes a deamination and an elimination yielding NH_3, α-ketobutyrate, and cysteine.

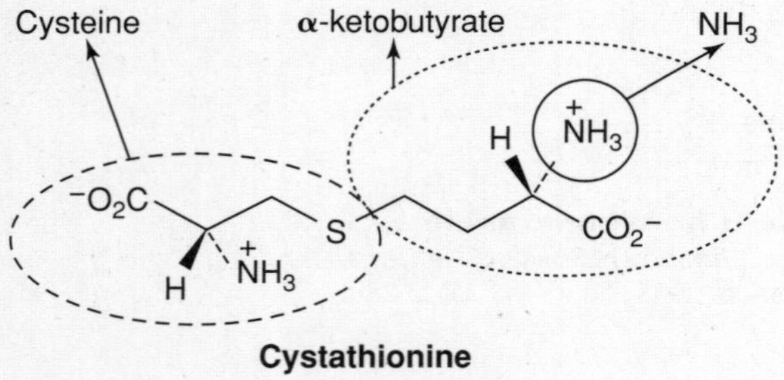

Figure 1-112. Cystathionine degradation to cysteine and α-ketobutyrate.

Figure 1-112 shows the sections of cystathionine from which each product is derived.

16.3.2. Amino Acids Derived from 3-Phosphoglycerate

Serine, glycine, and cysteine—all of which are nonessential amino acids—are derived from 3-phosphoglycerate. Cysteine will be discussed first to show its relationship to the common intermediate, cystathionine, in methionine biosynthesis.

16.3.2.1. Cysteine.

Cysteine is a nonessential amino acid, and the de novo synthesis of its carbon skeleton comes from 3-phosphoglycerate. The sulfur, however, still comes from methionine, so it is nonessential so long as there is sufficient methionine. A common intermediate in the synthesis of methionine and cysteine is cystathionine,

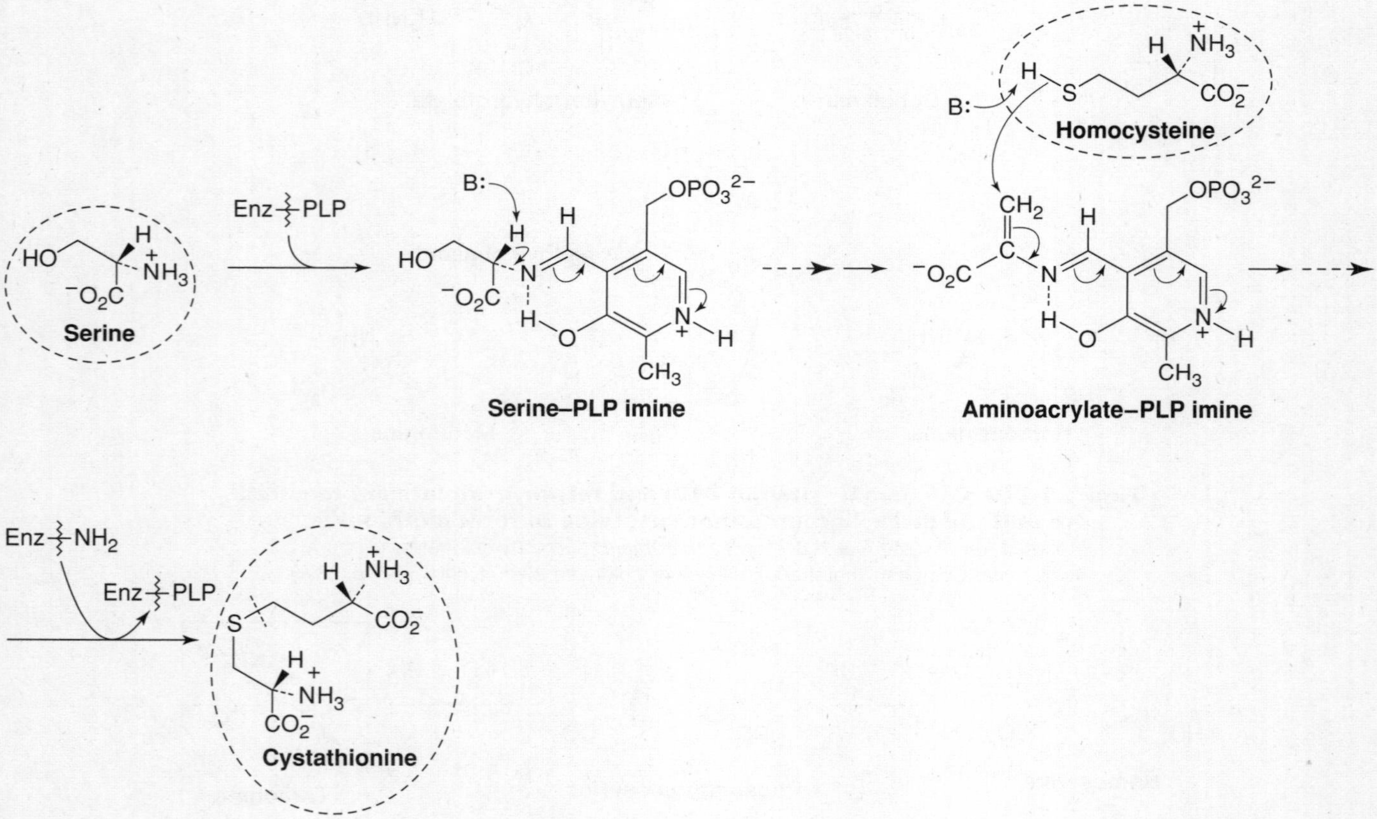

Figure 1-113. Cysteine formation from serine.
(Adapted from McMurry and Begley, T., *The Organic Chemistry of Biological Pathways*, Roberts and Company Publishers, Englewood, Colorado, 2005, Figure 1-5.23, p. 261.)

but the pathways for synthesis of cystathionine differ. The PLP-enzyme-intermediate necessary for methionine biosynthesis is homoserine-PLP-enzyme, whereas for cysteine biosynthesis, it is serine. A PLP-dependent enzyme is required in each case, and in each case, it is the hydroxy-amino acid that forms an enamine with PLP, and it is the molecule that contains the —SH group that displaces the —OH group. This —SH containing molecule is cysteine for methionine biosynthesis, and homocysteine for cysteine biosynthesis.

Reactions showing the exchange of sulfur between methionine and cysteine are important for the conservation of the sulfur atom in the amino acid pool or, perhaps, in mammals in general. Animals do not have sulfite reductase and therefore depend on bacteria and plants to supply reduced sulfur for synthesis of sulfur-

containing biomolecules necessary to support normal functions.

16.3.2.2. Serine.

The previous scheme (Figure 1-113) shows how carbons of serine are converted to cysteine. The carbon atoms of serine come from 3-phosphoglycerate. A scheme for its biosynthesis follows (Figure 1-114). It is a three-step process that involves a NAD^+-dependent oxidation to 3-phosphopyruvate, aminotransferase reaction to give 3-phosphoserine, and finally a phosphatase reaction that gives serine.

16.3.2.3. Glycine.

Serine is converted to glycine in a reversible reaction that requires, in addition to PLP, tetrahydrofolate

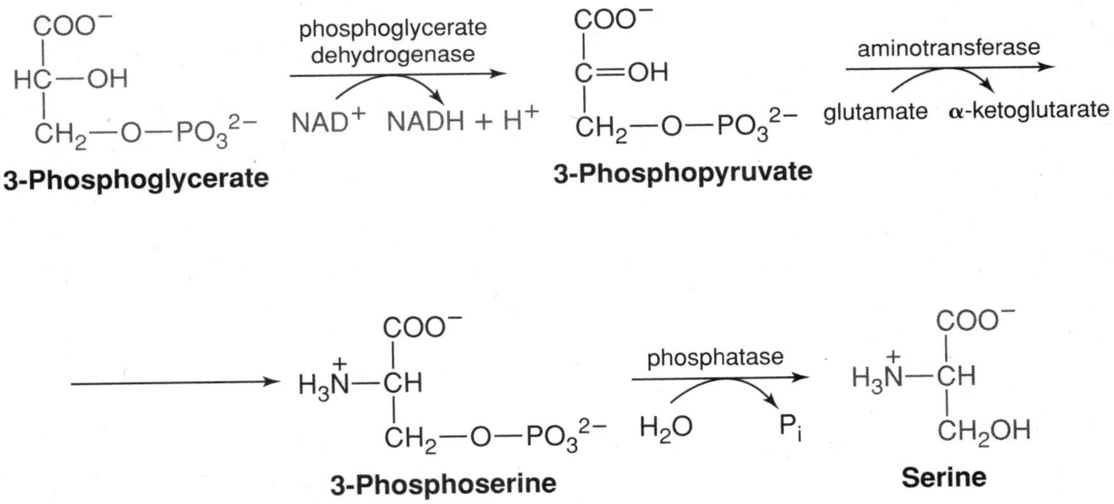

Figure 1-114. Serine biosynthesis from 3-phosphoglycerate.
(Adapted from Devlin, T. M., Editor, *Textbook of Biochemistry with Clinical Correlations*, Sixth Edition, Wiley-Liss, Hoboken, NJ, 2006, Figure 1-19.32, p. 757.)

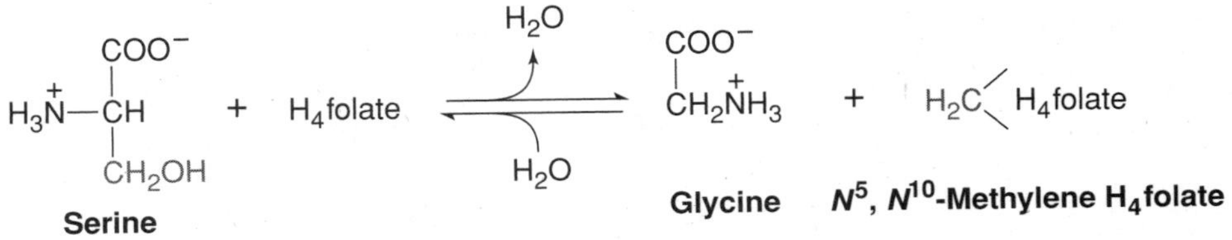

Figure 1-115. Interconversion of serine and glycine.
(Adapted from Devlin, T. M., Editor, *Textbook of Biochemistry with Clinical Correlations*, Sixth Edition, Wiley-Liss, Hoboken, NJ, 2006, Figure 1-19.38, p. 759.)

(THF or H_4folate). Products of the reaction are glycine and N^5,N^{10}-tetrahydrofolate (N^5,N^{10}-THF), as shown in Figure 1-115.

Folate has been shown to participate in another reaction of amino acid biosynthesis. It participates in one-carbon transfer reactions, and the one-carbon group can be at various oxidative states, from methyl to formyl. The following diagrams (Figure 1-116 and Figure 1-117) show the structures of folate and its various one-carbon carrier forms.

16.3.3. Amino Acids Derived from Pyruvate

Pyruvate is the carbohydrate metabolic intermediate from which the synthesis of the branch chain amino acids isoleucine, leucine, and valine is initiated. Figure 1-118 shows abbreviated pathways leading to their synthesis. Thiamin pyrophosphate is involved in the first step of their synthesis. For isoleucine, the second step involves a condensation reaction with α-ketobutyrate and with pyruvate for leucine and valine. Leucine biosynthesis branches off from that of valine biosynthesis at α-ketoisovalerate. Arrows with dashed lines indicate that there are several intermediate steps involved between the metab-

olites shown. The heavy arrows indicate final steps where the PLP-dependent aminotransferase reaction occurs.

16.3.4. Amino Acids Derived from α-Ketoglutarate

In addition to glutamate, these are glutamine, proline, and arginine (see Figure 1-119). They are all nonessential amino acids. The special condition for arginine has been mentioned and its synthesis is discussed in more detail along with reactions of the urea cycle. Glutamine biosynthesis has been discussed earlier in this section.

16.3.5. Amino Acids Derived from Phosphoenolpyruvate and Erythrose-4-phosphate:

The aromatic amino acids tryptophan, phenylalanine, and tyrosine are in this category. The first two are essential. Tyrosine is derived from phenylalanine, and since there are mammalian enzymes capable of catalyzing its formation, it is not an essential amino acid. Mammals do not have enzymes capable of making the aromatic ring structures of tryptophan and phenylalanine.

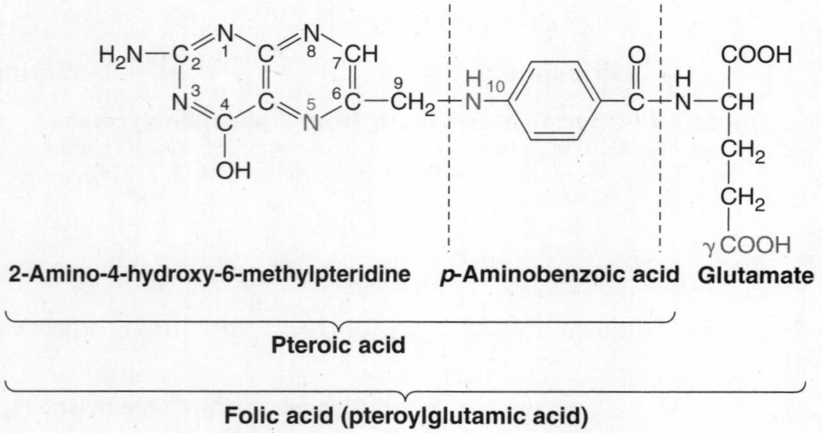

Figure 1-116. Structure of folic acid.
(Adapted from Devlin, T. M., Editor, *Textbook of Biochemistry with Clinical Correlations*, Sixth Edition, Wiley-Liss, Hoboken, NJ, 2006, Figure 1-19.41, p. 761.)

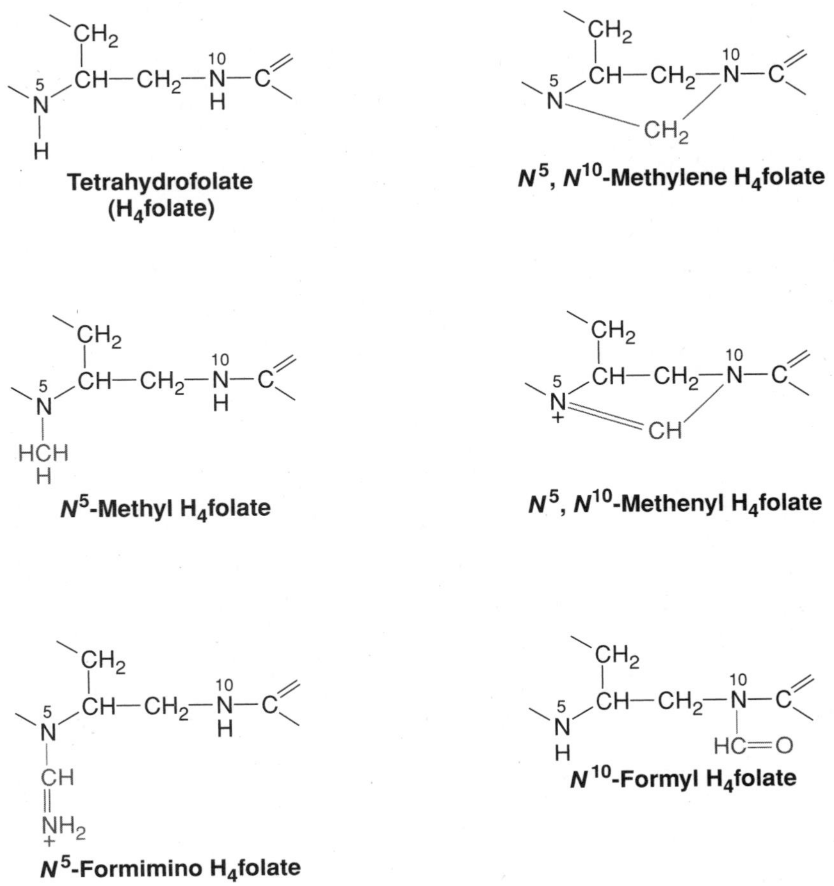

Figure 1-117. Structures of methyl-folate with the methyl group in various stages of oxidation.
(Adapted from Devlin, T. M., Editor, *Textbook of Biochemistry with Clinical Correlations*,
Sixth Edition, Wiley-Liss, Hoboken, NJ, 2006, Figure 1-19.42, p. 761.)

The first step in the biosynthesis of the aromatic amino acids is the addition of phosphoenolpyruvate (PEP) to erythrose-4-phosphate to produce 2-keto-3-deoxyarabinoheptulosonate-7-phosphate, which cyclizes to form the hemiacetal (DAHP) shown in the diagram of Figure 1-120. The next series of reactions produce chorismate.

Chorismate is the branch point in the pathway and the metabolite from which both tryptophan and phenylalanine are synthesized (Figure 1-121).

Intermediates between chorismate and tryptophan are anthranilate, N-(5′-phosphoribosyl)-anthranilate, indol-3-glycerol phosphate, and indole. The nitrogen of the indole ring derives from glutamine, two of the carbons from the ribosyl group, and the side chain along with the α-amino group of tryptophan from serine.

Phenylalanine can be made from chorismate in two steps where the intermediates are prephenate and phenylpyruvate (Figure 1-122). The amino group of phenylalanine comes from glutamate by an aminotransferase reaction.

In some bacteria, tyrosine can be formed directly from chorismate (Figure 1-123).

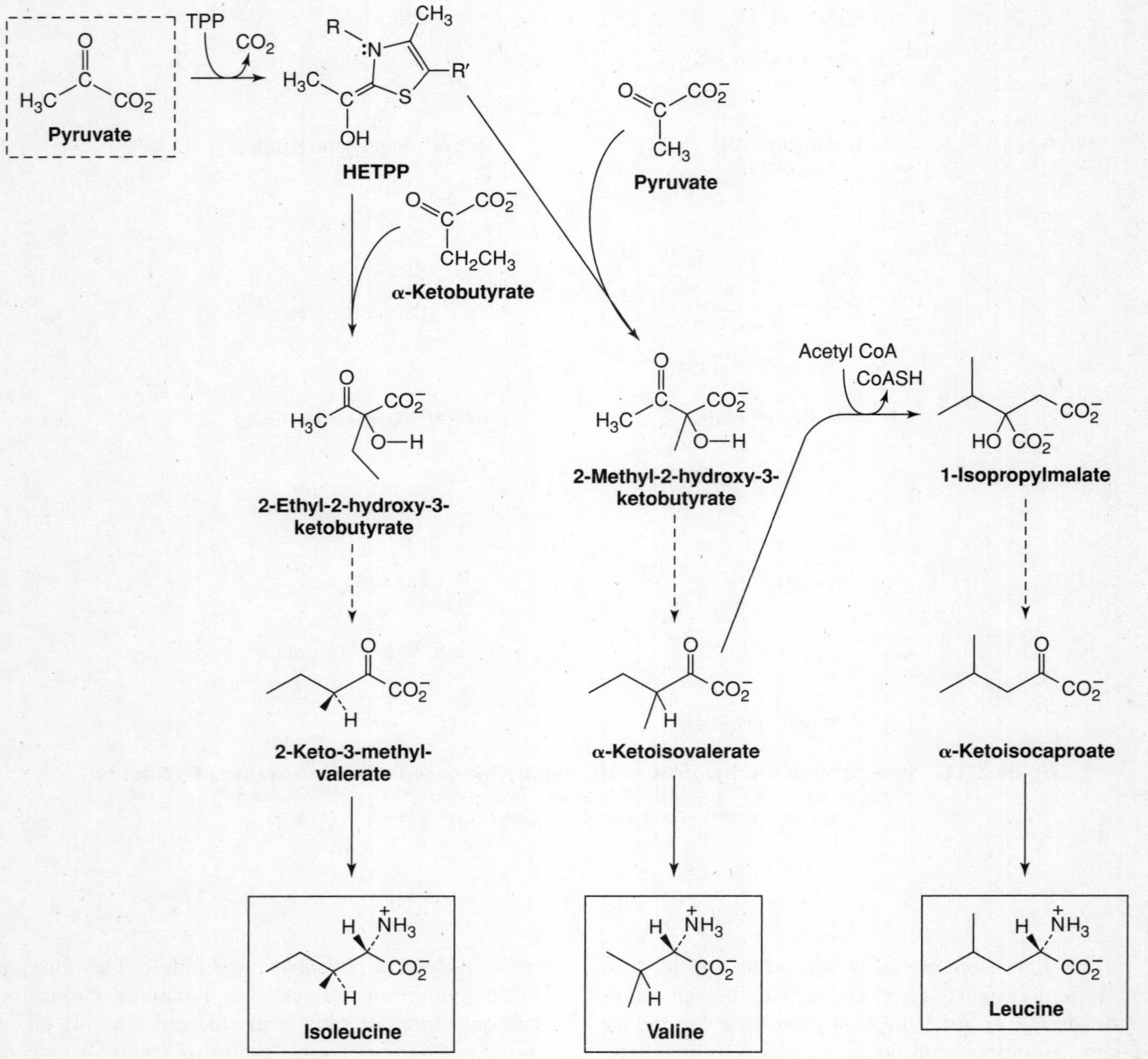

Figure 1-118. Branch chain amino acids are synthesized from pyruvate.
(Adapted from McMurry and Begley, T., *The Organic Chemistry of Biological Pathways*, Roberts and Company Publishers, Englewood, Colorado, 2005, Figures 5.39, 5.40, and 5.41, pp. 284–286).

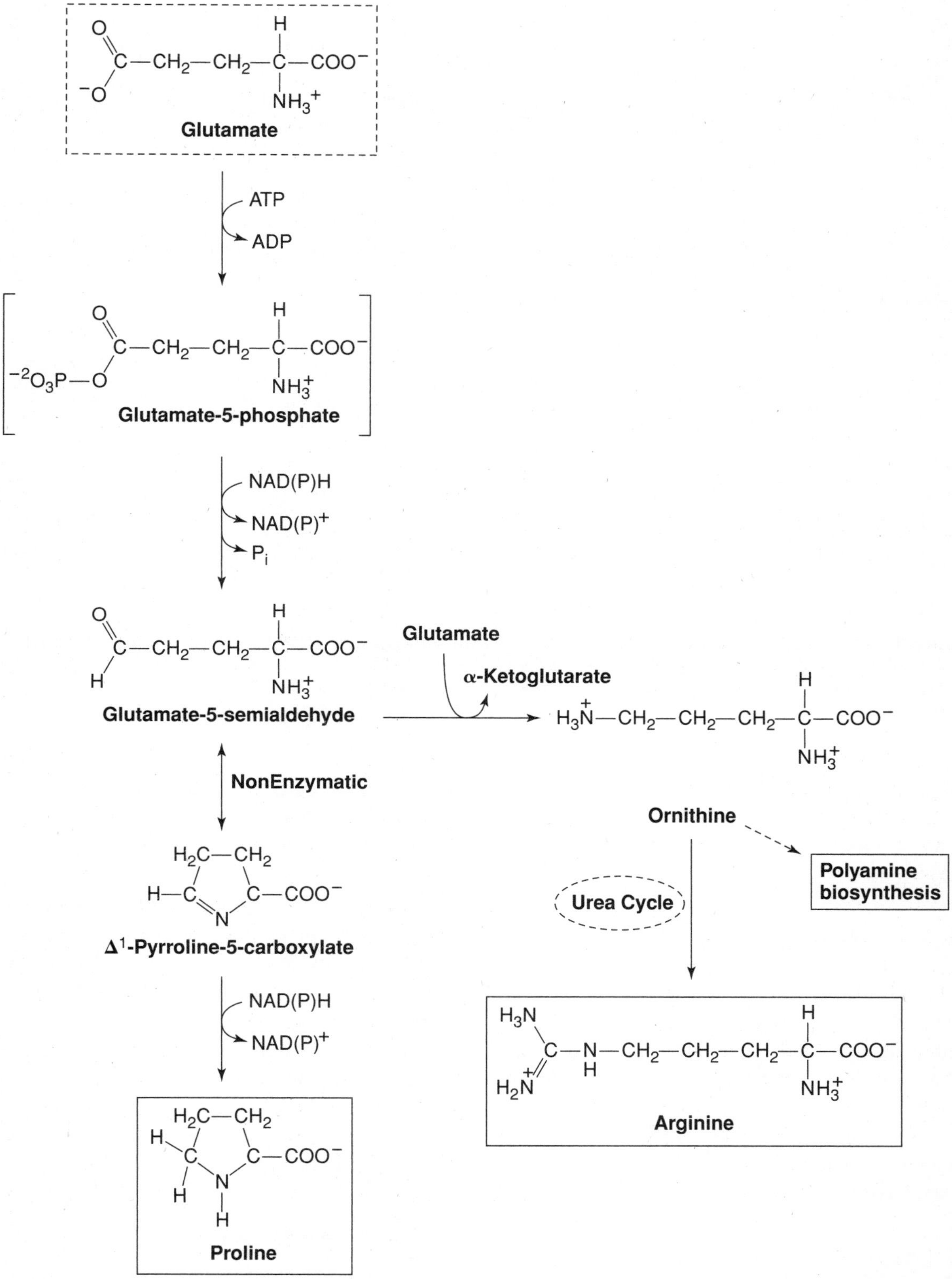

Figure 1-119. Amino acids derived from glutamate.
(Adapted from Voet, D. and Voet, J. D., *Biochemistry*, John Wiley & Sons, New York, 1990, Figure 1-24.43, p.718).

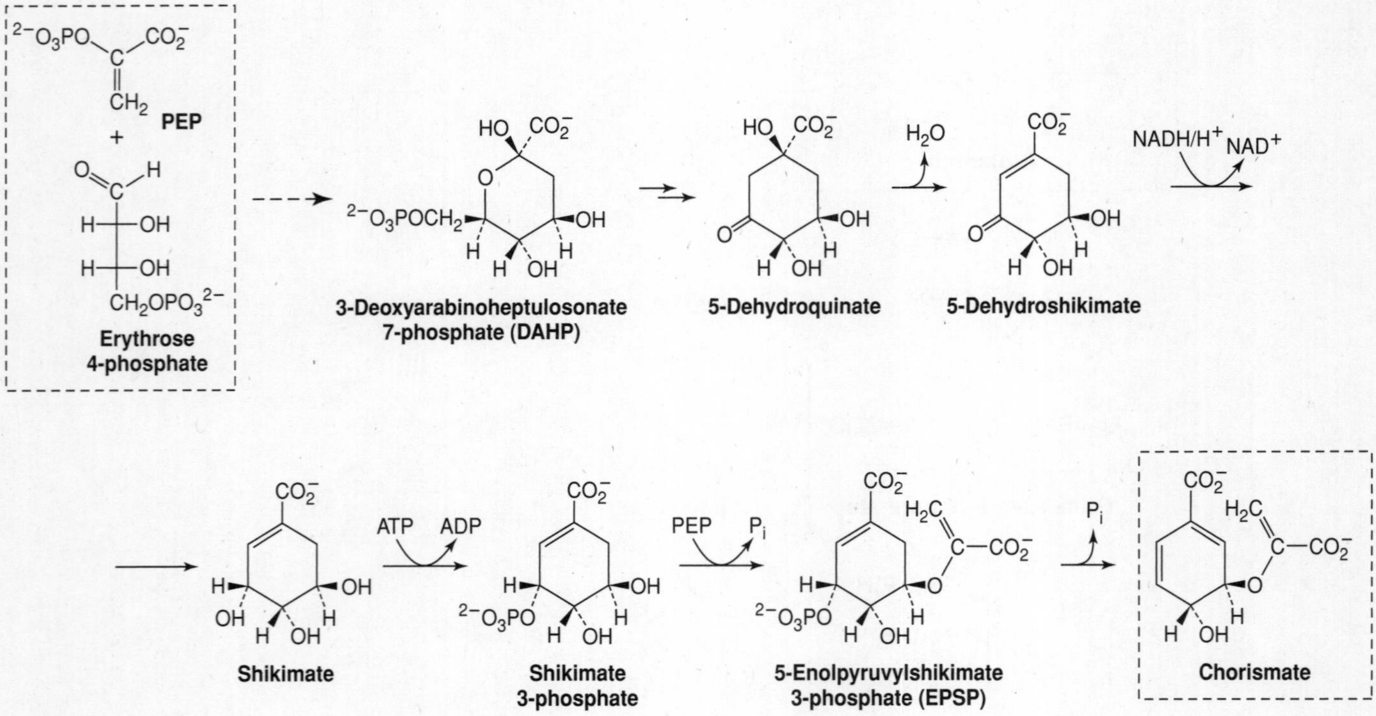

Figure 1-120. Synthesis of chorismate from phosphoenolpyruvate (PEP) and erythrose-4-phosphate.
(Adapted from McMurry, J. and Begley, T., *The Organic Chemistry of Biological Pathways*, Roberts and Company Publishers, Englewood, Colorado, 2005, Figure 1-5.42, p. 287.)

In mammalian systems, however, it is formed by hydroxylation of phenylalanine by phenylalanine hydroxylase.

16.3.5.1. Histidine.

Histidine is formed from ribose-5-phosphate. The first metabolite formed is 5-phosphoribosyldiphosphate (PRPP). One of the nitrogen atoms in the imidazole ring comes from adenine, and the other comes from glutamine. An imidazole acetol phosphate is the recipient of the α-amino group to produce histidinol phosphate. Reactions of a phosphatase and an NAD^+-dependent dehydrogenase eventually produce histidine. These reactions are shown in Figure 1-124.

16.4. Degradation of Amino Acids

To have an understanding of the catabolism of amino acids, it is necessary to know the disposition of the carbon skeletons, nitrogen, and other specific constituents such as sulfur.

Sulfur has been dealt with to some extent during discussions of methionine and cysteine biosynthesis. There, it was shown how sulfur is exchanged between those two amino acids through the intermediate cystathionine depending on which side of the sulfur cleavage occurs; cysteine is formed when cleavage occurs on one side, and homocysteine when it occurs on the other side. Reference to the synthesis of these two amino acids, however, shows that the process is more complex than depicted in Figure 1-125.

16.4.1. Methionine.

Methionine, after activation to yield S-adenosyl-methionine (AdoMet or SAM), is an active donor of methyl groups. The α-aminobutyrate part of the mol-

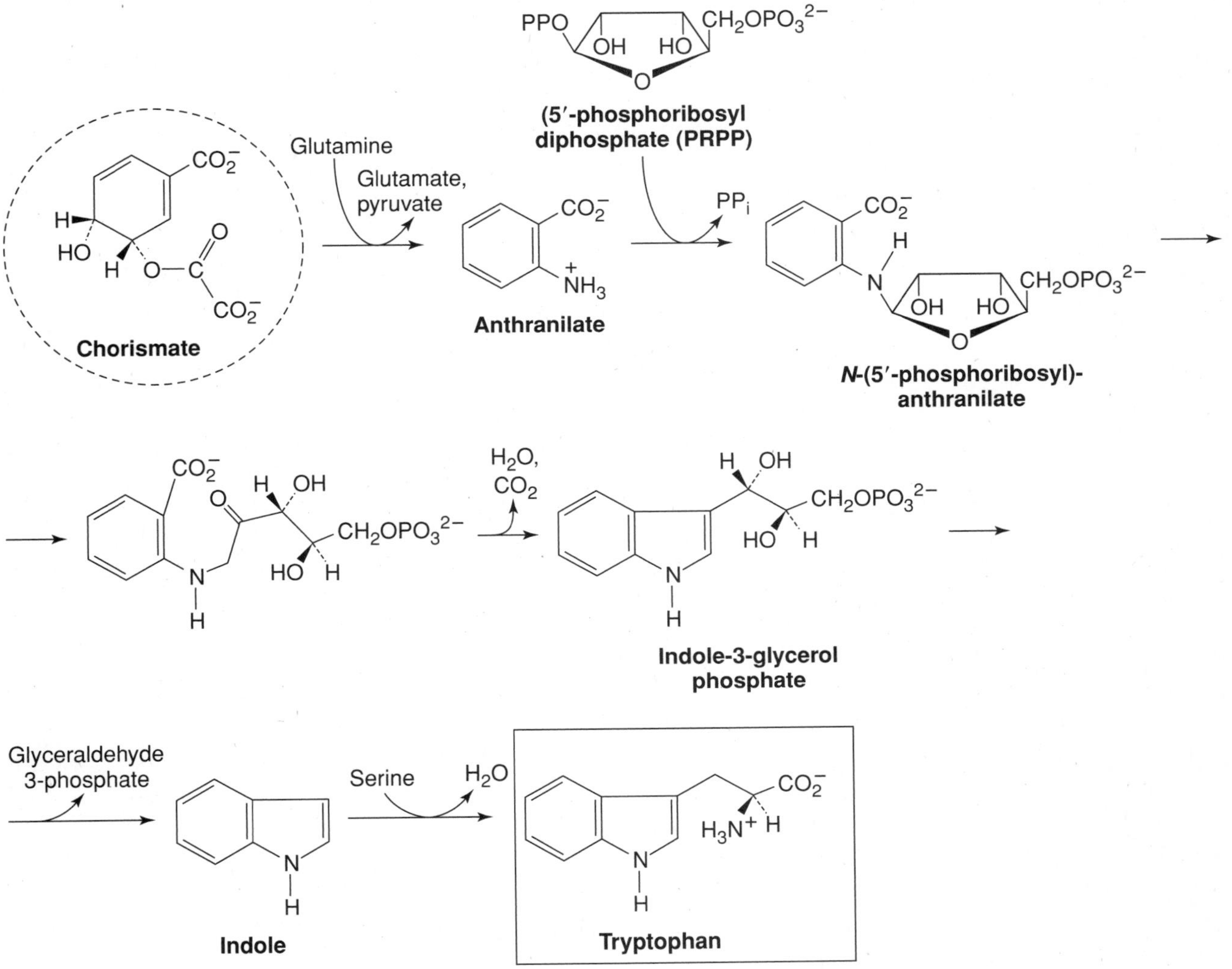

Figure 1-121. Tryptophan biosynthesis from chorismate.
(Adapted from McMurry, J. and Begley, T., *The Organic Chemistry of Biological Pathways*, Roberts and Company Publishers, Englewood, Colorado, 2005, Figure 1-5.45, p. 290.)

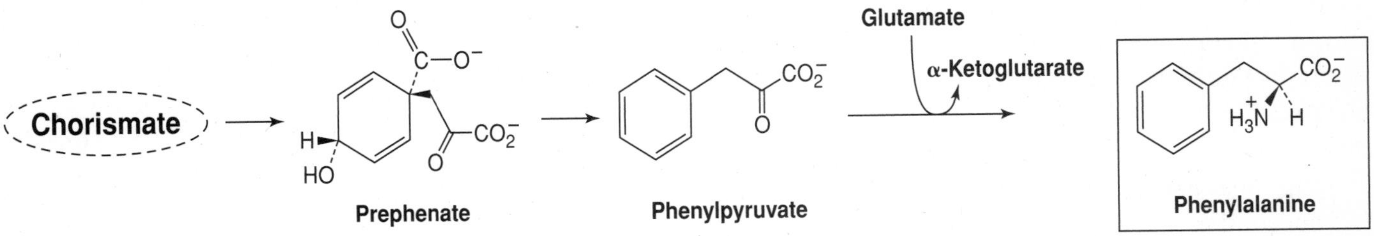

Figure 1-122. Biosynthesis of phenylalanine from chorismate.
(Adapted from McMurry, J. and Begley, T., *The Organic Chemistry of Biological Pathways*, Roberts and Company Publishers, Englewood, Colorado, 2005, Figure 1-5.47, p. 294.)

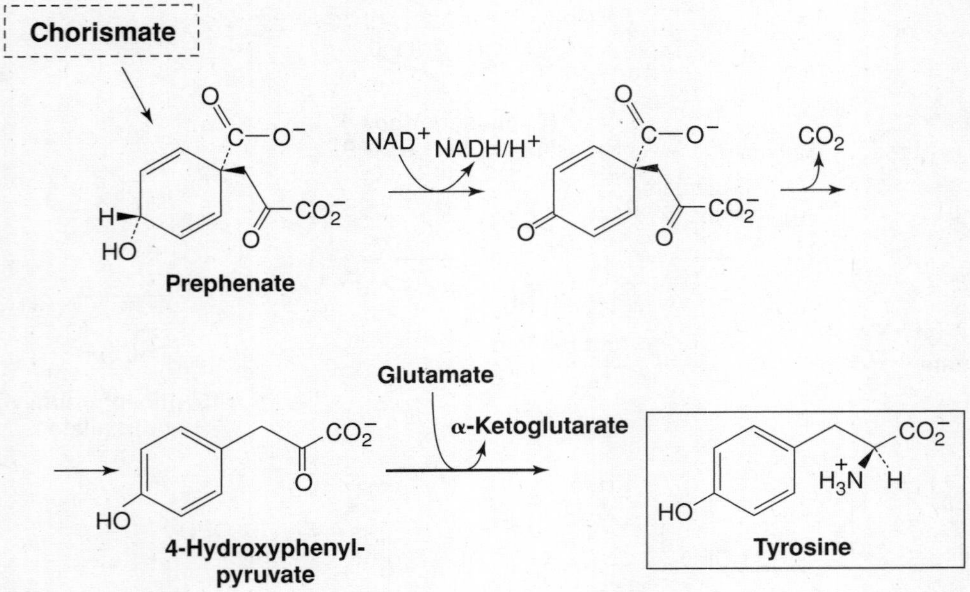

Figure 1-123. Direct synthesis of tyrosine from chorismate.
(Adapted from McMurry, J. and Begley, T., *The Organic Chemistry of Biological Pathways*,
Roberts and Company Publishers, Englewood, Colorado, 2005, Figure 1-5.48, p. 295.)

ecule is also a good leaving group and participates in the formation of polyamines. Formation and structure of AdoMet are shown in Figure 1-126. Either the adenosylhomocysteine or the methylthioadenosine that remains after the transfer can be used to regenerate methionine.

Sulfur from cysteine can be converted to other sulfur containing compounds—cysteinesulfinate, hypotaurine, taurine and bisulfite—which can be converted to sulfate (see Figure 1-127).

Sulfate can be activated through its conversion to 3′-phosphoadenosine-5′-phosphosulfate (PAPS), as shown in Figure 1-128. This is "activated" sulfate that is now in a form that can be transferred to other biomolecules.

The first step in the degradation of amino acids, in almost all cases, is the removal of nitrogen by aminotransferase. Exceptions are serine, threonine, and lysine. Serine and threonine accomplish the same end results from action of the enzymes serine dehydratase and threonine dehydratase, producing pyruvate and α-ketobutyrate, respectively. Lysine catabolism involves, first, formation of an imine between the ε-amino group of lysine and the keto group of α-ketoglutarate. This is a reductive amination reaction catalyzed by the enzyme saccharopine dehydrogenase, a NADPH-requiring reaction. The ε-amino group of lysine eventually becomes the α-amino group of glutamate. The original lysine carbons, α-aminoadipic semialdehyde, are converted through a series of steps to acetoacetyl coenzyme A (Figure 1-129).

17. THE UREA CYCLE

Excess nitrogen is eliminated from mammalian sources primarily through the urea cycle. Only five enzymes are involved in the urea cycle: (1) carbamoyl phosphate synthetase I (CPSI), (2) ornithine transcarbamoylase, (3) arginosuccinate synthetase, (4) arginosuccinate lyase, and (5) arginase. These reactions are shown in Figure 1-130. This is a "true" cycle since all of the carbon atoms of ornithine at the start of the cycle are the same atoms in ornithine at the end of the cycle.

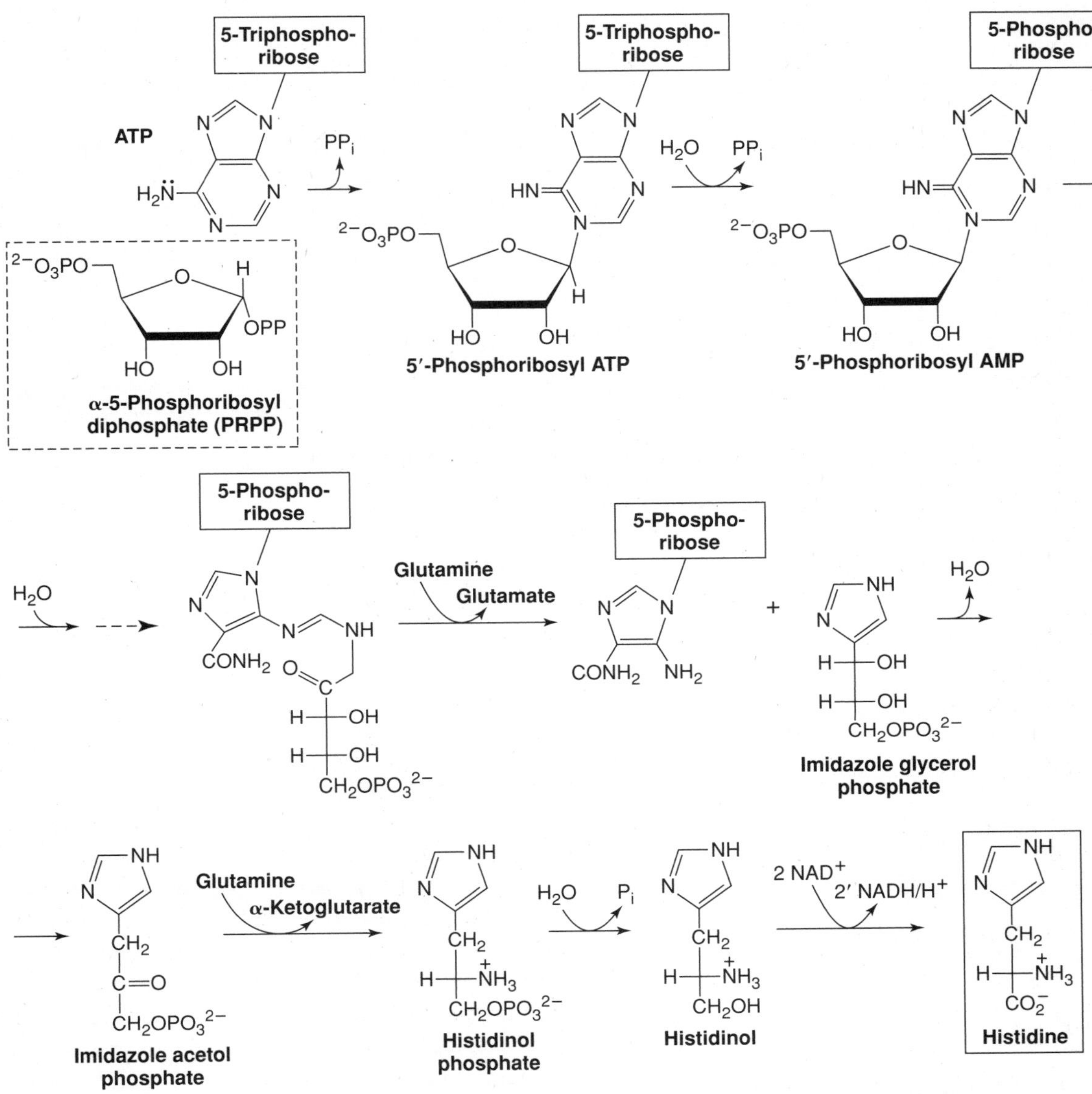

Figure 1-124. Synthesis of histidine from 5-phosphoribosyl-1-diphosphate (PRPP).
(Adapted from McMurry, J. and Begley, T., *The Organic Chemistry of Biological Pathways*,
Roberts and Company Publishers, Englewood, Colorado, 2005, Figure 1-5.49, p. 296.)

The synthesis of ornithine from glutamate was demonstrated earlier. The cleavage of arginosuccinate by argininosuccinate lyase forms arginine. This is its origin from (originally) glutamate. The final reaction of the cycle is catalyzed by arginase, which produces urea and ornithine. The two nitrogen atoms in urea come from free ammonium ions through carbamoyl phosphate and from aspartate. Fumarate produced by the cleavage of argininosuccinate enters the TCA cycle and can be oxidized for energy production or converted to glucose

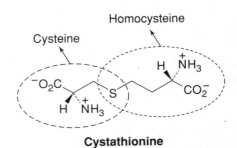

Figure 1-125. Cystathionine and sulfur exchange between cysteine and methionine.

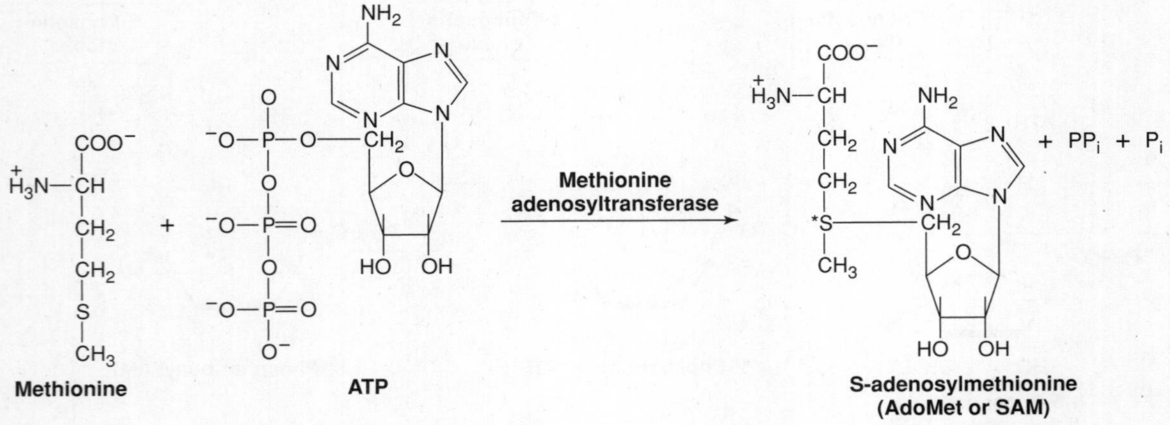

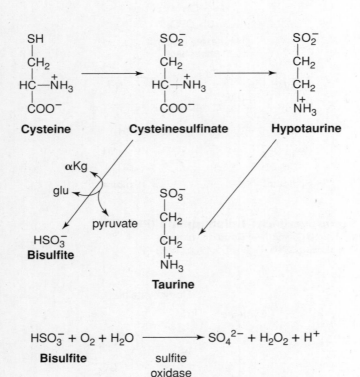

Figure 1-126. Formation of S-adenosylmethionine.
(Adapted from Devlin, T. M., Editor, *Textbook of Biochemistry with Clinical Correlations*,
Sixth Edition, Wiley-Liss, Hoboken, NJ, 2006, Figure 1-19.54, p. 768.)

by way of oxaloacetate and phosphoenolpyruvate (PEP) produced by PEP carboxykinase.

Carbon skeletons of the amino acids can be further metabolized to produce energy and/or stored as lipids or as glucose, depending on the end products of their degradation. Degradation products of the amino acid skeletons will end up as one or some combination of seven intermediary metabolites of carbohydrate metabolism. These include the following: acetoacetate, acetyl-CoA, α-ketoglutarate, fumarate, oxaloacetate, pyruvate, and succinyl-CoA. Whereas all of these metabolites can be metabolized directly for energy production, two of them, leucine and lysine, produce either acetyl CoA and/or acetoacetate only and are only capable of making lipids so far as energy reserve/storage is concerned. Thus, amino acids whose end products are only acetyl CoA and acetoacetate are strictly *lipogenic* (ketogenic). Lysine and leucine are the only two amino acids that fit into that category. All of the others have catabolic products that are *glucogenic* (capable of being converted to glucose), or they have products that are both glucogenic and lipogenic. Figure 1-131 summarizes the fate of each amino acid relative to whether it is glucogenic, lipogenic, or both.

Figure 1-127. Formation of taurine and bisulfite.
(Adapted from Devlin, T. M., Editor, *Textbook of Biochemistry with Clinical Correlations*, Sixth Edition, Wiley-Liss, Hoboken, NJ, 2006, Figure 1-19.61, p. 771.)

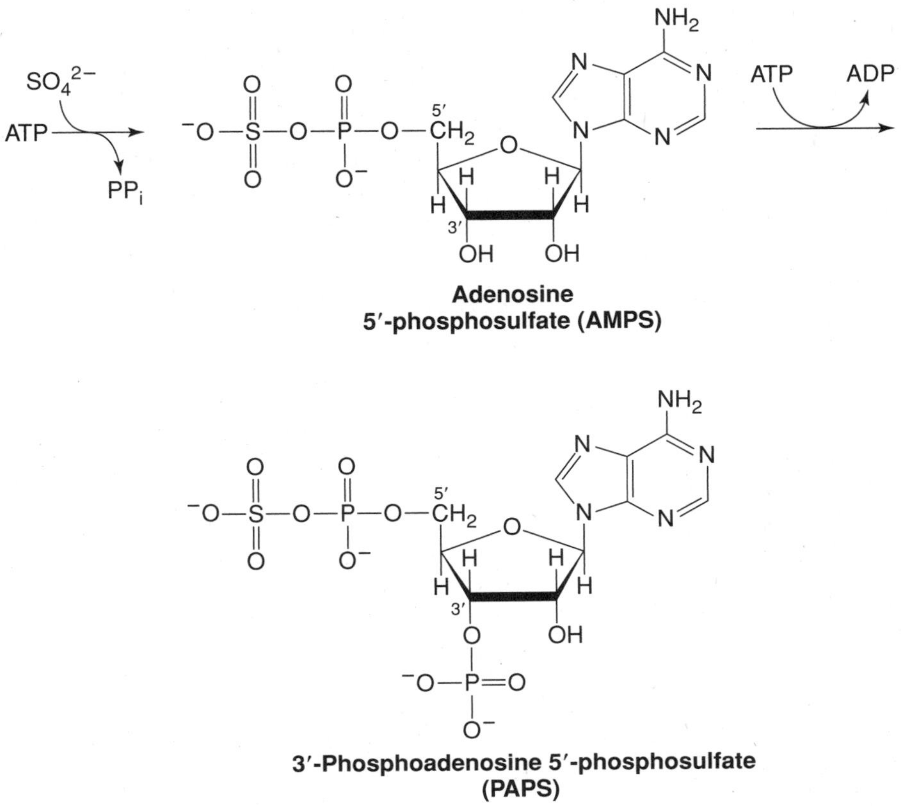

Figure 1-128. Formation of 3'-phosphoadenosine-5'-phosphosulfate (PAPS) from sulfate and ATP.

(Adapted from Devlin, T. M., Editor, *Textbook of Biochemistry with Clinical Correlations*, Sixth Edition, Wiley-Liss, Hoboken, NJ, 2006, Figure 1-19.62, p. 773.).

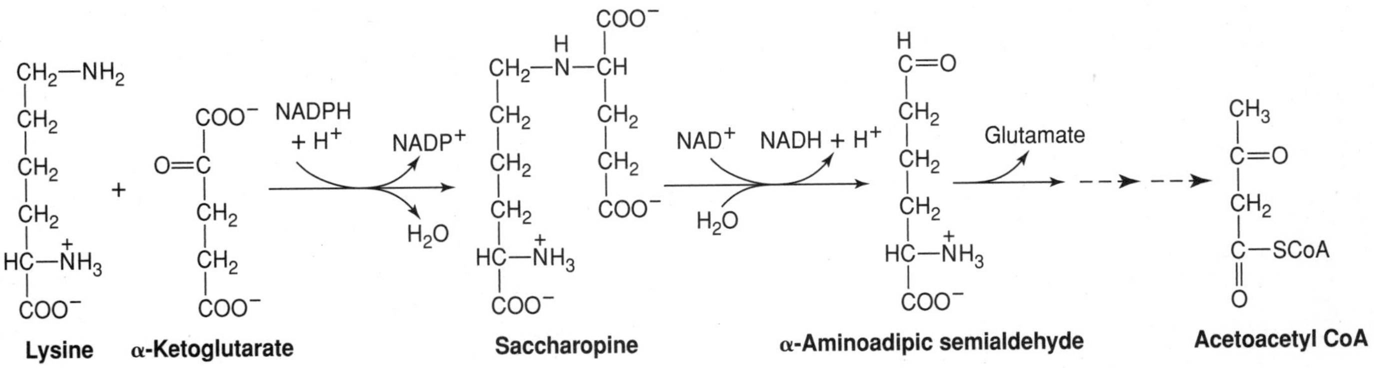

Figure 1-129. Lysine degradation.

(Adapted from Devlin, T. M., Editor, *Textbook of Biochemistry with Clinical Correlations*, Sixth Edition, Wiley-Liss, Hoboken, NJ, 2006, Figure 1-19.72, p. 779.)

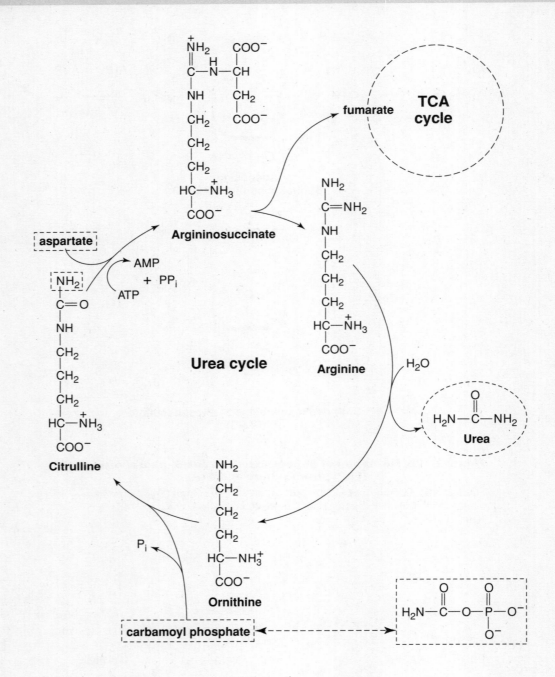

Figure 1-130. The urea cycle.
(Adapted from Devlin, T. M., Editor, *Textbook of Biochemistry with Clinical Correlations*, Sixth Edition, Wiley-Liss, Hoboken, NJ, 2006, Figure 1-19.24, p. 752.)

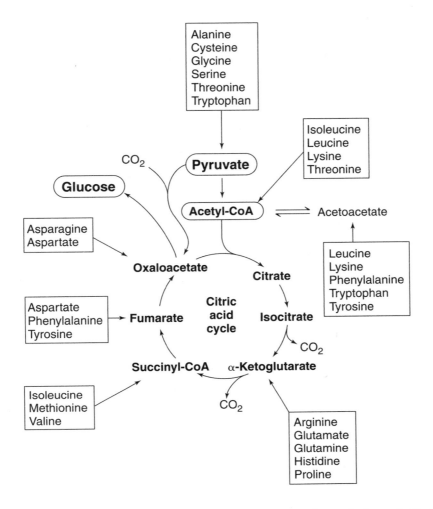

Figure 1-131. Summary of the fate of carbon atoms resulting from degradation of all of the amino acids.

(Adapted from Figure 1-20-13, p. 697, Voet, D., Voet, J. D., and Pratt, C. W., *Fundamentals of Biochemistry: Life at the Molecular Level*, Second Edition, John Wiley & Sons, New York, 2006.)

18. NUCLEOTIDE STRUCTURE AND METABOLISM

Purine and pyrimidine nucleotides play important roles in practically every aspect of function in biological species, including, but not limited to, photosynthesis, nitrogen fixation, energy metabolism, and regulation of various types of metabolic processes. They are integral components of enzymes (ribosymes) and coenzymes, and they are the base units of DNA and RNA. Purine and pyrimidine bases found in DNA and RNA are adenine (A), guanine (G), cytosine (C), thymine (T), and uracil (U). The corresponding nucleotides of A, G, C, and T in their 2′-deoxy forms are found in DNA. Nucleotides found in RNA are A, G, C, and U; and they exist in their ribose-phosphate forms. Linear polymers of DNA and RNA are linked together through phosphodiester bonds in a 3′–5′ configuration. DNA can exist in several conformations, the most common of which is a double-stranded helix in which the bases of the helices are paired, A with T, and G with C. The A:T and G:C pairs are held together by hydrogen bonds as shown in Figure 1-132.

The DNA double helix is formed with the bases on the inside of the molecule and the phosphodies-

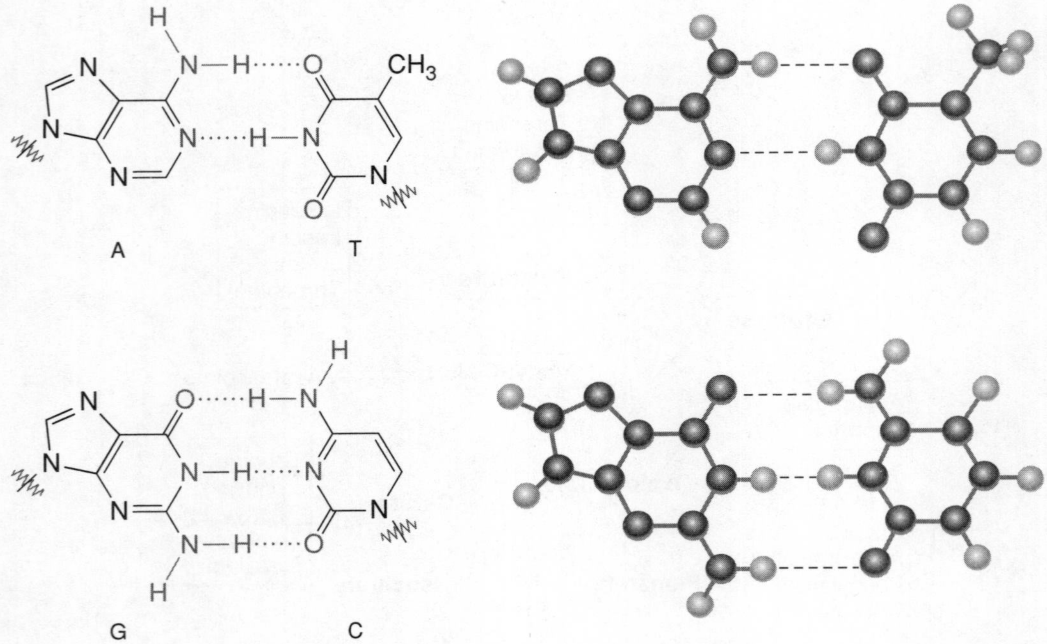

Figure 1-132. Hydrogen bonds in DNA base pairs.
(Adapted from McMurray and Begley, *The Organic Chemistry of Biological Pathways*, Fig. 2.13, p. 75.)

ter backbone on the outside. In this conformation, the DNA molecule is 20 Å wide, and it forms two groves, a minor grove of 6 Å and a major grove of 12 Å along the length of the DNA. The major grove allows some interactions with the nucleotide bases. A structure of this conformation is shown in Figure 1-134.

RNA is single stranded, however, it can form loops, and bases can pair with others, but the pairing will be A:U and G:C. Among the better examples of base pairing in RNA exist in tRNA molecules. A representation of the structure of yeast serine tRNA is shown in Figure 1-135.

The remainder of this section is divided into five parts: (1) synthesis of purines, (2) degradation of purines, (3) synthesis of pyrimidines, (4) synthesis of deoxyribonucleotides, and (5) degradation of pyrimidines.

18.1. Synthesis of Purines

Figure 1-133 shows the purine ring structure and the metabolic intermediates that contribute specific atoms to that structure.

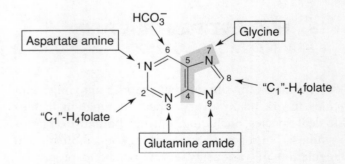

Figure 1-133. Sources of atoms for the purine ring.
(Adapted from Devlin, T. M., Editor, *Textbook of Biochemistry with Clinical Correlations*, Sixth Edition, Wiley-Liss, Hoboken, NJ, 2006, Figure 1-20.3, p. 794.)

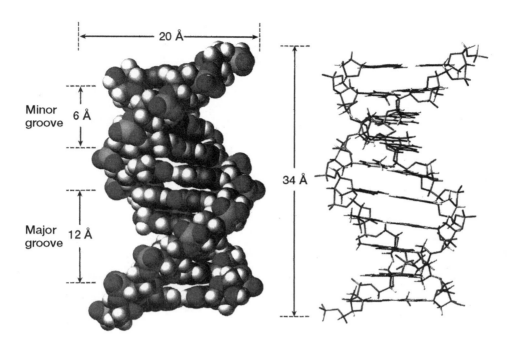

Figure 1-134. DNA molecule.

(Adapted from McMurray and Begley, *The Organic Chemistry of Biological Pathways*, Fig. 2.14, p. 76. McMurray, J. and Begley, T., *The Organic Chemistry of Biological Pathways*, Roberts and Company Publishers, Englewood, Colorado, 2005.)

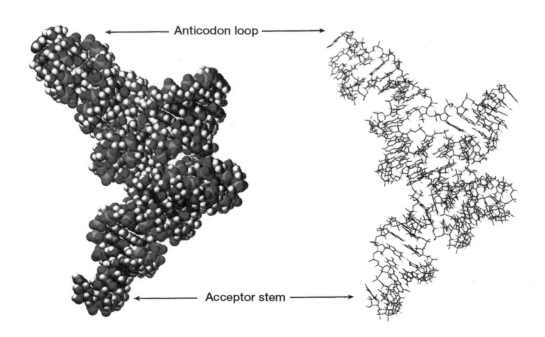

Figure 1-135. Structure of yeast serine tRNA.

(Adapted from McMurray and Begley, *The Organic Chemistry of Biological Pathways*, Fig. 2.15, p. 77.)

The first product of the metabolic pathway that leads to synthesis of purine nucleotides in a host of biological species, from bacteria to humans, is inosine monophosphate (IMP). The ultimate goal, however, is the formation of adenosine monophosphate (AMP) and guanosine monophosphate (GMP) (Figure 1-136).

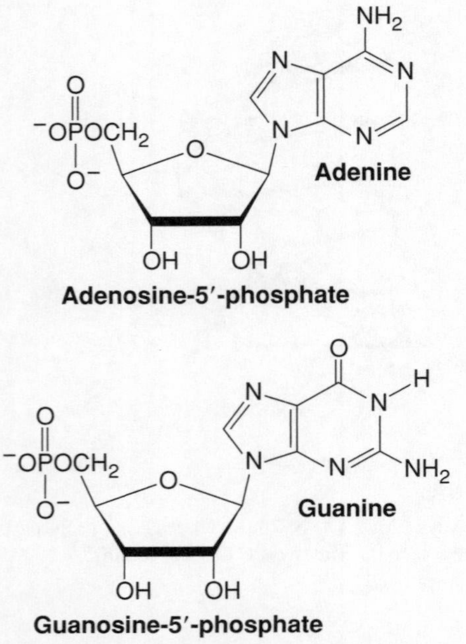

Figure 1-136. Structures of adenosine monophosphate (AMP) and guanosine monophosphate (GMP).

Eleven enzyme-catalyzed reactions are required for synthesis of IMP, and they start with an intermediary metabolite of the pentose phosphate pathway, α-D-ribose-5-phosphate.

The first reaction is formation of phosphoribosyl-1-pyrophosphate (Figure 1-137).

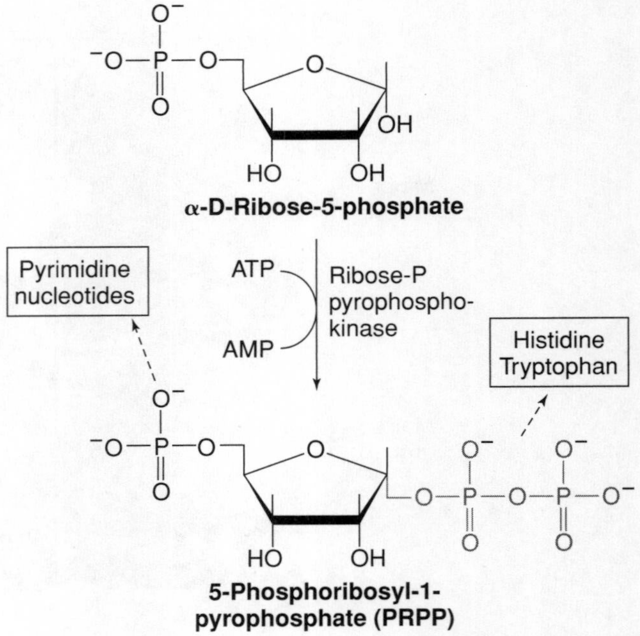

This is not the committed step for purine biosynthesis since this intermediate is required for synthesis of other metabolites such as pyrimidine nucleotides, histidine, and tryptophan. The first reaction unique to purine biosynthesis and, therefore, the **committed step** (step 2 in Figure 1-138) is formation of 5-phosphoribosylamine catalyzed by amidophosphoribosyl transferase. This

Figure 1-137. Synthesis of 5-phosphoribosyl-1-pyrophosphate (PRPP).

—NH_2 group comes from the amide group of glutamine and will become the nitrogen group at position 9 of IMP. This and the following nine steps in the biosynthesis of IMP are shown in Figure 1-138. There are, therefore, ten reactions directly involved in synthesis of the purine ring structure of IMP.

The committed step of the pathway, formation of β-5-phosphoribosylamine (PRA), occurs with inversion of configuration at the 1-position of ribose, and the amino group added from glutamine is in the β-position, the correct position for building the remainder of the ring system. In step 3, an ATP-dependent reaction, a glycine amide is formed with the amino group of PRA to produce glycinamide ribotide (GAR). This is the only step in which a single compound contributes more than one atom to formation of the purine ring structure. Further, glycine carbons form the junction between the two rings contributing atoms 4, 5, and 7 of purine. In step 4, carbon 8 is added from N^{10}-formyl-THF to the glycine nitrogen

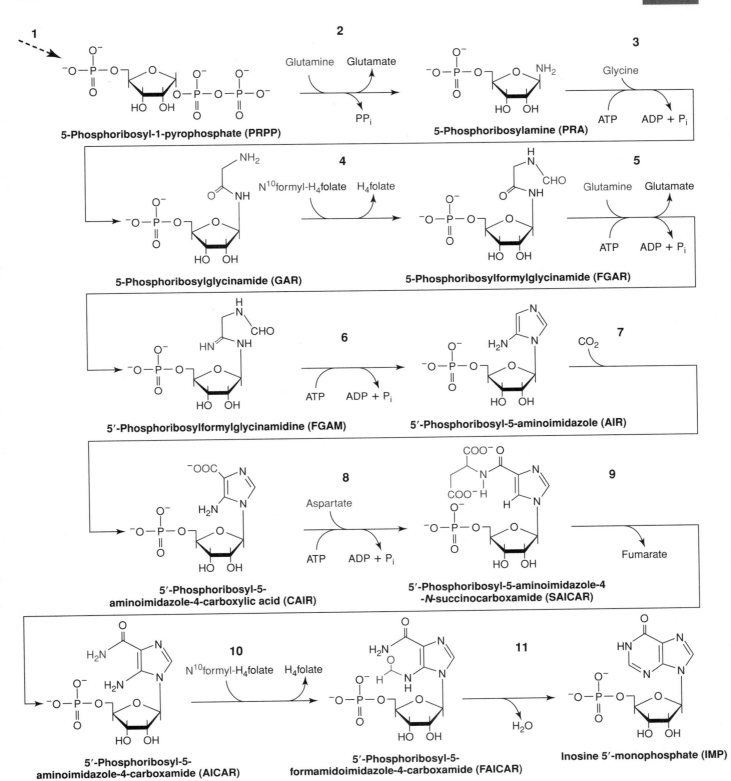

Figure 1-138. Pathway for synthesis of inosine monophosphate (IMP).
(Adapted from Devlin, T. M., Editor, *Textbook of Biochemistry with Clinical Correlations*,
Sixth Edition, Wiley-Liss, Hoboken, NJ, 2006, Figure 1-20.1, p. 793.)

of GAR to form formylglycinamide ribotide (FGAR). In a third ATP-requiring reaction (step 5), a second nitrogen group (9NH) from glutamine replaces the oxygen of the amide linkage formed upon initial formation of GAR (back in step 3). Aminoimidazole ribotide (AIR) synthetase catalyzes closure of the ring to form 5-aminoimidazole ribotide (step 6). The sixth position of the purine ring is added in step 7—a carboxylation reaction producing carboxyaminoimidazole ribotide (CAIR).

This is also an ATP-requiring reaction. The enzyme that carries out this reaction is a two-protein complex, each protein derived from separate genes. Even though the carboxylation reaction can occur with only one of these proteins, the combination of the two reduces the K_m for bicarbonate to the 0.1 mM range, permitting the reaction to occur under physiological conditions. ATP is required for this reaction. Step 8 is catalyzed by 5-aminoimidazole-4-(N-succinylocarboxamide)ribotide (SAICAR) synthetase, also an ATP-requiring reaction, in which the α-amino group of aspartate is added in an amide linkage to the carboxyl group of CAIR. Adenylosuccinate lyase (step 9) removes the carbon atoms of aspartate as fumarate. N^{10}-formyl-THF, in a reaction catalyzed by AICAR transformylase (step 10), adds a formyl group to the free —NH$_2$ that was added from glutamine. The formyl carbon will become the 2-position of the purine ring. The final step (step 11) is catalyzed by IMP cyclohydrolase, which eliminates a water molecule and closes the ring.

18.1.1. Summary of Key Points About Purine Biosynthesis

Synthesis of the purine ring structure is a ten-step process, including the committed step. Only one compound, glycine, adds more than one consecutive atom to the purine ring. Including formation of PRPP, the equivalent of six molecules of ATP are required, four of which are used after the committed step.

AMP and GMP are formed from IMP in accordance with the following scheme in Figure 1-139.

Both AMP and GMP are synthesized from IMP by two-step pathways. The two reactions involved in GMP synthesis are catalyzed by IMP dehydrogenase and GMP synthetase. IMP dehydrogenase uses NAD^+ and H_2O to introduce a carbonyl group in xanthosine monophosphate at position 2 by reactions that are not immediately obvious. The mechanism involves use of a thiol (—SH) group on the enzyme, which first reacts with the purine ring to form a conjugate addition (a tetrahedryl intermediate—covalent catalysis) at position 2, which is oxidized by NAD^+ to give NADH + H$^+$. This regenerates a double bond between positions 2 and 3 in the purine ring of the thiol adduct. The thiol-enzyme adduct is hydrolyzed by H_2O to regenerate the enzyme with its free —SH group and produce xanthosine monophosphate. In the second step, an amino group from glutamine is added, displacing the oxygen atom at position 2. This reaction is driven by energy derived from the hydrolysis of ATP to AMP and PP$_i$, which is hydrolyzed to 2P$_i$, ensuring irreversibility of the reaction. The final purine product is GMP.

The first step in AMP synthesis from IMP involves formation of adenylosuccinate by addition of aspartate to the carbonyl group of IMP in a reaction similar to that of step 8 in IMP synthesis. Cleavage of adenylosuccinate by adenylosuccinate lyase in the second step gives fumarate and AMP. Nucleoside monophosphate kinases and nucleoside diphosphate kinases generate the respective diphosphates and triphosphates, respectively, of GMP and AMP.

Biosynthesis of GMP and AMP is regulated by allosteric mechanisms. PRPP is a positive modifier of amidophosphoribosyl transferase, which catalyzes the first committed step in IMP synthesis, whereas AMP and GMP are negative modifiers. GMP is also

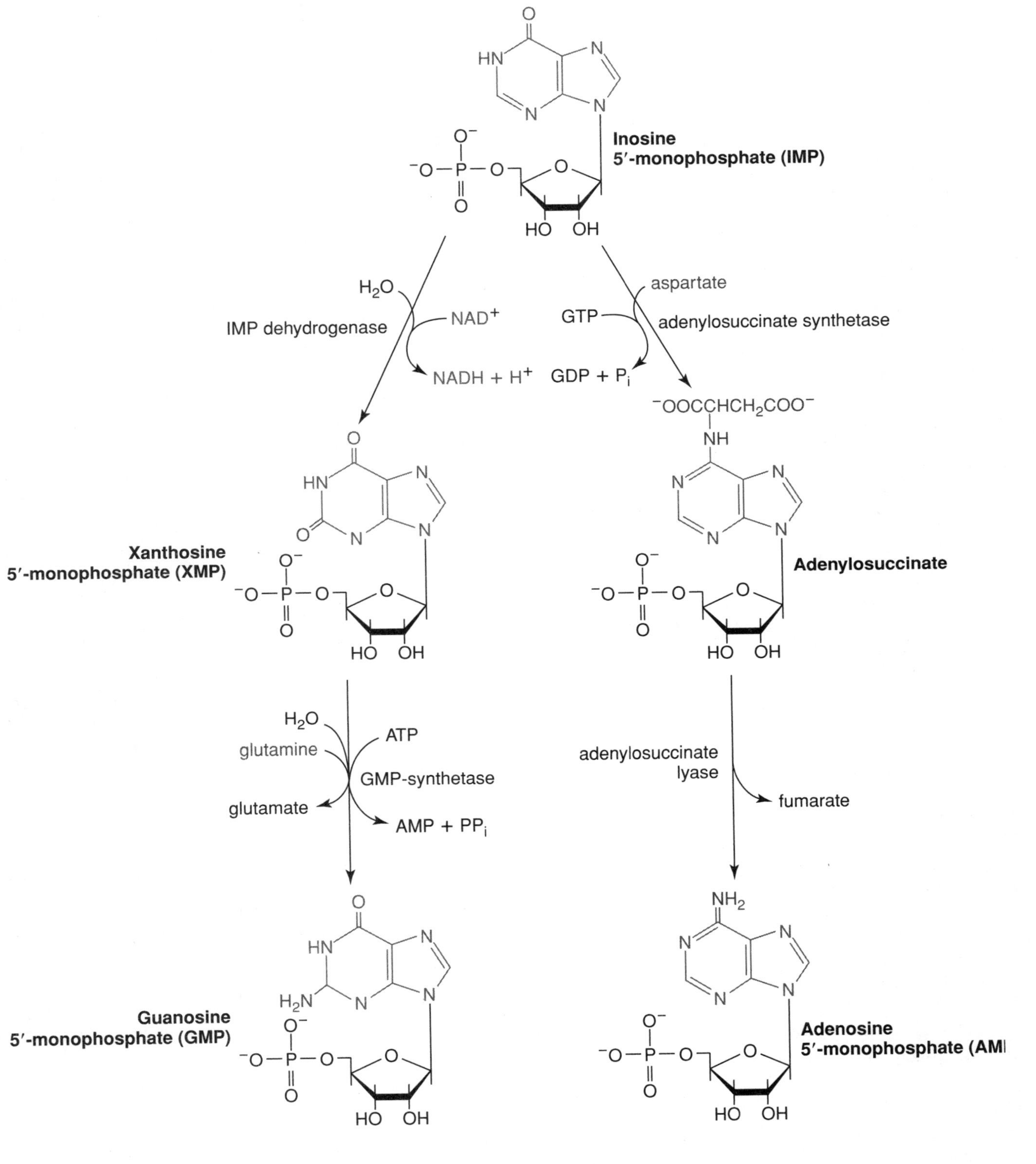

Figure 1-139. Formation of AMP and GMP from IMP.

(Adapted from Devlin, T. M., Editor, *Textbook of Biochemistry with Clinical Correlations*, Sixth Edition, Wiley-Liss, Hoboken, NJ, 2006, Figure 1-20.4, p. 794.)

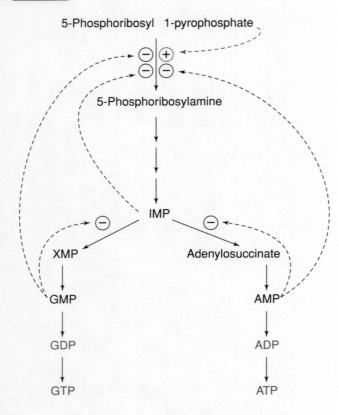

Figure 1-140. Regulation of GMP and AMP biosynthesis.
(Adapted from Devlin, T. M., Editor, *Textbook of Biochemistry with Clinical Correlations*, Sixth Edition, Wiley-Liss, Hoboken, NJ, 2006, Figure 1-20.7, p. 795.)

a negative modifier of IMP dehydrogenase and AMP is a negative modifier of adenylosuccinate synthetase. These regulatory mechanisms are shown in the diagram of Figure 1-140.

18.2. Degradation of Purines

The end product of purine metabolism in animals is uric acid, which may be metabolized to other products in other species. The pathway for degradation of purines to uric acid is shown in Figure 1-141.

The first step in catabolism of nucleotide monophosphates is conversion to nucleosides by nucleo-

tidase. AMP, however, may first be converted to IMP by AMP deaminase, or adenosine produced by the action of nucleotidase may undergo deamination by adenosine deaminase to inosine. Inosine, xanthosine, and guanosine are converted to their free bases and ribose-1-phosphate by purine nucleoside phosphorylase (PNP). At this stage, guanine is deaminated to give xanthine. The action of PNP on inosine produces hypoxanthine as the major nucleotide product. Hypoxanthine and xanthine are both metabolized by xanthine oxidase to produce uric acid. Hypoxanthine, however, is first converted to xanthine before being converted to uric acid. Xanthine oxidase is a complex protein that functions very much like an internal electron transport system. It contains FAD, two Fe-S-clusters and a molybdenum (Mo(VI)) cofactor in which the molybdenum oscillates between the Mo(VI) and the Mo(IV) states. During the process of oxidizing xanthine/hypoxanthine to uric acid, it produces H_2O_2, which can be toxic to cells. This toxicity is minimized by the action of catalase that converts hydrogen peroxide to water and oxygen:

$$2H_2O_2 \xrightarrow{\text{catalase}} 2H_2O + O_2.$$

In several other species, uric acid may be further metabolized to other excretory nitrogen-containing compounds. A diagram showing metabolic transformations that lead to formation of some of those excretory compounds, and some of the species in which these reactions occur, is presented in Figure 1-142.

18.3. Synthesis of Pyrimidines

In pyrimidine biosynthesis, the ring structure is synthesized first, and ribose phosphate is added last. The source of ribose phosphate for pyrimidines is PRPP. The overall biosynthetic pathway for pyrimidine biosynthesis is less complicated than that for purines, and it requires fewer steps—six as opposed to eleven (or ten starting with the committed step)—for purine biosynthesis.

Only three sources of carbon contribute atoms of the pyrimidine ring structure: aspartate, the amide group of glutamine, and bicarbonate. The following

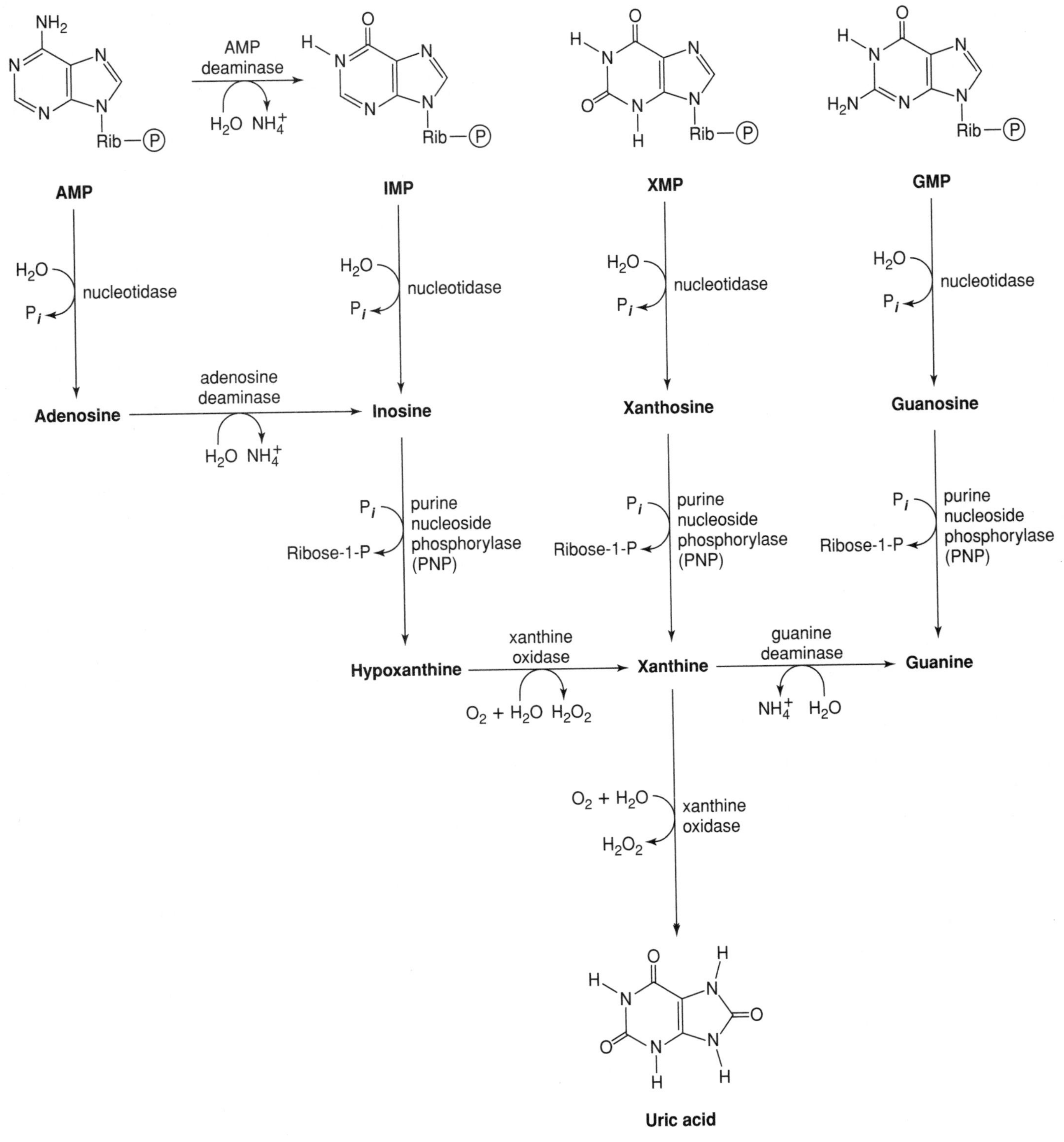

Figure 1-141. Pathway for degradation of purines to uric acid.

(Adapted from Voet, D., Voet, J.D., and Pratt, C. W., *Fundamentals of Biochemistry: Life at the Molecular Level*, Second Edition, John Wiley & Sons, New York, 2006, Figure 1-22.18, p. 809.)

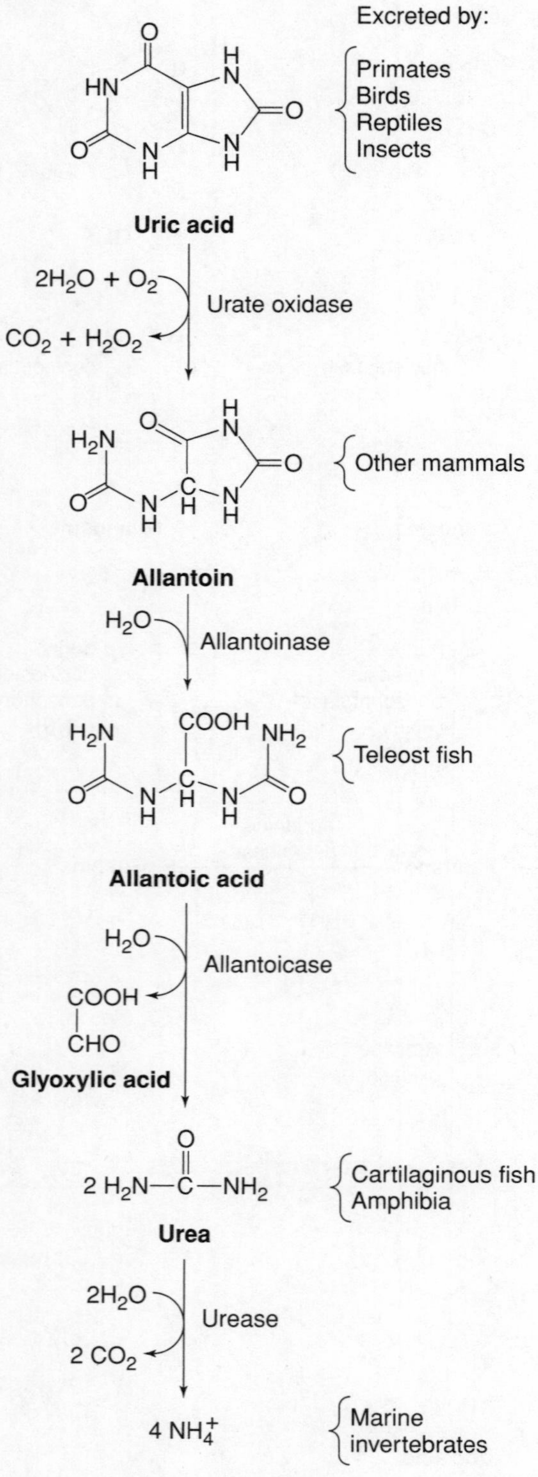

Uric acid

Excreted by:

Primates
Birds
Reptiles
Insects

$2H_2O + O_2$ ⟶ Urate oxidase

$CO_2 + H_2O_2$

Other mammals

Allantoin

H_2O ⟶ Allantoinase

Teleost fish

Allantoic acid

H_2O ⟶ Allantoicase

COOH
CHO

Glyoxylic acid

$2 H_2N-\overset{O}{\underset{}{C}}-NH_2$

Cartilaginous fish
Amphibia

Urea

$2H_2O$ ⟶ Urease

$2 CO_2$

$4 NH_4^+$

Marine
invertebrates

**Figure 1-142. End products of uric acid
metabolism in several other species of animals.**
(Adapted from Voet, D., Voet, J.D., and Pratt, C. W., *Fundamentals
of Biochemistry: Life at the Molecular Level*, Second Edition,
John Wiley & Sons, New York, 2006, Figure 1-22.21, p. 812.)

diagram (Figure 1-143) shows where these occur in the pyrimidine ring.

The ultimate goal is biosynthesis of three compounds (Figure 1-144).

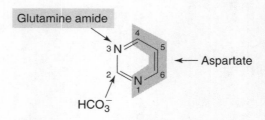

**Figure 1-143. Sources of carbon atoms
for the pyrimidine ring.**
(Adapted from Devlin, T. M., Editor, *Textbook of Biochemistry
with Clinical Correlations*, Sixth Edition, Wiley-Liss,
Hoboken, NJ, 2006, Figure 1-20.17, p. 805.)

The first step in the synthesis of pyrimidines is synthesis of carbamoyl phosphate by cytosolic carbamoyl phosphate synthetase II. Carbamoyl phosphate is synthesized from ATP, HCO_3^-, and glutamine with water also involved in its synthesis. Species that also have the urea cycle synthesize carbamoyl phosphate using carbamoyl phosphate synthetase I, a mitochondrial enzyme. In the latter case, NH_4^+ instead of glutamine is the nitrogen source. A diagrammatic representation of the pathway for UMP biosynthesis is shown in Figure 1-145.

The second step in pyrimidine biosynthesis is carbamoyl aspartate by condensation of aspartate with carbamoyl phosphate catalyzed by aspartate transcarbamoylase. Some aspects of the structure and regulation of this enzyme have been discussed earlier in the section on enzymes. It is one of the key regulatory enzymes for this pathway.

All of the components for the pyrimidine ring have been linked, but ring closure has not occurred. This is accomplished in the third step by action of dihydroorotase to form dihydroorotic acid.

In the fourth step, dihydroorotic acid is reduced to orotic acid by dihydroorotiate reductase in an irreversible manner by an FAD-dependent enzyme that also

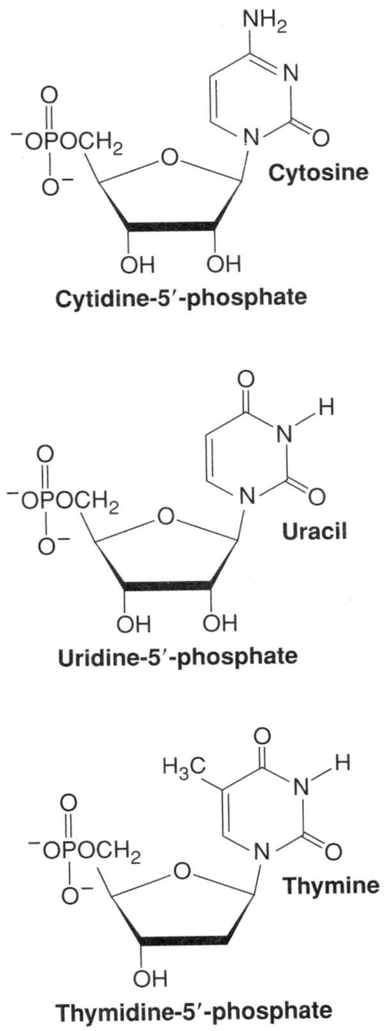

Figure 1-144. Structures of pyrimidine nucleotides.

Cytidine nucleotide is formed by amination of uridine triphosphate. UTP is made by a combination of the actions of nucleoside monophosphate kinase and nucleoside diphosphate kinase.

$$UMP + ATP \leftrightarrow UDP + ADP$$

$$UDP + ATP \leftrightarrow UTP + ADP$$

UTP is converted to CTP by CTP synthetase. The amine group of CTP comes from glutamine. This is an energy requiring reaction in which the energy is supplied by ATP. The reaction catalyzed by CTP synthetase is shown in Figure 1-146.

Thymidine only occurs in DNA as the 2'deoxy form. It is synthesized from deoxy-uridine monophosphate. Synthesis of TMP will be discussed later.

Some of the physical characteristics of the enzymes responsible for catalyzing reactions in pyrimidine biosynthesis differ in prokaryotes and eukaryotes. There is a trend in eukaryotes for some of the enzymes to exist in multienzyme complexes and/or to be multifunctional. In prokaryotes, they are generally separate proteins. The anabolic pathway is regulated in both cases by feedback inhibition and in some cases by feed-forward activation, but not always by the same metabolites. Figure 1-147 compares regulatory mechanisms for *E. coli* pyrimidine biosynthesis and animal pyrimidine biosynthesis.

18.4. Synthesis of Deoxyribonucleotides

With the exception of thymidine, deoxyribonucleotides are synthesized from their nucleotide diphosphate counterparts.

The mechanism of the reactions involved in effecting this transformation is much more complex than indicated in the simplified scheme shown in Figure 1-148. The intent of that reaction scheme is meant only to show that the process of generating deoxyribonucleotides from ribonucleotides occurs at the diphosphate level and that free radical reactions are part of the overall scheme for the transformations. The diagram of

uses a quinone as a reductant, producing reduced quinone. In mammalian species, this activity is associated with mitochondria.

The fifth step is catalyzed by orotate phosphoryl transferase that utilizes PRPP to produce orotidine-5'-monophosphate (OMP) and PP_i. As in many reactions where PP_i is a product, the reaction is forced into irreversibility by the hydrolysis of PP_i to 2 molecules of P_i.

Finally, in the sixth step OMP is converted to UMP by OMP decarboxylase. Each of these reactions is summarized in Figure 1-145.

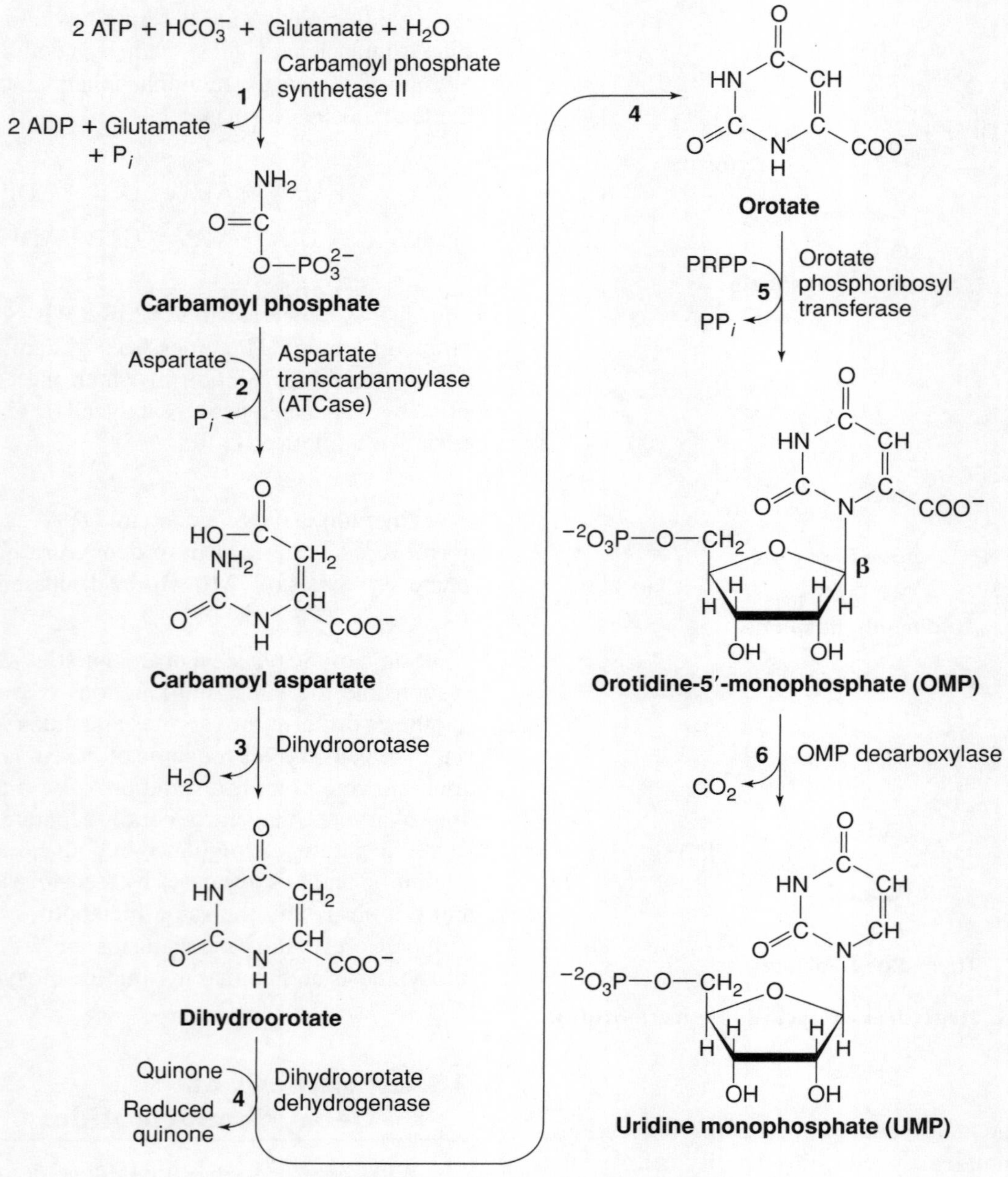

Figure 1-145. Biosynthetic pathway for UMP.
(Adapted from Voet, D., Voet, J. D., and Pratt, C. W., *Fundamentals of Biochemistry: Life at the Molecular Level*, Second Edition, John Wiley & Sons, New York, 2006, Figure 1-22.5, p. 796.)

Figure 1-149 is included to illustrate the complexity of the reaction. The more important points to remember are that reduction occurs when the nucleotides are in their diphosphate forms, ribonucleotide reductase operates through a free radical mechanism, and that dTMP is formed from dUMP, as will be shown later.

18.4.1. Regulation of Ribonucleotide Reductase Activity

Regulation of activity of ribonucleotide reductase is essential in order to ensure that deoxynucleotides are in sufficient balance for DNA synthesis. Its regulation is complex and occurs at several levels. Emphasis here

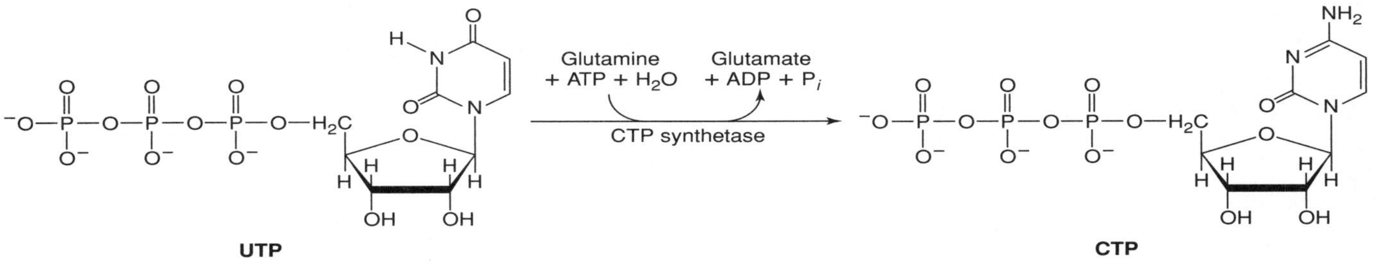

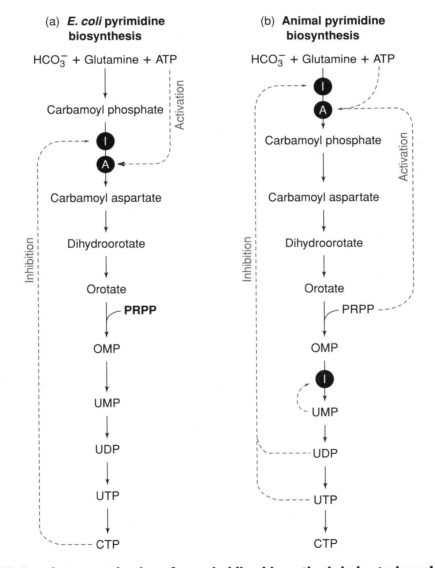

Figure 1-146. CTP synthetase reaction.
(Adapted from Modified from Voet, D., Voet, J. D., and Pratt, C. W., *Fundamentals of Biochemistry: Life at the Molecular Level*, Second Edition, John Wiley & Sons, New York, 2006, Figure 1-22.7, p. 798.)

Figure 1-147. Regulatory mechanisms for pyrimidine biosynthesis in bacteria and in animals.
(Adapted from Voet, D., Voet, J. D., and Pratt, C. W., *Fundamentals of Biochemistry: Life at the Molecular Level*, Second Edition, John Wiley & Sons, New York, 2006, Figure 1-22.8, p. 799.)

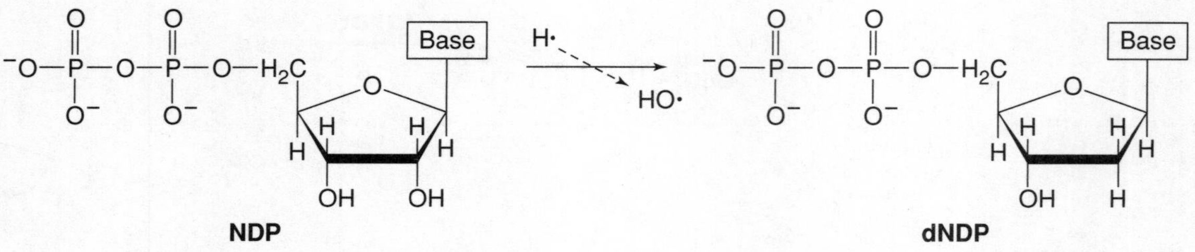

NDP

dNDP

Figure 1-148. General overall reaction for synthesis of deoxyribonucleotides.
(Adapted from Voet, D., Voet, J. D., and Pratt, C. W., *Fundamentals of Biochemistry: Life at the Molecular Level*, Second Edition, John Wiley & Sons, New York, 2006, p. 799.)

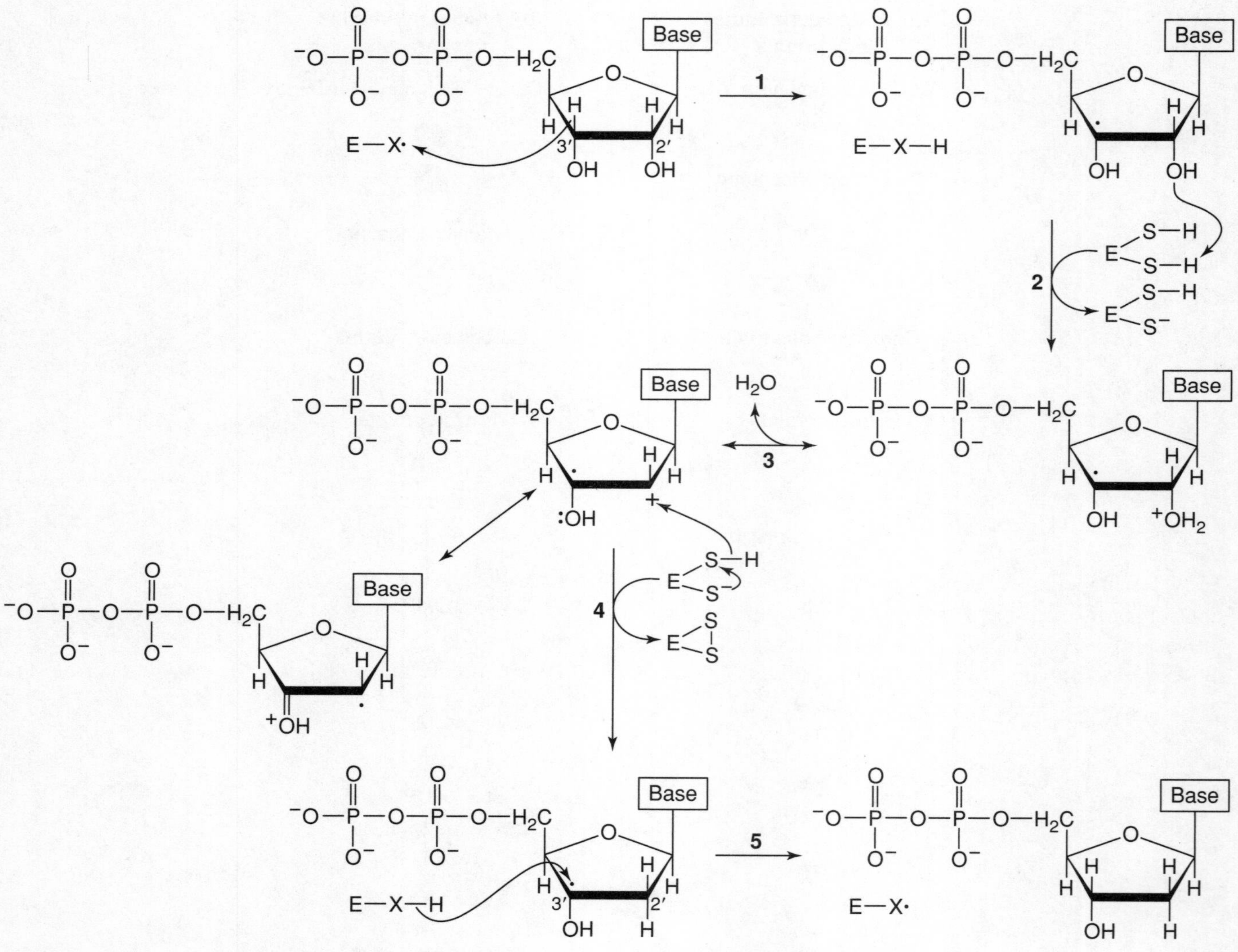

Figure 1-149. Mechanism of action of ribonucleotide reductase.
"The reaction occurs via a free radical-mediated process in which reducing equivalents are supplied by the formation of an enzyme disulfide bond (After Stubbe, J. A., *J. Biol. Chem.* 265, 5330 (1990). "
(Adapted from Voet, D., Voet, J. D., and Pratt, C. W., Figure 1-22-10, *Fundamentals of Biochemistry*, 2nd edition, p. 801.)

is only on the effects various nucleotides have on its activity. Some of those effects are summarized in the diagram of Figure 1-150. Those nucleotides below the arrows inhibit activity of ribonucleotide reductase, and those above the arrows stimulate its activity. Note that dATP inhibits reductase activity for all of its substrates, that ATP is the only non-deoxynucleotide that stimulates its activity, and that the activity it stimulates is for synthesis of deoxy-pyrimidine nucleotides.

CDP $\xrightarrow{\quad ATP \quad}$ dCDP
$\xleftarrow{\quad (dATP, dGTP, dTTP) \quad}$

UDP $\xrightarrow{\quad ATP \quad}$ dUDP
$\xleftarrow{\quad (dATP, dGTP, dTTP) \quad}$

ADP $\xrightarrow{\quad dGTP \quad}$ dADP
$\xleftarrow{\quad (dATP) \quad}$

GDP $\xrightarrow{\quad dTTP \quad}$ dGDP
$\xleftarrow{\quad (dATP) \quad}$

Figure 1-150. Summary of effects of various nucleotides on activity of ribonucleotide reductase.

18.5. Thymine Biosynthesis

Thymine is synthesized from dUMP by thymidylate synthase. The structural difference between dUMP and dTMP is that dTMP has a methyl group on position 5 of the pyrimidine ring. The source of the methyl group is N^5,N^{10}-methylenetetrahydrofolate. Structures and reactions of some of the methyl-THF analogs are discussed in the section on amino acids. The overall reaction catalyzed by thymidylate synthase is shown below (Figure 1-151).

18.6. Degradation of Pyrimidines

CMP, UMP, and dCMP are catabolized to uracil, and dTMP is catabolized to thymine as first steps in their degradation. The diagram on the next page (Figure 1-152) shows this series of reactions. Enzymes involved are deaminases, nucleotidases, and phosphorylases.

Uracil and thymine are then degraded to β-alanine and β-aminobutyrate, respectively. Those reactions are shown in Figure 1-153.

β-Alanine and β-aminobutyrate can undergo aminotransferase reactions to give malonyl-CoA and methylmalonyl-CoA, respectively. Malonyl-CoA can participate directly in fatty acid biosynthesis, and methylmalonyl-CoA can undergo a cobalamin-dependent mutase reaction to give succinyl-CoA and enter the TCA cycle for energy production or, through oxaloacetate, be converted to glucose.

19. HEME METABOLISM

19.1 Heme and Chlorophyll Biosynthesis

Heme and chlorophyll share several properties in common, and they are structurally very similar. Heme (structure *a*) has Fe^{2+} in coordination complex with nitrogen atoms of the pyrrole groups in its ring structure, whereas chlorophyll (structure *b*) has Mg^{2+} in that position. Chlorophyll also has a phytol group that

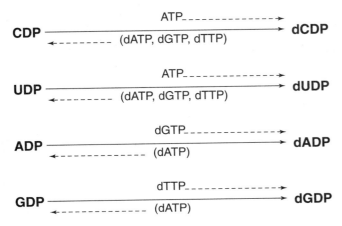

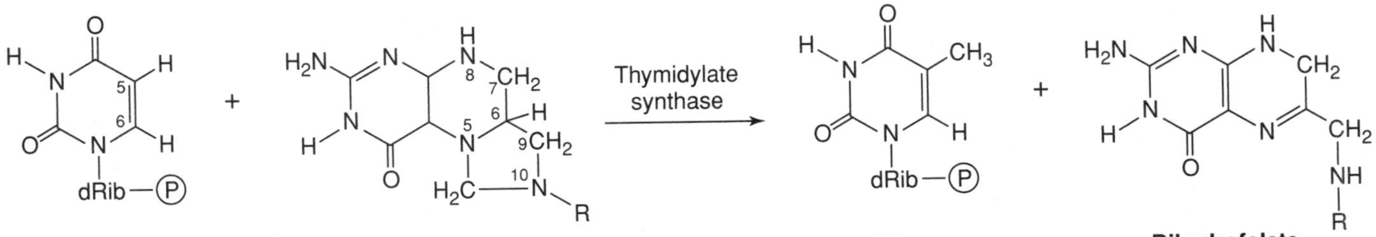

dUMP + N^5, N^{10}-**Methylenetetrahydrofolate** →[Thymidylate synthase] **dTMP** + **Dihydrofolate**

Figure 1-151. Reaction catalyzed by thymidylate synthase.
(Adapted from Voet, D., Voet, J. D., and Pratt, C. W., *Fundamentals of Biochemistry: Life at the Molecular Level*, Second Edition, John Wiley & Sons, New York, 2006, Text figure, p. 805.)

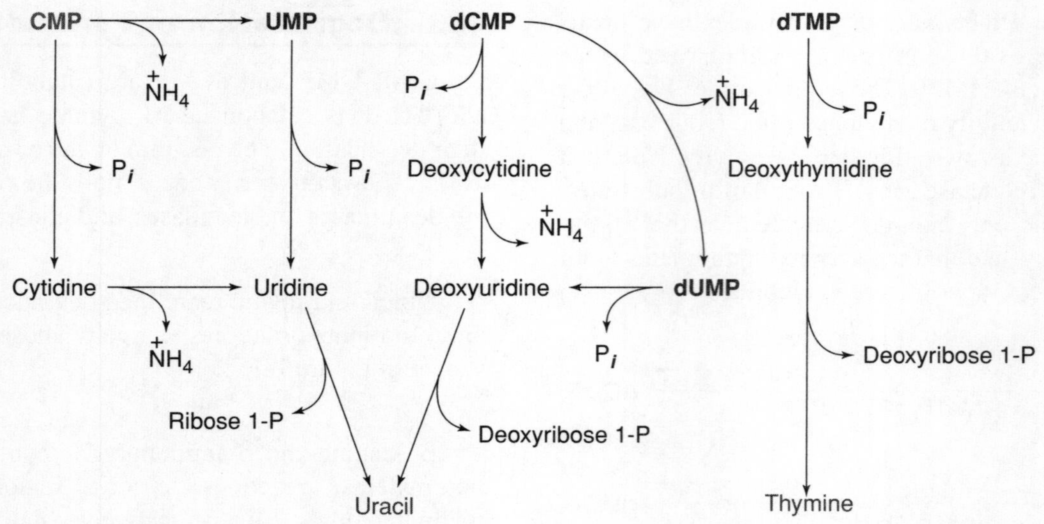

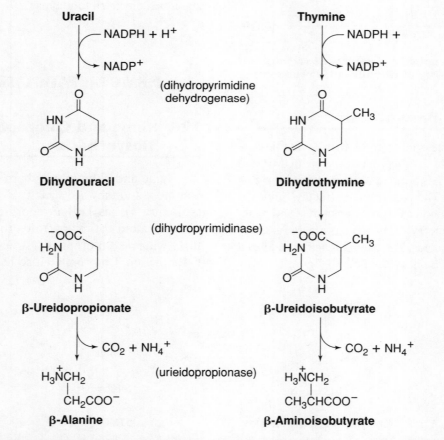

Figure 1-152. Initial steps in the degradation of pyrimidine nucleotides.
(Adapted from Devlin, T. M., Editor, *Textbook of Biochemistry with Clinical Correlations*,
Sixth Edition, Wiley-Liss, Hoboken, NJ, 2006, Figure 1-20.25, p. 809.)

Figure 1-153. Formation of β-alanine and β-aminoisobutyrate from uracil and thymine, respectively.
(Adapted from Devlin, T. M., Editor, *Textbook of Biochemistry with Clinical Correlations*,
Sixth Edition, Wiley-Liss, Hoboken, NJ, 2006, Figure 1-20.26, p. 809.)

helps anchor it to membrane structures. Figure 1-154 is a structural comparison of these two molecules.

Thus, it is not surprising that the committed step in the formation of heme and chlorophyll is the same, namely, synthesis of δ-aminolevulinic acid. In animals, some fungi, and bacteria, δ-aminolevulinic acid is synthesized from glycine and succinyl-CoA. In plants and some other species, all of its carbon atoms come from glutamate. Reaction sequence for the latter pathway is

$$\text{Glutamate} + \text{ATP} + \text{tRNA}^{Glu} \rightarrow \text{Glutamyl-tRNA}^{Glu} + \text{AMP} + \text{PP}_i$$

$$\text{Glutamyl-tRNA}^{Glu} + \text{NADPH/H}^+ \rightarrow \text{Glutamate-1-semialdehyde} + \text{tRNA}^{Glu} + \text{NADP}^+$$

$$\text{Glutamate-1-semialdehyde} + \text{Glutamate} \rightarrow \text{δ-Aminolevulinate} + \text{α-ketoglutarate}$$

and involves aminoacyl-tRNA synthetase, glutamyl-tRNA reductase, and aminotransferase.

In animals, some fungi, and bacteria, the pathway leading to the synthesis of porphobilinogen starts with glycine and succinyl-CoA (Figure 1-155).

The two pathways merge upon completion of synthesis of δ-aminolevulinic acid. From that point, reactions are the same, staring with ALA dehydrogenase through formation of protoporphyrin IX. At this step, either Fe^{2+} is added for heme formation, or Mg^{2+} is added for chlorophyll biosynthesis. There are several other modifications of the Mg^{2+} protoporphyrin com-

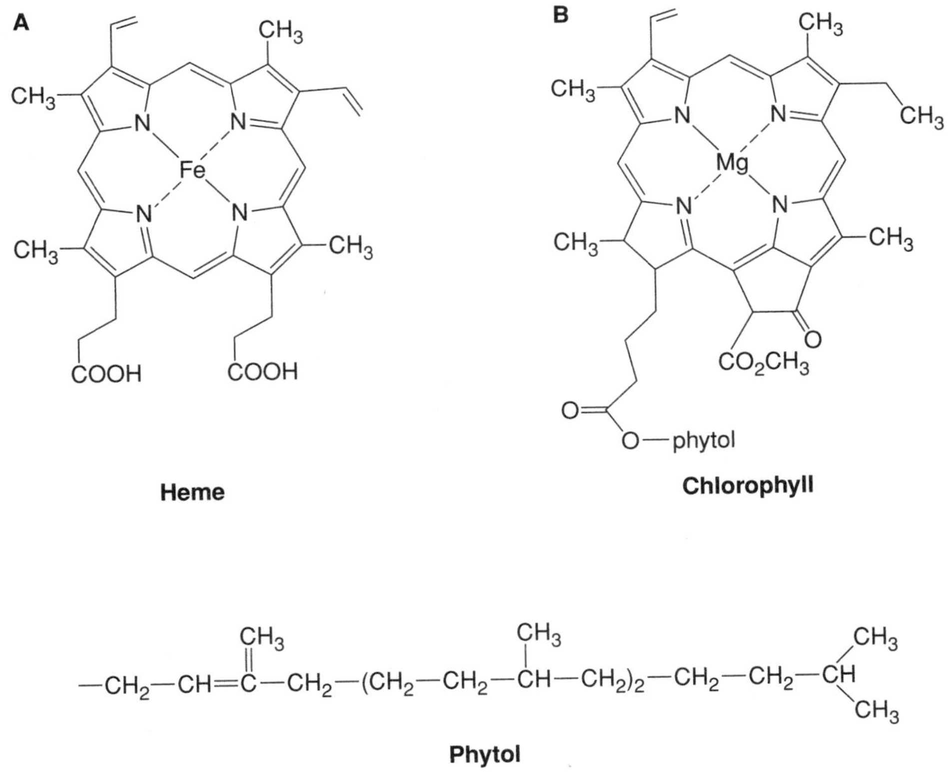

Heme

Chlorophyll

Phytol

Figure 1-154. Structures of heme and chlorophyll.
(Adapted from B. D. Hames et al., *Instant Notes in Biochemistry*, Bios Scientific Publishers, Leeds, UK, p. 240.)

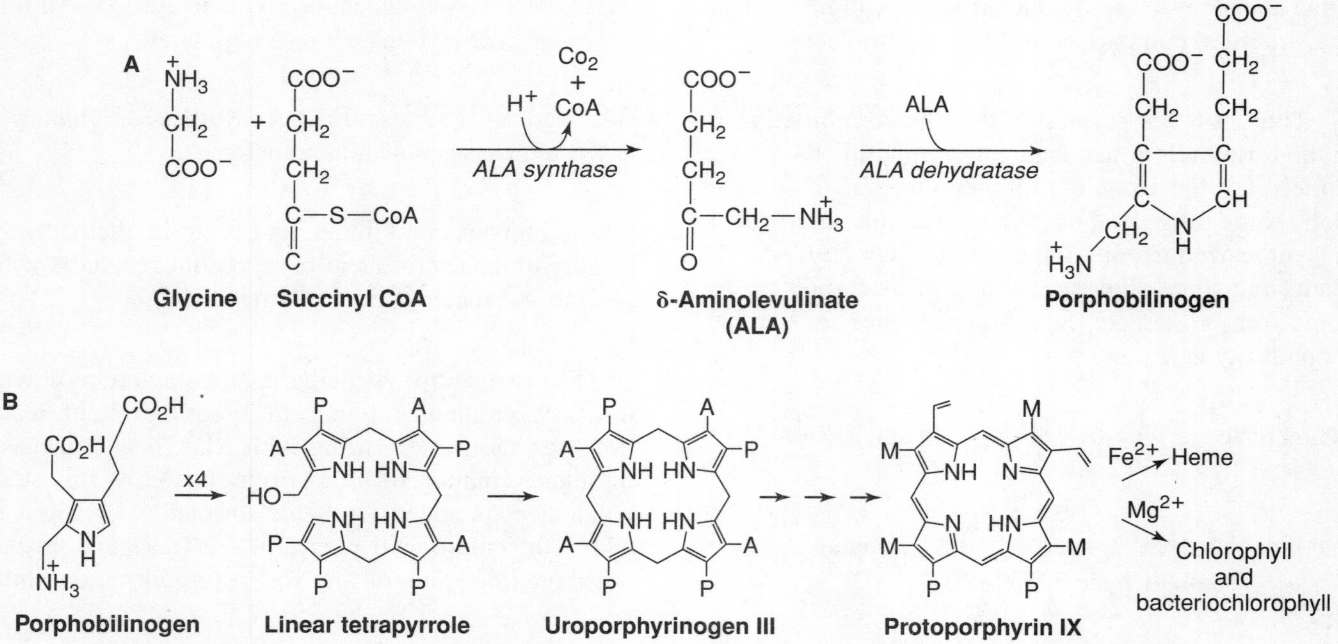

Figure 1-155. Pathway for biosynthesis of the porphyrin ring of heme and chlorophyll.
(Adapted from B.D. Hames et al., *Instant Notes in Biochemistry*, Bios Scientific Publishers, Leeds, UK, p. 336.)

plex prior to addition of phytol and completion of chlorophyll biosynthesis.

19.2. Heme and Chlorophyll Degradation

The highest concentration of heme in humans and in other mammals is in the red blood cells. The lifetime of red blood cells in humans is approximately 120 days, and the breakdown of heme is an active process in which the ring structure is cleaved and the product is made water soluble and excreted. In plants, the cyclic tetrapyrrole structure is also converted into molecules such as phytochromes, phycocyanin, and phycoerythrin where they function as ancillary light-harvesting pigments. In plants and animals, the initial reactions for catabolizing the cyclic tetrapyrrole ring structure follow the same scheme.

The first reaction is catalyzed by heme oxygenase, an enzyme of the cytochrome P450 class. This oxidation process requires $NADPH/H^+$ and O_2. Iron is released as Fe^{3+}, and CO is generated. This is the only known reaction in humans where carbon monoxide is produced. Some of the CO that is produced is exhaled, and measuring its amount is sometimes used as an indication of heme breakdown. The oxygen in CO is derived strictly from molecular oxygen as would be expected for a reaction catalyzed by a mixed function oxidase.

In the structures of Figure 1-156, M = (—CH$_3$), V = (—CH——CH$_2$), and P = (—CH$_2$CH$_2$CH$_2$OH). In mammals, bilirubin is made more water soluble by conjugation of the propionyl hydroxyl groups with glucuronic acid, with the enzyme bilirubin UDP glucuronyltransferase. The conjugate is excreted into bile and released in the ileum and large intestine where it is subjected to other metabolic conversions (urobilinogens and urobilins) by intestinal bacteria before being excreted in feces. The conjugation reaction is shown in Figure 1-157.

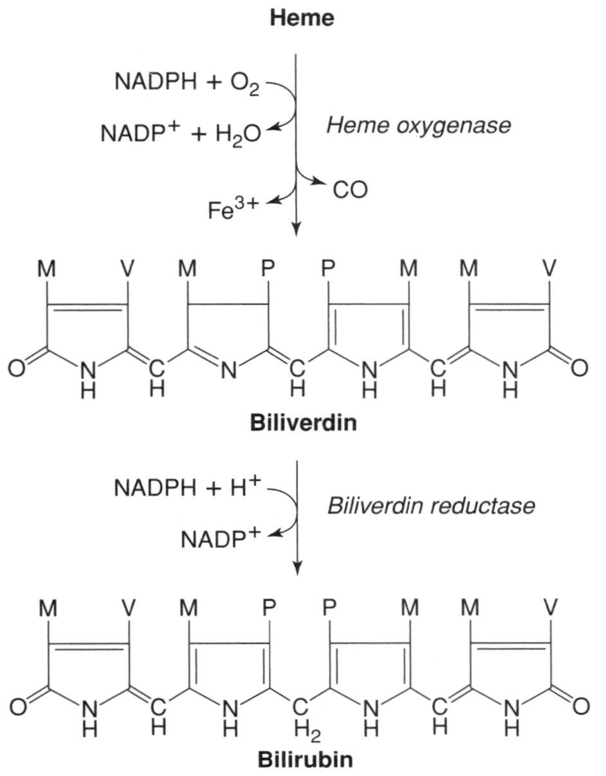

Heme

Figure 1-156. End products of the degradation of heme (and chlorophyll).
(Adapted in part from Voet, D., Voet, J. D., and Pratt, C. W., *Fundamentals of Biochemistry: Life at the Molecular Level*, Second Edition, John Wiley & Sons, New York, 2006, Figure 1-20-38, p. 729.)

20. LIPID METABOLISM

20.1. Fatty Acid Biosynthesis

Fatty acids are synthesized in the cytosol from acetyl coenzyme A (CoA) by the enzyme fatty acid synthase. They are synthesized from acetyl CoA, but butyryl CoA may also be a starting substrate. The end product from the initial synthesis of fatty acids is palmitic acid, a 16-carbon saturated fatty acid. All others are made from palmitate by elongation and desaturation reactions. Reactions involved in palmitate biosynthesis are shown in Figure 1-158, starting with the committed step, synthesis of malonyl CoA, followed by a series of reactions that result in completion of the first cycle of addition of a two-carbon fragment.

The two major substrates required for fatty acid synthesis are acetyl CoA and malonyl CoA. Acetyl CoA serves as the "primer," and its methyl group will become the methyl group of the final substrate, palmitate.

The committed step in fatty acid biosynthesis is the formation of malonyl CoA from acetyl CoA and bicarbonate by acetyl CoA carboxylase. This reaction is shown in the first line of Figure 1-158. Acetyl CoA carboxylase is a biotin-dependent enzyme, and it requires ATP. The reaction is similar to that of pyruvate carboxylase in that the first step is formation of carboxybiotin in an ATP-dependent reaction. Biotin is a prosthetic group for this enzyme. The carboxyl group from carboxybiotin is then transferred to acetyl CoA to form malonyl CoA.

Fatty acid synthase is a multienzyme complex. One of its components is *acyl carrier protein*, a small protein of approximately 77 residues (in bacteria). This protein has as a prosthetic group a phosphopantetheine moiety like that in coenzyme A. This group is attached to ACP by a phosphoester linkage to a serine residue. The structure of acetyl coenzyme A is in Figure 1-159. The portion of the molecule enclosed by the dashed line is the same in acetyl CoA and the acetyl-ACP complex. Thus, transfer of acyl group from one to the other is essentially energy neutral.

ACP-acetyltransferase and ACP-malonyltransferase each catalyze formation of acetyl-ACP and malonyl-ACP, respectively. The acetyl-ACP transfers the acyl group to an active —SH group on the enzyme. The carboxyl carbon of the acetyl group on the enzyme (Enz-SH) has electrophilic properties, and the α-carbon of malonyl-ACP becomes highly nucleophilic due to the ease of losing the nonesterified carboxyl group probably leaving a carbanion in the transition state. The result is loss of CO_2 and condensation of the remaining 2-carbon unit to acetyl CoA to form the β-ketoacyl-ACP complex, a 4-carbon unit (reaction 3b). CO_2 that is released from malonyl-ACP is the same as that used to form malonyl CoA, so all of the carbons in the newly formed fatty acid come from acetate. Also note that in the end, carbon atoms 15 and 16 of palmitate will be the

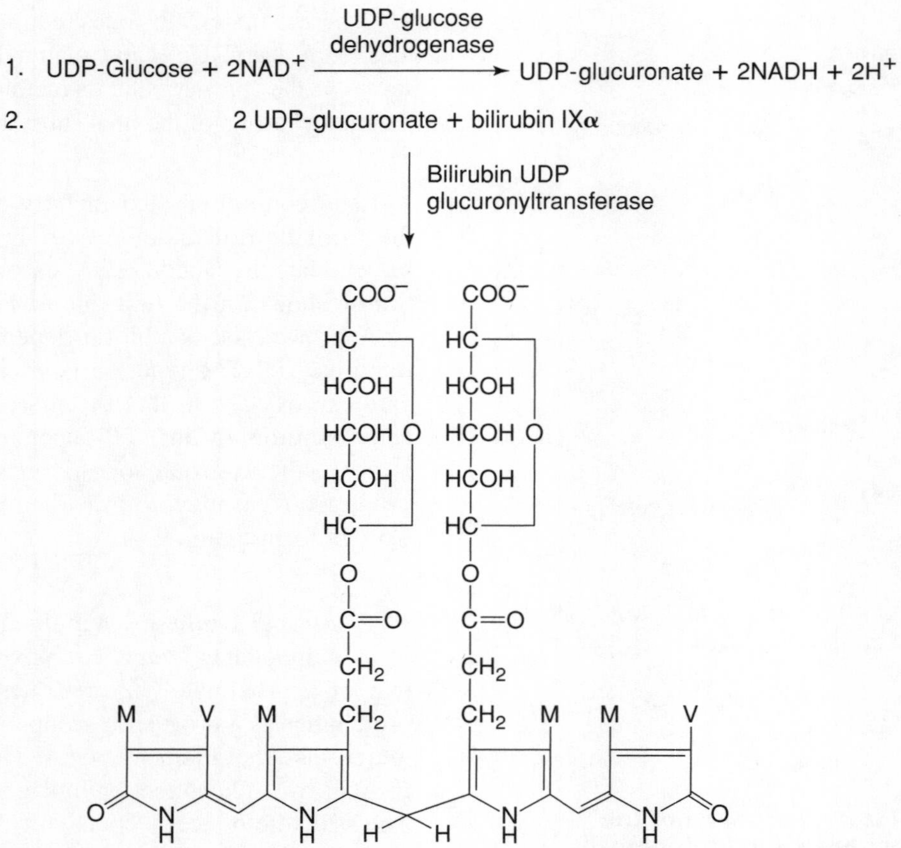

1. UDP-Glucose + 2NAD$^+$ $\xrightarrow{\text{UDP-glucose dehydrogenase}}$ UDP-glucuronate + 2NADH + 2H$^+$

2. 2 UDP-glucuronate + bilirubin IXα

Bilirubin UDP
glucuronyltransferase

Figure 1-157. Formation of the glucuronyl-billirubin conjugate by UDP gluronyltransferase.
(Adapted from Devlin, T. M., Editor, *Textbook of Biochemistry with Clinical Correlations*,
Sixth Edition, Wiley-Liss, Hoboken, NJ, 2006, Figure 1-20.13, p. 842.)

initial carbons of acetyl-ACP. The next step is reduction of the β-ketobutyryl-ACP by β-ketoacyl-ACP reductase using NADPH/H$^+$ to give β-hydroxybutyryl-ACP. The next step is dehydration of β-hydroxybutyryl-ACP by β-hydroxyacyl-ACP dehydratase to yield an enol-ACP complex, which is then reduced by (NADPH/H$^+$)—dependent enol-ACP reductase to a saturated butryl-ACP. This saturated acyl group is then transferred back to the active —SH group on the enzyme, and the process is repeated six more times. The product released from the fatty acid synthase complex is palmitate. No intermediate chain length fatty acids are released. The overall reaction is

AcCoA + 7 MalonylCoA + 14 NADPH + 14 H$^+$ →
Palmitate + 7 CO$_2$ + 14 NADP$^+$ + 8 CoASH + 6 H$_2$O.

When taking into account the energy required to make the seven molecules of malonyl CoA, the overall reaction becomes

8 AcCoA + 7 ATP + 14 NADPH + 14 H$^+$ →
Palmitate + 7 ADP + 7 P$_i$ + 14 NADP$^+$
+ 8 CoASH + 6 H$_2$O.

20.1.1. Elongation of Palmitic Acid

Elongation of palmitic acid (C-16) to stearic acid (C-18) occurs by enzymes (in mammals) located on the cytosolic side of the endoplasmic reticulum. Mechanism for the elongation reaction is essentially the same as it is for synthesis of palmitate in that the donor 2-carbon group comes from malonyl CoA.

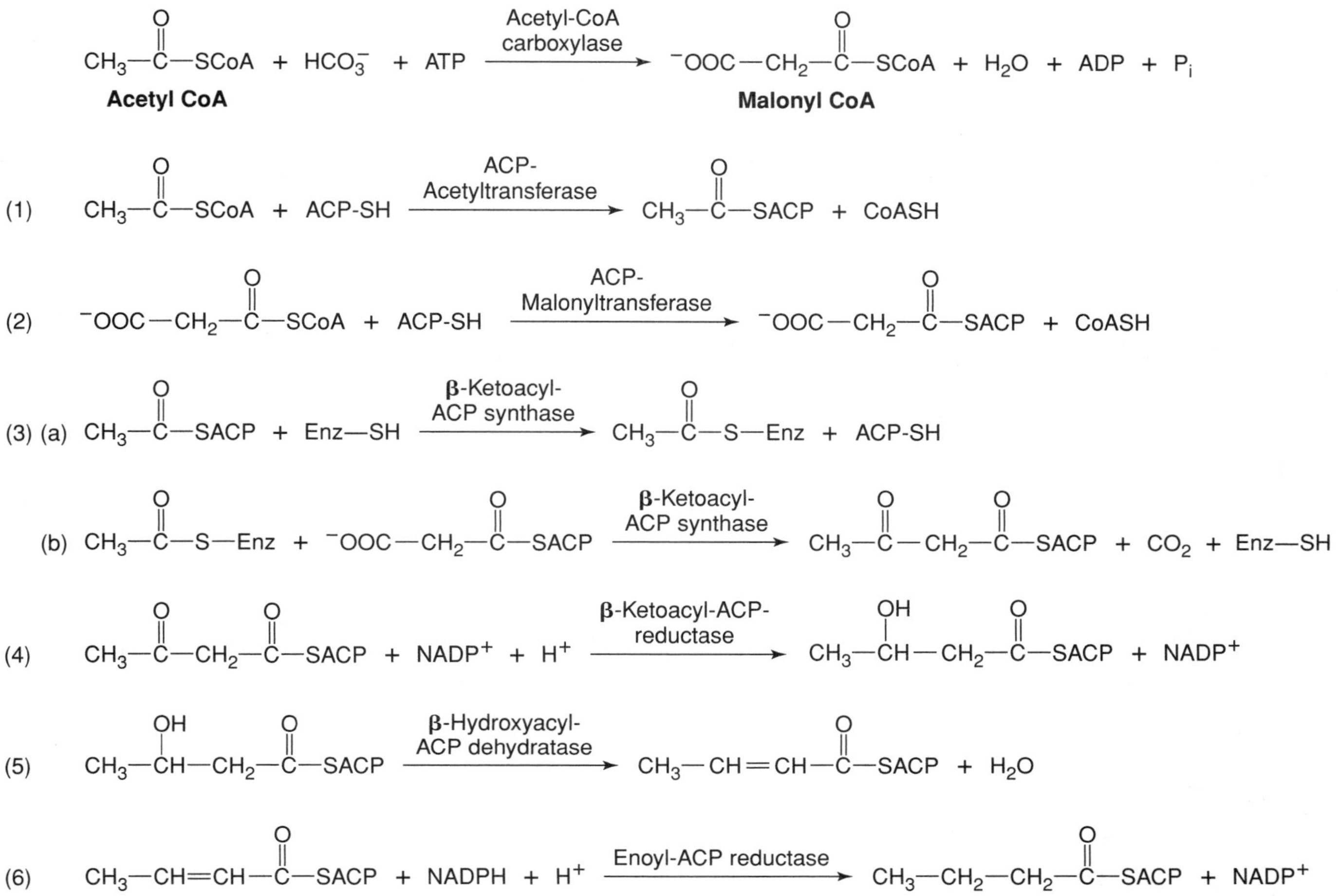

$$CH_3-\overset{\overset{O}{\|}}{C}-SCoA + HCO_3^- + ATP \xrightarrow{\text{Acetyl-CoA carboxylase}} {}^-OOC-CH_2-\overset{\overset{O}{\|}}{C}-SCoA + H_2O + ADP + P_i$$

Acetyl CoA   **Malonyl CoA**

(1) $$CH_3-\overset{\overset{O}{\|}}{C}-SCoA + ACP\text{-}SH \xrightarrow{\substack{\text{ACP-}\\\text{Acetyltransferase}}} CH_3-\overset{\overset{O}{\|}}{C}-SACP + CoASH$$

(2) $${}^-OOC-CH_2-\overset{\overset{O}{\|}}{C}-SCoA + ACP\text{-}SH \xrightarrow{\substack{\text{ACP-}\\\text{Malonyltransferase}}} {}^-OOC-CH_2-\overset{\overset{O}{\|}}{C}-SACP + CoASH$$

(3) (a) $$CH_3-\overset{\overset{O}{\|}}{C}-SACP + Enz-SH \xrightarrow{\substack{\beta\text{-Ketoacyl-}\\\text{ACP synthase}}} CH_3-\overset{\overset{O}{\|}}{C}-S-Enz + ACP\text{-}SH$$

(b) $$CH_3-\overset{\overset{O}{\|}}{C}-S-Enz + {}^-OOC-CH_2-\overset{\overset{O}{\|}}{C}-SACP \xrightarrow{\substack{\beta\text{-Ketoacyl-}\\\text{ACP synthase}}} CH_3-\overset{\overset{O}{\|}}{C}-CH_2-\overset{\overset{O}{\|}}{C}-SACP + CO_2 + Enz-SH$$

(4) $$CH_3-\overset{\overset{O}{\|}}{C}-CH_2-\overset{\overset{O}{\|}}{C}-SACP + NADP^+ + H^+ \xrightarrow{\substack{\beta\text{-Ketoacyl-ACP-}\\\text{reductase}}} CH_3-\overset{\overset{OH}{|}}{CH}-CH_2-\overset{\overset{O}{\|}}{C}-SACP + NADP^+$$

(5) $$CH_3-\overset{\overset{OH}{|}}{CH}-CH_2-\overset{\overset{O}{\|}}{C}-SACP \xrightarrow{\substack{\beta\text{-Hydroxyacyl-}\\\text{ACP dehydratase}}} CH_3-CH=CH-\overset{\overset{O}{\|}}{C}-SACP + H_2O$$

(6) $$CH_3-CH=CH-\overset{\overset{O}{\|}}{C}-SACP + NADPH + H^+ \xrightarrow{\text{Enoyl-ACP reductase}} CH_3-CH_2-CH_2-\overset{\overset{O}{\|}}{C}-SACP + NADP^+$$

Figure 1-158. Reaction pathway for palmitate biosynthesis.
(Adapted from Devlin, T. M., Editor, *Textbook of Biochemistry with Clinical Correlations*,
Sixth Edition, Wiley-Liss, Hoboken, NJ, 2006, Figures 17.7 and 17.8, pp. 669-670)

Malonyl CoA participates directly in reactions rather than first transferring the malonyl moiety to an ACP. These reactions are carried out by separate enzymes rather than by a multienzyme complex. CO_2 is eliminated in this reaction also in order to facilitate the chemical process of condensation to form a carbon-carbon bond. This process can make fatty acids up to chain lengths of 24.

20.1.2. Formation of Unsaturated Fatty Acids

Desaturation of fatty acids occurs in the endoplasmic reticulum of mammals. It occurs via a monooxygenase system that consists of NADPH-cytochrome b_5 reductase, cytochrome b_5, and the desaturase enzyme. This system is essentially an electron transport system using NADPH/H+ as the reductant and O_2 as the electron acceptor. The overall reaction is

$$R-CH_2-CH_2-(CH_2)_7-COOH + NADPH + H^+ + O_2 \rightarrow R-CH=CH-(CH_2)_7-COOH + NADP^+ + 2H_2O.$$

The enzyme is often referred to as stearoyl-CoA desaturase even though it will catalyze the formation of double bonds in palmitate and other fatty acids. Key to its function is the fact that the first double bond formed must be at C-9, and it cannot form dou-

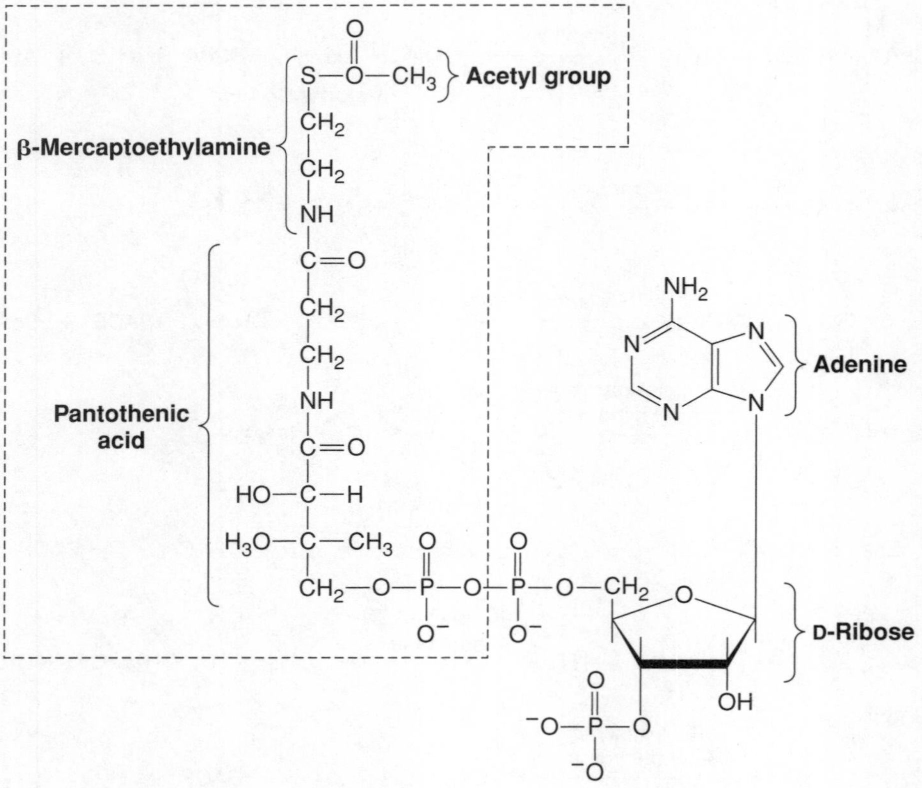

Figure 1-159. Structure of acetyl coenzyme A.
(Adapted from Devlin, T. M., Editor, *Textbook of Biochemistry with Clinical Correlations*, Sixth Edition, Wiley-Liss, Hoboken, NJ, 2006, Figure 1-14.12, p. 539.)

ble bonds in any fatty acids if there are fewer than six carbons beyond the first double bond formed. If the substrate is stearate, the product is oleic acid; if the substrate is palmitate, the product is palmitoleic acid. Each has a double bond at position 9. Palmitoleic acid can be elongated to 18 carbon atoms by the process described above. The product would be a C-18 carbon fatty acid that has a double bond at position 11. This compound is *cis*-vaccenate. Similarly, oleic acid can be elongated to a C-20 fatty acid with a double bond also at position 11. All of these are in the *cis* configuration.

20.1.3. Nomenclature and Other Positions Where Desaturases Function

Positions of double bonds in fatty acids are designated in the following manner. Oleic acid is (18:1 *cis*-Δ^9)

and palmitoleic is (16:1 *cis*-Δ^9). Elongation of palmitoleic by one 2-carbon unit gives (18:1 *cis*-Δ^{11}). Notations in parentheses indicate the ratio of the number of carbons to the number of unsaturated bonds; that they are in the *cis* configuration; and the position of the double bond counting from the carboxyl group, which is number one. Some polyunsaturated fatty acids that are considered to be nutritionally beneficial are designated as omega (ω) fatty acids, and the positions of double bonds are determined by counting from the methyl group (number 1) toward the carboxyl group. For example, oleic acid is ω-9, palmitoleic acid is ω-7, etc. Note that the number is for the carbon immediately before the double bond, whether counting from the carboxyl group or the methyl group.

The farthest position in which mammals can introduce double bonds into fatty acids is Δ^9. There are desaturases in humans, however, that can introduce double bonds at positions Δ^4, Δ^5, and Δ^6. There are also requirements in mammals for fatty acids that are poly-unsaturated in positions beyond position Δ^9. Linoleate (18:2 cis-Δ^9,Δ^{12}) and linolenate (18:3 cis-$\Delta^9, \Delta^{12}, \Delta^{15}$) are essential fatty acids and required in the diet. Note that linolenate is an ω-3 fatty acid, whereas linoleate is an ω-6 fatty acid.

20.2. Arachidonic Acid and Signaling/Regulatory Molecules

Several hormones and regulatory molecules are derived from arachidonic acid, which is derived from linoleic acid (18:2 cis-Δ^9,Δ^{12}). Among this class of compounds are prostaglandins, thromboxanes, leuco-trienes, and prostacyclins. Arachidonic acid is a C-20 polyunsaturated fatty acid, also known as eicosatetrae-noic acid (20:4 cis-$\Delta^5,\Delta^8,\Delta^{11},\Delta^{14}$). Compounds derived from this source are in a class called eicosanoids. Elongation of lineoleic acid and the introduction of two additional double bonds can produce arachidonic acid.

20.3. Cholesterol and Steroid Hormones Are Derived from Acetate

The first step in the synthesis of cholesterol is the formation of 3-hydroxy-3-methylglutaryl CoA (HMG-CoA) by HMG-CoA synthase. Substrates for the formation of HMG-CoA are acetoacetyl CoA and acetyl

CoA. The committed step in cholesterol biosynthesis is the conversion of HMG-CoA to mevalonic acid by HMG-CoA reductase. This reaction is shown below (Figure 1-160).

This enzyme is the target of drugs designed to reduce the blood level of cholesterol in humans. These drugs are known by the generic name of statins.

The next series of reactions result in the formation of farnesyl pyrophosphate (farnesyl-PP), a 15-carbon condensation product of three molecules of mevalon-ate. This is an ATP-dependent series of reactions in which decarboxylation and dehydration reactions are also involved.

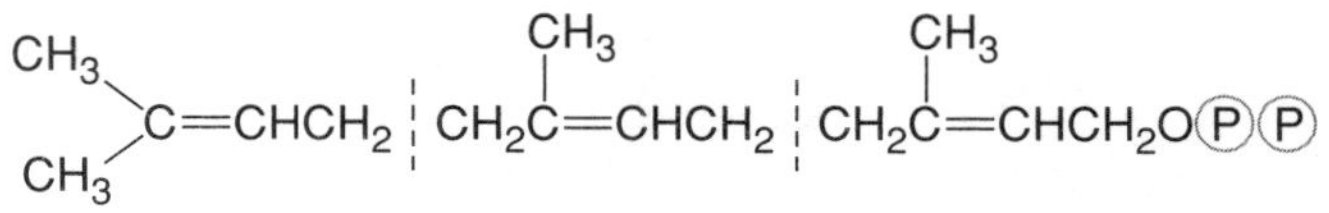

Squalene, a 30-carbon molecule, is formed by a reductive condensation reaction using two molecules of farnesyl–PP. The dashed line through squalene (Figure 1-161) shows positions of each of the two farnesyl molecules.

Squalene undergoes a series of reactions that leads to its cyclization to form lanesterol, which eventually yields cholesterol (Figure 1-162).

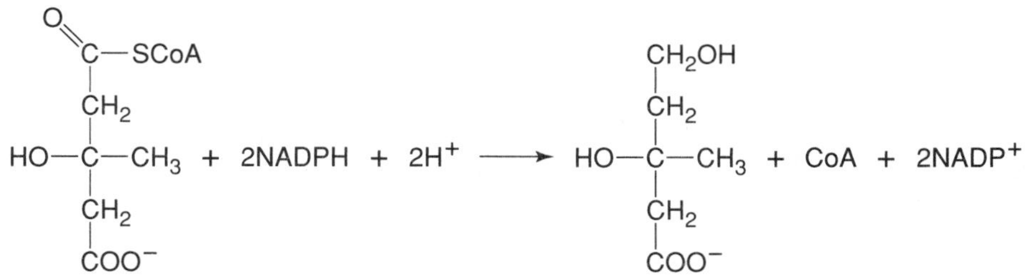

Figure 1-160. The committed step in cholesterol biosynthesis: HMG-CoA to Mevalonate. (Adapted from Devlin, T. M., Editor, *Textbook of Biochemistry with Clinical Correlations*, Sixth Edition, Wiley-Liss, Hoboken, NJ, 2006, Figure 1-18.31, p. 709.)

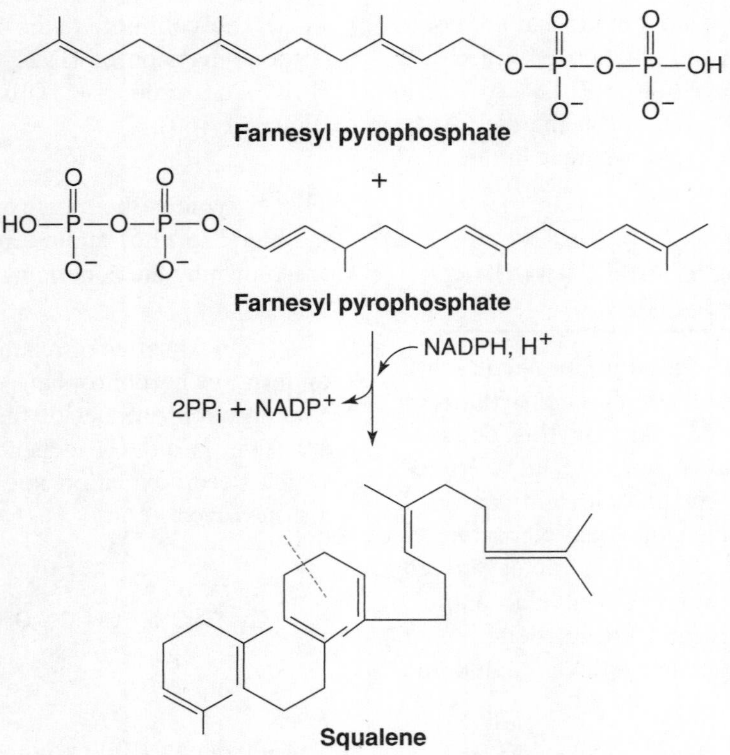

Farnesyl pyrophosphate

+

Farnesyl pyrophosphate

NADPH, H$^+$

2PP$_i$ + NADP$^+$

Squalene

Figure 1-161. Formation of squalene from farnesyl pyrophosphate.
(Adapted from Devlin, T. M., Editor, *Textbook of Biochemistry with Clinical Correlations*, Sixth Edition, Wiley-Liss, Hoboken, NJ, 2006, Figures 18.33 & 18.34, p. 710.)

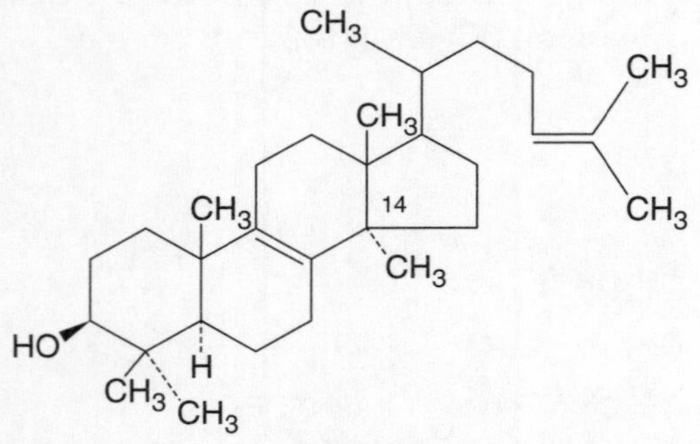

Lanosterol

Figure 1-162. Squalene is converted to lanosterol.
(Adapted from Devlin, T. M., Editor, *Textbook of Biochemistry with Clinical Correlations*, Sixth Edition, Wiley-Liss, Hoboken, NJ, 2006, Figures 18.35, p. 711.)

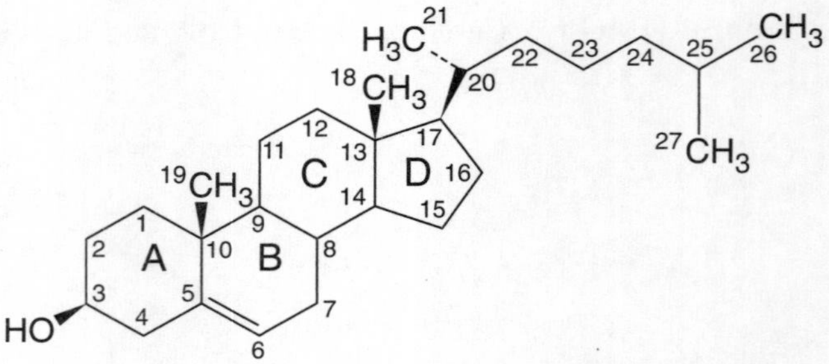

Figure 1-163. Numbering system for cholesterol.
(Adapted from Berg, J. M., Tymoczko, J. L., and Stryer, L. *Biochemistry*, Fifth Edition, W. H. Freeman and Company, 2002, Fig. 26.25, p. 733.)

This diagram (Figure 1-163) shows the numbering system for cholesterol and its derivatives.

The following hormones are derived from cholesterol: progesterone, 17β-estradiol, testosterone, dehydro-epiandrosterone, cortisol, aldosterone, and 1,25-dihydroxy-vitamin D$_3$.

20.4. Fatty Acids Are Stored as Triglycerides

Glycerol forms the basic alcoholic structure for triacylglycerols as well as phospholipids. The most common source for this glycerol phosphate for this purpose is dihydroxyacetone phosphate obtained from glycolysis; aldolase action on fructose-1,6-bisphosphate. Dihydroxyacetone phosphate is reduced to glycerol 3-phosphate. Another source is from phosphorylation of glycerol by glycerol kinase, which exists primarily in livers of mammalian species but is not highly expressed in other tissues.

Glycerol 3-phosphate is acylated first in the 1-position to form lysophosphatidic acid. A second fatty acid is added to the 2-position by acyltransferase to produce phosphatidic acid. Phosphatidate phosphatase removes the phosphate group, and the third fatty acid is added by acyltransferase. All fatty acids used in the transferase reactions are as their CoA derivatives. In almost all cases, the fatty acid in the 1-position is a saturated fatty acid, but those in the 2 and 3 positions are more likely to be unsaturated.

Phospholipids are synthesized from phosphatidic acids. As shown in Figure 1-164, phospholipids con-

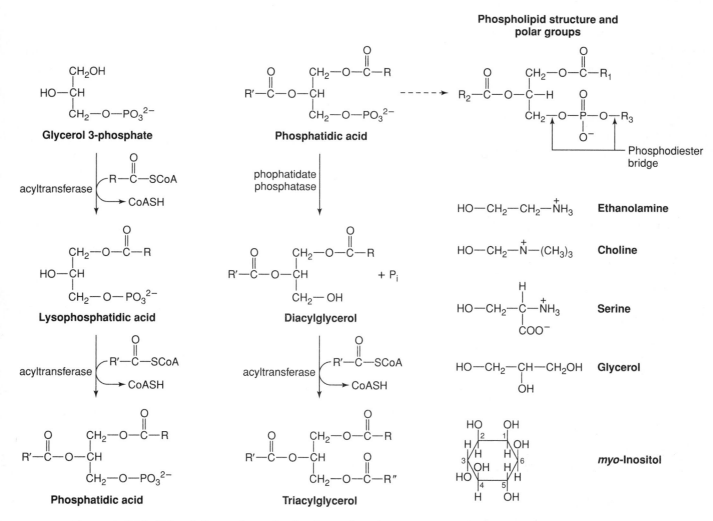

Figure 1-164. Triacylglycerol synthesis—branch point to phospholipids synthesis and structure.
(Adapted from Devlin, T. M., Editor, *Textbook of Biochemistry with Clinical Correlations*, Sixth Edition, Wiley-Liss, Hoboken, NJ, 2006, Figures 17.17 and 18.2, pp. 677 and 697.)

tain one of several types of bases in ester linkage with the phosphate group. Schematics of the synthesis and structures of triacylglycerols and structures of the various polar groups of phospholipids are shown in the following figure.

There is an additional energy requirement for synthesis of some of the phospholipids. Choline and ethanolamine are first phosphorylated by an ATP-requiring kinase to produce their respective phosphate derivatives, yielding ADP as a side product. Phosphocholine and phosphoethanolamine are first converted to CDP-choline and CDP-ethanolamine, respectively, by cytidyltransferase, which uses CTP as one of the substrates. PP_i is one of the products of this reaction. Transfer of the respective bases from their CDP-derivatives to phosphatidic acid results in formation of phosphatidylcholine and phosphatidylethanolamine and release of CMP. Phosphatidylcholine can also be made by the transfer of methyl groups to the amino group of phosphatidylethanolamine using AdoMet (SAM) as the methyl group donor. Phosphatidylserine can be made by base exchange between serine and phosphatidylethanolamine. Also, phosphatidylethanolamine can be derived from phosphatidylserine by a decarboxylation reaction.

Fatty acid residues in phospholipids are generally different in positions 1 and 2, with position 2 having a greater tendency of containing an unsaturated fatty acid.

Remodeling of the fatty acid composition of phospholipids is accomplished by the action of phospholipase A_1 and phospholipase A_2, which remove fatty acids by hydrolysis from positions 1 and 2, respectively, followed by reacylation catalyzed by an acyl-CoA transferase. Phospholipids with one acyl group removed is a lysophosphatide or lysophospholipid with the specific notation of either 2-acyl- or 1-acyl-lysophosphatide, depending on whether it was formed by the action of phospholipase A_1 or phospholipase A_2, respectively.

20.5. Sphingolipids

Sphingosine forms the base structure for sphingolipids. Sphingosine is synthesized from palmitoyl CoA and serine (see Figure 1-165). This is a condensation reaction accompanied by a decarboxylation to give 3-ketodihydrosphingosine. A PLP-dependent enzyme catalyzes the condensation reaction. The double bond that occurs in sphingosine is introduced only during formation of ceramide, another complex lipid.

Ceramide is an intermediate in the synthesis of other sphingolipids. It is formed by addition of a long-chain fatty acid, frequently a C-22 saturated fatty acid (behenic acid) to the amino group of sphingosine. Other long chain fatty acids, including unsaturated fatty acids, may occupy this position. Behenyl CoA and dihydrosphingosine and fatty acyl-CoA derivatives are substrates for this reaction. The products are CoA and dihydroceramide. The dihy-

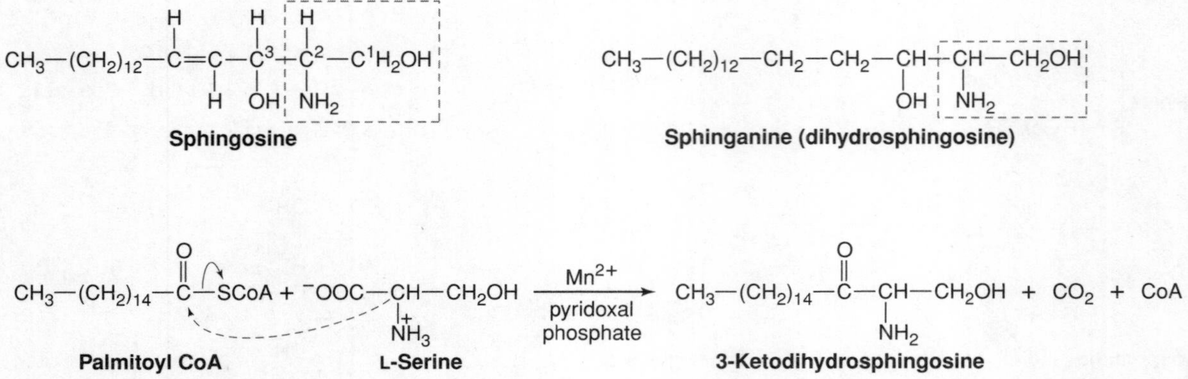

Figure 1-165. Sphingosine structure and some intermediates in its biosynthesis.
(Adapted from Devlin, T. M., Editor, *Textbook of Biochemistry with Clinical Correlations*, Sixth Edition, Wiley-Liss, Hoboken, NJ, 2006, Figures 18.48 and 18.45, pp. 721 and 720.)

drosphingosine moiety is oxidized by an FAD-dependent enzyme that introduces a double bond at position 4 and results in ceramide formation.

Ceramide

Ceramide is the basic structure for other sphingolipids such as the various carbohydrate derivatives. The following is a representative structure of galactocerebroside, where R represents the long chain (saturated) fatty acid. Several glucose and galactose derivatives may be added to produce several types of sphingolipids. In some cases, sulfur may be added to a hydroxyl group of the carbohydrate to produce sulfatides. Sulfur is added using PAPS as the sulfate donor (see section on amino acid metabolism).

Galactocerebroside

Sphingomyelin is also formed from this series of compounds. It contains phosphocholine esterified to the terminal —OH group instead of sugar molecules. Phosphocholine is transferred to ceramide from phosphatidylcholine.

Sphingomyelin

The R group is a long-chain fatty acid that may be palmitic (16:0), stearic (18:0), lignoceric (24:0), or nervonic (24:1 *cis*-Δ^{16}).

20.6. Fatty Acid Oxidation

Fatty acids are stored as triglycerides. They are released from the triglycerides by hydrolysis using a class of enzymes called *lipases*. The activity of lipases may be hormonally controlled dependent on the species of concern and the tissues in which they occur. Regardless of those possibilities, they are released as free fatty acids, but they are not transported to the tissues and cells where they are needed in the form of free acids. Instead, they are bound to albumin and/or a few other classes of circulating proteins. Once in the cell, they must be activated to the CoA derivatives before they can be utilized.

Activation of fatty acids for subsequent catabolism occurs in the cytosol and requires energy in the form of ATP. The first step in this process is formation of an acyl-adenylate complex as demonstrated below (Figure 1-166).

This reaction is made irreversible by the action of pyrophosphatase, which hydrolyzes pyrophosphate to inorganic phosphate.

β-Oxidation of fatty acids occurs in the mitochondria. Thus, the fatty acyl-CoA derivatives must cross the mitochondrial membrane. They are transported across the mitochondrial membrane as fatty acyl-carnitine derivatives. This is an active process that requires the action of two enzymes: **carnitine palmitoyl transferase I and carnitine palmitoyl transferase II.**

First, a note on the structure and origin of carnitine. Carnitine is 3-hydroxy-4-trimethylaminobutyrate. The carbons and nitrogen are derived from lysine. The methyl groups are transferred to lysine while it is still in peptide linkage in protein. It is not clear whether only specific proteins are capable of being trimethylated and how that process is controlled, but an enzyme system capable of trimethylating free lysine has not been described. Formation of carnitine from trimethyllysine is somewhat complex and involves four different enzymes. It is important to remember the source of car-

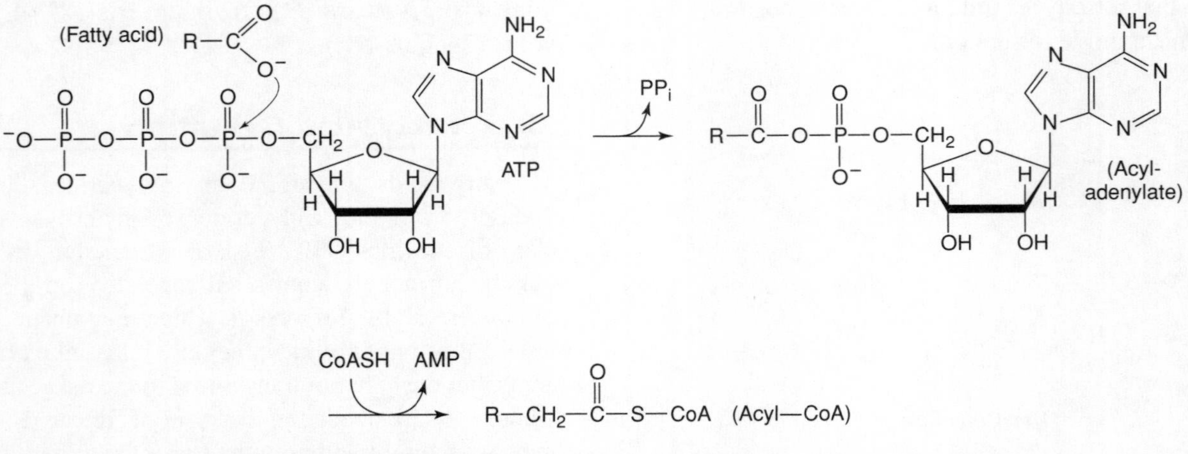

Figure 1-166. Activation of fatty acid and formation of fatty acyl-CoA.

bons, nitrogen, and methyl groups of carnitine. A diagram of carnitine biosynthesis from trimethyllysine is shown in Figure 1-167.

Carnitine-mediated transfer of fatty acids into the mitochondria for β-oxidation is essentially a three-step process. The first step (1) involves formation of fatty acyl-carnitine, a reaction catalyzed by carnitine palmitoyl transferase I. The second step (2) involves the transport of fatty acyl-carnitine across the inner mitochondrial membrane by carnitine acyltransferase, a reaction that is facilitated by an antiport transfer mechanism in which acyl-carnitine is transported into the mitochondrial matrix and free carnitine is transported out of the mitochondria into the cytosol. The final step (3) is transfer of the fatty acyl group from fatty acyl-carnitine to CoASH. This process is shown in Figure 1-168.

β-Oxidation is a cyclic four-step process. For a saturated fatty acid like palmitoyl-CoA, seven cycles are required for its complete oxidation to yield eight molecules of acetyl CoA.

As shown in Figure 1-169, the first step is catalyzed by the enzyme acyl-CoA dehydrogenase (reaction 1), which produces a double bond between the α- and β- carbons (carbon atom 2 and carbon atom 3). This enzyme is attached to the inner mitochondrial membrane and contains FAD as a prosthetic group. Nucleophilic groups on the enzyme facilitate removal of a proton from the α-carbon and transfer of electrons to FAD, which becomes reduced to $FADH_2$ after accepting a second proton. The net result is formation of a double bond in the substrate and production of one molecule of $FADH_2$. The second step is catalyzed by enol-CoA hydratase (reaction 2), which adds water across the double bond with the hydroxyl group residing on the β-carbon. The third reaction is catalyzed by 3-L-hydroxyacyl-CoA dehydrogenase (reaction 3) and results in oxidation of the β-hydroxy group to give the corresponding β-ketoacyl-CoA. The last reaction of the cycle is catalyzed by β-ketoacyl-CoA thiolase (reaction 4). This enzyme uses CoASH to cleave the molecule on the α-side of the keto group, producing acetyl-CoA and a fatty acyl-CoA molecule two-carbon atoms shorter than the starting one. This series of reactions would be repeated seven times for the complete oxidation of palmitate, giving the following overall stoichiometry:

$$\text{Palmitoyl-CoA} + 7\text{FAD} + 7H_2O + 7\text{NAD}^+ + 7\text{CoASH}$$
$$\longrightarrow 8\text{Acetyl-CoA} + 7\text{FADH}_2 + 7\text{NADH} + 7H^+.$$

20.7. Special Cases to Consider for β-Oxidation of Fatty Acids

Three special cases will be summarized here: (1) double bonds existing in the *cis-* configuration; (2) dou-

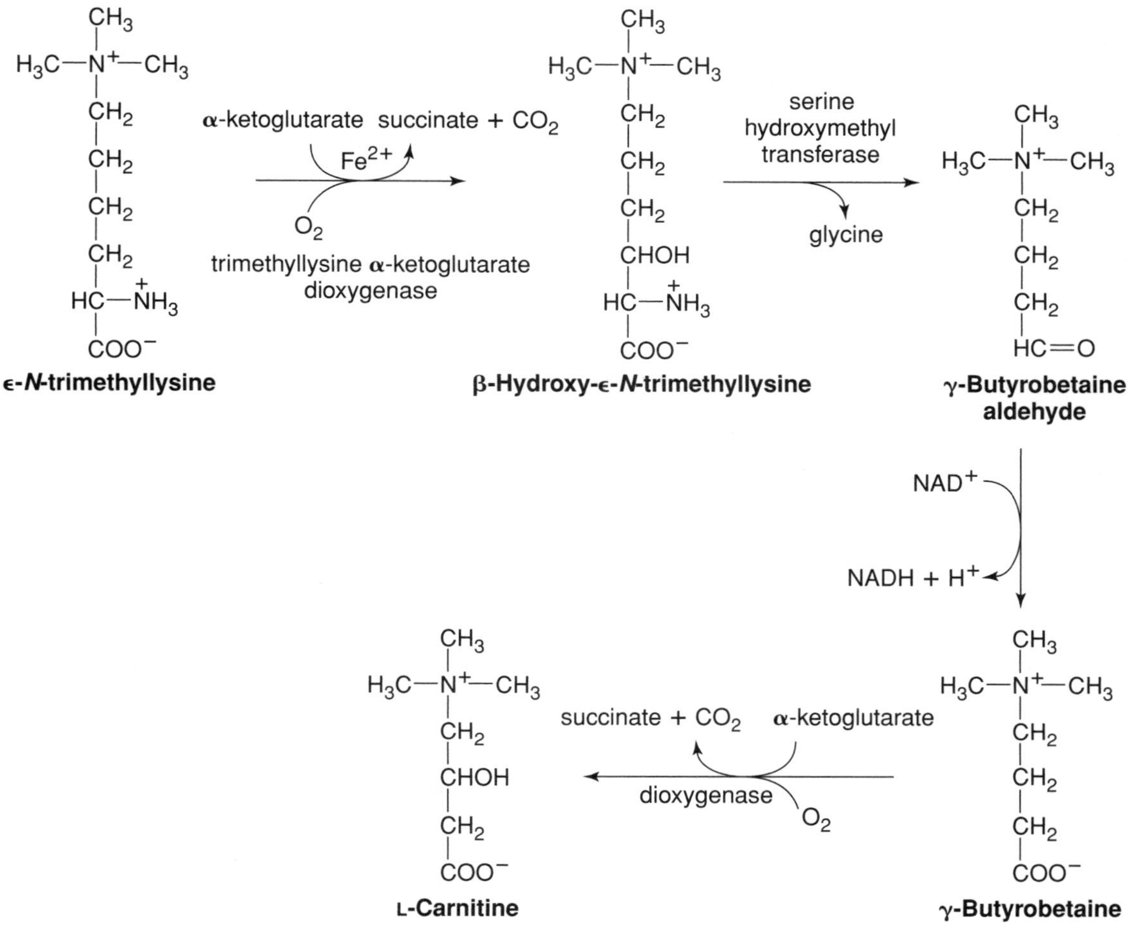

Figure 1-167. Biosynthesis of carnitine.
(Adapted from Devlin, T. M., Editor, *Textbook of Biochemistry with Clinical Correlations*, Sixth Edition, Wiley-Liss, Hoboken, NJ, 2006, Figure 1-19.74, p. 781.)

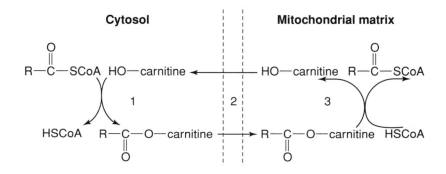

Figure 1-168. Carnitine-mediated transport of fatty acids into the mitochondria.

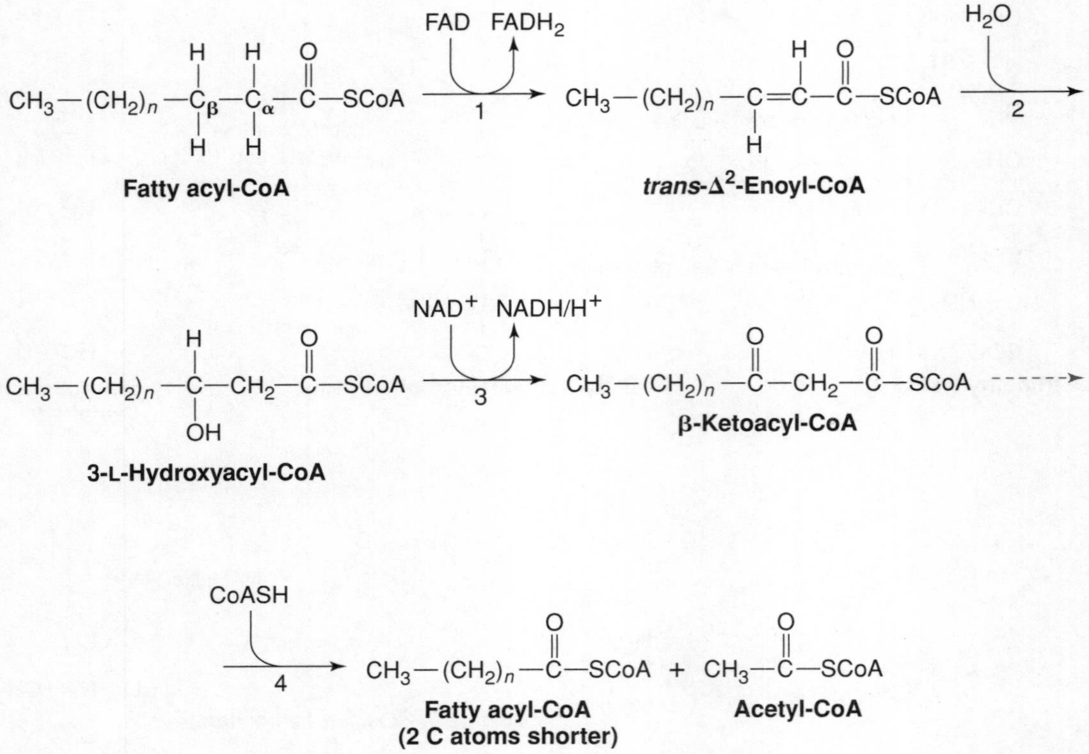

Figure 1-169. β-Oxidation of fatty acids.
(Adapted from Devlin, T. M., Editor, *Textbook of Biochemistry with Clinical Correlations*,
Sixth Edition, Wiley-Liss, Hoboken, NJ, 2006, Figures 17.21, p. 683.)

ble bonds that, upon β-oxidation, will appear in an incorrect position for reaction to occur; and (3) β-oxidation of odd chain fatty acids.

Double bonds introduced into fatty acids during β-oxidation are all in the *trans*-configuration. Double bonds that occur naturally from biosynthesis are in the *cis*-configuration. Thus, the intervention of additional enzymes is necessary for complete oxidation of some fatty acids. A consideration of the oxidation of linoleic acid (18:2 *cis*-$\Delta^9\Delta^{12}$) will illustrate solutions for cases 1 and 2. After release of 3 molecules of acetyl CoA (AcCoA) from linoleic acid, a *cis*-3-enol-CoA is formed (the first structure in Figure 1-170). This is converted to the *trans*-2-enoyl-CoA configuration by enoyl CoA isomerase (reaction 1 of the diagram). After another round of β-oxidation, a *cis*-4-enoyl-CoA compound is formed. Acyl CoA dehydrogenase (reaction 2) converts this compound to a *trans*-2,*cis*-4-enoyl-CoA

configuration. The latter compound is then reduced by 2,4-dienoyl CoA reductase (reaction 3) to a *trans*-3-enoyl-CoA configuration, which then undergoes isomerization by enoyl CoA isomerase (reaction 4) to the *trans*-2-enoyl-CoA configuration. β-Oxidation then proceeds normally.

Odd chain fatty acids will produce propionyl-CoA as the final product of β-oxidation. Propionyl-CoA is converted to methylmalonyl-CoA by propionyl CoA carboxylase. Methylmalonyl-CoA (in its L-configuration) can be converted to succinyl CoA by methylmalonyl CoA mutase, a B12/cobalamine-dependent enzyme. Succinyl CoA can take several metabolic routes: TCA cycle for energy production, conversion to oxaloacetate to phosphoenolpyruvate to glucose, to heme formation pathway. This is the only compound resulting from fatty acid oxidation that can lead to gluconeogenesis.

21. METHODS

Emphases on methods are found throughout various sections of this book. There are other general methods, however, that are useful in the study of biochemistry. A general discussion of some of those methods is presented in this section.

It was stated earlier in the section on regulation of enzyme activity that specific cellular organelles contain specific types of biochemical activities. This compartmentalization of activities facilitates biological processes and makes them more efficient by coordinate grouping of chemical processes that are designed to accomplish specific interrelated functions. The TCA cycle and fatty acid oxidation are localized largely in the mitochondria; many of the hydrolase activities, especially those pertaining to catabolic functions, are located within the lysosomes. Most of the enzymes of glycolysis and the urea cycle are in the cytosol. In addition, many proteins are being expressed through the use of various bioengineering techniques, and the importance of studying how proteins and other cellular constituents vary under various metabolic conditions is being recognized. Thus, it is important to be

able to separate individual proteins responsible for effecting those activities in order to quantify them and/or to characterize them and discover details of their modes of action. General techniques used to do so involve disruption of the tissue, cell membrane, or cell wall, depending on the type of cell whose constituents are to be analyzed. Some of those techniques will be listed but not necessarily discussed in detail. There are many sources from which details of methodologies can be obtained, including catalogs and handbooks of manufacturers of products used to effect some of the analyses and separations discussed. The chart in Figure 1-171, with several additions, mimics a similar diagram that occurs in the catalog of a commercial company. The diagram (Figure 1-171) serves as an outline for the first part of this discussion.

21.1. Methods for Cell Disruption

21.1.1. Mechanical Methods

Mechanical methods of cell disruption depend on shear forces to rupture cell membranes. These forces can be created using devices such as homogenizers, French pressure cells, sonicators, manual grinding (mortar and pestle), pressure bombs, ball mills, and so forth. The

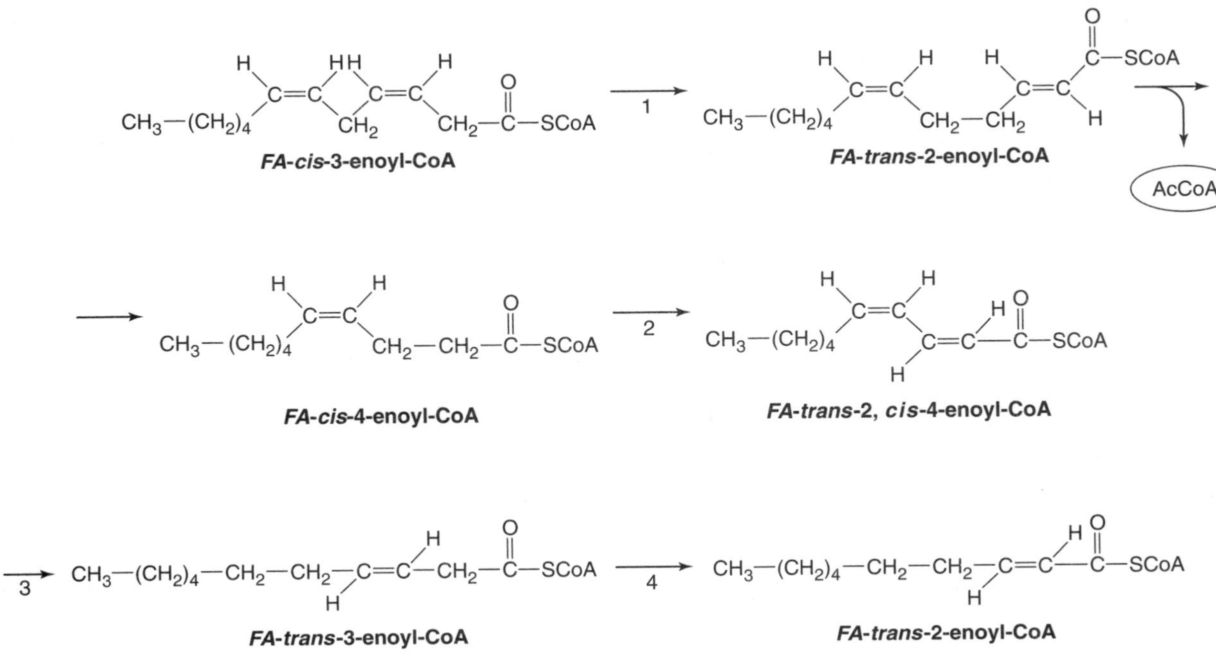

Figure 1-170. Oxidation of a fatty acids with a trans double bond.
(Adapted from Devlin, T. M., Editor, *Textbook of Biochemistry with Clinical Correlations*, Sixth Edition, Wiley-Liss, Hoboken, NJ, 2006, Figure 1-17.23 p. 685.)

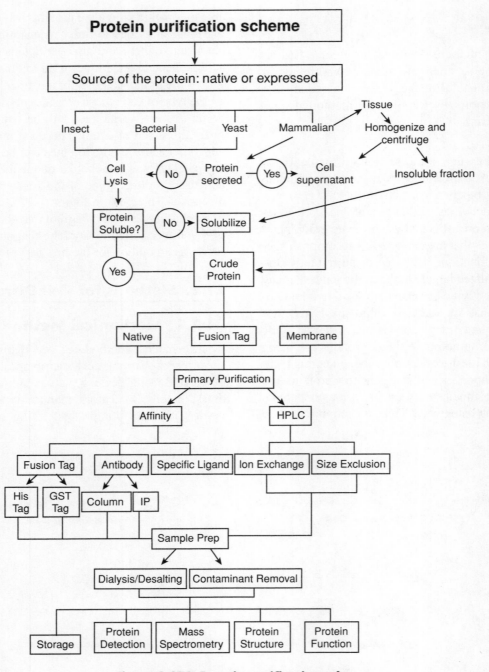

Figure 1-171. Protein purification scheme.
(Adapted from Pierce Chemical Company's website, http://www.piercenet.com.)

choice of a mechanism for cell disruption depends on what the investigator wishes to achieve. Some mechanical devices generally render harsher treatment to cells, and many of the intracellular structures are damaged, perhaps not completely, but sometimes sufficiently well enough to compromise analyses of intact cellular compartments such as lysosomes, peroxisomes, mitochondria, and others. Regardless of the type of homogenizer used, heating is a problem that must be dealt with by application of appropriate cooling procedures. Glass homogenizers, particularly the Dounce type shown in the right panel of Figure 1-172, are completely hand operated and are par-

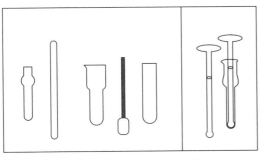

General glass-type homogenizers   Dounce-type

Figure 1-172. Glass-type tissue homogenizers.

ticularly good for homogenizing soft tissues with minimum damage to intracellular organelles.

Another problem encountered in tissue disruption is the release of proteases that can damage some of the proteins of interest. Proteases are of several types: serine, cysteine and calpain proteases, and metalloproteases. There are commercially available cocktails that can be added to homogenizing buffers prior to tissue disruption that will inhibit their action and allow isolation of undamaged or minimally damaged proteins.

Sonicators are generally good for small sample cell disruption, and Waring blenders for larger and tougher samples, particularly when used in the presence of very small abrasive agents such as acid-washed micro glass beads. These must meet certain criteria of size relative to the source material and cleanliness, hence, they are acid-washed.

Because cells and tissues have different characteristics, the type of liquid media used to suspend the cells prior to disruption will vary. For animal tissue such as liver, from which it is desirable to obtain intact mitochondria, 0.25 M sucrose buffered at a suitable pH and containing some of the preservatives mentioned above may be the medium of choice. A different medium would be used to obtain chloroplast from plant cells or mitochondria from yeast cells. Concentrations in the range of 1.15 M solutions of sorbitol and/or mixtures of sorbitol and mannitol may be necessary for use as a suspension medium for plant and yeast cells. It is also

necessary to wash cells grown in culture, generally with an isotonic solution, to eliminate contamination of the cell-free mixture by growth media.

21.1.2. Nonmechanical Methods of Cell Disruption

Nonmechanical methods of cell disruption include the use of detergents such as sodium lauryl (dodecyl) sulfate (SDS), Triton, Brig, and others. Some organic solvents such as toluene may also be used to make the cell membrane/wall permeable, thereby allowing some cellular constituents to exit through the holes that have been made in the membrane. All of the agents mentioned affect the integrity of membrane lipids by solubilizing or forming complexes with them and removing some from the membrane.

Enzymes such as lysozyme and Zymolase among others may be used to digest cellular wall structures and make it impossible for the cell to maintain proper internal osmotic balance. They will swell and rupture in hypotonic solutions.

21.1.3. Separation of Cellular Components by Centrifugation

The size, shape, and density of the particles to be separated contribute to their movement through a solution during centrifugation. Similarly, the density and viscosity of the solution through which they are moving also contribute to their rate of movement. Another important consideration is the relative centrifugal force created by the centrifuge during centrifugation. This force is expressed as relative centrifugal force (RCF) in terms of gravity (g); in other words, the increased force applied to the particle by the centrifuge relative to gravitational force. RCF can be calculated using the following formula:

$$RCF = 1.119 \times 10^{-5} \times rpm^2 \times radius \text{ (in cm)}.$$

For general purposes, the radius is usually measured from the center of rotation to the middle of the tube containing the sample. Information about distance from the center of rotation for various centrifuge rotors is available from the manufacturers of centrifuges and compatible rotors. Nomograms also exist on Web sites of these companies

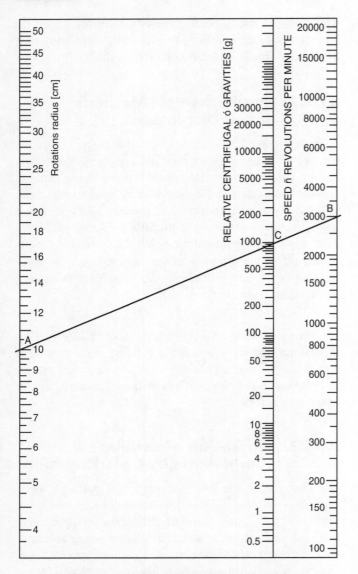

Figure 1-173. Nomogram for estimating relative centrifugal force (RCF).
(Adapted from *http://www.kimble-kontes.com/ pdfs/nomogram_centrifugal_forces.pd*f)

21.1.4. Centrifugal Force Required to Pellet Selected Cellular Components

The heavier of the cellular components are the nuclei and other cellular debris. These can be pelleted by centrifugation at $700 \times g$ for 10 minutes. Debris can be removed by resuspension of the pellet, filtration through several layers of cheesecloth, and repelleting.

Mitochondria can be pelleted in about 15 minutes at $5,000 \times g$. Succinate dehydrogenase can be used as a test for mitochondria in general, and the integrity of the inner membrane can be tested by the uptake of a fluorescent dye, carbocyanine.

Microsomes require the use of an ultra centrifuge in order to pellet them at $100,000 \times g$. The activity of NADPH cytochrome c reductase may be used as a measure of the presence of microsomes, which is synonymous with the smooth endoplasmic reticulum (ER).

The supernatant fraction remaining after these centrifugation steps is the cytoplasm. This fraction should be rich in lactate dehydrogenase.

Fractionation of subcellular components by differential centrifugation as stated above would not give pure subcellular fractions. Mitochondrial fractions will often contain peroxisomes and lysosomes. These can be detected by the presence of catalase and acid phosphatase, respectively. Mitochondria can be further purified by (isopycnic) sucrose gradient centrifugation. Mitochondria will form a band at a density of approximately 1.2 g/mL. In a sucrose gradient, that is the position where the density of the mitochondria and the sucrose gradient are equal, hence the term *isopycnic*. Chloroplasts from plants may be separated in a similar manner using Percoll as the gradient solute.

and allow for a quick estimation of the RCF. A representative nomogram is shown above (Figure 1-173).

In the example represented by the diagonal line, point "A" represents the distance from the center of rotation to a particular section of the centrifuge tube, "B" is the rpm (revolutions per minute), and "C" is the force times gravity at that point. It is important to use # × g values so that adjustments in rpm can be made if a different rotor or centrifuge must be used.

21.2. Purification of Soluble Proteins

Purification of native (as opposed to genetically engineered and expressed proteins) is a more arduous task and involves use of traditional methods of purification. Among them are ammonium sulfate precipitation, desalting (dialysis) and various steps involving chromatographic procedures. Ammonium sulfate competes with proteins for the water molecules that surround the proteins and keep them in solution. As ammonium sulfate concentration increases, it disrupts the shell of water surrounding proteins and the proteins aggregate and precipitate. The hydration sphere around different proteins is not the same. So at different concentrations of ammonium sulfate, different classes of protein will precipitate. The proteins can be redissolved and dialyzed or subjected to other procedures to remove excess salt if necessary. Additional purification procedures can then be used. Differential precipitation of proteins by ammonium sulfate is generally performed by adding small increments of finely ground ammonium sulfate to crude extracts of protein, separating the precipitated protein by centrifugation, and determining which fraction contains the activity of interest. A nomogram showing the amount of ammonium sulfate required to achieve various degrees of saturation is shown below (Figure 1-174).

A saturated solution of ammonium sulfate is 4.1 M at 25°C and 3.9 M at 0°C. In the nomogram, the initial concentration of ammonium sulfate is shown on the vertical axis, and the desired (final or next) concentration is

Initial concentration of ammonium sulfate, % saturation	Final concentration of ammonium sulfate, % saturation																
	10	20	25	30	33	35	40	45	50	55	60	65	70	75	80	90	100
	Grams solid ammonium sulfate to be added to 1L. of solution																
0	56	114	144	176	196	209	243	277	313	351	390	430	472	516	561	662	767
10		57	86	118	137	150	183	216	251	288	326	365	406	449	494	592	694
20			29	59	78	91	123	155	189	225	262	300	340	382	424	520	619
25				30	49	61	93	125	158	193	230	267	307	348	390	485	583
30					19	30	62	94	127	162	198	235	273	314	356	449	546
33						12	43	74	107	142	177	214	252	292	333	426	522
35							31	63	94	129	164	200	238	278	319	411	506
40								31	63	97	132	168	205	245	285	375	469
45									32	65	99	134	171	210	250	339	431
50										33	66	101	137	176	214	302	392
55											33	67	103	141	179	264	353
60												34	69	105	143	227	314
65													34	70	107	190	275
70														35	72	153	237
75															36	115	198
80																77	157
90																	79

Figure 1-174. Nomogram for determining the amount of ammonium sulfate necessary to achieve various % saturation.
(Adapted from Cooper, T. G., *The Tools of Biochemistry*, John Wiley & Sons, New York, 1977. Fig 10-6, p. 372., Modified from *Methods of Enzymology*, Vol. 1, Academic Press, NY, 1968, p. 76.)

Table 1-9.
Flow Chart for Recording Protein Purification Information

PROTEIN PURIFICATION TABLE					
Purification procedure	Total protein (mg)	Total activity (Units)	Specific activity (Units/mg)	% Yield (of activity)	Degree of purification
Step # 1	230,400	64,512	0.28	100.0	1.0
Step # 2	81,800	49,898	0.61	77.3	2.2
Step # 3	21,100		1.33		
Step # 4	5,660	27,904			17.6
Step # 5	1,185		16.75	30.8	
Step # 6	491		27.73		
Step # 7	57	5,023			314.8

shown on the horizontal axis. The point of intersection of the two lines is the amount of solid ammonium sulfate needed to achieve that final concentration.

It is important to collect sufficient data during the purification procedures to know for each step the degree of purification and the yield of the protein of interest. If in test trial runs, a particular procedure does not either improve purification or make the solution more suitable for the next step, that procedure should be eliminated. Also, if there is a large loss in the amount of protein of interest without a concomitant large increase in purity, it may be necessary to find an alternative method of proceeding. Table 1-9 is a convenient way of keeping track of this information. Some of the data have been eliminated. Filling in the missing data will facilitate understanding this process.

21.2.1. Chromatography

Chromatography employs a number of physical methods to separate and identify mixtures of chemical compounds. *Chroma* from Greek implies the separation of colored compounds. The invention of absorption chromatography is attributed to a Russian botanist, M. S. Tswett, who published on the separation of leaf pigments in 1903. Today, color is not a necessary criterion for detection of material separated in this manner

since there are many very sensitive methods of detecting chemicals that can be separated.

The basic principle of chromatography is similar to that of a simple distribution coefficient that describes the differential solubility of a solute in two immiscible solvents. The concentration of the solute in each solvent describes its distribution coefficient. If one solvent with its concentration of solute is removed (mobile phase) and a fresh aliquot of that same solvent is added to the other (stationary phase), the remaining solute will also distribute in accordance with the distribution coefficient. Continuous application of this process can effectively reduce the amount of solute in the stationary phase to an undetectable level. Chromatography expands this basic principle by the use of a solid matrix. Compounds to be separated are allowed to flow through this matrix and may be absorbed differentially by it. A mobile phase is forced to flow through this matrix, and as it does so, compounds undergo desorption, reabsorption throughout the length of the column until they are eluted at the end of the solid (immobile) matrix. Separation depends on the differential absorption and/or desorption between the two phases as dictated by the individual distribution properties of each component of the mixture. Each absorption, desorption process may be considered as one "theoretical plate." Thus, if a column has 10,000 theoretical plates, this process for the compounds in question will have undergone this absorption, desorption process 10,000 times.

21.2.1.1. Ion Exchange Chromatography.

Ion exchange chromatography depends on charge for separation. The immobile media may be either a weak or a strong ionic exchanger. Most protein separation techniques use weak ion exchangers like DEAE (diethylaminoethyl) cellulose or carboxymethyl cellulose. The active groups may be attached to support media other than cellulose. The choice of which media to use will depend on the ionic properties of the protein to be purified. If the pH of the sample containing the protein mixture and the elution buffer are above the pI (isoelectric point) of the proteins, the proteins will have a net negative charge, and an anion exchanger such as DEAE cellulose would be preferred. If the reverse is true, a cation exchanger like carboxymethyl (CM) cellulose would be preferred. A similar principle holds for separation of smaller, more stable molecules where strong anionic or cationic exchangers would be more effective.

21.2.1.2. Hydrophobic Interaction Chromatography.

Hydrophobic interaction chromatography depends on the interactions of hydrophobic groups of proteins with hydrophobic groups of the stationary phase of the column matrix. Some of the common types of groups that are attached to the stationary matrix include phenyl, octyl, and butyl. Proteins are generally placed on the column in a solution containing high salt concentrations and eluted using buffers of decreasing salt concentration. In many cases, the high salt concentration used in the column loading process is ammonium sulfate. Thus, if crude protein extracts were partially purified by ammonium sulfate precipitation, dialysis or other means of getting rid of salt before using this method may not be necessary.

21.2.1.3. Gel Filtration Chromatography.

Gel filtration chromatography separates molecules by size. It is also known as gel permeation or molecular exclusion chromatography. In this case, a column is filled with a rigid medium containing pores of various sizes. Proteins are layered on the column in as small a volume as practical, not more than one-tenth the volume of the internal liquid phase of the column. Proteins are pushed through the column and eluted with a buffer of a constant concentration. Large proteins that cannot penetrate the gel elute with the void volume, the volume of liquid in the column that does not include that within the pores of the beads. Other proteins are separated depending on the volume of liquid, external and internal to the pores, with which they equilibrate. Proteins that are small enough to equilibrate completely with the internal volume of the column will be eluted last. The process of gel filtration can be described by the following equation

$$V_r = V_o + KV_i$$

where V_r is the retention volume of the protein, V_o is the void volume of the column (i.e., that which is completely outside of the beads in the column), V_i is the volume of liquid inside the pores of the beads (internal volume), and K is the partition function of the protein (which should be between 0 and 1.0). Proteins elute from a gel filtration column in inverse proportion to their sizes.

21.2.1.4. Affinity Chromatography.

Many genetically engineered proteins are expressed with His-tags or as other fusion proteins where they can be purified by various affinity techniques directly and in high yield. Most manufacturers of biotech products provide manuals for conduct of such procedures. A diagram for purification of His-tag proteins is shown below (Figure 1-175). The immobilized ligand used for separation of most His-tagged proteins is either chelated nickel or cobalt. Histidine residues of the tagged protein bind to these metals rather tightly. Nontagged proteins are washed away and the His-tagged protein is eluted with imidazole buffers. Imidazole competes with the His-tagged protein for the metal ions and displaces it.

Proteins may be expressed with other proteins or fragments of proteins attached to them and then purified by affinity chromatography. Two examples of proteins used as fusion proteins are glutathione S-transferase (GST) and green fluorescent protein (GFP). For GST fusion proteins, reduced glutathione is attached to an

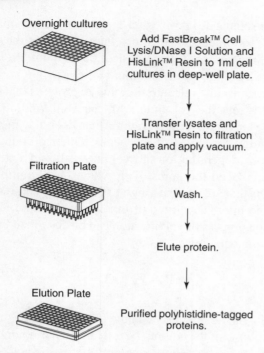

Overnight cultures

Add FastBreak™ Cell Lysis/DNase I Solution and HisLink™ Resin to 1ml cell cultures in deep-well plate.

Transfer lysates and HisLink™ Resin to filtration plate and apply vacuum.

Filtration Plate

Wash.

Elute protein.

Elution Plate

Purified polyhistidine-tagged proteins.

Figure 1-175. Procedure for affinity-labeled separation of genetically engineered proteins containing His-tags.
(Adapted from Promega Technical Bulletin TB342. Note: This is not an endorsement of this product.)

immobilized ligand. GST binds to it tightly, and the fusion protein is eluted from it using free reduced glutathione at neutral pH. The free glutathione competes for the ligand-bound glutathione and releases the fusion tagged protein. Similarly, GFP fusion proteins bind to an immobilized anti-GFP antibody and are eluted from it using an antibody/antigen elution buffer, such as buffers of low pH or that contain chaotropic salts. These are frequently one-step purification procedures. Tags are engineered to contain specific enzymatic cleavage sites so that the tags can be removed and the native protein studied by conventional or other methods as suggested by the bottom line of the protein purification chart at the beginning of this section.

21.2.1.5. High Performance Liquid Chromatography (HPLC).

HPLC began as a major separation tool in the mid-1970s with the development of columns and column-packing materials that could withstand high and constant pressure. This technique was aided also by the development of inline detectors. It is essentially the same in theory, and separate molecules in much the same way, as open-column techniques. Special types of affinity chromatography exist for HPLC that allows separation of molecules by their chirality (optical properties) in addition to bio-affinity separation. Some additional methods, however, include normal phase and reverse phase chromatography. In reverse phase chromatography, the more lypophilic compounds are eluted last, whereas in normal phase chromatography they are eluted first. HPLC assures improved efficiency, reliability, quantification, and separation speed.

21.3. Isotopes Used to Study Biological Systems

Two types of isotopes are used to study various biological processes: radioactive isotopes and stable isotopes. Radioactive isotopes are used in trace amounts and are more useful in determining the fate of metabolites in whole cell, tissues, and whole animal experiments. Stable isotopes are used frequently in enzymology to decipher mechanisms, but they are being used to a greater extent now to evaluate some metabolic products and pathways.

21.3.1. Radioactive Isotopes

Radioactive isotopes have been used in in vitro studies of nucleotide metabolism, to determine proteins that are covalently regulated by phosphorylation-dephosphorylation, and others. They have also been used to determine reaction rates in various types of experiments. Newer and sensitive methods are constantly being developed that minimize the necessity for the use of radioisotopes, but not eliminate their use.

The radioisotopes most commonly used in biological systems are tritium (^{3}H, t½ = 12.3 years), carbon-14 (^{14}C, t½ = 5730 years), phosphorus-32 (^{32}P, t½ = 14.3 days), sulfur-35 (^{35}S, t½ = 87.6 days), and iodine-125 (^{125}I, t½ = 60.1 days).

Radioisotopes are unstable atoms that emit particles during the process of being transformed to a more stable atom. Particles for the isotopes mentioned are either α-, β-, or γ-/X-rays, the latter two are those given of by the isotopes mentioned above during the process of disintegration. It is those particles that are detected by a Geiger counter, scintillation counter, or other device and used to measure the number of disintegration per min (dpm). None of these devices is 100 percent efficient, so counts per minute (cpm) are measured and converted to dpm using knowledge of the efficiency of the detection device in use.

Liquid scintillation counting employs use of fluorescent compounds of which the emission spectrum of one overlaps the excitation spectrum of the other. The first one absorbs energy from β-particles emitted from radioactive atoms, and they become excited by the displacement of electrons into a higher orbit. When the electrons fall back to the normal state, they emit light. Fluorescent light emitted from the first dye is absorbed by the second, which undergoes a similar process of excitation and light emission. It is the flashes of light from the second dye that are detected and counted. There are two detectors, and flashes of light are recorded as counts only when both detectors see flashes simultaneously.

Units of measurement for radioisotopes are Curie and/or Becquerel. One (1) Curie (Ci) = 3.7×10^{10} disintegrations per second (dps), and 1 Becquerel (Bq) = 1 disintegration per second (dps). The number of millicuries of a radioactive compound is the typical laboratory expression used and 1 millicurie = 2.2×10^9 disintegrations per minute (dpm) or 3.7×10^7 Bq, or 37 MBq; similarly, 1 microcurie = 2.2×10^6 dpm or 3.7×10^4 Bq, which equals 37 kBq.

The following isotopes, ^{3}H, ^{14}C, and ^{32}P, emit β-particles when they disintegrate. Each one of them is also transformed into a different atom: ^{3}H to lithium, ^{14}C to nitrogen, and ^{32}P to sulfur. Thus, the trace amounts of radioactive elements that are used in compounds result in their transformation into compounds with other atoms and make them unstable concomitant with the amount and rate of disintegration of the isotope they contain. This is not a major problem since the absolute number of radioactive atoms in a sample is very small. The molecules of interest, however, may also absorb some of the energy from emitted β-particles and become chemically unstable even if the molecules themselves do not contain radioisotopes.

The rate of decay of radioactive isotopes always follows first-order kinetics, and the rate is not affected by any physical conditions such as temperature and pressure.

$$-\frac{dn}{dt} = kn$$

Thus, the half-time for radioactive isotope decay is $0.693/k$, where k is a characteristic value for each isotope. From the $t\frac{1}{2}$ values given for some isotopes mentioned earlier, k values can be calculated; $t\frac{1}{2} = 0.693/k$. Thus, $k = 0.639/t\frac{1}{2}$.

21.3.2. Stable Isotopes

Stable isotopes are being used more frequently for many experimental procedures, including the study of enzyme mechanisms, metabolite distribution, and structural analyses. Stable isotopes, unlike radioactive isotopes, have stable nuclei, and they do not emit particles and become transformed. There is a natural abundance of stable isotopes in the environment, but for most laboratory experimental studies, they are used in as close to a pure form as possible. This is particularly true for ^{2}H (deuterium) and ^{13}C. Since these isotopes are heavier than their more naturally abundant counterparts, experimentalists find them useful in seeking answers for a variety of questions of interest. For example, as will be shown in another section, Meselson and Stahl used DNA labeled with ^{15}N in combination with ^{14}N-DNA to show that the replication of DNA is semiconservative.

Since stable isotopes are heavier, the frequency of their vibration is different from that of the lighter form of the same element, and breaking bonds that contain them requires more energy. In chemical reactions where breaking bonds containing heavy isotopes is the rate limiting step, an overall decrease in reaction rate is observed. Enzymologists often use kinetic isotope effects to decipher mechanisms of enzyme action. Table 1-10 lists some of the stable isotopes of major biological interest.

PART 1

BIOCHEMISTRY

Table 1-10.
List of Stable Isotopes of Biological Interest.

Natural Abundance of Stable Isotopes of Major Elements of Biological Interest		
Element	Isotope	% Abundance
Hydrogen	^1H	99.985
	^2H	0.015
Carbon	^{12}C	98.890
	^{13}C	1.110
Nitrogen	^{14}N	99.630
	^{15}N	0.370
Oxygen	^{16}O	99.759
	^{17}O	0.037
	^{18}O	0.204
Sulfur	^{32}S	95.000
	^{33}S	0.760
	^{34}S	4.220
	^{36}S	0.014

21.4. Relationship of Solute Concentration to Its Absorbance of Light

Determining reaction rates for the analyses of enzyme kinetics, it is desirable to be able to follow reactions continuously. If the reaction of interest does not contain a reactant or product that absorbs light at a convenient wavelength, it is desirable if possible to couple that reaction with another that does have a reactant or product that absorbs light at a convenient wavelength. The quantification of many biological molecules is done colorimetrically in many cases by producing chemically chromophores specific for the analyses being performed.

Many dehydrogenases use NAD^+ and $NADH/H^+$ as an oxidant or reductant. The absorbance spectra of NAD^+ and $NADH/H^+$ are shown in Figure 1-176. The spectra on the left are those of both NAD^+ in its oxidized form and $NADH/H^+$ the reduced form. It is clear that $NADH/H^+$ formation or oxidation changes the degree of absorbance at 340 nm. The spectra on the bottom are those of $NADH/H^+$ absorbance and fluorescence. During absorption of light, electrons are knocked into a higher orbit. When they return to the ground state, the energy absorbed to

get them into a higher orbit is released by several means; heat (nonradiative energy transfer) is one method, and fluorescence is another.

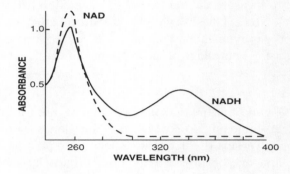

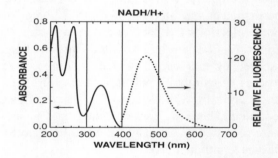

Figure 1-176. Absorbance spectra of NAD^+ and $NADH/H^+$ (top) and fluorescence excitation and emission spectra of $NADH/H^+$.

At a wavelength (λ) of 340 nm $NADH/H^+$ absorbs light, but NAD^+ does not. Thus, at 340 nm the absorbance of $NADH/H^+$ can be measured as a function of time and the rate of the reaction determined. Further, the absorbance can be converted to concentration and the reaction rate can be expressed as molar change per unit time. The molar absorbance value and the length of the pathway through which the light passes through the solution of $NADH/H^+$ must be known. The Lambert-Beer law describes this relationship, which can be applied to any absorbing species.

21.4.1. Absorbance of Light and the Lambert-Beer Law

When a quantum of light passes through a solution, there is a reasonable probability that some of that light will be absorbed by solute and effect a chemical reaction (as in photosynthesis) or it will be absorbed by the

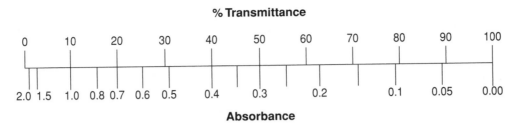

% Transmittance

| 0 | 10 | 20 | 30 | 40 | 50 | 60 | 70 | 80 | 90 | 100 |

| 2.0 1.5 | 1.0 0.8 0.7 | 0.6 0.5 | 0.4 | 0.3 | 0.2 | 0.1 | 0.05 | 0.00 |

Absorbance

Figure 1-177. Scale comparing % transmittance and absorbance.

solute and eventually dissipated as heat in some form. The absorption of a photon generally will displace electrons from a lower energy level to a higher energy level. The probability of the photon exciting a molecule and being absorbed is expressed mathematically by the following equation:

$$dI \,/\, I = -kcdb$$

where I is the intensity of light (the number of photons per square meter) and dI is the change in light intensity that results from some of it as it passes through a length of the solution (db), which is at a concentration c. The k term is a proportionality constant characteristic of the absorbing solute. The larger the value of k, the more light the solute absorbs per mole. Integrating the above equation between the limits I_0 when $l = 0$ (the point at which no light has entered the solution, incident light) and I at length b (length of the light path through the solution) gives

$$\int_{I_0}^{l} \frac{dI}{I} = -kc \int_{0}^{b} db$$

which gives

$$\ln \frac{I}{I_0} = 2.303 \log \frac{I}{I_0} = -kcb \,.$$

This can be written as

$$\log I_0 - \log I = A_s = \varepsilon cb \,.$$

If the incident light is 100 percent, the absorbance, A_s, is equal to the extinction coefficient for the solute, ε, times the concentration, times the solution path length. The extinction coefficient, ε, is defined as the amount of light absorbed while passing through 1.0 cm of a 1.0 Molar solution. Thus the unit designation of ε is $M^{-1}cm^{-1}$. The average spectrophotometer is designed for a 1.0 cm light path. Thus, path length is seldom a factor for most calculations.

The molar extinction coefficient for NADH/H$^+$ at 340 nm is 6.22×10^3 $M^{-1}cm^{-1}$. This value can be measured directly so appropriate dilution or an appropriate concentration of the solute must be made to obtain an accurate absorbance or percent transmission value. In this example, a 1×10^{-4} M solution of NADH/H$^+$ would have an absorbance of 0.622. What is the percent transmission at this absorbance value? Another example, if 90 percent of the incident light is absorbed by the solute, the absorbance is 1.0.

$$A_s = \log 100 - \log 10 = 2 - 1 = 1$$

The scale from a spectrophotometer (Figure 1-177) may illustrate this point better.

Percent transmittance on the top of the scale represents the amount of light absorbed. Absorbance is shown on the bottom scale. From the Beer-Lambert Law (Beer's Law) a linear relationship between concentration and absorbance holds only over a limited range where an amount of light being emitted from the sample is still sufficient to be measured accurately. Rearranging the equation for absorbance given above so that concentration can be calculated gives

$$c = \frac{A_s}{\varepsilon b} = \frac{0.622}{6.22 \times 10^3 \, M^{-1}} = 1 \times 10^{-4} \, M \, .$$

Numbers in this equation were added from the example given above.

A schematic of some of the main elements of a spectrophotometer are shown in the next diagram (Figure 1-178).

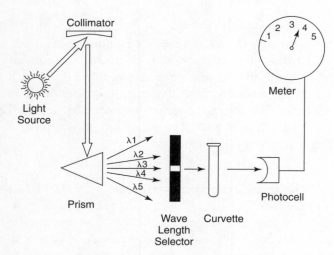

Figure 1-178. Schematic of main elements of a spectrophotometer.
(Adapted from *http://www.acad.carleton.edu/curricular/BIO/ classes/bio126/Documents/Lab_2.pdf*, Fig. 2.2)

The light source can be one that produces ultraviolet light or visible light. The Collimator focuses the light onto a prism as shown here, but it could be a gradient in some spectrophotometers. The purpose of the prism or gradient is to disperse the light beam into its component wavelengths, λ (nm). There is a device for selection of the wavelength that is to pass through the sample, a photocell to collect the light and a meter (perhaps like the percent transmission/absorbance scale shown above) to measure the amount of light absorbed. Some spectrophotometers are dual beam and permit the simultaneous measurement of the incident light (I_0) and the transmitted light (I). Another variation is the diode array spectrometer, which passes the full light spectrum through the sample simultaneously and photosensitive diodes detect the amount of light absorbed at each wavelength. Complete spectra are obtained with the diode array

spectrophotometer without the time dependent wavelength scanning.

21.5. Sample Analyses by Electrophoresis

Electrophoresis is a technique used for separation of macromolecules in an electric field. Separation depends on the properties of the macromolecule, the properties of the medium through which it must migrate, and the intensity of the applied electric field. Variations of this technique have been adapted to meet specific analytical requirements in order to characterize and/or determine specific properties of macromolecules. The technique as it applies only to proteins will be discussed in this section.

21.5.1. Polyacrylamide Gel Electrophoresis (PAGE)

Polyacrylamide is formed from condensation of units of $—CH_2—CH(CONH_2)—$. The condensation product can form cross-links with various degrees of porosity when polymerization is allow to occur in the presence of N,N′-methylene-bis(acrylamide). The size of the pores in a polyacrylamide gel can be controlled by controlling the concentration of acrylamide used and the degree of cross linking. It is an excellent support medium for electrophoresis of various macromolecules.

Proteins can be subjected to electrophoresis in their native forms or in a denatured state in the presence of SDS. In their native forms, the migration of proteins in an electric field is dependent on size, net charge on the protein, and the strength of the electric field applied across the migrating medium. The physical properties of the solid support medium and the buffer properties also play a role in determining migration rate.

21.5.1.1. Two-Dimensional Gel Electrophoresis.

Two dimensional gel electrophoresis is carried out in two stages: proteins are separated according to their isoelectric point and then in a SDS denaturing gel in an orientation 90 degrees from the first separation technique.

When proteins are run through a gel that has been constructed to maintain a pH gradient, they will migrate until they reach a point of electric neutrality (i.e., no charge). This process is called "isoelectric focusing." All proteins in the solution, regardless of size that have isoelectric points at the same pH will concentrate at that position. That strip or tube of isoelectrically separated proteins is then placed on a SDS-PAGE denaturing gel and subjected to electrophoresis in a second dimension. Proteins will then be separated by size. This is a very good procedure for separating individual proteins, and by using some of the more advanced techniques of removing individual spots and subjecting them to HPLC/mass spectrometry analyses, they can be further identified and characterized. Some of these techniques are, according to equipment manufacturers, capable of performing limited structural analyses with concentrations in the attamolar (10^{-18} M) concentration range.

It was P. H. O'Farrell who pioneered and initially perfected the technique of the two-dimensional gel shown below (Figure 1-179). The notation I.F. with the arrow at the top of the gel shows the direction of isoelectric focusing, and the notation SDS and the arrow on the right show the direction of size separation.

21.1.5.2. Determination of Molecular Mass Using SDS Denaturing Gels.

The general procedure for estimating molecular mass using SDS-PAGE involves reduction of disulfide bridges by treatment with 2-mercaptoethanol or dithiothreitol in the presence of SDS. SDS is an anionic detergent that essentially encapsulates proteins by binding to them in a relatively specific mass ratio of 1.4 to 1. All proteins will then have a negative charge of the same charge density and will move in an electric field directly in relation to size. Electrophoresis is performed in the presence of dye that establishes the leading edge of migrating material in the field. The relative position of movement of proteins is the ratio of the distance of movement of proteins of interest to that of the marker dye. Proteins of known molecular mass are used to establish a standard curve. This standard curve is constructed by plotting the distance of migration of known proteins (relative to the marker) versus the $\log_{10}$kDa (molecular mass). An example of a standard curve for a series of proteins is shown in the next diagram (Figure 1-180).

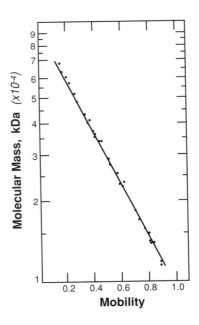

Figure 1-180. Standard curve for determining molecular mass from SDS-PAGE.
(Adapted from Cooper , T. G., *The Tools of Biochemistry*, John Wiley & Sons, New York, 1977, Figure 1-6-10 p. 207. The original was published by K. Weber and M. Osborn, *J. Biol. Chem.*, 244(1969): 4406.)

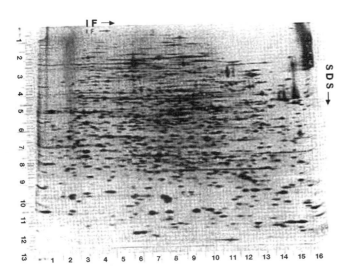

Figure 1-179. Two-Dimensional gel electrophoresis.
(Adapted from Cooper , T. G., *The Tools of Biochemistry*, John Wiley & Sons, New York, 1977, Figure 6-15 p. 212. The original was published by P. H. O'Farrell, *J. Biol. Chem.*, 250 (1975): 4007.)

PART

21.1.5.3. Western Blot Analysis.

Another technique for estimating the presence and amount of protein in a mixture makes use of specific antibodies for the protein of interest. A mixture containing the protein is first separated by SDS-PAGE. Proteins are then transferred from the SDS-PAGE gel to a nitrocellulose sheet, either by diffusion or electrophoretically. All proteins transferred adhere to the nitrocellulose. The nitrocellulose sheet is then soaked in a solution of a nonspecific protein like albumin, which will occupy all empty protein binding sites. Excess albumin is washed away, and the nitrocellulose sheet is soaked in a solution containing an antibody specific to the protein of interest. This is the primary antibody reaction, which binds tightly to the protein carrying its epitope. Excess of the primary antibody is removed; another antibody (secondary) that is specific to the first antibody is then allowed to bind to it on the nitrocellulose sheet. The secondary antibody has attached to it either a chromophore or an enzyme that can react to form a chromophore at the position of the band. This allows visualization of the position of the protein of interest only even in the presence of many other proteins (Figure 1-181).

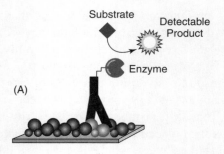

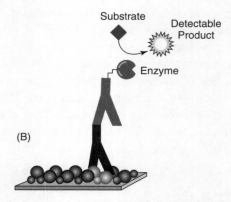

Figure 1-181. Schematic of the use of primary antibody (A) coupled to an enzyme for amplification and detection of a specific protein; and (B) use of a primary and secondary antibody.
(Adapted from Pierce Chemical Company's Catalog Website *http://www.piercenet.com*)

Cell Biology

PART 2

1. CELLULAR COMPARTMENTS OF PROKARYOTES AND EUKARYOTES

1.1. Organization, Dynamics, and Functions

1.1.1. Microscopy

Much of what we know about the structure of cells comes from the use of the microscope, which was invented in the seventeenth century and is still being improved today. The first microscopes were simple light microscopes, but now we have several different types.

Light microscopes, shown in Figure 2-1, have either one (monocular) or two (binocular) eyepieces at one end of a tube (magnification 10 X) and a lens housed in a short tube called an **objective** at the other end. A specimen for examination is placed on a glass slide, the slide is positioned on a stage illuminated from behind, and the specimen observed through both the eye piece and lens. The microscope is focused by coarse and fine control knobs. Objectives with lenses are available in various powers of magnification (usually 4 X to 100 X), but overall resolution (defined as the ability to distinguish between two objects) is limited by the wavelength of visible light, and a magnification of 1,000 X (the prod-

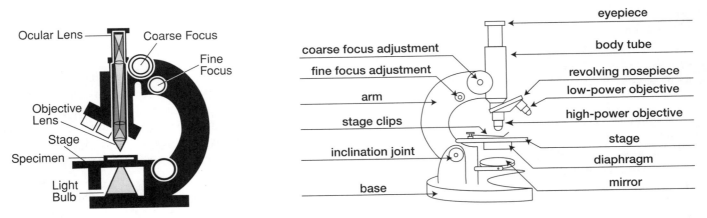

Figure 2-1. Diagrams of light microscopes.

153

uct of the magnification of the eyepiece and the objective) is the maximum attainable for light microscopy. This gives a resolution of approximately 0.2 μ. Resolution is the minimum size that can be seen as a discrete structure. Samples for the light microscope may be left unstained (to maintain the viability of living material) or can be "fixed" by soaking in solutions of chemicals to make them permeable for staining to enhance certain features. Specimens are generally observed only after placing another glass slide (coverslip) over the specimen. This ensures that the entire specimen is the same thickness and can be viewed without having to refocus the microscope on different parts of the specimen. Some samples are originally too thick for viewing and must be cut into thin slices before being placed between the slide and coverslip. Fragile samples must be embedded in a supporting medium before viewing. When necessary, samples are frozen and cut into sections with a cryostat. At 1,000 X magnification, the magnification commonly used for observing bacteria, a drop of mineral oil must be placed between the objective and the slide to maintain a constant refractive index in the system. Parfocal microscopes allow the objective lens to be changed to produce a different total magnification without refocusing. A form of microscopy with the illumination behind the sample is known as bright field. Dissecting microscopes have a large stage for the specimen that can be illuminated either from above or below, and the specimen can be dissected while looking at it under magnification. An inverted microscope has the light source above the specimen. This allows for viewing of samples such as bacteria in a petri dish or mammalian cells in a culture flask.

Fluorescence staining allows selected structures to be seen under a fluorescent microscope. One form of fluorescence microscopy is confocal microscopy. This involves the process of **optical sectioning**, whereby a series of mirrors and light apertures allow the viewer to focus selectively on different levels of the sample.

Living cells are best viewed by **phase contrast microscopy** or **differential interference contrast microscopy**. These two techniques exploit the variation in refractive index in different parts of the cell and result in a more nearly three-dimensional view of the specimen. **Dark field microscopes** have light sources that are at the side of the specimen so that only the light scattered by the specimen enters the objective and the specimen appears against a dark background. These three methods of microscopy allow one to see a dynamic cell undergoing various processes, such as mitosis.

Scanning electron microscopy uses electrons instead of light waves to visualize the specimen, which has to be fixed in a substance such as glutaraldehyde, sectioned into thin slices and shadowed with something like osmium tetroxide. Resolution by electron microscopy approaches 1 nanometer (200,000 X magnification) and allows identification of bilayer membranes and even large enzyme complexes. In older published material, the unit of measurement quoted may be an angstrom (Å), which is 1×10^{-10} meters (10 angstroms = 1 nanometer). A less commonly used type of microscopy is **X-ray microscopy**, which can be used with material that is not dehydrated and stained and for thicker sections than the electron microscope. The reader is referred to a good cell biology textbook for micrographs of cells and organelles.

1.1.2. General Introduction to Prokaryotes and Eukaryotes

Living things (not including viruses, which are not considered "living" by the normal definition), are divided into five kingdoms: Animalia, Plantae, Fungi, Protista (algae and flagellates), and Monera (bacteria). These are subdivided into phylum (called **division** when referring to plants and bacteria), class, order, family, genus, and species. The divisions can be visualized as a phylogenetic tree (dendrogram). Much of this taxonomy (the science of naming organisms) is attributed to an eighteenth-century scientist named Carolus Linnaeus (or Carl von Linné).

All organisms in the first four kingdoms listed above are **eukaryotes**, and organisms of the kingdom Monera are **prokaryotes**. The major difference between the cell types from these organisms is that prokaryotes lack membrane-bound organelles (such as mitochondria and nuclei), whereas the metabolic processes of eukaryotic cells are organized in such organelles. Evolutionary evidence indicates that prokaryotes existed before eukaryotes. As cells and organisms became more specialized, organization of cellular functions in confined spaces became necessary to support this more complex and demanding lifestyle. There is also evidence that during this evolution into eukaryotic cells, some prokaryotic cells became symbiotic (living in partnership with another organism) and became precursors of mitochondria and chloroplasts of eukaryotic cells.

Prokaryotes include bacteria and blue-green algae. They are single cell organisms delineated by a membrane and a cell wall. They have no membrane-bound organelles, but they do exhibit some degree of cytoplasmic organization. Prokaryotes are haploid (contain a single copy of genetic material). One circular, double-stranded chromosome is found in the majority of prokaryotic cells, and the cells replicate by binary (into two parts) fission. For the most part, they do not exhibit chromosomal recombination, although under some circumstances, they do exhibit changes in DNA sequence through the process of transformation, transduction, or conjugation (see the section on Molecular Biology).

Eukaryotic animal cells are surrounded by a cell (plasma) membrane, sometimes called a **plasmalemma**. Eukaryotic plant cells are surrounded by both a membrane and a cell wall. Eukaryotic cells have organelles, such as nuclei, mitochondria, lysosomes, peroxisomes, and chloroplasts, and some can reproduce either sexually or asexually.

1.1.3. Prokaryotes

As stated above, all prokaryotes belong to the kingdom Monera, which includes all bacteria and mycoplasma. There are approximately 2,500 types of bacteria that have been described, and it is estimated that there are 4 million yet to be studied. All are single-celled organisms, although some exist primarily as aggregates. For example *Diplococci* form pairs of cells, and *Streptococci* exist as chains of cells. Bacteria can be spherical (e.g., *Staphylococcus*), rod-shaped (e.g., *Bacillus*), or form an elongated spiral (e.g., *Spirillum*). Bacteria have both a cell membrane and a cell wall. These will be described in the following section on the structure and function of cellular components. Most bacteria are prototrophs (also referred to as autotrophs), meaning that they can live on simple sugars and inorganic substances alone. Those bacteria that require other organic molecules, such as amino acids and fatty acids, for survival

are called auxotrophs. Bacteria are approximately 1 to 10 microns in diameter.

Bacteria can be aerobic (using oxygen as the terminal electron acceptor), facultative anaerobes (using something other than oxygen, but able to live aerobically), or obligate anaerobes (unable to survive in an atmosphere containing oxygen). There are two groupings of bacteria, Eubacteria, the largest family, and Archaebacteria. The second family includes "extremophiles." These bacteria live under conditions that are inimical to most life forms. Some extremophiles live and flourish at very high temperatures, at low pH, and in high salt concentrations (halophiles). Some do not use oxygen as the terminal electron acceptor for respiration, but instead use sulfur or nitrogen. The first of this latter group produce hydrogen sulfide (H_2S), and the latter fix nitrogen as ammonia (NH_3). This contrasts with the production of water (H_2O) by cells that use oxygen. Some bacteria can reduce carbon dioxide to methane (methanogens).

A subset of Eubacteria contains blue-green algae, such as anabaena. These cells differ from other bacteria by having chlorophyll and fixing carbon dioxide (incorporating carbon dioxide into intermediary metabolites) by photosynthesis. Many blue-green bacteria exist in chains made up of individual, autonomous cells.

There are also prokaryotic cells called *Mycoplasma*. They are, at 0.15 microns, the smallest self-replicating cells. They have no cell wall, but are surrounded by a three-layer membrane that contains noncholesterol sterols. *Rickettsia, Chlamydia*, and *Proteobacteria* are also small prokaryotes (0.2–0.3 microns), but they are not capable of life and replication outside a host cell. Viruses and prions are not considered life forms since they are incapable of autonomous existence.

1.1.4. Eukaryotes

Most eukaryotes (possessing a nucleus and other intracellular organelles) are multicellular organisms, but some are single-celled organisms. The members of the eukaryotic, single-celled kingdom Protista include rhizopods such as amoeba (also spelled *ameba*), paramecium, euglena, and algae. Another type of single-celled eukaryote is yeast, in the kingdom Fungi. Yeast cells have cell walls as well as plasma membranes and are one of the organisms that can reproduce by fission as well as sexually. Wild-type yeasts are prototrophs. Yeasts can exist as single cells and also as multicellular mold. The ability to grow as one or multiple cells is known as **dimorphism**. Other dimorphic organisms include other fungi and slime molds.

Eukaryotic plant cells have a cell wall and a plasma membrane. Plants also have an additional organelle, the chloroplast, where photosynthesis (fixation of carbon dioxide into intermediary metabolites using energy derived from light; see Biochemistry section) takes place. Plant cells can grow using only carbon dioxide, light, and trace minerals found in water or soil. By contrast, eukaryotic animal cells do not have cell walls. The plasma membrane is the only structure that stands between their cytoplasm and the outside world. Animal cells must rely on a supply of organic molecules for fuel and maintenance of structural integrity.

Growth patterns of plants and animals differ. Most animal cells proliferate in all dimensions, whereas plant cells grow only in one direction, lengthening away from a group of cells at the tip of the stem or leaf, known as the apical meristem. If one carved one's initials on a tree trunk, the initials would remain at the same level above the ground even as the tree becomes much taller. This is different from the growth of animals. A child's knee does not stay at a fixed level from the ground as the child becomes an adult, but the distance between the ankle and knee becomes greater.

1.1.5. Cell Death

There are two distinct types of cell death: necrosis and apoptosis. **Necrosis** is the result of injury, and **apoptosis** is a planned event. One can distinguish between the two by examining the biochemistry and cell biology that occurs.

1.1.5.1. Apoptosis

Programmed cell death is needed to remove tissues that are no longer needed, such as the webbing between fingers and toes as development occurs or the sloughing off of the endometrial lining of the uterus when fertilization and implantation do not occur. It is also a protective mechanism used to destroy cells that have acquired damaged DNA or are infected with viruses and to clear cells after an immune response. Some treatments for cancer work by causing apoptosis of cancer cells. Frequently, apoptosis is induced by death activators, such as tumor necrosis factor (TNF), or by loss of growth factors necessary for cell survival. Apoptosis can be recognized by the development of blebs on the cell surface, degradation of DNA into oligonucleotides that form an orderly ladder pattern on electrophoresis, mitochondrial breakdown, cell shrinkage, and the release of cytokines to prevent local inflammation.

1.1.5.2. Necrosis

Necrosis affects groups of cells, and an external cause (such as ischemia or poison) can usually be identified. Necrosis is often accompanied by inflammation.

Ischemia (hypoxia) leads to a decrease in ATP production, after which cell membranes loose their integrity and allow external molecules to flow into the cell. Increased sodium and water inside the cell cause it to swell. Nuclei can lyse or shrink and become hyperchromatic (increased pigmentation). These nuclei are called **pyknotic nuclei**.

Liquefactive necrosis is caused by attraction of polymorphonucleocytes to a site of infection. The nucleocytes release bacteria-fighting enzymes that not only kill the infective agent but also destroy adjacent cells.

Two additional types of necrosis are caseus (in fungal and similar infections, and in tumor necrosis), a type of necrosis that produces cheese-like material; and fat necrosis, where fat is saponified by the action of lipases.

1.2. Cellular Membrane Systems (Structure and Transport)

1.2.1. Prokaryotic Cells, Plasma Membrane, and Cell Wall

Surrounding all cells is a cell membrane (plasma membrane; plasmalemma). The membrane is composed of phosphoglycerolipids arranged as a bilayer (see Figure 2-2). Each of the two lipid layers that make up the bilayer is called a leaflet.

Proteins with various functions are embedded in the membrane. Some are transport proteins, and some are enzymes, for example those that catalyze the synthesis of the cell wall and secretory proteins. On the internal surface of prokaryotic cell membranes are found the proteins of the electron transport system. Proteins and lipids can move with ease in the plane of the membrane, permitting it to be called a "fluid mosaic." Most membranes are 5–10 nm thick.

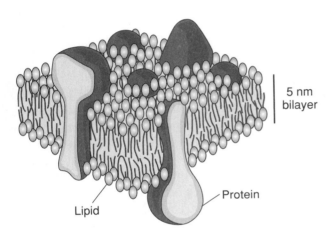

Figure 2-2. A membrane with a typical lipid bilayer structure.
(Adapted from Alberts, B., Bray, D., Lewis, J., Raff, M., Roberts, K., and Watson, J.D., *Molecular Biology of the Cell,* Second Edition, Garland Publishing, Inc., New York and London, 1989. Fig. 6-1.)

The membrane serves as a selectively permeable barrier between the outside environment and the cell cytoplasm (cytosol). Salts cannot cross freely, and this prevents uncontrolled osmosis from occurring. Large molecules such as proteins and hydrophilic molecules such as sugars cannot traverse this membrane without specialized transport systems, whereas water, carbon dioxide, and oxygen can diffuse freely from one side to the other.

Some bacteria, such as *Escherichia coli*, have two bilayer membranes (see Figure 2-3). The inner membrane is a phospholipid bilayer, but the outer membrane has lipopolysaccharides in the outermost leaflet.

Between the inner and outer membranes lies the periplasmic space. In *E. coli* the periplasmic space contains a mesh of peptidoglycan (murein). Murein is material made of proteins, polysaccharides, and lipids (lipopolysaccharide, abbreviated LPS). The peptidoglycan mesh is rigid and serves as a cell wall. Soluble proteins are also found in the periplasmic space.

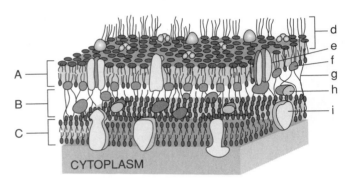

Figure 2-3. An *E. coli* membrane, including associated structures. The entire structure is approximately 25 nm in width: (A) outer lipid bilayer, (B) periplasmic space, (C) inner lipid bilayer, (d) lipopolysaccharides, (e) porin, (f) lipoprotein, (g) peptidoglycan, (h) soluble protein in periplasmic space, (i) transport protein.
(Adapted from Alberts, B., Bray, D., Lewis, J., Raff, M., Roberts, K., and Watson, J.D., *Molecular Biology of the Cell,* Second Edition, Garland Publishing, Inc., New York and London, 1989, Fig. 6-54.)

The outer of the two membranes together with the rigid periplasmic structure is considered to be the cell wall. Bacteria with this cell envelope structure are called **gram-negative** because they do not retain the purplish-blue dye used for the Gram stain after rinsing. The Gram stain has three steps: First the cells are stained with crystal violet or gentian violet and then treated with potassium iodide. Washing with ethanol or acid removes the dye deposits from gram-negative bacteria, but gram-positive bacteria retain the dye. Gram-negative cells, when placed in isotonic solution and treated with the enzyme lysozyme, lose part of the cell wall (outer membrane) and become spheroplasts, with the cell membrane being the major barrier to the outside world. Gram-positive organisms lose essentially all the cell wall under the same circumstances and become protoplasts.

Gram-positive bacteria have only a single membrane with an external cell wall. These cells stain purple with Gram stain. The cell wall is composed of peptidoglycan (murein); polysaccharides; and specialized organic acids, such as muramic, techoic, and teichuronic acids.

Some bacteria have yet another external layer of polysaccharide, known as a **capsule** or **glycocalyx**. This constitutes another layer of protection against phagocytosis (internalization by white cells).

Some bacteria, such as anthrax, can form spores in response to unfavorable growth conditions. Spores lack most of the water and protein found in the growing organism, but they have a rigid and protective outer shell. On exposure to favorable growth conditions, the dormant protein-synthesizing machinery in the cell is reactivated and the bacteria resume growth.

The cell walls of blue-green algae (cyanobacteria) are also made of murein, and the cells often aggregate into colonies surrounded by thick jelly-like coats. Beneath the cell wall is a typical bilayer plasma membrane made of phospholipids with embedded proteins.

1.2.2. Eukaryotic Plasma Membranes and Cell Walls

Protista can have many different types of cell walls that are usually made of pectin or cellulose, both of which are polysaccharides. Some may have no cell wall at all. Fungi have cell walls made from chitin (also a polysaccharide) and cellulose. Differences between the cell walls of fungi and amoeba-like organisms, and bacteria is one of the reasons why antibiotics, whose mechanism of action is often inhibition of bacterial cell wall synthesis, are ineffective against fungal infection.

Plant cells have a cell wall made largely of cellulose, a polymer of glucose, hemicellulose, lignin, pectin, and other polysaccharides. All animal cells have a plasma membrane, but no cell wall. Only animal cells have cholesterol in the membrane. Plants have other sterols, known as phytosterols, in their plasma membranes. Both plants and animal cells have sphingolipids as well as phosphoglycerolipids in their mem-

branes. The structure and synthesis of the membrane lipids is covered in the Biochemistry section of this study guide.

1.2.3. Membrane Biogenesis

Some components of membranes are inherited as cells divide. Sections of the parental plasma membrane, and some of the organelles, are shared between daughter cells during cell division (cytokinesis). Additional membranes and organelles are, of course, required, and these are synthesized de novo.

The synthesis of membrane lipids starts with synthesis of lipid "building blocks" on the cytosolic side of the endoplasmic reticulum. As this occurs, some of the lipids are transferred to the inner leaflet of the endoplasmic reticulum (ER) bilayer by translocator proteins called "flippases." Regulation of this lipid transfer prevents the inner leaflet of the ER membrane from accruing more lipid than the other leaflet. Transfer from the site of synthesis to the destination membrane (other organelle or plasma membrane) may be accomplished by several methods. These include packaging and transport in a vesicle that, upon reaching its destination, associates with the destination membrane and effects direct transfer of lipids. The enzymes involved in lipid trafficking are called lipid translocases, lipid transfer proteins, phospholipid transfer proteins, or phospholipid exchange proteins. Some of these are ATP-dependent, and some are ATP-independent.

Different eukaryotic membranes have different lipid compositions, including glycerophospholipids, cholesterol, and sphingolipids, and they also have different head groups and fatty acids as part of these complex lipids. Patches (called rafts) of a specific lipid type can be seen in many membranes. Some proteins embedded in a membrane are surrounded by specific lipids in a ring (annular lipids). The two leaflets of a single bilayer membrane are usually populated with different lipids. This reflects the function of each bilayer.

Membrane proteins are synthesized on endoplasmic-reticulum-associated ribosomes and transferred to their target membranes as described in the section on protein synthesis found later under the Molecular Biology sec-

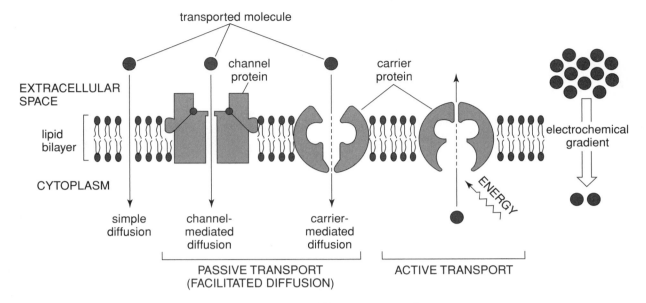

Figure 2-4. Diagram of different types of transport.
(Adapted from Alberts, B., Bray, D., Lewis, J., Raff, M., Roberts, K., and Watson, J.D.,
Molecular Biology of the Cell, Second Edition, Garland Publishing, Inc., New York and London, 1989, Fig. 6-44.)

tion. Turnover of membrane protein occurs by endocytosis of membrane patches, followed by intracellular proteolysis.

1.2.4. Membrane Transport

As stated above, some molecules, such as water, oxygen, and carbon dioxide, and small hydrophobic compounds such as ethanol, can diffuse across the cell membrane. All other molecules that cross the membrane have to be transported by facilitated transport, either inactive or active (see Figure 2-4). Active transport is defined as a transport mechanism that requires concomitant hydrolysis of a compound such as ATP that contains a high-energy bond.

1.2.4.1. Inactive Transport

In inactive transport, molecules are carried only from a compartment of higher concentration to lower concentration. Transport occurs through pores, channels, gap junctions, and carriers (transporters).

Pores and channels are gaps in the lipid bilayer, lined with pore or channel proteins (see Figure 2-5). Bacteria, mitochondria, and chloroplasts have relatively large pores. These permit entry of a variety of compounds, whereas animals and plants have pores and channels

that are smaller and more selective for molecules that are allowed to pass through.

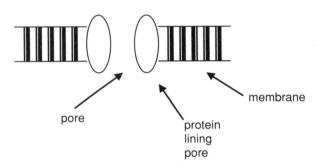

Figure 2-5. Arrangement of protein in a pore.

The passage of molecules through smaller channels is often regulated by compounds that cause channels to open and shut (see Figure 2-6). Some, such as those involved in propagation of an impulse or charge down a neuron, open and close in response to the local charge environment and are thus called **voltage-gated** channels. After opening, the channels assume a temporary inactive conformation that prevents the nerve impulse from flowing backward. Other channels, such as those at the postsynaptic side of a synapse, are ligand-gated, responding by opening or closing upon its interaction with a specific ligand, such as acetylcholine. Carrier

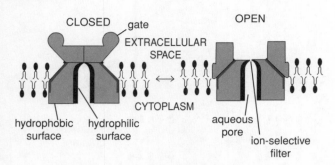

Figure 2-6. A gated channel.
(Adapted from Alberts, B., Bray, D., Lewis, J., Raff, M., Roberts, K., and Watson, J.D., *Molecular Biology of the Cell,* Second Edition, Garland Publishing, Inc., New York and London, 1989, Fig. 6-47.)

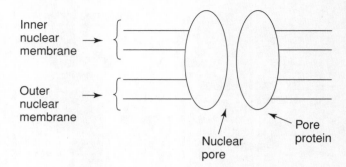

Figure 2-8. Diagram of a nuclear pore.

proteins behave like an air lock, allowing a compound to enter on one side of the membrane. The carrier protein then encloses the compound by shutting the entrance opening and then opens an exit to the other side of the membrane (see Figure 2-7).

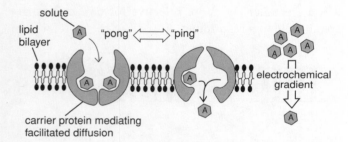

Figure 2-7. Mechanism of a carrier protein.
(Adapted from Alberts, B., Bray, D., Lewis, J., Raff, M., Roberts, K., and Watson, J.D., *Molecular Biology of the Cell,* Second Edition, Garland Publishing, Inc., New York and London, 1989, Fig. 6-56.)

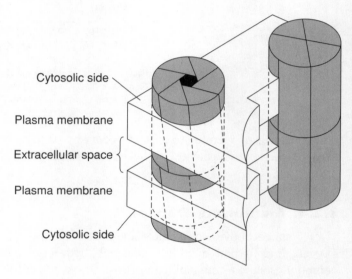

Figure 2-9. A gap junction.
(Adapted from Devlin, T.M., ed., *Textbook of Biochemistry with Clinical Correlations,* Fifth Edition, Wiley-Liss, New York, 2002, Fig. 12.37.)

The nuclear pore is a specialized pore, for it involves the adhesion of the inner and outer nuclear membranes on either side of the pore to form a continuous surface through the pore (see Figure 2-8). Nuclear pore proteins line the opening.

Another specialized pore is located in the eukaryotic cell membrane and is called a **gap junction** (see Figure 2-9). When two cells are in close proximity, these gap junctions span the plasma membrane of both cells and allow transfer of small ionic molecules and water between cells, thus allowing direct cell-to-cell communication.

Pores or channels cannot catalyze active transport, but the movement of molecules through them exhibits saturation kinetics and specificity, and the transport can be competitively inhibited (see Figure 2-10).

1.2.4.2. Active Transport
Active transport systems are also specific and, like facilitated (passive) systems, may be inhibited and saturated. Active transport systems have one additional characteristic: they can transport a molecule against a gradient. They do this by expenditure of energy, most often by hydrolysis of ATP but also

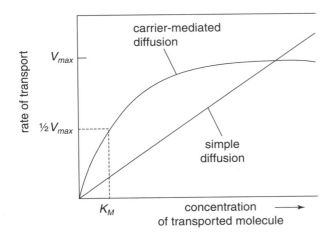

Figure 2-10. The difference between the kinetics of simple diffusion and carrier-mediated transport. (Adapted from Alberts, B., Bray, D., Lewis, J., Raff, M., Roberts, K., and Watson, J.D., *Molecular Biology of the Cell,* Second Edition, Garland Publishing, Inc., New York and London, 1989, Fig. 6-45.)

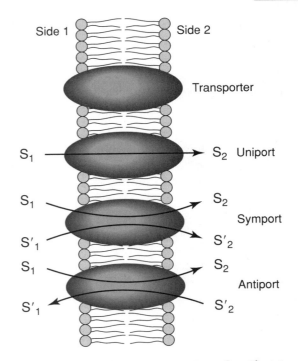

Figure 2-11. Uniport, symport, and antiport. (Adapted from Devlin, T.M., ed., *Textbook of Biochemistry with Clinical Correlations,* Fifth Edition, Wiley-Liss, New York, 2002, Fig. 12.33.)

by other mechanisms, such as using energy derived from an ion gradient.

The proteins that catalyze active transport of molecules across the membrane do so by changing their conformation. One model for a protein catalyzing active transport is that of a rotating door, with the material to be transported binding on one side and being carried to the other side as the protein rotates in the membrane. The transported material is then discharged on the other surface of the membrane.

Active transport can be effected by three general mechanisms: **uniport**, **symport**, or **antiport** (see Figure 2-11). In uniport, one molecule is carried across the membrane unidirectionally. In symport, two different molecules are transported in the same direction; and in antiport, two different molecules are transported in opposite directions.

Active uniport is primary active transport, with the use of energy providing the impetus for the transport of the molecule. Symport and antiport can be either primary active or secondary active transport. In secondary active transport, the transfer of one molecule is passive but depends on the active transport of its partner molecule. Figure 2-12 below shows transport of glucose in symport with sodium. Sodium

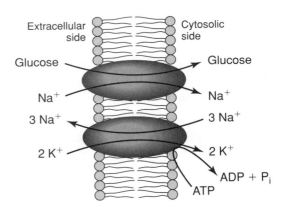

Figure 2-12. Secondary active transport. (Adapted from Devlin, T.M., ed., *Textbook of Biochemistry with Clinical Correlations,* Fifth Edition, Wiley-Liss, New York, 2002, Fig. 12.55.)

must be carried back across the membrane by active transport to be used for symport with another molecule of glucose. During the active transport stage, sodium and potassium undergo antiport. The two processes together are considered to be secondary active transport. Transport of glucose requires no energy but depends on the energy-driven transport of sodium back out of the cell.

Another type of transport is **group translocation**. This also requires energy and is rare in eukaryotes. It depends on covalent bond formation between the transported molecule and a molecule associated with the other side of the membrane. An example in eukaryotes is transport of amino acids in the kidney by the γ-glutamyl cycle. Prokaryotes, on the other hand, make great use of this mechanism for transport of sugars into the cell (see Figure 2-13). This is called **phosphotransfer**. In this mechanism, energy and phosphate are used to trap sugars as their phosphorylated derivatives inside the cell. Sugar transport systems, such as the phosphoenolpyruvate phosphotransferase system, are inducible.

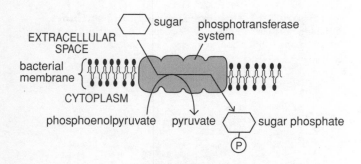

Figure 2-13. Sugar on the outside of a bacterial cell crosses the membrane and is trapped inside by addition of a phosphate donated by phosphoenolpyruvate.
(Adapted from Alberts, B., Bray, D., Lewis, J., Raff, M., Roberts, K., and Watson, J.D., *Molecular Biology of the Cell,* Second Edition, Garland Publishing, Inc., New York and London, 1989, Fig. 6-53.)

Many prokaryotic and eukaryotic transport systems are also inducible. One of the better-described eukaryotic systems that is regulated is the glucose transporters that respond to insulin by migrating from the cytoplasm to the cell membrane so that they can act to internalize glucose from the blood.

A single type of molecule can be transported by alternative mechanisms by different cell types in the same organism. For instance, glucose is transported by a facilitated mechanism in most tissues, but it enters intestinal cells by a secondary active mechanism.

1.2.4.3. Exo- and Endocytosis

Large molecules such as proteins and oligonucleotides can be transported from a cell across a cell membrane in vesicles that are derived from the cell membrane itself or from endoplasmic reticulum and Golgi. The process is called **exocytosis** and is used to release endogenous substances such as insulin and neurotransmitters from the cell (see Figure 2-14). As the molecules are synthesized and processed, they are packaged in secretory vesicles, which fuse with the cell membrane and are secreted. Molecules, such as insulin, that are continuously or constitutively secreted go directly to the cell membrane after synthesis. Other molecules, such as neurotransmitters or histamine from mast cells, that are only released as needed remain in the cell until a Ca^{++}-mediated signal occurs that causes the vesicles to move to the cell membrane. This is called **regulated secretion**.

Endocytosis may involve either the entry of water and solutes or of larger molecules such as microorganisms. The former is called **pinocytosis** ("cell drinking"

EXOCYTOSIS

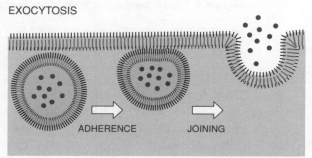

ENDOCYTOSIS

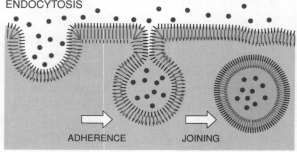

Figure 2-14. Mechanism of exo- and endocytosis.

in Greek), and the latter **phagocytosis** ("cell eating"). Pinocytosis occurs in smaller vesicles that are engulfed and transfer their contents to vesicles called endosomes. Endosomes then deliver their contents to lysosomes. Phagocytotic vesicles are larger (about 250 nm in diameter) and fuse directly with lysosomes to form phagolysosomes (Figure 2-14).

Under specific conditions, electron micrographs show sections of cell membrane that look dimpled like golf balls. The dimples are "coated pits" and are destined to be used for internalization during endocytosis. The coating is a protein called clathrin. The pits are constantly being internalized and emptied, and the membrane components are subsequently returned to the cell surface. These pits are also the site of receptor-mediated endocytosis of molecules such as the LDL receptor/LDL complex.

Phagocytosis is the property of specific phagocytic cells, such as macrophages and neutrophils, both of which are types of white blood cells. The particles to be phagocytosed bind to specific receptors on the surface of the white cells, and part of the plasma membrane surrounds the particles to form a phagosome. The particle-containing phagosome is then internalized. The phagosome fuses with a lysosome to form a phagolysosome. Phagolysosomes contain enzymes that digest the phagocytosed material. Anything that cannot be digested remains in the vesicle, which is then called a "residual body." Membrane fusion during exocytosis and endocytosis is mediated by proteins called "fusogenic" proteins.

1.3. Nucleus (Envelope and Matrix) and Chromosomes

1.3.1. Prokaryotic Cells—Chromosome

Prokaryotic cells do not have nuclei, but an area containing DNA, called a nucleoid, is associated with the inside of the plasma membrane and may be revealed by selective staining. DNA of prokaryotes is devoid of histones but is associated with polyamines and other basic proteins. Prokaryotes have only one chromosome, a circular, double-helical DNA structure. This chromosome has several million base pairs of nucleotides. Treatment of the double-stranded chromosome with

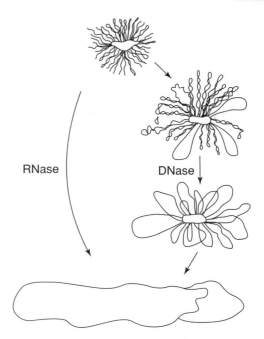

Figure 2-15. Unwinding of a bacterial nucleoid.
(Adapted from Devlin, T.M., ed., *Textbook of Biochemistry with Clinical Correlations,* Fifth Edition, Wiley-Liss, New York, 2002, Fig. 2.45.)

RNAse and DNAse releases a more relaxed structure (shown in Figure 2-15).

Cells generally reproduce by replication of the single chromosome followed by cell division. Each of the two resulting bacteria receives one of the copies of the chromosome. In the absence of any kind of recombination of genetic material, these daughter cells are identical and are called clones. Immediately prior to replication, part of the chromosome attaches to a specialized area on the inner surface of the plasma membrane. This area is an invagination called a mesosome. One of the strands of the double helix is nicked, and the 5' end of the broken strand attaches to another site on the membrane. The attachment of the DNA to two separate sites ensures that a complete chromosome is included in each of the two daughter cells. Replication of the entire chromosome can occur in as little as 20 minutes.

Bacteria also may contain smaller, closed circular DNA molecules whose base pairs number in the thousands. These are also double-stranded and are called plasmids. Plasmids often carry extrachromosomal genes that, when expressed, confer upon their host bacterial cells antibiotic resistance and the ability for toxin synthesis.

1.3.2. Eukaryotic Cells—Chromosomes and Nucleus

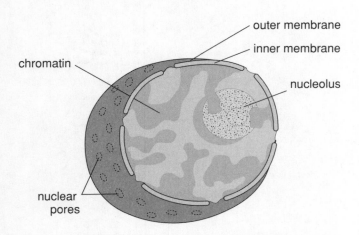

Figure 2-16. Diagram of a nucleus.
(Adapted from Alberts, B., Bray, D., Lewis, J., Raff, M., Roberts, K., and Watson, J.D., *Molecular Biology of the Cell,* Second Edition, Garland Publishing, Inc., New York and London, 1989, Fig. 1-18.)

The word *eukaryote* literally means "good nucleus." Thus eukaryotes by definition contain nuclei. The hereditary material in these cells, DNA, is contained within this organelle. Like prokaryotes, eukaryotes have double-stranded DNA, but unlike prokaryotes, the DNA is arranged in several linear chromosomes. Eukaryotes in general have much more DNA. For example, the smallest human chromosome has 50 million base pairs and is, by itself, ten times the size of an average bacterial genome. The number of chromosomes is dependent on the specific organism. For instance, humans have 23 different chromosomes (22 are somatic, and the other chromosome is the sex chromosome, X or Y), and roses have 7. In most eukaryotes, all chromosomes exist in duplicate (eukaryotes are generally diploid organisms), so humans have a total of 46 chromosomes. Plants exhibit a wider range of ploidy (number of copies of a given chromosome that exist in a cell). Most roses have 14 chromosomes, but some are triploid (21 chromosomes), and others are tetraploid (28 chromosomes). In diploid organisms, one of the pair of chromosomes is inherited from one parent, and the other from the other parent. This means that one chromosome can carry a gene for a red flower petal, and the other can carry a gene for a white petal. These pairs of genes are called **alleles**, because they code for proteins with the same or similar function, in this case flower color. Usually only one of the alleles is expressed at a time. There are exceptions to diploidy amongst eukaryotes. Yeast is a eukaryote and has varying ploidies. Some organisms, notably fruit flies (*Drosophila melanogaster*) have polytene chromosomes. These are also called "giant chromosomes" and result when chromatids do not separate after replication (see section on Molecular Biology). The cells end up with more and more chromatids at each round of replication—up to thousands of copies. Polytene chromosomes differ from cells that are polyploid, in that polyploid cells contain several copies of a chromosome, whereas polytene chromosomes have very thick structures made up of many layers of identical chromatids. Because of the thickness of polytene chromosomes, one can see distinct transverse banding patterns under the light microscope, and this allowed some of the earliest observations of the relationship between chromosome structure and phenotype. It was observed that during transcription, certain areas of a polytene chromosome become more loosely packed, and "puffs" were seen. These are called Balbiani rings. The placement of Balbiani rings could be correlated with an expressed phenotype.

The nucleus is approximately 5–10 microns in diameter and has a double membrane (see Figure 2-16). As mentioned earlier, the nuclear membrane has its own unique composition and includes a layer of filaments under the membrane (the nuclear lamina) that play a supportive role in maintaining the shape of the nucleus. Around the outside of the membrane there is another layer of filaments. Together, the filament layers and the membranes are called the **nuclear envelope**. There are pores in the membrane that allow RNA and proteins to leave the nucleus and enzymes and other nuclear proteins that have been synthesized in the cytoplasm to enter. The nuclear envelope is directly connected to the endoplasmic reticulum and is covered with ribosomes that engage in protein synthesis. Viewed under an electron microscope, a nucleus appears to have an amorphous content (nucleoplasm) with some small areas that are darker. The lighter area is euchromatin, where genes are capable of being transcribed (*chromatin* is the word used to describe DNA and its associated proteins). The darker areas are heterochromatin. Heterochromatin is made up of parts of the genome that are not available for transcription. One of the areas of heterochromatin in females that is located near the nuclear envelope is one of the copies of the X chromosome. This is called a Barr body and is not transcribed. The much larger dark area is the **nucleolus**. The nucleolus is not a separate structure but is the area where the rRNA genes reside on the chromosomes. Rapid and constant synthesis and processing of rRNA makes this area of the nucleus appear darker after preparation for electron microscopy. Just before cell division, condensed chromosomes can be seen in the nucleus even under a light microscope.

Nuclei, like other organelles within a eukaryotic cell, may be separated from other components using physical techniques such as **differential centrifugation**. Different types of organelles have different functions and contain different compliments of enzymes. One of the enzymes that is specific to the nucleus is 5′ nucleotidase. Thus an assay for this enzyme is used to indicate the presence of nuclei in a subcellular preparation.

Eukaryotic chromosomes exist as highly organized structures. The double-stranded DNA is wound around basic proteins called **histones**. There are five histones: H1, H2A, H2B, H3, and H4. Two copies each of the four histones, except H1, form the core of a nucleosome, around which the DNA is coiled (see Figure 2-17). The addition of the H1 histone to this complex gives a structure called a **chromatosome**. The resulting structure has been described as "beads on a string" and is visible under an electron microscope (see Figure 2-18).

DNA is attached to a protein scaffold followed by multiple layers of coiling and supercoiling. Together, all the DNA and associated proteins are known as **chromatin**. This structural organization permits the 2 meters of DNA contained in each nucleus to be packaged in the 5-micron diameter nucleus. In addition to histones, other proteins that are involved in replication and transcription are located in the nucleus.

DNA is also found in mitochondria and chloroplasts. This DNA also contains genes, and its structure is very similar to the DNA in prokaryotes.

1.4. Other Intracellular Structures, Including Mitochondria and Chloroplasts

1.4.1. Prokaryotes

The cytoplasm of prokaryotes contains two other distinct structures that can be seen with an electron microscope. These include ribosomes, where protein synthesis takes place, and insoluble granules. In blue-green algae (cyanobacteria), there is also chlorophyll. Prokaryotic cells also contain molecules that are necessary to support operation of biochemical pathways for energy production, structural maintenance, reproduction, and motility, but these are not arranged in identifiable structures.

1.4.2. Eukaryotes

Most eukaryotic cells have several other organelles and structures, the most prominent of which are **mitochondria** (singular *mitochondrion*). These are about 3 microns in diameter—the same size as many bacteria. It

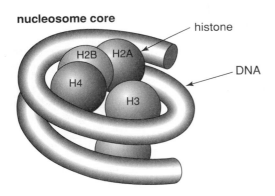

nucleosome core

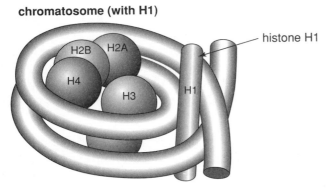

chromatosome (with H1)

Figure 2-17. The nucleosome core and a chromatosome.
(Adapted from Devlin, T.M., ed., *Textbook of Biochemistry with Clinical Correlations*, Fifth Edition, Wiley-Liss, New York, 2002, Fig. 2.47.)

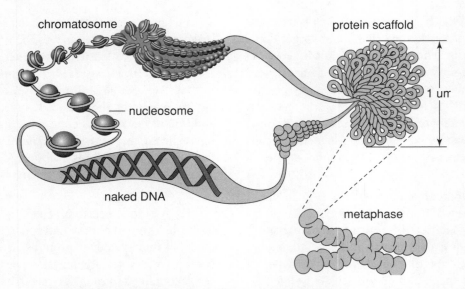

Figure 2-18. Various levels of organization of a chromosome.
(Adapted from Devlin, T.M., ed., *Textbook of Biochemistry with Clinical Correlations,* Fifth Edition, Wiley-Liss, New York, 2002, Fig. 2.46.)

is believed that mitochondria are descended from aerobic bacteria that invaded primitive cells and established a symbiotic relationship. Evidence cited for this theory includes the single, circular double-helical chromosome in mitochondria; the sensitivity of mitochondrial DNA replication and protein synthesis to the same antibiotics that affect bacteria; and similar ribosomal RNAs. (Note: These same criteria apply to the theory that chloroplasts originated as bacteria.) There is a notable exception to the general rule that eukaryotes possess mitochondria. This exception is the "petite" yeast cell that has lost its ability to respire and must derive all its energy from glycolysis. It is "petite" (small) because it is consequently less energy-efficient and does not grow as large.

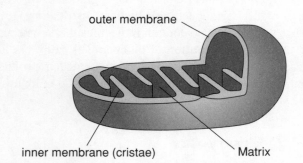

Figure 2-19. Diagram of a mitochondrion.
(Adapted from Alberts, B., Bray, D., Lewis, J., Raff, M., Roberts, K., and Watson, J.D., *Molecular Biology of the Cell,* Second Edition, Garland Publishing, Inc., New York and London, 1989, Panel 1-1.)

Mitochondria are surrounded by a double membrane (see Figure 2-19). The outer membrane is less selective than the inner membrane. It contains specific enzymes, such as monoamine oxidase, that may be used as markers for the outer membrane. The inner membrane has invaginations on the inner surface, called cristae (*crista* in the singular), and is the site of electron transport and oxidative phosphorylation. Between the inner and outer membranes is the intermembrane space. The area defined by the inner membrane is called the mitochondrial matrix. The membrane location of electron transport and oxidative phosphorylation in mitochondria is very important as it allows the creation of transmembrane pH (proton) gradients that drive energy formation. The gradients are also known as chemiosmotic gradients (see the Biochemistry section). Such gradients also function in energy-related pathways in chloroplasts, cyanobacteria, and flagella. Mitochondria reproduce by fission as cell division occurs.

Sperm cells contain very few mitochondria compared to the egg. The consequence of this is that almost all mitochondrial DNA comes from the mother (mitochondrial maternal inheritance). Mitochondrial DNA has proved very useful in following the evolutionary process because it mutates faster than chromosomal DNA and does not usually exhibit recombination.

The marker enzymes for mitochondrial structures are monoamine oxidase (for the outer membrane), the enzymes of electron transport (for the inner membrane), and the enzymes of the tricarboxylic acid cycle (also called the citric acid cycle or Krebs cycle) for the mitochondrial matrix. Mitochondria can synthesize DNA and some RNA and proteins, and the matrix contains the pathway for β-oxidation of fatty acids as well as part of the pathway of urea, pyrimidine, and heme synthesis. Synthesis of fatty acids, on the other hand, occurs in the **cytosol**, as does the glycolytic pathway, gluconeogenesis, glycogen metabolism, and the hexose monophosphate shunt (also called the pentose pathway).

Two other membrane-bound organelles are found in all eukaryotes, namely **lysosomes** and **peroxisomes** (see Figure 2-20). These two organelles have a single bilayer membrane and are approximately 0.5 microns in diameter. Lysosomes provide a compartment for hydrolase enzymes such as acid phosphatase that destroy macromolecules after transport into the lysosome. The pH inside lysosomes is very low, and all the hydrolase enzymes have acidic pH optima. This compartmentation in the lysosome prevents random destruction of cellular components by hydrolases. Peroxisomes contain enzymes that destroy toxic forms of oxygen as well as enzymes that catalyze reactions to oxidize lipids.

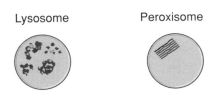

Figure 2-20. A lysosome and a peroxisome.
(Adapted from Alberts, B., Bray, D., Lewis, J., Raff, M., Roberts, K., and Watson, J.D., *Molecular Biology of the Cell,* Second Edition, Garland Publishing, Inc., New York and London, 1989, Panel 1-1.)

Other organized structures in eukaryotic cells include **endoplasmic reticulum** and **Golgi apparatus** (also called Golgi complex in animal cells, and dictyosomes in plants). Endoplasmic reticulum (ER) is a bilayer membrane formed as a tubular structure. It is described as either rough (RER) or smooth (SER), depending on its appearance in an electron micrograph as well as its structure. The "roughness" is a result of the presence of ribosomes associated with the membrane. It is in this area of endoplasmic reticulum that some protein synthesis takes place. The smooth ER contains the enzymes for metabolizing xenobiotics (molecules "foreign to life," such as therapeutic and street drugs, and pollutants). When endoplasmic reticulum is isolated the tubular structure breaks into small globules called microsomes. The commonly used marker enzyme for the ER is glucose 6-phosphatase. The Golgi apparatus is made up of layers of tubular membranes surrounding a lumen and is the site of much of the packaging and targeting of proteins for transport to other organelles or for secretion. The side of the Golgi stack closest to the ER is called the *cis*-Golgi, the middle of the stack is the *media*-Golgi, and the final side of the stack is the *trans*-Golgi. Targeting of proteins to specific membranes and organelles will be discussed later in the Molecular Biology Section.

Plant cells have two additional organelles, **chloroplasts** (one of the plastids found in plant cells) and **vacuoles**. Chloroplasts are surrounded by a double membrane (see Figure 2-21). In the chloroplast matrix are complex membrane systems called thylakoids. Thylakoids are the site of the photosynthetic apparatus. Areas where the thylakoid membranes are arranged in a multilayer structure are called grana, and the rest of the intrachloroplast space is called the stroma.

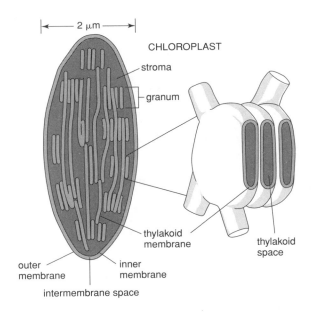

Figure 2-21. A diagram of a chloroplast.
(Adapted from Alberts, B., Bray, D., Lewis, J., Raff, M., Roberts, K., and Watson, J.D., *Molecular Biology of the Cell,* Second Edition, Garland Publishing, Inc., New York and London, 1989, Fig. 7-38.)

Vacuoles often appear as empty space in an electron micrograph of a plant cell. They are surrounded by a single membrane, called a tonoplast, and may occupy most of the space in a plant cell (see Figure 2-22). They contain enzymes that are involved in utilization of food-stuffs and also serve as "storehouses" for fuel molecules as well as waste products.

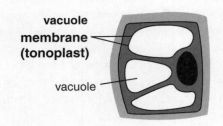

Figure 2-22. Diagram of a vacuole.
(Adapted from Alberts, B., Bray, D., Lewis, J., Raff, M., Roberts, K., and Watson, J.D., *Molecular Biology of the Cell*, Second Edition, Garland Publishing, Inc., New York and London, 1989, Panel 1-1.)

1.4.3. Specialized Structures and Other Characteristics

There are many other specialized cell structures, especially in single-celled organisms. About 50 percent of bacteria display **taxis**, which is a process of movement toward or away from an environmental stim-ulus, and they are also equipped for self-protection by stinging darts. Taxis requires flagella (for movement), sensory bristles and photoreceptors (for sensing the environment), and the contractile or water-expelling vesicles. The sensing structures endow cells with the ability for phototaxis (movement toward or away from a light source), chemotaxis (similar behavior in response to a chemical gradient), magnetotaxis (magnetism), aerotaxis (oxygen), and osmotaxis (osmotic pressure). Some cells also have stinging darts for self-protection.

Usually, bacteria move randomly using **flagella** to move in a straight line for a while and then to tumble. When moving in a straight line, the flagella spin counterclockwise, and during tumbling, they rotate clockwise (see Figure 2-23). Chemotaxis is controlled by "tumble frequency." When a chemical or other stimulant is present, the ratio of linear movement to tumbling changes, and the bacterium moves toward or away from the stimulus. If the stimulant is a chemical, it is sensed by receptors on the plasma membrane or by periplasmic substrate-binding proteins that then bind to receptors and results in methylation of the receptors. Methylation is the "sensing" mechanism. Tumble frequency is controlled by phosphorylation/dephosphorylation of proteins in response to the methylation signal. The "tubes"

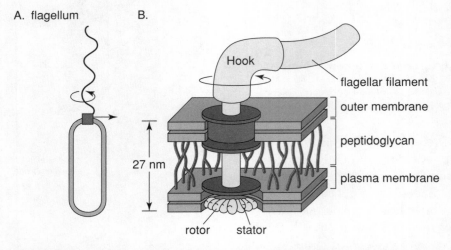

Figure 2-23. A diagram of a bacterial flagellum (A) and a diagram of the motor that drives its rotation (B). The rotating parts are in the lightest gray.
(Adapted from Alberts, B., Bray, D., Lewis, J., Raff, M., Roberts, K., and Watson, J.D., *Molecular Biology of the Cell*, Second Edition, Garland Publishing, Inc., New York and London, 1989, Fig. 12-42.)

of the flagellum are made from a protein called flagellin, and movement is mediated by a proton gradient across the membrane.

Like prokaryotes, eukaryotic cells can also have flagella. They are different from prokaryotic flagella and, together with cilia, will be discussed in the section on microtubules.

Cells with specialized functions also occur in multicellular organisms. For instance, intestinal cells have apical microvilli (membrane protrusions on their intestinal surface that function to increase the surface area of the cells), sensory cells in the ear have cilia to sense the sound waves, and mucosal epithelia have cilia that beat to move the sheets of mucous.

1.4.4. Cell Dynamics

Cells are not static, but exhibit plasticity (the ability to change) in many ways. The study of cell dynamics includes cell and organelle biogenesis, endo- and exocytosis, cell migration and remodeling, cell–cell interaction and signaling, interactions between organelles, and cell death amongst other things. These processes will be described at various points in the text.

2. CELL SURFACE AND CELL COMMUNICATION

2.1. Extracellular Matrix

Multicellular organisms have their cells organized functionally into tissues (e.g., epithelium), and groups of tissues are combined to form organs (e.g., liver, intestines, kidney). Tissues contain not only cells but also an extracellular matrix that helps to stabilize the tissue structure. Cells may connect with each other through intercellular junctions, and with the extracellular matrix through cell–matrix junctions.

2.1.1. The Extracellular Matrix of Connective Tissue

There are two major categories of tissue in mammals: **connective tissue** and **epithelial tissue**.

2.1.1.1. Connective Tissue

In connective tissue, the matrix material takes up most of the space, and the cells themselves are distributed sparsely in the matrix. For the most part, the cells do not touch each other but are surrounded by matrix material. The protein and polysaccharide components of the matrix are synthesized in the cells and then secreted. Each organ has a different amount of connective tissue. Brain has almost none, whereas connective tissue is a large component of skin and bone.

The cell types that secrete the matrix material all have names that end in *blast*. The general family name is fibroblast (for instance, fibroblasts secrete the extracellular matrix of the dermal layer of skin.) Cartilage and bone have specialized fibroblasts, known as chondroblasts and osteoblasts, respectively. The components of the matrix are designed to fulfill its various functions. The major functions are stabilization of the tissue and diffusion of nutrients and other molecules to the cells associated with the matrix. Molecules that promote stabilization are adhesive proteins such as fibronectin and laminin, and fibrous proteins such as elastin and collagen. Diffusion of small molecules is facilitated by the porous nature of the matrix. Molecules that contribute to the porosity are the glycosaminoglycans, polysaccharides that are often found as part of proteoglycans. Proteoglycans are molecules made of a peptide backbone to which are linked many polysaccharide chains. The family of polysaccharide glycosaminoglycans includes chondroitin sulfate, dermatan sulfate, heparan sulfate, heparan, hyaluronic acid, and keratan sulfate. These differ based both on their sugar components and also the number of sulfate groups. They are tissue-specific. The polysaccharide chains of the proteoglycans stretch out loosely from the peptide backbone, and the large number of negatively charged sulfate groups attracts cations such as Na^+. The influx of sodium into the matrix is accompanied by large amounts of water. The large water content of the matrix allows it to adapt to compression. This is particularly obvious in cartilage (try pressing on your earlobe). The stretched-out structure of the polysaccharides combined with the associated water molecules results in the resulting gel-like structure filling most of the space in the matrix of connective tissue, even though it composes only about one-tenth of the total weight. The rest of the weight is from the compactly folded embedded proteins.

2.1.1.2. The Proteins of Connective Tissue

The major protein of connective tissue is **collagen**. The family of collagens is the largest family of proteins in mammals (approximately 25% of all proteins). The amino acid composition of collagens is also unusual, being composed mostly of proline and glycine. Each collagen molecule is made of three intertwined chains, each of which is a polyproline II helix. This helix is different from the α-helix found in many proteins. For example, the polyproline II helix is left-handed, and the α-helix is right-handed. The structure is stabilized by hydrogen bonding between hydroxyproline residues, a vitamin C–dependent posttranslational modification of proline that is almost exclusively found in collagens. Three of these chains are in turn coiled around each other to form a superhelical structure. The glycines form an apolar edge on each polyproline II helix, and the three chains that are coiled together are stabilized by the hydrophobic surfaces formed by the glycine residues. There are over 20 different primary structures of the basic chain, and it is the different permutations as these chains are assembled into the three-coil structure (called procollagen) that gives rise to different types of collagen (see Figure 2-24). These differing collagen types are found in different tissues. Collagen polypeptides are synthesized intracellularly, assembled into procollagen trimers, secreted, and further modified extracellularly. After cleavage of both ends of the procollagen molecule, the final arrangement of collagen (also called tropocollagen) takes place. Fibrils are formed, consisting of repeating units of the trimeric collagen structure. The fibrils are visible under the electron microscope. Sometimes the fibrils aggregate into even larger arrays, called collagen fibers. Cross-linking of the fibrils and fibers occurs via covalent bonding involving an aldehyde derivative of lysine synthesized by copper-dependent lysine amino oxidase. This deaminated derivative is called allysine. Allysine can form a Schiff base with the ε-amino group of another lysine or form an aldol cross-link with another allysine. Collagen contains the modified amino acid hydroxylysine, and many of the collagens are glycoproteins.

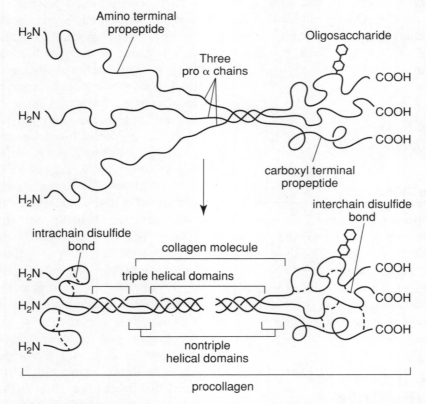

Figure 2-24. Diagram of the synthesis and assembly of procollagen.
(Adapted from Alberts, B., Bray, D., Lewis, J., Raff, M., Roberts, K., and Watson, J.D., *Molecular Biology of the Cell*, Second Edition, Garland Publishing, Inc., New York and London, 1989, Fig. 14-34.)

The different collagen types in different tissues are related to the function of the tissue. In skin, the collagen is arranged in a mesh that can resist stress in all directions, whereas in tendon, the molecules are arranged to be able to resist stress predominantly in one direction.

Elastin is another protein of connective tissue. It gives tissue elasticity and is found in tissues that must change shape, such as blood vessels, lungs, and skin. It is the major component of elastic fibers found in these tissues. It also has a large glycine and proline content but little hydroxyproline and no hydroxylysine. The random coil structure of elastin contains many cross links formed between allysine and lysine. These heterocyclic cross-linking structures are called desmosine. Elastin is associated with microfibrils containing a glycoprotein to form elastic fibers.

Fibronectin is one of the adhesive glycoproteins found in the extracellular matrix. Fibronectin has multiple globular domains that can bind noncovalently to collagen receptors on cell surfaces and to other molecules. This allows fibronectin to connect cells to the other components of the extracellular matrix. During embryonic development, fibronectin facilitates cell migration.

2.1.2. The Extracellular Matrix of Endothelial Tissue

In endothelial tissue, the extracellular matrix is in the form of **basal lamina** (layers). These are thin layers of a specific type of collagen, arranged as a mesh rather than fibrils, proteoglycans, and two glycoproteins called laminin and intactin (proteoglycans have more carbohydrate than protein, and glycoproteins have more protein than carbohydrate). The precise composition varies between tissues. In most cases, basal lamina serve to separate epithelial cells and the underlying connective tissue, but they are also sometimes found between sheets of cells. Basal lamina have an organizing roll in cell polarity and metabolism. They do this by influencing which proteins are found in each area of the cell membrane and by affecting cell differentiation.

Basal lamina has two layers: lamina rara and lamina densa (see Figure 2-25). Basement membrane includes

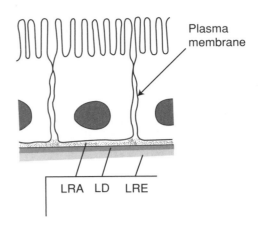

Figure 2-25. Arrangement of epithelial cells on the basal lamina. LRA is the lamina rara, LD is lamina densa, and LRE is lamina reticularis. (Adapted from Alberts, B., Bray, D., Lewis, J., Raff, M., Roberts, K., and Watson, J.D., *Molecular Biology of the Cell,* Second Edition, Garland Publishing, Inc., New York and London, 1989, Fig. 14-50.)

both these layers, plus a layer of reticular collagen fibers called lamina reticularis.

The lamina rara and lamina densa together are the basal lamina and are approximately 50 nm thick. All three laminae together are called the basement membrane.

2.1.3. Cell–Cell Interaction

2.1.3.1. Binding of Cells to the Extracellular Matrix

Fibronectin, one of the glycoproteins of the extracellular matrix that binds to cells, was described above. Cells have plasma membrane components that allow this binding to occur. These receptors are also glycoproteins, with a relatively low affinity for their ligands. They are, however, present in very high numbers. The members of this family of plasma membrane receptors are known as integrins.

2.1.3.2. Communication between Extracellular Matrix and Cytoskeleton

Extracellular matrix helps determine the shape of cells via communication with the cytoskeleton. Intracellular actin can influence the structure of the extracellular matrix. This two-way influence is mediated by fibronectin receptors, one of the family of integrin cell surface receptors. The fibronectin receptor is a transmembrane protein. Outside the cell, it binds fibronectin, and inside the cell, it binds intracellular proteins such as talin. Talin directs actin assembly.

2.1.3.3. Cell Adhesion and Junctions: Cell–Cell Communication

Cells form tissues in basically two ways. They can be created in a topographically discrete arrangement, or they can be made in separate places and migrate to form the tissue. In this latter case, there has to be in place a pathway to guide the cells to their final destination.

In either case, the cells that form a tissue need to be able to recognize each other. In multicellular organisms, such as vertebrates, cell–cell recognition is based on two types of mechanisms, one of which is calcium dependent, and one of which is calcium independent.

Calcium independent cell–cell recognition is mediated by membrane glycoproteins that belong to the immunoglobulin superfamily. Ca++-dependent recognition occurs through proteins that are not part of the immunoglobulin family. These proteins are called cadherins.

Cell–cell and cell–basal lamina adhesion can occur by junctional adhesion or nonjunctional adhesion mechanisms.

Cells that move in order to produce a tissue ("motile cells") do so by recognizing and following gradients of adhesiveness in the substratum. This is a form of chemotaxis and is mediated by the binding of the protein vinculin to talin. The ordering of cells in tissues through these signals is called the **morphogenetic code**. When cells are assembled in the appropriate tissue, the organization is stabilized by formation of **junctional contacts** between cells (see Figure 2-26).

Tight junctions form a barrier between cells that stops molecules diffusing from the bottom of the cell to the top along the side via the interstitial space. They are a type of "occluding junction" and play a major role in the asymmetrical exposure of intestinal epithelial

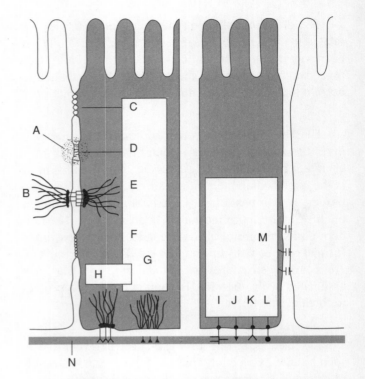

Figure 2-26. Different types of cell–cell and cell–matrix recognition. A, B, C, D, E, F, and M are points of cell–cell adhesion, and G, H, I, J, K, and L are points of cell–matrix adhesion: A) actin filaments, B) intermediate filaments, C) tight junctions, D) adhesion belt, E) desmosome, F) gap junction, G) focal contact, H) hemidesmosome, I) integral membrane proteoglycan, J) fibronectin receptor, K) collagen receptor, L) laminin receptor, M) nonjunctional cell–cell adhesions mediated by transmembrane adhesion proteins, and N) basal lamina. (Adapted from Alberts, B., Bray, D., Lewis, J., Raff, M., Roberts, K., and Watson, J.D., *Molecular Biology of the Cell,* Second Edition, Garland Publishing, Inc., New York and London, 1989, Fig. 14-68.)

cells to different environments. Adherens ("adhering") junctions have proteins within the cell that serve to anchor the junction actin filaments to the cytoskeletons of adjacent cells. Desmosomes and hemidesmosomes are similar to adherens junctions, but they have various types of intermediate filaments instead of actin as the link between cells. Focal contacts, which occur between cells and basal lamina, are bundles of actin that can pull the cell along the substratum. Gap junctions are communicating junctions that allow passage of ions and small molecules between cells. Gap junctions are particularly important in cell–cell signaling during embryogenesis. Other communicating junctions are chemical synapses, such as those between nerves and between nerves and muscle. Nonjunctional adhesion is mediated by receptors for fibronectin, collagen, or laminin. Plants have only one type of junction. This belongs to the communicating junction family, and the junctions are called plasmodesmata.

2.2. Signal Transduction and Receptor Function

Many cells interact with small molecules such as hormones and growth factors. Most of these molecules are incapable of crossing the cell membrane, and the information inherent in the hormone or growth factor signal must be transferred into the cell by a process called **signal transduction**. Inside the cell, a second messenger is activated, and the cell responds to the message.

2.2.1. Cell Membrane Receptors

Hydrophilic signaling molecules such as neurotransmitters, glucagon and other protein hormones, and growth factors mediate their effect by binding to **extracellular receptors** (these are proteins in the cell membrane). There are three ways in which the signal is transduced. One is by causing the opening of a channel. The second is by enzymatic activity of the receptor itself, which is discussed below in the section on tyrosine kinases. The third mechanism is via a change in receptor conformation after binding of the hormone/growth factor ligand. This conformation change alters the conformation of another molecule (a second messenger) on the inside surface of the membrane. These now will be discussed.

Binding of ligand to receptor is a saturable process (gives a hyperbolic curve when plotted) (see Figure 2-27). When binding of a radiolabeled ligand is observed in the presence of unlabeled ligand, a straight line is obtained. This represents the nonspecific binding (i.e., the ligand binds to something on the cell other than the receptor). Results from such experiments can be used to differentiate between specific and nonspecific binding. Nonspecific binding to the membrane is shown by experiments where large amounts of unlabeled ligand (in a ratio of about 1,000 unlabeled to 1 labeled) are added to an incubation containing increasing concentrations of labeled ligand bound to receptor. The unlabeled material will compete with ligand bound to specific sites but not to nonspecific sites, since these latter are not saturable. The difference between the nonspecific binding and the total binding is the true specific binding.

2.2.2. Second Messenger Systems

The internal molecules that sense the binding of ligand to receptor, with concomitant conformation change of the receptor, belong to a family of GTP-binding regulatory proteins (**G-proteins**). From the

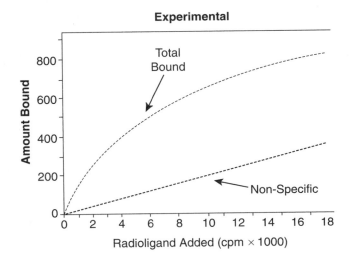

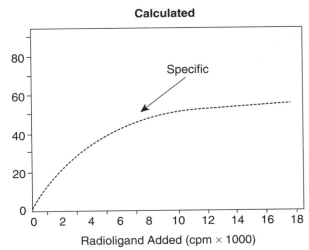

Figure 2-27. Plots of a binding experiment.
(Adapted from http://www.med.unc/pharm/receptor/lesson3.htm.)

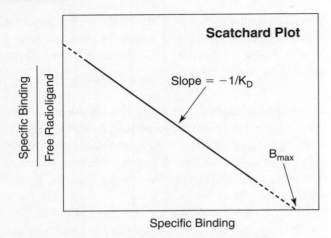

Scatchard Plot

Slope = $-1/K_D$

B_{max}

Specific Binding

Figure 2-28. Scatchard plot of the data shown in Figure 2-27. The ratio of ligand bound specifically to free ligand is plotted against the ratio of the ligand bound to free ligand. KD is the dissociation constant for the ligand, and B_{max} represents the total number of binding sites on the molecule to which the ligand binds.
(Adapted from *http://www.med.unc/pharm/ receptor/lesson3.htm.*)

G-proteins the signal is transmitted either through cyclic AMP (cAMP), phospholipase C (the inositol phosphate pathway), phospholipase A2, or ion channels.

G-proteins can be either stimulatory (G_s) or inhibitory (G_i). For example, working through cAMP, glucagon activates a G_s protein, whereas acetylcholine activates an inhibitory G-protein (G_i).

At this point, it is important to realize that the same chemical compound can have different effects in different cell types. The effect depends on the type of receptor that each cell type has. For instance, acetylcholine, as mentioned above, has an inhibitory effect when working through a G-protein that activates adenyl cyclase. In cells that have an acetylcholine receptor that works through the phospholipase C mechanism of signal transduction, acetylcholine is stimulatory. Inhibition and stimulation do not cancel each other out in a single cell because one cell type has only one type of receptor for a given ligand.

About half of all drugs target G-protein-linked receptors. The receptors themselves are proteins with seven trans-membrane helices (7-TMS receptors). The loops inside the cell formed as the helices weave in and out of the membrane form the domain that interacts with the G-protein.

2.2.2.1. The cAMP pathway

G-proteins are trimers, with three different subunits; α, β, and γ. In the inactive form, all three subunits are noncovalently associated, and a molecule of GDP is bound to the α subunit. On sensing the conformation change of the ligand-bound receptor, the G-protein dissociates into a separate α subunit and a βγ dimer. The GDP dissociates from the α subunit and is replaced by a GTP molecule. The GTP-bound α subunit is the active form of the G-protein. When the system is stimulatory, the G-protein is called G_s, and it activates adenylyl (also called adenyl) cyclase. This enzyme converts ATP to cAMP. In turn, cAMP acts as a positive regulator of protein kinase A. When the system is inhibitory, the G-protein is called G_i, and it causes the constitutive synthesis of cAMP to decrease.

In Figure 2-29, step 1 shows the resting state of the G-protein system; step 2 shows binding of hormone to receptor and association of the receptor with the trimeric G-protein. Step 3 shows the removal of GDP from the α subunit and its replacement with GTP. Step 4 shows the separation of the α-subunit from the βγ-dimer and its interaction with adenyl cyclase. Step 5 shows the synthesis of cAMP. Step 6 shows return to the resting state as GTP is hydrolyzed to GDP and the αβγ trimer reassociates.

Protein kinase A is activated by cAMP. Protein kinase A then phosphorylates other proteins, for instance glycogen synthase and glycogen phosphorylase in the glycogen pathway, hormone-sensitive lipase in the fatty acid mobilization pathway, as well as many other cAMP controlled systems, such as the synthesis and release of testosterone (FSH/LH) and thyroid hormone (TSH) from their respective sites of synthesis. The mechanism of activation of protein kinase A (PKA) is protein–protein interaction. Inactive PKA has four subunits: two are regulatory (R), and two catalytic (C), as shown in Figure 2-30. cAMP binds the regulatory subunits, causing the catalytic subunits to disassociate and become active.

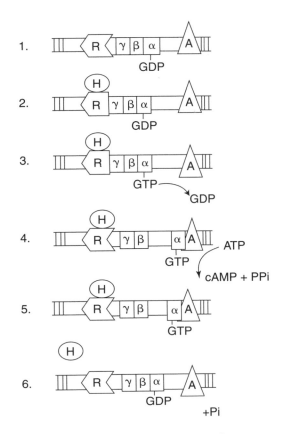

Figure 2-29. G-protein cycle and activation of protein kinase A.
(Adapted from Devlin, T.M., ed., *Textbook of Biochemistry with Clinical Correlations,* Fifth Edition, Wiley-Liss, New York, 2002, Fig. 21.17.)

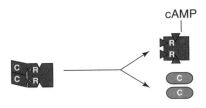

Figure 2-30. Activation of protein kinase A.
(Adapted from Devlin, T.M., ed., *Textbook of Biochemistry with Clinical Correlations,* Fifth Edition, Wiley-Liss, New York, 2002, Fig. 21.18.)

The signal is terminated by action of a phosphodiesterase that degrades cAMP to AMP. The phosphatase activity of the G-protein hydrolyzes the bound GTP to GDP, and the α, β, and γ subunits of the G-protein reassociate. As the GTP is hydrolyzed, the hormone recep-

tor decreases its affinity for the hormone, and the signal is halted.

This cAMP-mediated signal transduction cascade system responds to glucagon (liver, adipose), epinephrine (liver, cardiac muscle, kidney, skeletal muscle, adipose), serotonin (brain), and ACTH (adrenal cortex, adipose), as well as other hormones. Some transcription factors (e.g., CREB transcription factor) are also under the control of this second messenger pathway.

A similar system is involved in the visual cycle. The receptor analog is a protein called rhodopsin and the G-protein, also an αβγ-trimer, is called transducin. The enzyme that is regulated in this case is not a cyclase, but rather a phosphodiesterase that degrades cGMP to GMP and initiates the transfer of visual information to the brain.

Cholera and pertussis toxin work through the G-protein system by causing ADP-ribosylation of the α-subunit, which causes it to become permanently activated. Much of what is known about the G-protein mechanism of signal transduction comes from experiments using GTP analogs (i.e., nonhydrolyzable analogs), such as GTP with a thioester linkage between the last two phosphate groups, which leave the system permanently activated; or molecules similar to cAMP that can cross the membrane and activate the system in the absence of the hormone-receptor effect on adenyl cyclase.

2.2.2.2. The Phosphatidylinositol Pathway

An example of a hormone working through this pathway is gonatropin-releasing hormone. The first steps are the same as described above, but the G-protein activates phospholipase C instead of adenylyl cyclase. Phospholipase C hydrolyses phosphatidyl inositol in the cell membrane to inositol trisphosphate and diacylglycerol. Both inositol trisphosphate (IP_3) and the diacylglycerol have independent effects on the cell. Diacylglycerol is hydrophobic and recruits protein kinase C to the membrane to initiate a phosphorylation cascade. IP_3 is hydrophilic and moves to the cytosol to release Ca^{++} stores from endoplasmic reticulum and mitochondria. Ca^{++} frequently has its effect by binding to a protein called calmodulin. Ca^{++}-calmodulin regulates enzymes through protein–protein interaction. This type of signal cascade is terminated by further metabolism of IP$_3$ and reuptake of Ca^{++}.

2.2.2.3. G-Protein-Associated Ion Channels

Some, but not all, postsynaptic ligand-gated ion channels (see below) are controlled via G-proteins. In this case, a neurotransmitter such as acetylcholine binds its receptor, which activates a G-protein. The activated G-protein in turn causes the opening of channels such as K$^+$ channels.

2.2.2.4. Receptors That Are Enzymes

The third type of signal transduction across the cell membrane is mediated by the family of receptor tyrosine kinases, single pass membrane proteins. In this signal cascade, the membrane receptors act as enzymes. Tyrosine kinase can phosphorylate target proteins, inducing a change in conformation that is propagated to activate intracellular enzymes.

The membrane receptor tyrosine kinase can also autophosphorylate, providing a charged surface to which other proteins can bind. An example of such a protein is phospholipase C, which is thus activated and produces IP$_3$ and DAG from phosphatidyl inositol.

An important signaling cascade, the Ras pathway, is also responsive to binding to the transmembrane tyrosine kinase. The final result of this pathway is activation of transcription factors.

Insulin works through a receptor-tyrosine kinase. In this case, the signal transduction has two effects. One is the eventual production of transcription factors (the slow response), and the other is activation of protein phosphatases to effect lipid and carbohydrate metabolism (fast response). The mechanism of the fast-response cascade is still under investigation.

2.2.2.5. Steroid and Thyroid Hormones

Steroid and thyroid hormones can diffuse into the cell, and their receptors usually reside in the cytosol and nucleus, respectively. On binding of a steroid hormone to its intracellular receptor (also called a ligand-

activated response factor, LATF), the complex moves into the nucleus and binds to a specific region on the DNA (known as a hormone response element, HRE). Thyroid hormone diffuses to the nucleus and binds its LATF, followed by binding to an HRE. The final step of the response to steroid and thyroid hormones is transcription of mRNA and protein expression.

2.3. Excitable Membrane Systems

Excitable membranes are found in the nervous system and function to propagate an electrical signal from one end of a cell to the other. **Nerve cells** are made up of a cell body that contains the nucleus and two types of long processes that emanate from the cell membrane, as shown in Figure 2-31. One type of these processes is the **axon**, a large, thin membrane tube with a diameter of 1µ to 35 µ in humans, and up to 1 mm in squid. The axon can be from 1 mm to 1 meter in length. It is branched at the end, and carries messages away from the cell to other cells. The other type is the **dendrite**. One cell can have many dendrites, and they serve to increase the surface area of the cell membrane so that the cell can receive input from as many as 10^5 other cells.

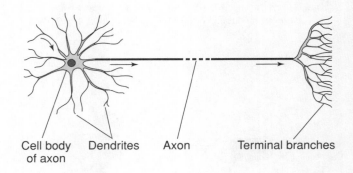

Figure 2-31. Cell body, axon, and dendrites. The axon may be between 1 mm to more than 1 m in length. The signal comes into the dendrites and leaves from the terminal branches. From there, it crosses a synapse and impinges on dendrites of other cells. (Adapted from Alberts, B., Bray, D., Lewis, J., Raff, M., Roberts, K., and Watson, J.D., *Molecular Biology of the Cell,* Second Edition, Garland Publishing, Inc., New York and London, 1989, Fig. 19-2.)

The cell body contains the nucleus, protein synthetic machinery, and most of the cell's mitochondria. Dendrites are in contact with axons from other cells, and when they receive a signal from a cell, the axon carries it from the cell body to the synaptic terminals. The synaptic terminals are, in turn, in contact with dendrites on another cell. This constitutes a network that can receive and transmit signals from cell to cell to cell.

The signal that initiates in the cell body and is carried along the axon is electric. It is propagated by the opening and closing of membrane channels that allow K^+ and Na^+ to cross the cell membrane. When the signal reaches the presynaptic terminal of the nerve (the terminal of the axon) the signal is converted to a chemical signal and uses a ligand-gated mechanism to cross the synapse (space) to the next nerve cell. The signal is then converted to an electrical signal again for propagation down the next axon.

Originally, the plasma membrane of the axon is more negatively charged on the inside surface of the axon and more positively charged on the outside. The transmembrane electrical potential is −70 mV. Under resting conditions, the membrane uses an ATPase to

pump sodium out of the cell and potassium into the cell by an antiport mechanism to maintain this membrane potential. When a signal is received (from entry of ions from the synapse into the postsynaptic terminal of the nerve), the potential across the membrane becomes less negative. When the potential is depolarized to some "threshold" potential, a **voltage-gated channel** opens (see Figure 2-32). This allows sodium to move down its concentration gradient into the cell, and potassium, whose concentration is higher in the cell, to move out. There is a very short period of time (milliseconds) during which the membrane polarization reverses to a positive potential, and this change in electrical potential causes the next channel down the axon to open, and the process is repeated down the length of the axon. The electrical impulse moves only in one direction because the first channel closes to an inactive conformation that resists reopening until a new signal is initiated from the postsynaptic terminal on the cell body. The ATPase is constantly pumping sodium and potassium across the membrane, quickly returning the local potential to −70 mV (see Figure 2-33).

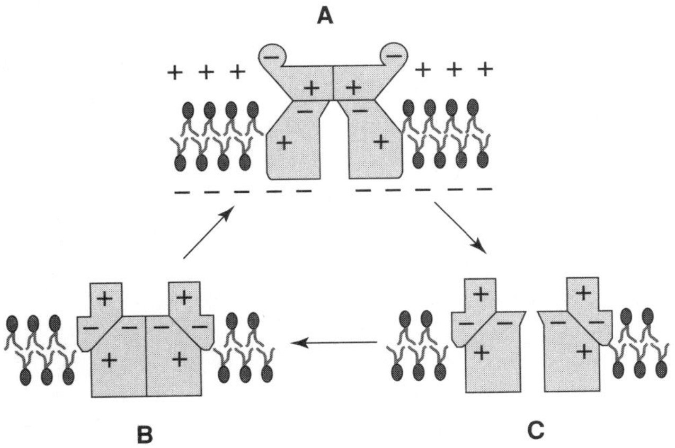

When the signal reaches the end of the axon (the presynaptic terminal), the electrical signal is transduced into a chemical signal. This is done by opening voltage-gated calcium channels in the membrane.

Synaptic vesicles in the presynaptic nerve contain **neurotransmitters** that have been synthesized in the cell body and have migrated along the axon to the presynaptic terminal. When the vesicles are not phosphorylated, they store neurotransmitters inside the presynaptic terminal by associating with the cytoskeleton.

As shown in Figure 2-34, when the electrical signal reaches the presynaptic terminal of the nerve cell, calcium enters the presynaptic neuron from the synaptic cleft, binds to calmodulin, and activates a kinase that phosphorylates proteins embedded in the membrane of synaptic vesicles. After phosphorylation, the vesicles are freed and move to the membrane, and their contents are released into the **synapse** (gap between nerve cells) by exocytosis.

On the postsynaptic membrane of the bodies of the cells receiving the signal are receptors that bind

Figure 2-32. Voltage-gated channel in its three possible conformations. A) Channel is closed but not inactivated (i.e., it is ready to respond to a signal). The membrane is polarized. C) The channel is open, and the membrane depolarized. B) Channel is inactivated (i.e., it is refractory to any further signal), and the membrane is still depolarized. (Adapted from Alberts, B., Bray, D., Lewis, J., Raff, M., Roberts, K., and Watson, J.D., *Molecular Biology of the Cell,* Second Edition, Garland Publishing, Inc., New York and London, 1989, Fig. 6-58.)

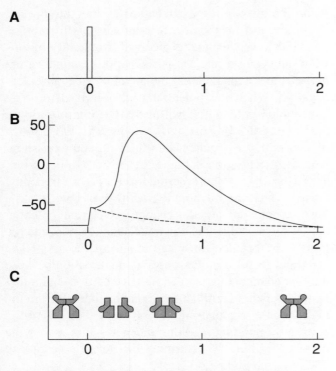

Figure 2-33. Movement of a nerve signal along a membrane. Panel A shows the stimulating current. Panel B shows the membrane potential in millivolts (mV). The stimulating current induces depolarization and a gradual return to the resting –70 mV. Panel C follows the state of the Na+ channels during the process.
(Adapted from Alberts, B., Bray, D., Lewis, J., Raff, M., Roberts, K., and Watson, J.D., *Molecular Biology of the Cell,* Second Edition, Garland Publishing, Inc., New York and London, 1989, Fig. 6-59.)

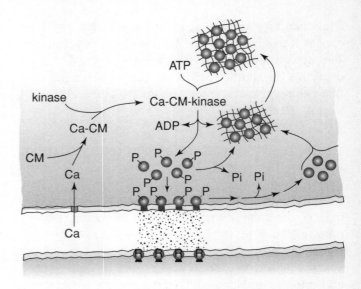

Figure 2-34. Release of chemical signal into the synapse.
(Adapted from Devlin, T.M., ed., *Textbook of Biochemistry with Clinical Correlations,* Fifth Edition, Wiley-Liss, New York, 2002, Fig. 23.7.)

the secreted neurotransmitters. These receptors are the mechanism by which the signal is transduced back into an electrical signal. The receptors bind neurotransmitters and cause opening of channels to allow the influx of sodium, potassium, or calcium into the postsynaptic cell. This initiates an impulse in the next neuron. The neurotransmitters that propagate the signal from one nerve cell to the next are called excitatory. There are also inhibitory neurotransmitters that inhibit propagation of the signal. They work by binding postsynaptic receptors that effect opening of chloride channels. Entry of negatively charged chloride makes the membrane potential even more negative (hyperpolarized) and prevents opening of ion channels down the axon.

To stop the signal, the neurotransmitters must be removed from the synapse. This occurs by reuptake into the presynaptic terminal (dopamine), metabolism in the synapse (acetylcholine), or metabolism in an associated cell (GABA [γ-aminobutyric acid]).

At synapses between nerves and muscles, the nerve signal is transduced to the muscle by acetylcholine, and this results in release of calcium from the sarcoplasmic reticulum (as endoplasmic reticulum is called in muscle) into the cytoplasm of the sarcomeres. Calcium stimulates initiation of muscle contraction.

3. CYTOSKELETON, MOTILITY, AND SHAPE

The eukaryotic cell has a complex network of protein filaments that gives it the ability to keep and change its shape and alter its intracellular organization. Collectively, these filaments are known as the **cytoskeleton**. The three types of filaments found in largest number are **actin filaments**, **microtubules**, and **intermediate filaments**.

3.1. Actin Filaments

Actin is one of a number of multigene families. At least six types of actin genes occur in mammals, and their gene products show considerable homology. Some actins are in skeletal muscle, some in smooth muscle, some in cardiac muscle, and some form part of the cytoskeleton.

Actin in the cytoskeleton is found predominantly just beneath the cell membrane, where it forms the cell cortex (*cortex* meaning the outside part). Actin is part of a network of proteins held together by actin-binding proteins, of which the most abundant is filamin. This network, or mesh, gives the cell shape. It is, however, another property of actin that allows cells to change shape and move along the basement membrane. This property is the ability to polymerize and depolymerize. The cell junction described earlier as a focal contact is made of actin. By polymerizing and depolymerizing, the actin in the focal contact allows a cell to "walk" along a substratum. Actin is synthesized in a globular form called G-actin. In the presence of magnesium and ATP, the G-actin molecules can polymerize to form filaments called F-actin.

3.1.1. Actin in Muscle Contraction

One of the other important roles of actin is in muscle contraction. The "pull" exerted on the muscle fibers comes as a result of interaction between actin, myosin, and several other proteins (see Figure 2-35). Muscle is made up of **myofilaments**, which are bundles of linked fibers. The myofilaments in turn are composed of repeating contractile units (Z-band to Z-band) called **sarcomeres**.

Myosin, also called the "thick filament," is the other major contractile filament. It has two heavy chain subunits that coil together and two light chains associated with the "head" of the molecule. Myosin molecules assemble into fibers in a head-to-tail organization. Shortening of the sarcomere occurs when the myosin "pulls" the actin filaments toward the center of the sarcomere. None of the filaments themselves change length, but the sarcomere shortens when the actin pulls the Z bands closer together (see Figure 2-36).

The "pulling" action is initiated by release of calcium from the sarcoplasmic reticulum into the sarcomere in response to a nerve signal. The calcium is subsequently pumped back into the sarcoplasmic reticulum to await the next signal to contract.

How does this sudden increase in calcium in the sarcomere initiate contraction? Two additional muscle proteins are necessary for this to happen. One is tropomyosin, and the other is the trimeric protein troponin. Tropomyosin in resting muscle is associated with F-actin to hide the sites on myosin that, when bound to actin, account for the "pull mechanism." To initiate the "pull," the tropomyosin has to change conformation and expose these sites. This conformation change comes via interaction with troponin. Troponin is also bound to tropomyosin through the Tn-T subunit. The Tn-I subunit (troponin-inhibitory) is the part of the troponin molecule that keeps tropomyosin in a conformation such that it prevents the binding of myosin to actin. Tn-C binds calcium. When Tn-C binds calcium released from the sarcoplasmic reticulum, it initiates a series of conformation changes in the troponin subunits and in tropomyosin that expose the actin-myosin binding sites, and contraction becomes possible.

The affinity of the binding of myosin to actin is also influenced by a conformation change in myosin caused by ATP to ADP hydrolysis. Myosin has an ATPase activity that results in an ADP-myosin complex with high affinity for actin. Muscle relaxation requires that the ADP be removed from myosin and replaced by ATP to lower the myosin-actin affinity.

3.2. Microtubules

Other frequent players in the movement of cells and cell components are microtubules. They, too, are filaments, made up of proteins called **tubulins**. Tubulin is a dimer of two globular subunits called α-tubulin and β-tubulin. When the two subunits associate, they form protofilaments. Thirteen protofilaments aligned parallel to one another make up a microtubule. There are two major types of microtubules, those in cilia and eukaryotic flagella, and those that help organize the cytoplasm.

Cilia are made from microtubules. They are hairlike appendages that protrude from the cell surface.

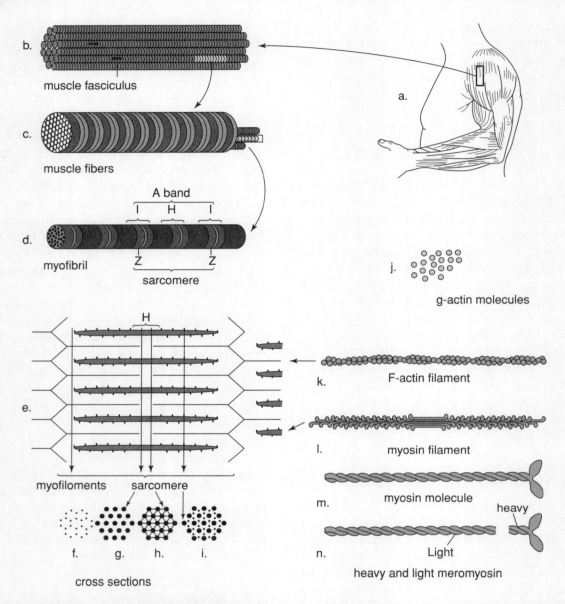

b. muscle fasciculus

c. muscle fibers

a.

A band

I   H   I

d. myofibril

Z   Z

sarcomere

j. g-actin molecules

H

e.

k. F-actin filament

myofilaments   sarcomere

l. myosin filament

m. myosin molecule

n. heavy and light meromyosin

heavy

Light

f.   g.   h.   i.

cross sections

Figure 2-35. Myofilaments associate to form an intact muscle. The "H" band is indicated in panels d and e. The "Z" band is shown as the heavy bands at the ends of sarcomeres in the same diagram, and the "I" (isotropic) band is made up of the Z band and the area on either side of it (panel d). Panels d and e both show that a complete segment between two Z bands is called the "A" band or sarcomere.
(Adapted from Devlin, T.M., ed., *Textbook of Biochemistry with Clinical Correlations,* Fifth Edition, Wiley-Liss, New York, 2002, Fig. 23.27.)

They "beat" in order to move fluid past the cell (such as in the gut) and also to move cells (such as protozoa). Flagella are similar in structure but much longer and have a more sinuous motion than the cilia, which move only back and forth like a whip. Flagella are found on sperm cells and protozoa. Note that bacterial flagella, described earlier, are different in structure and method of locomotion from eukaryotic flagella. Cilia and flagella both have a striking cross-sectional appearance (see Figure 2-37).

The entire central region containing the microtubules is called the axoneme. As seen in Figure 2-37, the microtubules are arranged in a "9 + 2" array. The two

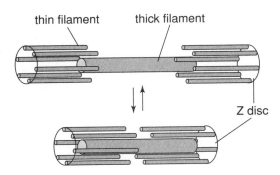

thin filament   thick filament

Z disc

**Figure 2-36. Actin filaments are pulled
along the myosin filaments.**
(Adapted from Alberts, B., Bray, D., Lewis, J., Raff, M., Roberts, K.,
and Watson, J.D., *Molecular Biology of the Cell,* Second Edition,
Garland Publishing, Inc., New York and London, 1989, Fig. 11-4.)

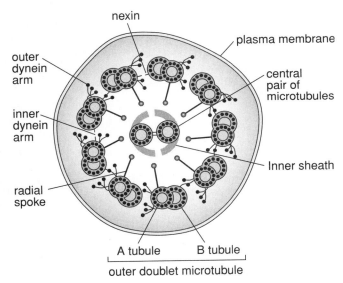

nexin

plasma membrane

outer
dynein
arm

central
pair of
microtubules

inner
dynein
arm

Inner sheath

radial
spoke

A tubule   B tubule

outer doublet microtubule

**Figure 2-37. Diagram of a cross section of
a cilium.** The diameter is about 250 nm.
(Adapted from Alberts, B., Bray, D., Lewis, J., Raff, M., Roberts, K.,
and Watson, J.D., *Molecular Biology of the Cell,* Second Edition,
Garland Publishing, Inc., New York and London, 1989, Fig. 11-53.)

tubules in the center are complete, but the nine tubules
that encircle this central structure each consist of one
complete and one partial microtubule. The outer pairs
of microtubules are connected by two types of protein,
dynein and nexin. Nexin holds the doublets together
but is flexible and allows the doublets to move up and
down. Dynein is the protein that effects the movement
of microtubules, with some similarities to the myosin/
actin sliding movement. The motion is ATP-driven.

At the base of each cilium is a centriole called a
basal body. It functions to anchor cilia to the cytoskeleton. The centriole has no central microtubules, and
the peripheral microtubules are arranged in groups of
three.

Centrioles also perform another function. As
described later in the section on mitosis, they are part of
the centrosome that organizes cell division.

Tubulin microtubules are also found in the cytoplasm in their role as organizers of the cell. More actin
fibers than tubulin fibers are present, and actin fibers
form a more complex network. Tubulin microtubules
play specific roles such as moving organelles. Microtubules are organized by the centrioles. They function
largely by "growing" (polymerizing) at one end and
"shrinking" (depolymerizing) at the other. Organelles
are known to move along microtubule "roads" at the
expense of the hydrolysis of ATP. The location of the
Golgi and endoplasmic reticulum is determined by
"stretching" along microtubules. The vesicles containing neurotransmitters (see above) also move along
microtubules down the axon.

3.3. Intermediate Filaments

The term *intermediate* was coined because these
filaments are intermediate in size between the thick and
thin fibers in muscle. They are made of protein "ropes"
and contribute stability to the cell. They surround the
nucleus and extend out into the cytosol and can also
extend from one cell to another via the desmosome.
Their function appears to be the provision of mechanical support to the cell. Intermediary filaments found in
epithelial cells and hair and nails belong to the Type I
(keratins) family. Type II are found in tissues originating
in mesenchymal tissue and include vimentin, desmin,
and glial fibrillary acidic protein. Type III are neurofila-
ment proteins found in nerve axons and dendrites, and
Type IV are nuclear lamins, which are discussed in the
section on mitosis.

All intermediate filaments share a homologous region
in the middle of their amino acid sequence. The amino-
and carboxyl-terminal sequences differ. All intermediate
filaments are oligomeric, with intertwined monomers that

overlap to form the ropelike structures. It appears that the filaments are associated in some way with microtubules since compounds that collapse the microtubule structure also destroy intermediate filaments.

3.4. Organization of the Cytoskeleton

All three of the types of structures described above (actin, microtubules, and intermediate filaments) together make up the cytoskeleton. The cytoskeleton is important in allowing cells to move, to change shape, and to organize their cytoplasm. Many of the cytoskeletal proteins are interlinked into a complex mesh, with the spaces filled with a "ground substance" of a high concentration of small molecules in solution. Organelles are also in the spaces and often appear to be attached to the cytoskeleton filaments. Cell migration is made possible by a pull exerted by filaments in a specific direction, and cell shape is also determined by movement and distribution of the filaments.

The cytoskeleton of one cell can influence the behavior and characteristics of another cell. When two cells migrate, the movement ceases when they touch. This is called **contact inhibition of movement**. A cell that shows polarity (such as a basal cell associated with an extracellular matrix) may secrete compounds unidirectionally. These compounds may serve to organize the orientation of other cells associated with the same matrix.

3.5. Cell Surface Structures of Prokaryotes

Many prokaryotes exhibit motility. This is accomplished by movement of protein appendages, called flagella, that are attached to the cell surface. Unlike eukaryotic flagella, prokaryotic flagella do not have the 9 + 2 arrangement of microtubules. Flagella are powered by a motor apparatus in the cell membrane. The energy for movement is derived from a chemiosmotic gradient across the membrane. Some prokaryotes have polar flagella (flagella originating at one or both ends of the cell) and others have a peritrichous (meaning "surrounded by hair") flagella protruding from all surfaces. Movement in prokaryotes is triggered by the need to swim toward nutrients or away from toxins (chemotaxis), or by physical stimuli (phototaxis, aerotaxis, magnetotaxis).

Cell–cell communication in prokaryotes is accomplished by a process called **quorum sensing**. This is the secretion of small molecules that are recognized by other cells. These signals allow prokaryotes to sense cell density, to react together to fight off antibiotics, and to organize spore and fruiting body formation.

Transfer of genetic information from one cell to another is mediated through protrusions made of protein. These are called **pili** or **fimbriae**. An example of such a pilus is the sex or F pilus of *E. coli*. Pili and fimbriae also function in attachment of bacteria to surfaces.

4. PROTEIN SYNTHESIS AND PROCESSING

Translation, posttranslational modification, and intracellular trafficking are all described in the section on Molecular Biology, and secretion and endocytosis have been described in the earlier section on membrane transport.

5. CELL DIVISION, DIFFERENTIATION, AND DEVELOPMENT

5.1. Bacterial Cell Division

Prokaryotes reproduce by **binary fission**. This means that each cell divides to form two daughter cells that are genetically identical to the parent cell. The rate at which this happens is known as generation time and is calculated from the average time it takes a population of bacterial cells to double in number. Note that the division of cells is not usually synchronous; thus the average time must be used. This time can be as short as 20 minutes under optimal circumstances. Doubling time depends on the bacterial species and the environment, especially the availability of nutrients. The various mechanisms by which bacteria duplicate their DNA will be discussed later. It is important to note, however, that for cell division to occur, all forms of DNA—extrachromosomal as well as chromosomal—must be duplicated.

As the bacterial chromosome replicates, the two copies become attached to two specific points on the cell. Cell division then occurs between these two attachment points, ensuring that each cell receives one chromosome.

5.2. Eukaryotic Cell Cycle

Eukaryotic cells undergo a cell cycle that starts with a diploid cell (2N), continues through DNA replication to produce a cell that is 4N, and ends with cell division producing two diploid cells (see Figure 2-38). The first stage is called G_1, or Gap 1, and is characterized by preparation for DNA replication. The second stage, S for synthesis, is the time during which DNA is replicated, and the cell becomes 4N. G_2 is preparation for cell division, and M, for **mitosis**, is when the cell division occurs. There is also a stage called G_0 that may last for a long period of time in cells that are not actively replicating. This stage interrupts the procession through G_1. Together, G_1, S, and G_2 are called interphase and make up most of the cell cycle. In a cell that is replicating every 24 hours, only 1–2 hours is taken up by mitosis. The cell cycle is controlled by a series of cyclins and kinases (see below).

The G_1 phase of the cell cycle has a "restriction point" (called START in yeast). Once the cell has passed this point in the cycle, it is committed to continue on through cell division. It is at the restriction point that the cell receives signals from the environment indicating the desirability of dividing or not, and the signal is transmitted by the activity of kinases. The length of the G_1 phase varies from cell type to cell type and determines the length of the cell cycle for each cell. The normal cycle can be anywhere from 12 hours to a year. Some cells never divide in the adult.

During the synthetic (S) phase of the cell cycle, DNA is replicated. This will be discussed later in the section on Molecular Biology. Each new chromosome, after replication, remains attached to the parent chromosome at the centromere in a binary structure called sister **chromatids** (see Figure 2-39). The sister chromatids are held together by proteins called cohesins at the kinetochore. A protein called separin (separase) catalyzes release of the cohesins, allowing the chromatids to separate.

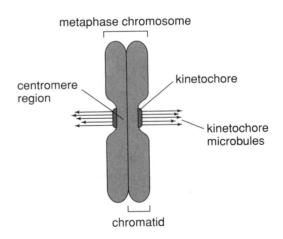

Figure 2-39. Conjoined sister chromatids in a metaphase chromosome.
(Adapted from Alberts, B., Bray, D., Lewis, J., Raff, M., Roberts, K., and Watson, J.D., *Molecular Biology of the Cell,* Second Edition, Garland Publishing, Inc., New York and London, 1989, Fig. 13-30.)

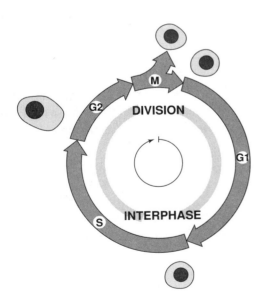

Figure 2-38. The cell cycle.
(Adapted from Alberts, B., Bray, D., Lewis, J., Raff, M., Roberts, K., and Watson, J.D., *Molecular Biology of the Cell,* Second Edition, Garland Publishing, Inc., New York and London, 1989, Fig. 13-1.)

The cells then enter another waiting period, the G_2 phase. In G_2, there is another restriction point that commits the cell to divide. This restriction point is regulated by a kinase, M phase promoting factor (MPF). The dimeric kinase is activated by dephosphorylation of its catalytic subunit, known as Cdc2. The regulatory subunit, necessary for kinase activity, can be cyclin A or cyclin B. It is degradation of this regulatory subunit that terminates the kinase activity. MPF can also phosphorylate many proteins and promote breakdown of the germinal vesicle (nucleus).

There are also several other checkpoints that act as controls on the cell cycle, allowing the cycle to continue when the two absolute criteria for successful cell division are present. Only when the cell has both adequate mass and duplicated DNA can the cell enter mitosis. The checkpoints are controlled, as described above, by the family of cdks (cyclin-dependent kinases) and their attendant cyclins. It has been found that many of these checkpoint proteins are products of tumor suppressor genes, so-called because mutations in these genes can lead to uncontrolled cell growth. Cyclin B is absolutely needed for exit from mitosis. There are also inhibitors of cdks, and these are called CKI proteins (cdk-cyclin kinase inhibitors).

5.3. Mitosis and Cytokinesis

The first indication that cells are entering mitosis is the condensation of the otherwise amorphous genetic material into structures that are visible under the light microscope. This condensation appears to be triggered by phosphorylation of the H1 histone by M phase kinase, MPK. This phase is called **prophase** and is the first of the four phases of mitosis (see Figure 2-40). Later in prophase, the nuclear envelope disappears. This is caused by dissolution of a network of fibers, the lamina, beneath the nuclear membrane into individual lamins (see Figure 2-41). Lamins are categorized as a type of intermediate filaments.

At this time, cytoskeleton microtubules are rearranged to form a spindle, which is anchored at the two ends (or poles) by MTOCs (microtubule organizing centers). This structure is called the mitotic spindle. The spindle poles are associated with arrangements of microtubules, called asters. These resemble stars (Latin *aster)* and will form the basis for the many microtubules that will pull the chromatids to either end of the nucleus. The polar MTOCs are associated with regions called centrosomes, and each centrosome contains two centrioles (see earlier).

The next stage is called **metaphase**. In metaphase, the chromosomes line up along the center of the cell, in a region known as the equatorial plate, and microtubules attach to a region of the centromere called the kinetochore, which is considered another type of MTOC. The microtubules will eventually be used to separate the sister chromatids (Figure 2-42).

In **anaphase**, the chromatids are pulled to each end (pole) of the nucleus to form the beginnings of two separate nuclei (see Figure 2-43).

The final stage is **telophase**. The microtubules of the spindle disaggregate, the chromatin (genetic material) once again becomes amorphous, and the nuclear envelope is resynthesized. There are now two nuclei, and the next stage of cell division, **cytokinesis**, can occur.

5.3.1. Cytokinesis

The very first evidence of cytokinesis can be seen during anaphase, when a puckering of the cell membrane becomes evident. The puckering (or furrowing) forms at a right angle to the mitotic spindle so that the resulting two cells each contain a set of chromosomes.

The intermediate filaments in the cell form a contractile ring around the center of the cell, and this ring becomes smaller, pinching the cell into two. The extra membrane needed to accomplish the task of surrounding two cells instead of one is synthesized and stored prior to cell division. The cell is finally divided into two daughter cells, which is called cytokinesis.

Other organelles must be replicated in order for each daughter cell to have an adequate number. Mitochondria (and chloroplasts in plant cells) are duplicated prior to cell division, and approximately half of the resulting population is included in each daughter cell. Golgi apparatus and endoplasmic reticulum are broken into small sections, and some sections go to each new cell. The centrosome, the organizing structure for microtubule assembly, is replicated in interphase, and becomes two spindle poles. After cell division, each daughter cell contains one spindle pole, which reverts back to a centriole.

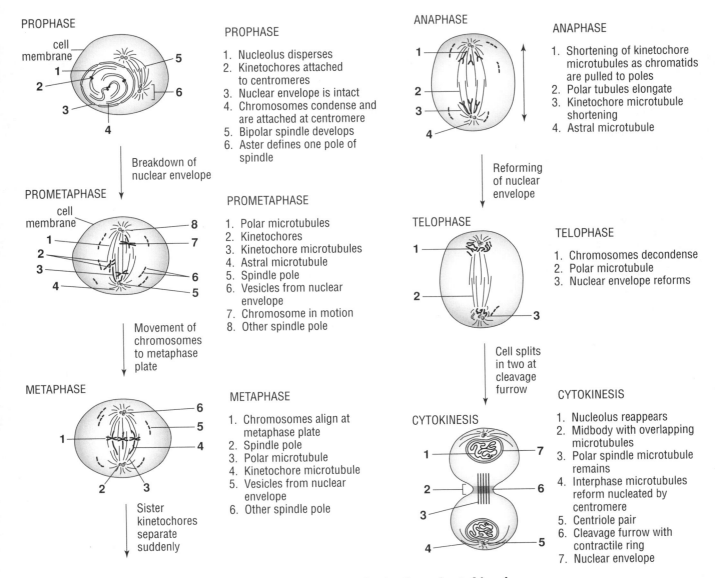

PROPHASE
cell membrane
1
2
3
4
5
6

PROPHASE
1. Nucleolus disperses
2. Kinetochores attached to centromeres
3. Nuclear envelope is intact
4. Chromosomes condense and are attached at centromere
5. Bipolar spindle develops
6. Aster defines one pole of spindle

Breakdown of nuclear envelope

PROMETAPHASE
cell membrane
1
2
3
4
8
7
6
5

PROMETAPHASE
1. Polar microtubules
2. Kinetochores
3. Kinetochore microtubules
4. Astral microtubule
5. Spindle pole
6. Vesicles from nuclear envelope
7. Chromosome in motion
8. Other spindle pole

Movement of chromosomes to metaphase plate

METAPHASE
1
2
3
6
5
4

METAPHASE
1. Chromosomes align at metaphase plate
2. Spindle pole
3. Polar microtubule
4. Kinetochore microtubule
5. Vesicles from nuclear envelope
6. Other spindle pole

Sister kinetochores separate suddenly

ANAPHASE
1
2
3
4

ANAPHASE
1. Shortening of kinetochore microtubules as chromatids are pulled to poles
2. Polar tubules elongate
3. Kinetochore microtubule shortening
4. Astral microtubule

Reforming of nuclear envelope

TELOPHASE
1
2
3

TELOPHASE
1. Chromosomes decondense
2. Polar microtubule
3. Nuclear envelope reforms

Cell splits in two at cleavage furrow

CYTOKINESIS
1
2
3
4
7
6
5

CYTOKINESIS
1. Nucleolus reappears
2. Midbody with overlapping microtubules
3. Polar spindle microtubule remains
4. Interphase microtubules reform nucleated by centromere
5. Centriole pair
6. Cleavage furrow with contractile ring
7. Nuclear envelope

Figure 2-40. Diagram of mitosis and cytokinesis.
(Adapted from Alberts, B., Bray, D., Lewis, J., Raff, M., Roberts, K., and Watson, J.D., *Molecular Biology of the Cell,* Second Edition, Garland Publishing, Inc., New York and London, 1989, Panel 13-1.)

5.3.2. Growth Factors

Cells divide in response to external signals called **growth factors**. Some of these are platelet-derived growth factor (PDGF), epidermal growth factor (EGF), insulin-like growth factors (IGF-I and IGF-II), and interleukins (IL). Some growth factors act predominantly by up- or down-regulating the cell's response to other growth factors (for instance TGF-β [transforming growth factor β]).

Growth factors are named for the tissue where their presence was initially found, but many of them are synthesized in many other tissues as well. Several are also known by a variety of names, and a standardized nomenclature is yet to be developed. The factors act by binding to protein tyrosine kinases in the cell membrane, as described earlier, which then trigger a cascade of the Ras pathway, or a similar signal-amplifying pathway. Many tumors grow in response to

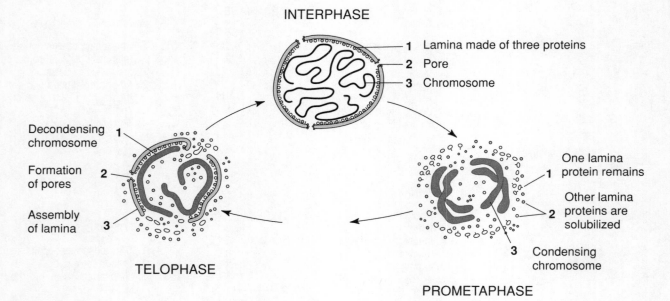

Figure 2-41. Cycle of the nuclear membrane during mitosis.
(Adapted from Alberts, B., Bray, D., Lewis, J., Raff, M., Roberts, K., and Watson, J.D.,
Molecular Biology of the Cell, Second Edition, Garland Publishing, Inc., New York and London, 1989, Fig. 13-36.)

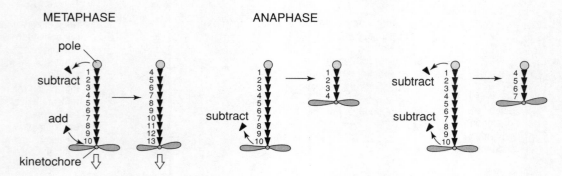

Figure 2-42. Diagrams of the way in which microtubules can be pulled in a given direction by polymerization and depolymerization. The open arrows indicate the direction of tension.
The shortening of microtubules may occur in either of the ways indicated.
(Adapted from Alberts, B., Bray, D., Lewis, J., Raff, M., Roberts, K., and Watson, J.D.,
Molecular Biology of the Cell, Second Edition, Garland Publishing, Inc., New York and London, 1989, Fig. 13-60.)

excess growth factor or to the permanent activation of receptor-kinases.

5.4. Meiosis and Gametogenesis

Eukaryotes have more than one copy of each chromosome and reproduce by producing **gametes**, typically sperm and egg cells. In diploid organisms, one member of each pair of chromosomes must be packaged in a gamete.

The resulting gametes contain a "random" or **independent assortment** of chromosomes (see Figure 2-44). This means that one gamete may have maternal chromosome 1 and paternal chromosome 2, and another gamete might have both chromosomes 1 and 2 from the father. As each parent has 23 pairs of chromosomes, the variety in the maternal/paternal chromosome complement in gametes is great. The Punnett square described in the section on Molecular Biology diagrams independent assortment.

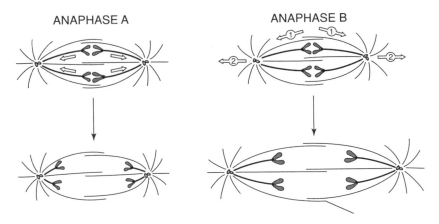

ANAPHASE A   ANAPHASE B

Figure 2-43. Chromatids being pulled to the two poles.
(Adapted from Alberts, B., Bray, D., Lewis, J., Raff, M., Roberts, K., and Watson, J.D.,
Molecular Biology of the Cell, Second Edition, Garland Publishing, Inc., New York and London, 1989, Fig. 13-59.)

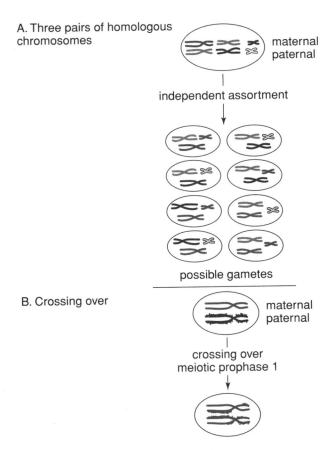

A. Three pairs of homologous chromosomes

maternal
paternal

independent assortment

possible gametes

B. Crossing over

maternal
paternal

crossing over
meiotic prophase 1

**Figure 2-44. Independent assortment
and crossing-over during gametogenesis.**
(Adapted from Alberts, B., Bray, D., Lewis, J., Raff, M., Roberts, K.,
and Watson, J.D., *Molecular Biology of the Cell,* Second Edition,
Garland Publishing, Inc., New York and London, 1989, Fig. 15-9.)

The process whereby chromosomes are incorporated into gametes is known as **meiosis**. During meiosis, one of each pair of chromosomes (homologues) replicates to form sister chromatids, analogous to the initial events of mitosis (see Figure 2-47). These chromatids (of which there are now four) together are known as a bivalent (see Figure 2-45).

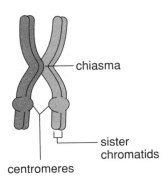

chiasma

sister
chromatids

centromeres

**Figure 2-45. Paired homologous
chromosomes showing four chromatids.**
(Adapted from Alberts, B., Bray, D., Lewis, J., Raff, M., Roberts, K.,
and Watson, J.D., *Molecular Biology of the Cell,* Second Edition,
Garland Publishing, Inc., New York and London, 1989, Fig. 15-10.)

There are two cell divisions that occur during meiosis. The prophase of the first meiotic division is itself divided into stages. These are diagrammed in Figure 2-46.

So far, division I of meiosis has occurred. The cell then goes through the rest of the process analogous to

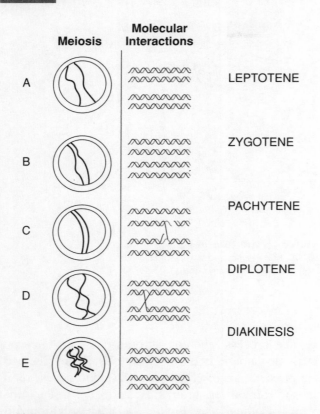

Meiosis   **Molecular Interactions**

A   LEPTOTENE

B   ZYGOTENE

C   PACHYTENE

D   DIPLOTENE

E   DIAKINESIS

Figure 2-46. Diagram of meiosis, indicating the stages at which exchange of genetic information can occur. A) LEPTOTENE: Chromosomes condense and attach to the nuclear envelope. Replicated chromosomes are called sister chromatids. B) ZYGOTENE: Chromosomes begin to pair. Recombination initiated by strand nicking. C) PACHYTENE: Synaptonemal complex extends along whole length of chromosomes, and single strand exchanges occur. D) DIPLOTENE: Separated chromosomes linked at chiasmata, and region of exchanged strands is extended. E) DIAKINESIS: Further condensation of chromosomes, which detach from envelope. All four chromatids are visible, and chiasmata persist. The recombination event reaches resolution.
(Adapted from Devlin, T.M., ed., *Textbook of Biochemistry with Clinical Correlations,* Fifth Edition, Wiley-Liss, New York, 2002, Fig. 15-4.)

mitosis (division II) and divides (see Figure 2-47). The new cells are still diploid, but the two copies of each set of information are the same, unlike a normal diploid cell that has maternal and paternal copies of each chromosome.

In division II the sister chromatid pairs line up on the spindle, and one chromatid is pulled to each end of the cell. Each of these two cells is identical. From one

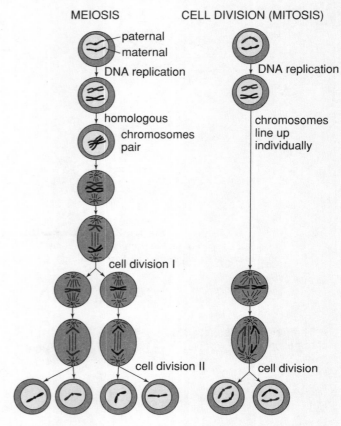

MEIOSIS   CELL DIVISION (MITOSIS)

paternal
maternal

DNA replication   DNA replication

homologous chromosomes pair   chromosomes line up individually

cell division I

cell division II   cell division

Figure 2-47. Comparison of meiosis with mitosis.
(Adapted from Alberts, B., Bray, D., Lewis, J., Raff, M., Roberts, K., and Watson, J.D., *Molecular Biology of the Cell,* Second Edition, Garland Publishing, Inc., New York and London, 1989, Fig. 15-8.)

diploid cell, four haploid cells have been produced, with two of one genotype and two of another.

During the close association of pairs of sister chromatids in meiosis I, there is a possibility that genetic material may be exchanged between chromatids (see Figure 2-48). This results in recombination, a variation from the strict linkage one expects from Mendelian genetics.

5.5. Fertilization and Early Embryonic Development

Following meiosis, cells are haploid, and two must be merged to form a diploid **zygote** (a single cell). This process is called **fertilization**. Diploid organisms have an advantage over haploid organisms because a muta-

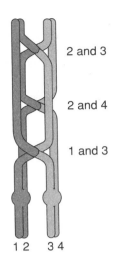

Figure 2-48. Diagram of multiple exchange points between four chromatids. The pairs of numbers at the chiasmata indicate the chromatids involved in each crossover.
(Adapted from Alberts, B., Bray, D., Lewis, J., Raff, M., Roberts, K., and Watson, J.D., *Molecular Biology of the Cell,* Second Edition, Garland Publishing, Inc., New York and London, 1989, Fig. 15-12.)

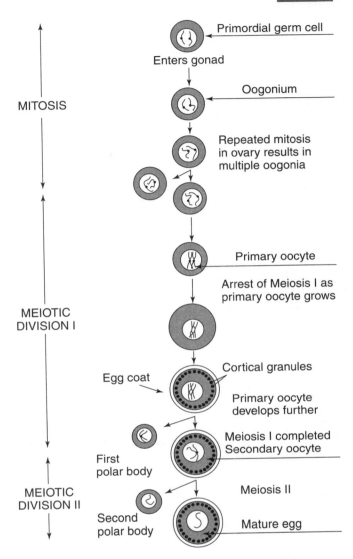

Figure 2-49. Formation of the female gamete.
(Adapted from Alberts, B., Bray, D., Lewis, J., Raff, M., Roberts, K., and Watson, J.D., *Molecular Biology of the Cell,* Second Edition, Garland Publishing, Inc., New York and London, 1989, Fig. 15-25.)

tion in one of the two copies of a gene is not necessarily harmful and may in fact be advantageous.

The gamete known as an egg (oocyte) is larger than most cells. It develops by a process called **oogenesis**. During development of an organism, germ cells go to the gonad (in mammals and many organisms this is the ovary). The oogonium, differentiated from the primordial germ cell, undergoes mitosis to produce even more oogonia, which in turn can become mature oocytes by meiosis. The female is born with all her immature oogonia in place. As the cells mature, they go through the first stage of meiosis to become primary oocytes. When sexual maturity is reached, meiosis resumes at the second stage. The first division produces two cells with a pair of sister chromatids in each. The two cells are of vastly different sizes. One is very small, called a polar body, and the other is large. In turn, the large cell undergoes another unequal division. Oogenesis results finally in the production of three haploid cells, two of which are polar bodies, and one of which is a fully developed egg (see Figure 2-49).

In animals that need to reach maturity before sexual reproduction, maturation of the primary oocyte is con-

trolled by hormones, including a gonadotropin called luteinizing hormone (LH), progesterone, and follicle stimulating hormone (FSH). The egg is surrounded by follicle cells, which communicate with the egg by passing small molecules through gap junctions. The egg itself has a glycocalyx called the zona pellucida (or vitelline layer in nonmammalian eggs) surrounding the plasma membrane. This layer serves as mechanical protection for the egg. Another feature of the egg is a layer of cortical granules just beneath the membrane. On entry of the sperm into the egg, these granules secrete chemicals that alter the glycocalyx layer to prevent a second sperm from penetrating the egg plasma membrane.

The sperm cell (spermatozoon, plural *spermatozoa*) is a very small cell, with a haploid nucleus in the "head" at one end and a flagellum as a tail that propels the sperm toward the egg. The area between the head and the tail is called the midpiece and contains mitochondria to produce energy for the sperm's motion. The head has a coat around it called the acrosome, which contains hydrolytic enzymes. These enzymes break down the egg's outer coat, allowing the sperm to penetrate.

The development of the sperm is very different from that of the egg. **Spermatogenesis** starts only when the organism has reached maturity and occurs in seminiferous tubules in the testes. Immature germ cells are called spermatogonia, and they divide continually during the life of the organism. When needed, some of the spermatogonia stop dividing and go through differentiation to form primary spermatocytes. Sister chromatids are formed in the first round of meiosis, and two daughter cells result. Each daughter cell contains a set of 22 sister chromatids, representing half the genetic component of the parental cells, plus a pair of either X or Y chromatids. During meiosis stage II, each of these daughter cells divides, with half of each pair of chromatids going to each new cell. The spermatid cells are now haploid. Unlike oogenesis, where it is important to maintain the size of the oocyte and polar bodies are formed and sacrificed to this end, all four spermatids are allowed to mature into spermatozoa (see Figure 2-50).

At puberty, release of the gonadotropin called luteinizing hormone stimulates Leydig cells in the testes to produce testosterone. Testosterone is responsible for initiating spermatogenesis.

5.5.1. Fertilization

As sperm meets egg, a process is activated whereby the acrosomal vesicle on the head of the sperm releases its contents in a mechanism analogous to the calcium-mediated release of neurotransmitters from a nerve cell. The released molecules include hydrolases that dissolve the zona pellucida surrounding the egg. This allows the

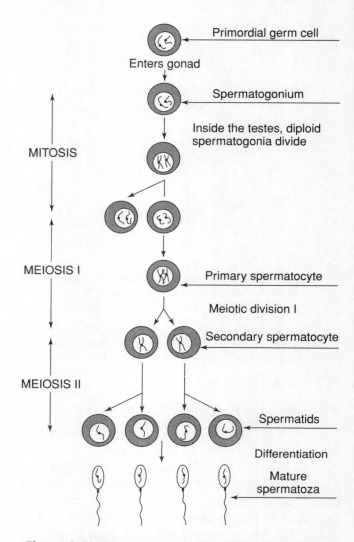

Figure 2-50. Spermatogenesis. It differs in three ways from oogenesis: new cells enter meiosis continually after puberty; each cell generates four mature gametes; a process of differentiation is needed to produce mature sperm. (Adapted from Alberts, B., Bray, D., Lewis, J., Raff, M., Roberts, K., and Watson, J.D., *Molecular Biology of the Cell,* Second Edition, Garland Publishing, Inc., New York and London, 1989, Fig. 15-37.)

genetic material of the sperm to enter the egg. Any eggs or sperm that have not been used in fertilization die within minutes to hours.

The egg, once fertilized, changes its outer membrane to prevent entry of a second sperm, and the process of egg activation is triggered. This occurs via a G-protein–inositol phosphate signaling system (see previous section on signal transduction) and is regulated by ions, particularly calcium and sodium.

5.5.2. Embryogenesis

After fertilization, the first rounds of cell division the cell cycle are shorter than normal because there is little increase in total cellular content (except in mammals, where the protected intrauterine environment allows development to proceed in a more leisurely fashion). The first two to four rounds of cell division are accompanied by use of preexisting maternal mRNA. Only subsequently does paternal mRNA become transcribed, and this is considered the final stage of fertilization. In nonmammals, each cell division results in smaller and smaller cells. In the first stage of **embryogenesis**, the egg divides repeatedly (up to 12 times) with very little gain in total mass. The resulting small cells are called blastomeres and form into a ball known as a **blastula**. When there are about 16 cells present, the blastula has become hollow, and the space inside the ball is called the blastocoel (see Figure 2-51). Eventually (after 12 or so cell divisions), transcription begins to speed up, and the mass of each subsequent cell starts to increase. This is the midblastula transition.

The outside layer of the blastula becomes an epithelial cell sheet of about a thousand cells that can now go through the process of forming a **gastrula**. **Gastrulation** is the mechanism by which an organism gains its multilayered form. The initial step is the migration of a few cells, called primary mesenchyme cells, into the hollowed middle of the blastula ball. These cells migrate to specific sites in the interior of the blastocoel by "walking along" using projections called filopodia. When the cells stop migrating, they become secondary mesenchyme cells. At the same time, the blastula begins to invaginate. Eventually, this invagination makes contact with the inside of the epithelial layer at the opposite side of the blastula. The three embryonic layers are now in place. The invaginated tube is the **endoderm**, the original epithelial layer that remains on the outside is the **ectoderm**, and the mesenchymal cells are the **mesoderm**.

Eventually, the endoderm will become the gut (and associated tissues such as liver and lungs), the ectoderm will give rise to the epidermis (and the neural system), and the mesoderm will become connective tissue (and muscle, urogenital tissue, and the vasculature).

Two more important events now occur. They define the center of the body and also "organize" the development of the **neural tube** (see Figure 2-52). A group of mesodermal cells moves to the center top of the gastrula to form the notochord. In primitive animals, the notochord goes on to form a substitute for the vertebrae; but in more advanced animals, it becomes mesenchyme, which in turn is the source of connective tissue, including cartilage and bone, dermis, muscle, and the vascular system. The ectoderm at the top of the gastrula thickens and forms the neural plate. This folds inward and is pinched off to form a tube, known as the neural tube. The general organization of the organism is now in place.

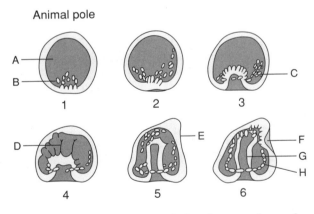

Animal pole

Figure 2-51. Formation of the three embryonic layers. Cells break loose from the vegetal pole of blastula and migrate up the inner wall, and the vegetal pole invaginates. The invaginated epithelium forms the gut tube, and connection of the end of the tube with the epithelium forms the site of the future mouth. A) blastocoel, B) primary mesenchyme cells, C) migrating primary mesenchyme cells, D) filopodia pulling epithelial sheets, E) ventral side, F) future mouth, G) gut tube, and H) future skeleton. (Adapted from Alberts, B., Bray, D., Lewis, J., Raff, M., Roberts, K., and Watson, J.D., *Molecular Biology of the Cell,* Second Edition, Garland Publishing, Inc., New York and London, 1989, Fig. 16-6.)

5.5.3. Early Mammalian Development

In mammals (by definition animals that are viviparous), early differentiation has a component not found in other organisms, for the mammalian embryo must produce an amniotic sac and a placenta. For the first rounds of division, the zona pellucida remains as a protective coat. At the 8- to 16-cell stage, the cell aggregate is called a **morula** (Latin for *blackberry*). The inside of the ball of cells becomes larger to form a blastocyst. One side of the blastocyst develops a multicellular layer,

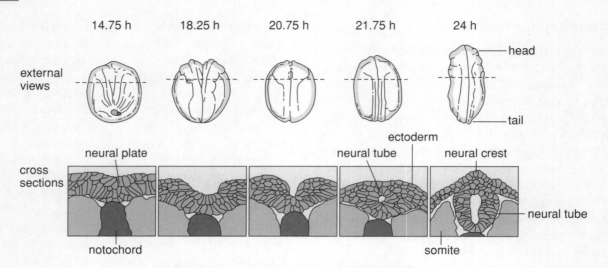

Figure 2-52. Formation of the neural tube.
(Adapted from Alberts, B., Bray, D., Lewis, J., Raff, M., Roberts, K., and Watson, J.D.,
Molecular Biology of the Cell, Second Edition, Garland Publishing, Inc., New York and London, 1989, Fig. 16-13.)

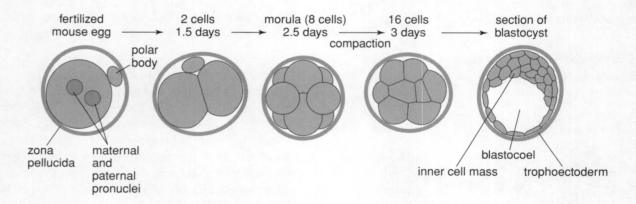

Figure 2-53. Formation of the trophoectoderm (future placenta).
The egg is about 50 microns in diameter.
(Adapted from Alberts, B., Bray, D., Lewis, J., Raff, M., Roberts, K., and Watson, J.D.,
Molecular Biology of the Cell, Second Edition, Garland Publishing, Inc., New York and London, 1989, Fig. 16-23.)

called the inner cell mass, and the other side remains in a single cell layer (the trophoectoderm), as shown in Figure 2-53.

The trophoectoderm makes contact with the uterine wall and gives rise to the placenta. The embryo itself is derived from the inner cell mass, as are the other extra-embryonic structures. The process of gastrulation and formation of notochord and neural tube is similar to that described above for other vertebrates.

5.5.4. From Gastrula to Fully Developed Organism

Now begins the process of **differentiation**. All the cells present at this stage have essentially the same genotype, and various processes must occur in the right places at the right time to produce a fully differentiated organism. Much of this differentiation relies on the positioning of the cells. In the eggs of nonmammalian organisms, the egg has two poles, called the animal and the vegetal poles. Gradients of small molecules, called morphogens, determine the path that a cell developing at a certain place in the gradient will take (see Figures 2-54 and 2-55).

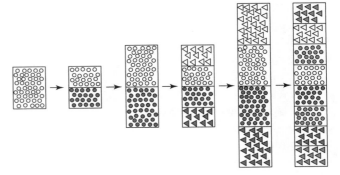

Figure 2-55. Interaction of adjacent groups of cells to produce new types of morphogens. Each symbol represents a positional value. Note that as the cell grows the positional values increase, allowing for more and more differentiation. (Adapted from Alberts, B., Bray, D., Lewis, J., Raff, M., Roberts, K., and Watson, J.D., *Molecular Biology of the Cell,* Second Edition, Garland Publishing, Inc., New York and London, 1989, Fig. 16-43.)

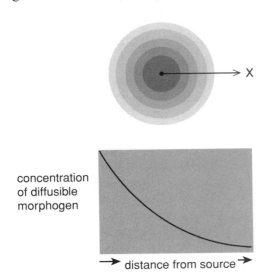

concentration of diffusible morphogen

→ distance from source →

Figure 2-54. Diagram of a two-dimensional version of a morphogen gradient. "X" indicates the initial point from which the gradient radiates. Because the gradients occur in all four directions, each point in the egg has a unique combination of concentrations of small molecules. As soon as morphogens have directed formation of different populations of cells, differentiation becomes guided by a process called induction. Two adjacent groups of cells can organize the production of a third type of cell, and this process can be repeated many times. This organization is mediated by excretion of growth factor morphogens. (Adapted from Alberts, B., Bray, D., Lewis, J., Raff, M., Roberts, K., and Watson, J.D., *Molecular Biology of the Cell,* Second Edition, Garland Publishing, Inc., New York and London, 1989, Fig. 16-42.)

Once a cell has been chosen for a given fate, it must remain in that developmental pathway. A cell in a committed pathway of differentiation is called "determined." At first, the cell may have few, if any, characteristics of the cell type it will eventually become; but with time, the differentiation process will be completed, and all cells derived from this cell will be of the same type. The commitment to a given path seems to occur at some point during gastrulation. At this point, the genes that will be expressed in the final cell type are programmed

to stay active, and those that will not be needed are given instructions to become silenced.

5.5.5. Positional Information

The gradients described above provide gradual concentration transitions. There appears to be a threshold effect in the gradients, however. When a certain critical point on the concentration is achieved, a positional value is imprinted on a cell. A combination of positional values acquired at various time points during development directs further development of the cell. Thus, a cell destined to become a muscle cell can eventually be directed into functioning as a leg muscle cell or an arm muscle cell, depending on the positional information it receives. Positional information has been studied in detail in the fruit fly. Here there are three distinct stages of positional effects. The first is mediated by morphogen gradients. The second stage involves expression of "segmentation genes," which use the morphogen gradient information to put in place the different segments of the fly. The third stage is under control of "homeotic selector genes." The gene products of homeotic genes are transcription factors that control, in the fruit fly, transcription of groups of genes to express a body part, such as a leg or a wing. Analogs of homeotic genes have been found in mammals by looking for genetic similarities, even though at this time there is no evidence of "segmentation" during embryogenesis. A subset of homeotic genes are called homeobox (HOX) genes. These genes encode proteins that contain a homeodomain of about 60 amino acids. Groups of genes that work together (e.g., genes for transcription factors that control development of the heart) code for the same homeobox domain. This domain functions as a DNA-binding domain. Homeotic genes are a functional group (i.e., they are genes that control development), and all homeobox genes code for the homeobox domain. Not all homeotic genes have this domain, and not all homeobox proteins have a homeotic function. Some cancers have been shown to be caused by mutations in homeobox genes.

During development, one also sees differential expression of members of multigene families. An example of a multigene family is the series of genes for globin.

5.5.6. Nuclear/Cytoplasmic Interactions

Interaction between cytosol and nucleus has been shown during oocyte maturation, entry of a zygote into mitosis, and other aspects of development. This has become very apparent during cloning experiments where nuclear transfer occurs. Apoptosis also exhibits nuclear/cytoplasmic interactions.

During regular cell metabolism and growth, communication between nucleus and mitochondria and chloroplasts allows for coordinated expression of nuclear- and organelle-coded proteins.

5.5.7. Tissue-Specific Expression

As tissues and organs develop, cells become dedicated to different functions. This results in large sections of the genome ceasing to be expressed. The expression of a specific complement of proteins in a given tissue is under the control of tissue-specific transcription factors. About 75 percent of all transcribed genes are the same in most cells, but the rest are not. A good example of this is the expression of hemoglobin in reticulocytes. Reticulocyte tissue-specific factors build up complexes to which RNA polymerase binds, and these complexes control transcription of hemoglobin genes. Different tissues may share some of the same factors found in the reticulocyte transcription factor complex, but not all of the factors. It is the unique nature of the complex determined by the presence of specific factors that regulates gene expression. The complement of factors in a given tissue is determined during differentiation.

Molecular Biology

Much of molecular biology is an understanding of vocabulary and jargon. It is suggested that one good study aid is making a list of all the words and word phrases given. If the meaning of anything is not clear in the material given here, you can consult a text or use a search engine on a computer. You will find mostly three types of sites: (1) published research papers probably have the most correct information, but are lengthy and sometimes hard to read; (2) anything on a site with the domain name "edu" is likely to be correct: and (3) descriptions of techniques from the major manufacturers of molecular biology products are also a good and reliable source of information.

1. MENDELIAN AND NON-MENDELIAN INHERITANCE

The first recorded description of genetic inheritance was made by Gregor Mendel in the middle of the nineteenth century. He started his experiments by studying characteristics of growing peas. By ensuring that they were not randomly or self-fertilized, he could follow their genetic **phenotypes** (observable characteristics). Amongst other things, he found that when he applied pollen from a long-stemmed plant to the pistil of a short-stemmed plant and planted seeds from the resulting plants (called F_1, or $Filial_1$, to indicate that they are the first generation derived from an experimental cross), all grew as long-stemmed. These offspring are called **hybrids** and are defined as the offspring of two parents with disparate characteristics. By cross-pollination between these second-generation plants, he produced peas (F_2 generation) that grew in a ratio of 1 short to 3 long-stemmed organisms (see Figure 3-1). Below is an example of results of crossing two plants that are both **homozygous** (both copies of the gene are the same in each organism), but one plant is homozygous recessive and the other is homozygous dominant. The short-stemmed gene is recessive, which means that any time one or both of the genes in an organism is a dominant gene for long stems, the phenotype of plant will be long-stemmed (note that the dominant gene is usually shown as an upper case initial, and the recessive in lower case.)

From many such experiments, Mendel inferred that discrete "units" of heredity controlled phenotypic expression. In the middle of the twentieth century, Avery, McLeod, and McCarty, using bacteria; and Hershey and Chase, using viruses, showed that the genetic material transmitting these characteristics is DNA.

Today, we know that these units described by Mendel are sections of DNA called **genes**, and that the genetic sequence of each organism is called its **genotype**. The

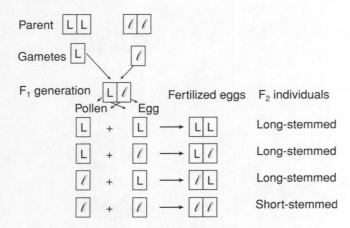

Figure 3-1. Monohybrid cross between a homozygous long-stemmed plant (L) and a homozygous short-stemmed plant (l). All the F1 generation progeny are long-stemmed, and the F2 generation shows a 3:1 ratio of phenotypes.

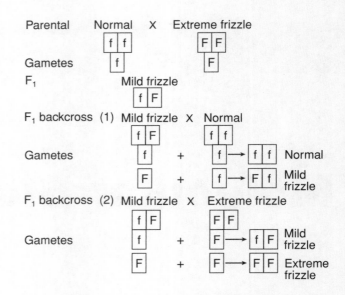

Figure 3-2. Incomplete dominance.
The diagram shows the cross between two homozygotes, the backcross between the mild frizzle offspring and a normal parent, and the backcross between a mild frizzle offspring and an extreme frizzle parent.

two genes at the same locus (place) in each of the two paired chromosomes of an organism are called **alleles** (in the case described above the alleles are for "short-stemmed" and "long-stemmed"). The long-stemmed gene is dominant, because it determines the characteristic of the plant when it is paired with a short-stemmed gene. The short-stemmed gene is considered to be recessive because its expression is dominated by the long-stemmed gene. When an organism has two identical alleles (e.g., long-stemmed and long-stemmed), it is called homozygous. When it has one of each, it is considered **heterozygous**.

Some genes exhibit **incomplete dominance**. In the diagram below (Figure 3-2), one can follow the genotype of chickens that show "normal" and "extreme frizzle" feathers, and also the heterozygote (one dominant and one recessive gene) that gives a "mild frizzle" phenotype. The backcross of the mild frizzle chicken from the F₁ generation with each of the parents confirms the original genotype of each parent by yielding one offspring genetically identical to the parent used in the backcross, and one identical to the F₁ organism.

Codominance is found for some traits, for instance blood groupings. The gene for the *A* red blood cell antigen and the *B* blood cell antigen can both be expressed in the same person, resulting in a person with AB blood.

Every organism is the result of the expression of many genes. Mendel also showed that inheritance of each gene is independent of other genes. We now know that there are exceptions to this rule, and these will be discussed later. To look at these more complicated cases, the **Punnett square** is a useful tool. Below is a simple example of this methodology using only one trait, *B* and *b*. The parents are both heterozygous (Bb), and the phenotypic ratio of offspring is 3:1.

2. PUNNETT SQUARE DIAGRAMS

Two organisms, both heterozygotes for the gene *B* are crossed. Each organism can make two types off gametes, *B* or *b*. The gametes from one parent are listed on the horizontal axis, and those from the other parent on the vertical axis. The combinations of gametes are put in squares, and the genotypes noted (see Figure 3-3).

This gives a ration of one homozygous dominant organism (BB) to one homozygous recessive organism (bb) to 2 heterozygous organisms (Bb). Since the genotype *Bb* has the same phenotype as the genotype BB, the phenotypic ratio observed is 3:1.

	B	b
B	BB	Bb
b	bB	bb

Figure 3-3. Punnett square diagram of a monohybrid cross.

More complicated, and more useful, is a Punnett square of a cross involving genes *A* and *B*. Each parent has an *AaBb* genotype and can produce gametes *AB*, *Ab*, *aB*, and *ab*. All possibilities of the genotypes of male and female gametes are placed on the vertical and horizontal axes, respectively. The resulting F$_1$ generation is determined by placing the combination of gametes in the table (see Figure 3-4). In this case, both parents are heterozygous for both traits.

AaBb

		AB	Ab	aB	ab
	AB	AABB	AAbB	aABB	aAbB
	Ab	AABb	AAbb	aABb	aAbb
AaBb	aB	AaBB	AabB	aaBB	aabB
	ab	AaBb	Aabb	aaBb	aabb

Figure 3-4. Punnett square diagram of a dihybrid cross.

Examination of the results shows that there are 9 combinations with one or both genes *A* and *B* occurring in the dominant form. These will have the dominant phenotype of both genes. Three have at least one dominant *A* and no dominant *B*; these will have a phenotype of dominant *A* and recessive *b*. Similarly, one will see 3 organisms with a dominant *B*, recessive *a* phenotype. Only one organism will be recessive for both traits. The ratio is thus 9:3:3:1.

The above diagrams show the principle of **segregation**. This states that two alleles are separated when germ cells are formed. The corollary to this is the principle of **independent assortment**, the fact that genes for different characteristics are not necessarily inherited together.

In other words, an organism that has the genetic makeup *AaBb* can produce germ cells that are *AB*, *Ab*, *aB*, or *ab*. Some exceptions to this rule are linked genes (genes on the same chromosome), such as genes linked to maleness, called holandric genes; and epistasis, a situation where one gene influences the expression of another. An example of epistasis is the control of coat color in several species, including some cats and some mice. Let us call the gene that codes for pigmentation in fur *F*. An *FF* or *Ff* genotype results in a colored coat, and *ff* results in an albino coat. The gene *C* controls whether the coat is black or brown. *CC* and *Cc* are black, and *cc* is brown. However, when the genotype is *ff*, there is no color at all. So in this case, it makes no difference whether the genotype is *CC* (black), *Cc*, or *cc* (brown); the animal is still albino, and a dihybrid cross gives 9/16 black, 3/16 brown, and 4/16 albino. Compare this with the 9:3:3:1 ratio of the normal dihybrid cross. In this particular example, gene *F* codes for the first enzyme in a pathway leading to the formation of pigment. When both genes are *f*, no pigment can be made, so any instructions for black or brown color are irrelevant.

Mendelian genetics becomes more difficult to analyze when combinations of more than one gene are required for a single trait, such as eye or hair color. These traits are called **polygenic**. Simple Mendelian inheritance patterns are also lost in the case of **pleiotropic genes**. These are genes that have more than one effect. An example of this is the case of a gene controlling a given phenotype and also controlling fitness of an organism. This happens in certain mice where a gene for yellow coat is also lethal. This means that the expected occurrence of yellow coats is not seen in live offspring.

For the most part, any gene has a set incidence (frequency) of dominant and recessive forms in the population. If the dominant allele forms 60 percent of the population of a gene, then 40 percent of the alleles are recessive. The incidence is stated as 0.6 (*p*) and 0.4 (*q*), respectively, and the two probabilities (*p* + *q*) add up to 1. How can one calculate these percentages? The key is to look at the incidence of the recessive phenotype in a population and then apply the Hardy-Weinberg equation. The Hardy-Weinberg equation is the expansion of the binomial $(p + q)^2$, where *p* is the incidence of the dominant gene, and *q* is the incidence of the recessive gene. The expansion is $p^2 + 2pq + q^2$, where p^2 is the number of homozygous dominant individuals, $2pq$ is the number of heterozygotes, and q^2 is the number of homozygous recessive individuals.

For example, if in a population of 1,000, there are 300 individuals that are phenotypically recessive for some trait, x, that means 0.3 is the value of q^2, and q is $\sqrt{0.3}$ (or 0.54). Since $p + q$ must equal 1, then $p = 0.46$. The frequency of homozygous dominant individuals (p^2) is therefore $(0.46)^2$, which equals 0.2, or 200 individuals. And the frequency of heterozygotes is $2pq$, or 0.5 (500 individuals).

Non-Mendelian inheritance is caused by the presence of genes that are not in the nucleus but reside for instance in the mitochondrion. This is an example of "epigenetics" (the inheritance of characteristics that are not coded for by nuclear DNA). In animals, essentially all mitochondria are acquired from the cytoplasm of the egg. This is called **maternal inheritance**. Since there is no reassortment of genes when mitochondria reproduce, the only way in which mitochondrial genetic material can vary is by mutation. Analyses of maternally inherited genes allow for construction of genetic trees and hypotheses on the age and origins of humans and other organisms. In plants, chloroplasts also have DNA and participate in this extranuclear pattern of inheritance, sometimes called **cytoplasmic inheritance**. In some lower organisms where both gametes contribute chloroplasts and mitochondria, the organelles can assort stochastically (randomly and independently), resulting in cells that have organelles from both parents. Other mechanisms for non-Mendelian inheritance, such as those caused by recombination, will be discussed throughout the text.

3. TRANSFORMATION, TRANSDUCTION, AND CONJUGATION

Bacteria do not form gametes and reproduce sexually. Instead, they duplicate their single chromosome and then divide into two daughter cells. There are, however, other mechanisms for reassortment of genetic material. The three ways in which this can happen are transformation, transduction, and conjugation.

Transformation is defined as the uptake and expression of foreign DNA by a cell. It occurs when bacterial cells take up naked DNA and does not require cell–cell contact. In vivo, this DNA is usually a **plasmid**. After the plasmid enters the cell, it can be replicated (as long as it has an origin of replication) and transferred into daughter cells during cell division. Its genes can be also be expressed in its host cell. These are frequently genes for antibiotic resistance, and this is a major mechanism by which populations of bacteria gain antibiotic resistance. Certain bacteria, such as *Bacillus* and *Neisseria*, are readily transformed in vivo. Transformation in cell culture is the process by which naked DNA is introduced into cells that have been rendered "competent" to take up DNA. This is done by exposing the cells to heat shock or incubating them with calcium chloride. The ability to make cells competent is especially important when using *E. coli* for genetic engineering, since *E. coli* is not a strain that can be transformed in vivo. Transformed cells are called hybrids or **recombinants**. The experiments by Avery, Macleod, and McCarty that showed DNA as the "transforming factor" were done in 1944.

Transduction refers to the introduction of exogenous DNA into a bacterial cell by a bacteriophage. The bacteriophage growing in the host cell sometimes packages its own replicated DNA into a bacteriophage coat before release from a cell. Sometimes it also packages a mixture of a portion of the host cell DNA along with its own phage DNA. On infection of a new cell, the phage DNA (either just phage-specific or phage plus co-packaged DNA from the previous host) is integrated into the DNA of the infected cell and reproduced as the cellular DNA undergoes cell division. Transduction is also the name used for the process whereby viruses (including tumor viruses) insert their DNA into a eukaryotic cell.

Conjugation, like transformation, is the process of transfer of a plasmid from one bacterial cell to another, but unlike transformation and transduction, conjugation requires direct cell–cell contact. The plasmid to be transferred from one gram-negative cell to another carries genes for a structure called a sex pilus (plural *pili*), a tube connecting two cells to facilitate transfer of the plasmid. Gram-positive cells can produce adhesive materials that anchor the two cells together. During transfer, a single-stranded copy of the plasmid is transferred to the recipient cell, where the complementary strand is synthesized to give a double-stranded plasmid.

In *E. coli*, conjugation often involves duplication and transfer of the F (fertility) factor from an F⁺ cell to an F⁻ cell, thus making the recipient cell F⁺ also (see Figure 3-5).

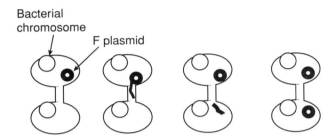

Figure 3-5. Transfer of F factor between cells.
In the first figure, the bacterium containing the F plasmid is called F⁺, and the other, which has no F plasmid, is F⁻. The second two figures show a single strand copy of the plasmid traversing the pilus between the two cells. After synthesis of the second strand of the plasmid in the recipient cell, that cell also becomes F⁺.

Sometimes the factor integrates into the chromosome, creating what is known as an *Hfr* cell (high frequency recombination). Conjugation between an Hfr cell and a F⁻ cell results in replication and transfer of only part of the F factor attached to a segment of adjacent host DNA (see Figure 3-6). The recipient cell is

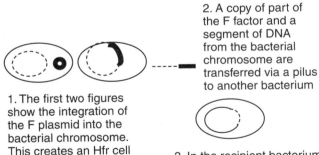

1. The first two figures show the integration of the F plasmid into the bacterial chromosome. This creates an Hfr cell

2. A copy of part of the F factor and a segment of DNA from the bacterial chromosome are transferred via a pilus to another bacterium

3. In the recipient bacterium, the part of the F factor is discarded, and the piece of foreign DNA is integrated into the chromosome

Figure 3-6. Conjugation between an Hfr and an F⁻ cell.

still F⁻, since it still does not contain a complete F factor gene, but it has acquired new genetic material from the previous host and is now a recombinant.

4. RECOMBINATION AND COMPLEMENTATION

The term **recombination** in genetics is defined as moving pieces of DNA without the loss or addition of even one base pair. The mechanisms for recombination will be described below in the section on DNA recombination.

Complementation in genetics implies that a gene that is defective on one allele can be "complemented" by another allele that is not defective. In complementation, the wild-type activity is restored without any cleavage and splicing of the DNA. In eukaryotes, natural complementation occurs when one copy of a chromosome carries a defective gene and the other does not. In fact, the complementation test can be used to determine whether defects occur in the same or different genes (see Figure 3-7). The test is done by mating organisms with mutations to produce hybrid offspring.

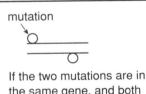

mutation

If the two mutations are in the same gene, and both alleles produce mutant protein, no functional protein is produced. The mutations are said to be "trans".

Here the two mutations are in the same allele. One allele produces mutant protein, and the other wild-type. The mutations are "cis".

Figure 3-7. Two alleles of a single gene, indicating trans and cis mutations.

When the results of cross-breeding indicate that the mutations appear to be in the same gene, this is called **functional allelism** or **putative allelism,** even if the mutations are actually not in the same gene. For mutations in different genes, a *trans* configuration produces one organism with a wild type, and one with a mutant gene.

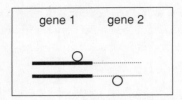

Figure 3-8. Two genes, each with one mutant allele.

The phenotype for the organism shown above would be wild type for both genes, since it carries one wild type gene for each trait (see Figure 3-8). The complementation test thus allows comparison of the products from DNA with *trans* mutations and assignment of the mutations to a single gene or two different genes.

Complementation tables can be created to aid with determination of the locus of a mutation. For example, one could diagram a set of organisms thus:

Genotype	Phenotype
A− B+ C+ crossed with A− B+ C+	A− B+ C+
A+ B− C+ crossed with A+ B− C+	A+ B− C+
A+ B+ C− crossed with A+ B+ C−	A+ B+ C−
A− B+ C+ crossed with unknown	A+ B+ C+
A+ B− C+ crossed with unknown	A+ B− C+
A+ B+ C− crossed with unknown	A+ B+ C+

A comparison of the crosses with known genotypes allows easy identification of the mutation in the unknown as in this case in the B complementation group.

In multimeric proteins (proteins with more than one subunit), a mutation in one allele produces some monomers that are wild type, and some that are mutant. When a mixed oligomer is formed, the mutated monomer often prevents the wild-type monomer from functioning. This is called negative complementation. In prokaryotes complementation can be effected by transforming a cell carrying a defective protein with a plasmid carrying a gene for a functional protein.

5. MUTATIONAL ANALYSIS

Mutational analysis is the study of the relationship of mutations in the genotype and the observation of the resulting phenotype. It can be considered in two ways. The first is where a mutation already exists, and the genetic basis of the mutation is sought. The other is where a new mutation is introduced into a wild-type gene to study the effect of the mutation on the function of the protein. This latter, called directed mutagenesis, is used most frequently when studying the characteristics and mechanism of action of a protein. This will be discussed in the section on Methodology.

How can we study a gene with a preexisting mutation? The most definitive way is to isolate and sequence the gene. There are other more rapid ways of comparing wild-type and mutant genes, however. These include restriction fragment length polymorphism (RFLP) and microarrays (also discussed in the Methodology section).

There are various types of mutations, including **point mutations**, as well as a group of mutations that involve larger changes in the DNA. Point mutations are a change in one base pair. The change creates a different codon, but sometimes the new codon codes for the same amino acid as in the wild-type codon. This is called a silent or neutral mutation, as it produces a wild-type protein. A mutation that results in the insertion of an amino acid with characteristics very similar to the wild-type amino acid (e.g., leucine for valine) is called a conservative mutation, and the resulting protein is often fully functional. A more drastic change, say insertion of lysine instead of aspartate, frequently leads to an inactive or otherwise functionally altered protein. This type is called a missense mutation. Nonsense mutations describe point mutations that create a stop codon and code for a truncated protein. Here are the definitions of various point mutations.

Wild-type codon	TTA	(leucine, a hydrophobic amino acid)
Point mutation	TTG	(still leucine, a silent or neutral mutation)
Point mutation	ATA	(isoleucine, a conservative mutation)
Point mutation	TCA	(serine, a hydrophilic amino acid, a missense mutation)
Point mutation	TAA	(termination codon, a nonsense mutation)

At the level of the bases, point mutations can be divided into two types, **transition** and **transversion**. A transition occurs when a base pair of a purine (adenine or guanine) and a pyrimidine (thymine or cytosine) are changed to another purine and pyrimidine, and transversion is the exchange of a purine/pyrimidine pair for a pyrimidine/purine pair.

Transition	Transversion
NNNANNN to NNNGNNN	NNNANNN to NNNCNNN
NNNTNNN NNNCNNN	NNNTNNN NNNGNNN

(*A* stands for the purine base adenine; *C* stands for the pyrimidine base cytosine; *G* stands for the purine base guanine; *N* stands for any nucleotide; and *T* stands for the pyrimidine base thymine.)

Other types of mutations are caused by deletion or insertion of one or more bases, leading to a frameshift in coding. These mutations may also lead to proteins that are nonfunctional. Mutations also occur by rearrangement of DNA sequences and intron/exon splicing errors.

The most accurate and definitive test for mutations is DNA sequencing. This is, however, time-consuming and expensive, and more rapid tests have been developed. RFLP can be used. **Polymorphism** in DNA sequences is defined as sequences that exist in several different forms from organism to organism within a single species. The test detects changes in restriction sites due to polymorphism. When polymorphic genes are cut by restriction endonucleases, fragments of different lengths occur because differences in sequence lead to differences in presence or absence of restriction endonuclease sites. These fragments can be separated by polyacrylamide gel electrophoresis (PAGE). Gene microarrays are used extensively for medical diagnosis of mutations, such as those that predispose people to breast cancer, and polymerase chain reaction (PCR) is used to detect mutations in several ways. All three of these techniques are described in the section on Methodology.

6. GENETIC MAPPING AND LINKAGE ANALYSIS

Crossing-over (see material on Cell Biology) often results in more than one gene moving from one chromatid to another (see Figure 3-9). It may be assumed that any two genes that move in concert are close together or "linked." An analysis of this phenomenon gives rise to the concept of **genetic linkage**, and can be used as a first approximation for **genetic mapping**. The recombination (crossing-over) event may be measured in one of two ways. The first is analysis of phenotypic expression of mutations found on the section of DNA in question, and the second is by tracing changes in restriction patterns. In the first case (genetic mapping), a trait, such as the occurrence of cystic fibrosis, is examined in a number of people in a family. It is noted whether the cystic fibrosis "gene" always appears linked to some other phenotypic trait or marker (for instance light-colored eyes). If it does, it may be reasonably assumed that the two genes (cystic fibrosis and light-colored hair) are close enough that even with the occurrence of crossing-over, the two traits are inherited together. The distance between genes is measured in units of "morgans," (one centimorgan is the equivalent to approximately a million base pairs) named after a pioneer (Thomas Hunt Morgan) of the study of genetic mapping using fruit fly phenotypes. The sequencing of the human genome has been of great benefit to listing as many markers as possible. A further refinement of this process is the gathering of data for the ongoing HapMap (haplotype map, a **haplotype** being the genetic characteristics of only one of each pair of chromosomes).

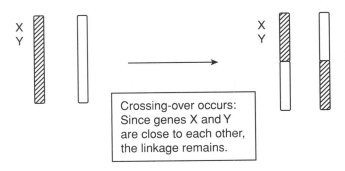

Crossing-over occurs: Since genes X and Y are close to each other, the linkage remains.

Figure 3-9. Crossing-over.

The other method (called physical mapping), is to perform restriction endonuclease digestions. Analysis of overlaps places the resulting fragments in order (see RFLP in the Methodology section). Each fragment can also be sequenced. This method can also identify single nucleotide polymorphisms (SNPs). These are a change in a single nucleotide.

7. CHROMATIN AND CHROMOSOMES

7.1. Karyotypes

Each eukaryotic organism has its own characteristic number of pairs of chromosomes. For instance, humans have 23 pairs (22 are autosomal, and one pair has the X and Y sex chromosomes), for a total of 46 chromosomes. Cats have a total of 38 chromosomes, and many plants have 18 (9 pairs).

Chromosomes are normally diffuse and difficult to count, but administration of colchicine, a drug that inhibits microtubule (spindle fiber) formation and stops mitosis (see Cell Biology section) at a stage called c-metaphase, permits individual chromosomes to be visualized. This can be done in cell culture (or the intact organism), and the cells can be harvested and displayed on a glass slide. In humans, the cells of choice for karyotyping are lymphocytes. For prenatal diagnosis, cells from amniotic fluid or biopsies of chorionic villi may be used. Stains are applied to c-metaphase chromosomes, and this allows visualization of specific banding patterns on the chromosomes. The slide is photographed, and images of individual chromosomes may be cut from the picture and arranged in pairs. This enables identification of gender, chromosomal abnormalities such as trisomy 21 (Down syndrome), and other mutations that alter the banding patterns. Today, automatic methodology and computer technology facilitate karyotyping.

The human haploid genome contains 3,000,000,000 DNA nucleotide pairs, divided among 22 pairs of autosomal chromosomes and 1 pair of sex chromosomes. See Figure 3-10 for a representation of human chromosomes.

Prokaryotes, mitochondria, and chloroplasts have a single circular chromosome. As a result, karyotyping is not applicable to these organisms and organelles.

7.2. Translocations, Inversions, Deletions, and Duplications

Over time, exons and entire genes can be duplicated. This has an evolutionary advantage because a mutation

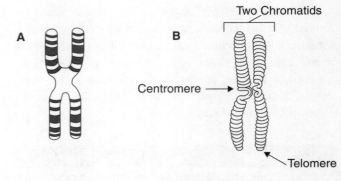

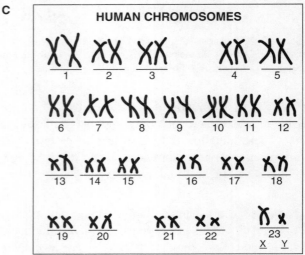

Figure 3-10. Representation of the 23 paired chromosomes of the human male. a) Stained chromosomes. b) Structure of a chromosome (typical metaphase chromosome). c) Karyotype of a male. This cartoon of a photomicrograph is adapted from K. F. Jorgenson, J. H. van de Sande, and C. C. Lin, *Chromosoma 68* (1978): 287–302. Source for a-c is http://www.accessexcellence.org/RC/VL/GG/human.html.

in one copy of the sequence on a chromosome can be compensated for by the wild-type copy on the same chromosome. In a million years this occurs for a given gene with approximately a 1 percent probability. The copied sequence sometimes accumulates changes, leading to divergence where the organism acquires different characteristics. Some copies become pseudogenes that are not expressed. An example of duplication and divergence can be seen in the gene families (see Figure 3-11) for the globin chains of hemoglobin (α and β) and myoglobin, and for rRNAs (ribosomal RNAs). Sometimes genes are deleted. If this is not a lethal event, the deletion is perpetuated in subsequent generations.

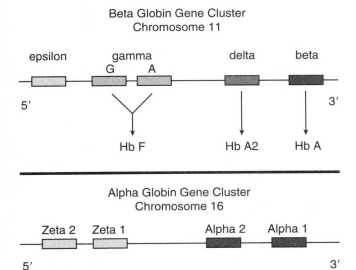

Beta Globin Gene Cluster
Chromosome 11

epsilon gamma delta beta
G A

5′ 3′

Hb F Hb A2 Hb A

Alpha Globin Gene Cluster
Chromosome 16

Zeta 2 Zeta 1 Alpha 2 Alpha 1

5′ 3′

Figure 3-11. Gene families.
(Adapted from http://sickle.bwh.harvard.edu/hbsynthesis.html.)

If the duplicated DNA sequence is moved to another chromosome, this is called a translocation. **Translocations** are often facilitated by a transposon (see later). Sometimes the duplicated material is inserted in the opposite direction from the original DNA sequence. This duplication is considered an **inversion**.

All of the above events lead to evolutionary changes that add to the benefit of sexual reproduction and introduce hybrid vigor, an advantage endowed by variation in the gene pool.

7.3. Aneuploidy and Polyploidy

Mammals are generally **diploid** or 2N (2 copies of each chromosome). This is called **euploidy**, meaning a good number. A cell with only one copy of each chromosome is called haploid.

Under certain circumstances, a cell may lose or gain a chromosome. This is known as **aneuploidy**, and examples are Down syndrome (trisomy 21, or three copies of chromosome 21); Turner's syndrome (monosomy, or only one copy of the X chromosome and no Y chromosome); Klinefelter's syndrome (XXY); trisomy X, or triple X syndrome (XXX); and XYY syndrome. These examples of **triploidy** are gen-

erally caused by nondisjunction of the chromosomes during meiosis.

Other examples of triploidy occur when the organism has three copies of each chromosome caused by fertilization of an egg by two sperm, and this is almost inevitably fatal in animals. Only if the organism is a mosaic (having cells with different chromosome complements or genes) with most of the cells being normal can such an organism survive.

Some plants, however, are bred to be triploid, as this gives them characteristics desirable to the consumer (size, lack of seeds). An autopolyploid organism has three chromosome copies that are all the same, whereas an allopolyploid organism has three copies, two the same and one different. This breeding technique has been exploited to create organisms such as apriums and pluots. These two fruits are derived from apricots and plums and have many copies of their chromosomes.

7.4. Structure

The hierarchy of structure in the chromosomes of eukaryotes begins with the double helix formed by the polymer of phosphates, sugars, and bases in DNA. In Figure 3-12A a simplified depiction of a DNA polymer is shown. Note that the 3′ hydroxyl group on the sugar (deoxyribose) is the site of chain lengthening during replication (see later). Also to be noted is that deoxyribose has no 2′ hydroxyl on the sugar, whereas ribose (in RNA) has both 2′ and 3′ hydroxyl groups. The presence of two hydroxyl groups makes RNA labile to alkaline hydrolysis whereas DNA is resistant to alkaline hydrolysis.

The helices form grooves on the outside as they twist around. The grooves are alternately larger and smaller and are called the major and minor grooves (see Figure 3-12B). The grooves present binding sites for DNA-associated molecules. The double-helical structure is stabilized by hydrophobic interactions between stacked bases on the inside of the helix and by hydrogen bonding between paired bases (see Figure 3-12C). The phosphate groups are on the outside of the helix and add to the stabilization by charge repulsion.

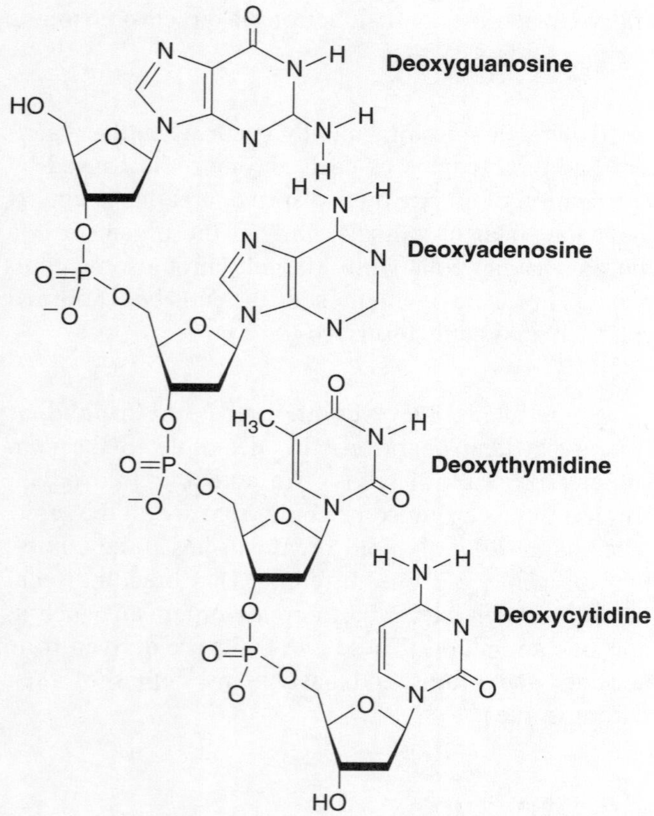

Deoxyguanosine

Deoxyadenosine

Deoxythymidine

Deoxycytidine

3'-terminus

Figure 3-12A. A single strand of DNA.
(Adapted from Devlin, T.M., ed., *Textbook of Biochemistry with Clinical Correlations*, Fifth Edition, Wiley-Liss, New York, 2002, Fig. 2.8.)

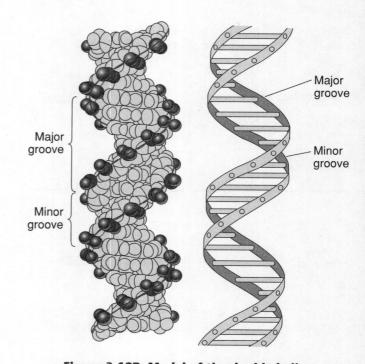

Figure 3-12B. Model of the double helix, showing the major and minor grooves.
(Adapted from Devlin, T.M., ed., *Textbook of Biochemistry with Clinical Correlations*, Fifth Edition, Wiley-Liss, New York, 2002., Fig. 2.17)

it may be involved in regulation of gene transcription. The section on Cell Biology covers further information on DNA structure.

This same negative charge allows the DNA to interact with basic proteins called histones that contain a high percentage of lysines and arginines. This is discussed in the Cell Biology section on the nucleus. Other small molecules that are highly positively charged are associated with DNA. These include polyamines (putrescine, spermidine, and spermine). DNA, when complexed with its associated proteins, is called **chromatin**.

The DNA double helix occurs in several conformations. The A and B forms are both right-handed helices, and in the A form, the bases are stacked more tightly with the base pairs at an angle to the sugar-phosphate backbone. The A form is found under conditions of low humidity. The B form is the usual form. Its base pairs are at a right angle to the backbone. Z-DNA is left-handed and found in sections of DNA with alternating purines and pyrimidines. Its function is not known, but

The ratio of bases obeys Chargaff's rules: [A] = [T] and [C] = [G] and [purines] = [pyrimidines]. This is a result of the pairing of bases, each pair always containing one purine and one pyrimidine. Different species have different ratios of A/T (paired by two hydrogen bonds) and G/C (paired by three hydrogen bonds). This can be observed by examining the hyperchromicity following denaturation of DNA of various species. DNA absorbs ultraviolet light at 260 nm. Double-stranded DNA has a smaller absorption coefficient at that wavelength than single-stranded DNA (or RNA) because the light-absorbing bases are partially obscured in the compact DNA structure. Monitoring absorption, therefore, can be used to examine the fraction of DNA remaining in a double helix at a given temperature. This allows calculation of the percent of G/C pairs in a DNA sample. The triple hydrogen bonds between guanine and cytosine require the input of more heat to break than the double hydrogen-bonded adenine/thymine pairs. The temperature at which the absorption value reaches 50 percent of

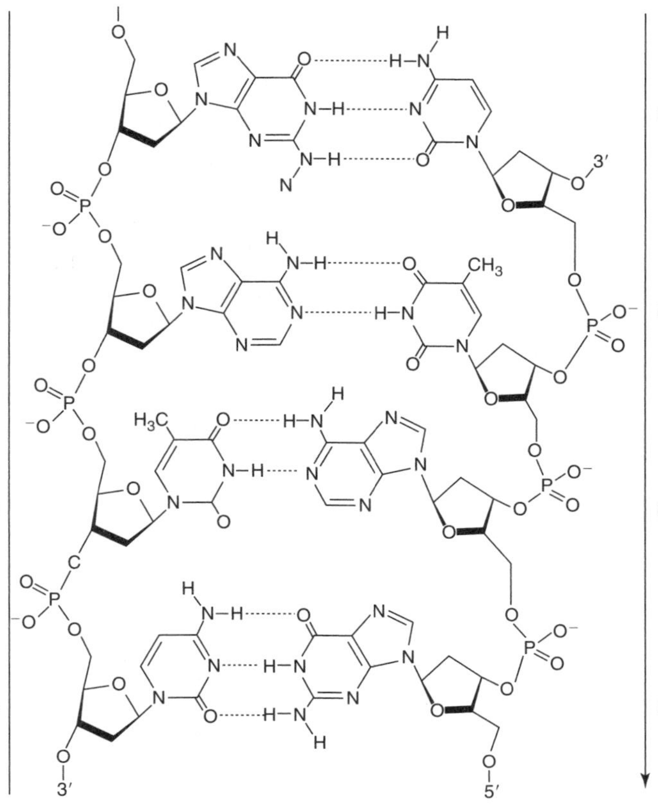

Figure 3-12C. Double-stranded DNA showing base pairing.
(Adapted from Devlin, T.M., ed., *Textbook of Biochemistry with Clinical Correlations,* Fifth Edition, Wiley-Liss, New York, 2002, Fig. 2.18.)

its maximum is called the "melting" temperature (T_m), as shown in Figure 3-13.

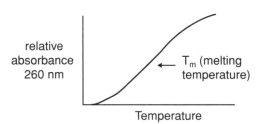

Figure 3-13. Melting curve.

8. GENOMICS

8.1. Genome Structure

A **genome** is the complete set of genes of an organism (a transcriptome includes only those genes that are transcribed). The number of base pairs in the genome of an organism ranges from 10^6 (mycoplasma) to greater than 10^{11} (some plants and amphibians). The minimum size of a genome increases as the phylum becomes more complex (i.e., mammals have a larger minimum genome size than birds); but apart from this general rule, there appears to be no correlation between complexity of a particular organism and genome size. This may be explained by the fact that much DNA appears to be noncoding, for example introns, and therefore the total size of the genome does not reflect the number of genes.

8.2. Repeated DNA and Gene Families

An examination of the number of copies of genes and other DNA sequences reveals that the genome can be divided into three groups: (1) single copy (nonrepetitive) DNA, (2) moderately repetitive DNA, and (3) highly repetitive DNA (also called simple sequence

DNA). The amount of repetitive DNA increases as organisms become more complex. The term *reiterated* is also used to describe DNA sequences that are repeated. *Reiterated* is a qualitative term and usually applies to sequences that are longer than those that are considered repetitive. C_ot curves (C_ot annealing depends on both *concentration* and *time*) are used to measure the proportion of the three groups of genes. To do this, DNA from an organism is denatured and sheered into small pieces. The pieces are allowed to reanneal, and the absorbance at 260 nm is monitored. Some of the pieces (those that are present in large numbers of copies) find partners at a lower C_ot value and hybridize to each other. Moderately repetitive sequences take longer to hybridize, and the single-copy DNAs take the longest (see Figure 3-14).

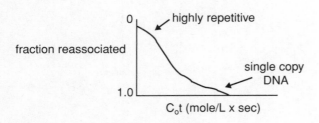

Figure 3-14. Cot curve.

Similar hybridization experiments can be used to determine the closeness or relatedness of two species. For these experiments, DNA from both species is sheered and allowed to rehybridize. The more similarity there is between the DNA from the two species, the lower the C_ot value at which the DNA will hybridize. Some highly repetitive sequences are called satellite DNA, because after shearing, they break into small lengths that migrate to a different place from the rest of the DNA on centrifugation in a CsCl density gradient.

Single-copy DNA sequences include both active genes and pseudogenes and make up about half of the human genome. Much of it is found at the centromeres of chromosomes, where it remains permanently condensed in a form of DNA called **heterochromatin**. This is different in structure from that of most DNA that is found in the amorphous, euchromatin structure. Moderately repetitive sequences are repeated up to several thousand times, and are interspersed between single-copy sequences.

Examination of the sequence of DNA leads to identification of **open reading frames** (orfs). These start with the initiation codon and end with a stop codon, signaling the beginning and end of sequences coding for proteins. Before and after the sequence that codes for a protein are untranslated regions (5' and 3' UTRs). In eukaryotes, many genes are "split," that is they have sequences called **exons** that code for protein, and **introns** that are interspersed. Introns are copied into mRNA (messenger RNA) together with exons but are then cleaved from the mRNA before translation. There are specific DNA sequences that signal the intersection of introns and exons. This will be covered in the section on protein synthesis.

It should be noted that mutations in different exons coding for the same protein, even though far apart, cannot complement one another, since they are still in the same gene (complementation group). Gene families (also discussed earlier) are sets of genes whose exon sequences are related. They are derived from gene duplication with subsequent divergence of sequence. Sometimes there are two or more identical genes (e.g., the gene for the α chain of hemoglobin) on the same chromosome. These are called nonallelic copies. Families of genes usually code for proteins with the same function, such as the different types of actin found in different tissues of the body. The protein products of these genes may share a functional domain, such as a DNA-binding domain.

Families are found within one organism. *Orthologs* are genes that are analogous in different organisms.

DNA also has inverted repeats, or palindromes. Short palindromic sequences act as specific restriction endonuclease target sites (see Methodology section). Longer inverted repeats in eukaryotes can form stable hairpin structures.

8.3. Centromeres and Telomeres.

Centromeres are regions found approximately in the middle of chromosomes. In condensed chromosomes, they form the site of attachment of the kinetochore (see Cell Biology section) during mitosis and meiosis. In stained mitotic chromosomes, they appear as nodes joining the two chromatids together. The chromosome arms on either side of the centromere are known as the *p* and *q* arms.

Telomeres are the outer ends of the chromosomes, and are made up of repeating sequences. The progressive shortening of the telomeres with each replication of the chromosome, caused by the inability to replace the RNA primer at the end of the lagging strand (see later discussion of DNA replication), appears to contribute to the "aging" clock. There is some evidence that cancer cells may retain an enzyme called telomerase that can keep replacing the telomeres and provide another mechanism for making cells immortal. Telomerase adds a short DNA sequence (TTAGGG in vertebrates). It acts as a **reverse transcriptase** that carries its own RNA template for this sequence.

8.4. Gene Identification

Genes can be identified by using sequence data and searching for open reading frames, with their attendant promoter regions, and for splice sites. The extensive information produced from the various genome projects and the use of computer software has made this possible. The use of computers and databases has introduced the term *in silico* to the vocabulary of the life scientist. Sequences can be compared to known genes from other species, and *motif* searches used to determine the possible function of a gene. Motifs, found in expressed proteins, can be either similar short stretches of primary structure or similar secondary structure arrangements, such as a helix-loop-helix. A good way to determine gene organization on the chromosome is by comparing the chromosome with unknown gene order to a chromosome from another species that has already been characterized. This tendency of gene order to be conserved from species to species is called **synteny**.

8.5. Transposable Elements

Transposons (transposable elements) are pieces of DNA that can move on their own from one place to another. They are the driving mechanism behind most evolutionary change. They can also move other pieces of DNA with them, are not restricted to insertion at any particular site on the DNA, and occur both in prokaryotes and eukaryotes. In prokaryotes, each transposon codes for all the genes used in its movement (the enzymes are called transposases), whereas many eukaryotic transposons have

lost that ability and have to rely on "moving" enzymes coded for by other transposons. Transposon movement can cause deletions, insertions, and inversions. A single transposon may insert at two or more different places, causing gene duplication. Unequal crossing-over between the two copies can produce gene rearrangements.

Recombination by transposons and insertion sequences does not necessitate matching sequences in the target DNA. Human DNA has many long interspersed elements (LINES) and short interspersed sequences (SINES) that originated as transposons. The genome contains numerous Alu sequences, and these are examples of SINES. The term *Alu* refers to the presence of an Alu restriction site in the roughly 300 base pair mobile elements. Alu sequences are also examples of a group of transposons called **retrotransposons** because it is believed that they were reverse-transcribed from mRNA into DNA by reverse transcriptase before insertion. They may retain introns from the unprocessed mRNA.

A transposon is made up of an insertion sequence (IS) flanked by inverted repeats. The site of insertion is a specific short sequence of nucleotides. During insertion of the transposon, these nucleotides are caused to repeat in the same direction as diagrammed in Figure 3-15.

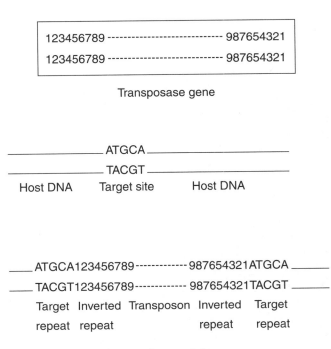

Figure 3-15. A bacterial transposon.

Figure 3-15 shows the product of transposon insertion. The dashed line represents the insertion sequence (IS). In bacteria this includes the gene(s) necessary for insertion. At either end of the IS, the numbers represent the inverted terminal repeats. After insertion, the target sequence is duplicated, and these sequences are direct repeats. The length of the transposon can vary, as can the insertion sites, and these characteristics are described by the nomenclature, such as IS2 or IS50R. Composite transposons (also called composite elements) carry other genes. For example the Tn series of bacterial transposons carry genes for antibiotic resistance. Transposons cause gene rearrangement by several mechanisms, including addition and deletion of genes.

9. GENE MAINTENANCE

9.1. DNA Replication

As we discuss DNA replication, repair, and recombination we shall see that there are many **DNA polymerases** involved. For reference, here is a table (Table 3-1) of the polymerases and their functions.

All DNA is double stranded. It is assumed that this is a safeguard against damage to one strand. A damaged strand can be repaired by using the undamaged strand as a template. DNA replication has to copy both strands, sometimes referred to as the "Watson and Crick" strands. The mechanism is semiconservative and was first described by Meselson and Stahl in a classic experiment where they grew bacteria in a medium containing "heavy" nitrogen (N^{15} ━━━) and then replaced the medium with one containing the common "light" nitrogen (N^{14} ———). They then grew the bacteria for several generations; isolated DNA after each cell doubling; and used density centrifugation to determine whether the DNA contained light or heavy nitrogen, or some intermediate between the two. The original DNA showed both strands to be heavy, but after a round of replication in the light medium, the DNA showed a band with density intermediate between light and heavy. On the second round, there were two bands: light and intermediate. This showed the semiconservative nature of DNA replication, defined as each new double-stranded helix having one parental strand and

**Table 3-1.
Polymerases and Their Functions**

Prokaryotic (*E. coli*)	
Pol I	Completion of Okazaki fragment, DNA repair
Pol II	DNA repair, damage bypass
Pol III	Major enzyme for replication
Pol IV	Damage bypass
Pol V	Damage bypass
Eukaryotic	
Pol α	"Primase" for replication
Pol β	Base excision repair
Pol γ	Mitochondrial DNA synthesis
Pol δ	Major enzyme for replication
Pol ε	Not determined
Pol ξ	Damage bypass
Pol η	Damage bypass
Pol ι	Damage bypass

one new daughter strand. This is diagrammed in Figure 3-16.

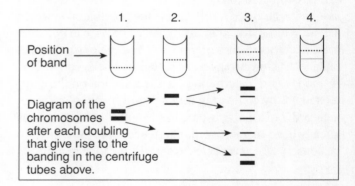

Figure 3-16. Centrifugation of DNA shows semiconservative replication.

In tube 1 (Figure 3-16), the banding of the original heavy chromosomes is shown. Tube 2 shows an intermediate band after the first doubling, indicating that the daughter chromosomes are composed of one heavy strand and one light strand. Tube 3 shows the banding after two doublings. There is an equal mixture of the heavy/light chromosomes and the completely light chromosomes. After numerous doublings, the two chromosome pairs that are heavy/light will persist, but all other chromosomes will be completely light. This is diagramed in tube 4, where only a residual intermediate band is shown.

9.2. The Challenges of DNA Replication

There are three major problems to be solved in order for DNA to be replicated successfully. One is the condensed and twisted structure of the DNA molecule. The second is the fact that DNA polymerases (DNA-dependent DNA-polymerases), the enzymes that synthesize DNA, can only work in one direction. Since DNA is antiparallel, that would seem to necessitate that synthesis would start at a different end of each strand and move in opposite directions. The third problem is that DNA polymerases cannot start synthesis of a DNA strand without a primer. We will look at each of these three problems and their solutions.

Problem 1 is due to the tightly packed nature of chromatin. This hinders binding of enzymes necessary for DNA replication, so the structure must be opened up to allow access. This is accomplished by topoisomerases. These enzymes break a phosphodiesterase bond in the DNA and anchor the free end via formation of a phosphodiesterase bond to the primary structure of the topoisomerase itself. By covalently attaching the DNA to its active site, the topoisomerase ensures the genome does not become unstable. The DNA can then be rejoined in an unwound form by creating a new phosphodiesterase link in the DNA. Topoisomerases Type I make a break in one strand, and topoisomerases Type II break both strands. Another enzyme involved in minimizing the supercoiled structure is DNA gyrase. Once the DNA superstructure has been simplified, the strands are separated by binding to enzymes called helicases. As these enzymes move along, opening more DNA, single-stranded DNA binding proteins (SSBs) bind to the single-stranded DNA to prevent it from reannealing.

The second problem in DNA replication is the problem of copying the DNA in both directions (i.e., one strand must be synthesized in the 5′–3′ direction, and the other in the 3′–5′ direction), as illustrated in Figure 3-17. DNA polymerase will only synthesize DNA 5′–3′ (see Figure 3-18). This problem is overcome by contin-

uous synthesis of one strand (the leading strand) 5′–3′, and the other (lagging strand) discontinuously in small sections 5′–3′ but in the effective overall order 3′–5′ (see Figure 3-19). This accomplishes the aim of replicating both strands in the same area simultaneously.

Figure 3-17. Antiparallel arrangement of the DNA double helix.

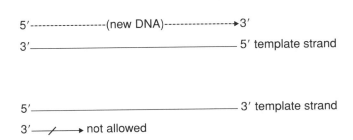

Figure 3-18. Replication of the above double strand does not occur in the 5′–3′ direction.

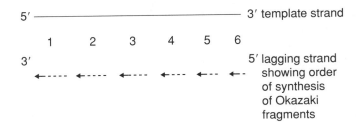

Figure 3-19. Solution to problem of prohibition of 3′–5′ synthesis. Although the individual Okazaki fragments are synthesized 5′–3′, the overall result is synthesis of the entire strand in the 3′–5′ direction.

As shown in Figure 3-19, the synthesis of the continuous, leading strand presents no problems, and the synthesis of the other strand occurs in the same direction by making small segments in the 5′ to 3′ direction at a time. These segments are called **Okazaki fragments**. Eventually, the Okazaki fragments (100–1,000 nucleotides long) are ligated together to form an unbroken DNA strand. This will be discussed later.

The third problem mentioned above is the inability of DNA polymerases to start synthesis of a DNA strand without a primer. How can a primer be made if the DNA polymerase will not synthesize it? The answer is to use, in prokaryotes, an RNA polymerase called a primase, which does not require a primer, to make a short complementary RNA strand. From this, DNA polymerase can begin copying the template DNA. In eukaryotes, the priming function is fulfilled by an RNA-synthesizing primase/DNA polymerase α complex that synthesizes the RNA primer (Figure 3-20). The short RNA strand is later removed and replaced with DNA. Both leading and lagging strands require this RNA primer. The primer is from 1 to 60 nucleotides long, depending on the organism.

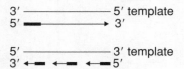

Figure 3-20. Use of an RNA primer (▬▬▬) for the leading and the lagging strand.

What else is needed to replicate DNA? So far we have discussed unwinding, the bidirectional nature of synthesis, and the need for an RNA primer.

DNA synthesis starts at defined locations on DNA. Eukaryotes have many of these sites, called *ori* (origin of replication). The circular prokaryotic genome has only one. In eukaryotes, this means that many areas of DNA are being replicated at one time, and this results in "bubbles" in the DNA with a replication fork at each end of the bubble. Figure 3-21 shows multiple origins of replication in a length of eukaryotic DNA.

In eukaryotes, synthesis ceases when a new strand from one bubble meets the strand being copied from the adjacent bubble, or when the strand reaches the end of the chromosome. In prokaryotes, synthesis ends when the entire circular chromosome has been replicated.

At this point, the new strands, both leading and lagging, still have RNA primers (---) attached at the 5′ end, and the lagging strand still consists of Okazaki fragments with RNA primers attached. The diagram below shows a diagram of the 5′–3′ strand in Figure 3-21.

To finish the synthesis, the RNA primers must be removed, as shown.

The resulting gaps in the DNA are filled in using the free 3′ hydroxyls as starting points.

In prokaryotes, the same polymerase (polymerase I) removes the RNA primer and synthesizes the fill-in DNA. In eukaryotes, two enzymes are required to remove the RNA: RNAse H and flap endonuclease I (FENI). DNA polymerase δ then fills in the gap. In both prokaryotes and eukaryotes, the disconnected DNA sequences are joined by DNA ligase.

During DNA synthesis, it is important that the polymerase stay attached to the DNA template and not fall off. This ability is called processivity, and it is enabled by the presence, in eukaryotes, of a sliding clamp called

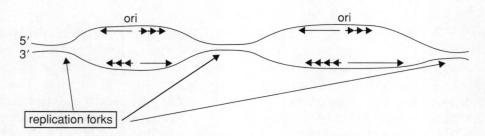

Figure 3-21. Multiple origins of replication.

a proliferating cell nuclear antigen (PCNA) that encircles the DNA and keeps the polymerase bound to the DNA template.

On the lagging strand, the attachment and release of the clamp occurs as each Okazaki fragment is synthesized. The clamp is attached by an ATP-dependent clamp loading factor, also called replication factor C (RFC).

DNA polymerases can (fortunately rarely) make mistakes and insert the incorrect base. The newly synthesized strand must be proofread and edited to replace these incorrect bases. The DNA polymerases responsible for DNA synthesis have this ability. They have a 3′–5′ exonucleolytic function that can remove newly added bases that are incorrect and replace them with the correct bases.

As stated above, DNA replication stops when replication forks meet. In prokaryotes, this is 180° from the origin of replication, and the circle is closed by the action of a ligase. In eukaryotes, DNA is divided into linear chromosomes. This leaves the DNA strands incomplete at the ends of the chromosome (see Figure 3-22).

Figure 3-22. Two DNA strands immediately after replication is almost completed.

At the ends of both strands (Figure 3-22) are tandem repeats of six nucleotides, called telomeres, with the G-rich strand extending slightly longer. The shorter strand becomes even more truncated after removal of the primer. It cannot be extended by DNA polymerase as the gap to be filled is 3′ to 5′.

The enzyme telomerase has a short stretch of RNA (complementary to the repeated sequence at the end of the DNA) as part of its structure, and it uses this as a primer. The enzyme works as a reverse transcriptase and synthesizes DNA that is homologous to the template. It can then dissociate, move along the strand, and continue making more copies of the repeated sequence (see Figure 3-23).

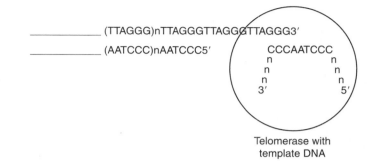

Figure 3-23. Telomerase.

Cells that have differentiated and are destined to divide only a few more times do not contain telomerase. As these cells age, the telomeres shorten. This gives the DNA a finite life. A mark of cancer cells is that they start to synthesize telomerase that replaces the telomeres, endowing the cells with immortality.

The final step as DNA synthesis proceeds is restoration of the superstructure by topoisomerases and gyrases. Actions of these enzymes result in DNA in a form that can be repackaged in the nuclei of the daughter cells.

9.3. DNA Damage and Repair

DNA can be damaged by several mechanisms. A single base pair mutation (point mutation) may occur because of insertion of the incorrect base during replication or by chemical mutagenesis, such as deamination of cytosine to form uracil, adenine to hypoxanthine, or guanine to xanthine. Other mutations result in depurination (removal of a purine base) to form abasic sites (apurinic, or AP sites) or in oxidation or alkylation of a base. Some mutagens can form cross-links between strands. Sometimes intrastrand dimers of bases occur, most commonly dimerization of adjacent thymines, caused by ultraviolet radiation from sunlight (both natural and artificial). Different mechanisms of repair are used for different types of DNA damage.

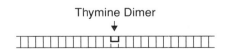

Figure 3-24. Thymine dimer.

Thymine dimers (Figure 3-24) can be removed by photoreactivation in which the covalent bond between the two bases is removed by a photoactivated enzyme called photolyase. This is common in prokaryotes but rare in mammals. Higher organisms generally repair pyrimidine dimers using excision repair. Mutations in the enzymes for excision repair cause xeroderma pigmentosum, a disease characterized by sensitivity to light and susceptibility to cancer.

Mismatch repair is used for mutations where the two bases opposite each other are no longer complementary due to a replication error. It is important that the repair occurs on the strand with the incorrect base, and not the correct strand. To enable this, the repair must occur immediately after the DNA is replicated and before site-specific methylation occurs, catalyzed by a "maintenance methylase." Mismatch repair is carried out by enzymes known as the *mut* family. This involves the same mechanism as excision repair.

Excision repair (see Figure 3-25) is used in cases of base damage, such as deamination or unwanted methylation. Either one base (base excision repair, BER) or a sequence of several nucleotides (nucleotide excision repair, NER) on either side of the mutation is removed, and a new sequence complementary to the other DNA strand is synthesized.

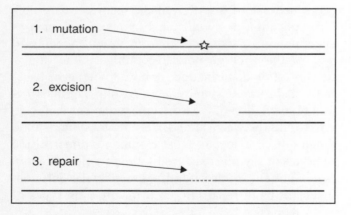

Figure 3-25. Excision repair. In base-excision repair, only one base is removed; in nucleotide excision repair, several nucleotides are removed.

The first step in BER is the cleavage of the incorrect or damaged base from the deoxyribose by a glycosylase.

Two enzymes cut the sugar-phosphate, one on either side, to remove the rest of the nucleotide. These enzymes are an endonuclease and a lyase. The single nucleotide gap is filled in by a polymerase (pol II in *E. coli* and pol β in eukaryotes), and a ligase joins the two DNA sequences.

For NER, the base is not removed first, but rather a single enzyme complex introduces strand breaks (the incision step) several nucleotides away on both sides of the damaged base. This section is removed (in the excision step by a 5'–3' exonuclease), the gap is filled in by a DNA polymerase, and the DNA is joined by a ligase. It should also be noted that methyl groups adventitiously added to guanine can also be removed directly by a methylase.

In cases where a base(s) is replaced, removed, or restored directly, as in thymidine dimer repair or removal of a single base prior to excision of the sugar-phosphate, the base must be "flipped" to the outside of the double helical structure for the action of the repair enzymes. This is called *base flipping*.

When a section of damaged DNA is not removed before DNA replication occurs, the damage can sometimes cause the DNA polymerase to leave a gap in the new complementary strand that is synthesized (Figure 3-26). The gap is filled by migration and excision of the matching DNA segment from the other parental strand. The new gap created can now be filled correctly by a polymerase. Excision repair can now occur on the original lesion. This is called **daughter strand gap repair** and is a recombination event. Recombination repair requires a family of proteins called the *Rec* proteins, of which *RecA* is the best studied. As in any recombination event, recombination repair requires the new daughter strand containing the gap to line up with the parent strand containing the correct sequence for the transfer of the "patch" to occur.

After the segments from the parental DNA have been used to fill the gap, the gap now left in the parental strand is filled in (dotted arrow in Figure 3-26) using the daughter strand as template. Sometimes, DNA replication simply stops when a damaged area is reached, and the replication fork collapses, allowing reannealing of the parental strands and repair of the damage. The process of replication then resumes.

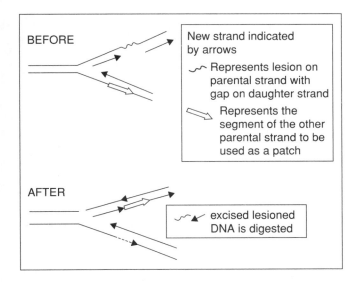

Figure 3-26. Daughter strand gap repair.

An alternative method of reading through lesions such as those described above is by "bypass" synthesis. This uses a polymerase without stringent proofreading characteristics. This polymerase often puts in the wrong base, resulting in introduction of a permanent mutation. Fortunately, this is rare since bypass enzymes are distributive, meaning that they lack processivity and are only transiently bound to the DNA.

Double strand breaks between repeated sequences, caused for example by irradiation, are repaired by **single strand annealing (SSA)**, shown below (Figure 3-27).

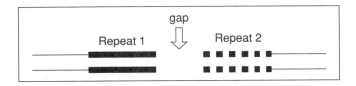

One strand of the DNA slides along until it matches the previous repeat.

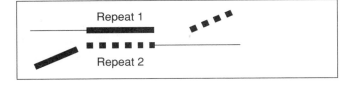

Overhangs are excised, DNA polymerase fills in the gaps (indicated by the dotted lines), and the strands are sealed by a ligase. The net result is an intact double strand containing one fewer repeat of the repeated sequence.

Figure 3-27. Single strand annealing.

In eukaryotes the two most common methods of repair of double strand breaks are homologous repair (Figure 3-28) and non-homologous end-joining.(Figure 3-29). Homologous repair is far the more accurate of the two methods, but it requires the availability of a homologous sequence of DNA.

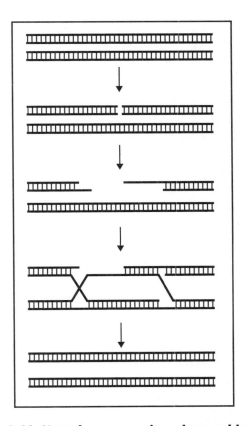

Figure 3-28. Homologous repair and recombination.
The strand with the double break is trimmed to form overhanging ends. "D loops" form as the strands from the two double strands cross over and are used as templates for new strands.

213

Non-homologous end-joining (NHEJ) is the more common mechanism for repairing double strand breaks, since it does not require that homologous DNA be present. It consists of four steps, the first of which is recognition of the broken ends by a heterodimeric protein called *Ku*. The ends are then trimmed and any gaps are filled and finally ligated (Figure 3-29).

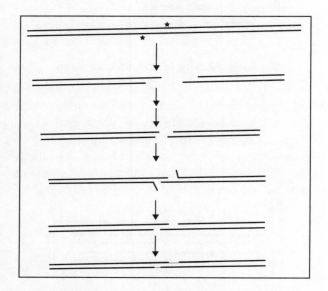

Figure 3-29. Non-homologous end-joining.

How do cells know that repair is necessary? This is best understood in *E. coli* where a group of genes arranged in **operons** (see below) controls what is called the SOS response. Because all the operons share a common repressor (*LexA*), they are considered to be part of a **regulon**. The exact signal for repair initiation is not known, but one requirement is a single-stranded length of DNA. The SOS signal cascade is initiated by the *RecA* protein. *RecA* causes cleavage of the *LexA* protein, rendering it incapable of repressing the repair regulon.

9.4. DNA Modification

DNA can be modified by **methylation**. The methylating enzymes ("maintenance methylases") are active only immediately after replication. These enzymes require that one strand be already methylated for activity. When only one strand is methylated, it is called hemimethylation. The methyl donor is S-adenosylmethionine (AdoMet, also called SAM). The methylation serves in prokaryotes as a "self-recognition" system.

For instance, the DNA of *E. coli* is methylated at the recognition sites of the Eco R family of endonucleases and prevents the bacterial cell from destroying its own DNA. Foreign DNA is methylated at different sites and can be recognized and cleaved by *E. coli* restriction endonucleases.

In eukaryotes, methylation, particularly of cytosine to form methylcytosine (mC), is a signal that the gene that is methylated is not to be transcribed. The methylated sequences are recognized by regulatory proteins that suppress transcription and frequently also aid in a tighter folding of the DNA. A deficiency in a DNA methylase can cause hereditary metabolic disease. In some cases, only one of the allelic genes (either maternal or paternal) will normally be expressed. This departs from normal Mendelian expectations of inheritance. Methylation is the mechanism for silencing of the unwanted gene and is one mechanism of "imprinting." *Imprinting* is the term used for the decision that only one of the two alleles will be expressed. A failure of this methylation results in both genes being expressed. Mutations in methylases are also causative in some cancers, cardiovascular disease, and immune disorders. Aging can alter methylation patterns and give rise to some of the conditions we associate with this condition. Modifications of DNA other than methylation are rare and generally found only in parasites.

9.5. DNA Recombination and Gene Conversion

Homologous (general) **recombination** in eukaryotes and **gene conversion** occurs at the 4 chromosome (8 chromatid) stage of meiosis (first meiotic prophase)—see the earlier discussion of meiosis in the Cell Biology section. The exchange of genetic information is done at the chiasmata that are formed at the end of pachytene and diplotene during gametogenesis in both females and males. It can occur at any position in the DNA but is absolutely precise so that each chromatid retains the same amount of DNA after the exchange as before. It can involve a single base pair or a longer sequence, but the exchange is always between alleles. Recombination involves numerous proteins, many of which are part of the *Rec* and *Ruv* protein families. The series of diagrams in Figure 3-30 follows this process in a stepwise manner.

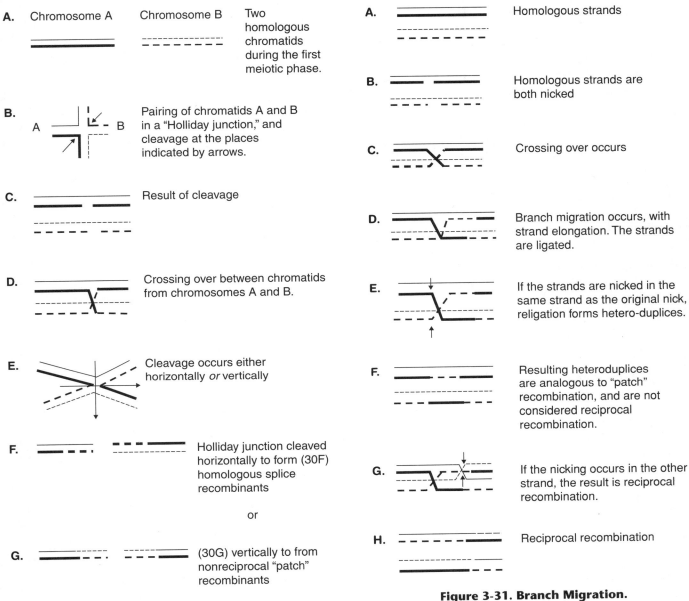

Figure 3-30. DNA recombination.

Figure 3-31. Branch Migration.

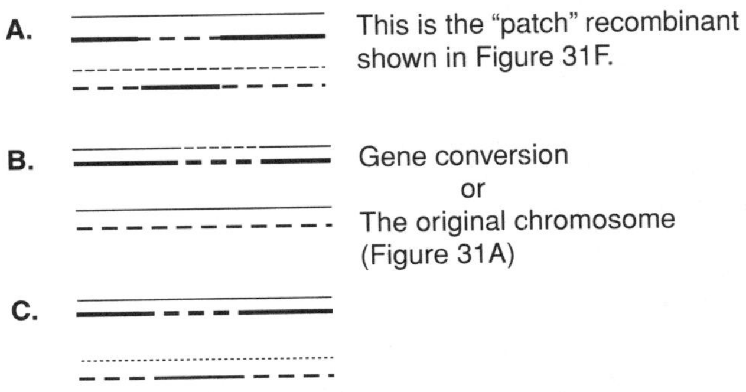

Figure 3-32. Gene Conversion.

9.6. Branch Migration

Branch migration can occur during recombination This starts with homologous sequences on two chromosomes. This process is diagrammed in Figure 3-31.

9.7. Gene Conversion

Another event that can follow the above processes is **gene conversion**, diagrammed in Figure 3-32.

Other similar models have been proposed for homologous recombination, but all are based on the initial formation of a Holliday junction. Lambda phage integration and recombination occurs by an analogous mechanism catalyzed by an integrase, but requires association with a protein called IHF (integration host factor) to form a structure called an intosome.

Non-homologous recombination (specialized recombination) in prokaryotes can be site-specific. This occurs when a phage carries a short DNA sequence that matches a sequence on the bacterial chromosome. The enzyme that catalyzes insertion (an integrase or recombinase) can also remove the sequence. Site-specific recombination is mediated by staggered strand breakage and re-ligation. The breaks form staggered ends, similar to the staggered ends found in cleavages by restriction endonucleases.

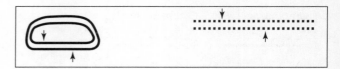

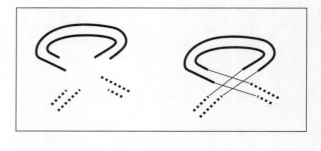

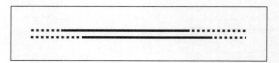

Figure 3-33. Integration of bacteriophage lambda into the *E. coli* chromosome.

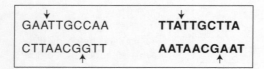

Cleavage and re-ligation at the points indicated by the arrows results in the following:

Because some phages are circular, such re-ligation can result in integration of the phage into the bacterial genome (see Figure 3-33).

An unusual case of recombination occurs in some RNA viruses, where the RNA polymerase can switch from strand to strand of the double-stranded template, making a hybrid product.

9.8. The Genetic Code

As described in the Biochemistry section, DNA is a double helix made up of antiparallel complementary strands. Shortly after the discovery of its structure by

James Watson, Francis Crick, and Rosalind Franklin in 1953, Marshall Nirenberg discovered that the coding for amino acids resides in triplets of bases. He did this by synthesizing stretches of oligonucleotides and placing them in a mixture of amino acids and all the other machinery necessary for translation. He found that a sequence of *U*'s coded for a polypeptide consisting entirely of phenylalanine. But when he synthesized a polymer of alternating *U*'s and *A*'s, he got incorporation of alternate isoleucine and tyrosine. He deduced that:

AUAUAUAUAUAU

was read as:

AUA UAU AUA UAU

and that either UAU or AUA coded for isoleucine. He could then use:

AAUAAUAAUAA
(read as either AAU AAU, etc. or AUA AUA, etc.).

		U	C	A	G	
	U	UUU ⎤ Phe UUC ⎦ UUA ⎤ Leu UUG ⎦	UCU ⎤ UCC ⎥ Ser UCA ⎥ UCG ⎦	UAU ⎤ Tyr UAC ⎦ UAA ⎤ Stop UAG ⎦	UGU ⎤ Cys UGC ⎦ UGA Stop UGG Trp	U C A G
5′	C	CUU ⎤ CUC ⎥ Leu CUA ⎥ CUG ⎦	CCU ⎤ CCC ⎥ Pro CCA ⎥ CCG ⎦	CAU ⎤ His CAC ⎦ CAA ⎤ Gln CAG ⎦	CGU ⎤ CGC ⎥ Arg CGA ⎥ CGG ⎦	U C A G	3′
	A	AUU ⎤ AUC ⎥ Ile AUA ⎦ AUG Met	ACU ⎤ ACC ⎥ Thr ACA ⎥ ACG ⎦	AAU ⎤ Asn AAC ⎦ AAA ⎤ Lys AAG ⎦	AGU ⎤ Ser AGC ⎦ AGA ⎤ Arg AGG ⎦	U C A G
	G	GUU ⎤ GUC ⎥ Val GUA ⎥ GUG ⎦	GCU ⎤ GCC ⎥ Ala GCA ⎥ GCG ⎦	GAU ⎤ Asp GAC ⎦ GAA ⎤ Glu GAG ⎦	GGU ⎤ GGC ⎥ Gly GGA ⎥ GGG ⎦	U C A G

Figure 3-34. The genetic code.
(Adapted from Alberts, B., Bray, D., Lewis, J., Raff, M., Roberts, K., and Watson, J.D.,
Molecular Biology of the Cell, Second Edition, Garland Publishing, Inc., New York and London, 1989, Fig. 3-15.)

This coded for incorporation of isoleucine and asparagine, showing that AUA codes for isoleucine, UAU codes for tyrosine, and AAU codes for asparagine. Following a series of experiments of this general type, the entire code was determined (Figure 3-34).

The first letter of the codon (5′) is read down the left side, the second across the top, and the third down the right side of each group of four codons. For example, aspartate is coded by GAC. It may be seen that there are 64 codons (4 letters arranged in sets of three (4^3 is 64), and that three codons are indicated as "stop" codons (sometimes called termination or nonsense codons, and known as amber, ochre, and umber). These codons cause termination of protein synthesis. For some amino acids (e.g., alanine) there are two or more codons, and because of this the code is called degenerate. The 5′ codon in an expressed mRNA sequence at the beginning of the open reading frame codes for the first amino acid to be inserted into a polypeptide (i.e., it codes for the amino acid at the N-terminus of a polypeptide). The mRNA and the polypeptide are considered "co-linear."

As stated above, several amino acids have more than one codon. For instance, phenylalanine is coded for by UUU and UUA. The tRNA that carries the **anti-codon** (see discussion later) often has an inosine (I) in the position that pairs with the 3′ *U* or *A* of the codon. *I* can pair with both *U* and *A*, so the same anticodon can serve to match both codons:

Anticodon   3′ AAI 5′   or   3′ AAI 5′

Codon   5′ UUU 3′   5′ UUA 3′

This phenomenon is called the "wobble hypothesis," as it requires that the base on the anticodon at the 5′ position be associated less firmly with the corresponding base in the codon than in the normal pairing. Because of the wobble, there are fewer tRNAs (the carriers of the anticodons) than the 61 that would be needed for an exact match of every codon. The number of codons per amino acid is not related to the frequency of occurrence of that amino acid in proteins, and in fact, the codon usage frequency for a particular amino acid varies from species to species.

The genetic code is not quite universal. Exceptions to the code shown above occur in mitochondria and some more primitive species of organisms. Additionally, there is at least one case where certain cells can adapt a codon to give a different response from normal; for instance, under certain circumstances the stop codon UGA can be used to instruct the protein synthetic machinery to insert selenocysteine into a protein.

9.9. Transcription

Before we start our discussion of transcription, let us look at the various characteristics of **RNA polymerases** (see Table 3-2).

Transcription is the process by which RNA is synthesized as a complementary copy of the DNA code. The enzymes responsible are called DNA-dependent RNA polymerases. Only specific lengths of DNA (genes) are used as templates at any one time, and which are used is originally determined by cell type and the environment (e.g., presence of hormones) and other regulators. This will be discussed later.

The sections of DNA to be used as templates are indicated by methylation of the DNA and its associated histones, which serves to repress transcription of the methylated sequence, and by acetylation of histones, which acts to reverse gene repression. Sometimes the methylases, demethylases, acetylases, and deacetylases are considered to be transcription factors (see later discussion) since they help regulate transcription.

Once a section of DNA to be transcribed is identified, two related types of signals are necessary for initiation of transcription. The first family of signals are sequences within the DNA itself, called **promoters**, control elements, and **enhancers**. The second related

set of signals lies with molecules, called **transcription factors**, which bind to the sequences on DNA.

First, let us consider the DNA sequences. Promoters are sequences that begin "upstream" from the start of transcription. There are also other sequences that are not called promoters but that also facilitate transcription initiation. Enhancer sequences that increase the number of transcripts synthesized lie either "upstream" or "downstream" of the start of transcription.

Promoters are sequences of about 6 nucleotides. The nature of these sequences was identified by searching for sequences that were present upstream from several genes. When several such sequences were identified, this suggested that they might be promoters, and they were called "consensus sequences" because they were identified by sequence similarity. Subsequently, cloning and mutation experiments have confirmed that these sequences are indeed promoters. In prokaryotes, the two most common promoters are the **Pribnow box** and the **−35 sequence**. The Pribnow box is about 10 nucleotides upstream from the start of transcription and has the sequence T*A*TAAT*, where the bases followed by asterisks are the most conserved from gene to gene and species to species. The other common sequence, the −35 sequence, is T*T*G*ACA. The asymmetry and directionality of the promoter sequences ensure that transcription can only proceed in one direction. Tran-

**Table 3-2.
RNA Polymerases**

	Eukaryotic I (A)	Eukaryotic II (B)	Eukaryotic III (C)	Mitochondrial	Prokaryotic
Location	Nucleolus	Nucleus	Nucleus		
Function	rRNA	mRNA, viral RNA	tRNA, 5S rRNA	All mitochondrial RNA	All RNA
Sensitivity to α-amanitin	Insensitive	Very sensitive	Intermediate sensitivity	None, but sensitive to rifampicin	Sensitive to rifampicin

scription usually starts 5–8 nucleotides beyond the last *T* of the Pribnow box and generally starts at a purine base.

In eukaryotes, the promoter sequences are the **TATA box** (TATA(A/T)(A/T)A, where (A/T) means that the nucleotide can be either an *A* or a *T*, and the **CAAT box** (GG(T/C)CAATCT). The TATA box is about 25 nucleotides upstream from the start of transcription, and the CAAT box precedes it at about −75. Other short conserved sequence elements can be involved, including the *GC box* (GGGCGG) at −90. This can be present in multiple copies. A specialized family of promoters is the family of hormone response elements (HRE) to which hormone/receptor complexes bind. HREs include the estrogen response element (ERE) and the glucocorticoid response element (GRE).

Both prokaryotes and eukaryotes also have sequences called enhancers that increase the rate of transcription up to 100-fold. These sequences can reside upstream or downstream of the start of transcription, and the sequences may appear in either direction.

The sequences described above serve as recognition and binding sites for the proteins necessary for transcription. First, we shall consider the binding of proteins other than the RNA polymerases, for it is these proteins that largely determine when a particular gene will be transcribed. These proteins bind to the DNA at the promoter regions. They include the transcription factors of the TFII family (in the case of polymerase II that transcribes mRNA), and factors that are specific for the tissue, such as the HNF (hepatocyte nuclear factors) that regulate the genes specific to liver function. Another common transcription factor is SP1. It binds to the GC box. After recruitment of the RNA polymerase to the DNA/proteins complex, the multiprotein aggregation is called the basal transcription apparatus.

The frequency of transcription is regulated by the binding of activators to short consensus sequences, either in the promoter region or in the enhancer. This enables formation of the basal transcription apparatus. Examples of such activators are the hormone-receptor complexes (also called ligand-activated transcription factors, or LATF) that bind to hormone response ele-

ments. Coactivators are proteins that bind to both the proteins of the basal activation complex proteins, and to the activators, to link them.

Another group of regulatory transcription factors are the "silencers" that prevent assembly of the basal transcription apparatus and prevent transcription. There are also proteins called "insulators" that bind to the DNA to prevent binding of transcription factors and enhancers.

How do all these proteins interact with the DNA? They do so by the presence in their structures of special motifs designed to fit into or around the helical DNA. These include zinc "fingers," which are looplike stretches of amino acids stabilized by zinc molecules. These fingers fit into the major grooves of the DNA. Other motifs are the helix-turn-helix and the helix-loop-helix, which also fit in the major groove of the DNA helix. Leucine zippers are protein motifs consisting of two leucine-rich alpha helices. These fit along the length of the DNA like two blades of a pair of scissors. Many transcription factors have a domain of 60 amino acids known as a homeodomain. A factor may have one or many of the above domains and motifs (see section on Cell Biology).

As stated above, much of the regulation of genes to be transcribed occurs by methylation and acetylation of DNA and histones. Transcription factors themselves can also be activated and inactivated. The best example of this is the family of ligand activated transcription factors that bind DNA only when complexed to the activating ligand, usually a steroid hormone.

Once the basal transcription apparatus is in place, a DNA-dependent RNA polymerase can initiate synthesis of RNA. In eukaryotes which polymerase transcribes a given gene depends on whether the gene codes for a protein, in which case a polymerase II (B) transcribes mRNA. Other polymerases transcribe tRNA and rRNA genes (see Table 3-2).

In *E. coli*, there is only one RNA polymerase, and it synthesizes all RNA. It has five subunits (β, β', α, ω, and σ). The first four subunits listed constitute the core enzyme and are together capable of RNA synthesis, but at random start points. Addition of the σ subunit forms the holoenzyme and restricts the polymerase to initiation at a promoter. This is a more common type of transcriptional regulation for prokaryotes than is formation of a basal transcription apparatus (the more common mechanism for transcriptional regulation in eukaryotes). There is a family of σ subunits with specificity for different types of genes. The difference between prokaryotic and eukaryotic RNA polymerases has been exploited for antibiotic therapy. For instance, rifampicin (rifampin) inhibits only the prokaryotic enzyme, stopping expression of bacterial genes while allowing transcription of eukaryotic genes to continue.

Synthesis of RNA proceeds as described for DNA synthesis with some notable exceptions: (1) Only one strand is copied, and therefore discontinuous synthesis is not needed; (2) no primer is necessary; (3) substrates are ribonucleotides, not deoxyribonucleotides; (4) *U* is inserted instead of *T*; and (5) only discrete segments of DNA are transcribed.

Synthesis of a transcript in prokaryotes comes to an end at the appropriate place either by ρ-dependent termination or by ρ-independent termination. Rho-independent termination occurs when the RNA being synthesized has a sequence such that it folds back on itself to form a stem and loop structure. Rho-dependent termination is mediated by the Rho protein. The Rho protein appears to facilitate termination by winding the RNA around itself to stop transcription. Messenger RNA is rarely processed in prokaryotes, and since there is no nucleus, ribosomes can attach to mRNA as it is synthesized and begin synthesis of protein even before the RNA transcript is finished. This is called simultaneous or coupled transcription/translation.

Eukaryotes have several RNA polymerases. There is one in mitochondria that is responsible for all transcription in that organelle. In the nucleus, there are three RNA polymerases. RNA polymerase II (pol II) transcribes mRNA; polymerase III (pol III) transcribes 5S rRNA and tRNA; and polymerase I (pol I), located in the nucleolus, transcribes the remaining rRNAs. The binding of RNA polymerases to DNA in eukaryotes is nearly always controlled by the formation of the basal

transcription apparatus. The three eukaryotic nuclear RNA polymerases can be differentiated by their sensitivity to the mushroom-derived poison, α-amanitin. Pol II is inhibited by very small amounts of the poison, pol III only by higher concentrations, and pol I is almost completely insensitive.

It is the extensive synthesis of rRNA that makes the nucleolus look darker than the rest of the nucleus. The area where the rRNA genes are located is called the nucleolar organizer, and it contains hundreds of copies of the genes for the 28S, 5.8S, and 18S rRNAs separated by spacer sequences. Initiation of transcription by pol I is regulated by the binding of class I transcription factors and pol I to sequences in these spacer regions.

Initiation of transcription of the 5S rRNA by pol III also has a unique characteristic. The site of binding for the transcription factor IIIA is actually located within the sequence of the gene itself.

The stop signals for transcription in eukaryotes are different from those of prokaryotes. Transcripts formed by pol I and pol III may be terminated in one of two ways. Sometimes the polymerase recognizes a specific sequence and is released from the DNA template. Alternately, the polymerase continues synthesizing RNA beyond the desired end of the transcript, and an endonuclease clips off the excess RNA. Pol II termination is less well understood. The polymerase can read and transcribe more than a 1,000 nucleotides beyond the desired end of the transcript. In higher eukaryotes, the excess is then cleaved just beyond a sequence AAUAAA in the newly synthesized RNA. At this point, all three RNAs in eukaryotes need to be processed since they all have excess nucleotides.

When messenger RNA has been transcribed from DNA, it contains both the open reading frame (orf) as well as UTRs (untranslated regions) that lie before and after the orf. The orf is the segment of the RNA that actually codes for a protein. The UTRs will serve other roles. Immediately after synthesis, the entire transcript is called pre-mRNA and must be processed before it can leave the nucleus. In eukaryotes, three essential events need to occur: (1) capping, (2) addition of a poly-A tail, and (3) splicing.

The first modification of mRNA occurs during transcription. A "cap" is added to the 5' end. The first nucleotide put in place by pol II is either *A* or *G* (purines) All three phosphates remain attached. This makes the start of the transcript look like the following:

$$5'ppp(A/G)pNpNpN$$

Then pppG is added to the 5' end by an enzyme called guanylyl transferase. It is added in the 3'–5' orientation, and three phosphates are hydrolyzed in the process. The cap and the start of the transcript then looks like the following:

$$3' \quad 5'5' \qquad 3'$$

$$Gppp(A/G)pNpNpN$$

Methylation of the guanine cap and the first base of the original transcript then occurs. Further methylation is possible in some cases. The 5' end is now protected from exonuclease digestion.

The addition of a poly-A tail at the 3'end of the mRNA transcript is initiated by binding of a specificity component called CPSF (cleavage-polyadenylation specificity factor) to the AAUAAA sequence. This organizes the cleavage of the excess RNA (see above), binding of poly (A) polymerase that can add up to 200 *A* residues, and also association of poly (A) binding protein (PABP). PABP binds to the poly-A tail in the process of its synthesis, and keeps the poly (A) polymerase from dissociating totally from the complex before the poly-A tail has reached its required length. A few mRNAs are not polyadenylated, but instead have a hairpin loop at the 3' end.

All RNA found in the nucleus is larger than the final form (see later discussion of rRNA and tRNA processing) and is known as heterogeneous RNA (hnRNA) since it is of widely different lengths. It is associated with proteins, and the complexes are called heterogeneous ribonucleoprotein particles (hnRNP).

We have already talked about poly-A tails and capping of mRNA, now we will cover **splicing**. Genes

of higher eukaryotes are called "interrupted genes" because they are composed of introns and exons. *Intron* is short for "intervening sequence" and is a sequence that does not code for part of a protein, and *exon* is short for "expressed sequence." The initial mRNA transcript is called pre-mRNA because the introns that have been transcribed must be removed before the final mRNA is transported out of the nucleus for protein synthesis. The most common mechanism for the removal of introns is that found in higher eukaryotes, where a "spliceosome" is assembled at the ends of the introns. There are short conserved sequences that delineate the splice sites (boundaries) between exons and the introns that separates them. The first two nucleotides of the intron are always GU, and the last two are AG. An additional important base is an A that is located in the intron and indicates the branch site. The first step in splicing is cleavage of pre-mRNA at the GU site. The intron then curves around toward the next exon, and forms a 5'–2' link to the *A* in the intron. This results in a structure called a **lariat**. The lariat is removed, and the two exons are joined together by an esterification reaction (see Figure 3-35).

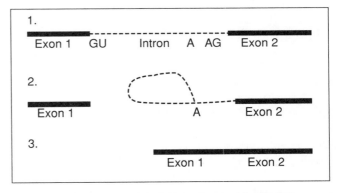

Figure 3-35. Lariat formation and splicing.

The machinery used for the splicing process consists of both proteins and small RNAs that exist as ribonucleoprotein particles called snRNPs (pronounced *snurps*). They are U1, U2, U4, U5, and U6. U1 binds the 5' splice site, U2 and associated proteins bind the branch site and recruit U4, U5, and U6 to form a spliceosome that goes through various conformational changes and eventually results in excision of the intron and the joining of the two exons. The final mRNA transcript contains a 5' UTR (untranslated region) and a 3' UTR on either side of the gene transcript. These RNA sequences will not be used to code for the protein to be made, but they do serve other functions, to be discussed later. A defect in splicing can cause diseases. There is also a phenomenon called "alternative splicing sites" where an organism can choose different splice sites. Somehow, viruses such as HIV have exploited this ability to increase the number of different proteins they can synthesize. Prokaryotes do not have introns in their pre-mRNA but do have introns that serve other purposes (see later discussion).

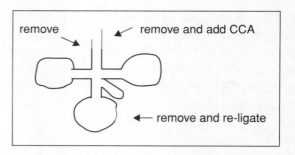

Figure 3-36. Processing of a tRNA.

The processing of rRNA differs between prokaryotes and eukaryotes. In eukaryotes three of the four ribosomal rRNAs (18S, 5.8S, and 28S) are transcribed as a single chain called the 45S rRNA precursor. The three separate rRNAs are cleaved by an **endonuclease** and processed by **exonucleases** to truncate both ends. Small nucleolar RNAs (snoRNAs, or snoRNPs when associated with protein) are also associated with the processing and further modification of eukaryotic rRNA. There are multiple tandem repeats of the gene for the 45S precursor, just as there are repeats of the 5S precursor that is situated elsewhere. Even in yeast, where the 5S gene is adjacent to the 45S gene, it is transcribed independently. In prokaryotes, tRNA genes are interspersed with the rRNA genes and must also be removed and processed.

Processing of tRNA involves several different steps (Figure 3-36). Both the 5′ and 3′ ends must be trimmed. The 5′ end is removed by ribonuclease P, an endonuclease, whereas the 3′ end is trimmed by an exonuclease. The CCA trinucleotide shared by all tRNAs on the 3′ end is added by an enzyme called tRNA nucleotidyl transferase. Many tRNAs also have an intron. The mechanism for its removal is different from the mechanism used for mRNA. In tRNA, the cleavage and ligation of the RNA are separate events and do not involve lariat formation. The necessary enzymes are a phosphodiesterase (cleavage), polynucleotide kinase (to add phosphate), and adenylate synthetase for ligation. The final modification of tRNAs is the extensive modification of the bases to form unusual bases such as pseudouridine (symbol ψ).

An analysis of the mechanism of RNA processing led to the discovery of **ribozymes**. These are RNAs with catalytic activity. They are found associated with processing of eukaryotic pre-mRNA as well as the so-called Group I introns (bacteria, eukaryotic organelles, and the nuclei of lower eukaryotes) and Group II introns (bacteria and organelles). These latter two groups often serve as mobile gene elements. The splicing of these introns is also an autocatalytic event. The process is called autosplicing, or self-splicing. Groups I and II introns can also code for endonucleases that allow the intron to be mobile and to insert, like transposons, into sites elsewhere in the genome. These sites are specific, and the process is called "intron homing." Group I introns migrate as DNA, but Group II introns migrate as RNA sequences and code for a reverse transcriptase that allows them to make DNA and insert into the genome. The activity of ribozymes in vivo seems to be associated with protein, but it has been proved that the catalytic activity belongs to the RNA itself. It has been theorized that RNAs may have been the first class of catalytic molecules to exist.

The final stage of expression (DNA to RNA to protein) is **translation**. In prokaryotes, this is linked to transcription, but in eukaryotes, mRNA must first be transferred from the nucleus to the cytoplasm. In both prokaryotes and eukaryotes, the site of protein synthesis is the **ribosome**.

Ribosomes are large RNA-protein complexes. Eukaryotic ribosomes are organized into two subunits: 40S (34 proteins, 18S rRNA) and 60S (50 proteins, 28, 5.8. and 5S rRNAs). The *S* refers to a Svedberg unit and describes the rate of centrifugation. Together, the two subunits constitute the 80S ribosome. Prokaryotes also have ribosomes with two subunits: 30S (21 proteins, 16S rRNA) and 50S (34 proteins, 23 and 5S rRNAs).

The two-subunit prokaryotic ribosome is 70S. The ribosomes of mitochondria and chloroplasts are similar to prokaryotic ribosomes. Ribosomes in eukaryotes can be found free in the cytosol (so-called free ribosomes) or associated with the rough endoplasmic reticulum (ER). Indeed, it is the presence of ribosomes that makes this part of the ER look rough. The membrane-bound microsomes are responsible for proteins that are to be secreted or targeted to other organelles.

The third major component of protein synthesis (in addition to ribosomes and mRNA) is the family of tRNAs. **Transfer RNA** has been described earlier. It functions to transduce the genetic code into protein by being able to recognize a codon in mRNA and insert the cognate amino acid into a protein. This requires each tRNA (remember, there are fewer than 61 tRNAs because of the "wobble" phenomenon) to have an anticodon that recognizes a codon and also have a recognition site for the enzyme that will attach its cognate amino acid. Where the recognition signal for the correct amino acid resides on each tRNA varies. Sometimes the anticodon is involved, and sometimes it is not. The lack of obligate involvement of the anticodon in substrate recognition has been shown by studying "suppressor mutations," where the anticodon has a mutation, but the tRNA (suppressor tRNA) still binds the originally intended amino acid. This complexity of specific recognition sites is further complicated by the fact that the number of aminoacyl tRNA synthetases, the enzymes that join the amino acid and the tRNA with a covalent bond, is the same as the number of amino acids and not the number of tRNAs. This means that one synthetase may have to recognize as many as six (for leucine) tRNAs. A tRNA for leucine is called $tRNA^{leu}$ when uncharged, and leucyl $tRNA^{leu}$ when bound to its cognate amino acid.

The process of forming a covalent bond ("charging") between the 2′ or 3′ hydroxyl of the terminal adenine residue in the tRNA and the carboxyl group of the amino acid (an ester bond) occurs with hydrolysis of ATP to AMP and pyrophosphate. The energy inherent in the resulting ester (acyl) bond between tRNA and amino acid will eventually provide the energy needed for synthesis of a peptide bond. In cases where there is not much difference in the structure of two or more amino acids—for instance, the hydrophobic amino acids valine, leucine, and isoleucine—a checking (sieving) mechanism occurs. The respective aminoacyl tRNA

synthetases for these three amino acids have a second recognition site that enables the enzyme to proofread (or edit) the products of its own catalysis.

With ribosomes, aminoacyl tRNAs, mRNA, and various other expression factors ready, protein synthesis can be initiated. The first step in protein synthesis in eukaryotes is the binding of GTP to eukaryotic initiation factor 2a (eIF-2A). GTP-eIF-2a binds to met-$tRNA_i^{met}$. Methionine is the mandatory first amino acid in the synthesis of a protein (in prokaryotes, this ternary complex is made up of GTP, initiation factor 2 (IF-2), and formylmet-$tRNA_i^{met}$, which is synthesized from a charged methionyl $tRNA^{met}$ by a transformylase). The subscript i indicates that this is a tRNA specific for initiation. At this stage, the 40S ribosome is still bound to eIF-3 (an anti-association factor) that prevents it from binding to the 60S subunit. The initiating amino-acyl tRNA complex, mRNA, and various other initiation factors are then bound to the 40S (30S in prokaryotes) ribosomal subunit. The positioning of the mRNA in prokaryotes is determined by a sequence on mRNA about 10 bases upstream from the AUG (start codon that binds formylmethionine tRNA in prokaryotes, and methionyl tRNA in eukaryotes) called the ribosome-binding site or, in prokaryotes, the Shine-Delgarno sequence. In eukaryotes, the 5′ cap and the poly-A tail position the mRNA in the correct position on the ribosome. The "preinitiation complex" is now in place.

The second stage of initiation starts with the removal of anti-association factor eIF-3; binding of more initiation factors; and hydrolysis of the GTP bound to eIF-2a, promoting its release; and a final association of the 40S subunit with the 60S subunit to form an 80S ribosome/aminoacyl-tRNA/mRNA complex (the initiation complex), as shown in Figure 3-37.

It should be noted that the eIF-2a now loses its GDP and binds a GTP to position itself for a new round of initiation. This exchange of GTP for GDP is catalyzed by a guanine nucleotide exchange factor.

Elongation can now begin. In this step, the peptide chain grows by sequential addition of amino acids. The mRNA is read 5′ to 3′, and the protein is synthesized from the N-terminal to the C-terminal end. The peptide

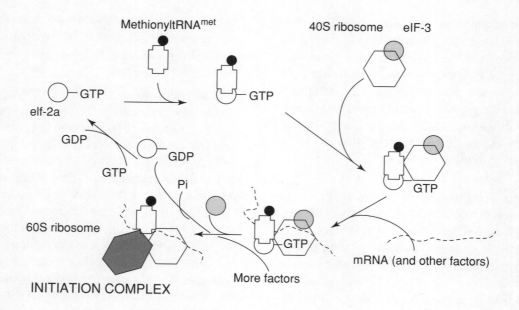

Figure 3-37. Formation of the initiation complex. On the right is shown formation of the eIF-2a-GTP-Met-tRNA$_i^{met}$ complex and its binding to form the 43S initiation complex. Messenger RNA then binds, and eIF3 dissociates, as does eIF-2a after hydrolysis of GTP.

bonds themselves are catalyzed by peptidyltransferase, an enzyme that needs no additional energy input, since the amino acids have been "activated" by esterification to the tRNA terminal adenine residue. Energy in the form of GTP is used, however, at other stages in the elongation process, including the selection of the appropriate aminoacyl tRNA and movement of mRNA along the ribosome as the peptide chain grows. Many protein elongation factors are involved in these processes.

The ribosome has three distinct sites for amino acid interaction called the *A* (aminoacyl) site, the *P* (peptidyl) site, and the *E* (exit) site. The *A* and *P* sites span the two ribosomal subunits, and the *E* site is on the large subunit.

The first tRNA carrying methionine (or formylmethionine in prokaryotes) associates with the AUG start codon in the *P* site. The positioning of the next aminoacyl tRNA in the *A* site is dependent on hydrolysis of GTP associated with elongation factor 1α (EF-1α), EF-Tu in prokaryotes. A peptide bond is formed between the methionine (f-met) and the second amino acid. The methionine is cleaved from its tRNA, and the dipeptide stays attached to the second tRNA, which moves to the *P* site. The free tRNA$^{met\,(fmet)}$ moves into the *E* site. Even though the peptide bond formation requires no energy, the movement does, and this is accomplished by hydrolysis of GTP associated with EF-2 (EF-G, or G-factor in prokaryotes). EF-1α (EF-Tu) now brings the third aminoacyl tRNA into the *A* site, a bond is formed, and everything moves again, releasing the first tRNA from the E site and replacing it with the second tRNA.

The sequence of diagrams below shows the insertion of the initiating methionine followed by valine and glycine.

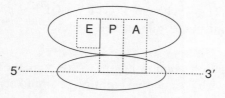

1. Methionyl-tRNA^{met} binds the *P* site.

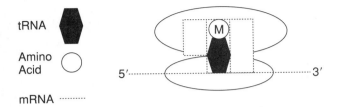

tRNA

Amino
Acid

mRNA

2. Valyl-tRNA^{val} binds the *A* site, and a peptide bond is formed.

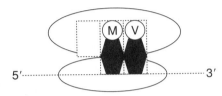

3. The methionylRNA^{met} moves to the *E* site, where the tRNA is cleaved and disassociates from the ribosome. The methionine is still peptide-bonded to the valyl-tRNA^{val}, which now is translocated to the *P* site. This leaves the *A* site free to bind to a glycyl-tRNA^{gly} to elongate the growing peptide chain.

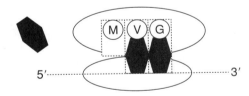

When a termination codon (UGA, UAA, or UAG) is reached, a release factor (eRF in eukaryotes) binds to the stop codon in the *A* site where a charged tRNA would normally bind. Peptidyltransferase now uses its hydrolytic function to cleave the completed peptide from the last tRNA located in the *P* site. The ribosome rebinds the anti-association factor (eIF-3 or its prokaryotic equivalent), causing the two ribosomal subunits to dissociate in preparation for the next round of synthesis.

In prokaryotes, there are two "class 1" release factors, called RF1 and RF2. They have different specific-

ity for the three stop codons. The release factors in turn must be released by release factor 3 (RF3).

As a protein is synthesized, it is folded into its three-dimensional shape. Some proteins do this spontaneously in the presence of proteins called "chaperones" that protect the protein as it folds. "Heat shock proteins" are chaperones and were discovered many years ago after it was noticed that several proteins were synthesized in response to changing cell culture temperature. Some proteins require a more active assistance for folding. This is provided by the ATP-dependent family of chaperonins. Proteins that are not correctly folded are usually degraded.

Proteins that are for export (secretory) or for transfer to organelles are made by ribosomes associated with the rough endoplasmic reticulum. Initiation and elongation start on free ribosomes. About 8–12 residues centered in the first 15–30 amino acids of these proteins are hydrophobic and form the middle of the signal peptide (or leader sequence). This leader sequence binds a signal recognition particle (SRP) made up of proteins and a small RNA molecule. This temporarily halts protein synthesis, and the ribosome and attached molecules moves to the cytosolic side of the ER where it attaches to a "docking" protein (SRP receptor). The ribosome then is moved to a translocon, a transmembrane receptor that allows the signal peptide to cross into the lumen of the endoplasmic reticulum followed by the rest of the nascent protein. As the ribosome is transferred from the SRP receptor to the translocon, the SRP dissociates, and protein synthesis resumes. On the luminal surface of the ER, there is an integral membrane protein called signal peptidase that cleaves the signal peptide as it appears on the other side of the ER membrane. Folding and further processing of the protein can now occur in the lumen of the ER.

Processing of secretory proteins prepares them for targeting to organelles as well as for insertion in the plasma membrane or secretion. **Glycosylation** increases stability of proteins to be excreted (e.g., immunoglobulins) and also serves as a marker for transport of proteins to a specific place in the cell. Glycosylation is catalyzed by a family of glycosyltransferases that can add one or more carbohydrate residues to serine or threonine (*O*-linked glycosylation) or asparagine (*N*-linked glycosylation). N-glycosylation starts cotranslationally, that is as the protein is synthesized, and is finished in the Golgi apparatus. O-glycosylation starts after protein synthesis is complete, and the protein has been transported to the Golgi apparatus. Carbohydrate residues that can be added include galactose, glucose, mannose, N-acetylgalactosamine, N-acetylglucosamine, and N-acetylneuraminic acid (sialic acid). The individual sugars are added by transferases using phosphate sugars as substrates. Building the core of the N-linked carbohydrate structure is initiated on a molecule called dolichol phosphate, and the carbohydrate chain then transferred to asparagine residues for completion of synthesis. The O-linked chain is assembled entirely on the protein. Several diseases occur because of deficiencies in glycosylation, for example I-cell disease. In this disease, mannose 6-phosphate is not added to hydrolases bound for lysosomes, and these hydrolase enzymes are found in extracellular fluid where they can destroy necessary metabolites.

Another stabilizing posttranslational modification, especially for secreted proteins, is the formation of disulfide bonds. Proteins can also be modified by cleavage. Insulin is a good example of these two types of processing, since it is synthesized as preproinsulin in the ER lumen. The signal peptide is cleaved to give proinsulin, and it is then packaged in granules. Before release from the cell, it is further cleaved in two places to yield its final form (the *A* and *B* chains joined by two disulfide bridges) and a C-peptide that is secreted with it but has no activity.

The figure below shows the posttranslational processing of insulin. The areas shown as dotted lines are removed. The *A* and *B* chains stay linked through covalent disulfide bonds.

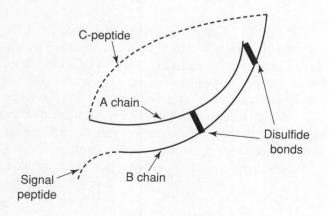

As the protein processing occurs in the *cis-*, *medial-*, and *trans*-Golgi, the proteins are sorted for transport to various parts of the cell based on glycosylation and amino acid sequences. Families of SNARE (soluble NSF [N-ethylmaleimide-sensitive fusion protein] attachment protein receptor) proteins recognize proteins to be targeted to membranes and organelles. Final packaging of the proteins occurs in the *trans*-Golgi. The v-SNARE proteins are in the membrane of the vesicles that bud off from the Golgi and are used to transport the proteins to their target membrane, and t-SNARE proteins are the recognition molecules similar to receptors on the target membrane. The two types of SNARE proteins interact to bring vesicle and membrane into close proximity, facilitating the transfer of the protein into the membrane.

The *trans*-Golgi network can both export and import proteins. Vesicles that leave go to the endosome, the lysosome, to plasma membrane for secretion (such as regulated secretory granules), and to axons or dendrites. Vesicles that are imported are from endosomes or from plasma membrane for recycling. The mannose-6-phosphate-lysosome signaling system (see above), which directs proteins to lysosomes and endosomes, has a mannose-6-phosphate receptor on the *trans*-Golgi membrane associated with clathrin (a protein) on the membrane. After the vesicle buds, clathrin is removed before fusion of the vesicle with the destination organelle. There may also be other vesicle coating proteins that are used instead of clathrin in other cases. As well as carbohydrate residues described above, palmitate and myristate can be covalently linked to protein.

Other modifications occur posttranslationally (after the amino acids have been incorporated into protein). The amino terminal methionine (or formylmethionine in prokaryotes) is usually removed, and sometimes the amino terminus is acetylated or has other groups added to it. The carboxyl terminus can be methylated or be joined to a glycosyl-phosphatidylinositol anchor for insertion in a membrane.

Individual amino acids can be methylated (predominantly the two acidic and three basic amino acids); hydroxylated (lysine and proline); or phosphorylated (serine, threonine, tyrosine, hydroxyproline, and hydroxylysine). Some more unusual modifications include prenylation by isoprenoids (these are formed in the cholesterol synthetic pathway) and formation of allysine for cross-linking of fibrous proteins. Glutamate in blood clotting factors is γ-carboxylated to allow it to chelate calcium. Another unusual amino acid found in proteins is selenocysteine, first discovered in glutathione peroxidase. This is not strictly a posttranslational modification because selenium is added to a serine residue esterified to a tRNA, and the selenocysteine incorporated into protein by the normal ribosomal-based process.

The amino acid cystine is not a naturally occurring amino acid, but is rather the name given to two cysteines forming a disulfide bridge. Cystine can be obtained in its disulfide bridge form by proteolysis of some proteins under nonreducing conditions, but it is not used in this form in protein synthesis (i.e., there is no codon or tRNA for the insertion of cystine into protein).

An unusual type of protein modification, found only in some prokaryotes, is protein splicing. The piece of the protein that is removed is called an *intein*, and the remaining polypeptides that are spliced together are called *exteins* (analogous to introns and exons). Inteins have inherent splicing catalytic activity, and some inteins also serve as "homing endonucleases" that can create a cut in DNA to allow for insertion of DNA coding for the intein. This introduces regions coding for inteins into genes that lack them.

Much of the regulation of protein expression occurs at the level of transcription, but translation can also be regulated. One of the best described regulatory systems is the inactivation of eIF-2a (eukaryotic initiation factor 2a) by phosphorylation. The phosphorylated form binds the limiting eIF-2b (the guanine nucleotide exchange factor) tightly, thus sequestering it from replacing GDP on eIF-2a and preventing formation of the initiation complex. This method of regulation is active in situations such as starvation and is also the mechanism by which globin synthesis is inhibited when heme is not available.

Some mitochondrial and chloroplast proteins, such as mitochondrial NADH oxidase, have some subunits coded for by the nuclear DNA, and some by mitochondrial or chloroplast DNA. These subunits are synthe-

sized in the cytoplasm and the organelles respectively. Coordinate regulation of expression of proteins encoded by the nuclear and mitochondrial/chloroplast genomes is not, however, well understood. Most of the regulation appears to occur at the level of entry into the organelle of posttranscriptional regulatory proteins, such as RNA processing enzymes, that are encoded in the nucleus and synthesized in the cytosol.

10. GENE REGULATION IN PROKARYOTES

10.1. Positive and Negative Control of the Operon

Prokaryotes have groups of genes that code for enzymes in a metabolic pathway and are under the control of a single promoter. These genes are called **operons**. The purpose of operons is to put the organism in a position to respond quickly to changes in the environment. Among the best studied are the *lac* operon and the *trp* and *his* operons. The *lac* operon is made up of genes that allow the use of lactose as a sole carbon source, and the *trp* and *his* operons code for proteins that synthesize tryptophan and histidine when these amino acids are not available exogenously. Eukaryotes have relatively few genes that are coordinately regulated, since eukaryotic organisms are rarely prone to radical shifts in nutrient availability.

The *lac* operon in *E. coli* was the earliest operon to be described. It is arranged as shown in Figure 3-38.

Figure 3-38. The *lac* operon.

The three genes *lac*Z, *lac*Y, and *lac*A code for three proteins either in the metabolic pathway for lactose or related in some way to it. They are, respectively, β-galactosidase that can cleave galactose to lactose and glucose, a permease that facilitates entry of lactose into the cell, and a transacetylase whose function is not known. The mRNA for these three proteins is transcribed as a continuous polycistronic mRNA. Even though the three genes are transcribed together, there are different amounts of each of the proteins that they code for. This is regulated by the rate of translation of each of the three segments of the mRNA.

In the presence of glucose, the preferred carbon source, there is no need for expression of the *lac* operon. This is controlled by binding of the *lac*I repressor protein, transcribed from the gene indicated in Figure 3-38. The expression of this protein is constitutive. It binds to the operator *lac*O site (indicated as *O* in Figure 3-38). The repressor protein is large enough that this binding partially blocks the promoter *lac*P (*P* in the diagram) site and prevents transcription of the three genes *lac*Z, *lac*Y, and *lac*A. The fact that the *lac*I gene product is synthesized and then diffuses to the operator means that this is a *trans* effect. A *trans* effect occurs when the product of a gene regulates a gene that is not contiguous to the gene that codes for the regulator molecule. It may, in fact, be on a different chromosome. This is different from a *cis* effect, where the location of the regulatory element is closely related to the location of the gene. The *lac* promoter is an example of a *cis* effect.

How does the cell know when to initiate transcription of the *lac* operon? In the presence of lactose, the repressor binds lactose, changes conformation, and dissociates from the operator. Now, RNA polymerase can bind to the promoter, and transcription can occur. It was originally believed that lactose itself bound the repressor protein, causing it to change conformation and be released from the operator. It is now known that the actual inducer molecule is allolactose. This is, like lactose, a dimer of glucose and galactose, but with a different type of covalent glycosidic linkage. Under noninducing conditions, there is always a small amount of the β-galactosidase present, and in addition to cleavage of the glycosidic linkage of lactose, it also has an activity that allows it to turn lactose into allolactose.

The *lac* operon can be induced by certain other small molecules, the best known being isopropylthiogalactoside (IPTG), which is a "gratuitous inducer" in that it induces β-galactosidase but is not itself metabolized by the enzyme. This property is exploited in genetic engineering, as will be described later.

So far we have discussed the fact that in the presence of glucose the cell prefers to use glucose as a carbon source, but when lactose is the only carbon source, it can switch to using lactose. What happens when both glucose and lactose are present, and the cell still prefers to use glucose? As part of the promoter, there is a region (labeled *CAP* in the Figure 3-38) that ensures the use of glucose when both glucose and lactose are present. It is the binding site for a protein known either as CAP (Catabolite Activator Protein) or CRP (cAMP receptor protein). The CAP site must be occupied for transcription to occur. In the presence of glucose, the cell produces little cAMP, and the CAP protein is not bound to the CAP site on the DNA. This would be the situation whether glucose is present alone or together with lactose. This ensures that glucose is the fuel that is used, because, with no CAP bound, the *lac* operon is not transcribed. If glucose is withdrawn, the amount of cAMP rises. The CAP protein binds the cAMP and changes conformation to facilitate binding to the CAP site. Now the operon can be transcribed.

In summary, three things need to happen for the operon to be transcribed: (1) binding of allactose to the *lac*I gene product to release it from the operator site, (2) binding of the CAP-cAMP complex to the CAP site, and (3) binding of RNA polymerase to the promoter site. Catabolite repression (lack of cAMP, keeping CAP from binding the CAP site) also regulates the galactose and arabinose operons.

The lactose operon is transcribed in the presence of lactose. Operons for the synthesis of amino acids, such as *trp* (tryptophan operon) are the reverse (Figure 3-39). They are not transcribed in the presence of the molecule for which they are named. This operon exists because it would be inefficient for the cell to make tryptophan if the amino acid were available in the environment.

| P/O/a | *trp*E | *trp*D | *trp*C | *trp*B | *trp*A |

Figure 3-39. Tryptophan operon.

There are five metabolic steps in the synthesis of tryptophan from its chorismate precursor. The steps are catalyzed by three enzymes, two of which are bifunctional. The *trp*A through *trp*E genes code for these three enzymes (*trp*E and *trp*D for two subunits of a bifunctional enzyme, *trp*C for a monomeric bifunctional enzyme, and *trp*B and *trp*A for a dimeric monofunctional enzyme).

In the *lac* operon, the repressor binds the operator in the absence of inducer. In the *trp* operon, the opposite happens: the repressor binds the operator only when bound to tryptophan. This prevents synthesis of the enzymes in the tryptophan synthetic pathway, and the cell saves energy by using exogenous tryptophan. When the *corepressor* (as tryptophan is called to differentiate it from the repressor protein) is not present, the operon is "derepressed" (i.e., the repressor is removed from the operator site), and expression of the operon occurs. The operator is not a separate sequence of DNA, as it is for the *lac* operon, but is an integral part of the promoter.

There is a second promoter site between the *trp*D and *trp*C genes. This promoter is not regulated, and so *trp*C, *trp*B, and *trp*A gene products are synthesized constitutively at a very low rate. *Trp*B and *trp*C gene products are the only proteins of the five that contain tryptophan in their primary structure. It is hypothesized that they are always present at a low level so that in the total absence of tryptophan the synthetic pathway is not stopped completely by the inability to make two of the necessary components of the pathway. This is a form of **attenuation**. The area indicated as *a* in Figure 3-39 is an attenuation site and represents a sequence of 14 codons starting with a start codon, and ending with a stop codon. Preceding this sequence is a sequence known to be recognized by RNA polymerase. The attenuation serves as a "brake" on polymerases that have begun to transcribe the operon even in the presence of tryptophan. The mechanism for the attenuation involves the coordinated transcription/translation function found in prokaryotes. The sequence of 14 amino acids in the attenuator site includes two adjacent codons for tryptophan. When tryptophan is present, translation of the mRNA transcribed from these codons can continue. This causes the mRNA to assume a conformation that is a termination signal for RNA polymerase. When there is no tryptophan present, the transcription stalls temporarily as translation is slowed by the low availability of tryptophanyl-tRNA^{trp}. Under these conditions,

the transcription eventually resumes, and the operon is expressed (Figure 3-40).

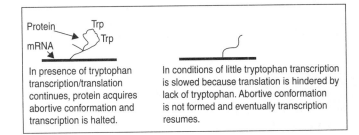

Figure 3-40. Attenuation of trp operon.

Attenuation cannot occur in eukaryotes because it requires simultaneous transcription/translation. Attenuation is found in many of the operons for amino acid synthesis in prokaryotes. For the *his* operon, it is the major mechanism of control.

There are also instances of structurally similar amino acids attenuating transcription. For instance, isoleucine and threonine can act as attenuators of the *thr* operon, and three related hydrophobic amino acids—isoleucine, leucine, and valine—can all act as attenuators of the shared *ilv* (isoleucine, leucine, valine) operon.

A related regulatory phenomenon is **antitermination**. This is effected by an antitermination protein that binds to RNA polymerase and allows it to "read through" a termination site. Antitermination was first recognized in phages. Phage genes are arranged in such a way that the phage can exploit the host transcription and translation enzymes to initiate reproduction of the phage. To do this, the "early genes" (also called immediate early) are expressed. The host RNA polymerase recognizes a termination site that allows only this group of genes to be expressed. One of the gene products is the phage's own RNA polymerase, and another product is an antitermination factor. In the presence of the antitermination factor, the phage polymerase can now read through the initial termination site and allow expression of a set of middle or delayed early genes.

The signal for antitermination lies upstream of the terminator site. In phage lambda, the antitermination factors (antiterminators) are called *pN* and *pQ*. The initial antitermination site is called *nut* (for *N* utilization). It signals pN to bind to RNA polymerase and cause transcription termination. There is also a family of *nus* genes (*N*-utilization substance). The *nus* gene products bind the antitermination proteins and prevent them from attenuating transcription by binding to RNA polymerase.

Since prokaryotes have these gene groupings (operons) and also linked transcription-translation, a mutation in one gene can cause the cessation of transcription or translation in all the associated genes. These are called polar mutations (i.e., they are directional).

11. GENE REGULATION IN EUKARYOTES

11.1. Cis- and *Trans*-Acting Regulatory Elements

Eukaryotes, like prokaryotes, have two families of regulatory elements. The **cis-acting regulatory elements** are DNA sequences such as promoters, enhancers, hormone response elements, and any sequence of DNA that is regulatory and located near a gene and is on the same piece of DNA. **Trans-acting regulatory elements** are proteins such as transcription factors, RNA polymerase, repressors, and ligand-activated transcription factors.

11.2. Gene Rearrangements and Amplification

Additional contributions to eukaryotic gene regulation are made by gene rearrangements and amplification. Certain eukaryotic genes can rearrange in order to provide a greater variety of related proteins without the need to have a different gene for each of the proteins. A good example of this is the production of immunoglobulins.

An organism can synthesize up to 10^8 different immunoglobulins. Each one has two identical light chains (κ or λ) and two identical heavy chains (γ, α, μ, δ, or ε). Kappa and lambda are from two different gene families; the heavy chains are from a single family. Genes for heavy (one family, *H*) and light (two families, λ and μ) gene segments all reside on different chromosomes. The primary structure of each chain can be divided into two different domains that are considered constant (C) and variable (V). The large number of different molecules are synthesized by joining *C* gene segments (there are about 10 different gene segments for the *C* region), and *V* segments (several hundred gene segments). The *V* regions contain the antigen recognition site.

Light chain *V* gene segments have a 3′ leader sequence (L) and *C* gene segments have a 3′ joining sequence (J). Heavy chains have the same *L*, *V*, *J*, and *C* gene segments, but they also have an additional short sequence of amino acids called the diversity segment (D). Recombination of these segments results in the very high variability in immunoglobulin sequences.

During splicing of gene segments, several mechanisms come into play, including a cleavage reaction similar to that of a transposase. This is catalyzed by enzymes called RAG1 and 2 that anchor the cleaved DNA by forming a covalent phosphodiesterase bond to themselves. The non-homologous end-joining mechanism is used to join the segments. During these processes, nucleotides can be deleted or inserted, introducing even more variation into immunoglobulin diversity.

After gene rearrangement, each antibody-producing cell is left with only one intact gene for a light chain and one intact gene for a heavy chain. This immortalization of one particular genotype for an immunoglobulin in each cell is called clonal selection. However, further changes of genotype in a cell can occur. All lymphocytes start by producing immunoglobulins of the IgM class. As a cell reproduces, it can undergo "class switching," where the heavy chain region gene segment can be changed, keeping the specificity for antigen the same, but altering the class (γ, α, μ, δ, or ε chains give rise to IgG, IgA, IgM, IgD, and IgE, respectively).

Transcriptional regulation controls the amount of transcript synthesized. Eukaryotes have an additional mechanism called **gene amplification**. This is the process of producing additional copies of a gene. An example of this is the acquisition of methotrexate resistance by amplification of the gene that codes for dihydrofolate reductase (*dhfr*). This enzyme is the target for methotrexate, and synthesis of more copies of the enzyme allows the cell to overcome resistance to the drug. There are two types of gene amplification. One involves the synthesis of "double-minute chromosomes," which are small chromosomes carrying two to four copies of the *dhfr* gene. The double-minute chromosomes cannot replicate and are often lost as cells divide. This form of gene amplification is thus unstable. For creation of a stable cell line, the amplified *dhfr* genes must be incorporated into the chromosome itself. The amplified genes reside as tandem arrays next to the original *dhfr* gene. Only one of the two *dhfr* alleles is amplified, and the difference in the length of the two homologous chromosomes can become so great that it can be seen after staining. The mechanism of gene amplification is not well understood.

12. BACTERIOPHAGES AND ANIMAL AND PLANT VIRUSES

12.1. Genome Replication and Regulation

Bacteriophages and viruses display many different types of replicative mechanisms. Bacteriophages have two forms of life cycle, lytic and lysogenic. In the lytic cycle, the host cell dies, and in the lysogenic cycle, it survives.

In the lytic mode, the phage attaches to the bacterial cell, and DNA is injected into the cell. The "early" genes of the phage are transcribed and translated by existing host proteins. Production of phage RNA and proteins commences, and expression of host proteins is inhibited by degradation of host DNA by phage-encoded proteins. This early period, before all the phage proteins are present and new phage is produced, is called the eclipse period. During the maturation phase, new phage are assembled, and phage-encoded lysozyme is synthesized. This enzyme potentiates destruction of the cell wall, and new phages are released. T-even phages reproduce by the lytic mechanism.

The temperate phages, such as bacteriophage lambda (λ), can reproduce by the lytic mechanism but are also capable of reproduction by the lysogenic mechanism. The linear phage DNA can form a circle after insertion into the cell and be reproduced independently, much like a plasmid. Alternatively, the DNA can insert into the bacterial chromosome, at which point it is called a prophage. As the cell doubles, so does the prophage. Some later event, such as exposure to ultraviolet light, can activate removal of the prophage from the host DNA and initiate the lytic cycle.

Animal viruses follow a cycle much like that of bacteriophage. However, the entire virus enters the cell by endocytosis or by fusion with the cell membrane, and the surrounding capsule is removed in the cytoplasm of the host cell. DNA-containing viruses generally enter the nucleus and are integrated into DNA, and transcription of the viral genes occurs. Sometimes the "early" genes are transcribed using host enzymes, but some viruses carry their own synthetic enzymes as part of the virus. Translation of the mRNA and synthesis of the capsule (capsid) proteins occur in the cytosol. Meanwhile, the viral DNA is being replicated in the nucleus, and the cytosol-translated proteins migrate into the nucleus where DNA and protein is assembled into a complete virus. The new viruses can now be released from the cell.

RNA-viruses have many modes of replication. They all need to make copies of their RNA genome and proteins to form new capsids around these RNAs. In some single-stranded RNA viruses, the infecting strand is the sense (+) strand. It functions like processed mRNA and is translated on host ribosomes. The product is a single polyprotein. This is cleaved as the polyprotein chain is synthesized by a virally encoded protease. One of the proteins released is the viral RNA-dependent RNA polymerase (also called a replicase). This, aided by host proteins, makes antisense (−) RNA, which in turn is used as a template to make more infectious (+) strands. The (+) strand can be used as a template for many more copies of polyproteins and RNA strands. Eventually, new virions are packaged into capsids and released from the cell. The entire process takes place in the cytosol. The polio virus is a positive-strand RNA virus.

The second type of RNA virus is the negative (−) strand virus. Some of these are segmented, and some are nonsegmented. The nonsegmented negative RNA virus carries its own RNA-dependent polymerase, since it must first make sense mRNA using the viral RNA as template. This mRNA is polycistronic. The mRNA is then translated on host ribosomes. The same enzyme transcribes viral RNA to make more copies. It functions as both a transcriptase and a replicase. Transmembrane proteins for insertion into new virion envelopes are made on ribosomes associated with host endoplasmic reticulum. An example of a negative-strand nonsegmented RNA virus is the rhabdovirus that causes rabies.

Hantavirus and the influenza viruses are examples of segmented negative-strand RNA viruses. The RNA genome is composed of several short RNA sequences. On infection of a cell, the RNA and capsid are transported into the nucleus of the host cell, and mRNA and new viral RNA is synthesized by a viral polymerase that is part of the original virion. Because this occurs in the nucleus, the individual RNA segments can be spliced in a "mix-and-match" mechanism by the host splicing enzymes, resulting in more proteins than could be coded by the individual RNA segments alone. Newly synthesized mRNA goes to the cytosol. Viral proteins are synthesized there, and some of these proteins, to be used for synthesis of more viral RNA, return to the nucleus for more RNA-dependent RNA synthesis. The other viral proteins go to the host cell membrane. Final assembly of new virions occurs on the host cell membrane.

Double-stranded RNA viruses also have segmented RNA. There are variations in the mechanism of replication among this type of virus, and the one described here is a common one. Neither strand functions as mRNA, so the first thing that occurs during viral replication is synthesis of mRNA by a polymerase that is part of the virion, followed by processing by other viral enzymes. The mRNA is then extruded from the viral capsid. The mRNA is translated into capsid proteins on host ribosomes, and assembled into a precapsid (an immature capsid). The mRNAs are enclosed into this capsid and copied into double-stranded RNA. This new RNA is used as a template for more mRNA, which once again is translated on host ribosomes and repackaged into more capsids. Eventually, the capsids move to the host cell endoplasmic reticulum where they acquire a temporary membrane by budding into the lumen. The membrane is eventually lost as the viruses mature and are released

from the host cell. The rotaviruses that cause gastroenteritis are double-stranded RNA viruses.

There is another type of RNA-containing virus called a **retrovirus**. The best-known example of this is HIV (human immunodeficiency virus), the causative agent for AIDS (acquired immunodeficiency disease). This family of viruses carries its own RNA-dependent DNA polymerase, called **reverse transcriptase (RT)**. This will be referred to again later in the section on methodology. Additionally, the virus has two copies of its RNA genome and two tRNAs that serve as primers. Remember, regular DNA synthesis by DNA-dependent polymerase requires RNA primers, and reverse transcriptase is no exception. The RNA genome has direct repeats at either end of the sequence.

The replication of the genome is a very complex process and involves two "jumps" of newly synthesized DNA segments to form new primers, and DNA synthesis to form a double strand. An integrase enzyme that was contained in the original viral capsule can now ligate the DNA into the host genome. One of the direct repeats that has been copied from the RNA genome includes a promoter to regulate transcription of viral genes. The other direct repeat occasionally serves as a promoter to regulate host genes that are downstream from insertion.

12.2. Virus-Host Interactions

Both DNA and RNA viruses can become **transforming (tumor) viruses**. For DNA tumor viruses that invade "permissive" cells, the entire viral genome is expressed, and this leads to host cell lysis and death. In "nonpermissive" cells, viral DNA is integrated into the host genome, and only a small fraction of the viral genome is expressed. No new viruses are made. The mechanism of **tumorigenesis** by DNA viruses varies. For instance some viral oncogenes or gene products cause chromosome breakage; some bind and inactivate cell cycle control proteins, such as *p53*; and some stimulate host cell DNA synthesis. There are no cellular homologues of DNA viral tumorigenic genes.

We shall now discuss transforming RNA viruses, the retroviruses. Retroviruses transform a cell, and they can also be replicated each time the cell divides. This allows them to transmit oncogenic potential from generation to generation. A usual (nondefective) retrovirus has three genes: *pol*, for the RNA-dependent DNA polymerase; *gag*, for group specific antigens; and *env*, for envelope. These viruses can become oncogenic by integrating into the host genome and activating or inactivating a cellular gene. This happens when the virus serves as a strong promoter for a cellular gene or inactivates a cellular gene by inserting itself in the middle of the gene (insertional inactivation). These viruses act slowly and are typified by viruses that cause leukemia.

First, let us consider the difference between retroviral oncogenic genes (*v-onc*) and their cellular homologues (*c-onc*). The cellular genes usually code for genes involved in regulation, such as receptors, transcription factors, and growth factors. They are called proto-oncogenes. Some retroviruses lose *gag* or *env* and instead carry a copy of a *c-onc* (a normal cellular gene). This is now called a *v-onc*, and readily acquires mutations during its transfer to new cells. If the viral oncogene comes from a different animal source than the cell that is transformed (e.g., the *src* gene that is found in humans but originated in chickens), the gene resembles that found in the source animal.

The reasons that the viral oncogenes are tumorigenic, and the cellular proto-oncogenes are not, vary. They include changes in the protein product as a result of mutations, or insertion together with viral promoters that result in overexpression. The place where the oncogene inserts can also make the viral oncogene tumorigenic. Insertion downstream from a strong host promoter, such as an immunoglobulin promoter, can lead to overexpression of the gene product. Insertion in the middle of a type of cell cycle control gene called a tumor repressor gene results in loss of control of the cell cycle and proliferation of cells.

It is believed that the oncogene-carrying defective virus is formed at the point that RNA is transcribed from an integrated virus. One or both of the normal genes (*gag* or *env*) is deleted from the transcript, and an adjacent host gene is spliced into the RNA. The evidence for this mechanism is that the host gene (*c-onc*) has introns, whereas the analogous *v-onc* (viral oncogene) has no introns, suggesting that processed RNA is its source. As indicated above, oncogenes are analogs of naturally occurring genes, for instance a kinase or receptor gene. Some of these genes are *myc*, *src*, *ras*, and *sis*. The only way a defective virus can replicate is if a helper virus is present. Helper viruses are called acute transforming viruses.

13. METHODOLOGY

13.1. Restriction Maps

In the late 1960s, an explosion of activity in the field of molecular biology occurred, powered by the development of new biochemical techniques. One of the most basic of these techniques is the harnessing of enzymes called **restriction endonucleases** to produce usable short segments of DNA. These segments can then be used for cloning, sequencing, **restriction fragment length polymorphism (RFLP)**, and other DNA manipulation.

Restriction endonucleases are enzymes that cleave DNA at specific sequences. Most DNAses have no such specificity, but are rather general endo- or exonucleases. Restriction endonucleases function in nature as a mechanism to protect a cell, usually bacterial, against foreign DNA. They function as a primitive immune system. As mentioned above in the section on DNA methylation, as DNA is replicated, it is methylated. Each bacterial species has a maintenance methylase that methylates its new DNA at sites specific to the particular type of bacterium. This allows the cell to recognize its own DNA. When DNA from another organism that lacks this protective methylation pattern specific to its host organism invades the cell, it is recognized by host cell's endonucleases and cleaved.

Restriction endonucleases are named for their *in vivo* hosts. For instance, the first restriction endonuclease enzyme discovered in *E. coli* is called Eco RI. Cleavage of DNA by endonucleases may leave blunt or overhanging ends on the DNA products. For example, *Bal* I cuts thusly to form blunt ends:

```
      ↓
TGGCCA      TGG      CCA
         →
ACCGGT      ACC      GGT
      ↑
```

The product of *Aat* II cleavage, on the other hand, gives overhanging "sticky" or "cohesive" ends:

```
      ↓
GACGTC      GACTG      C
         →
CTGCAG      C      TGCAG
      ↑
```

The cleavage recognition sites are usually "palindromes" in the sense that one strand reads the same 5′ to 3′ as the other strand reads 5′ to 3′. The *E. coli* methylation/cleavage site is GAATTC. Note that the palindrome does not mean that the sequence reads the same backwards and forwards, as in the usual definition of palindrome, but rather that complementary strands have sequences that are palindromic to each other. Most restriction endonuclease recognition sites are six base pairs long, but there are also some that recognize four and five nucleotide-long sequences. Because the shorter sequences occur more frequently, some endonucleases that recognize these sites are called "frequent cutters." Some restriction endonucleases cut DNA at the same place as other endonucleases. These are called isoschizomers. The enzymes have stringent ionic strength and metal ion requirements, and some recognize different sites when incubated under different conditions.

After the target DNA has been cleaved, the fragments are separated on an agarose gel containing ethidium bromide. This fluorescent dye is bright orange when intercalated into DNA. This allows visualization of the fragments and comparison with a standard curve derived from known fragment lengths.

A simple example of a plasmid with restriction endonuclease recognition sites is drawn below in Figure 3-41.

The following table (Table 3-3) indicates the length of the fragments produced by digestion with each endonuclease and with combinations of the enzymes.

Table 3-3.
Length of Fragments
Produced by Digestion with Enzymes

Enzyme(s) used	Size of fragment(s) (bp)
Eco RI	5,500
Bam HI	5,500
Hind III	5,500
Eco RI and Bam HI	2,000; 3,500
Eco RI and Hind III	2,500; 3,000
Bam HI and Hind III	1,000; 4,500
All three enzymes	1,000; 2,000; 2,500

When the restriction digest map is not known, the DNA can be subjected to digestion by several restriction endonucleases, and the map deduced. Here is a table (Table 3-4) showing fragments produced by digestion by another plasmid. It may be used to practice plasmid mapping. *Note:* The plasmid has two Eco RI sites. The answer is at the end of the Methodology section.

It is important to note the difference between the product(s) of digestion of circular DNA and of linear DNA. Circular DNA results in the same number of fragments as cuts, and a linear DNA gives the same number plus one. The diagram below shows that two cuts in a linear segment yield three fragments.

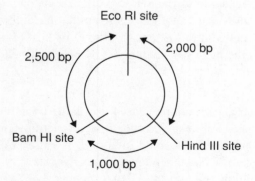

Figure 3-41. A plasmid restriction map.

```
1        2        3
```

**Table 3-4.
A Practice Example of
Restriction Endonuclease Mapping**

Enzyme(s) used	Size of fragment(s) (bp)
Bam HI	4,000
Hind III	4,000
Eco RI	1,500; 2,500
Hind III and Eco RI	300; 1,500; 2,200
Bam HI and Eco RI	1,000; 1,500; 1,500
Bam HI and Hind III	1,200; 2,800
All three enzymes	300; 1,000; 1,200; 1,500

One of the more important applications of restriction endonucleases in the laboratory is for amplification of a gene or other DNA sequence, and/or construction of a clone for overexpression of a protein by insertion of a restriction digest fragment into a plasmid. The resulting plasmid is called a **recombinant DNA molecule**.

13.2. DNA Cloning in Prokaryotes and Eukaryotes

The first step in cloning a sequence of a gene is the identification of the gene. Methods to do this will be covered later. Once the gene has been identified, it must be excised before it can be placed in a vector (usually a plasmid or a phage). The vector itself must be cut to receive the gene. The choice of restriction endonuclease is of vital importance. It must be specific for the locations at or near each end of the DNA to be inserted into the vector, and it should only cut the vector once (Figure 3-42).

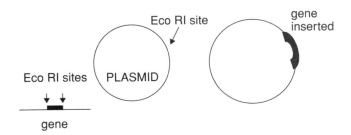

Figure 3-42. Insertion of a DNA fragment into a plasmid.

The vector plus inserted gene (a recombinant plasmid) are now placed into a suitable host, such as *E. coli*, by transformation. The bacterial cells are allowed to replicate and divide until adequate amounts of the gene are produced. The plasmid, which has replicated itself every time the bacterial cells double, is harvested, and the gene, now existing in many copies, can be excised by using the same restriction endonuclease that was originally used to excise it from the donor DNA. The earliest cloning (about 1970) was done in *E. coli* using plasmids like pBR322. There are now hundreds of specialized plasmids and host cells.

One of the useful characteristics of pBR322 that has been adapted in many subsequent plasmids is the phenomenon of antibiotic resistance. There are two absolute requirements for successful cloning. One is the creation of a recombinant plasmid, and the other is the transformation of the recombinant plasmid into the host cell. Both these processes carry with them the chance of failure. To check for the successful completion of both processes, biological tests are utilized. The plasmid pBR322, for example, has a site for Bam H1 cleavage in the sequence that confers tetracycline resistance (the *tet* gene), as pictured in Figure 3-43. The plasmid also has a gene for β-lactamase, the gene that confers resistance to ampicillin (*amp*). Together, tetracycline and ampicillin resistance can be used as a test of success with both the recombination and transformation steps. A bacterium with no plasmid at all will be *tet*^{s} and *amp*^{s} (i.e., sensitive to tetracycline and ampicillin), because it does not contain the plasmid that confers resistance to the two antibiotics. A bacterium containing a plasmid with no insert will be tetracycline resistant and ampicillin resistant (*tet*^{r} and *amp*^{r}). A bacterium with a plasmid bearing an insert at the *Bam* HI site has an interrupted *tet* resistance gene due to the presence of the insert (this is an example of insertional inactivation) and is *tet*^{s} but remains *amp*^{r} because it still has the intact β-lactamase gene.

Bacteria that are sensitive to one of the antibiotics will die when cultured in the presence of the antibiotic. Thus, the bacteria that have not been successfully transformed will die in the presence of both ampicillin and/or tetracycline. Bacteria transformed with the "empty" plasmid will grow in the presence of both antibiotics. The desired product, diagrammed as the third circle above (Figure 3-43), will be sensitive to tetracycline but

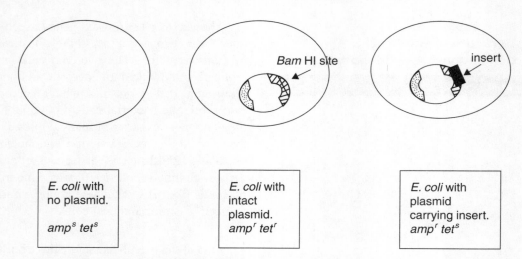

Figure 3-43. Use of antibiotic resistance as a measure of successful cloning.
The dotted area is the *amp* resistance gene; the crosshatched area is the tet resistance gene.

resistant to ampicillin. These latter may be identified by "replica plating" (see Figure 3-44). A group of colonies is "blotted" from one petri dish containing medium with ampicillin as a biological test of successful transformation. This is done with a soft cloth (for example velvet), and the adhering bacteria placed on a second petri dish. As the new colonies grow up on the agar, they form a potentially identical arrangement of colonies. The second plate has medium containing tetracycline and ampicillin, and the plates are compared. Those that grow on the plate minus tetracycline, but do not grow on the plate with this antibiotic, are identified as *tet*^{s} and *amp*^{r}, and can be further cultured to obtain the gene of interest.

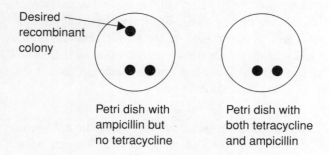

Figure 3-44. Result of replica plating.

There are alternative biological tests for identifying successfully transformed organisms, such as the "blue-white" test. One of the advantages of this technique is that it does not require replica plating. The plasmid contains part of the lac operon, including the operator region and the β-galactosidase gene. The gene to be cloned is inserted into the gene for β-galactosidase. The bacteria are cultured in medium containing a dye called X-gal. On metabolism by β-galactosidase, this dye turns blue, and the whole bacterial colony has a blue tinge. The "gratuitous inducer" IPTG (see the section on the *lac* operon) is added to the medium also, and colonies with a plasmid with a complete promoter/β-galactosidase sequence metabolize the dye and appear blue. White colonies have an interrupted β-galactosidase gene and cannot metabolize X-gal to its blue product. When combined with an antibiotic resistance marker, the blue-white test distinguishes successful cloning from failure.

It was stated above that there are many hundreds of vectors now commercially available. What other modifications have been engineered into these vectors? Many plasmids are now available with multiple cloning sites. These are "cassettes" of sites that have been added next to each other in the plasmid sequence. This allows for a gene to be excised from a sequence of DNA using two endonucleases and then placed in a plasmid in a particular direction (see Figure 3-45).

The direction of the gene will depend on whether plasmid *A* or *B* is used. This becomes important when

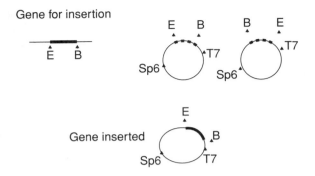

Figure 3-45. Example of multiple cloning cassettes with restriction endonuclease sites in opposite order.

the desired product is not more copies of the DNA, but rather RNA or protein. For RNA to be transcribed, the plasmid must have a site that codes for the initiation of RNA synthesis (i.e., a promoter). Frequently, when the desired product is RNA, the site is a viral promoter code, often either the T7 or SP6 virus (or both). These can be engineered into the plasmid so that one is situated that initiates transcription in one direction, and the other in the reverse direction. Figure 3-45 shows that the direction of insertion of the gene will determine whether SP6 or T7 polymerase is used for its expression. The plasmid must also contain inducible genes for the viral RNA polymerases for transcription to occur in a bacterial cell.

Transcription can also be catalyzed by endogenous bacterial promoters. Frequently a promoter such as that for the *lac* or arabinose operon is used. The level of expression is initially kept low (see glucose catabolite-dependent repression above). Enhanced production is initiated later by addition of an inducer to the medium. This allows the cells to use most of its initial energy for doubling rather than production of the cloned protein. Only when a large population of cells is available is expression induced.

RNA and protein can also be purified from in vitro systems. After amplification, the plasmid is purified and RNA transcribed after incubation in the presence of an in vitro transcription system. In vitro translation systems can be used when the final product desired is the protein gene product and are often also used for the

study of regulation of transcription or translation. One such system involves the use of the chloramphenicol acetyl transferase (CAT) gene. In this system, a hypothesized promoter is engineered into a plasmid upstream from the CAT gene, and the expression of CAT used as a reporter enzyme for confirmation that the sequence is a promoter. Acetylchloramphenicol can be detected fluorometrically. The CAT gene in this instance is called a reporter gene.

Various problems are inherent in bacterial expression systems. One problem is that when a gene is inserted into a plasmid for the purposes of expression, there is only a one-in-three chance that it will be inserted "in frame" downstream from a promoter and will be expressed as the desired protein, due to the fact that each codon has three nucleotides. There is a one-in-two possibility that the insert will be oriented in the correct direction. This gives only a one-in-six probability of productive insertion. Another very common problem is that overexpression can result in inclusion bodies that are insoluble masses of protein. Yet another problem occurs when the recombinant plasmid is engineered for expression of proteins that are toxic to the cell. A way around this is to insert the gene of interest after a promoter that responds to a high temperature. The cells carrying the plasmid are grown at a lower temperature, and the cells are heat shocked immediately before harvesting the protein in order to potentiate the expression of the toxic protein.

The amount of protein produced from any recombinant plasmid depends on the strength of the promoter as well as the number of plasmids. Some plasmids have a low copy number in a given cell (only one or a few plasmids per cell), which limits the amount of product. There is also a limit on the size of the recombinant plasmid and the insert (some plasmids will accept an insert of up to 10 kb). Additionally, bacteria cannot posttranslationally modify many eukaryotic proteins.

How can we clone larger proteins and proteins that can be posttranslationally modified? Various ways have been devised. They include the use of bacteriophage λ, which can carry inserts up to 15,000 bp. Another is use of a vector such as a cosmid. Cosmids are plasmids that contain both prokaryotic and eukaryotic regulatory sequences and can be shuttled between prokaryotic cells and eukaryotic cells. They can be amplified in prokaryotes with a short doubling time, isolated, and transferred to eukaryotic cells, where expression occurs together with posttranslational modification. Large sections of eukaryotic DNA can be cloned into yeast artificial chromosomes (YACS). YACS can carry up to 500 kbp. They have telomeres and centromeres, and after introduction into a yeast cell, they replicate like a normal yeast chromosome.

Two things that have not been discussed are the isolation of the DNA to be inserted into the plasmid and harvest of a plasmid from host cells. There are several ways of isolating genes. An example of this is to isolate poly-A-containing RNA (i.e., mRNA) from a cell where a large amount of the desired mRNA is produced. The classic example of this approach is the isolation of Hb mRNA from reticulocytes. Isolated RNA from the cells is applied to an oligo-dT column (polydT isolation). This is a chromatography column with sequences of repeated thymines bound to a solid support. Poly-A–containing RNA will hybridize to the column. This can then be eluted with a solution containing short polyT sequences. From a reticulocyte source, most of the mRNA will code for globin and can be reverse-transcribed into cDNA (complementary or copy DNA) by reverse transcription using reverse transcriptase.

Another way is to isolate mRNA by using antibodies. In this technique, ribosomes are isolated from cells that express the protein of interest by using antibodies against the desired protein (an antigen). The antibody binds the antigenic protein. The antigen-antibody complex is precipitated by centrifugation. Since the nascent protein is still attached to the ribosome/mRNA complex, mRNA for the desired protein is part of the resulting pellet. The mRNA can be removed from the complex and reverse transcribed into cDNA.

The last topic related to cloning to be discussed is the isolation of the plasmid, both before and after insertion of recombinant DNA and amplification. This is a relatively easy procedure unless an extremely pure preparation is required for the next phase of experimentation. Bacterial cells are lysed in a buffer, usually containing lysozyme and EDTA to promote lysis of the cell wall and to protect against nucleic acid degradation, respectively. The lysate is then treated with sodium dodecyl sulfate at a low pH to precipitate protein and chromosomal DNA. The protein and chromosomal DNA are then pelleted by centrifugation. The plasmid remains in the supernatant, whose pH must be neutralized, and plasmid DNA is isolated by use of an anion exchange column and precipitation in ethanol, or by chloroform/phenol extraction.

13.3. Other Uses of Restriction Endonucleases

Restriction endonucleases have many other uses. The human genome has recently been mapped by using restriction endonuclease digests and sequencing. By cleaving DNA segments with several different endonucleases, sequencing them, and searching for overlaps in sequence, the entire genome has been sequenced. The following is an example to work through.

A piece of DNA with the sequence

AAAGGTTTCCCATTTCCGTTAAATGTCAA

is subjected to three separate digests with three restriction endonucleases, with the following results:

Digest 1 yields	CCCATTTCCGT
	AAAGGTTT
	TAAATGTCAA

Digest 2 yields	AAAG
	ATTTCCGTTAAA
	TGTCAA
	GTTTCCC

Digest 3 yields	TTAAATGTCAA
	AAAGGT
	TTTCCG
	TTCCCA

When the sequences from the above three digests are overlapped, a unique ordering of the sequence can be determined. Can you see how?

RFLP (restriction fragment length polymorphism) involves use of restriction endonucleases, but no DNA sequencing. A DNA sample is digested by restriction endonucleases followed by electrophoresis. This technique is used to determine identity or for diagnosis (see below). Each individual has genetic polymorphism that results in addition or deletion of restriction sites. Digestion of DNA with various restriction enzymes can therefore distinguish between individuals or organisms.

Restriction endonucleases are also used in the creation of DNA libraries. There are two types of DNA libraries, genomic libraries and cDNA libraries. Each has its specific usefulness.

Genomic libraries are populations of bacteria into which have been cloned plasmids carrying fragments of genomic DNA. These fragments include promoters, introns, and other untranslated regions. Some bacteria in the library harbor complete genes because of the randomness of DNA fragment generation, and others only fragments of genes. The identity of a gene carried in each bacterium can be learned by growing bacterial colonies on solid medium and probing each colony with a DNA probe, or by sequencing the insert. Genomic DNA libraries are used when preserving genes for the study of posttranscriptional processing or for other studies that require the gene to be in its original form.

cDNA libraries are created in a similar way, but instead of fragmented genomic DNA, they contain cDNA sequences obtained by isolating total mRNA and reverse- transcribing it into cDNA. cDNA libraries are obtained in order to study which genes are being transcribed at a particular time in a particular tissue.

13.4. Nucleic Acid Blotting and Hybridization

Visualization of a specific segment of DNA relies on hybridization with a complementary sequence (called a **probe**) that is labeled in such a way that it is visible. The label on the complementary strand is usually radioactive (labeled by adding a P^{32}-containing phosphate group to the 3′ hydroxyl of the DNA probe) or fluorescent (covalently bound to a fluorophore). Or it may be labeled with biotin that can later be visualized by incubation with fluorescently labeled avidin.

The first step in nucleic acid blotting is fragmentation of the DNA of interest by restriction endonucleases or some other method. The fragments are then separated by electrophoresis on an agarose or acrylamide gel. After separation, the fragments are not visible to the naked eye and must be hybridized to the labeled probe. The gel matrix in which electrophoresis has occurred is too fragile for this visualization procedure, so the DNA is transferred to a membrane that resembles a piece of paper but is made of a substance such as nylon. This process of transfer is called **blotting** because it is analogous to the use of blotting paper to dry liquid ink used for writing. The blotting is done by placing the membrane onto the gel and keeping the membrane wet under a pile of damp paper towels. A weight is placed on the top of the gel/membrane "sandwich." After the desired time has passed, the membrane can be removed. The mirror image of the DNA fragmentation pattern is now attached to the membrane and can be linked more firmly to the membrane by cross-linking in the presence of ultraviolet light or by heating to denature the DNA. On the membrane, the DNA can be incubated in a solution containing the probe. The probe will hybridize only to DNA on the membrane to which it is complementary (Figure 3-46).

This technique can be used for tests of paternity, for forensics such as rape and murder cases, and in prenatal diagnostics. These tests are examples of the RFLP analysis. Here is an example of a test for sickle-cell anemia.

A sample of fetal blood or blood from the placenta (genetically identical to the fetus) is taken. Lymphocytes are isolated and cultured, and DNA extracted. The DNA is then cleaved with one or more restriction endonucleases, and the fragments are separated by electrophoresis. They are blotted on to a membrane, and the membrane is probed with the hemoglobin gene that has been previously labeled as described above. This process is diagrammed in detail below (Figure 3-47).

After digestion, there are many DNA fragments, but, as stated above, only three out of all the DNA fragments contain part of the Hb gene. All the fragments are separated by electrophoresis, transferred to a membrane, and probed with labeled DNA gene that has previously been isolated and that is full length (Figure 3-48). The probe is labeled either with radioactivity or a fluorescent dye.

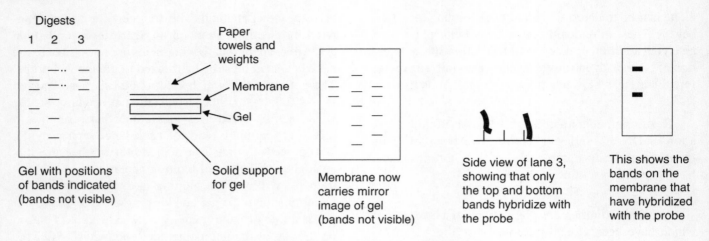

Digests
1 2 3

Gel with positions of bands indicated (bands not visible)

Paper towels and weights

Membrane

Gel

Solid support for gel

Membrane now carries mirror image of gel (bands not visible)

Side view of lane 3, showing that only the top and bottom bands hybridize with the probe

This shows the bands on the membrane that have hybridized with the probe

Figure 3-46. Schematic of Southern blotting.

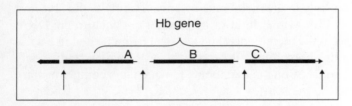

Hb gene

A   B   C

Figure 3-47. A diagram of a hemoglobin gene showing restriction sites. Total DNA is fragmented by an endonuclease that cuts at the arrows and leaves fragments A, B, and C that contain segments of the Hb gene. Only the Hb gene and its flanking sequences are shown.

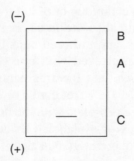

(−)

B

A

C

(+)

Figure 3-48. A diagram of a gel showing separation of hemoglobin restriction fragments by electrophoresis, followed by transfer to a membrane and Southern blotting. The shortest fragment (C) migrates the farthest toward the anode.

How can all three fragments be hybridized to the one probe? Even though only part of the probe is hybridized to each of the three fragments, there is enough affinity that the entire probe is fixed on the membrane, and the location of all three fragments can be visualized (Figure 3-49).

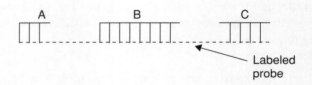

A   B   C

Labeled probe

Figure 3-49. All three fragments can bind to the probe.

How can this be used for diagnosis of sickle-cell disease or trait? The mutation that causes sickle-cell disease is located such that a restriction endonuclease site is lost. We can diagram the mutated gene thus (Figure 3-50):

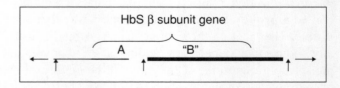

HbS β subunit gene

A   "B"

Figure 3-50. A diagram of a sickle hemoglobin gene showing restriction sites.

Digestion with restriction endonuclease yields only two fragments that are recognized by the Hb gene probe.

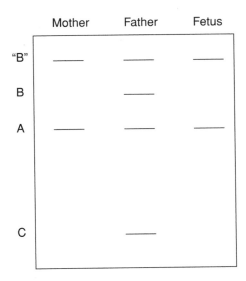

Figure 3-51. Southern blot of the hemoglobin gene from a mother with sickle-cell anemia, a father who is a sickle-cell carrier, and their unborn child.

The mother has a pattern that indicates that she has sickle-cell disease (only A and "B"). Father has the trait (A, B, and C, but also "B"). This gives the fetus a 50/50 chance of having the trait or the disease. The blot diagrammed (Figure 3-51) reveals that the child has the disease. Blots of DNA fragments probed with labeled DNA are called **Southern blots** after the scientist who devised the technology, Edwin M. Southern.

Southern blotting can also be used in situ by placing a membrane on top of colonies on a petri dish. This picks up bacteria from each colony. The bacteria are lysed on the membrane, and the DNA probed. Any colonies that hybridize with the probe on the membrane can be picked from the original dish and cultured. This is used, for instance, when checking for a point mutation in a gene. Identification of a colony carrying a mutated gene is done by using various degrees of "stringency" in probing. After transfer to the membrane and incubation with the probe, the membrane is washed at low stringency (with a buffer that allows DNA that is hybridized relatively loosely to remain on the membrane). Under these conditions, all genes, wild-type and mutated, will respond to the probe. The membrane is rewashed under conditions that allows only exact matches of gene and probe to remain on the membrane. The colonies carrying the mutated gene that previously hybridized to the probe will no longer do so, while exact matches still hybridize. This allows isolation from the relevant colonies containing the mutant gene for expression and permits expression and further study of the mutated protein.

There are also other blots, the most popular being **Northern blots** and **Western blots**. Northern blots start with isolation of mRNA, electrophoresis, and transfer to a membrane. The probe used is a labeled, selected known segment of DNA. If the probe hybridizes to an RNA fragment on the membrane, it demonstrates that this particular segment of DNA is being transcribed. Western blots use antibodies or other ligands to probe for the presence of a particular protein.

Microarrays are a recent technology that are also based on probe hybridization. Many DNA or RNA sequences can be bound to a small "chip" similar to a computer chip. The DNA or RNA that is being tested is incubated with the chip, and probe hybridization visualized. Microarrays are being used, among other things, for tracking of different mutation sites in the same gene.

13.5. PCR

Cloning of a gene for amplification was discussed above. Another method that is used for amplification of a gene is the **polymerase chain reaction (PCR)**. This is faster than in vivo cloning but produces less DNA than cloning. It is also more likely to introduce mistakes. Nonetheless it has become the method of choice for amplification for forensic investigation. It is generally necessary for use of PCR to know DNA sequences that flank the desired DNA sequence (there are also more advanced techniques that use a known segment at only one end or ligate known sequences at the ends of the sequence of interest). It also requires a DNA polymerase that can withstand the heat used to denature DNA.

The method is based on the regular mechanism of DNA replication, in which a template, primers (in vivo these are made of RNA, but in vitro they can be synthesized chemically directly as DNA), DNA polymerase, deoxyribonucleotides, and other components are needed. The DNA that is to be amplified is denatured (Step 1 in Figure 3-52). Two primers (forward and

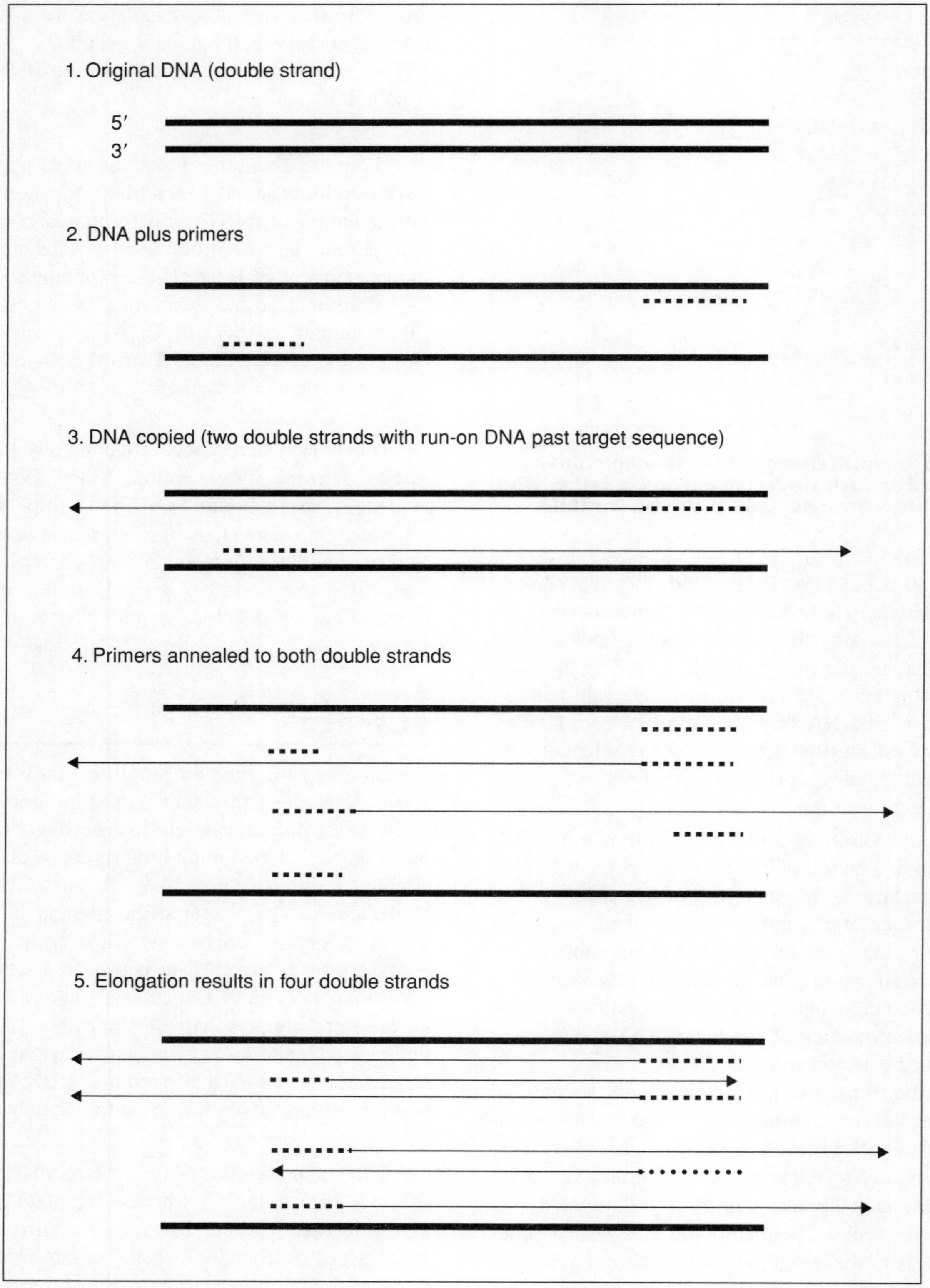

1. Original DNA (double strand)

5′
3′

2. DNA plus primers

3. DNA copied (two double strands with run-on DNA past target sequence)

4. Primers annealed to both double strands

5. Elongation results in four double strands

Figure 3-52. Two rounds of PCR.
(▬▬▬) original DNA. (———) newly synthesized DNA. (■ ■ ■ ■) primers.

reverse) are added to the reaction mixture and allowed to anneal (Step 2). DNA polymerase then uses the primers and the template DNA to synthesize copies of the target DNA (Step 3). This process is repeated (usually up to 30 times) by temperature cycling. The temperature is raised to denature the DNA, lowered enough to allow primer to anneal (Step 4), and changed again to the optimal temperature for DNA polymerase to synthesize new DNA (Step 5).

The above schematic shows the mechanism of PCR (Figure 3-52). Only in the third round of PCR are the newly synthesized fragments exactly the desired length (i.e., fragments with no overhang), and these fragments will continue to be made in ever larger amounts with each round of PCR. Restriction endonuclease sites can be included at the ends of the primers to allow easy digestion of the PCR fragment for ligation into a plasmid.

What can PCR be used for? As mentioned, forensic analysis of blood and other body fluids often uses PCR. It can also be used to introduce small mutations (site-directed mutagenesis) by the use of mismatched primers. The mutant proteins can be used in vivo for characterization of enzyme structure and mechanisms. RT-PCR combines reverse transcription of RNA into DNA followed by PCR, and can be used, for example, as a method of quantification of the amount of a specific RNA being transcribed under a given circumstance.

13.6. Sequencing and Analysis

The earliest method for DNA sequencing involved use of chemicals to cleave the DNA at different nucleotides. Today, DNA sequencing is usually performed by an in vitro method similar to PCR, but only one round of amplification occurs, and only one strand is copied. This method is called dideoxy-DNA sequencing and is sometimes called the **Sanger procedure**, in honor of the person who devised it. It is based on the premise that if synthesis of the strand can be stopped at the same type of base but at different places in the sequence, and the sizes of the resulting fragments measured, then it is possible to determine where those bases belong in the sequence. Synthesis stops at the position of dideoxynucleotide (ddNTP) incorporation because there is no 3' hydroxyl group for the next esterification to occur (Figure 3-53).

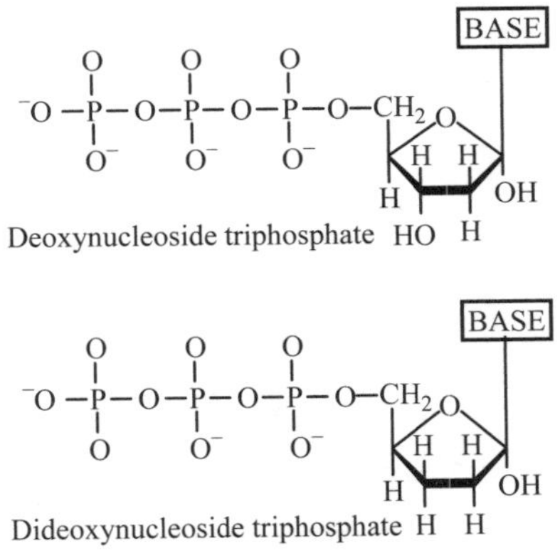

Figure 3-53. A regular dNTP and a ddNTP (the dideoxy analogue).
(Adapted from Devlin, T.M., ed., *Textbook of Biochemistry with Clinical Correlations,* Fifth Edition, Wiley-Liss, New York, 2002, Fig. 7.4.)

Below is a primer and template ready for sequencing by dideoxynucleotide sequencing.

5'   TTGCCG

3'   AACGGCTAAGCTCCGTAACCTTA

Samples of the template and primer are put into four separate test tubes, and to each one, all four dNTPs (dATP, dTTP, dCTP, dGTP), polymerase, and all the other necessary components are added. To each of the four test tubes, one of the four ddNTP analogues is also added.

The diagram below demonstrates how inclusion of ddATP in a reaction mixture results in random termination of DNA synthesis.

5'TTGCCGATTCGA* 3'AACGGCTAAGCTCCGTAACCTTA	12 base pairs
5'TTGCCGATTCGAGGCATTGGA* 3'AACGGCTAAGCTCCGTAACCTTA	21 base pairs
5'TTGCCGA* 3'AACGGCTAAGCTCCGTAACCTTA	7 base pairs
5'TTGCCGATTCGAGGCA* 3'AACGGCTAAGCTCCGTAACCTTA	16 base pairs

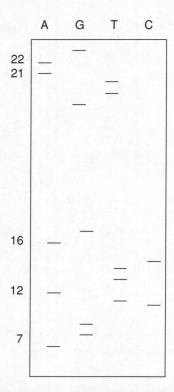

Figure 3-54. Samples from the above sequencing reaction are separated by electrophoresis.
A, G, T, C along the top of the gel designate which ddNTP had been included in each reaction mixture.

The next inserted dideoxynucleotide will be a ddA, to give a fragment of 22 base pairs. Repeating this with each of the ddNTP analogues added to a sequencing reactions results in synthesis of different length products (Figure 3-54).

Note that the sequence (see Figure 3-54) is read from the bottom up by going from column to column, because the smallest piece of DNA is that which was "stopped" first by a ddNTP. Compare the sizes of the fragments in the lane marked "A" with the results of the dideoxynucleotide sequencing shown above. The other lanes contain fragments from incubations in the presence of the other three dideoxynucleotides. The final sequence read from the gel is that of the strand that is complementary to the original template strand. Visualization of the DNA in the gel is either by using radiolabeled or fluorescently labeled nucleotides, or by staining. The order of nucleotide wells (AGCT) is used by convention and originated as a necessary characteristic of an earlier chemical method of DNA sequencing.

13.7. Protein-Nucleic Acid Interaction

Discussed earlier are several of the types of proteins that bind to DNA and RNA, such as hormone-receptor complexes (LATFs), repressor proteins, and modifying enzymes. How can one determine experimentally whether the role of a given protein involves binding to DNA or RNA?

An initial type of experiment might be a **gel shift assay** (see Figure 3-55). When a nucleic acid sequence is bound to a protein, it will migrate less rapidly through a nondenaturing electrophoretic gel than a segment that is not bound to protein. DNA is placed in a well of a nondenaturing gel. DNA that has been preincubated with the hypothesized binding protein is also added to the gel. DNA segments that show retarded migration can be reisolated from the gel, and more detailed studies done to identify the exact sequence to which the protein is bound. DNA can only be visualized if previously labeled.

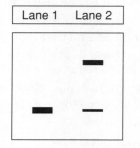

The diagram to the left shows: Lane 1, DNA without added cell extract; and Lane 2, DNA plus cell extract. The upper band in Lane 2 shows that migration is retarded when the DNA is bound by a protein in the cell extract.

Figure 3-55. Gel shift assay

For a more detailed protein-DNA binding study, **DNAse** or **RNAse protection assays** (also called DNA or RNA footprinting) are used. The oligonucleotide with the proposed binding site is incubated with the protein of interest and then exposed to a nuclease, such as DNAse I, which cuts the DNA at all exposed phosphodiester bonds, or to a chemical that cleaves exposed nucleic acid sequences. The section of the DNA that is protected by the bound protein is not cleaved. Removal of the binding protein and electrophoresis of the nucleotide fragments, both from the "protected" strand and from a strand that has not been incubated with the protein, allows identification of the protein-nucleic acid interaction site by comparison to one another.

Many promoter and enhancer consensus sequences were discovered using techniques like those described above.

13.8. Site-Directed Mutagenesis

Mutations in proteins have been very useful in delineating which residues are important in the activity or regulation of the protein. Originally these mutations were either identified by natural occurrence or were induced by treatment of a cell with a chemical mutagen, such as a nitrogen mustard, that had the potential for changing the DNA sequence of a gene. With the discovery of the modern techniques of molecular biology, sophisticated strategies have been developed that allow insertion of a specific mutation into a gene and subsequent expression of a mutated protein. These mutations can be introduced in several ways, for example, by isolating DNA containing the desired mutation site and using PCR primers that have a base substitution to make copies of the DNA with a mutation.

A very useful way to introduce several amino acid changes at one place in a protein is by use of in vivo suppression of amber codons. A stop (amber) codon is introduced at the desired mutation site, and the plasmids containing the amber codon are transformed into several strains of host cells. Each strain of bacteria carries an amber suppressor tRNA carrying a different amino acid. As the protein is expressed, the specific suppressor tRNA in each strain inserts a different amino acid into the mutated site. The result is a collection of bacterial clones, each carrying a different mutation at the same site. This is a very efficient way of synthesizing families of proteins with different amino acid replacements at the site of interest.

13.9. Answer to Mapping Problem

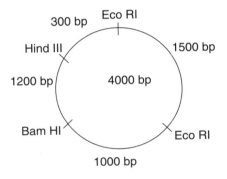

Part 4

PRACTICE EXAMS

Both Practice Exams are also on CD-ROM in our special interactive GRE Biochemistry, Cell and Molecular Biology TEST*ware*®. It is highly recommended that you first take this exam on computer. You will then have the additional study features and benefits of enforced timed conditions and instant, accurate scoring. See page xv for guidance on how to get the most out of our GRE Biochemistry, Cell and Molecular Biology software.

Answer Sheet: Practice Exam 1

1. (A) (B) (C) (D) (E)
2. (A) (B) (C) (D) (E)
3. (A) (B) (C) (D) (E)
4. (A) (B) (C) (D) (E)
5. (A) (B) (C) (D) (E)
6. (A) (B) (C) (D) (E)
7. (A) (B) (C) (D) (E)
8. (A) (B) (C) (D) (E)
9. (A) (B) (C) (D) (E)
10. (A) (B) (C) (D) (E)
11. (A) (B) (C) (D) (E)
12. (A) (B) (C) (D) (E)
13. (A) (B) (C) (D) (E)
14. (A) (B) (C) (D) (E)
15. (A) (B) (C) (D) (E)
16. (A) (B) (C) (D) (E)
17. (A) (B) (C) (D) (E)
18. (A) (B) (C) (D) (E)
19. (A) (B) (C) (D) (E)
20. (A) (B) (C) (D) (E)
21. (A) (B) (C) (D) (E)
22. (A) (B) (C) (D) (E)
23. (A) (B) (C) (D) (E)
24. (A) (B) (C) (D) (E)
25. (A) (B) (C) (D) (E)
26. (A) (B) (C) (D) (E)
27. (A) (B) (C) (D) (E)
28. (A) (B) (C) (D) (E)
29. (A) (B) (C) (D) (E)
30. (A) (B) (C) (D) (E)

31. (A) (B) (C) (D) (E)
32. (A) (B) (C) (D) (E)
33. (A) (B) (C) (D) (E)
34. (A) (B) (C) (D) (E)
35. (A) (B) (C) (D) (E)
36. (A) (B) (C) (D) (E)
37. (A) (B) (C) (D) (E)
38. (A) (B) (C) (D) (E)
39. (A) (B) (C) (D) (E)
40. (A) (B) (C) (D) (E)
41. (A) (B) (C) (D) (E)
42. (A) (B) (C) (D) (E)
43. (A) (B) (C) (D) (E)
44. (A) (B) (C) (D) (E)
45. (A) (B) (C) (D) (E)
46. (A) (B) (C) (D) (E)
47. (A) (B) (C) (D) (E)
48. (A) (B) (C) (D) (E)
49. (A) (B) (C) (D) (E)
50. (A) (B) (C) (D) (E)
51. (A) (B) (C) (D) (E)
52. (A) (B) (C) (D) (E)
53. (A) (B) (C) (D) (E)
54. (A) (B) (C) (D) (E)
55. (A) (B) (C) (D) (E)
56. (A) (B) (C) (D) (E)
57. (A) (B) (C) (D) (E)
58. (A) (B) (C) (D) (E)
59. (A) (B) (C) (D) (E)
60. (A) (B) (C) (D) (E)

61. (A) (B) (C) (D) (E)
62. (A) (B) (C) (D) (E)
63. (A) (B) (C) (D) (E)
64. (A) (B) (C) (D) (E)
65. (A) (B) (C) (D) (E)
66. (A) (B) (C) (D) (E)
67. (A) (B) (C) (D) (E)
68. (A) (B) (C) (D) (E)
69. (A) (B) (C) (D) (E)
70. (A) (B) (C) (D) (E)
71. (A) (B) (C) (D) (E)
72. (A) (B) (C) (D) (E)
73. (A) (B) (C) (D) (E)
74. (A) (B) (C) (D) (E)
75. (A) (B) (C) (D) (E)
76. (A) (B) (C) (D) (E)
77. (A) (B) (C) (D) (E)
78. (A) (B) (C) (D) (E)
79. (A) (B) (C) (D) (E)
80. (A) (B) (C) (D) (E)
81. (A) (B) (C) (D) (E)
82. (A) (B) (C) (D) (E)
83. (A) (B) (C) (D) (E)
84. (A) (B) (C) (D) (E)
85. (A) (B) (C) (D) (E)
86. (A) (B) (C) (D) (E)
87. (A) (B) (C) (D) (E)
88. (A) (B) (C) (D) (E)
89. (A) (B) (C) (D) (E)
90. (A) (B) (C) (D) (E)

Continued

Answer Sheet: Practice Exam 1 (Continued)

91. Ⓐ Ⓑ Ⓒ Ⓓ Ⓔ
92. Ⓐ Ⓑ Ⓒ Ⓓ Ⓔ
93. Ⓐ Ⓑ Ⓒ Ⓓ Ⓔ
94. Ⓐ Ⓑ Ⓒ Ⓓ Ⓔ
95. Ⓐ Ⓑ Ⓒ Ⓓ Ⓔ
96. Ⓐ Ⓑ Ⓒ Ⓓ Ⓔ
97. Ⓐ Ⓑ Ⓒ Ⓓ Ⓔ
98. Ⓐ Ⓑ Ⓒ Ⓓ Ⓔ
99. Ⓐ Ⓑ Ⓒ Ⓓ Ⓔ
100. Ⓐ Ⓑ Ⓒ Ⓓ Ⓔ
101. Ⓐ Ⓑ Ⓒ Ⓓ Ⓔ
102. Ⓐ Ⓑ Ⓒ Ⓓ Ⓔ
103. Ⓐ Ⓑ Ⓒ Ⓓ Ⓔ
104. Ⓐ Ⓑ Ⓒ Ⓓ Ⓔ
105. Ⓐ Ⓑ Ⓒ Ⓓ Ⓔ
106. Ⓐ Ⓑ Ⓒ Ⓓ Ⓔ
107. Ⓐ Ⓑ Ⓒ Ⓓ Ⓔ
108. Ⓐ Ⓑ Ⓒ Ⓓ Ⓔ
109. Ⓐ Ⓑ Ⓒ Ⓓ Ⓔ
110. Ⓐ Ⓑ Ⓒ Ⓓ Ⓔ
111. Ⓐ Ⓑ Ⓒ Ⓓ Ⓔ
112. Ⓐ Ⓑ Ⓒ Ⓓ Ⓔ
113. Ⓐ Ⓑ Ⓒ Ⓓ Ⓔ
114. Ⓐ Ⓑ Ⓒ Ⓓ Ⓔ
115. Ⓐ Ⓑ Ⓒ Ⓓ Ⓔ
116. Ⓐ Ⓑ Ⓒ Ⓓ Ⓔ
117. Ⓐ Ⓑ Ⓒ Ⓓ Ⓔ
118. Ⓐ Ⓑ Ⓒ Ⓓ Ⓔ
119. Ⓐ Ⓑ Ⓒ Ⓓ Ⓔ
120. Ⓐ Ⓑ Ⓒ Ⓓ Ⓔ

121. Ⓐ Ⓑ Ⓒ Ⓓ Ⓔ
122. Ⓐ Ⓑ Ⓒ Ⓓ Ⓔ
123. Ⓐ Ⓑ Ⓒ Ⓓ Ⓔ
124. Ⓐ Ⓑ Ⓒ Ⓓ Ⓔ
125. Ⓐ Ⓑ Ⓒ Ⓓ Ⓔ
126. Ⓐ Ⓑ Ⓒ Ⓓ Ⓔ
127. Ⓐ Ⓑ Ⓒ Ⓓ Ⓔ
128. Ⓐ Ⓑ Ⓒ Ⓓ Ⓔ
129. Ⓐ Ⓑ Ⓒ Ⓓ Ⓔ
130. Ⓐ Ⓑ Ⓒ Ⓓ Ⓔ
131. Ⓐ Ⓑ Ⓒ Ⓓ Ⓔ
132. Ⓐ Ⓑ Ⓒ Ⓓ Ⓔ
133. Ⓐ Ⓑ Ⓒ Ⓓ Ⓔ
134. Ⓐ Ⓑ Ⓒ Ⓓ Ⓔ
135. Ⓐ Ⓑ Ⓒ Ⓓ Ⓔ
136. Ⓐ Ⓑ Ⓒ Ⓓ Ⓔ
137. Ⓐ Ⓑ Ⓒ Ⓓ Ⓔ
138. Ⓐ Ⓑ Ⓒ Ⓓ Ⓔ
139. Ⓐ Ⓑ Ⓒ Ⓓ Ⓔ
140. Ⓐ Ⓑ Ⓒ Ⓓ Ⓔ
141. Ⓐ Ⓑ Ⓒ Ⓓ Ⓔ
142. Ⓐ Ⓑ Ⓒ Ⓓ Ⓔ
143. Ⓐ Ⓑ Ⓒ Ⓓ Ⓔ
144. Ⓐ Ⓑ Ⓒ Ⓓ Ⓔ
145. Ⓐ Ⓑ Ⓒ Ⓓ Ⓔ
146. Ⓐ Ⓑ Ⓒ Ⓓ Ⓔ
147. Ⓐ Ⓑ Ⓒ Ⓓ Ⓔ
148. Ⓐ Ⓑ Ⓒ Ⓓ Ⓔ
149. Ⓐ Ⓑ Ⓒ Ⓓ Ⓔ
150. Ⓐ Ⓑ Ⓒ Ⓓ Ⓔ

151. Ⓐ Ⓑ Ⓒ Ⓓ Ⓔ
152. Ⓐ Ⓑ Ⓒ Ⓓ Ⓔ
153. Ⓐ Ⓑ Ⓒ Ⓓ Ⓔ
154. Ⓐ Ⓑ Ⓒ Ⓓ Ⓔ
155. Ⓐ Ⓑ Ⓒ Ⓓ Ⓔ
156. Ⓐ Ⓑ Ⓒ Ⓓ Ⓔ
157. Ⓐ Ⓑ Ⓒ Ⓓ Ⓔ
158. Ⓐ Ⓑ Ⓒ Ⓓ Ⓔ
159. Ⓐ Ⓑ Ⓒ Ⓓ Ⓔ
160. Ⓐ Ⓑ Ⓒ Ⓓ Ⓔ
161. Ⓐ Ⓑ Ⓒ Ⓓ Ⓔ
162. Ⓐ Ⓑ Ⓒ Ⓓ Ⓔ
163. Ⓐ Ⓑ Ⓒ Ⓓ Ⓔ
164. Ⓐ Ⓑ Ⓒ Ⓓ Ⓔ
165. Ⓐ Ⓑ Ⓒ Ⓓ Ⓔ
166. Ⓐ Ⓑ Ⓒ Ⓓ Ⓔ
167. Ⓐ Ⓑ Ⓒ Ⓓ Ⓔ
168. Ⓐ Ⓑ Ⓒ Ⓓ Ⓔ
169. Ⓐ Ⓑ Ⓒ Ⓓ Ⓔ
170. Ⓐ Ⓑ Ⓒ Ⓓ Ⓔ
171. Ⓐ Ⓑ Ⓒ Ⓓ Ⓔ
172. Ⓐ Ⓑ Ⓒ Ⓓ Ⓔ
173. Ⓐ Ⓑ Ⓒ Ⓓ Ⓔ
174. Ⓐ Ⓑ Ⓒ Ⓓ Ⓔ
175. Ⓐ Ⓑ Ⓒ Ⓓ Ⓔ
176. Ⓐ Ⓑ Ⓒ Ⓓ Ⓔ
177. Ⓐ Ⓑ Ⓒ Ⓓ Ⓔ
178. Ⓐ Ⓑ Ⓒ Ⓓ Ⓔ
179. Ⓐ Ⓑ Ⓒ Ⓓ Ⓔ
180. Ⓐ Ⓑ Ⓒ Ⓓ Ⓔ

Practice Exam 1

DIRECTIONS: Choose the best answer for each question and mark the letter of your selection on the corresponding answer sheet.

1. $\Delta G = \Delta H - T\Delta S$, which of the following conditions indicates that a reaction is spontaneous?

    (A) ΔG is positive
    (B) ΔH is negative
    (C) $\Delta H - T\Delta S$ is positive
    (D) $\Delta H - T\Delta S$ is zero
    (E) $T\Delta S$ is positive

2. What are alleles?

    (A) Genes at the same locus on a pair of chromosomes
    (B) Genes from two different organisms that serve the same function
    (C) Homologous chromosomes
    (D) Neighboring genes
    (E) Palindromic sequences in chromosomes

3.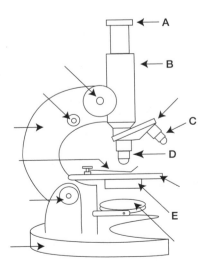

In the above diagram which letter indicates the eyepiece?

4. Answer this question using the letters placed at various points on the diagram. Which point on the curve represents the mean distance between two nuclei in a chemical bond?

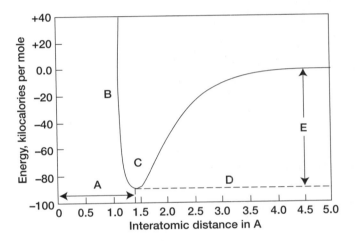

5. What is epistasis?

    (A) A gene expressed only in the male
    (B) A gene is only expressed if another one is also expressed
    (C) A heterozygous condition
    (D) Hereditary information not carried on chromosomal DNA
    (E) Two alleles the gene products of which are both expressed

6. What is the name of the instrument that cuts thin slices of a specimen for light microscopy?

    (A) Cryostat
    (B) Diaphragm
    (C) Interferometer
    (D) Scanner
    (E) Sectioner

7. If the reaction FAD $\rightarrow$ FADH$_2$ has an E_0' in Volts of -0.22, which of the reactions shown in this list is most capable of passing electrons to FAD?

   (A) Cytochrome $c^{+3} \rightarrow$ Cytochrome c^{+2} $(+0.22)$
   (B) Dehydroascorbate $\rightarrow$ Ascorbate $(+0.08)$
   (C) Ferredoxin$_{ox} \rightarrow$ Ferredoxin$_{red}$ (-0.43)
   (D) Fumarate $\rightarrow$ Succinate $(+0.03)$
   (E) Pyruvate $\rightarrow$ Lactate (-0.19)

8. What is necessary for transduction to occur in bacteria?

   (A) Bacteriophage
   (B) Fertility factor
   (C) Heat shock
   (D) Lysogeny
   (E) Pilus formation

9. Which of the following terms describes a condition, as in the Henderson-Hasselbalch equation, where $pH = pK_a$?

   (A) $[A^-] = [HA]/2$
   (B) $[A^-] = 2[HA]$
   (C) $[A^-]/[HA] = 0.5$
   (D) $[A^-]/[HA] = 1.0$
   (E) $[HA]/[A^-] = 10.0$

10. Given the following complementation table, which complementation group(s) carry(ies) a mutation?

Genotype	Phenotype
A−B+C+ crossed with A−B+ C+	A−B+C+
A+B−C+ crossed with A+B−C+	A+B-C+
A+B+C− crossed with A+B+C−	A+B+C−
A−B+C+ crossed with unknown	A+B+C+
A+B+C+ crossed with unknown	A+B+C+
A+B+C− crossed with unknown	A+B+C−

   (A) A
   (B) A + B
   (C) B
   (D) B + C
   (E) C

11. All of the following types of microscopy allow the researcher to look at live specimens EXCEPT

   (A) dark field
   (B) differential contrast
   (C) electron
   (D) fluorescent
   (E) phase contrast

12. The pKa for one amino group of a dibasic amino acid is 9.2 and the pKa of the other amino group is 10.8. The pKa of the carboxyl group is 2.2. The isoelectric point (pI) is

   (A) $(9.2 + 2.2)/2$
   (B) $(10.8 + 9.2)/2$
   (C) $(10.8 + 2.2)/2$
   (D) $(10.8 + 9.2 - 2.2)/2$
   (E) $(10.8 + 9.2 + 2.2)/3$

13. What type of genetic abnormality is Down syndrome?

   (A) Aneuploidy
   (B) Diploidy
   (C) Euploidy
   (D) Haploidy
   (E) Polyploidy

14. Which cellular substructure probably originated in the kingdom Monera?

   (A) Endoplasmic reticulum
   (B) Golgi
   (C) Lysosome
   (D) Mitochondrion
   (E) Nucleus

15. Here is a representative peptide bond between two amino acids.

$$R^1 - \underset{\underset{H_2N^4}{|}}{\overset{\overset{H^2}{|}}{C^3}} - \overset{\overset{O^5}{\|}}{C^6} - \underset{\underset{H^8}{|}}{N^7} - \underset{\underset{H}{|}}{\overset{\overset{R^9}{|}}{C^{10}}} - C^{11} \overset{O^{12}}{\underset{O^-}{}}$$

If these were in a protein in a *trans* configuration, which atoms would lie in a plane?

(A) 2,3,4,5,6,7
(B) 3,4,5,6,7,10
(C) 3,4,6,7,8,10
(D) 3,5,6,7,8,10
(E) 3,6,7,8,9,10

16. All of the following terms describe genes that can be expressed EXCEPT

(A) allelic gene
(B) divergent gene
(C) duplicated gene
(D) exonic gene
(E) pseudogene

17. What is the shape of a bacterium of the type *Bacillus*?

(A) Chains of round cells
(B) Elongated spiral
(C) Pairs of round cells
(D) Rod-shape
(E) Single round cells

18. What type of interaction occurs predominantly between DNA and histones?

(A) Covalent
(B) Hydrogen bonding
(C) Hydrophobic
(D) Ionic
(E) Van der Waals

19. Amino acids frequently found in proteins where there is a change in direction (β-turn of the polypeptide chain) are

(A) Cys, Val
(B) Gly, Pro
(C) His, Met
(D) Phe, Trp
(E) Tyr, Leu

20. If the base composition of DNA is 30% purine and 20% thymine, what percentage is guanine?

(A) 10%
(B) 15%
(C) 20%

(D) 30%
(E) 50%

21. In what environment do halophiles live?

(A) Extreme cold
(B) Extreme heat
(C) High pH
(D) High salt
(E) Low salt

22. A first-order reaction carried out at constant temperature, pressure, and $[H^+]$, will have a rate constant that

(A) changes as the amount of product increases
(B) has units of t^{-1}
(C) increases logarithmically as product is removed
(D) is nonvariant only during initial rate measurements
(E) varies with the concentration of reactants

23. What is the definition of T_m (melting temperature) of DNA?

(A) Temperature at which all DNA is denatured.
(B) Temperature at which all the G-C bases are denatured.
(C) Temperature at which half the DNA is denatured.
(D) Temperature at which half the G-C and half the A-T bases are denatured.
(E) Temperature at which DNA starts to denature.

24. Enzymes enhance reaction rates by a combination of mechanisms that stabilize the transition states of reactants. Serine proteases use a combination of which mechanisms to enhance reaction rates?

(A) Acid-base and covalent catalysis
(B) Acid-base and proximity (binding of substrates)
(C) Acid-base and strain and distortion.
(D) Proximity (orientation and covalent catalysis)
(E) Strain and distortion and proximity (orientation of substrates)

25. What is the definition of a transcriptome?

(A) All the genes in an organism
(B) All the exons in an organism
(C) All the mRNA in an organism
(D) All the proteins in an organism
(E) All the transcribed genes in an organism

26. What is a prototroph?

(A) A cell that can live on simple sugars and inorganic ions alone.
(B) A cell that can photosynthesize.
(C) A cell that cannot live in the presence of oxygen.
(D) A cell that reproduces by binary fission or sexually.
(E) A cell that uses carbon dioxide to form methane.

27. The class of enzymes that catalyzes the formation of oxaloacetate from pyruvate, CO_2, and ATP is a (an)

(A) Hydrolase
(B) Isomerase
(C) Ligase
(D) Oxidoreductase
(E) Transferase

28. During the transformation of substrate to product for an enzymatic reaction, the system is capable of performing work as long as

(A) ΔS (entropy) remains constant
(B) direct interaction of the substrate with a specific region of the enzyme forms a stable irreversible complex
(C) it is in a nonequilibrium state
(D) the energy required to reach the transition-state is the same as for the uncatalyzed reaction.
(E) the K_{eq} for the catalyzed reaction differs from that of the uncatalyzed reaction.

29. The Michaelis-Menten equation for a competitive inhibitor is

$$v = \frac{V_{max}[S]}{K_m\left(1 + \dfrac{[I]}{K_i}\right) + [S]}$$

If $[I] = K_i$ and $[S] = 2K_m$, what fraction of enzyme is in the ES complex?

(A) 0.20
(B) 0.25
(C) 0.50
(D) 0.67
(E) 0.75

30. What is the sign that a cell has undergone apoptosis?

(A) Destruction of adjacent cells
(B) DNA in an orderly ladder
(C) Inflammation
(D) Lipase action
(E) Pyknotic nuclei

31. All of the following can be estimated from a $C_o t$ curve EXCEPT

(A) genetic complexity
(B) number of repetitive copies of DNA sequences
(C) percentage G-C in genomic DNA
(D) percentage single-copy DNA
(E) similarity between species

32. Which of the reactions in the following diagram would best demonstrate the mechanism of the overall reaction between a mechanism-based inhibitor of an enzyme and its normal substrate?

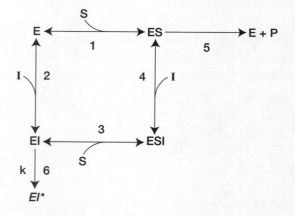

(A) 1 and 5
(B) 1, 2, 5, and 6
(C) 1, 2, and 3
(D) 2 and 3
(E) 2 and 6

33. Which amino acid in a protein can NOT be glycosylated?

   (A) Arginine
   (B) Asparagine
   (C) Hydroxyproline
   (D) Serine
   (E) Threonine

34. Which letter indicates lipopolysaccharides in the diagram of an *Escherichia coli* membrane shown below?

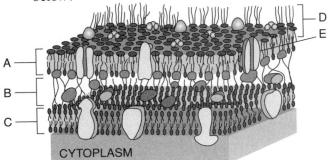

35. A two-substrate enzyme-catalyzed reaction in which product is produced from a ternary complex

   (A) follows a sequential mechanism
   (B) has a $\Delta G°$ for the uncatalyzed reaction lower than that for the catalyzed reaction
   (C) has a K_{eq} that depends upon the starting ratio of the concentration of reactants
   (D) has a transition-state that is achieved when the first substrate binds
   (E) must have one of the products of the reaction leave before final product is formed

36. What is the term for genes that are similar between one organism and another?

   (A) Alleles
   (B) Analogs
   (C) Heterologs
   (D) Homologs
   (E) Orthologs

37. What do Gram-positive cells become when treated with an isotonic solution and lysozyme?

   (A) Glycocalyx
   (B) Mitoplasts
   (C) Periplasts
   (D) Porins
   (E) Protoplasts

38. Which of the following single-stranded DNA sequence is NOT part of a double-stranded palindromic sequence?

   (A) ACTAGT
   (B) TGTACA
   (C) ACTACT
   (D) AGTACT
   (E) CGTACG

39. The γ-phosphate group of ATP and the β-phosphate group of ADP are considered to be high-energy phosphate compounds because

   (A) each of the phosphate atoms has a partial positive charge that enhances its ability for nucleophilic attack on more positive centers in molecules
   (B) electrostatic repulsion of negative charges on those phosphate groups makes them less stable
   (C) formal negative charges on the oxygen atoms make them good chelating agents for divalent metal ions
   (D) the size of the adenosine moiety of ATP and ADP together with the γ- and β-phosphates provide steric hindrance to their interaction at enzyme active sites
   (E) there are more resonance forms for those phosphate groups in ATP and ADP than for free phosphate

40. Which is the major enzyme for DNA replication in prokaryotes?

   (A) Pol I
   (B) Pol II
   (C) Pol III
   (D) Pol IV
   (E) Pol V

41. What is the role of a "flippase"?

    (A) Addition of carbohydrate to membrane proteins
    (B) Insertion of proteins into a membrane
    (C) Transfer of lipids between organelles
    (D) Transfer of lipids from one cell membrane to another
    (E) Transfer of lipids from one leaflet of a membrane to the other

42. The end product of glucose metabolism by glycolysis under anaerobic conditions is

    (A) acetate
    (B) carbon dioxide
    (C) lactate
    (D) malate
    (E) pyruvate

43. Which is the major enzyme for mitochondrial DNA replication?

    (A) Pol α
    (B) Pol β
    (C) Pol γ
    (D) Pol δ
    (E) Pol ε

44. Which of the membrane transport mechanisms shown below is a channel?

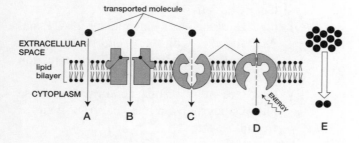

45. The first high-energy compound formed in glycolysis is

    (A) 1,3-bisphosphoglycerate
    (B) 3-phosphoglycerate
    (C) dihydroxyacetone 3-phosphate
    (D) glyceraldehyde 3-phosphate
    (E) phosphoenolpyruvate

46. This diagram represents chromosomes during replication where the organism was originally grown in medium containing nitrogen-15 (█████) and then shifted to medium containing nitrogen-14 (——)

Which sucrose gradient centrifugation banding pattern best represents these chromosomes?

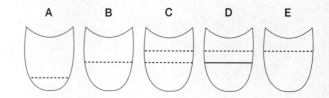

47. Which reaction is responsible for the first substrate-level production of ATP in glycolysis?

    (A) 1,3-bisphosphoglycerate → 3-phosphoglycerate
    (B) 2-phosphoglycerate → phosphoenolpyruvate
    (C) 3-phosphoglycerate → 2-phosphoglycerate
    (D) glyceraldehyde 3-phosphate → 1,3-bisphosphoglycerate
    (E) phosphoenolpyruvate → pyruvate

48. What is a characteristic of active transport and NOT a characteristic of passive transport?

    (A) Sigmoidal plot of transport rate versus concentration of solute
    (B) Competition between solutes for transport
    (C) Movement of solute against a concentration gradient
    (D) Saturability
    (E) Specificity of solute to be transported

49. Because one of the major functions of glycolysis is rapid production of energy, the inhibitory effect of citrate and H⁺ on phosphofructokinase-1 activity can be rationalized by

   (A) decreased fatty acid oxidation
   (B) deficiency of glucose for other metabolic functions
   (C) increased activity of the TCA cycle and oxidative phosphorylation
   (D) low energy charge [AMP/(ATP+ADP) ratio] of the cell
   (E) reduced need for phosphoenolpyruvate for aromatic amino acid biosynthesis

50. DNA synthesis requires a primer. What is it, and how is this made in prokaryotes?

   (A) DNA, by a special DNA polymerase
   (B) DNA, by DNA polymerase III
   (C) DNA, by reverse transcriptase
   (D) RNA, by an RNA polymerase
   (E) RNA, by reverse transcriptase

51. Pyruvate dehydrogenase requires each of the following coenzymes to effect its action EXCEPT

   (A) FAD
   (B) Lipoic acid
   (C) NAD⁺
   (D) Pyridoxal phosphate
   (E) Thiamin pyrophosphate

52. What is the definition of pinocytosis?

   (A) Movement of a solid out of a cell
   (B) Movement of liquid in a vesicle into a cell
   (C) Secondary active transport
   (D) Simple diffusion across a membrane
   (E) Targeting of a protein to an organelle

53. What serves as a template for telomerase?

   (A) DNA made by a DNA polymerase
   (B) RNA associated with the enzyme
   (C) RNA made by reverse transcriptase
   (D) RNA synthesized by an RNA polymerase
   (E) The complementary strand on the DNA

54. This TCA cycle enzyme catalyzes a substrate level phosphorylation.

   (A) α-Ketoglutarate dehydrogenase
   (B) Isocitrate dehydrogenase
   (C) Malate dehydrogenase
   (D) Succinate dehydrogenase
   (E) Succinyl-CoA synthetase

55. What is the name given to the "puffs" shown on the polytene chromosomes of fruit flies?

   (A) Balbiani rings
   (B) Barr bodies
   (C) Euchromatin
   (D) Nucleosomes
   (E) Scaffolds

56.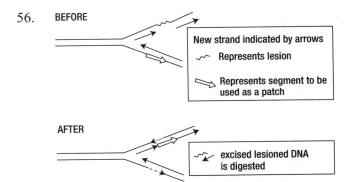

What type of repair does the above diagram show?

   (A) Base excision repair
   (B) Daughter strand gap repair
   (C) Mismatch repair
   (D) Nucleotide excision repair
   (E) Photoreactivation

57. Isocitrate dehydrogenase is one of the enzymes of the TCA cycle the activity of which is regulated by intermediary metabolites. Which of the following is an activator of this enzyme?

   (A) ADP
   (B) ATP
   (C) FADH₂
   (D) GTP
   (E) NADH/H⁺

58. What is the name of the chromosomal structure diagrammed below?

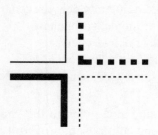

(A) Holliday junction
(B) Nonhomologous end-joining structure
(C) Single strand annealing
(D) SOS signal
(E) Thymine dimers

59. What information can be obtained by amniocentesis when Barr bodies are seen?

(A) Proteins are being expressed
(B) rRNA transcription is occurring
(C) The fetus has Down syndrome
(D) The fetus is female
(E) The fetus is nonviable

60. During oxidative phosphorylation, ATP is generated when

(A) a pH gradient across the outer mitochondrial membrane occurs
(B) hydrogen ions are pumped from the matrix of mitochondria into the intermembrane space
(C) hydrogen ions are pumped into the matrix by complex IV
(D) hydrogen ions are pumped out of the matrix through complex I
(E) hydrogen ions flow through the F_1F_0 protein complex of the inner mitochondrial membrane

61. All of the following are subunits of the prokaryotic apoenzyme RNA polymerase EXCEPT

(A) α
(B) β
(C) β'
(D) ω
(E) σ

62. All of the following are characteristic of a nucleosome EXCEPT

(A) DNA wound around histones
(B) histone H1
(C) histones H2a and H2b
(D) histone H3
(E) histone H4

63. If the inner mitochondrial membrane is made permeable to H^+ by compounds like 2,4-dinitrophenol the

(A) electron potential (E_0^1) between the substrate and the terminal electron acceptor decreases
(B) overall reaction becomes endothermic
(C) rate of generation of a membrane potential increases
(D) rate of oxygen utilization increases
(E) rate of synthesis of ATP increases

64. Which RNA polymerase would be expected to direct synthesis of RNA of 5.8S, 28S, and 18S?

(A) Eukaryotic RNA polymerase I (A)
(B) Eukaryotic RNA polymerase II (B)
(C) Eukaryotic RNA polymerase III (C)
(D) Mitochondrial RNA polymerase
(E) Prokaryotic RNA polymerase

65. Which of the following is an intermediate in the oxidative phase of the pentose phosphate pathway?

(A) 2-Keto-l-gulonolactone
(B) 6-Phosphogluconate
(C) Fructose-6-phosphate
(D) L-Gluconate
(E) Xylitol

66. Which amino acid is prominent in the "zipper" motif found in many DNA-binding proteins?

   (A) Alanine
   (B) Cysteine
   (C) Isoleucine
   (D) Leucine
   (E) Valine

67. The function of the many glycines in collagen is to

   (A) direct the procollagen molecules out of the cell
   (B) form a nonpolar edge for hydrophobic stabilization
   (C) form the globular structures at the ends of procollagen
   (D) promote helix formation
   (E) serve as carbohydrate receptors

68. Regulation of EIF-2a is one way of regulating translation. How is the factor regulated?

   (A) Allosterically
   (B) Methylation
   (C) Phosphorylation
   (D) Protein-protein interaction
   (E) Zymogen cleavage

69. The pentose phosphate pathway is controlled primarily by

   (A) activation of glucose 6-phosphate dehydrogenase by sedoheptulose 7-phosphate
   (B) feedback inhibition of glucose 6-phosphate dehydrogenase by ribose 5-phosphate
   (C) feedback inhibition of glucose 6-phosphate dehydrogenase by xylulose 5-phosphate
   (D) the availability of NADP+
   (E) the ratio of NAD+/NADPH(H+)

70. For what does ACAUGCCCAACGTT code in a finished and processed protein?

1st position (5′ end) ↓	2nd position				3rd position (3′ end) ↓
	U	**C**	**A**	**G**	
U	Phe	Ser	Tyr	Cys	U
	Phe	Ser	Tyr	Cys	C
	Leu	Ser	STOP	STOP	A
	Leu	Ser	STOP	Trp	G
C	Leu	Pro	His	Arg	U
	Leu	Pro	His	Arg	C
	Leu	Pro	Gin	Arg	A
	Leu	Pro	Gin	Arg	G
A	Ile	Thr	Asn	Ser	U
	Ile	Thr	Asn	Ser	C
	Ile	Thr	Lys	Arg	A
	Met	Thr	Lys	Arg	G
G	Val	Ala	Asp	Gly	U
	Val	Ala	Asp	Gly	C
	Val	Ala	Glu	Gly	A
	Val	Ala	Glu	Gly	G

   (A) His-ala-glu-arg
   (B) Met-ala-glu-arg
   (C) Met-cys-pro
   (D) Pro-asn-val
   (E) Thr-cys-pro-thr

71.

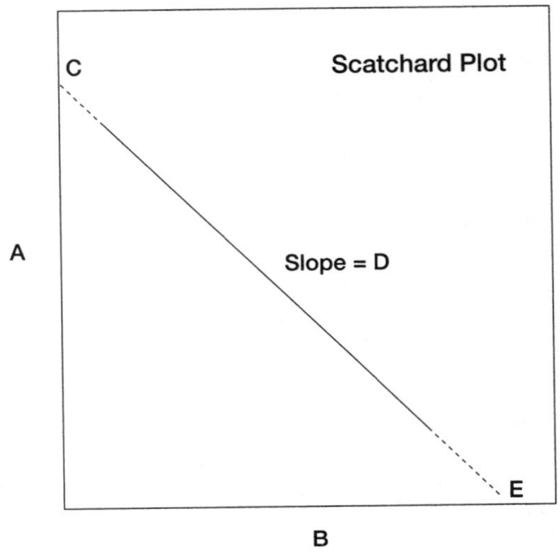

In the Scatchard Plot shown above, which letter indicates the total number of binding sites for the ligand on each cell?

72. Free glucuronic acid in humans may be metabolized

    (A) by an aldolase to give glycerol and glycerate
    (B) by reduction to glucose directly and then phosphorylated to glucose 6-phosphate
    (C) to diketo-L-gulonate and excreted
    (D) to D-xylulose 5-phosphate and enter the pentose phosphate pathway
    (E) to myoinositol and participate in signal transduction pathways

73. What is the first step in eukaryotic messenger RNA processing?

    (A) Addition of a polyA tail
    (B) Addition of the cap
    (C) Methylation of the cap
    (D) Splicing
    (E) Transport out of the nucleus

74. In G-protein–mediated cell signaling, what is the final step that brings the system back to its resting state?

    (A) Adenyl cyclase is activated.
    (B) Cyclic AMP is synthesized.
    (C) GTP replaces GDP by addition of a phosphate.
    (D) The hormone associates with the receptor.
    (E) The three subunits of the G-protein reassociate.

75. After cleavage of the 45S rRNA precursor, what transcripts are found?

    (A) 5.8S, 18S, and 28S
    (B) 5.8S, 18S, and 30S
    (C) 5S, 18S, and 28S
    (D) 5S, 5.8S, and 18S
    (E) 5S, 5.8S, and 28S

76. Alanine and ATP stimulate gluconeogenesis by inhibiting

    (A) aldolase
    (B) glyceraldehyde 3-phosphate dehydrogenase
    (C) phosphofructokinase I
    (D) phosphoglycerate kinase
    (E) pyruvate kinase

77. What is the role of ribonuclease P in RNA processing?

    (A) Cleavage of the 45S rRNA precursor
    (B) Degradation of mRNA
    (C) Removal of introns in mRNA
    (D) Removal of the intron in tRNA
    (E) Trimming of 5′ end of tRNA

78. The nucleation center (core molecule) for initiating glycogen synthesis is a

    (A) lipopolysaccharide with a terminal glucose in a 1,6-linkage
    (B) polynucleotide with a terminal UDP-glucose
    (C) small dimeric protein
    (D) small branched chain carbohydrate
    (E) truncated form of UDP-glucose pyrophosphorylase that adds the first ten glucose units of the core structure

79. Where are most mitochondria and the nucleus located in a nerve cell?

    (A) Axon
    (B) Cell body
    (C) Dendrite
    (D) Synaptic terminals
    (E) Terminal branches

80. The mechanism of coordinate control of glycogen synthesis and degradation involves

    (A) activation of glycogen phosphorylase by dephosphorylation
    (B) activation of glycogen synthase by dephosphorylation and phosphorylase activation by phosphorylation
    (C) activation of glycogen synthase by phosphorylation
    (D) glycogen synthase and phosphorylase activation by phosphorylation
    (E) glycogen synthase and phosphorylase activation by dephosphorylation

81. Each of the following is a correct pairing of the functions of mitochondria during active electron transport and active photosynthesis during the light phase EXCEPT

	Mitochondria	Chloroplast
(A)	$[H^+]$ greater outside of matrix	$[H^+]$ greater inside the thylakoid space
(B)	ATP is made inside matrix	ATP is made outside of the thylakoid lumen
(C)	H^+ generated from oxidation	H^+ generated from photon interaction
(D)	NADH/H^+ is oxidized	NADH/H^+ is made
(E)	O_2 is used	O_2 is generated

82. In the Z-system of photosynthesis, electron flow follows which general pathway (some components are omitted for simplicity)?

    (A) P680→cytochrome bf→(plastoquinone→ plastocyanin→P700
    (B) P680→pheophytin→(plastoquinone)→ cytochrome bf→P700
    (C) P680→plastocyanin→(plastoquinone)→ cytochrome bf→P700
    (D) P700→plastocyanin→(plastoquinone)→ cytochrome bf→P680
    (E) P700→plastocyanin→cytochrome bf→ (plastoquinone→pheophytin →P680

83. What ensures that an electrical signal is transmitted uni-directionally down the membrane of a nerve cell?

    (A) Degradation of the gated channel after closing
    (B) Efflux of sodium from the cell
    (C) Inactivation of an ATPase
    (D) Opening of the next gated channel in series
    (E) Temporary inactivation of each gated channel in turn

84. The chloroplast compartment where NADPH/H^+ and ATP are synthesized is

    (A) on the stroma lamellae
    (B) on the stroma side of the inner membrane
    (C) on the stroma side of the thylakoid membrane
    (D) within the inner space of the grana
    (E) within the space between the inner and outer membranes

85. There are 64 codons, but many fewer tRNAs. All of the following are contributory to this discrepancy EXCEPT

    (A) fewer than 61 codons code for an amino acid
    (B) the binding of the first base in the anticodon is less stringent than the binding of the other two bases
    (C) some tRNAs recognize more than one codon
    (D) three codons are stop codons
    (E) wobble

86. Energy conserved from PSI and PSII during the "light" reactions of photosynthesis is used for synthesis of which metabolite during the "dark" reactions?

    (A) 1,3-bisphosphoglycerate
    (B) 3-Phosphoglycerate
    (C) Dihydroxyacetone phosphate
    (D) Glyceraldehyde 3-phosphate
    (E) Glycerol phosphate

87. Which neurotransmitter is metabolized in the synapse?

    (A) Acetylcholine
    (B) Dopamine
    (C) Epinephrine
    (D) GABA
    (E) Norepinephrine

88. A special requirement for plants that use the C-4 photosynthetic mechanism is that they have

   (A) a high photorespiration by ribulose 1,5-bisphosphate carboxylase
   (B) a special cellular arrangement that separates enzymes involved in initial CO_2 trapping from those involved in fixation of CO_2
   (C) a special transport mechanism for ribulose 1,5-bisphosphate
   (D) an effective means of generating ATP, since it is not done by the light reactions
   (E) adapted for use of low light intensity to make CO_2 trapping more efficient

89. How many aminoacyl tRNA synthetases are there?

   (A) 4
   (B) 12
   (C) 20
   (D) 61
   (E) 64

90. The enzyme that converts atmospheric nitrogen into a biologically usable form is

   (A) amino acid oxidase
   (B) amino transferase
   (C) glutamate dehydrogenase
   (D) glutamine synthetase
   (E) nitrogenase

91. Which amino acid is the first in every protein made on eukaryotic ribosomes?

   (A) Alanine
   (B) Cysteine
   (C) Glycine
   (D) Methionine
   (E) Serine

92. In the following diagram of a sarcomere, which letter represents the Z-line?

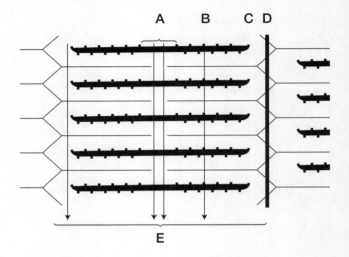

93. Each of the following amino acids is essential in mammals under all conditions EXCEPT

   (A) Arginine
   (B) Histidine
   (C) Lysine
   (D) Phenylalanine
   (E) Threonine

94. The carbon skeleton of which group of amino acids is derived from both the glycolytic scheme and the pentose phosphate pathway?

   (A) Alanine, aspartate, and cysteine
   (B) Arginine, glutamine, and proline
   (C) Methionine, threonine, and lysine
   (D) Phenylalanine, tyrosine, and tryptophan
   (E) Valine, leucine, and isoleucine

95. Each step in protein synthesis requires energy EXCEPT

   (A) charging of tRNA
   (B) formation of the initiation complex
   (C) formation of the peptide bond
   (D) movement of the mRNA on the ribosome
   (E) termination

96. Where is the calcium that triggers muscle contraction stored?

    (A) Lysosome
    (B) Mitochondrion
    (C) Outside the cell
    (D) Sarcoplasmic reticulum
    (E) Vacuole

97. Obligatory intermediates in asparagine biosynthesis are

    (A) aspartate and $(NH_4)_3PO_4$
    (B) aspartyl-β-ADP and NH_4^+
    (C) aspartyl-β-AMP and glutamine
    (D) aspartyl-β-phosphate and glutamine
    (E) aspartyl-β-phosphate and NH_4^+

98. In what kind of array are microtubules in a cilium arranged?

    (A) 7 +2
    (B) 8 +2
    (C) 8 +3
    (D) 9 +2
    (E) 9 +3

99. In the *de novo* synthesis of methionine, the direct source of the methyl group on sulfur is

    (A) methylcobalamin
    (B) N^{10}-formyl-THF
    (C) N^5,N^{10}-methylene-THF
    (D) N^5,N^{10}-methynyl-THF
    (E) N^5-methyl-THF

100. What is the name of the protein that takes the signal sequence of a protein across the endoplasmic reticulum membrane?

    (A) Chaperonin
    (B) Flippase
    (C) Signal recognition particle (SRP
    (D) SRP receptor
    (E) Translocon

101. From where does the energy for movement of prokaryotic flagella come?

    (A) Chemiosmotic gradient
    (B) Conformation change
    (C) Electric stimulation
    (D) Hydrolysis of Acetyl CoA
    (E) Mitochondrially synthesized ATP

102. Atoms, other than the α-amino group, of this amino acid come predominantly from adenine and ribose

    (A) Arginine
    (B) Asparagine
    (C) Glutamine
    (D) Histidine
    (E) Tryptophan

103. The incidence of dominant gene A in the population is 0.8. What is the incidence of recessive gene a?

    (A) 0.1
    (B) 0.2
    (C) 0.4
    (D) 0.6
    (E) 0.8

104. During which phase of cell division do cells become 4N?

    (A) G_1
    (B) G_0
    (C) S
    (D) G_2
    (E) M

105. Sixteen % of a population show a homozygous recessive phenotype. What percentage of the population are heterozygotes?

    (A) 16
    (B) 32
    (C) 36
    (D) 48
    (E) 84

GRE BIOCHEMISTRY, CELL AND MOLECULAR BIOLOGY

106. Each of the following is an intermediate in the synthesis of steroid hormones EXCEPT

(A) 3-hydroxy-5-methylglutaryl CoA
(B) acetoacetyl CoA
(C) farnesyl pyrophosphate
(D) geranyl pyrophosphate
(E) mevalonic acid

107. In a cross between Aa and AA genotypes what percent of the offspring are Aa?

(A) 10
(B) 25
(C) 50
(D) 75
(E) 100

108.

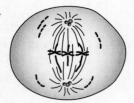

Which stage of mitosis does the above diagram represent?

(A) Anaphase
(B) Cytokinesis
(C) Metaphase
(D) Prophase
(E) Telophase

109. Interaction of regulatory and/or other molecules with bases of double stranded DNA may occur

(A) at the vertical linear alignment of each turn of the helix
(B) through direct interaction since bases are aligned in the helix on the outside of the phosphodiester bonds
(C) through interaction with the major grove of the double helix

(D) through interaction with the minor grove of the double helix
(E) when palindromic sequences exist at the innermost section of the minor grove

110. When are oogonia synthesized in the female?

(A) After sexual intercourse
(B) At first menstruation
(C) Before birth
(D) During late puberty
(E) In infancy

111. Which of the following is a positive allosteric modifier of purine biosynthesis

(A) Adenosine monophosphate
(B) Adenosine triphosphate
(C) Guanosine monophosphate
(D) Inosine monophosphate
(E) Phosphoribosyl-1-pyrophosphate

112. A plasmid cut with Eco RI gives two fragments of 2 kb and 0.3 kb. Cut with Hind III there are fragments of 1 kb and 1.3 kb. When cut simultaneously with both enzymes the fragments derived are 0.1 kb, 0.2 kb, 0.8 kb, and 1.2 kb. Which of the plasmid maps is correct?

(A)

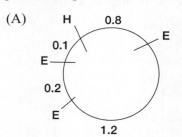

(B)

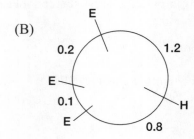

(C)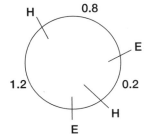

(D)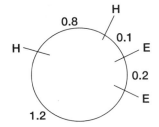

(E)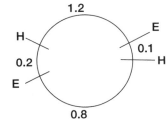

113. Which cells result from the meiotic phase of oogenesis?

(A) One polar body and one egg
(B) One polar body and two eggs
(C) Two polar bodies and one egg
(D) Two polar bodies and two eggs
(E) Three polar bodies and one egg

114. Which combination describes the preinitiation complex in protein synthesis?

(A) 40S ribosome subunit, mRNA, GTP
(B) 40S ribosome subunit, mRNA, GTP, methionyl-tRNA^{met}
(C) 40S ribosome subunit, mRNA, methionyl-tRNA^{met}
(D) 60S ribosome subunit, mRNA, GTP
(E) 60S ribosome subunit, mRNA, GTP, methionyl-tRNA^{met}

115. Which of the following is LEAST likely to be associated with the regulation of enzyme activity?

(A) Cooperative subunit-subunit interaction of enzymes
(B) Covalent modification of enzymes
(C) Feedback inhibition of metabolic pathways
(D) Interconversion of metabolites such as lactate and pyruvate
(E) Synthesis and degradation of enzymes

116. By what treatment can bacterial cells be rendered competent?

(A) Bacteriocide
(B) Calcium chloride
(C) Freezing
(D) Lysozyme
(E) Sodium dodecyl sulfate

117. What is the name of the 16-cell developing organism at the hollow ball stage?

(A) Blastula
(B) Embryo
(C) Fetus
(D) Gastrula
(E) Ovum

118. All of the following mutations are transitions EXCEPT

(A) AAATTT → AAATCT
(B) AAATTT → AGATTT
(C) AAATTT → AAACTT
(D) AAATTT → AAAGTT
(E) AAATTT → GAATTT

119. Thymine is synthesized from

(A) dUDP by methylation of the 5-position using AdoMet
(B) dUDP by methylation of the 5-position using N^5,N^{10}-THF
(C) dUMP by methylation of the 5-position using AdoMet
(D) dUMP by methylation of the 5-position using methyl cobalamin
(E) dUMP by methylation of the 5-position using N^5,N^{10}-methylene-THF

120. What results from a nonsense mutation?

  (A) Elongated protein
  (B) Protein misdirected to the wrong cellular compartment
  (C) Protein not expressed
  (D) Protein with an amino acid replacement
  (E) Truncated protein

121. For what type of proteins do "homeotic" genes code?

  (A) Apoptotic factors
  (B) Histones
  (C) Ribosomal proteins
  (D) Transcription factors
  (E) Translation factors

122. Where is a CAAT box found?

  (A) In eukaryotes at transcription initiation site -25
  (B) In eukaryotes at transcription initiation site -75
  (C) In eukaryotes in the middle of the transcribed sequence
  (D) In prokaryotes at transcription initiation site -10
  (E) In prokaryotes at transcription initiation site -35

123. Which fatty acid is essential (required in diets of mammals) and serves as a precursor of arachidonic acid?

  (A) Eicosatetraenoic acid
  (B) Linoleic acid
  (C) Linolenic acid
  (D) Oleic acid
  (E) Palmitoleic acid

124. Where is the signal peptidase located?

  (A) Cytosol
  (B) Cytosolic side of the endoplasmic reticulum (ER)
  (C) Golgi
  (D) Lumen of the ER
  (E) Luminal side of the ER membrane

125. Phosphatidylcholine is made from phosphatidic acid and choline. Choline is activated by which of the following reactions before it is added to phosphatidic acid?

  (A) Choline and ATP to choline-P plus CTP to CDP-choline
  (B) Choline and ATP to choline-P plus UTP to UDP-choline
  (C) Choline and CTP to CDP-choline
  (D) Choline and UTP to UDP-choline
  (E) Choline and GTP to GDP-choline

126. Each of the following is an intermediate in the biosynthesis of sphingomyelin EXCEPT

  (A) ceramide
  (B) palmitoyl CoA
  (C) phosphatidate
  (D) phosphatidylcholine
  (E) serine

127. Complete β-oxidation of palmitoyl CoA would theoretically produce how many equivalents of ATP? Assume 3 equivalents for each NADH/H$^+$ produced and 2 equivalents for each FADH$_2$.

  (A) 72
  (B) 88
  (C) 96
  (D) 117
  (E) 131

128. Choose the correct formula for determining the requested information concerning purification of an enzyme. The starting amount of soluble protein is assigned the value "A," total number of units of activity is "B," specific activity is "C," % yield is "D," and the degree of purification is "E." The starting specific activity can be calculated from

  (A) $A \div B = C$
  (B) $A \times B = C$
  (C) $B \div A = C$
  (D) $B \times D = C$
  (E) $B = C$

129. An enzymatic assay gave a rate change of NADH/H⁺ at 340 nm through a 1-cm light path of 0.0622/min. How many units of activity are contained in 1 ml of reaction mixture? [Note: A unit is defined as a change of 1.0 micromole/min. Also, $A_s = \varepsilon cb$, where ε = molar absorbance coefficient, b = light path, and c = concentration. ε for NADH is 6.22×10^3.]

(A) 0.001
(B) 0.010
(C) 0.100
(D) 1.000
(E) 10.00

Answer questions 130 and 131 based on your knowledge of collagen synthesis.

Addition to Fibroblast Culture	Collagen Synthesized
Nothing	Abnormal
Fe⁺³	Abnormal
Fe⁺²	Normal
Reduced vitamin C (ascorbate)	Normal
Oxidized vitamin C (dehydroascorbate)	Abnormal
Cu⁺²	Abnormal

130. Where does the deficiency or mutation appear to be?

(A) Dehydroascorbate reductase
(B) Iron reductase
(C) Lysine oxidase
(D) Lysyl hydroxylase
(E) Prolyl hydroxylase

131. Why are no disulfide bonds found in collagen?

(A) No disulfides are made as procollagen is synthesized.
(B) There are no cysteines in procollagen.
(C) The disulfides are oxidized as part of extracellular maturation into collagen.
(D) The region with disulfides are cleaved during maturation.
(E) The sulfurs of collagen are in iron-sulfur centers.

For questions 132–136 match the letter with the stage or event occurring at that stage. Letters may be used more than once.

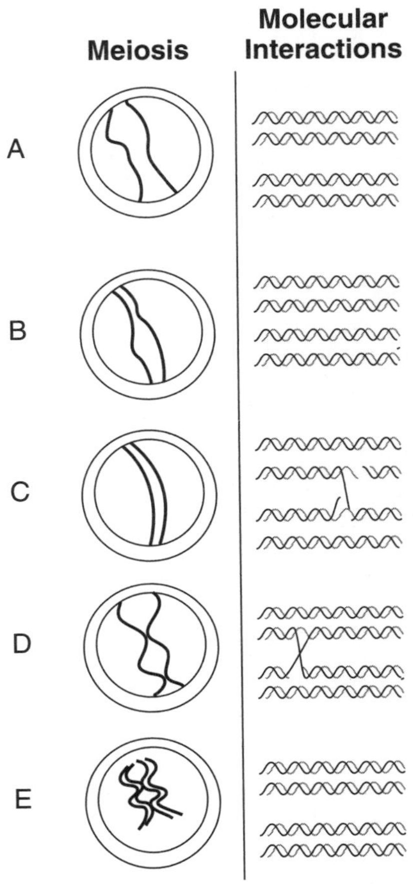

132. Diakinesis

133. Chromosomes begin to pair

134. Chromosomes detach from membrane

135. Pachytene

136. Region of exchanged strands extended

For questions 137–142 match the letter to the type of cell junction. For questions 137–139 use the letters on the left cell; for questions 140–142 use the letters on the right cell.

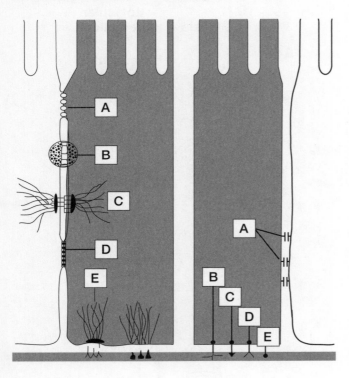

To answer questions 137–139 use the letters on the cell to the left.

137. Tight junctions

138. Adhesion belt

139. Desmosome

To answer questions 140–142 use the letters on the cell to the right.

140. Integral membrane proteoglycan

141. Transmembrane adhesion proteins

142. Laminin receptor

Questions 143–145 address a new genetic code.

An unusual primitive organism was discovered. After attempts to understand its translational apparatus failed, it was suggested that it might use a genetic code different from that of the majority of previously known organisms. Templates for translation were synthesized, and the following results were obtained.

Experiment Number	Template	Major Amino Acids Incorporated
1	All A	Tyr
2	All U	Ala
3	All C	Lys
4	All G	Glu
5	Alternating G and C	Met and ser
6	Alternating A and U	Phe and val
7	Alternating G and U	Leu and his
8	Alternating C and U	Ile and asp
9	Mixture of equal amounts of all four bases	All amino acids

143. How many codons are potentially possible from only A and U?

   (A) 2
   (B) 3
   (C) 4
   (D) 6
   (E) 8

144. Experiment 5 yields large amounts of met and ser, but also smaller amounts of cys and arg, and trace amounts of lys and glu. What might be the code for cys or arg?

   (A) CCC
   (B) CGC
   (C) GCG
   (D) GGC
   (E) GGG

145. Who first suggested the above method for deciphering the genetic code?

(A) Crick
(B) Meselson
(C) Nirenberg
(D) Stahl
(E) Watson

Use the family tree to answer questions 146–148.

The diagram below is a family tree. Circles are females, squares are males, diamonds are either sex, and a dot inside a shape indicates a heterozygote. Clear is unaffected and solid is affected.

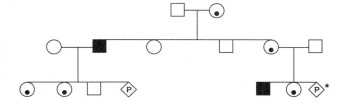

146. What type of inheritance is indicated above?

(A) Autosomal dominant
(B) Autosomal recessive
(C) Multifactorial
(D) X-linked
(E) Y-linked

147. What is the probability of the proband (person) indicated by the asterisk being affected?

(A) Zero affected if male
(B) Zero affected if female
(C) 50% affected if male
(D) 100% affected if male
(E) 100% carrier if female

148. What condition is most likely illustrated by the above?

(A) Blood type
(B) Color blindness
(C) Eye color
(D) Flower color
(E) Frizzle

Following is a list of nitrogen-containing compounds. For questions 149–151, choose the most appropriate answer from this list. An option may be used more than once.

(A) Alanine
(B) Aspartate
(C) Glutamate
(D) Glutamine
(E) Glycine

149. All of the atoms of this compound are incorporated into guanine during its biosynthesis.

150. This compound contributes two-thirds of the ring structure of cytidine.

151. This compound provides the γ-nitrogen for asparagine biosynthesis.

152. This compound is a product of arginase action.

(A) Allantoin
(B) Ammonium
(C) Glycine
(D) Urea
(E) Uric acid

Use the information on the lac operon to answer questions 153–156.

The mechanism and structure was elucidated by Jacob and Monod. Gene I codes for a protein called lacI. In the absence of lactose, lacI binds the operator site (O) and prevents the polymerase from binding the promoter (P) and initiating transcription of the structural genes, Z, Y, and (A). When lactose is present it binds to lacI protein, and lacI leaves the operator site and transcription occurs.

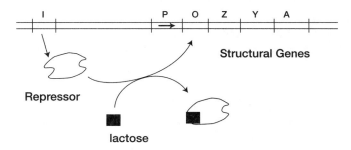

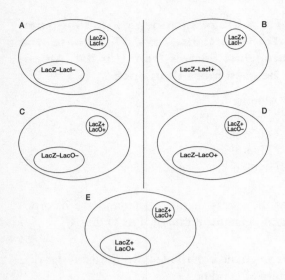

The above diagram shows bacteria transfected with a plasmid bearing the entire lac operon, and a chromosome also bearing the entire lac operon. Wild-type and mutant genes are indicated by a + or − sign. All other genes in the operon that are not indicated are wild-type.

Remembering that there are two types of mutation, *cis* and *trans*, determine which bacterium fits the criteria listed below. For example, in figure B there would be no expression of lacZ on the chromosome in the presence or absence of lactose because it is mutated. Expression on the plasmid of lacZ in the presence of lactose because the lacI gene product from the chromosome can diffuse to the plasmid.

Choose from Figures A, B, C, and D to answer the questions.

153. No lacZ expression on either plasmid or chromosome either in the presence or absence of lactose

154. LacZ is regulated normally by lactose on the plasmid, but not expressed in the chromosome either in the presence or absence of lactose.

155. No expression of lacZ on the chromosome, no expression on the plasmid of LacZ in the absence of lactose, but expression after addition of lactose.

156. If the Z gene is mutated, all three of the structural genes become inactivated. What is this type of mutation called?

(A) Abortive
(B) Designated
(C) Lateral
(D) Polar
(E) Reverse

Answer questions 157–159 using the following graph. A lettered answer may be used more than once.

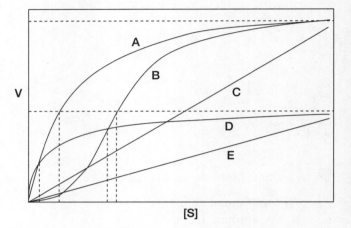

A set of kinetic data for an enzyme was plotted using the following equation

$$\log\left(\frac{v}{V_{max}-v}\right) = n\log[S] - \log K_{eq}$$

157. A straight line was obtained with a slope of 2.5. The shape of the v_i *vs.* [S] plot most likely resembled which curve?

158. A straight line was obtained with a slope of 0.5. The shape of the v_i *vs.* [S] plot most likely resembled which curve?

159. Data for an allosteric enzyme in the presence of saturating concentrations of a positive modifier was plotted using the above equation. The v_i *vs.* [S] plot of the original data most likely resembled which of the above curves?

Questions 160–162 concern a mutant form of an enzyme.

An enzyme (W⁺) is activated by fructose 6-phosphate (F6P). A mutant (mut) lacks response to F6P. Both forms are inhibited by aspartate.

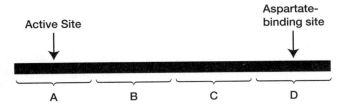

To investigate the location of the mutant F6P binding site, chimeras were constructed. Sections from the mutant are indicated by a thin line.

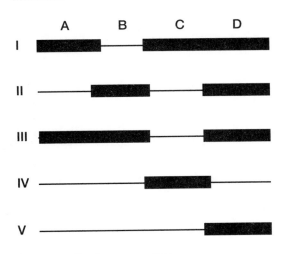

Construct I, phenotype W⁺
Construct II, phenotype mutant
Construct III, phenotype mutant
Construct IV, phenotype W⁺
Construct V, phenotype mutant

160. In which segment of the gene does the mutation lie?

161. If there were a mutation in the wild-type active site and aspartate binding site, which construct would give activity and still be responsive to fructose 6-phosphate?

(A) I
(B) II

(C) III
(D) IV
(E) V

162. After sequencing of the fragment carrying the F6P mutation, five changes were noticed.

	Wild-type sequence	Mutant sequence
A	GAU	GAA
B	GAC	GAU
C	AUU	GUU
D	UUU	UCU
E	CCC	CCG

1st position (5′ end) ↓	2nd position				3rd position (3′ end) ↓
	U	**C**	**A**	**G**	
U	Phe	Ser	Tyr	Cys	U
	Phe	Ser	Tyr	Cys	C
	Leu	Ser	STOP	STOP	A
	Leu	Ser	STOP	Trp	G
C	Leu	Pro	His	Arg	U
	Leu	Pro	His	Arg	C
	Leu	Pro	Gin	Arg	A
	Leu	Pro	Gin	Arg	G
A	Ile	Thr	Asn	Ser	U
	Ile	Thr	Asn	Ser	C
	Ile	Thr	Lys	Arg	A
	Met	Thr	Lys	Arg	G
G	Val	Ala	Asp	Gly	U
	Val	Ala	Asp	Gly	C
	Val	Ala	Glu	Gly	A
	Val	Ala	Glu	Gly	G

Which of the mutations would you test first to confirm that this is the relevant mutation in the loss of F6P sensitivity?

The diagram shown below is a schematic representation of a mock metabolic pathway. Refer to it to answer questions 163–165.

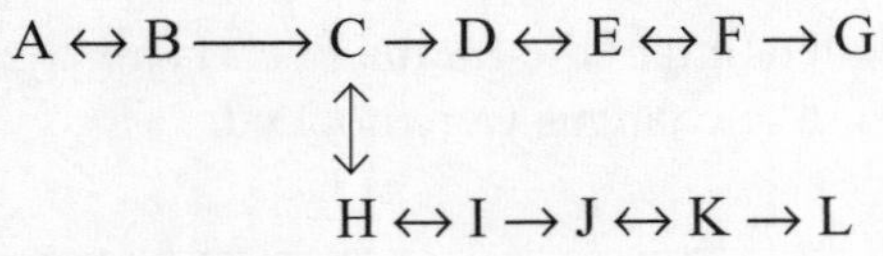

$$A \leftrightarrow B \longrightarrow C \to D \leftrightarrow E \leftrightarrow F \to G$$
$$\updownarrow$$
$$H \leftrightarrow I \to J \leftrightarrow K \to L$$

163. Under cellular conditions where the concentration of G is in excess of needs, which reaction in the pathway is most likely going to be inhibited by a feedback allosteric mechanism?

(A) A to B
(B) B to C
(C) C to D
(D) C to H
(E) D to E

164. Under cellular conditions where the concentration of L is in excess of needs, which reaction in the pathway is most likely going to be inhibited by a feedback allosteric mechanism?

(A) B to C
(B) C to H
(C) H to I
(D) I to J
(E) J to K

165. If the concentrations of both L and G are in excess, which reaction in the pathway is most likely going to be inhibited by a feedback allosteric mechanism?

(A) A to B
(B) B to C
(C) C to D
(D) H to I
(E) I to J

Questions 166–168 concern DNA sequencing.

A short sequence of DNA was sequenced using the dideoxy method. The fragments were run on a gel, stained, and are shown below.

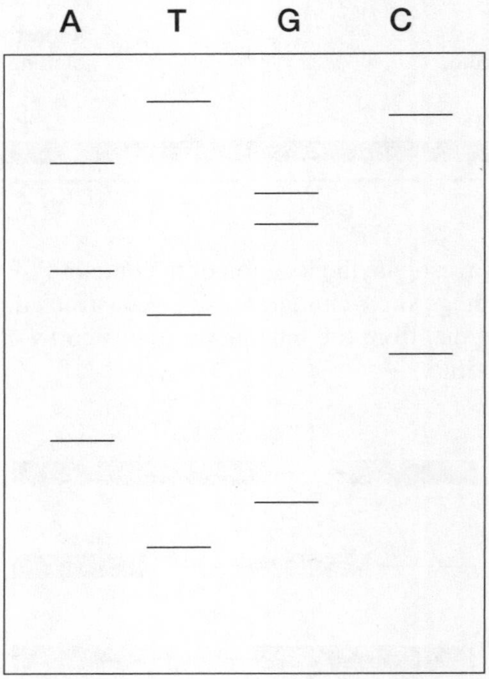

166. What is the sequence of the DNA?
(A) 3′-TGACTAGGACT-3′
(B) 5′-ATCGGCATATG-3′
(C) 5′-TCAGGATCAGT-3′
(D) 5′-TGACTAGGACT-3′
(E) 5′-ACTGATCCTGA-3′

167. Prior to the use of dideoxy sequencing the Maxam-Gilbert chemical method of sequencing was used. The bases were chemically altered, the base then removed, and the strand cleaved.

Base specificity	Base alteration	Base removal
G	Dimethylsulfate	Piperidine
A + G	Acid	Acid
C + T	Hydrazine	Piperidine
C	Alkali	Piperidine

A/G   G   C/T   C

What is the sequence shown on the above gel, obtained after chemical cleavage of DNA?

(A) 5′-ACGCAGTC-3′
(B) 5′-AGCTCAGGCTCAGAGGCTCTC-3′
(C) 5′-CTCTCGGAGACTCGGACTCGA-3′
(D) 5′-CTGACGCA-3′
(E) 5′-CCTGGACCGGCCA-3′

168. Nearest Neighbor Analysis can be used to examine identity between DNA fragments from two or more different sources. The DNA is copied four times, using a different αP^{32}-labeled NTP each time. The four resulting labeled DNA strands are then cleaved with an endonuclease that cuts on the 3′ side of the phosphate group. This results in the transfer of the label to the nucleoside that is the 5′ nearest neighbor of the NTP that provided the label.

For example, in a strand 5′ CAT 3′ labeled using P^{32}ATP, endonuclease cleavage would give a labeled C.

In the sequence shown on the gel in question 166, what would be the results of using labeled CTP in the Nearest Neighbor Analysis?

(A) Labeled A and labeled T
(B) Labeled A only

(C) Labeled C and labeled A
(D) Labeled T only
(E) Labeled A and G

For questions 169–171 use the peptides shown below.

The following two peptides exist in the same solution. They must be separated and characterized. [Note: pKa values for histidine are 2.3, 6.0, and 9.6.]

I.   R—A—M—K—K—M—G—T—I—W—M—S—R—K
II.   A—R—E—G—K—M—G—S—L—P—M—T—H—K

169. What are the approximate net charges of each of these peptides at pH 8.0?

(A) +2 and +3
(B) +3 and +5
(C) +5 and +2
(D) +5 and +3
(E) +6 and +4

170. At pH 7.0 and low ionic strength, what is the most appropriate chromatographic method to use for separation of these two peptides?

(A) Affinity
(B) Anion exchange
(C) Cation exchange
(D) Gel filtration
(E) Hydrophobic interaction

171. How many total fragments would be expected after complete digestion with trypsin?

(A) 3
(B) 4
(C) 5
(D) 6
(E) 8

All of the terms listed are involved in DNA repair, DNA expression, or viruses. For questions 172–176 match the term with the appropriate activity.

    (A) a-amanitin
    (B) Catabolite activator protein
    (C) Integrase
    (D) Lariat
    (E) Pribnow box

172. Inhibition of RNA polymerase

173. Insertion of lambda phage

174. Regulation of the lac operon

175. Splicing of mRNA

176. Transcription initiation

All of the terms listed are involved in DNA repair, DNA expression, or viruses. For questions 177–180 match the term with the appropriate activity.

    (A) CAAT box
    (B) Rec protein
    (C) Reverse transcriptase
    (D) Rho factor
    (E) Thymine dimers

177. Photoreactivation

178. Replication of RNA viruses

179. SOS response

180. Termination of transcription

Answer Key

1. B	31. C	61. E	91. D	121. D	151. D
2. A	32. B	62. B	92. D	122. B	152. D
3. A	33. A	63. D	93. A	123. B	153. D
4. C	34. D	64. A	94. D	124. E	154. A
5. B	35. A	65. B	95. C	125. A	155. C
6. A	36. E	66. D	96. D	126. C	156. D
7. C	37. E	67. B	97. C	127. E	157. B
8. A	38. C	68. C	98. D	128. C	158. D
9. D	39. B	69. D	99. A	129. B	159. A
10. C	40. C	70. D	100. E	130. B	160. C
11. C	41. E	71. E	101. A	131. D	161. D
12. B	42. C	72. D	102. D	132. E	162. D
13. A	43. C	73. B	103. B	133. B	163. C
14. D	44. B	74. E	104. C	134. E	164. D
15. D	45. A	75. A	105. D	135. C	165. B
16. E	46. C	76. E	106. B	136. D	166. D
17. D	47. A	77. E	107. C	137. A	167. D
18. D	48. C	78. C	108. C	138. B	168. E
19. B	49. C	79. B	109. C	139. C	169. C
20. A	50. D	80. B	110. C	140. B	170. C
21. D	51. D	81. D	111. E	141. A	171. E
22. B	52. B	82. B	112. C	142. E	172. A
23. C	53. B	83. E	113. C	143. E	173. C
24. A	54. E	84. C	114. B	144. D	174. B
25. E	55. A	85. A	115. D	145. C	175. D
26. A	56. B	86. D	116. B	146. D	176. E
27. C	57. A	87. A	117. A	147. C	177. E
28. C	58. A	88. B	118. D	148. B	178. C
29. C	59. D	89. C	119. E	149. E	179. B
30. B	60. E	90. E	120. E	150. B	180. D

Practice Exam 1

Detailed Explanations of Answers

1. (B)

In most cases, constant temperature is assumed and for the equation

$$\Delta G = \Delta H - T\Delta S$$

ΔG is negative if ΔH is negative or if the numerical value of $T\Delta S$ is larger than that for ΔH. The latter is not likely to occur and, therefore, a negative value of ΔH will almost certainly ensure that the reaction is spontaneous.

2. (A)

Genes with the same function from two organisms are orthologs, homologous chromosomes are members of the pair of chromosomes, neighboring genes are simply genes that are next to each other on the chromosome, and palindromic sequences in chromosomes are frequently restriction endonuclease sites.

3. (A)

The eyepiece is the "piece where one puts one's eye." The other important parts of the microscope are C and D (objectives), the stage (shown above E [the diaphragm]), the mirror or other light source (shown below the diaphragm), and the various focusing knobs.

4. (C)

The nuclei are not a fixed distance apart but oscillate about a mean distance r_o. If the nuclei are closer together than r_o there is repulsion; if they are farther apart than r_o, but within a certain range, there is attraction.

5. (B)

A gene expressed only in the male is holandric, a heterozygous condition is self-described, hereditary information not carried on chromosomal DNA is epigenetic, and two alleles the gene products of which are both expressed are codominant.

6. (A)

Specimens must be frozen ("cryo" means cold) before they can be cut as thinly as is needed to be transparent.

7. (C)

The flow of electrons is from the more negative to the more positive. If a compound has a negative reduction potential, its reduced form has a much lower ability to accept electrons. The only value in the table that is more negative than the $FAD/FADH_2$ pair is the ferredoxins.

8. (A)

Fertility factor is a piece of DNA that is transferred between bacterial cells by conjugation, heat shock is used as part of making cells competent, lysogeny describes the condition wherein a virus or phage is incorporated into a bacterial chromosome, and pilus formation is necessary for conjugation and transfer of DNA.

9. (D)

[HA] is the concentration of the conjugate acid and [A⁻] is the concentration of the conjugate base. When [HA] = [A⁻], the value of the ratio is 1.0, and since the log of 1 = 0, pH = pK_a.

10. (C)

A+B+C- genotype crossed with unknown yields phenotype A+B+C-. Because the defective phenotype of the unknown mutant is not complemented by the C⁻

gene of the cross with the known genotype, it may be concluded that the defective gene in the unknown is C.

11. (C)

Of the choices only electron microscopy requires that all water be removed from the specimen. This renders the cell nonviable.

12. (B)

At the isoelectric point or pH, there is an equal number of positive and negative charges. At a pH half way between the pK values of the two amino groups, each would be ½ charged and the carboxyl group would be fully charged. Thus, the net charge would be 0.

13. (A)

"An" means "not," and "euploidy" means a good number of chromosomes. Diploidy refers to two copies of each chromosome, haploidy means one copy of each chromosome, and polyploidy means several copies of each chromosome.

14. (D)

There are two organelles—mitochondria and chloroplasts—that share characteristics with bacteria, such as size and a single circular chromosome.

15. (D)

Six atoms of the *trans* conformation of a peptide bond lie within the same plane: the two alpha carbons, the carboxyl carbon and its attached oxygen, as well as the nitrogen and its attached hydrogen atom. This is the primary conformation of peptide bonds found in proteins.

16. (E)

Pseudogenes are copies of genes that are missing promoter regions and are not expressed. Allelic genes are the analogous genes on the pairs of chromosomes; divergent genes are copied genes that have acquired changes, but are still expressed; duplicated genes are also often expressed; and exons are segments of genes that are expressed.

17. (D)

Bacilli are rod shaped. Examples of bacteria that form chains of round cells are streptococci; elongated

spirals include *Spirillum*; pairs of round cells are diplococci; most bacteria are single round cells.

18. (D)

The many arginines and lysines in histones have positive charges that form ionic interactions with the negative phosphates on DNA.

19. (B)

Four amino acid residues generally makeup this turn and consist of *glycine* residues, *proline* residues, an amino acid, and one or more hydrophilic amino acid residues that would permit interaction with the aqueous environment at the surfaces and/or those capable of post-translational modification such as asparagine, serine, and residues with formal positive or negative charges.

20. (A)

If 20% is thymine, 20% is adenine. Adenine plus guanine are purines (30%). 30% minus 20% is 10%.

21. (D)

"Halo" means salt, "phil-" means love. Different types of extremophiles are found under all the other conditions listed.

22. (B)

From this equation,

$$k = \frac{2.303}{t} \log \frac{[A]_0}{[A]}$$

the log of the ratio of concentrations is dimensionless. Thus, the dimension of k for a first-order rate constant is expressed in units of reciprocal time, t^{-1}.

23. (C)

Temperature at which all DNA is denatured depends on %GC, and is shown as the highest point on the melting curve; heating at low temperatures does not denature bases. A-T bases are denatured at lower temperatures than are G-C; temperature at which DNA starts to denature is at the lowest point on the melting curve.

24. (A)

Enzymes of this type facilitate reactions by altering the pathway and using some of its acidic and basic groups to catalyze release of the acyl group from the enzyme. Covalent catalysis in this case is also accompanied by acid-base catalysis. In all serine proteases, there is a specific serine within the protein structure that has high propensity for ester bond formation.

25. (E)

All the genes in an organism are a genome; all the exons in an organism are the potential but not necessarily expressed sections of DNA. All of the mRNA does not include rRNA and tRNA. All the proteins in an organism are the proteome.

26. (A)

Prototrophs can live on simple carbon compounds and inorganic salts alone. Plant cells that are photosynthetic are a specialized subset of prototrophs called autotrophs. Cells that live in the presence of oxygen are aerobes or facultative aerobes. Cells that have two mechanisms of reproduction usually have sexual and asexual reproduction, and cells that use carbon dioxide as terminal electron acceptor are methanogens.

27. (C)

This class of enzymes catalyzes the linking of two molecules, coupled with the utilization of energy obtained from the breaking of a "high energy" bond such as in ATP and/or its equivalent. An enzyme of this class that uses also a vitamin as a cofactor is pyruvate carboxylase (EC 6.4.1.1, pyruvate:CO_2 ligase [ADP]). The vitamin is biotin, which is attached to the enzyme by a peptide linkage involving the carboxyl group of biotin and an ε-amino group of a lysine residue of the enzyme. Biotin is a prosthetic group of this enzyme.

28. (C)

A reaction (system) is capable of doing work until the reaction reaches equilibrium. For example, if Q is defined as the ability to do work and is related to the following expression

$$\ln\left(\frac{k_r[C][D]}{k_f[A][B]}\right)$$

It is performing work until the forward and reverse reaction rates reach the same value. At that point, the value of Q is 0.

29. (C)

Because a competitive inhibitor changes the apparent K_m by the factor $(1 + ([I]/K_i))$, the equation is the logical extension of that fact. Also, because the amount of enzyme in the ES complex is related directly to v_i and the total amount of enzyme is directly related to V_{max}, substituting the relative values into the equation and solving for the ratio of v_i/V_{max} will give the correct answer.

30. (B)

The hydrolysis of DNA into fragments that form a regularly spaced pattern when subjected to electrophoresis is the key diagnostic for apoptosis. Destruction of adjacent cells, inflammation, and pyknotic (shrunken and hyperpigmented) nuclei are indications of necrosis. Lipases are involved in fat necrosis.

31. (C)

Percentage G-C in genomic DNA is measured by a melting curve.

32. (B)

Reactions 1, 2, and 5 represent the reactions for a competitive inhibitor in the presence of substrate. In this case, a mechanism-based inhibitor is involved, which leads to irreversible inhibition by reaction 6 at a rate defined by the rate constant, k.

33. (A)

Asparagine can be *N*-glycosylated. Serine, threonine, and hydroxyproline can be *O*-glycosylated.

34. (D)

The outer lipid membrane is A, the periplasmic space is B, the inner lipid membrane is C, and E is an embedded (integral) protein.

35. (A)

The one thing that is common among sequential mechanisms is that reaction occurs only from a ternary complex. For random sequential reactions, it does not matter which substrate binds first or which product leaves first. However, there is a definite order of binding of substrates and a definite order of release of products for ordered sequential mechanisms.

36. (E)

Alleles are the two analogous genes on a pair of chromosomes; heterologs are entitites that differ; homologs are similar genes in the same species.

37. (E)

Gram-positive cells lose essentially all the cell wall with this treatment. Gram-negative cells lose only the outer membrane (cell wall), and become spheroplasts. Mitoplasts are derived from mitochondria, the extracellular glycocalyx is a capsule, and porins are membrane proteins that serve in transport.

38. (C)

Restriction endonuclease sites are "palindromes." The complementary sequence to the sequence in answer C, written 5′-3′, is AGTAGT.

39. (B)

ATP is classified as a "high-energy" compound because the terminal phosphate groups (of ATP and ADP) contain negatively charged oxygen atoms on the phosphate groups that contribute to electrostatic repulsion and increased destabilization. Hydrolysis of the terminal (γ) phosphate yields inorganic phosphate, which has an increased number of resonance forms and is more stable. The difference in energy between the two forms of that phosphate group is approximately −7.3 kcal/mole. The terminal (β) phosphate on ADP fits essentially the same category and also releases approximately −7.3 kcal/mole upon hydrolysis.

40. (C)

Pol I completes Okazaki fragments and does DNA repair; Pol II does repair and damage bypass; Pols IV and V do damage bypass.

41. (E)

Membrane lipids are synthesized inside the cell. Initially they are incorporated in the inner leaflet and are transferred to the outer leaflet by enzymes called "flippases."

42. (C)

The net reaction for glycolysis under anaerobic conditions is:

$$\text{Glucose} + 2\text{ADP} + 2\text{P}_i \rightarrow 2\text{Lactate} + 2\text{ATP} + 2\text{H}_2\text{O}$$

$NADH/H^+$ that is generated in the glyceraldehyde-3-phosphate dehydrogenase reaction must be regenerated for glycolysis to continue. This is accomplished by reduction of pyruvate to lactate.

43. (C)

Pol α is a replication primase, Pol β does base excision repair, Pol γ is mitochondrial, and the function of Pol ε is unknown.

44. (B)

Simple diffusion is shown in A, a carrier in C, active transport is D, and E is transport down an electrochemical gradient.

45. (A)

Glyceraldehyde-3-phosphate dehydrogenase catalyzes synthesis of the first "high-energy" compound in glycolysis. The product, 1,3-bisphosphoglycerate, is a "high-energy" compound, even though the reaction is easily reversible.

46. (C)

A shows a single heavy band, B is a single hybrid band, C shows equal bands that are light and hybrid, D has overwhelmingly light bands, and E has only light bands.

47. (A)

Phosphoglycerate kinase catalyzes formation of the first molecule of ATP in glycolysis. $\Delta G°$ for this reaction is −8.22 kJ mol^{-1} or approximately −2 kcal mole^{-1}.

48. (C)

Energy is required to overcome the directional pressure of a concentration gradient. All of the other four characteristics are shared by mediated passive and active transport.

49. (C)

If sufficient ATP is present, the necessity for operation of glycolysis is diminished. High citrate and H^+ in the cytosol would be indicative of sufficient operation of the TCA cycle and of active oxidative phosphorylation to supply cellular needs for energy.

50. (D)

In eukaryotes the primer is made by a RNA-synthesizing primase/DNA polymerase α complex.

51. (D)

Pyridoxal phosphate is not required for this reaction. The four required coenzymes are thiamin pyrophosphate (TPP), lipoyl lysine (lipoic acid as a prosthetic group), FAD, and NAD^+. In general, three enzymes are involved: pyruvate dehydrogenase (E_1), dihydrolipoyl transacetylase (E_2), and dihydrolipoyl dehydrogenase (E_3). An intermediate in the reaction is $TPP\text{-}CHOH\text{-}CH_3$, α-hydroxyethylthiamine pyrophosphate.

52. (B)

"Pino" means "drink" and "cytosis" refers to a cell. Solids are eaten (phagocytosis). Both activities require formation of a vesicle. The others do not necessarily involve entrance or exit into or from a cell.

53. (B)

The complementary strand on the DNA cannot be used, since there is no place for a primer. The enzyme has to bring its own attached template.

54. (E)

Succinyl CoA synthetase catalyzes a substrate-level phosphorylation in the TCA cycle. The enzyme requires GDP and produces GTP, an ATP equivalent.

55. (A)

Balbiani rings are observed in fruit fly chromosomes in areas of active transcription. Barr bodies are the condensed second X chromosome. Euchromatin is the diffuse form of the interphase chromosomes. Nucleosomes are structures made up of DNA wound around a histone core, with histone H1 missing, and a scaffold is a protein to which chromosomes are attached.

56. (B)

The other daughter strand provides the patch for the repair of the daughter strand with the lesion.

57. (A)

ADP stimulates activity of this enzyme consistent with the overall indication of the cellular requirement for energy.

58. (A)

During recombination two homologous chromosomes hybridize in a Holliday junction that can be cleaved in two different planes to produce either homologous splice recombinants or nonreciprocal patch recombinants.

59. (D)

The Barr body is a condensed inactive X chromosome, visible by electron microscopy. Protein synthesis occurs in the cytosol. The nucleolus is the site of rRNA synthesis. Down syndrome is diagnosed by karyotyping, and observation of three copies of chromosome 21. The photomicrograph gives no information about viability.

60. (E)

The energy generated by the flow of H^+ through the ATP synthase complex from the inner membrane space to the matrix provides the energy necessary to effect synthesis of ATP from ADP and P_i. Complexes I, III, and IV are involved in moving protons from the matrix into the intermembrane space.

61. (E)

The first four subunits listed constitute the core, or apoenzyme, and together are capable of RNA synthesis, but at random start points. Addition of the σ subunit forms the holoenzyme and restricts the polymerase to initiation at a promoter.

62. (B)

Both nucleosomes and chromatosomes have DNA wound around histones. H1 is the only histone found in a chromatosome and not in a nucleosome.

63. (D)

2,4-Dinitrophenol is an uncoupler of oxidative phosphorylation. It is a weak acid that binds to protons in the intermembrane space and carries them across the membrane into the matrix where it releases them due to the higher pH and lower proton concentration.

64. (A)

Eukaryotic RNA polymerase II (B) makes mRNA and eukaryotic RNA polymerase III (C) makes tRNA. Mitochondrial RNA polymerase and prokaryotic RNA polymerase both make ribosomal RNA of different lengths.

65. (B)

The second NADPH/H$^+$ is produced by reductive decarboxylation of 6-phosphogluconate by 6-phosphogluconate dehydrogenase to give ribulose-5-phosphate.

66. (D)

The other motifs found frequently in DNA-binding proteins are the zinc finger, the helix-turn-helix, and the helix-loop-helix.

67. (B)

Collagen is made of three polyproline II helices. The three helix structure is stabilized by hydrophobic interactions of the small glycine R-chains. The collagen is secreted from the cell only if prolines are hydroxylated; the polyproline helix is stabilized by hydrogen bonding with hydroxyprolines. Glycine cannot be covalently bound via the R-group to carbohydrate, and the globular structure contains an average mixture of amino acids.

68. (C)

Phosphorylated eIF-2a binds eIF-2b (guanine nucleotide exchange factor) tightly, preventing formation of the initiation complex.

69. (D)

The pentose phosphate pathway is controlled primarily by the availability of NADP$^+$.

70. (D)

The first amino acid must be methionine. The next is coded for by CCC (proline), AAC (asparagine), and GTT (valine). The methionine is removed after translation.

71. (E)

The Y axis is the ratio of specifically bound ligand to free ligand. C is simply the maximum value on the Y axis. D is the inverse of the dissociation constant, and the X axis is specifically bound ligand.

72. (D)

Free glucuronic acid is metabolized to L-xylulose, where it can be converted through a series of reactions to D-xylulose, phosphorylated by xylulose kinase to xylulose-5-phosphate, and further metabolized by the pentose phosphate pathway and eventually back to glucose.

73. (B)

After the cap is added it is methylated. The poly-A tail is added and splicing occurs. All this precedes transport of the mRNA from the nucleus.

74. (E)

At the return to resting state the α-subunit recombines with the βγ-subunits. Adenyl cyclase activation occurs early in propagation of the signal, and the result is the synthesis of cAMP. GDP replaces GDP as an entire molecule and not via addition of a phosphate. Both this replacement and binding of hormone to receptor occur at the start of the process.

75. (A)

The 5S rRNA is coded for on another chromosome.

76. (E)

Pyruvate kinase catalyzes the formation of pyruvate and ATP from phosphoenolpyruvate. The alanine cycle in animals is one mechanism for getting pyruvate into liver for gluconeogenesis. If pyruvate kinase is inhibited, phosphoenolpyruvate carboxykinase reaction can be facilitated and metabolites used for gluconeogenesis rather than for more energy production.

77. (E)

The 3′ end is shortened by an exonuclease. The CCA trinucleotide shared by all tRNAs on the 3′ end is added by an enzyme called tRNA nucleotidyl transferase. Many tRNAs also have an intron. The mechanism for its removal is different from the mechanism used for mRNA. In tRNA the cleavage and ligation of the RNA are separate events and do not involve lariat formation. The necessary enzymes are a phosphodiesterase (cleavage), polynucleotide kinase (to add phosphate), and adenylate synthetase for ligation subunit is coded for on another chromosome.

78. (C)

Glycogenin, an initiator protein for glycogen synthesis, is a small protein that functions as a dimer. It, like glycogen synthase, requires UDP-glucose as the activated source of glucose units. Glycogenin also requires Mn^{2+} and the muscle form attaches glucose units to a tyrosine residue (Tyr194) in each subunit. Approximately 10 units of glucose are added before glycogen synthase takes over.

79. (B)

The cell body is responsible for synthesis of housekeeping proteins and neurotransmitters. These molecules are then transported to other parts of the cell.

80. (B)

Glycogen synthase is active in its dephosphorylated form, whereas glycogen phosphorylase is inactive. Conversely, glycogen synthase is inactive in its phosphorylated form, whereas glycogen phosphorylase is active. The phosphorylation-dephosphorylation activities are under hormonal control; however, there are also other allosteric effectors that interact with these enzymes.

81. (D)

$NADPH/H^+$ is made in the stroma of plant cells during light-dependent reactions of photosynthesis.

82. (B)

An electron transport system involving the cytochrome bf complex, plastoquinones, and a copper-containing protein, plastocyanin, crosses the thylakoid membrane diagonally and links PSII to PSI, figuratively referred to as the Z-system in photosynthesis.

83. (E)

Immediately after closing, a channel is temporarily refractory to reopening. Sodium is constantly pumped out of the cell by an ATPase. The channel is not degraded, since it will later be restored to its normal state. The opening of the next channel does not affect the previous channel.

84. (C)

NADPH and ATP are formed in the stroma where the light-independent (dark) reactions of photosynthesis occur: the Calvin cycle.

85. (A)

There are indeed 61 different codons for amino acids and three stop codons. However, tRNA that carries the anticodon often has an inosine (I) in the position that pairs with the 3′ "U" or "A" of the codon. "I" can pair with both "U" and "A", so the same anticodon can serve to match both codons. This is called wobble.

86. (D)

The second stage of the Calvin cycle involves the reductive formation of glyceraldehyde-3-phosphate. This series of reactions requires use of ATP and NADPH that were formed during the light-requiring phase of photosynthesis.

87. (A)

Acetylcholine is hydrolyzed by acetylcholine esterase; norepinephrine and dopamine are removed from the synapse by reuptake into the presynaptic terminal, and GABA is metabolized in associated cells.

88. (B)

Plants that use the C-4 mechanism require a special type of anatomy called Kranz (the German word for wreath) anatomy. Bundle sheath cells are surrounded by a layer of mesophyll cells in a wreath-like configuration.

The bundle sheath cells contain large amounts of chlorophyll, RubisCO, and organelles. CO_2 is fixed in the mesophyll cells by the enzyme phosphoenolpyruvate carboxylase, which forms oxaloacetic acid. The oxaloacetic acid is quickly converted to malate, where it is transported to the bundle sheath cells and reconverted to CO_2, generally by an NADP-dependent malic dehydrogenase.

89. (C)

The number of aminoacyl tRNA synthetases, the enzymes that join the amino acid and the tRNA with a covalent bond, is the same as the number of amino acids, and not the number of tRNAs. This means that one synthetase may have to recognize as many as 6 (for leucine) tRNAs.

90. (E)

The overall reaction of nitrogen fixation is $N_2 + 3H_2 \rightarrow 2NH_3$ and it is generally carried out by some bacteria and archaea. The enzyme system responsible for effecting nitrogen fixation is the nitrogenase complex (EC 1.18.6.1).

91. (D)

In prokaryotes formylmethionine is the initiating amino acid.

92. (D)

A is the H band, B does not have a common band name, C and D together are the I band, and E is the A band.

93. (A)

Arginine is listed as an essential amino acid; however, adults are generally able to obtain sufficient quantities of this amino acid from the urea cycle, but growing infants and children cannot.

94. (D)

Amino acids derived from phosphoenolpyruvate and erythrose-4-phosphate are the aromatic amino acids tryptophan, phenylalanine, and tyrosine. The first two are essential but tyrosine is not; it is derived from phenylalanine.

95. (C)

The energy for this step comes from the hydrolysis of the high energy bond between amino acid and tRNA. Charging of tRNA requires ATP and the other steps require GTP.

96. (D)

The sarcoplasmic reticulum (SR) is the equivalent of the endoplasmic reticulum. In response to a nerve signal, calcium is released from the SR stores; it is moved back into the SR by pumping.

97. (C)

For the synthesis of asparagine, a 4-carboxyl-AMP derivative of aspartate is formed with release of inorganic pyrophosphate. Asparagine is formed directly by transfer of an amide group of glutamine accompanied by release of AMP.

98. (D)

Note that the arrangement is different from that of the basal body (centriole). The centriole has nine triplet arrays but no central microtubules.

99. (A)

The methyl group for synthesis of methionine is first transferred from N-methyl-THF to cobalamin to yield methylcobalamin, where it is then transferred to homocysteine to yield methionine.

100. (E)

Some proteins require a more active assistance for folding. This is provided by the ATP-dependent family of chaperonins.

101. (A)

In cilia, dynein effects movement by an ATP-dependent mechanism. Flagella are driven by a motor that responds to a chemiosmotic gradient.

102. (D)

Histidine is formed from ribose-5-phosphate. The first metabolite formed is 5-phosphoribosyldiphosphate (PRPP). One of the nitrogen atoms in the imidazole ring comes from adenine and the other comes from glutamine.

103. (B)

The probability of there being one or other of the alleles present is 1. Therefore A plus a equals 1.

104. (C)

During the S phase, DNA is replicated and the cell becomes 4N. It remains 4N during the G_2 phase, and as the cell is divided in the M phase each daughter cell becomes 2N.

105. (D)

The distribution of genotypes is $A^2 + 2Aa + a^2$. The square root of 0.16 is 0.4; therefore, A = 0.6, and 2Aa = 0.48, or 48%.

106. (B)

Cholesterol and steroid hormones are derived from acetate. The first step in the biosynthesis of cholesterol is formation of 3-hydroxy-3-methylglutaryl CoA (HMG-CoA) by HMG-CoA synthase.

107. (C)

	A	A
A	AA	AA
a	aA	aA

108. (C)

"Meta" means "in the midst of." Metaphase can be recognized by the movement of the condensed chromosomes to the middle of the cell and the metaphase plate.

109. (C)

The DNA double helix molecule is 20Å wide and it forms two grooves, a minor grove of 6Å and a major groove of 12Å along the length of the DNA. The major grove allows some interactions with the nucleotide bases.

110. (C)

Current accepted belief is that females are born with all the eggs they will ever have. There is some evidence that this belief may change.

111. (E)

Biosynthesis of GMP and AMP is regulated by allosteric mechanisms. PRPP is a positive modifier of amidophosphoribosyl transferase, which catalyzes the first committed step in IMP synthesis.

112. (C)

The plasmid is 2.3 kb total. Hind III produces a fragment of 1 kb, and the only two fragments from the double digest that add up to 1 kb are 0.2 and 0.8 kb. Therefore, Eco RI must cut within the 1-kb Hind III fragment.

113. (C)

In the meiotic phase of oogenesis the cell divides twice. The first division produces a secondary oocyte and a small polar body. The secondary oocyte divides again into the mature egg and another small polar body.

114. (B)

40S ribosomal subunit, mRNA, GTP, methionyl-tRNA[met] is the preinitiation complex.

115. (D)

The interconversion of metabolites such as lactate and pyruvate is essentially an equilibrium catalyzed reaction that follows Michaelis-Menten kinetics. This reaction is not regulated by intermediary metabolites.

116. (B)

A bacteriocide is an agent that kills bacteria; freezing may or may not have a long-term affect but definitely does not make them competent; lysozyme breaks down the cell wall; and sodium dodecyl sulfate solubilizes the lipids in the membrane. The last two kill bacteria.

117. (A)

Division of the fertilized egg four times results in 16 cells. The "ball" formed by these cells is known as a blastula. The ovum (egg) precedes the blastula, and the gastrula, embryo, and fetus are the result of further development of the blastula.

118. (D)

A transition is purine to purine or pyrimidine to pyrimidine. In choice D, the change of T to G is a pyrimidine to a purine. This is a transversion.

119. (E)

Thymine is synthesized from dUMP by thymidylate synthase. The methyl group on position 5 of the pyrimidine ring comes from N^5,N^{10}-methylenetetrahydrofolate.

120. (E)

A nonsense mutation occurs when a mutation introduces a stop codon. A mutation that changed a stop codon to a codon for an amino acid would result in an elongated protein. A mutation in the promoter could cause nonexpression of a protein, and a point mutation is usually the cause of insertion of the wrong amino acid. Misdirection of a protein could come from a mutation leading to a change in the amino acid that is glycosylated, or the loss of the enzyme that adds the carbohydrate residue to the protein.

121. (D)

After body segments are formed under control of morphogen gradients, the appropriate body parts develop in each segment under control of a group of transcription factors. The genes for these factors are called homeobox genes.

122. (B)

CAAT boxes are found in eukaryotes. At -25 is the TATA box, and an enhancer is found in the middle of the gene itself.

123. (B)

Several hormones and regulatory molecules are derived from arachidonic acid, which is derived from linoleic acid (18:2 cis-Δ^9,Δ^{12}).

124. (E)

As the protein begins to appear on the luminal side of the endoplasmic reticulum the signal sequence is cleaved.

125. (A)

Choline is first phosphorylated by an ATP-requiring kinase to produce its respective phosphate derivative yielding ADP as a side product. Phosphocholine is then converted to CDP-choline with release of PP_i. Transfer of the CDP-derivatives to phosphatidic acid results in formation of phosphatidylcholine and release of CMP.

126. (C)

Phosphatidic acid is diacylglycerol-3-phosphate. It is an intermediate in the biosynthesis of triacylglycerol and phospholipids, but not sphingomyelin.

127. (E)

Solution of this problem requires a calculation of the total number of ATP equivalents produced for each NADH/H^+ and $FADH_2$ during β-oxidation plus one substrate-level (GTP) for each acetate that goes through the cycle as well as for each NADH/H^+ and $FADH_2$ produced during acetate oxidation. As stated in the text, however, the yield for NADH/H^+ is ~2.5 and for $FADH_2$ is ~1.5 rather than 3 and 2 as used in this question.

128. (C)

Refer to the purification chart in this book. When all blank spaces are filled in correctly, the answer will be obvious.

129. (B)

All information needed to solve this problem is in the stem except knowledge of the fact that a 1 M solution contains 1 mmole/ml of solute; a 1 mM solution contains 1 μmole/ml of solute.

130. (B)

Ascorbate only works here as a cofactor in the reduced form. During the hydroxylation of proline, ascorbate is oxidized to dehydroascorbate. Re-reduction to ascorbate occurs at the expense of Fe^{+2}. Because Fe^{+3} has no effect on the system, it must be the enzyme that reduces iron that is not functioning correctly.

131. (D)

Most proteins that are secreted from the cell have disulfide bond to increase stability. The disulfides in collagen are in the globular regions that are cleaved after the procollagen leaves the cell.

132. (E)

DIAKINESIS. Further condensation of chromosomes, which detach from envelope. All 4 chromatids are visible, and chiasmata persist. The recombination event reaches resolution.

133. (B)

ZYGOTENE. Chromosomes begin to pair. Recombination initiated by strand nicking.

134. (E)

DIAKINESIS. Chromosomes detach from envelope.

135. (C)

PACHYTENE. Synaptonemal complex extends along whole length of chromosomes, and single strand exchanges occur.

136. (D)

DIPLOTENE. Separated chromosomes linked at chiasmata, and region of exchanged strands is extended.

137. (A)

Tight junctions cause adherence of adjacent epithelial cells to each other, and prevent transfer of most molecules from one cell to another.

138. (B)

Adherens junctions occur in epithelia, where they often form a continuous adhesion belt just below the tight junctions, encircling each of the interacting cells in the sheet.

139. (C)

Desmosomes link the intermediate filaments of adjoining cells.

140. (B)

The long carbohydrate chains attached to the protein indicate that this is a proteoglycan.

141. (A)

These proteins do not form tight adhesions between cells. They may serve to allow traction between cells without totally immobilizing one cell in relation to another.

142. (E)

The laminin receptor allows cells to adhere to basal lamina. The other types of nonjunctional adhesion mechanisms between cell and basal lamina are integral membrane proteoglycans, fibronectin receptors (shown as (C)) and collagen receptors (shown as D).

143. (E)

$2^3 = 8$

AAU, UUU, UAA, AAA, AUA, AUU, UUA, UAU

144. (D)

CCC is lys, GGG is glu, CGC is either met or ser, GCG is either met or ser.

145. (C)

Watson and Crick discovered that DNA was a double helix, and Meselson and Stahl that DNA replication is semiconservative.

146. (D)

Autosomal dominant, all carriers are affected; autosomal recessive requires two carrier parents; multifactorial has a much more complex pattern of inheritance, and Y-linked does not occur, since there are very few genes on the Y chromosome and there is always an X chromosome to complement.

147. (C)

A male child could inherit the normal or the mutant gene from the mother.

148. (B)

Blood type is codominance, eye color is multifactorial, and both flower color and frizzle are codominance.

149. (E)

In an ATP-dependent reaction, a glycine amide is formed with the amino group of phosphoribosylamine to produce glycinamide ribotide. This is the only step in which a single compound contributes more than one atom to formation of the purine ring structure.

150. (B)

Only three sources of carbon contribute atoms of the pyrimidine ring structure and they are aspartate, the amide group of glutamine, and bicarbonate.

151. (D)

Asparagine is formed directly by transfer of the amide group of glutamine to aspartyl β-AMP. It is important to note that the carboxyl group to which the amide is transferred must first be activated. This is done in a reaction with ATP with concomitant loss of inorganic pyrophosphate.

152. (D)

This is the final step in the urea cycle that leads to urea formation. The original ornithine, the first intermediate of this cycle, is regenerated.

153. (D)

The plasmid is *lacO-*, so no transcription of lacZ can occur. The chromosome is *lac Z-*, so there is no gene to transcribe.

154. (A)

The plasmid is lacI+ lacZ+, so transcription of Z is regulated by inducer. The chromosome is lacI-, but the protein product of the lacI gene on the plasmid can diffuse to the chromosome and regulation of lacZ expression occurs.

155. (C)

The plasmid is lacO+ so transcription occurs, and is regulated. The chromosome is both lacO- and lacZ-, so no transcription occurs.

156. (D)

Since prokaryotes have these gene groupings (operons) and also linked transcription-translation, a mutation in one gene can cause the cessation of transcription or translation in all the associated genes. These are called polar mutations (i.e., they are directional).

157. (B)

A plot of $\log(v/(V_{max}-v))$ versus $\log[S]$ would give a straight line, the slope of which is "n," the "Hill coefficient." If there is no cooperativity as in Michaelis-Menten kinetics or for other conditions that give hyperbolic plots, n = 1.0. If there is negative cooperativity, n <1.0. If there is positive cooperativity, n is >1.0. Positive cooperativity almost always leads to plots with n values greater than one and v_i vs. [S] plots are sigmoidal, as is the case for this problem.

158. (D)

In this case negative cooperativity is observed, since n <1.0 and the rectilinear plot would show characteristics like those of curve D. Even though at first glance it may appear that the curve is hyperbolic, it is not. It rises more steeply at the beginning and increases more slowly toward Vmax. In fact, it would take a concentration of 81^2-fold (or 6561-fold) increase in concentration to increase the enzyme's activity from 10% to 90%.

159. (A)

In this case, the curve is made hyperbolic by the addition of a saturating concentration of a positive allosteric modifier. So, essentially only the active form of the enzyme—the form that binds substrate with higher affinity—is present and the kinetic pattern resembles Michaelis-Menten and a Hill plot has a slope of approximately 1.0.

160. (C)

Constructs I and IV have wild-type phenotypes. They both have the wild-type C segment.

161. (D)

For functional active site, need the mutant segment A; for functional aspartate inhibition, need mutant segment D; and for a functional F6P site; need wild-type segment C.

162. (D)

UUU-UCU is phe to ser (nonconservative), GAU-GAA is asp to glu (conservative), AUU-GUU is ile to val (conservative), GAC-GAU is asp to asp (silent), and CCC-CCG is pro to pro (silent).

163. (C)

Feedback allosteric regulation of metabolic pathways by end products of that pathway would frequently manifest itself by inhibition of the first unique irreversible step leading to that end product. In this example, if G is in sufficient supply, inhibition of the conversion of C to D would be expected, since that is the first unique irreversible step leading to G formation.

164. (D)

This is very similar to question 163 and the same rationale holds. The conversion of I to J is the first unique irreversible step in the pathway to L formation. There should be no waste of intermediates, since all other steps back to C are reversible.

165. (B)

In cases in which there is a branch point leading to formation of two different products, it is expected that end products of both pathways would inhibit formation of the intermediary metabolite at the branch point. In this case, conversion of B to C would be inhibited by G and L. It would be expected that neither G nor L alone would be able to completely inhibit formation of C. Each would inhibit that conversion partially and only the combination of both would be able to give an inhibition pattern that approached complete inhibition of the enzyme responsible for that conversion.

166. (D)

Read from the bottom up to get 5′-3′

167. (D)

The key to reading this sequence is to realize that a band in A/ G that is also in G is a G, and a band in A/G that is NOT in G is an A.

168. (E)

On the 5′ side of the two internal C's are a G and an A.

169. (C)

Both peptides have net positive charges at pH 8.0. The second peptide contains histidine, which in its free state has a pI of 7.8 ((6.0 + 9.6)/2). Internally situated within the peptide, however, only the imidazole group should be considered. At pH 8.0, an insignificant amount of the imidazole residue would be protonated and its charge would be essentially zero. Thus, the net charge on peptide II is approximately +2.

170. (C)

Both peptides have net positive charges at pH 8.0; therefore, cation exchange chromatography would be appropriate. Peptide I has the more positive charge and would be expected to have greater affinity for the exchange media and should elute last. Hydrophobic interaction chromatography is ruled out, since low salt conditions are specified. Most protein separation techniques use weak ion exchanger like DEAE (diethylaminoethyl) cellulose or carboxymethyl (CM) cellulose. The active groups may be attached to support media other than cellulose. The choice of which media to use will depend upon the ionic properties of the protein to be purified. If the pH of the sample containing the protein mixture and the elution buffer are above the pI (isoelectric point) of the protein, the protein will have a net negative charge and an anion exchanger such as DEAE cellulose would be preferred.

171. (E)

Trypsin cleaves peptide linkages on the carboxyl side of arginine and lysine residues. Five fragments would be expected from peptide I (2 peptides and 3 amino acids) and three fragments from peptide II (all peptides). Thus the total number from both peptides would be eight. Other notes and observations about these peptides: (1) Peptide I will have significant absorbance at 280 nm due to the presence of tryptophan, which none of the others have. (2) Peptide II has phenylalanine, which does not have significant absorbance at 280 nm. (3) The mass and structure of these peptides could be determined using a combination of liquid chromatography and tandem mass spectrometry, LC/MS/MS, a common proteomics technique that was not discussed in the text, but should be checked out from other sources.

172. (A)

The three eukaryotic nuclear RNA polymerase can be differentiated by their sensitivity to the mushroom-derived poison, α- amanitin. Pol II is inhibited by very small amounts of the poison, pol III only by higher concentrations, and pol I is almost completely insensitive.

173. (C)

The linear lambda phage DNA can form a circle after insertion into the cell, and be reproduced independently, much like a plasmid.

174. (B)

As part of the lac operon promoter there is a region (labeled "CAP" in the diagram above) that ensures the use of glucose when both glucose and lactose are present. It is the binding site for a protein known either as CAP (Catabolite Activator Protein) or CRP (cAMP receptor protein). The CAP site must be occupied for transcription to occur. In the presence of glucose the cell produces little cAMP, and the CAP protein is not bound to the CAP site on the DNA. This would be the situation whether glucose is present alone, or together with lactose. This ensures that glucose is the fuel that is used, because, with no CAP bound, the lac operon is not transcribed. If glucose is withdrawn the amount of cAMP rises. The CAP protein binds the cAMP and changes conformation to facilitate binding to the CAP site. Now the operon can be transcribed.

175. (D)

The most common mechanism for the removal of introns is that found in higher eukaryotes, where a "spliceosome" is assembled at the ends of the introns. There are short conserved sequences that delineate the splice sites (boundaries) between exons and the introns that separates them. The first two nucleotides of the intron are always GU, and the last two are AG. An additional important base is an A that is located in the intron and indicates the branch site. The first step in splicing is cleavage of pre-mRNA at the GU site. The intron then curves around towards the next exon, and froms a 5'-2' link to the A in the intron. This results in a structure called a lariat. The lariat is removed and the two exons joined together by an esterification reaction.

176. (E)

In prokaryotes the two most common promoters are the "Pribnow box", and the "–35 sequence". The Pribnow box is about 10 nucleotides upstream from the start of transcription and has the sequence T*A*TAAT*, where the bases followed by asterisks are the most conserved from gene to gene and species to species.

177. (E)

Some mutagens can form cross links between strands. Sometimes intrastrand dimers of bases occur, most commonly dimerization of adjacent thymines, caused by ultraviolet radiation from sunlight (both natural and artificial).

178. (C)

There is another type of RNA-containing virus, called a retrovirus. The best known example of this is HIV (human immunodeficiency virus), the causative agent for AIDS (acquired immunodeficiency disease). This family of viruses carries its own RNA-dependent DNA polymerase, called reverse transcriptase (RT).

179. (B)

In *E. coli* a group of genes arranged in operons (see below) control what is called the SOS response. Because all the operons share a common repressor (LexA) they are considered to be part of a "regulon". The exact signal for repair initiation is not known, but one requirement is a single stranded length of DNA. The SOS signal cascade is initiated by the RecA protein. RecA causes cleavage of the LexA protein, rendering it incapable of repressing the repair regulon.

180.

(D) Synthesis of a transcript in prokaryotes comes to an end at the appropriate place either by ρ-dependent termination or by ρ-independent termination. Rho-independent termination occurs when the RNA being synthesized has a sequence such that it folds back on itself to form a stem and loop structure. Rho-dependent termination is mediated by the Rho protein.

Answer Sheet: Practice Exam 2

1. (A) (B) (C) (D) (E)
2. (A) (B) (C) (D) (E)
3. (A) (B) (C) (D) (E)
4. (A) (B) (C) (D) (E)
5. (A) (B) (C) (D) (E)
6. (A) (B) (C) (D) (E)
7. (A) (B) (C) (D) (E)
8. (A) (B) (C) (D) (E)
9. (A) (B) (C) (D) (E)
10. (A) (B) (C) (D) (E)
11. (A) (B) (C) (D) (E)
12. (A) (B) (C) (D) (E)
13. (A) (B) (C) (D) (E)
14. (A) (B) (C) (D) (E)
15. (A) (B) (C) (D) (E)
16. (A) (B) (C) (D) (E)
17. (A) (B) (C) (D) (E)
18. (A) (B) (C) (D) (E)
19. (A) (B) (C) (D) (E)
20. (A) (B) (C) (D) (E)
21. (A) (B) (C) (D) (E)
22. (A) (B) (C) (D) (E)
23. (A) (B) (C) (D) (E)
24. (A) (B) (C) (D) (E)
25. (A) (B) (C) (D) (E)
26. (A) (B) (C) (D) (E)
27. (A) (B) (C) (D) (E)
28. (A) (B) (C) (D) (E)
29. (A) (B) (C) (D) (E)
30. (A) (B) (C) (D) (E)

31. (A) (B) (C) (D) (E)
32. (A) (B) (C) (D) (E)
33. (A) (B) (C) (D) (E)
34. (A) (B) (C) (D) (E)
35. (A) (B) (C) (D) (E)
36. (A) (B) (C) (D) (E)
37. (A) (B) (C) (D) (E)
38. (A) (B) (C) (D) (E)
39. (A) (B) (C) (D) (E)
40. (A) (B) (C) (D) (E)
41. (A) (B) (C) (D) (E)
42. (A) (B) (C) (D) (E)
43. (A) (B) (C) (D) (E)
44. (A) (B) (C) (D) (E)
45. (A) (B) (C) (D) (E)
46. (A) (B) (C) (D) (E)
47. (A) (B) (C) (D) (E)
48. (A) (B) (C) (D) (E)
49. (A) (B) (C) (D) (E)
50. (A) (B) (C) (D) (E)
51. (A) (B) (C) (D) (E)
52. (A) (B) (C) (D) (E)
53. (A) (B) (C) (D) (E)
54. (A) (B) (C) (D) (E)
55. (A) (B) (C) (D) (E)
56. (A) (B) (C) (D) (E)
57. (A) (B) (C) (D) (E)
58. (A) (B) (C) (D) (E)
59. (A) (B) (C) (D) (E)
60. (A) (B) (C) (D) (E)

61. (A) (B) (C) (D) (E)
62. (A) (B) (C) (D) (E)
63. (A) (B) (C) (D) (E)
64. (A) (B) (C) (D) (E)
65. (A) (B) (C) (D) (E)
66. (A) (B) (C) (D) (E)
67. (A) (B) (C) (D) (E)
68. (A) (B) (C) (D) (E)
69. (A) (B) (C) (D) (E)
70. (A) (B) (C) (D) (E)
71. (A) (B) (C) (D) (E)
72. (A) (B) (C) (D) (E)
73. (A) (B) (C) (D) (E)
74. (A) (B) (C) (D) (E)
75. (A) (B) (C) (D) (E)
76. (A) (B) (C) (D) (E)
77. (A) (B) (C) (D) (E)
78. (A) (B) (C) (D) (E)
79. (A) (B) (C) (D) (E)
80. (A) (B) (C) (D) (E)
81. (A) (B) (C) (D) (E)
82. (A) (B) (C) (D) (E)
83. (A) (B) (C) (D) (E)
84. (A) (B) (C) (D) (E)
85. (A) (B) (C) (D) (E)
86. (A) (B) (C) (D) (E)
87. (A) (B) (C) (D) (E)
88. (A) (B) (C) (D) (E)
89. (A) (B) (C) (D) (E)
90. (A) (B) (C) (D) (E)

Continued

Answer Sheet: Practice Exam 2 (Continued)

91. Ⓐ Ⓑ Ⓒ Ⓓ Ⓔ
92. Ⓐ Ⓑ Ⓒ Ⓓ Ⓔ
93. Ⓐ Ⓑ Ⓒ Ⓓ Ⓔ
94. Ⓐ Ⓑ Ⓒ Ⓓ Ⓔ
95. Ⓐ Ⓑ Ⓒ Ⓓ Ⓔ
96. Ⓐ Ⓑ Ⓒ Ⓓ Ⓔ
97. Ⓐ Ⓑ Ⓒ Ⓓ Ⓔ
98. Ⓐ Ⓑ Ⓒ Ⓓ Ⓔ
99. Ⓐ Ⓑ Ⓒ Ⓓ Ⓔ
100. Ⓐ Ⓑ Ⓒ Ⓓ Ⓔ
101. Ⓐ Ⓑ Ⓒ Ⓓ Ⓔ
102. Ⓐ Ⓑ Ⓒ Ⓓ Ⓔ
103. Ⓐ Ⓑ Ⓒ Ⓓ Ⓔ
104. Ⓐ Ⓑ Ⓒ Ⓓ Ⓔ
105. Ⓐ Ⓑ Ⓒ Ⓓ Ⓔ
106. Ⓐ Ⓑ Ⓒ Ⓓ Ⓔ
107. Ⓐ Ⓑ Ⓒ Ⓓ Ⓔ
108. Ⓐ Ⓑ Ⓒ Ⓓ Ⓔ
109. Ⓐ Ⓑ Ⓒ Ⓓ Ⓔ
110. Ⓐ Ⓑ Ⓒ Ⓓ Ⓔ
111. Ⓐ Ⓑ Ⓒ Ⓓ Ⓔ
112. Ⓐ Ⓑ Ⓒ Ⓓ Ⓔ
113. Ⓐ Ⓑ Ⓒ Ⓓ Ⓔ
114. Ⓐ Ⓑ Ⓒ Ⓓ Ⓔ
115. Ⓐ Ⓑ Ⓒ Ⓓ Ⓔ
116. Ⓐ Ⓑ Ⓒ Ⓓ Ⓔ
117. Ⓐ Ⓑ Ⓒ Ⓓ Ⓔ
118. Ⓐ Ⓑ Ⓒ Ⓓ Ⓔ
119. Ⓐ Ⓑ Ⓒ Ⓓ Ⓔ
120. Ⓐ Ⓑ Ⓒ Ⓓ Ⓔ

121. Ⓐ Ⓑ Ⓒ Ⓓ Ⓔ
122. Ⓐ Ⓑ Ⓒ Ⓓ Ⓔ
123. Ⓐ Ⓑ Ⓒ Ⓓ Ⓔ
124. Ⓐ Ⓑ Ⓒ Ⓓ Ⓔ
125. Ⓐ Ⓑ Ⓒ Ⓓ Ⓔ
126. Ⓐ Ⓑ Ⓒ Ⓓ Ⓔ
127. Ⓐ Ⓑ Ⓒ Ⓓ Ⓔ
128. Ⓐ Ⓑ Ⓒ Ⓓ Ⓔ
129. Ⓐ Ⓑ Ⓒ Ⓓ Ⓔ
130. Ⓐ Ⓑ Ⓒ Ⓓ Ⓔ
131. Ⓐ Ⓑ Ⓒ Ⓓ Ⓔ
132. Ⓐ Ⓑ Ⓒ Ⓓ Ⓔ
133. Ⓐ Ⓑ Ⓒ Ⓓ Ⓔ
134. Ⓐ Ⓑ Ⓒ Ⓓ Ⓔ
135. Ⓐ Ⓑ Ⓒ Ⓓ Ⓔ
136. Ⓐ Ⓑ Ⓒ Ⓓ Ⓔ
137. Ⓐ Ⓑ Ⓒ Ⓓ Ⓔ
138. Ⓐ Ⓑ Ⓒ Ⓓ Ⓔ
139. Ⓐ Ⓑ Ⓒ Ⓓ Ⓔ
140. Ⓐ Ⓑ Ⓒ Ⓓ Ⓔ
141. Ⓐ Ⓑ Ⓒ Ⓓ Ⓔ
142. Ⓐ Ⓑ Ⓒ Ⓓ Ⓔ
143. Ⓐ Ⓑ Ⓒ Ⓓ Ⓔ
144. Ⓐ Ⓑ Ⓒ Ⓓ Ⓔ
145. Ⓐ Ⓑ Ⓒ Ⓓ Ⓔ
146. Ⓐ Ⓑ Ⓒ Ⓓ Ⓔ
147. Ⓐ Ⓑ Ⓒ Ⓓ Ⓔ
148. Ⓐ Ⓑ Ⓒ Ⓓ Ⓔ
149. Ⓐ Ⓑ Ⓒ Ⓓ Ⓔ
150. Ⓐ Ⓑ Ⓒ Ⓓ Ⓔ

151. Ⓐ Ⓑ Ⓒ Ⓓ Ⓔ
152. Ⓐ Ⓑ Ⓒ Ⓓ Ⓔ
153. Ⓐ Ⓑ Ⓒ Ⓓ Ⓔ
154. Ⓐ Ⓑ Ⓒ Ⓓ Ⓔ
155. Ⓐ Ⓑ Ⓒ Ⓓ Ⓔ
156. Ⓐ Ⓑ Ⓒ Ⓓ Ⓔ
157. Ⓐ Ⓑ Ⓒ Ⓓ Ⓔ
158. Ⓐ Ⓑ Ⓒ Ⓓ Ⓔ
159. Ⓐ Ⓑ Ⓒ Ⓓ Ⓔ
160. Ⓐ Ⓑ Ⓒ Ⓓ Ⓔ
161. Ⓐ Ⓑ Ⓒ Ⓓ Ⓔ
162. Ⓐ Ⓑ Ⓒ Ⓓ Ⓔ
163. Ⓐ Ⓑ Ⓒ Ⓓ Ⓔ
164. Ⓐ Ⓑ Ⓒ Ⓓ Ⓔ
165. Ⓐ Ⓑ Ⓒ Ⓓ Ⓔ
166. Ⓐ Ⓑ Ⓒ Ⓓ Ⓔ
167. Ⓐ Ⓑ Ⓒ Ⓓ Ⓔ
168. Ⓐ Ⓑ Ⓒ Ⓓ Ⓔ
169. Ⓐ Ⓑ Ⓒ Ⓓ Ⓔ
170. Ⓐ Ⓑ Ⓒ Ⓓ Ⓔ
171. Ⓐ Ⓑ Ⓒ Ⓓ Ⓔ
172. Ⓐ Ⓑ Ⓒ Ⓓ Ⓔ
173. Ⓐ Ⓑ Ⓒ Ⓓ Ⓔ
174. Ⓐ Ⓑ Ⓒ Ⓓ Ⓔ
175. Ⓐ Ⓑ Ⓒ Ⓓ Ⓔ
176. Ⓐ Ⓑ Ⓒ Ⓓ Ⓔ
177. Ⓐ Ⓑ Ⓒ Ⓓ Ⓔ
178. Ⓐ Ⓑ Ⓒ Ⓓ Ⓔ
179. Ⓐ Ⓑ Ⓒ Ⓓ Ⓔ
180. Ⓐ Ⓑ Ⓒ Ⓓ Ⓔ

Practice Exam 2

DIRECTIONS: Choose the best answer for each question and mark the letter of your selection on the corresponding answer sheet

1. Net energy consumed in the decomposition of a molecule of water is 118 kcal. If the energy for an H-H bond is 103 kcal and for an H-O bond is 110 kcal, the energy released upon formation of a molecule of water (in kcal) is

   (A) −118
   (B) −206
   (C) −220
   (D) −440
   (E) −646

2. Which of the following is NOT spherical or spiral?

   (A) *Bacillus*
   (B) *Diplococcus*
   (C) *Spirillum*
   (D) *Staphylococcus*
   (E) *Streptococcus*

3. What is a "gratuitous inducer"?

   (A) A co-inducer that requires another molecule for activity
   (B) A molecule that binds a promoter to inhibit transcription
   (C) A repressor protein
   (D) An enzyme that degrades the inducing molecule
   (E) An inducing molecule that cannot be metabolized

4. The relative high boiling point of water compared to chemical compounds of relatively similar molecular weight is due to the

   (A) angle between H-O-H bonds in water
   (B) dissociation of H-O-H to $H^+ + OH^-$
   (C) fact that the van der Waals radius for oxygen is greater than it is for H–
   (D) formation of a large array of intermolecular hydrogen bonds
   (E) length of H-O- bonds

5. What is a characteristic of organisms that are dimorphic?

   (A) Divide by binary fission
   (B) Exist as a single cell and a multicellular organism
   (C) Facultative anaerobes
   (D) Have more than one terminal electron acceptor
   (E) Reproduce sexually and asexually

6. A type of secondary structure in proteins is

   (A) α-helix
   (B) disulfide bond
   (C) peptide bond
   (D) salt bridge
   (E) van der Waals bond

7. What happens to the transcription of the *trp* operon when there is very little tryptophan present?

   (A) Transcription cannot be initiated.
   (B) Transcription cannot be terminated.
   (C) Transcription is accelerated.
   (D) Transcription is slowed and then resumes.
   (E) Transcription undergoes premature termination.

8. When do bacterial spores form?

   (A) After addition of new medium
   (B) Before apoptosis
   (C) During conjugation
   (D) Just prior to fission
   (E) Under unfavorable conditions

9. What is the purpose of the "antitermination factor" in phage?

   (A) To allow transcription of delayed early (middle) genes
   (B) To bind to the rho factor
   (C) To limit the number of transcripts produced
   (D) To promote cleavage of polycistronic RNA
   (E) To promote synthesis of immediate early genes

10. One type of bond generally involved in stabilizing the quaternary structure of proteins is a (an)

    (A) disulfide
    (B) ester
    (C) hydrophobic
    (D) peptide
    (E) phosphodiester

11. How do RAG 1 and 2, the enzymes that catalyze cleavage and rearrangement of immunoglobulin genes, ensure that the two ends to be joined stay in place?

    (A) A lariat formation occurs between the two pieces of DNA to be joined.
    (B) A phosphodiester bond is formed between the DNA and a separate docking protein.
    (C) A phosphodiester bond is formed between the DNA and the enzyme.
    (D) The enzyme binds DNA by hydrophobic interaction.
    (E) The enzyme binds DNA by ionic interaction.

12. All of the following classes of molecules are found in animals EXCEPT

    (A) amino acid
    (B) cellulose
    (C) lipid
    (D) nucleic acid
    (E) protein

13. According to the theory of absolute reaction rates, all chemical reactions

    (A) are not directly dependent upon complexes that are not in the transition state
    (B) are related directly to the number of reactants involved regardless of whether all have reached transition-state energy level
    (C) have a reaction order consistent with the number of reactants
    (D) must have at least one of the reactants for a two-reactant process in its transition state
    (E) show a first-order dependence on the concentration of molecules in the transition state

14. What makes a lytic phage able to destroy its host cell?

    (A) It causes the cell to become hypertonic.
    (B) It causes the cell to undergo apoptosis.
    (C) It degrades host DNA.
    (D) It inhibits DNA polymerase.
    (E) It makes detergent-like molecules.

15. What term is applied to lipids that surround a protein in a membrane?

    (A) Adventitious
    (B) Aggregated
    (C) Amphipathic
    (D) Annular
    (E) Axillary

16. A serine residue in serine proteases becomes a better nucleophile through a charge relay type interaction involving two additional amino acids, which are

    (A) Asn and His
    (B) Asp and His
    (C) Gln and His
    (D) Glu and Arg
    (E) Glu and Lys

17. What kind of polymerase is reverse transcriptase?

    (A) DNA-dependent DNA polymerase
    (B) DNA-dependent RNA polymerase
    (C) RNA-dependent DNA polymerase
    (D) RNA-dependent RNA polymerase
    (E) Template-independent DNA polymerase

18. Which statement best describes the function of a coenzyme that serves as a prosthetic group?

    (A) Acetyl-coenzyme A is used as an acyl group carrier in fatty acid biosynthesis with release of coenzyme A.
    (B) Ascorbic acid is a cofactor in several hydroxylation reactions in which it often becomes oxidized and is regenerated in its free form in another reaction.
    (C) Biotin is covalently linked to pyruvate carboxylase and serves to accept and deliver CO_2 to pyruvate to produce oxaloacetate.
    (D) Folic acid accepts methyl groups from specific compounds during metabolism and delivers them to other compounds in different enzymatic reactions.
    (E) NAD^+ is reduced to $NADH/H^+$ by glyceraldehyde 3-phosphate dehydrogenase and oxidized by lactate dehydrogenase.

19. All of the following characteristics are common to passive and active transport EXCEPT

    (A) ability to be inhibited
    (B) facilitation
    (C) requirement for energy
    (D) saturability
    (E) specificity

20. The Michaelis-Menten equation for a competitive inhibitor is

$$v = \frac{V_{max}[S]}{K_m\left(1 + \dfrac{[I]}{K_i}\right) + [S]}$$

If $[I] = \frac{1}{2}K_i$ and $[S] = 1\frac{1}{2}K_m$, what fraction of enzyme is in the ES complex?

    (A) 0.20
    (B) 0.25
    (C) 0.50
    (D) 0.67
    (E) 0.75

21. What is the evidence that *v-onc* genes were derived from mRNA and not DNA?

    (A) Lack of introns
    (B) Presence of ribose
    (C) Presence of unusual bases
    (D) Presence of uracil
    (E) Sensitivity to alkali

22. Which series of reactions in the following diagram would best demonstrate the mechanism of the interaction of a noncompetitive inhibitor of an enzyme in the presence of its normal substrate?

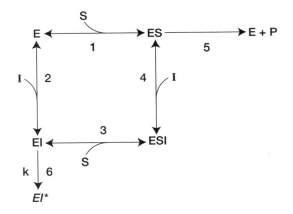

    (A) 1 and 5
    (B) 1, 2, 3. 4, and 5
    (C) 1, 2, 5, and 6
    (D) 2 and 3
    (E) 2 and 6

23. What is the function of a "gap junction"?

    (A) Entry of nucleotides into nucleus
    (B) Site for attachment of carbohydrate
    (C) To form a space between two leaflets of a membrane
    (D) Transfer of small molecules between cells
    (E) Transport of RNA out of the nucleus

24. For what purpose would a cDNA library be useful?

    (A) Determination of a cell's genome
    (B) Determination of a cell's metabolome
    (C) Determination of a cell's proteome
    (D) Determination of a cell's transcriptome
    (E) Study of promoter function

25. Each of the following is a metabolite of the glycolytic scheme EXCEPT

    (A) 2-phosphoglycerate
    (B) glyceraldehyde 3-phosphate
    (C) glycerol 3-phosphate
    (D) phosphoenolpyruvate
    (E) pyruvate

26. A recombinant plasmid carrying genes for tet and amp resistance, with an insert in the *tet* gene, is transformed into a bacterium that is sensitive to both antibiotics. What are the characteristics of a bacterial cell that has been successfully transformed with this plasmid?

    (A) Tet resistant amp resistant
    (B) Tet resistant amp sensitive
    (C) Tet sensitive amp resistant
    (D) Tet sensitive amp sensitive
    (E) Lytic

27. The reaction that commits glucose metabolism to glycolysis is

    (A) fructose 1,6-bisphosphate → glyceraldehyde 3-phosphate + dihydroxyacetone 3-phosphate
    (B) fructose 6-phosphate → fructose 1,6-bisphosphate
    (C) fructose 6-phosphate → fructose 2,6-bisphosphate
    (D) glucose → glucose 6-phosphate
    (E) glucose 6-phosphate → fructose 6-phosphate

28. What type of transport is shown in the diagram below?

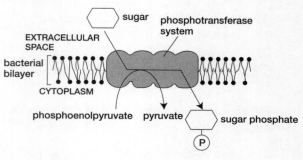

    (A) Antiport
    (B) Diffusion
    (C) Group translocation
    (D) Secondary active transport
    (E) Symport

29. What studies are often connected to the use of the chloramphenicol acetyltransferase gene as a reporter gene?

    (A) Antibiotic sensitivity
    (B) Promoters
    (C) Replication
    (D) Splicing
    (E) Termination

30. What is the name of the region in prokaryotes where DNA is attached to the membrane?

    (A) Mesosome
    (B) Nucleoid
    (C) Nucleolus
    (D) Nucleosome
    (E) Nucleus

31. What defines cosmids?

    (A) Having both eukaryotic and prokaryotic initiating signals
    (B) They are used in the blue/white recognition system.
    (C) They confer antibiotic resistance.
    (D) They have T7 and SP6 transcription initiation sites.
    (E) Use in the yeast two hybrid system

32. Which of the following transformations produces NADH/H$^+$ as a product?

    (A) 1,3-bisphosphoglycerate → 3-phosphoglycerate
    (B) 2-phosphoglycerate.→ phosphoenolpyruvate
    (C) 3-phosphoglycerate.→ 2-phosphoglycerate
    (D) glyceraldehyde 3-phosphate → 1,3-bisphosphoglycerate
    (E) glyceraldehyde 3-phosphate → dihydroxyacetone 3-phosphate

33. All of the following techniques use DNA EXCEPT

    (A) footprinting
    (B) gel shift
    (C) RFLP
    (D) Southern blot
    (E) Western blot

34. How many chromosomes does a diploid human nucleus contain?

    (A) 22
    (B) 23
    (C) 44
    (D) 45
    (E) 46

35. In the monohybrid cross (AA x aa), where a genotype containing at least one A confers a dominant phenotype, what is the ratio of dominant phenotype to recessive phenotype?

    (A) 0:4
    (B) 1:3
    (C) 2:2
    (D) 3:1
    (E) 4:0

36. Which enzyme catalyzes formation of the second high-energy compound in glycolysis?

    (A) Enolase
    (B) Glyceraldehyde 3-phosphate dehydrogenase
    (C) Phosphoglycerate kinase
    (D) Phosphoglycerate mutase
    (E) Pyruvate kinase

37. What is the total length of DNA in a diploid human nucleus?

    (A) 1 inch
    (B) 1 foot
    (C) 3 feet
    (D) 6 feet
    (E) 20 feet

38. In eukaryotic cells, most enzymes of the TCA cycle are located in the

    (A) cytosol
    (B) inner side of the outer mitochondrial membrane
    (C) intermembrane space of mitochondria
    (D) mitochondrial matrix
    (E) outer mitochondrial membrane

39. In the cross (AA × Aa), what is the ratio of AA: Aa:aa genotype?

    (A) 0:4:1
    (B) 1:3:2
    (C) 2:2:0
    (D) 3:1:1
    (E) 4:0:2

40. All of the following are associated exclusively with plant cells EXCEPT

    (A) chloroplasts
    (B) grana
    (C) mitochondria
    (D) thylakoid membranes
    (E) vacuoles

41. The equivalent number of atoms of carbon from the first molecule of acetyl-CoA that enters the TCA cycle released as CO_2 during a second turn of the cycle is(are)

    (A) 0.0
    (B) 0.5
    (C) 1.0
    (D) 1.5
    (E) 2.0

42. A red blood cell may be AO, AA, AB, etc. What is this type of inheritance called?

    (A) Co-dominance
    (B) Epistasis
    (C) Holandry
    (D) Incomplete dominance
    (E) Synteny

43. Two enzymes of the TCA cycle catalyze reactions that result in the release of CO_2. They are

    (A) aconitase and malic dehydrogenase
    (B) fumarase and succinate dehydrogenase
    (C) isocitrate dehydrogenase and α-ketoglutarate dehydrogenase
    (D) malic dehydrogenase and succinyl-CoA synthetase
    (E) succinyl-CoA synthetase and aconitase

44. What is the role of an osteoblast?

    (A) Closing of the bone plates of the skull
    (B) Crosslinking of collagen
    (C) Mineralization of bone
    (D) Removing calcium from bone
    (E) Synthesis of bone matrix

45. What is the term used to describe genes linked to maleness?

    (A) Co-dominance
    (B) Epistasis
    (C) Holandry
    (D) Incomplete dominance
    (E) Synteny

46. Pyruvate dehydrogenase is inhibited by

    (A) acetyl CoA
    (B) AMP
    (C) FAD
    (D) GMP
    (E) NAD^+

47. Twenty-five percent of a population is homozygous dominant for a given trait. What percentage of the population is heterozygous?

    (A) 10
    (B) 25
    (C) 30
    (D) 40
    (E) 50

48. Each of the following components of the electron transport chain of mitochondria pumps electrons out of the mitochondrial matrix EXCEPT

    (A) Coenzyme Q
    (B) Complex I
    (C) Complex II
    (D) Complex III
    (E) Complex IV

49. Which amino acid is NOT found in mature collagen?

    (A) Cysteine
    (B) Glycine
    (C) Isoleucine
    (D) Leucine
    (E) Valine

50. What is required for bacterial conjugation to occur?

    (A) A phage
    (B) A pilus
    (C) An ori
    (D) Being gram positive
    (E) Competence

51. Which protein(s) constitute ATP synthase?

    (A) Complex IV
    (B) Complexes I/II
    (C) Complexes II/III
    (D) Cu^{2+}/cytochrome oxidase
    (E) F_1/F_0

52. What is the situation called when a mutation in one monomer of an oligomeric protein causes the whole protein to be nonfunctional?

   (A) A nonsense mutation
   (B) Functional allelism
   (C) Negative complementation
   (D) Synteny
   (E) *Trans* configuration

53. Which letter indicates a desmosome?

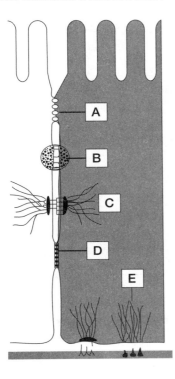

54. Which compound is an intermediate/product in both the oxidative and reductive phase of the pentose phosphate pathway?

   (A) 3-keto-l-gulonate
   (B) L-xylulose
   (C) ribose 5-phosphate
   (D) ribulose 5-phosphate
   (E) xylulose 5-phosphate

55. All of the following mutations could cause a nonsense mutation EXCEPT

1st position (5' end) ↓	2nd position				3rd position (3' end) ↓
	U	**C**	**A**	**G**	
U	Phe	Ser	Tyr	Cys	U
	Phe	Ser	Tyr	Cys	C
	Leu	Ser	STOP	STOP	A
	Leu	Ser	STOP	Trp	G
C	Leu	Pro	His	Arg	U
	Leu	Pro	His	Arg	C
	Leu	Pro	Gin	Arg	A
	Leu	Pro	Gin	Arg	G
A	Ile	Thr	Asn	Ser	U
	Ile	Thr	Asn	Ser	C
	Ile	Thr	Lys	Arg	A
	Met	Thr	Lys	Arg	G
G	Val	Ala	Asp	Gly	U
	Val	Ala	Asp	Gly	C
	Val	Ala	Glu	Gly	A
	Val	Ala	Glu	Gly	G

   (A) ....TTTTTGTCT to ......TCCATTTGT
   (B) ....TTTTTGTCT to ......TCCTAGTAT
   (C) ....TTTTTGTCT to ......TTCTGACCT
   (D) ....TTTTTGTCT to ......TTTTAATCT
   (E) ....TTTTTGTCT to ......TTTTAGTCT

56. All of the following are components of second messenger signaling systems EXCEPT

   (A) cAMP
   (B) Ca^{++}
   (C) diacylglycerol
   (D) glucuronidation
   (E) phosphorylation

57. What is represented in the following figure?

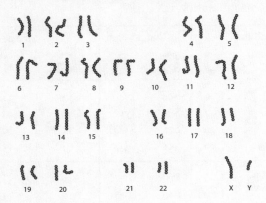

(A) Allotype
(B) Genotype
(C) Ideotype
(D) Karyotype
(E) Phenotype

58. Glucuronic acid is formed by oxidation of

(A) ADP-glucose
(B) CDP-glucose
(C) GDP-glucose
(D) glucose 1-phosphate
(E) UDP-glucose

59. What is the genotype of Turner syndrome?

(A) Trisomy 21
(B) Trisomy X
(C) XO
(D) XXY
(E) XYY

60. Some restriction sites on a DNA sequence are recognized by more than one restriction endonuclease. What are such endonucleases called?

(A) Isoligases
(B) Isolyases
(C) Isonucleases
(D) Isophosphodiesterases
(E) Isoschizomers

61. The enzymatic reactions in glycolysis that cannot participate in gluconeogenesis are

(A) enolase, phosphoglucomutase, hexokinase
(B) glyceraldehyde 3-phosphate dehydrogenase, phosphoglycerate kinase, hexokinase
(C) phosphoglucoisomerase, aldolase, hexokinase
(D) pyruvate kinase, phosphofructokinase I, hexokinase
(E) triophosphate isomerase, phosphoglucose isomerase, hexokinase

62. Which two amino acids are found more frequently in histones than in other proteins?

(A) Asp and glu
(B) Lys and arg
(C) Met and cys
(D) Trp and pro
(E) Val and ile

63. How many transmembrane helices do most cell receptors have?

(A) 2
(B) 3
(C) 5
(D) 6
(E) 7

64. The mechanism of glucagon stimulation of gluconeogenesis involves

(A) decreased phosphatase activity of the bifunctional phosphofructokinase II/fructose-2,6-bisphosphatase
(B) formation of a complex with phosphofructokinase I that inhibits its activity
(C) formation of a complex with the bifunctional phosphofructokinase II/fructose-2,6-bisphosphatase and stimulation of phosphatase activity
(D) second messenger stimulation of protein kinase and subsequent phosphorylation of phosphofructokinase II
(E) stimulation of adenylate kinase, which leads to a decrease in cAMP concentration

65. One of the genes that may be missing from a defective virus is env. What is the other?

(A) Gag
(B) Myc
(C) Ras
(D) Sis
(E) Src

66. The structure of glycogen consists of

(A) linear polymers of glucose in 1,4-linkages
(B) linear polymers of glucose with inositol at every tenth position where branching occurs
(C) mixed polymers of glucose and galactose
(D) mixed polymers with alternating linkages of glucose and lactose
(E) polymers of glucose with linear 1,4-linkages and branches with 1,6-linkages

67. What is the mechanism by which protein kinase A is activated?

(A) Allosteric interaction
(B) Compartmentation
(C) Induction
(D) Protein-protein interaction
(E) Zymogen cleavage

68. The light reactions of photosynthesis take place in which substructure of chloroplasts?

(A) Inner membrane
(B) Intermembrane space
(C) Outer membrane
(D) Stroma
(E) Thylakoid membrane

69. Both light and heavy chains of immunoglobulins have V, C, J, and C sequences. The heavy chain has also has a segment called "D." What does "D" stand for?

(A) Degenerate
(B) Dense
(C) Differentiation
(D) Diversity
(E) Duplicated

70. Which pathway is stimulated by the binding of insulin to its receptor?

(A) Gag
(B) Myc
(C) Ras
(D) Sos
(E) Src

71. Analysis of a double-stranded DNA shows that 25% of the bases are adenine. What percentage of the bases are pyrimidines?

(A) 10
(B) 20
(C) 25
(D) 40
(E) 50

72. Photochemistry (photosynthesis) occurs upon absorption of light (photons). Light absorption by which of the following initiates O_2 production?

(A) Cytochrome bf
(B) Photosystem I
(C) Photosystem II
(D) Plastocyanin
(E) Plastoquinone

73. Upon shearing, some highly-repetitive DNA sequences break into fragments that show a unique migration pattern on sedimentation in a CsCl density gradient. What are these fragments called?

(A) Alu sequences
(B) Nucleosomes
(C) Polysomes
(D) Pseudogenes
(E) Satellite DNA

74. What ion pours out of nerve cells when a voltage-gated channel opens?

(A) Calcium
(B) Chloride
(C) Magnesium
(D) Potassium
(E) Sodium

75. DNA codes for "UTRs." What are these?

   (A) Codons for addition of the polyA tail
   (B) Regions containing uracil
   (C) Ribosomal sequences
   (D) Sequences on the transcript that are unexpressed
   (E) Splicing sequences

76. The first stable compound produced in the Calvin cycle upon fixation of CO_2 is a three-carbon compound. The acceptor molecule for CO_2 in the Calvin cycle that leads to formation of that C-3 compound is

   (A) acetylphosphate
   (B) ribose 5-phosphate
   (C) ribulose 1,5-bisphosphate
   (D) ribulose 5-phosphate
   (E) xylulose 1,5-bisphosphate

77. A chromosome has a region toward the middle called a centromere. What are the names given to the arms of the chromosome on either side?

   (A) A and b
   (B) Left and right
   (C) P and q
   (D) Up and down
   (E) X and y

78. What does this figure represent?

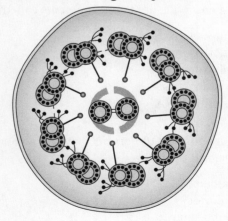

   (A) Basal body
   (B) Flagellum
   (C) Kinetochore

   (D) Spindle fiber
   (E) Pilus

79. One of the ways that the C-4 photosynthetic mechanism differs from the C-3 mechanism is that

   (A) CO_2 is initially incorporated into oxaloacetate by phosphoenolpyruvate carboxylase
   (B) major metabolites for carbohydrate biosynthesis start with production of two molecules of 3-phosphoglycerate
   (C) O_2, ATP, and NADPH/H^+ are products of the light reaction of photosynthesis
   (D) ribulose 1,5-bisphosphate carboxylase is required for CO_2 fixation into carbohydrate
   (E) ribulose 1,5-bisphosphate is regenerated by the reductive phase of the pentose phosphate pathway

80. What serves as a template for telomerase?

   (A) A DNA sequence that is part of the enzyme
   (B) An RNA sequence that is part of the enzyme
   (C) DNA on the other strand of the double-stranded DNA
   (D) DNA synthesized by a primase
   (E) RNA synthesized by a primase

81. CAM photosynthesis is a hallmark of succulents such as cactuses and is characterized by the fact that those type plants

   (A) are best suited for forest-type rather than desert-type environment
   (B) can conserve water by closing the stroma during the day
   (C) open the stroma during the night to facilitate photorespiration
   (D) release O_2 to the atmosphere more rapidly when the stroma is closed
   (E) use the basic photosynthetic mechanism of C-3 plants

82. The specific order of genes on a chromosome is often preserved between species. What is this phenomenon called?

   (A) Co-dominance
   (B) Epistasis

(C) Holandry
(D) Incomplete dominance
(E) Synteny

83. The carbon skeleton of which of the following amino acids is biosynthesized largely from an intermediate of the pentose phosphate pathway?

(A) Cysteine
(B) Glutamine
(C) Histidine
(D) Lysine
(E) Valine

84. All of the following prokaryotic DNA polymerases catalyze repair EXCEPT

(A) I
(B) II
(C) III
(D) IV
(E) V

85. One of the required intermediates in glutamine biosynthesis is

(A) γ-carboxyglutamate
(B) γ-glutamyl-ADP
(C) γ-glutamyl-AMP
(D) γ-glutamylphosphate
(E) $(NH_4)_3PO_4$

86. At which point does the cell become 4N?

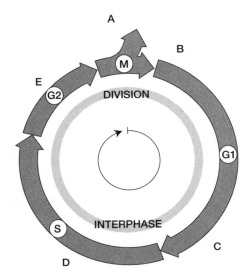

87. Which enzyme in eukaryotes is responsible for synthesizing the primer for replication?

(A) pol α
(B) pol β
(C) pol γ
(D) pol δ
(E) pol ε

88. Methionine is an essential amino acid in mammals because mammals have enzymes capable of catalyzing the synthesis of each of the following EXCEPT

(A) cystathionine
(B) homocysteine
(C) homoserine
(D) O-succinylhomoserine
(E) phosphohomoserine

89. What is the function of SNARE proteins?

(A) Acting as docking proteins for translocation of proteins into the ER
(B) Catalysis of addition of carbohydrate residues to proteins
(C) Checking fidelity of a newly-synthesized protein
(D) Recognition of proteins for targeting to membranes and organelles
(E) Synthesis of clathrin

90. Which compound is a branch-point intermediate in aromatic amino acid biosynthesis?

(A) 5-Dehydroquinate
(B) 5-Dehydroshikimate
(C) Anthranilate
(D) Chorismate
(E) Prephenate

91. One compound produced by the urea cycle is also an intermediary metabolite of the TCA cycle. The carbon skeleton for that metabolite is derived from

(A) arginine
(B) asparaginine
(C) aspartate
(D) glutamate
(E) glutamine

92. What is the name of the protein that attaches the sister chromatids during the 4N stage of cell division?

    (A) Cadherin
    (B) Cohesin
    (C) Desmin
    (D) Elastin
    (E) Spindle fiber

93. How many origins of replication does the bacterial chromosome have?

    (A) 1
    (B) 2
    (C) 4
    (D) 10
    (E) Depends on size of genome

94. The committed step in purine biosynthesis is formation of

    (A) 5-phosphoribosylamine
    (B) 5-phosphoribosyl-1-pyrophosphate
    (C) 5-phosphoribosyl-1-glycinamide
    (D) 5'-phosphoribosyl-5-aminoimidazole
    (E) inosine-5'-monophosphate

95. What is the name of the characteristic of DNA polymerases that allows them to continue DNA synthesis without falling off the template?

    (A) Fidelity
    (B) Processivity
    (C) Progressivity
    (D) Redundancy
    (E) Sieving

96. Which enzyme catalyzes the first essential step in degradation of all purine nucleotides?

    (A) Adenosine deaminase
    (B) Allantoinase
    (C) Nucleotidase
    (D) Purine nucleoside phosphorylase
    (E) Xanthine oxidase

97. What is the product of deamination of cytosine?

    (A) Adenine
    (B) Guanine
    (C) Inosine
    (D) Thymine
    (E) Uracil

98. In the first stage of mitosis a histone is phosphorylated by M phase kinase. Which histone is this?

    (A) H1
    (B) H2A
    (C) H2B
    (D) H3
    (E) H4

99. How does an organism protect its own DNA from cleavage by the restriction endonucleases that it synthesizes?

    (A) Binding of protective proteins
    (B) Compartmentation
    (C) Lack of the target sequences
    (D) Methylation
    (E) Tight coiling

100. The committed step in pyrimidine biosynthesis in *E. coli* is catalyzed by

    (A) aspartate transcarbamolase
    (B) carbamoyl phosphate synthetase II
    (C) dihydrooratase
    (D) orate phosphoribosyl transferase
    (E) orotidine-5-monophosphate decarboxylase

101. In base excision repair, what enzyme catalyzes the first step?

    (A) Deaminase
    (B) Demethylase
    (C) Glycosylase
    (D) Phosphodiesterase
    (E) Photolyase

102. Mechanism for formation of deoxyribonucleotide involves

    (A) reduction of the 2'-position of their corresponding diphosphate forms

(B) reduction of the 2′-position of their corresponding monophosphate forms

(C) reduction of the 2-position of phosphoribosylpyrophosphate prior to addition of their respective bases

(D) reduction of the 2′-position of their corresponding triphosphate forms

(E) synthesis of 2-deoxyribose followed by its activation to 2-deoxyphosphoribosylpyrophosphate and its addition to the bases

103. If AUAUAUAUAAU codes for the insertion of isoleucine and tyrosine, and AAUAAUAAUAA codes for isoleucine and asparagine, what codes for isoleucine?

(A) AAU
(B) AUA
(C) AUU
(D) UAU
(E) UUA

104. Ultimate degradation product(s) of pyrimidines is (are)

(A) β-alanine and β-aminoisobutyrate
(B) β-ureidoisobutyrate
(C) β-ureidopropionate
(D) dihydrouracil and dihydrothymine
(E) uracil and thymine

105. What does the presence of the zinc finger motif in a protein suggest about its function?

(A) It binds DNA.
(B) It binds NADH.
(C) It is an SNRP.
(D) It is a zymogen.
(E) It is ribosomal protein.

106. Which is the correct designation for the normal product produced by fatty acid synthase in which a single double bond has subsequently been introduced?

(A) 16:1 cisΔ^9
(B) 16:1 *cis*Δ^7
(C) 16:1 *trans*Δ^9
(D) 18:1 *cis*Δ^9
(E) 18:1 *trans*Δ^9

107. Which stage of meiosis is diakinesis?

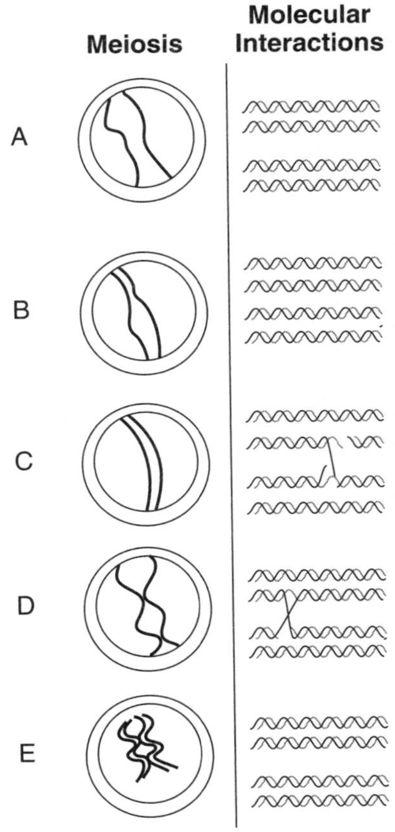

108. What is the mechanism by which rho-independent termination of transcription is effected?

(A) Addition of a cap structure
(B) Addition of a polyA tail
(C) Binding of sigma factor to RNA polymerase
(D) Formation of a stem/loop structure in the RNA
(E) Recognition of a stop codon

109. Which compound is the product of the enzyme that catalyzes the committed step in cholesterol biosynthesis?

(A) Farnesylpyrophosphate
(B) HMG-CoA
(C) Lanosterol
(D) Mevalonate
(E) Squalene

110. How are the two ends of exons held in proximity during excision of an intron?

(A) A lariat formation occurs between the two pieces of RNA to be joined.
(B) A phosphodiester bond is formed between the RNA and a separate docking protein.
(C) A phosphodiester bond is formed between the RNA and the enzyme.
(D) The enzyme binds RNA by hydrophobic interaction.
(E) The enzyme binds RNA by ionic interaction.

111. What are the projections on primary mesenchyme cells that allow them to migrate into the blastocele?

(A) Cilia
(B) Filopodiae
(C) Flagella
(D) Peduncles
(E) Pili

112. The sequence of reactions leading to formation of triacylglycerol is

(A) glyceraldehyde-3-phosphate → glycerol → monoacylglycerol → diacylglycerol → triacylglycerol
(B) glyceraldehyde-3-phosphate → phosphatidic acid → lysophosphatidic acid → diacylglycerol → triacylglycerol
(C) glycerol → monoacylglycerol → diacylglycerol → triacylglycerol
(D) glycerol → monoacylglycerol → lysophosphatidic acid → phosphatidic acid → diacylglycerol → triacylglycerol
(E) glycerol-3-phosphate → lysophosphatidic acid → phosphatidic acid → diacylglycerol → triacylglycerol

113. All of the four eukaryotic ribosomal RNAs are transcribed together EXCEPT

(A) 5S
(B) 5.8S
(C) 18S
(D) 28S
(E) 40S

114. The base structure of sphingolipids, sphingosine, is formed from

(A) palmitoleic acid and threonine
(B) palmitoleic acid and cysteine
(C) palmitoleic acid and serine
(D) palmitoyl CoA and serine
(E) palmitoyl CoA and threonine

115. Which will become the skeleton?

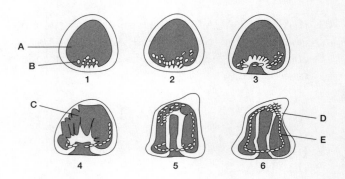

116. What is the role of tRNA nucleotidyl transferase in RNA processing?

(A) Adds three nucleotides to the 3′ end
(B) Adds unusual bases
(C) Removes a segment at the 5′ end
(D) Removes an intron
(E) Removes nucleotides at the 3′ end

117. Fatty acid oxidation occurs in the

(A) cytosol
(B) Golgi
(C) microsomes
(D) mitochondria
(E) peroxisomes

118. Each of the following terms denotes a function of the state of reactants and products EXCEPT

(A) ΔE^0
(B) ΔG
(C) ΔG^0
(D) ΔH^0
(E) ΔS^0

119. What is the probability of a spontaneous mutation occurring in a specific gene?

    (A) 1% in 10^{15} years
    (B) 1% in 10^{12} years
    (C) 1% in 10^{9} years
    (D) 1% in 10^{6} years
    (E) 1% in 10^{3} years

120. Which type of molecule can diffuse freely across the plasma membrane?

    (A) Amino acid
    (B) Protein
    (C) Salt
    (D) Sugar
    (E) Water

121. Which of the following is NOT a mechanism used by enzymes for rate enhancement?

    (A) Acid-base catalysis
    (B) Covalent catalysis
    (C) Lowering of ΔG^0
    (D) Proximity and orientation
    (E) Strain and distortion

122. Which of the following would result from insertion of a transposon?

    (A) inverted repeat-target repeat-transposon-target repeat
    (B) inverted repeat-target repeat-transposon-target repeat-inverted repeat
    (C) target repeat-inverted repeat-transposon-inverted repeat
    (D) target repeat-inverted repeat-transposon-inverted repeat-target repeat
    (E) target repeat-inverted repeat-transposon-target repeat-inverted repeat

123. Where would one find a cell wall made predominantly of cellulose?

    (A) Animals
    (B) Birds
    (C) Plants
    (D) Rickettsia
    (E) Salmonella

124. The source of oxygen in photosynthesis results from chemical activity directly involving the interaction of the

    (A) chlorophyll-pheophytin and H_2O
    (B) cytochrome bf and CO_2
    (C) cytochrome bf and H_2O
    (D) manganese center with CO_2
    (E) manganese center with H_2O

125. Which of the following promoter-type sequences are found in both eukaryotes and prokaryotes?

    (A) CAAT box
    (B) Enhancer
    (C) GC box
    (D) Pribnow box
    (E) TATA box

126. Of what does the basement membrane consist?

    (A) All three lamina (densa, rara, and reticularis)
    (B) Lamina densa and lamina rara
    (C) Lamina densa only
    (D) Lamina rara and lamina reticularis
    (E) Lamina reticularis and lamina densa

127. Where on DNA does a ligand-activated transcription factor bind?

    (A) -35 sequence
    (B) Enhancer
    (C) GC box
    (D) Hormone response element
    (E) SP1 site

Use the information below to answer questions 128–130.

A scientist studying fate maps (these show which embryonic cells will give rise to which structures) takes cells from an embryo of one organism with a mutation, and transfers them into an embryo without the mutation. The mutation allows identification at a later stage of the cells origin. The mutated cells are shown as black dots.

128. What structure will develop from these cells?

   (A) Mouth
   (B) Muscle
   (C) Neural tube
   (D) Placenta
   (E) Skin

129. Two micromeres (cells from an embryo at the 8-cellstage), A and C, are removed from the embryo one at a time, and in neither case do eyes develop. Removal of cell D alone also causes loss of eyes.

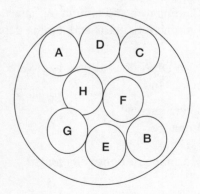

What is likely to be the reason for the above results?

   (A) A and D, but not C, are needed to become part of the eye structure

   (B) Both A and C contribute to eye structure, and D is necessary to produce molecules to organize A and C to become eyes
   (C) Only A forms part of the eye structure
   (D) Only C forms part of the eye structure
   (E) Only D forms part of the eye structure

130. Beatrice Mintz performed a key experiment in embryology. In her experiments she took a four-cell embryo from a black mouse and fused it with a four-cell embryo from a white mouse. This formed a chimeric 8-cell embryo. It was known that each cell can either go on to form the placenta or to form the inner cell mass that is destined to become the animal itself. At this time it was not known how many of the cells out of the eight were destined to become the inner mass. The number of cells that become part of the inner mass could be calculated by looking at the ratio of solid color mice to mosaic (chimeric) mice. For instance, if the answer had been four, then the percentage would be 87.5. (WWWW, WWWB, WWBW, WBWW, BWWW, WWBB, WBWB, BWBW, BWWB, BBWW, BBBW, BBWB, BWBB, WBBB, BBBB) (13 out of 15). For two cells the percentage of chimeras would be 50. The actual result found was that it needed three cells to make the inner mass.

What percentage of chimeric mice would this yield?

   (A) 20
   (B) 25
   (C) 35
   (D) 75
   (E) 80

Use the following information to answer questions 131–133.

A scientist has isolated a cell-line in which G-protein–linked signaling activity is extremely low. He also has a cell line with normal G-protein–signaling activity. Results from experiments to locate the mutation in the abnormal cells are shown below. Butyryl CoA is a cAMP analog that can cross cell membranes. "Activity" is the activity of protein kinase A after addition of hormone. Caffeine inhibits phosphodiesterase that breaks down cAMP. PPNG is a non-hydrolyzable analog of GTP.

	Experiment	Wild-type Cells	Mutant Cells
1	Scatchard plot	As expected	Same as wild-type
2	Add butyryl CoA	High activity	High activity
3	Add caffeine	High activity	Low activity
4	Add additional hormone	High activity	Low activity
5	Add PPNG	High activity	Low activity
6	Add rotenone	Low activity	Low activity
7	Add succinate	High activity	Low activity

131. Where is the defect in the mutant cells?

(A) Adenyl cyclase
(B) ATP availability
(C) GTP stability
(D) Hormone receptor
(E) Phosphodiesterase

132. Which experiments show that the problem does not lie with the affinity of the receptor for the hormone?

(A) 1 and 2
(B) 1 and 3
(C) 1 and 4
(D) 2 and 4
(E) 5 and 6

133. What term is used for intracellular signaling over long distances?

(A) Autocrine
(B) Endocrine
(C) Juxtacrine
(D) Paracrine
(E) Synaptic

For questions 134–136 use the information given below.

Transport of citrulline out of the mitochondrion occurs as part of the urea cycle. To study the phenomenon further a liposome was made that incorporated the transporter.

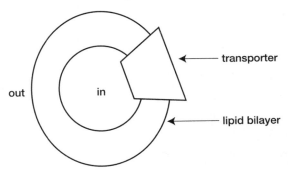

The following chemicals were added to the liposome suspension (outside) or incorporated into the liposome lumen during preparation of the liposome (inside).

Results after the system was allowed to come to equilibrium are shown below.

Chemical Added	Outside after incubation	Inside after incubation
Citrulline outside	Citrulline	—
Ornithine outside	Ornithine	—
Citrulline outside, ornithine inside	Citrulline	Ornithine
Ornithine outside, citrulline inside	Ornithine and citrulline	Ornithine and citrulline
Citrulline outside, arginine inside	Citrulline	Arginine

134. What type of transport mechanism may be inferred from the above data?

(A) Uniporter
(B) Diffusion
(C) Symporter
(D) Passive antiporter
(E) Active antiporter

135. On one day the liposomes were prepared by a graduate student instead of the laboratory technician. The experiment above was repeated, but the results were different.

Added	Outside after incubation	Inside after incubation
Citrulline outside	Citrulline	
Ornithine outside	Ornithine	
Citrulline outside, ornithine inside	Citrulline and ornithine	Citrulline and ornithine
Ornithine outside, citrulline inside	Ornithine	Citrulline
Ornithine and citrulline outside	Ornithine and citrulline	

What could account for this result?

(A) Activation of a lipase
(B) Lack of energy source
(C) Proteolytic cleavage of the transporter
(D) Transporter inserted with incorrect orientation
(E) Wrong mixture of lipids used to make the liposomes

136. What technique would be best to use in these transport experiments?

(A) Chromatography
(B) Electrophoresis
(C) Fluorometry
(D) Radioactive labeling of substrates
(E) Spectrophotometry

Use the information given to answer questions 137–139.

Analysis of total membrane lipid in a culture of yeast showed an unexpectedly high amount compared to the normal of phosphatidylethanolamine (PE) and phosphatidylserine (PS) compared to phosphatidylcholine (PC). In order to investigate this further the cell was fractionated into subcellular fractions, and the membranes from each analyzed. PM, plasma membrane; MT, mitochondria; MC, microsomes; VC, vacuoles.

Subcellular fraction	Phospholipid	Normal	Mutant
PM	PC	21	4
	PE	18	29
	PS	23	30
MT	PC	39	38
	PE	26	25
	PS	2	3
MC	PC	53	53
	PE	10	9
	PS	8	9
VC	PC	41	41
	PE	17	17
	PS	4	4

137. What appears to be the problem with this mutant?

(A) Degradation of PC
(B) Degradation of PS
(C) Inability to make the choline head group
(D) Inability to make PS
(E) Lack of transport of PC to the plasma membrane

138. To be sure that the subcellular membrane fractions have been correctly identified, enzyme assays are used. What is a good marker for the plasma membrane?

(A) Glucose 6-phosphatase
(B) Monoamine oxidase
(C) NADH-dependent cytochrome c reductase
(D) NADPH-dependent cytochrome c reductase
(E) 5′ nucleotidase

139.

Membrane protein	Regulatory lipid	Effect
Mitochondrial ADP exchange	Cardiolipin	Necessary for nucleotide exchange
Na^+/K^+-ATPase	Cholesterol	Necessary for activity
Anion transport (Band 3)	Cholesterol	Necessary for activity
Ca^{2+}-ATPase in muscle sarcoplasmic reticulum	Phosphatidyl-ethanolamine	Necessary for activity
Glycophorin	Phosphatidylino-sitol	Necessary for activity
Glycophorin	Phosphatidylino-sitol phosphates	Promotes binding to cytoskeleton
β-Hydroxybutyrate dehydrogenase	Phosphatidyl-choline	Necessary for activity

Which protein is most likely to be affected in the mutant?

(A) ADP exchanger
(B) Anion transporter
(C) Glycophorin
(D) β-Hydroxybutyrate dehydrogenase
(E) Sodium/potassium ATPase

For questions 140–147 match the letter with the stage of mitosis pictured or the transition during which certain events occur.

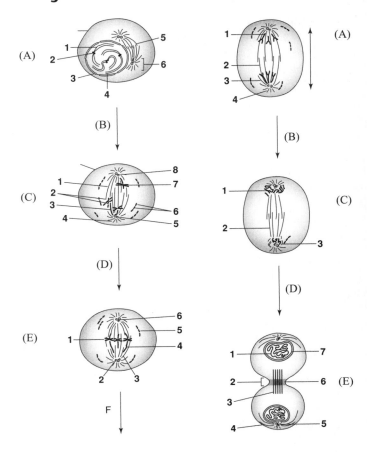

For questions 140–143 use the left side of the above diagram.

140. Astral microtubule forms

141. Chromosomes align at metaphase plate

142. Vesicles from nuclear membrane form

143. Prophase

For questions 144–147 use the right side of the diagram.

144. Nuclear envelope reforms

145. Cleavage furrow forms

146. Anaphase

147. Cytokinesis

The following vignette and diagram provide information for consideration in order to answer questions 148–151.

Ethylene glycol toxicity in mammals occurs as a result of its metabolism by liver alcohol dehydrogenase (ADH). The rate of its metabolism will decrease in the presence of ethanol.

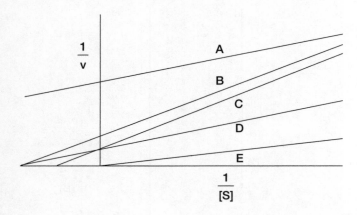

148. If line D in the diagram reflects a kinetic plot expected when ADH metabolizes ethylene glycol alone, which line would reflect metabolism of ethylene glycol in the presence of ethanol?

149. Which combination of numbers taken from the diagram below defines the mechanism of the interaction between ADH, ethylene glycol, and ethanol?

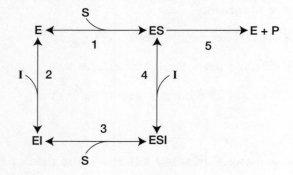

(A) 1 and 5
(B) 1, 2, 3, 4, and 5
(C) 1, 2, 3, and 4
(D) 1, 2, and 5
(E) 1, 4, and 5

150. Which of the following equations defines the reaction of ADH in the presence of both ethylene glycol and ethanol?

(A) $\dfrac{1}{v} = \left(\dfrac{K_m}{V_{max}}\right)\dfrac{1}{[S]} + \left(\dfrac{1}{V_{max}}\right)$

(B) $\dfrac{1}{v} = \left(\dfrac{K_m}{V_{max}}\right)\left(1 + \dfrac{[I]}{Ki}\right)\dfrac{1}{[S]} + \left(\dfrac{1}{V_{max}}\right)$

(C) $\dfrac{1}{v} = \left(\dfrac{K_m}{V_{max}}\right)\left(1 + \dfrac{[I]}{Ki}\right)\dfrac{1}{[S]} + \left(\dfrac{1}{V_{max}}\right)\left(1 + \dfrac{[I]}{Ki}\right)$

(D) $\dfrac{1}{v} = \left(\dfrac{K_m}{V_{max}}\right)\dfrac{1}{[S]} + \left(\dfrac{1}{V_{max}}\right)\left(1 + \dfrac{[I]}{Ki}\right)$

(E) $\dfrac{1}{v} = \dfrac{K_m}{V_{max}[S]} + \dfrac{1}{V_{max}} + \dfrac{[I]}{K_i V_{max}}$

151. The reaction catalyzed by this enzyme is of the following general type

$$R\text{-}H_2COH + NAD^+ \leftrightarrow R\text{-}CHO + NADH + H^+$$

Thus, the enzyme may be classified as a(n)
(A) hydrolase.
(B) isomerase.
(C) ligase
(D) oxidoreductase.
(E) transferase.

Use the sequence to answer questions 152–154.

A researcher wishes to clone and express a gene. In the following gene sequence N_x denotes an unspecified sequence.

5′-AATCGCCGAGCTCGGTTACGN$_x$
TAGGCATCTCGAGCCTAGG-3′

152. The restriction endonucleases to be used for this project are SacI and XhoI. The recognition site for XhoI is CTCGAG. What is the recognition site for SacI?

(A) ATCGCC
(B) CGCCGA
(C) CCGACT
(D) GAGCTC
(E) GCCGAC

153. Which vector would be most appropriate?

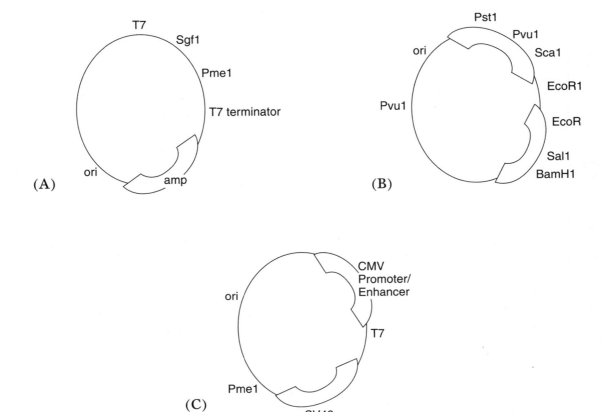

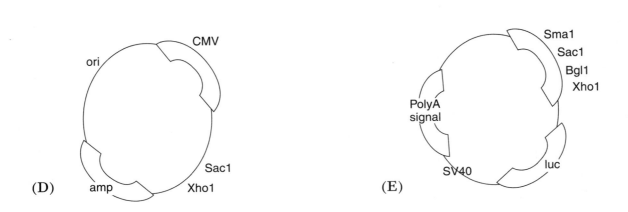

154. Which pair of primers will be effective for PCR-amplification of the gene?
   - (1 AATCGCC
   - (2 ATCCGTA
   - (3 TAGGCAT
   - (4 TTAGCGG
   - (5 CCTAGGC

   (A) 1 and 2
   (B) 1 and 3
   (C) 1 and 5
   (D) 2 and 3
   (E) 4 and 2

Use information in this vignette to answer questions 155–157.

A chemical plant, upon inspection of its storage facility, discovered that one of its tanks had a slow leak that deposited chemicals into the soil near a neighborhood playground. The company agreed to pay for cleanup and for damages, but they also needed to know whether individuals had this chemical in their bodies in a detectable form, but an assay was not available to them. A bioorganic chemist at a local university had been conducting experiments on the enzymatic degradation of xenobiotics. The compound spilled by the company, coincidentally, was one on which he had some data showing that its degradation followed Michaelis-Menten mechanism, namely,

$$E + S \leftrightarrow ES \rightarrow E + P,$$

where the double arrow represents k_1 for the forward and k_2 for the reverse reactions, respectively, and the single arrow represents k_3. Data reported by the chemist were: $k_1 = 1 \times 10^{12}$ M^{-1}min^{-1}, $k_2 = 1 \times 10^6$ min^{-1}, and $k_3 = 1 \times 10^3$ min^{-1}. In order to use this enzyme in an analytical assay, a first-order rate constant must be obtained from them. Answers to the following questions lead to that approximation. For the first two questions choose the most appropriate answer from the following list.

(A) 1×10^{-3}
(B) 1×10^{-6}
(C) 1×10^{-9}
(D) 1×10^3
(E) 1×10^6

155. What is the approximate numerical value for K_m for the reaction of this xenobiotic with this enzyme?

156. What is the approximate numeric value for the affinity constant of the xenobiotic for this enzyme?

157. Which of the following terms best defines the first-order rate constant that can be used to perform an enzymatic assay for this xenobiotic?

(A) $\dfrac{k_2 + [E]k_3}{k_1}$

(B) $\dfrac{k_2 + [E]k_1}{k_3}$

(C) $\dfrac{k_2 + k_3}{k_1[E]}$

(D) $\dfrac{[E]k_3}{(k_2 + k_3)/k_1}$

(E) $\dfrac{[E]k_3}{k_1/(k_2 + k_3)}$

Use the following information about a questioned paternity to answer question 158–160.

A mother (M) admits to the possibility that one of four men (P1, 2, 3, and 4) could possibly be the father of her child (C). Below is a simplified diagram of a RFLP analysis of DNA from mother, child, and all four possible fathers.

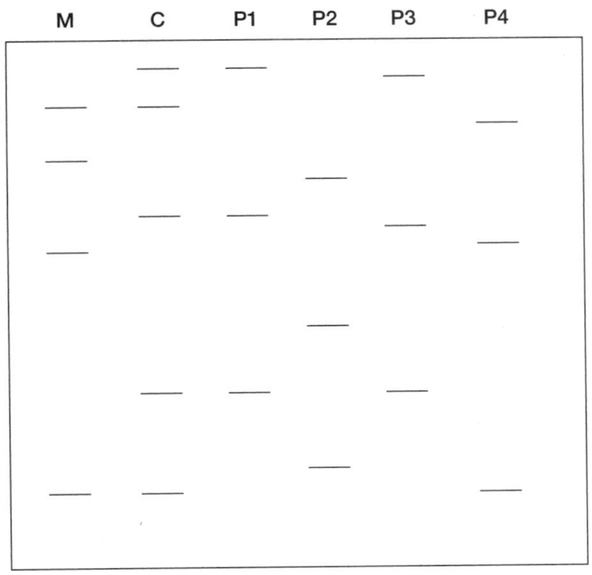

158. Which two men could be the father?

(A) 1 and 2
(B) 1 and 3
(C) 1 and 4
(D) 2 and 3
(E) 2 and 4

159. How could one determine which of the two is actually the father?

(A) Run the gel under different conditions.
(B) Sequence the DNA fragments that are the same.
(C) Use a different detection method.
(D) Use different restriction endonucleases.
(E) Use larger volumes of sample.

160. One of the two potential fathers refused to cooperate further, even though there was no more DNA available for the test. How best could one obtain a sample of his DNA without drawing more blood?

(A) A karyotype he had done several years earlier
(B) Finger nail clippings
(C) Fingerprints on a cup
(D) Hair shaft after a haircut
(E) Saliva on a cigarette butt

Use the information given to answer questions 161—163.

Fixation of CO_2 during photosynthesis is catalyzed by ribulose-1,5-bisphosphate (RubisP) carboxylase (RubisCO). Stoichiometry of the reaction is: one molecule of RubisP plus one molecule of CO_2 yield two molecules of 3-phosphoglyceric acid (3-PGA). When the reaction is conducted in the laboratory using ^2H_2O (deuterium oxide) as solvent and CO_2 containing trace amounts of $^{14}CO_2$ (500 dpm/nmole), it was observed that one atom of deuterium and one atom of $^{14}CO_2$ are incorporated into the two molecules of 3-PGA. 3-PGA was converted chemically to glycolate, which was oxidized enzymatically and stereospecifically (with respect to proton removal) to glyoxylate as shown in the following diagram.

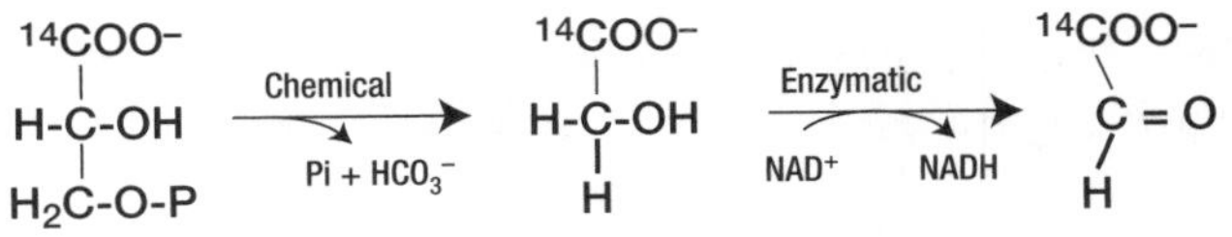

A 1.0-ml aliquot of the reaction mixture was removed each minute, absorbance of NADH/H$^+$ recorded, glyoxylate isolated, and its amount and specific radioactivity determined.

A Minutes	B Absorbance	C nmoles	D dpm	E Specific activity of ^{14}C
0	0.0	0	0	...
1	0.062	10	1,250	125
2	0.124	20	5,000	250
3	0.186	30	14,400	480
4	0.248	40	19,600	490
5	0.310	50	24,750	495

161. If 1.0 International unit of enzyme activity is defined as the amount required to catalyze the conversion of 1.0 µmole of substrate to product per minute, how many units of enzyme were used in this experiment?

    (A) 0.001
    (B) 0.010
    (C) 0.100
    (D) 0.200
    (E) 0.500

162. Specific radioactivity (^{14}C) was calculated from which column(s)?

    (A) A and D
    (B) A+B and D
    (C) A+C and D
    (D) B and D
    (E) C and D

163. Which column in the table above provides data from which a conclusion can be drawn about whether CO_2 and the H^+ from water are incorporated into the same molecule of 3-PGA?

Use the following information on a metabolic pathway to answer questions 164–166.

The following series of reactions can occur in a metabolic pathway and they have $\Delta G^{0'}$ values as shown. Rearrange all or any one of them as may be required and answer the following 3 questions. [Note: $\Delta G = \Delta G^{0'} + 2.303RT \log_{10} K_{eq}$ and $2.303RT = 1.36$ kcal.]

Reactions	$\Delta G^{0'}$
$A + B \leftrightarrow C + D$	+4.25
$B + E \leftrightarrow C + F$	+8.36
$D + K \leftrightarrow F + J$	+2.75

164. $\Delta G^{0'}$ for the reaction $A + K \leftrightarrow E + J$ is

    (A) –2.72
    (B) –1.36
    (C) 0.0
    (D) 1.36
    (E) 2.72

165. At equilibrium, the ratio of products to reactants is

    (A) 0.05
    (B) 0.10
    (C) 1.00
    (D) 5.00
    (E) 10.0

166. If $\Delta G^{0'}$ is the value determined in question 164 and K_{eq} is as determined in question 165, what is ΔG, i.e., work potential?

    (A) –2.72
    (B) –1.36
    (C) 0.0
    (D) 1.36
    (E) 2.72

Use the following information to answer questions 167–169.

DNA from a newly discovered organism (A) is compared with control DNA from a similar organism (B) using a melting curve and a CoT curve.

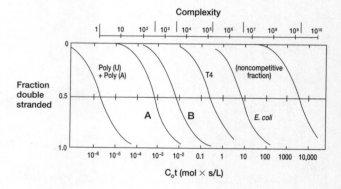

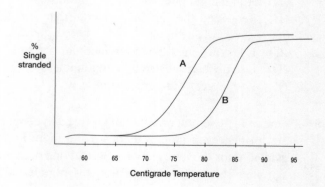

167. What can be learned from the above two curves?

    (A) The sample has lower A-T than the control.
    (B) The sample DNA is less complex than DNA from the control.
    (C) The sample is more likely to come from a hot spring than the control.
    (D) The sample is more stable than the control.
    (E) The two organisms are the same.

168. How are single- and double-stranded DNA usually measured in these experiments?

    (A) Electrophoresis
    (B) HPLC
    (C) Autoradiography
    (D) Spectrometry
    (E) Western blotting

169. What technique could you use to see whether proteins from one organism interact with DNA from the other species?

    (A) Centrifugation
    (B) Gel shift assay
    (C) Fluoroscopy
    (D) Radioautography
    (E) Spectrophotometry

For questions 170–171, choose the most appropriate answer from the following list.

    (A) Allantoin
    (B) Aminoisobutyrate
    (C) Orotatylglucuronate
    (D) Urea
    (E) Uric acid

170. This compound is an excretory product of AMP and GMP degradation in mammals.

171. This compound is a product of the action of xanthine oxidase.

For questions 172–173, choose the most appropriate answer from the following list.

    (A) Aspartate
    (B) Cysteine
    (C) Glutamate
    (D) Glutamine
    (E) Lysine

172. This compound is a necessary intermediate for the biosynthesis of methionine.

173. Complete catabolism of this amino acid gives only ketogenic metabolites.

Use the information on Southwestern blotting to answer questions 174–176.

A 2D variant of "blotting" allows for the study of interaction between DNA-binding proteins, and DNA. This technique requires that the proteins are loaded on a gel in a well that is the width of the gel, so that they run as wide bands through the gel as they are separated. DNA fragments are similarly separated, and then the DNA gel is turned 90° and transferred to a membrane. This membrane is then exposed to the protein gel. Subsequent staining for the protein shows which proteins bound DNA, and to which fragment they bound.

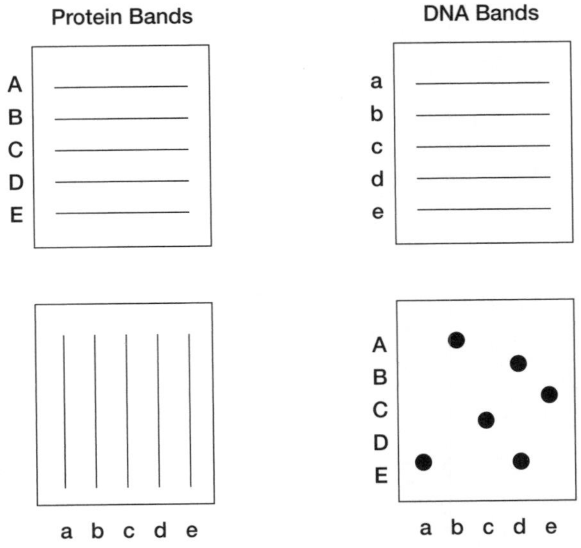

Protein Bands

DNA Bands

Orientation of DNA gel after 90° turn

Staining for protein on blot

174. To which DNA band does protein A bind?

(A) a
(B) b
(C) c
(D) d
(E) e

175. Which protein binds to two different bands?

(A) A
(B) B
(C) C
(D) D
(E) E

176. What experiment could you do to examine these results further?

(A) Gel Shift electrophoresis
(B) Northern blot
(C) RFLP
(D) Southern blot
(E) Western blot

For questions 177–179, choose the most appropriate answer from the following list. An answer may be chosen more than once.

(A) Complex I
(B) Complex II
(C) Complex III
(D) Complex IV
(E) Ubiquinone

177. In the presence of Antimycin A, electron transport through this molecular structure will be inhibited.

178. In the presence of Rotenone, electron transport will not be affected when succinate is the substrate because electrons enter the electron transport chain at this site.

179. A key component of this molecular structure is inhibited by potassium cyanide.

180. Each of the following is a correct pairing of the functions of mitochondria during active electron transport and active photosynthesis during the light phase EXCEPT

	Mitochondria	Chloroplast
(A)	$[H^+]$ greater inside the matrix	$[H^+]$ greater outside thylakoid space
(B)	ATP is made inside the matrix	ATP is made outside of the thylakoid lumen
(C)	H^+ generated from oxidation	H^+ generated from photon interaction
(D)	NADH/H^+ is oxidized	NADPH/H^+ is made
(E)	O_2 is used	O_2 is generated

Answer Key

1. A	31. A	61. D	91. C	121. C	151. D
2. A	32. D	62. B	92. B	122. D	152. D
3. E	33. E	63. E	93. A	123. C	153. E
4. D	34. E	64. D	94. A	124. E	154. C
5. B	35. E	65. A	95. B	125. B	155. B
6. A	36. A	66. E	96. C	126. A	156. E
7. D	37. D	67. D	97. E	127. D	157. D
8. E	38. D	68. E	98. A	128. A	158. B
9. A	39. C	69. D	99. D	129. B	159. D
10. C	40. C	70. C	100. A	130. D	160. E
11. C	41. C	71. D	101. C	131. A	161. B
12. B	42. A	72. C	102. A	132. C	162. E
13. E	43. C	73. E	103. A	133. B	163. E
14. C	44. E	74. D	104. A	134. D	164. B
15. D	45. C	75. D	105. A	135. D	165. E
16. B	46. A	76. C	106. A	136. D	166. C
17. C	47. E	77. C	107. E	137. E	167. B
18. C	48. C	78. B	108. D	138. E	168. D
19. C	49. A	79. A	109. D	139. D	169. B
20. C	50. B	80. B	110. A	140. B	170. E
21. A	51. E	81. B	111. B	141. E	171. E
22. B	52. C	82. E	112. E	142. B	172. B
23. D	53. C	83. C	113. A	143. A	173. E
24. D	54. D	84. C	114. D	144. B	174. B
25. C	55. A	85. D	115. E	145. D	175. E
26. C	56. D	86. D	116. A	146. A	176. A
27. B	57. D	87. A	117. D	147. E	177. C
28. C	58. E	88. B	118. B	148. C	178. B
29. B	59. C	89. D	119. D	149. D	179. D
30. A	60. E	90. D	120. E	150. B	180. A

Practice Exam 2

Detailed Explanations of Answers

1. (A)

As much energy is released in breaking a chemical bond as is consumed in making it, the reverse reaction of making water from two molecules of hydrogen and one of oxygen would result in the release of -118 kcal of energy $((206+116) - 440)$.

2. (A)

Bacilli are rod-shaped, diplococci are pairs of round cells, spirilla are spiral, and staphylococci are single round cells.

3. (E)

It is sometimes advantageous to use an inducer that cannot be metabolized and therefore persists indefinitely in the sample. For example, allolactose, the normal inducer of the lac operon, can be metabolized, and this removes the induction of the operon. IPTG (isopropylthiogalactoside) is not metabolized, and induction persists.

4. (D)

Water has an extensive hydrogen-bonding network. This highly organized structure contributes to many of the physical properties of water including its high boiling point. Compare the boiling point of water with that of methane; both are close to the same mass but methane does not have the ability to form the type of intermolecular interactions that water does.

5. (B)

Dimorphic means "two forms." All the other answers have two different conditions, but only dimorphic answers the question.

6. (A)

The α-helix is one of the major secondary structures found in proteins. For L-α-amino acids, the helical structure is right handed; if held in the right hand with the right hand with

fingers pointing in the direction of the turns, the pitch (as in the turn of a screw) of the helix would be in the direction of the thumb. There are 3.6 amino acid residues per turn, and the pitch of the helix (linear distance between turns) is 5.4 Å.

7. (D)

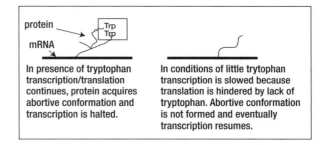

In presence of tryptophan transcription/translation continues, protein acquires abortive conformation and transcription is halted.

In conditions of little trytophan transcription is slowed because translation is hindered by lack of tryptophan. Abortive conformation is not formed and eventually transcription resumes.

8. (E)

Spores require no water for survival in their dormant state.

9. (A)

Phage genes are arranged in such a way that the phage can exploit the host transcription and translation enzymes to initiate reproduction of the phage. To do this the "early genes" (also called immediate early) are expressed. The host RNA polymerase recognizes a termination site that allows only this group of genes to be expressed. One of the gene products is the RNA polymerase of the phage, and another product is an antitermination factor. In the presence of the antitermination factor the phage polymerase can now read through the initial termination site and allow expression of a set of middle or delayed early genes.

10. (C)

The quaternary structure of a protein is defined by the interaction and arrangement of subunits of a protein. These subunits are held together by noncovalent bonds, one type of which is hydrophobic.

11. (C)

During splicing of gene segments several mechanisms come into play, including a cleavage reaction similar to that of a transposase. This is catalyzed by enzymes called RAG1 and 2 that anchor the cleaved DNA by forming a covalent phosphodiesterase bond to themselves.

12. (B)

Cellulose, like starch and glycogen, is a chain of glucose molecules. Cellulose has β1-4 glycosidic bonds, whereas the other two have α1-4 bonds. Cellulose is found only in plants and microorganisms.

13. (E)

It is important to recognize that the frequency factor in the Arrhenius equation is dimensionless and has the same units as those for first-order reactions, $time^{-1}$. The overall rate of the reaction depends upon the concentration of molecules in the activated state and there is equilibrium between those in the activated state and those that are not. This is also consistent with Eyring's theory of absolute reaction rates.

14. (C)

In the lytic mode the phage attaches to the bacterial cell and DNA is injected into the cell. The "early" genes of the phage are transcribed and translated by existing host proteins. Production of phage RNA and proteins commences, and expression of host proteins is inhibited by degradation of host DNA by phage-encoded proteins.

15. (D)

Annulus means a "ring." Ring describes the formation of the lipids around a protein in a membrane.

16. (B)

In all serine proteases, there is a specific serine within the protein structure that has a specific affinity for ester bond formation. For chymotrypsin, it is serine-195. Its hydroxyl group, as in others, is made more chemically active through interaction with a "catalytic triad" consisting (almost exclusively) of *aspartate*, *histidine*, and serine.

17. (C)

Reverse transcriptase nullified the dogma that DNA to RNA to protein is a one-way event. It synthesizes DNA using RNA as a template.

18. (C)

Pyruvate carboxylase [EC 6.4.1.1, Pyruvate:CO_2 ligase(ADP)] contains the vitamin biotin, which is attached to the enzyme by a peptide linkage involving the carboxyl group of biotin and an ε-amino group of a lysine residue of the enzyme. Biotin is a prosthetic group of this enzyme.

19. (C)

Only active transport requires energy. All facilitated transport has the other four characteristics.

20. (C)

Solution of this problem requires recognition of the fact that the ratio v_i/V_{max} is the same as $[ES]/[E]_T$, which can be obtained by dividing both sides of the Michaelis-Menten equation by V_{max}. Next, it is necessary to know that a competitive inhibitor gives an apparent K_m that differs from the true K_m by the factor $(1 + [I]/K_i)$. The value of v_i/V_{max} can then be obtained by substituting into the altered equation the relative values of [S] and [I].

21. (A)

It is believed that the oncogene-carrying defective virus is formed at the point that RNA is transcribed from an integrated virus. One of the normal genes (*gag* or *env* or both) is deleted from the transcript, and an adjacent host gene is spliced into the RNA. The evidence for this mechanism is that the host gene (*c-onc*) has introns, whereas the analogous *v-onc* (viral oncogene) has no introns, suggesting that processed RNA is its source.

22. (B)

Reactions 1, 2, 3, 4, and 5 represent the reactions for a noncompetitive inhibitor. Noncompetitive inhibitors react with any form of the enzyme because they bind at a site different from the substrate, and their binding is independent of the presence of substrate. A noncompetitive inhibitor effectively removes some of the enzyme from the active pool. Enzyme left in the active pool reacts normally. Thus, the K_m for that pool of enzyme does not change.

23. (D)

Gap junctions form bridge-like tunnels between cells through which molecules may pass.

24. (D)

A cDNA library is made by using reverse transcriptase to synthesize DNA using RNA as a template. This means that the library contains only those genes that are actively transcribed in the cells from which the library has been made.

25. (C)

Glycerol 3-phosphate is required for triacylglycerol formation. It is formed by reduction of dihydroxyacetone phosphate, which takes it out of the glycolytic scheme.

26. (C)

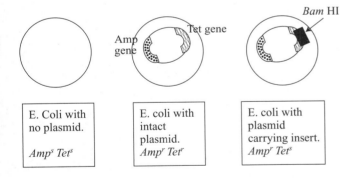

27. (B)

The transformation that commits metabolism of glucose to glycolysis is the conversion of fructose 6-phosphate to fructose 1,6-bisphosphate by the enzyme phosphofructokinase. The ΔG° value for this reaction is -5.56 kcal mol^{-1}. It is the first irreversible step along this pathway and its activity in many species is under allosteric and/or hormonal control.

28. (C)

Antiport, secondary active transport, and symport require movement of more than one molecule, and diffusion does not involve a protein.

29. (B)

In vitro translation systems can be used when the final product desired is the protein gene product, and are often also used for the study of regulation of transcription or translation. One such system involves the use of the chloramphenicol acetyl transferase (*CAT*) gene. In this system a hypothesized promoter is engineered into a plasmid upstream from the *CAT* gene, and the expression of CAT used as a reporter enzyme for confirmation that the sequence is a promoter. Acetylchloramphenicol can be detected fluorometrically. The *CAT* gene in this instance is called a reporter gene.

30. (A)

A nucleoid is the DNA structure itself, the nucleolus is the area in the nucleus where rRNA is transcribed in eukaryotes, and nucleosomes are DNA/protein structures in eukaryotes.

31. (A)

Cosmids are plasmids that contain both prokaryotic and eukaryotic regulatory sequences and can be shuttled between prokaryotic cells and eukaryotic cells. They can be amplified in prokaryotes with a short doubling time, and isolated and transferred to eukaryotic cells, where expression occurs together with posttranslational modification.

32. (D)

Glyceraldehyde 3-phosphate dehydrogenase catalyzes this reaction. The substrate forms a thiolhemiacetyl with the enzyme. The substrate is then oxidized by NAD$^+$ producing NADH/H$^+$ as one of the products.

33. (E)

In a Western blot, protein is electrophoresed and probed with an antibody or other ligand.

34. (E)

Humans have 22 pairs of autosomal chromosomes and a pair of sex chromosomes, either XY or XX.

35. (E)

One parent can only produce a gamete of genotype A. Thus all offspring will have an A allele and have an A phenotype.

36. (A)

Enolase catalyzes formation of the second "high-energy" compound in glycolysis. This enzyme fits the general category of lyases since it catalyzes the removal of a molecule of water and produces a product with a double bond. The relationship of the double bond to the phosphate group and the resonance structure created in the product, phosphoenolpyruvate, makes it a "high-energy" compound.

37. (D)

Figure 2-18 in the Cell Biology section of the text illustrates how approximately 2 m of DNA is packaged in the nucleus.

38. (D)

The TCA cycle is a catabolic pathway, and all enzymes for its operation are located in the mitochondrial matrix except succinate dehydrogenase, which is located in the inner membrane of mitochondria.

39. (C)

In the cross (AA x Aa), what is the ratio of AA: Aa:aa genotypes?

	A	A
A	AA	AA
a	aA	aA

40. (C)

Eukaryotic cells have mitochondria. The other four are characteristic of plant cells alone.

41. (C)

During the first turn of the cycle, neither of the original carbons of acetyl-CoA is lost as CO_2. Instead, both molecules of CO_2 come from the original oxaloacetate. Two of the subsequent dicarboxylic acid molecules in the cycle, succinate and fumarate, are symmetrical compounds and the positions of the carboxyl groups become indistinguishable to the enzymes that produce malate and oxaloacetate. Thus, the second turn of the cycle results in the lost of approximately one-half of the label from the original acetyl-CoA.

42. (A)

In co-dominance both alleles are expressed. Epistasis is the case in which a gene can be expressed only if another gene is also expressed. Holandric genes are male-related; incomplete dominance is mixed expression (e.g., pink from a red and a white parent), and synteny describes the case in which the order of genes on a chromosome is the same in two different organisms.

43. (C)

Result of the action of isocitrate dehydrogenase is production of α–ketoglutarate by an oxidative decarboxylation reaction with loss of CO_2. In a similar manner, CO_2 is lost from α–ketoglutarate during formation of succinyl CoA.

44. (E)

Cells with names ending in "blast" are involved in synthesis, and those ending in "clast" are involved in destruction.

45. (C)

In co-dominance both alleles are expressed. Epistasis is the case in which a gene can be expressed only if another gene is also expressed. Incomplete dominance is mixed expression (e.g., pink from a red and a white parent); synteny describes the case in which the order of genes on a chromosome is the same in two different organisms.

46. (A)

Pyruvate dehydrogenase is an enzyme complex composed of five different activities, and it uses an equivalent number of cofactors. It is inhibited by acetyl CoA and, in eukaryotes, its activity is also controlled by a pyruvate dehydrogenase kinase, which inactivates it upon phosphorylation; and a phosphatase, which activates it by removing the phosphate group.

47. (E)

The square root of 0.25 is 0.5; this is the incidence in the population of the dominant gene. Therefore the incidence of the recessive gene is also 0.5. (0.5 × 0.5) multiplied by 2 is 0.5, and 50% of the population is heterozygous.

48. (C)

Protons are pumped into the intermembrane space through complexes I, III, IV, and through reactions of the Q cycle. Complex II is the entry point for electrons from other intermediary metabolites such as succinate.

49. (A)

All cysteines in the preprocollagen are found in the globular region that is cleaved after secretion from the cell.

50. (B)

Conjugation, like transformation, is the process of transfer of a plasmid from one bacterial cell to another, but unlike transformation and transduction, conjugation requires direct cell–cell contact. The plasmid to be transferred from one gram-negative cell to another carries genes for a structure called a sex pilus (plural pili), a tube connecting two cells to facilitate transfer of the plasmid.

51. (E)

ATP synthase is a transmembrane protein designated as F_1/F_0 complex. It has a "controlled" pore through the center that permits H^+ to flow and to dissipate the proton gradient. Energy captured in this process is used to synthesize ATP. This is a very complex protein and the process of ATP synthesis is not a simple one. F_0 resides in the membrane and F_1 consists of several subunits and is on the matrix side. It actually rotates during the process of ATP synthesis, putting into position the subunit responsible for the actual ATP synthesis.

52. (C)

A nonsense mutation is the insertion of a nucleotide to form a stop codon, functional allelism is a description

of experimental results that indicate that two mutations are in the same allele even though they are not. Synteny describes genes being in the same order on chromosomes in different species, and a *trans* configuration of mutations means that two mutations are not in the same gene and that they produce a wild-type phenotype.

53. (C)

A indicates a tight junction, B an adhesion belt, D a gap junction, and E a focal contact.

54. (D)

Ribulose 5-phosphate is the final decarboxylation product of the oxidative phase and it is involved in the reductive phase with several of the isomerase and transferase enzymes.

55. (A)

Only A does not contain a stop codon (TAA, TAG, or TGA). Note that the genetic code table shows U, but the original mutation would be in DNA; therefore, the sequences are shown with Ts.

56. (D)

cAMP is formed as a result of the activation of adenylcyclase. Calcium and diacylglycerol are second messengers in the phosphatidylinositol pathway. Phosphorylation can occur as the result of activation of protein kinase A or C, or by autophosphorylation of a tyrosine kinase receptor. Glucuronidation is a process that makes compounds more hydrophilic and facilitates secretion.

57. (D)

Karyon is "nucleus" in Greek. Allotype and ideotype are terms used in describing antibodies, and genotype and phenotype relate the existence of certain genes to the resulting physical expression of these genes.

58. (E)

Glucuronic acid is formed by oxidation of UDP-glucose by a NAD^+-dependent UDP-glucose dehydrogenase.

59. (C)

Down syndrome is trisomy 21, and XXY is Klinefelter syndrome.

60. (E)

Most restriction endonuclease recognition sites are six base pairs long, but there are also some that recognize sequences of four and five nucleotides. Because the shorter sequences occur more frequently, some endonucleases that recognize these sites are called "frequent cutters." Some restriction endonucleases cut DNA at the same place as other endonucleases. These are called isoschizomers.

61. (D)

Three reactions in glycolysis are irreversible and in order to form glucose, other enzymatic steps are necessary to get around them. The irreversible reactions are hexokinase, phosphofructokinase (PFK), and pyruvate kinase.

62. (B)

The positive charge that results from lysines and arginines can neutralize the negative charge on DNA.

63. (E)

The seven helices are a common motif of membrane receptors.

64. (D)

The mechanism of glucagon's effect on gluconeogenesis is G-protein–dependent stimulation of adenyl cyclase to increase formation of cAMP. cAMP activates protein kinase, which phosphorylates phosphofructokinase2.

65. (A)

A usual (nondefective) retrovirus has three genes. *Pol* for the RNA-dependent DNA polymerase, *gag* for group specific antigens, and *env* for envelope.

66. (E)

Glycogen synthase adds a glucose residue to the 4-position of preexisting glycogen molecules. The chains of glucose molecules in glycogen always end with the 4-position (nonreducing end) free. After the chain has grown to approximately ten units, branching enzyme will cleave about seven units and transfer them to the 6-position of another chain at about five glucosyl residues from the end, thereby creating a branch point with an α-1-6-linkage.

67. (D)

Protein kinase A has two catalytic subunits and two regulatory subunits. When the four subunits are in a tetramer, the catalytic subunits are inactive. The binding of cAMP promotes dissociation of the subunits, and the monomeric catalytic subunits are active.

68. (E)

In green plants, it is within the thylakoid membrane that the photosensitive structures lie and where the light-dependent reactions take place.

69. (D)

Light chain V gene segments have a 3′ leader sequence (L) and C gene segments have a 3′ joining sequence (J). Heavy chains have the same L, V, J, and C gene segments, but they also have an additional short sequence of amino acids called the diversity segment (D).

70. (C)

Autophosphorylation of the receptor tyrosine kinase initiates the Ras cascade.

71. (D)

In a double-stranded DNA the ratio of purines to pyrimidines is always 1:1.

72. (C)

The wavelength of maximum absorbance of light by PSI is approximately 700 nm and that of PSII is approximately 680 nm. Even though both are exposed to light and absorb it simultaneously, the flow of electrons that normally initiates the phototransduction process is initiated by PSII.

73. (E)

Some highly repetitive sequences are called satellite DNA because after shearing they break into small lengths that migrate to a different place from the rest of the DNA on centrifugation in a CsCl density gradient.

74. (D)

Potassium concentration inside the cell is greater than outside. Opening of a voltage-gated channel in response to a nerve signal allows potassium to flow out down a concentration gradient.

75. (D)

Sequences on the transcript that are unexpressed are found both upstream and downstream from the open reading frame of a gene. These are called "untranscribed regions." They contain many regulatory sequences such as promoters.

76. (C)

The acceptor molecule for CO_2 in the Calvin cycle is ribulose-1,5-bisphosphate. CO_2 is added to the 2-position of ribulose-1,5-bisphosphate (Ru-1,5-P_2) to produce on the enzyme the intermediate, 2′-carboxy-3-keto-D-arabinitol-1,5-bisphosphate which is hydrated and cleaved to produce two molecules of 3-phosphoglycerate; the first stable compounds formed in this cycle.

77. (C)

These are accepted names for the two arms of the chromosome.

78. (B)

The central microtubules indicate that this is a flagellum (or a cilium). A basal body has two central microtubules. Kinetochores and spindle fibers are associated with mitosis, and a pilus is a tube through which DNA can pass from one bacterium to another.

79. (A)

C-4 photosynthetic mechanism involves the initial incorporation of CO_2 into C-4 compounds in one type of plant cell and transport of the C-4 compound to another type of cell within the plant where RubisCO resides. CO_2 is fixed in the mesophyll cells by the enzyme phosphoenolpyruvate carboxylase that uses (PEP) as the other substrate and produces oxaloacetic acid.

80. (B)

Telomerase adds a short DNA sequence (TTAAGGG in vertebrates). It is a reverse transcriptase that carries its own RNA template for this secquence.

81. (B)

The photosynthetic mechanism used by CAM plants is of the C-4 type, but they are distinguished by the fact that they conserve water by opening the stomata at night and storing CO_2 in C-4 acids. During the day, CO_2 is released to RubisCO where photosynthesis can take place.

82. (E)

In co-dominance both alleles are expressed. Epistasis is the case in which a gene can be expressed only if another gene is also expressed. Holandric genes are male-related; incomplete dominance is mixed expression (e.g., pink from a red and a white parent), and synteny describes the case in which the order of genes on a chromosome is the same in two different organisms.

83. (C)

Histidine is formed from ribose-5-phosphate. The first metabolite formed is 5-phosphoribosyldiphosphate (PRPP).

84. (C)

Pol III is the major enzyme for replication. See section on Gene Maintenance in the Molecular Biology section of the text.

85. (D)

A second ammonium ion may be incorporated into glutamate using glutamine synthetase to form glutamine.

$$\text{Glutamate} + NH_4^+ + ATP \rightarrow \text{Glutamine} + ADP + P_i + H^+$$

The γ–position of glutamate is first activated in a reaction requiring ATP resulting in formation of the intermediate γ–glutamyl phosphate.

86. (D)

During the S phase, DNA is replicated and the cell becomes 4N. It remains 4N during the G_2 phase, and as the cell is divided in the M phase each daughter cell becomes 2N.

87. (A)

Pol β does base excision repair, γ is mitochondrial, δ is the major enzyme for replication, and the role of pol ε is undetermined.

88. (B)

Mammals lack the ability to synthesize the carbon chain (homocysteine) of methionine; hence it is an essential amino acid.

89. (D)

As the protein processing occurs in the *cis-*, medial-, and *trans*-Golgi, the proteins are sorted for transport to various parts of the cell based on glycosylation and amino acid sequences. Families of SNARE soluble NSF (*N*-ethylmaleimide-sensitive fusion protein) attachment protein receptor proteins recognize proteins to be targeted to membranes and organelles. Final packaging of the proteins occurs in the *trans*-Golgi. The v-SNARE proteins are in the membrane of the vesicles that bud off from the Golgi and are used to transport the proteins to their target membrane, and t-SNARE proteins are the recognition molecules similar to receptors on the target membrane. The two types of SNARE proteins interact to bring vesicle and membrane into proximity, facilitating the transfer of the protein into the membrane.

90. (D)

One of the steps in formation of aromatic amino acids is production of chorismate. Chorismate is the branch point in the pathway and the metabolite from which both tryptophan and phenylalanine are synthesized: tryptophan from anthranilate and phenylalanine from prephenate. Tyrosine is made by hydroxylation of phenylalanine.

91. (C)

Argininosuccinate is made from citrulline and aspartate. Argininosuccinate lyase produces fumarate, which can enter the TCA cycle, and arginine. Carbons of fumarate come from aspartate.

92. (B)

Cadherins are calcium-dependent proteins that keep cells together, desmin is an intermediate filament, elastin is a fibrous protein found in connective tissues, and spindle fibers pull the nuclei in mitosis.

93. (A)

Prokaryotes have only one origin of replication, whereas eukaryotes have many "ori's" that can be worked on by many copies of DNA polymerase.

94. (A)

The committed step of the pathway, formation of β-5-phosphoribosylamine (PRA), occurs with inversion of configuration at the 1-position of ribose and the amino group added from glutamine is in the β-position, the correct position for building the remainder of the ring system.

95. (B)

Processivity is promoted by a sliding clamp called a PCNA (proliferating cell nuclear antigen).

96. (C)

The first step is catalyzed by nucleotidase. In the case of adenosine, however, adenosine deaminase reaction may precede nucleotidase, but regardless of which comes first, further degradation occurs only after nucleotidase action.

97. (E)

Removal of the amino group leaves a carbonyl group, which is uracil.

98. (A)

Condensation of chromosomes is triggered by phosphorylation of histone H1, the histone that is not part of the nucleosome core.

99. (D)

As DNA is replicated in bacteria it is methylated at the sites that would otherwise be target sites of its own endonucleases.

100. (A)

The committed step in pyrimidine biosynthesis is the formation of carbamoyl aspartate by condensation of aspartate with carbamoyl phosphate catalyzed by aspartate transcarbamoylase.

101. (C)

The first step in BER is the cleavage of the incorrect or damaged base from the deoxyribose by a glycosylase. Two enzymes cut the sugar-phosphate, one on either side, to remove the rest of the nucleotide. These enzymes are an endonuclease and a lyase. The single nucleotide gap is filled in by a polymerase (pol II in *E. coli* and pol β in eukaryotes) and a ligase joins the two DNA sequences.

102. (A)

The biochemical mechanism for formation of 2-deoxyribonucleotides is somewhat complex. Important points to remember are that reduction occurs when the nucleotides are in their diphosphate forms, ribonucleotide reductase operates through a free radical mechanism, and dTMP is formed from dUMP.

103. (A)

AUA and UAU must code for isoleucine and tyrosine (which is unknown). In the second strand, AUA must code for one or the other, and in fact it codes for isoleucine. So the code for tyrosine must be AAU or UAA.

104. (A)

Uracil and thymine are eventually degraded to β-alanine and β-aminoisobutyrate, respectively. β-Alanine and β-aminoisobutyrate can undergo aminotransferase reactions to give malonyl-CoA and methylmalonyl-CoA, respectively. Malonyl-CoA can participate directly in fatty acid biosynthesis, and methylmalonyl-CoA can undergo a cobalamin-dependent mutase reaction to give succinyl-CoA and enter the TCA cycle for energy production or through oxaloacetate to glucose.

105. (A)

Other motifs in DNA-binding are the leucine zipper, helix-loop-helix, and helix-turn-helix.

106. (A)

Palmitoleic acid is the product. It would be represented by the notation (16:1 *cis*-Δ⁹). Notations in parentheses indicate the number of carbons to the number of unsaturated bonds and that they are in the *cis* configura-

tion, and the position of the double bond counting from the carboxyl group, which is number one.

107. (E)

The term "dia" indicates separation. In diakinesis the chromosomes detach from the nuclear envelope.

108. (D)

Synthesis of a transcript in prokaryotes comes to an end at the appropriate place either by ρ-dependent termination or by ρ-independent termination. Rho-independent termination occurs when the RNA being synthesized has a sequence such that it folds back on itself to form a stem and loop structure. Rho-dependent termination is mediated by the Rho protein. The Rho protein appears to facilitate termination by winding the RNA around itself to stop transcription.

109. (D)

The compound is mevalonate and it is produced from HMG-CoA by HMG-CoA reductase.

110. (A)

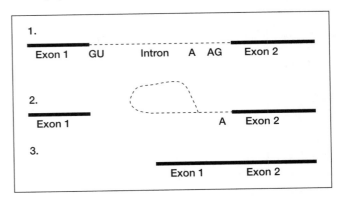

111. (B)

Cilia and flagella are microtubules, pili form between bacterial cells, and a peduncle is a stalk-like structure.

112. (E)

Glycerol 3-phosphate is acylated first in the 1-position to form lysophosphatidic acid. A second fatty acid is added to the 2-position by acyltransferase to produce phosphatidic acid. Phosphatidate phosphatase removes the phosphate group and the third fatty acid is added by acyltransferase.

113. (A)

The processing of rRNA differs between prokaryotes and eukaryotes. In eukaryotes three of the four ribosomal rRNAs (18S, 5.8S, and 28S) are transcribed as a single chain called the 45S rRNA precursor. The three separate rRNAs are cleaved by an endonuclease and processed by exonucleases to truncate both ends. Small nucleolar RNAs (snoRNAs, or snoRNPs when associated with protein) are also associated with the processing and further modification of eukaryotic rRNA. There are multiple tandem repeats of the gene for the 45S precursor, just as there are repeats of the 5S precursor that is situated elsewhere. Even in yeast, where the 5S gene is adjacent to the 45S gene, it is transcribed independently. In prokaryotes tRNA genes are interspersed with the rRNA genes and must also be removed and processed.

114. (D)

Sphingosine forms the base structure for sphingolipids. Sphingosine is synthesized from palmitoyl CoA and serine. This is a condensation reaction accompanied by a decarboxylation to give 3-ketodihydrosphingosine. A PLP-dependent enzyme catalyzes the condensation reaction.

115. (E)

See Cell Biology section of the text, Figure 1-51.

116. (A)

The CCA trinucleotide shared by all tRNAs on the 3′ end is added by an enzyme called tRNA nucleotidyl transferase.

117. (D)

β-Oxidation of fatty acids occurs in the mitochondria. Thus, the fatty acyl-CoA derivatives must cross the mitochondrial membrane. They are transported across the mitochondrial membrane as fatty acyl-carnitine derivatives. This is an active process that requires the action of two enzymes: carnitine palmitoyl transferase I and carnitine palmitoyl transferase II.

118. (B)

ΔG is related to the work potential for a reaction and can have different values depending upon the varying concentrations of reactants. Metabolic reactions are driven by changes in values of ΔG^0, which is related to the state function ΔG^0 by the following equation.

$$\Delta G = \Delta G^0 + RT\ln K_{eq}$$

119. (D)

1% in 10^6 years. This low rate of mutation is due to both fidelity of DNA replication and to efficacy of DNA repair.

120. (E)

All the others are large and/or hydrophilic. Proteins, amino acids, and sugars have regulated transport systems. The transport of salts is also regulated to prevent osmotic changes and to regulate nerve conductance.

121. (C)

$\Delta G^0 = -RT\ln K_{eq}$, which shows that it is directly related to K_{eq}. Because enzymes do not change Keq for a reaction, it also follows that they will not change ΔG^0.

122. (D)

The transposon, which is flanked by inverted repeats, is inserted between duplicated target site sequences.

123. (C)

Plants can synthesize 1-4β linkages between glucose molecules. The resulting chains are cellulose. Starch and glycogens have 1-4β linkages.

124. (E)

There is a manganese center (cluster) consisting of 4 manganese ions on the lumen side of PSII in the thylakoid membrane. Manganese of this cluster can exist in several oxidation states. H_2O is associated with this center, and it is here that the oxidation of $2H_2O$ to $4H^+$ and O_2 occurs.

125. (B)

Prokaryotes have the Pribnow box and eukaryotes have CAAT, GC, and TATA boxes.

126. (A)

All three layers make up the basement membrane. Lamina rara and lamina densa together form the basal lamina.

127. (D)

A ligand-activated transcription factor is an intracellular receptor that can bind a hormone and the complex then binds to a section of DNA called a hormone response element.

128. (A)

See Figure 1-51 in the Cell Biology section of the text.

129. (B)

Removal of A, C, and D all result in loss of eye structure.

130. (D)

WWW, WWB, WBW, BWW, BWB, BBW, WBB, BBB. Six out of 8 constructs are mixed; therefore, 75%.

131. (A)

With no addition of a cAMP analog the mutant system shows no responsiveness. Experiments 6 and 7 address the need for energy to make GTP (from ATP). PPNG has no effect; therefore, it is not hydrolysis of GTP that has an effect. Caffeine is an inhibitor of phosphodiesterase, reinforcing the fact that it is not the breakdown of GTP that has the inhibitory effect.

132. (C)

Both the Scatchard plot, which allows determination of the Ka for ligand, and the additional hormone added in experiment 4 show that the affinity of receptor for ligand is not changed.

133. (B)

All four of the other hormone types have their effect on cells next to the cell making the cell, or (autocrine) on the actual cell making the hormone.

134. (D)

The only experiment that showed movement across the membrane was the one with ornithine outside and citrulline inside. This indicates an antiport mechanism.

135. (D)

Because the results are the reverse of those in the original experiment, and we know that transport requires one substrate on one side, and the other substrate on the other side, the transporter must be inserted in the liposome backward.

136. (D)

If either ornithine and citrulline are labeled with a radioisotope it is easy to determine where the molecule ends up. In the case where both move, one can be labeled with ^{3}H, and the other with ^{14}C.

137. (E)

All the other membranes have normal PC; therefore, B and C are not correct. PS is slightly elevated, so making of PS is not inhibited, and there is no increased degradation of PS.

138. (E)

Glucose 6-phosphatase is a marker for endoplasmic reticulum, as is NADPH-dependent cytochrome c reductase. Monoamine oxidase is in the mitochondrial outer membrane, and NADH-dependent cytochrome c reductase in the inner mitochondrial membrane.

139. (D)

β-hydroxybutyrate dehydrogenase is the only enzyme listed that is regulated by PC.

140. (B)

Astral microtubule forms between prophase and prometaphase.

141. (E)

This shows metaphase with chromosomes aligned at the metaphase plate.

142. (B)

Vesicles from nuclear envelope between prophase and prometaphase.

143. (A)

Prophase is the first stage in mitosis.

144. (B)

Nuclear envelope reforms between anaphase and telophase.

145. (D)

Cleavage furrow forms between telophase and cytokinesis.

146. (A)

In anaphase chromatids are pulled to poles.

147. (E)

Final splitting into two cells occurs in cytokinesis.

148. (C)

Ethylene glycol and ethanol are both substrates for alcohol dehydrogenase. Each competes with the other for the active site. In this problem, ethylene glycol is assigned the role of substrate and ethanol that of a competitive inhibitor. Lines D and C in this Lineweaver-Burk plot reflect that situation. Note that V_{max} does not change for the competitive inhibitor. This means that the intercept on the Y axis remains the same but the slope changes and hence the "apparent" K_m.

149. (D)

Reactions 1 and 5 represent the normal course of reaction and would give a straight line in the Lineweaver-Burk plot as discussed. Reactions 1, 2, and 5 would represent the case for a competitive inhibitor.

150. (B)

This is a typical Lineweaver-Burk plot for a competitive inhibitor. Note that V_{max} does not change for the competitive inhibitor. This means that the intercept on the Y axis remains the same but the slope changes and hence the "apparent" K_m. The apparent K_m differs from the actual K_m by the factor $(1 + ([I]/K_i))$, which is

the factor that alters the slope in equation B. Compare this equation with the one for a straight line, namely, $y = mx + b$.

151. (D)

This is an oxidation-reduction reaction, hence the type enzyme catalyzing it is an oxidoreductase.

152. (D)

GAGCTC CTCGAG is a palindrome.

153. (E)

It is the only plasmid with both Xho I and Sac I site. It also has a SV40 promoter, which allows it to act as an expression vector in eukaryotes.

154. (C)

AATCGCC will act in a forward direction
5'-AATCGCCGAGCTCGGTTACGN$_x$
TAGGCATCTCGAGCCTAGG-3'
In the backward direction   CGGATCC-5'.

155. (B)

Derivation of the Michaelis-Menten equation shows that K_m is defined as $(k_2 + k_3)/k_1$. Substituting the chemist's values for these constants into this equation gives $1.001 \times 10^6/1 \times 10^{12} = \sim 1 \times 10^{-6}$ M. Constants added in the numerator are first-order and that in the denominator is second-order. Reciprocal time cancels and the correct unit of molar concentration is obtained.

156. (E)

The affinity constant is equivalent to the reciprocal of the dissociation constant (K_S) for the ES complex. $K_S = k_3/k_1 = 1 \times 10^6/1 \times 10^{12} = 1 \times 10^{-6}$, the reciprocal of which is 1×10^6. In this case, K_m is not the true dissociation constant, since it differs by 0.001, the numeric value of k_3.

157. (D)

The ratio of V_{max}/K_m has units that are the same as units for a first-order rate constant, $(Mt^{-1})/M = t^{-1}$. Because $V_{max} = k_3[E]_{total}$ and $K_m = (k_2 + k_3)/k_1$, D is the only correct answer.

158. (B)

Lanes P1 and P3 in the gel have bands that match those bands of the child that do not match the mother.

159. (D)

The bands shown were produced by endonucleases that have restriction sites shared by two possible fathers. To find sites that are different, other endonucleases must be used.

160. (E)

Saliva contains nucleated cells. Finger nails and hair shafts are not cellular, and fingerprints are mostly oil and enucleated surface keratinocytes. Karyotypes show only the gross structure of the chromosomes.

161. (B)

A 1.0 molar solution contains 1.0 millimole/mL and a 1.0 mM solution contains 1.0 μmole/mL. If the absorbance index (ε) is 6.2×10^3, the mM ε = 6.2. The absorbance change is 0.062 per minute. Thus, 0.062/6.2 = 0.01 μmole/mL and is the same as the number of international units (IU) of enzyme activity.

162. (E)

Specific radioactivity was calculated from columns C and D, (D/C), and is expressed as dpm/nmole.

163. (E)

Column E shows that the specific radioactivity of the product starts out lower than the specific radioactivity of the reactant (500 dpm/nmole). This means that there was a kinetic isotope effect for the enzymatic removal of a proton from glycolate. Because one-half of the glycolate formed had ^{2}H-C-H and the other half had H-C-H, the latter was oxidized faster than the former and if ^{14}C and ^{2}H are in the same molecule, the one with ^{14}C will be oxidized more slowly and the product formed will initially have a lower specific radioactivity. These data suggest that both ^{14}C and ^{2}H were added to the same molecule of PGA.

164. (B)

When the direction of the middle reaction is reversed, its $\Delta G^{0'}$ value becomes –8.36 kcal. The results of adding the three reactions together gives the reaction in question with a $\Delta G^{0'}$ of –1.36 kcal. Reactants and products that show up on opposite sides of the double-arrow cancel each other.

165. (E)

Because $\Delta G_{0'} = -RT\ln K_{eq} = -2.303RT\log_{10}K_{eq} = -1.36 \log_{10}K_{eq}$, $\log_{10}K_{eq}$ for the reaction is –1.36/–1.36 = 1.0 and K_{eq} is 10.

166. (C)

$\Delta G = \Delta G^{0'} + RT\ln K_{eq} = -1.36 + 1.36\log_{10}K_{eq} = -1.36 + 1.36 = 0$. Thus, since ΔG is zero, the system is at equilibrium.

167. (B)

The melting curve shows that the sample (A) has more AT (melts at a lower temperature), is less stable, and less likely to be from a hot spring. The Cot curve going from left to right indicates an increase in complexity of the DNA.

168. (D)

The difference between single- and double-stranded DNA is generally measured using the hyperchromic effect, that is, that single-stranded DNA absorbs more light at 260 nm than double-stranded.

169. (B)

Gel shift assays show interaction between proteins and DNA.

170. (E)

The end product of purine catabolism in animals is uric acid. Other products may be formed from uric acid in other species: allantoic acid in teleost fish, urea in cartilaginous fish and amphibia, and ammonium in marine invertebrates.

171. (E)

Purines are catabolized first to xanthine and then to uric acid. The enzyme that catalyzes the conversion of xanthine to uric acid is xanthine oxidase.

172. (B)

An intermediate in the biosynthetic pathway for methionine is cystathionine. Cystathionine is formed from *O*-succinyl-homoserine and cysteine, which provides the sulfur atom of methionine.

173. (E)

Only two amino acids are catabolized exclusively to ketogenic (lipogenic) products. They are lysine and leucine.

174. (B)

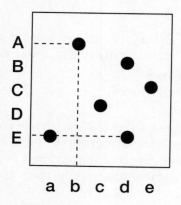

175. (E)

See answer to Question 174.

176. (A)

Northern blot is RNA. Southern and Western are used in the "Southwestern" technique. RFLP does not tell you which proteins are bound.

177. (C)

Antimycin is an antibiotic that inhibits electron transport through complex III by binding to cytochrome heme and inhibiting electron transfer to ubiquinone.

178. (B)

Rotenone is an inhibitor of electron transport. It is an insecticide that binds to complex I and prevents reduction of ubiquinone. Succinate oxidation will not be inhibited in intact mitochondria by Rotenone because electrons from succinate enter the electron chain through FAD to coenzyme Q to complex III, a point in the chain beyond the blockage by Rotenone.

179. (D)

Potassium cyanide inhibits the mitochondria electron transport chain at complex IV. Cyanide binds to heme a_3 (Fe^{+3}) of this complex and prevents electron transfer beyond this point to reduce O_2 to water.

180. (A)

During active oxidative phosphorylation, protons (H^+) are pumped *out of the matrix* into the intermembrane space. ATP is made in the matrix by the flow of protons back into the matrix through F_1/F_0 ATPase accompanied by dispersion of the chemiosmotic gradient. The chemiosmotic gradient buildup in chloroplast during active photosynthesis is in the opposite direction. Protons are pumped into the thylakoid space (lumen). ATP is synthesized in the stroma when the gradient is dispersed by the flow of protons through C_1/C_0 ATPase, the chloroplast counter part to mitochondrial F_1/F_0 ATPase.

Index

A

Abzymes, 40
Acetylcoenzyme
    formation of, 56–57
Acid-base catalysis, 24–25
Acids
    buffers, 12–13
    defined, 11
    Henderson-Hasselbalch equation, 12
    pH, 12
    strong and weak, 12
    titration curve of weak, 12–13
Actin filament, 178
Acyl carrier protein, 127
Adaptive photosynthetic mechanisms, 86–87
Adenosine monophosphate (AMP), 112
    formation of, 114–116
AdoMet
    formation of, 104, 106
Affinity chromatography, 145–146
Alanine, 91
    structure of, 15
Alcohol
    oxidation of, 26–27
Aldolase
    glycolysis, 50
Alleles, 164, 196
Allosteric regulation, 40, 41–45
α-helix, 16–17
α-ketoglutarate
    amino acids derived from, 98
Amino acids
    biosynthesis of, 89–102
        from alphaα-ketoglutarate, 98
        from three3-phosphoglycerate, 96–98
        from oxaloacetate/aspartate, 91–96
        phosphoenolpyruvate and erythrose-4-phosphate,
            98–102
    as building block of proteins, 13–14
    configuration of, 13–14
    degradation of, 102, 104
    essential and nonessential, 89–91

    general structure for, 13
    lipogenic or glucogenic, 106, 109
    metabolic sources of carbon for all, 92
    primary structure of proteins and, 14
    pyridoxyl phosphate reactions and, 88–89
    structures and names of, 15
Amino-aromatic bond, 7
Aminotransferase
    biosynthesis of amino acids and, 91, 92
    ping-pong reaction, 38
Ammonia
    nitrogen fixation, 88
Ammonium sulfate precipitation, 142–143
Amphiphilic, 10
Anabolism, 3
Anaphase, 184, 185
Anaplerotic reactions, 61–62
Aneuploidy, 203
Anthrax, 158
Antibodies
    as catalysts, 38–40
Anticodon, 217
Antiport, 161
Antitermination, 229–230
Apoptosis, 156
Arachidonic acid
    signaling/regulating molecules, 131
Archaebacteria, 155
Arginine, 91
    biosynthesis of, 98, 101
    structure of, 15
    in urea cycle, 104–109
Aromatic-aromatic bond, 7
Arrhenius equation, 21
Ascorbic acid
    coenzyme form, 26
Asparagine
    biosynthesis of, 91–92, 93
    structure of, 15
Aspartate, 91
    amino acids derived from, 91–96
    structure of, 15

Aspartate transcarbamoylase, 42–43
Atomic bonds, 7
ATP
    energy levels of various compounds compared to, 47
    as high-energy compound, 46–47
Attenuation, 229
Auxotrophs, 155
Axon, 176
Axoneme, 180

B

Bacteria
    antibiotic resistance, 198
    cell division, 182–183
    flagella, 168
    gram-negative bacteria, 157
    overview of, 155
    replication of chromosomes, 163
    taxis, 168
Bacteriophages
    genome replication and regulation, 231–233
Balbiani rings, 164
Barr body, 165
Basal body, 181
Basal lamina, 171
Base flipping, 212
Bases
    buffers, 12–13
    defined, 11
    Henderson-Hasselbalch equation, 12
    pH, 12
    strong and weak, 12
Becquerel, 147
Beer-Lambert Law, 149–150
β-pleated sheets, 16–17
β-pleated turns, 16–18
Bilirubin, 126, 127
Binary fission, 182
Biochemistry, 3
Biotin, 29
    coenzyme form, 26
    mechanism of action, 29
Bisulfite
    formation of, 104, 106
Blastula, 191
Blotting, 239
Branch migration, 215
Buffers, 12–13

C

CAAT box, 219

Cahn-Ingold-Prelog priority rule, 13
Calvin cycle, 82–85
    Rubis CO reaction, 84
    second stage of, 84–85
    summary of stages of, 83
    transport system in plants for moving
        triosephosphates, 85
cAMP, 40–41
    glucagon effect on, 56
CAM photosynthesis, 87
cAMP pathway, 174–175
Capsule, 158
Carbon
    metabolic sources for amino acids, 92
Carbonate dehydratase
    quaternary structure of, 18–19
    tertiary structure of, 18
Carnitine
    biosynthesis, 136, 137
Carnitine palmitoyl transferase I, 135–136
Carnitine palmitoyl transferase II, 135–136
Carrier protein, 159–160
Catabolism, 3
Catalytic antibodies, 40
Cell adhesion, 172–173
Cell cycle, 183–184
Cell death
    apoptosis, 156
    necrosis, 156
Cell division, 182–194
    bacterial, 182–183
    eukaryotic cell cycle, 183–184
    fertilization and early embryonic development,
        188–194
    meiosis and gametogenesis, 186–188
    mitosis and cytokinesis, 184–186
Cell membrane receptors, 173–176
Cell membrane systems, 158
    endocytosis, 162–163
    eukaryotes, 159
    exocytosis, 162
    gram-negative bacteria, 157
    membrane biogenesis, 158–159
    membrane transport
        active, 160–162
        inactive, 159–160
    prokaryotes, 156–158
Cells
    cell-cell interaction, 171–173
    cell surface and cell communication
        excitable membrane systems, 176–178
        extracellular matrix, 169–171
        signal transduction and receptor function, 173–176

cytoskeleton, motility and shape, 178–182
eukaryotes, 154–156
methods for disruption of, 139–142
nerve cells, 176–178
prokaryotes, 154–155
structure
  cellular membrane, 156–163
  mitochondria, 165–167
  nucleus and chromosomes, 163–165
Centrifugation
  force required to pellet components, 142
  relative centrifugal force, 141–142
  separation of cellular components of, 141–142
Centromeres, 206–207
Ceramide, 134–135
Chargaff's rule, 204
Chemical bonds, 3–12
  acid-base reactions, 11–12, 11–13
  buffers, 12–13
  common types of bonds, 4
  energy conservation and, 3–4
  potential energy curve, 7–8
  redox states, 8–9
  summary of types of bonds, 7
  thermodynamics and, 4–7
  water, 10–11
Chemical reaction mechanism
  enzymatic reaction mechanisms, 22–25
  factors that influence, 21–22
  first-order reaction, 20
  reaction rate, 20
  second-order reaction, 20–21
Chemiosmotic mechanism, 63
Chlamydia, 155
Chlorophyll, 76
  absorption spectra of, 79
  biosynthesis of, 123–126
  degradation of, 126–127
  as intracellular structure prokaryotes, 165
  structure of, 78–79, 125
Chloroplast, 156
  structure and function of, 77–78, 167
Cholesterol
  derived from acetate, 131–132
Chromatids, 183
Chromatin, 164, 165, 204–205
Chromatography, 144–146
  affinity, 145–146
  gel filtration, 145
  high performance liquid, 146
  hydrophobic interaction, 145
  ion exchange, 145
  overview of, 144

Chromatosome, 165
Chromosomes
  aneuploidy and polyploidy, 203
  centromeres, 206–207
  chromatin, 204–205
  eukaryotes, 164–165
  karyotypes, 202
  overview of, 202
  polytene, 164
  prokaryotes, 163
  structure of, 203–205
  telomeres, 207
  translocation, inversions, deletions, and duplications, 202–203
  various levels of organization, 165, 166
Chymotrypsin
  covalent catalysis by, 22–24
Cilia, 179–180
Citric acid cycle, 57
Claissen rearrangement, 39
Coarse control mechanism, 40
Codominance, 196
Codons, 217
Coenzymes
  defined, 25
  function of, 25
  vitamins and coenzyme forms, 26
Cofactors, 25
Collagen
  structure and synthesis of, 170–171
Committed step, 112
Compartmentation, 40
Competitive inhibitors, 36–37
Complementation, 199–200
Concerted model of allosteric regulation, 41–44
Conjugation, 198–199
Connective tissue
  extracellular matrix, 169–171
  overview of, 169
  proteins of, 170–171
Contact inhibition of movement, 182
Covalent bonds, 3
  common types of bonds, 4
  energy conservation and, 3–4
  potential energy curve, 7–8
  redox states, 8–9
  thermodynamics and, 4–7
Covalent catalysis, 22–24
Covalent modification, 40
C-4 photosynthesis, 86–87
Crick, Francis, 216
Cristae, 166
Curie, 147

Cysteine
  biosynthesis of, 96–97
  structure of, 15
Cytochrome *bf*, 79, 81
Cytokinesis, 184–185
Cytoplasmic inheritance, 198
Cytoskeleton
  actin filament, 178
  communication with extracellular matrix, 171–172
  defined, 178
  intermediate filaments, 181–182
  microtubules, 178–181
  organization of, 182
Cytosol, 167
  transport system in plants for moving triosephosphates to, 85

D

Dark field microscope, 154
Dark reactions, 75
Daughter strand gap repair, 212
D configuration, 13
Dendrite, 176
Deoxyribonucleotides
  synthesis of, 119–120
Diels-Alder reaction, 39
Differential centrifugation, 165
Differential interference contrast microscopy, 154
Differentiation, 192–193
Dimer, 18, 20
Dimorphism, 156
Dipeptide, 14
Diploid, 203
Dipole moment
  defined, 11
  of methanol, 11
  of water, 11
Divisions, 154
DNA
  branch migration, 215
  cloning, 235–238
  configuration of, 109–110
  damage and repair, 211–214
  gene conversion, 215–216
  genetic code, 216–218
  mitochondrial, 166
  modification, 214
  recombination and gene conversion, 214–215
  repeated DNA and gene families, 205–206
  replication, 208–211
  replication of, in prokaryotes, 163

sequencing and analyzing, 243–244
  structure of, 203–205
  transcription, 218–227
DNA cloning, 235–238
DNA polymerase, 208
DNAse, 244
Dominant gene, 196
Double-displacement reactions, 38
Down syndrome, 203
Dynein, 181

E

Ectoderm, 191
Einstein of photons, 77
Elastin, 171
Electrochemical cell, 8–9
Electrolysis, 8
Electron transport chain
  TCA (tricarboxyclic acid) cycle, 63–66
Electron volt, 77
Electrophiles, 25
Electrophoresis, 150–152
Embryogenesis, 191
Embryonic development
  early mammalian development, 191–192
  embryogenesis, 191
  from gastrula to fully developed organism, 192–193
  nuclear/cytoplasmic interactions, 194
  positional information, 193–194
  tissue-specific expression, 194
Endocytosis, 162–163
Endoderm, 191
Endonuclease, 222
Endoplasmic reticulum, 167
Endothelial tissue
  extracellular matrix, 171
Energy conservation, 3–4
Energy of activation, 21
Enhancers, 218
Enolase
  catalyzes second "high-energy" compound in, 51, 53
Enthalpy, 4–5
Entropy, 5–6
Enzyme inhibitors
  classification of, 34–37
  competitive inhibitors, 36–37
  mechanism-based inhibitors, 37
  noncompetitive inhibitors, 36–37
  reversible inhibitors, 34–35
Enzymes
  acid-base catalysis, 24–25

classification of
    hydrolases, 27
    isomerases, 28
    ligases, 29–30
    lyases, 27–28
    oxidoreductases, 26–27
    transferases, 27
coenzymes, 25
covalent catalysis, 22–24
defined, 20
enzyme kinetics, 30–37
    classification of enzyme inhibitors, 34–37
    Lineweaver-Burk plots, 34
    Michaelis-Menten equation, 31, 32
    overview of, 30–33
    practical aspect of initial velocity measurement,
        33–34
function of, 20
holoenzyme, 25
proximity and orientation, 22
regulation of enzymatic activity, 40–45
serine proteases, 24
strain and distortion, 24
Epigenetics, 198
Erythrose-4-phosphate
    amino acids derived from, 98–102
Escherichia coli
    cell membrane of, 157
Eubacteria, 155
Eukaryotes
    cell cycle, 183–184
    characteristics of, 155–156
    compared to prokaryotes, 154–155
    cytoskeleton, 178–182
    defined, 154
    DNA cloning in, 235–238
    gene regulation in, 230–231
    overview of, 154–155
    structures of
        chloroplasts and vacuoles, 168
        chromosomes and nucleus, 164–165
        endoplasmic reticulum, 167
        Golgi apparatus, 167
        mitochondria, 165–167
Euploidy, 203
Excision repair, 212
Excitable membrane systems, 176–178
Exocytosis, 162
Exons, 206, 221
Exonuclease, 222
Exothermicity, 5
Extein, 227

Extracellular matrix, 169–171
    binding of cells to, 171
    communication with cytoskeleton, 171–172
    connective tissue, 169–171
    endothelial tissue, 171
Extracellular receptors, 173

F

Faraday's constant, 9
Fatty acids
    biosynthesis, 127–128
    formation of unsaturated fatty acids, 129–130
    oxidation, 135–136
    special cases for β-oxidation of, 136–138
    stored as triglycerides, 133–134
Fertilization, 188, 190
Fibrils, 170
Fibronectin, 171
Fimbriae, 182
First law of thermodynamics, 4–5
First-order reaction, 20
Flagella, 168, 180, 182
Folate
    biosynthesis of amino acids and, 98–99
Folic acid
    coenzyme form, 26
Follicle stimulating hormone (FSH), 189
Franklin, Rosalind, 216
Functional allelism, 199–200
Fungi
    cell wall, 158

G

GABA transaminase, 37
Gamete, 189
Gametes, 186
Gametogenesis, 186–188
Gap junctions, 160, 172
Gastrula, 191
Gastrulation, 191
Gel filtration chromatography, 145
Gel shift assay, 244
Gene amplification, 230–231
Gene conversion, 214, 215–216
Genes
    defined, 195
    identification, 207
    maintenance
        bacteriophage and viruses, 231–233
        branch migration, 215

DNA damage and repair, 211–214
DNA modification, 214
DNA recombination and gene conversion, 214–215
DNA replication, 208–211
gene conversion, 215–216
gene regulation, 227–231
genetic code, 216–218
transcription, 218–227
Genetic code, 216–218
Genetic linkage, 201
Genetic mapping, 201
Genetics
  bacteriophages and animal/plant viruses, 231–233
  chromatin and chromosomes, 202–205
  gene maintenance, 208–227
  gene regulation, 227–231
  genetic mapping and linkage analysis, 201
  genomics, 205–208
  Mendelian and non-Mendelian inheritance, 195–196
  methodology, 233–245
  mutational analysis, 200–201
  Punnett square diagrams, 196–198
  recombination and complementation, 199–200
  transformation, transduction and conjugation, 198–199
Genome
  defined, 205
  structure of, 205
Genomics
  centromeres and telomeres, 206–207
  gene identification, 207
  genome structure, 205
  repeated DNA and gene family, 205–206
  transposable elements, 207–208
Genotype, 195
Gibbs free energy, 5
Gla residue, 30
Glucagon
  effect on cAMP, 56
Glucogenic amino acids, 106, 109
Gluconeogenesis
  compared to glycolysis, 68–70
  summary of entry points in TCA cycle that lead to, 70–72
Glucuronic acid oxidative pathway, 68
Glutamate
  biosynthesis of, 98, 101
  nitrogen fixation, 88
  structure of, 15
Glutamine
  nitrogen fixation, 88

structure of, 15
Glyceraldehyde 3-phosphate dehydrogenase (GAPDH)
  reaction, 51
Glycerol, 133
Glycine
  biosynthesis of, 97
  structure of, 15
Glycocalyx, 158
Glycogenesis, 72–75
Glycogenin, 72
Glycogen metabolism
  glycogenesis, 72
  glycogenolysis, 72–73
  regulation of, 73–75
Glycogenolysis, 72–75
Glycogen phosphorylase, 72–75
Glycogen synthase, 72–75
Glycolysis, 47–56
  aldolase, 50
  enolase catalyzes second "high-energy" compound in, 51, 53
  functions of, 47
  gluconeogenesis, 68–72
  glyceraldehyde 3-phosphate dehydrogenase reaction, 51
  net reaction for, 47
  overall scheme of pathway, 48
  phosphoglycerate kinase reaction, 51, 53
  phosphoglycerate mutase reaction, 51, 53
  reactions that regulate, 55–56
  reaction that commits glucose metabolism to, 49–50
  summary of, 54–56
  triose phosphate isomerase (TIM), 50
Glycosylation, 225–226
Golgi apparatus, 167
Gonadotropin-releasing hormone, 175–176
G-proteins, 173–175
Grana, 78
Group translocation, 162
Growth factors, 185–186
Guanosine monophosphate (GMP), 112
  formation of, 114–116

H

Hantavirus, 232
Haplotype, 201
Hardy-Weinberg equation, 197–198
Hatch-Slack cycle for C-4 carbon fixation, 86
Heat of activation, 21
Helix dipole, 7

Heme
  biosynthesis of, 123–126
  degradation of, 126–127
  structure of, 125
Henderson-Hasselbalch equation, 12
Heterochromatin, 164, 206
Heterozygous, 196
High performance liquid chromatography, 146
Hill coefficient, 45
Hill equation, 45
Histidine
  biosynthesis of, 102, 105
  structure of, 15
Histone, 165
Holoenzyme, 25
Homeotic genes, 193–194
Homologous recombination, 214
Homologous repair, 213
Homozygous, 195
Hormones
  derived from cholesterol, 132
Hybrid, 195
Hydrogen bonds
  characteristics of, 7
  structure of water, 10–11
Hydrolase, 27
Hydrophhobic interaction chromatography, 145
Hydrophilic, 10
Hydrophobic, 10
Hydrophobic bonds, 7

I

Imprinting, 214
Inactive transport, 159–160
Incomplete dominance, 196
Independent assortment, 186, 197
Influenza virus, 232
Inosine monophosphate (IMP)
  synthesis of, 112–114
Insulin, 176
Integrins, 171
Intein, 227
Intermediate filaments, 181–182
Interrupted genes, 221
Intron, 221
Introns, 206
Inversion, 203
Ion exchange chromatography, 145
Ion pair, 7
Ischemia, 156
Isoleucine

biosynthesis of, 98, 100
  structure of, 15
Isomerase, 28
Isotopes
  decay rate, 147
  radioactive, 146–147
  stable, 147

J

Junctional contacts, 172

K

Karyotypes, 202
Kinetics, 3
Klinefelter's syndrome, 203
Kranz anatomy, 86

L

LaChâtelier's principle, 6
Lactate
  in glycolysis, 47, 50
Lactone ring formation, 39
Lanesterol, 131–132
Lariat, 221
Law of mass action, 6
L configuration, 13
Leguminous plants, 88
Leucine
  biosynthesis of, 98, 100
  structure of, 15
Ligand-gated channels, 159–160
Ligase
  defined, 26
  reaction of, 29–30
Light
  absorbance of, and solute concentration, 148–150
  Beer-Lambert Law, 149–150
Light absorption in photosynthesis, 77
Light reactions, 75
Lineweaver-Burk plots
  classification of enzyme inhibitors, 34–37
  defined, 34
  diagnostic value of, 34–37
Linkage analysis, 201
Linnaeus, Carolus, 154
Lipase, 135
Lipid metabolism, 127–138
  arachidonic acid and signaling/regulating molecules, 131

cholesterol and steroid hormones derived from acetate, 131–132
elongation of palmitic acid, 128–129
fatty acid biosynthesis, 127–128
fatty acid oxidation, 135–136
fatty acids stored as triglycerides, 133–134
formation of unsaturated fatty acids, 129–130
nomenclature and other positions where desaturases function, 130–131
special cases for β-oxidation of fatty acids, 136–138
sphingolipids, 134–135
Lipogenic amino acids, 106, 109
Lipoic acid
coenzyme form, 26
Luteinizing hormone (LH), 189
Lyase
defined, 26
reaction of, 27–28
Lysine
biosynthesis of, 92–94
catabolism, 104, 107
structure of, 15
Lysosomes
structure and function of, 167
Lysozyme, 24

M

Maternal inheritance, 198
Mechanical methods of cell disruption, 139–141
Mechanism-based inhibitors, 37
Meiosis, 186–188
Mendel, Gregor, 195
Mendelian inheritance, 195–198
Mesoderm, 191
Metabolism
cartoon view of metabolic chart, 45
forms of conserved energy in, 46–47
glycolysis, 47–56
overview of, 45–46
Metaphase, 184, 185
Methionine
biosynthesis of, 95
structure of, 15
Methodology
for biochemistry, 139–152
for cell disruption, 139–142
chromatography, 144–146
electrophoresis, 150–152
isotopes to study biological systems, 146–147
purification of soluble proteins, 142–146
solute concentration and absorbance of light, 148–150

spectrophotometer, 148–150
for molecular biology
DNA cloning, 235–238
nucleic acid blotting and hybridization, 239–241
polymerase chain reaction (PCR), 241–243
protein-nucleic acid interaction, 244–245
restriction maps, 233–235
sequencing and analysis, 243–244
site-directed mutagenesis, 245
uses of restriction endonucleases, 238–239
Methylation, 214
Michaelis-Menten equation, 31, 32
Microarrays, 241
Microscope
overview of use of, 153–154
types of, 154
Microtubules, 178–181
Mismatch repair, 212
Mitochondria
diagrammatic representation of mitochondrial compartments, 58
structure and function, 165–167
structure of, and electron transport chain, 66
Mitosis, 183–185
Mitotic spindle, 184
Molecular mass
determining using SDS denaturing gels, 151–152
Monera, 154, 155
Morphogenetic code, 172
Morphogens, 193
Morula, 191
Muscle contraction
actin in, 179–181
Mutational analysis, 200–201
Mycoplasma, 155
Myofilaments, 179
Myosin, 179

N

NAD⁺
in glycolysis, 50, 52, 54
Necrosis, 156
Negative modifier, 42
Nerve cells, 176–178
structure and function of, 176–177
Neural tube, 191
Neurotransmitters, 177–178
Nexin, 181
Nicotinic acid
coenzyme form, 26
Nirenberg, Marshall, 216

Nitrogen fixation, 87–88
Nitrogen metabolism, 87–104
    biosynthesis of amino acids, 89–102
    nitrogen fixation, 87–88
    pyridoxyl phosphate reactions relative to amino acid
        metabolism, 88–89
Noncompetitive inhibitors, 36–37
Non-homologous end-joining (NHEJ), 214
Non-homologous recombination, 216
Nonmechanical methods of cell disruption, 141
Non-Mendelian inheritance, 198
Northern blots, 241
Nuclear envelope, 164
Nuclear pore, 160
Nucleic acid blotting and hybridization, 239–241
Nucleoid, 163
Nucleolus, 165
Nucleophiles, 25
Nucleotide structure and metabolism, 109–123
    degradation of purines, 116
    degradation of pyrimidines, 123
    overview of, 109–110
    regulation of ribonucleotide reductase activity,
        120–123
    synthesis of deoxyribonucleotide, 119–120
    synthesis of purines, 110–116
    synthesis of pyrimidines, 116–119
    thymine biosynthesis, 123

O

Objective, microscope, 153
O'Farrell, P. H., 151
Okazaki fragments, 209
Oogenesis, 189
Open reading frames, 206
Operons, 214
    positive and negative control of, 227–230
Optical sectioning, 154
Ordered sequential reactions, 37–38
Ori, 210
Oxaloacetate/aspartate
    amino acids derived from, 91–96
Oxidation, 8
Oxidative phosphorylation, 62–66
Oxidoreductases, 26–27

P

Palmitate
    biosynthesis, 127, 129
Palmitic acid
    elongation of, 128–129

Pantothenic acid
    coenzyme form, 26
Partial charges
    characteristics of, 7
PCR, 241–243
Pentose phosphate pathway, 66–68
    functions of, 66
    nonoxidative phase of, 67–68
    oxidative phase of, 67
Peptide bond
    planar arrangement of atoms in, 14, 16
    resonance structure of, 14
Peroxisomes
    structure and function of, 167
Petite yeast cell, 166
pH
    Henderson-Hasselbalch equation, 12
Phagocytosis, 163
Phase contrast microscopy, 154
Phenotype, 195
Phenylalanine
    biosynthesis of, 98, 103
    structure of, 15
Phosphatidylinositol pathway, 175–176
Phosphoenolpyruvate
    amino acids derived from, 98–102
Phosphofructokinase, 55, 68
Phosphoglycerate kinase reaction, 51, 53
Phosphoglycerate mutase reaction, 51, 53
Phospholipids, 133–134
Phosphotransfer, 162
Photosynthesis, 75–87
    adaptive photosynthetic mechanisms, 86–87
    Calvin cycle, 82–85
    CAM photosynthesis, 87
    chlorophylls, 76
    chloroplast structure, 77–78
    dark reactions, 75
    defined, 75
    essential tasks of, 75–76
    Hatch-Slack cycle for C-4 carbon fixation, 86
    Kranz anatomy, 86
    light reactions, 75
    overall reaction, 75
    photochemical considerations of light absorption
        and energy generation, 77–82
    photosystem II (PSII), 79–82
    photosystem I (PSI), 79–82
    schematic overview of, 78
    Z-system of photosynthesis, 81
Photosystem I (PSI), 79–82
Photosystem II (PSII), 79–82
Pili, 182

Ping-pong reactions, 38
Pinocytosis, 162
Plasmalemma, 155
Plasmids, 163, 198
Plastoquinone, 79–81
Pleiotropic gene, 197
Point mutations, 200
Polyacrylamide gel electrophoresis (PAGE), 150
Polygenic, 197
Polymerase chain reaction (PCR), 241–243
Polymorphism, 201
Polyploidy, 203
Polytene chromosomes, 164
Positional information, 193–194
Positive modifier, 44
Potential energy curve, 7–8
Pribnow box, 218
Primary structure of proteins, 14–15
Probe, 239
Prokaryotes
    cell division, 182–183
    cell surface structures, 182
    characteristics of, 155
    chlorophyll, 165
    compared to eukaryotes, 154–155
    defined, 154
    DNA cloning in, 235–238
    gene regulation in, 227–230
    overview of, 154–155
    structures of
        cell wall and membrane, 157–158
        chromosomes, 163
        ribosomes, 165
Proline
    biosynthesis of, 98, 101
    structure of, 15
Promoters, 218
Prophase, 184, 185
pro-R, 27
pro-S, 27
Protease, 141
Protein-nucleic acid interaction, 244–245
Protein-protein interaction, 40–41
Proteins
    α-helix, 16–17
    amino acids as building blocks of, 13–14
    β-pleated sheets, 16–17
    β-pleated turns, 16–18
    connective tissue, 170–171
    enzymes, 20
    overview of structure and names of amino acids, 15
    primary structure of, 14

purification of soluble proteins, 142–146
    quaternary structure of, 18–19
    secondary structure, 16–18
    tertiary structure of, 18
Proteobacteria, 155
Protista, 155
Prototrophs, 155
Punnett square, 196–198
Purification of soluble proteins, 142–144
Purines
    biosynthesis of, 110–116
    degradation of, 116
    role of, 109
Putative allelism, 199–200
Pyknotic nuclei, 156
Pyridoxine
    coenzyme form, 26
Pyridoxyl phosphate
    reactions relative to amino acid metabolism, 88–89
Pyrimidines
    biosynthesis of, 116–119
    degradation of, 123–124
    role of, 109
Pyruvate
    amino acids derived from, 98
    in glycolysis, 50
    metabolism and formation of acetylcoenzyme A, 56
Pyruvate carboxylase, 29
Pyruvate kinase, 55

Q

Quaternary structure of proteins, 18–19
Quorum sensing, 182

R

Radioactive isotopes, 146–147
R amino acids, 13–14
Random sequential reactions, 37–38
Ras pathway, 176
Reaction rate
    defined, 20
    factors that influence, 21–22
Recessive gene, 195, 196
Recombinants, 198
Recombination, 199
Rec proteins, 212
Redox states, 8–9
Reduction, 8
Reduction potentials, 9
Regulated secretion, 162

Regulatory mechanisms
  of enzyme activity, 40–45
Regulon, 214
Reiterated, 206
Relative centrifugal force, 141–142
Restriction endonucleases
  defined, 233
  other uses of, 238–239
  restriction maps, 233–235
Restriction fragment length polymorphism (RFLP),
    233
Restriction maps, 233–235
Retrotransposons, 207
Retrovirus, 232
Reverse transcriptase (RT), 232
Reversible inhibitors, 34–35
Riboflavin
  coenzyme form, 26
Ribonucleotide reductase
  regulation of, 120–123
Ribosome, 222–223
  prokaryotes, 165
Ribozymes, 20, 222
Rickettsia, 155
RNA
  configuration of, 109–110
RNA polymerase, 218, 219–220
RNAse protection assay, 244
Rubis CO reaction, 84

S

S amino acids, 13–14
Sanger procedure, 243
Sarcomeres, 179
Scanning electron microscope, 154
Secondary structure of proteins, 16–18
Second law of thermodynamics, 5–6
Second-order reaction, 20–21
Segmentation genes, 193–194
Segregation, 197
Sequencing and analysis, 243–244
Sequential model of allosteric regulation, 41–44
Sequential reactions, 37–38
Serine
  biosynthesis of, 97
  catabolism, 104
  structure of, 15
Serine proteases, 24
Sickle-cell disease, 240–241
Signal transduction, 173–176
Single strand annealing (SSA), 213

Site-directed mutagenesis, 245
Southern blots, 241
Spectrophotometer, 148–150
Sperm, 190
Spermatogenesis, 190
Sphingolipids, 134–135
Splicing, 221
Squalene, 131–132
Stable isotopes, 147
Stage, 153
Statins, 131
Steroid hormones
  derived from acetate, 131–132
  signal transduction, 176
Stop codon, 217
Stroma
  transport system in plants for moving
      triosephosphates from, 85
Substrate-level phosphorylation, 47
Sulfur
  biosynthesis of amino acids, 96
  catabolism of amino acids and, 102, 104
Symport, 161
Synapse, 177–178
Synthases, 29
Synthetases, 26, 29

T

TATA box, 219
Taurine
  formation of, 104, 106
Taxis, 168
TCA (tricarboxyclic acid) cycle, 57–66
  anaplerotic reactions, 61–62
  diagrammatic representation of mitochondrial
      compartments, 58
  electron transport chain, 63–66
  functions of, 57
  gluconeogenesis entry points, 68–72
  overview of, 58–61
  oxidative phosphorylation, 62–66
  regulation of, 61
Telomeres, 207
Telophase, 184, 185
Temperature jump experiments, 6
Tertiary structure of proteins, 18
Thermodynamics, 3
  enthalpy, 4–5
  entropy, 5–6
  first law of, 4–5
  Gibbs free energy, 5

LaChâtelier's principle, 6
law of mass action, 6
second law of, 5–6
Thiamin
coenzyme form, 26
35 sequence, 218
3-phosphoglycerate
amino acids derived from, 96–98
Threonine
biosynthesis of, 94–95
catabolism, 104
structure of, 15
Thymine
biosynthesis, 123
Thyroid hormone
signal transduction, 176
Tissue-specific expression, 194
Topoisomerase, 209
Trans-acting regulatory elements, 230
Transcription, 218–227
Transcription factors, 218
Transduction, 198
Transferase, 27
Transfer RNA, 223–224
Transformation, 198
Transforming (tumor) virus, 232
Transition, point mutations, 201
Translation, 222
Translocation, 203
Transposons, 207–208
Transversion, point mutations, 201
Tricarboxyclic acid cycle. See TCA (tricarboxyclic acid) cycle
Triglycerides
fatty acids stored as, 133–134
Triose phosphate isomerase (TIM), 50
Triosephosphates
transport system in plants for moving, 85
Tripeptide, 14
Triple X syndrome, 203
Triploidy, 203
Trisomy X, 203
Trophoectoderm, 192
Tropinin, 179
Tropomyosin, 179
Tryptophan
biosynthesis of, 98
structure of, 15
Tubulins, 179
Tumorigenesis, 232–233
Turner's syndrome, 203
Two-dimensional gel electrophoresis, 150–151

Two-substrate reactions
antibodies as catalysts, 38–40
ping-pong or double-displacement reactions, 38
sequential reactions, 37–38
Tyrosine
biosynthesis of, 98, 104
structure of, 15
Tyrosine kinase, 176

U

Uniport, 161
Unsaturated fatty acids, 129–130
Urea cycle, 104–109
Uric acid
degradation of purines to, 116–117
end products of metabolism of, 118

V

Vacuoles, 168
Valine
biosynthesis of, 98, 100
structure of, 15
Van der Waals
characteristics of, 7
Van der Waals envelope, 10
Vergabatrin, 37
Viruses
genome replication and regulation, 231–233
transforming (tumor) virus, 232
Vitamin A, 26
Vitamin B_{12}, 26
Vitamin D, 26
Vitamin E, 26
Vitamin K, 26
mechanism of action, 30
Vitamins
coenzyme forms, 26
Voltage-gated channel, 159–160, 177

W

Water
acid-base reactions, 11–12
boiling point of, 10
decomposition of, 4, 5
diagram of, 10
dipole moment, 11
orientation of water molecules in solvation of ions, 11
properties of, 10
structure of, 10–11

Watson, James, 216
Western Blot analysis, 152
Western blots, 241
Wobble hypothesis, 217

X

X-ray microscope, 154
XYY syndrome, 203

Y

Yeast, 50, 155–156

Z

Zero potential, 9
Z-system of photosynthesis, 81
Zygote, 188

INSTALLING REA's TESTware®

SYSTEM REQUIREMENTS

Pentium 75 MHz (300 MHz recommended) or a higher or compatible processor; Microsoft Windows 98 or later; 64 MB available RAM; Internet Explorer 5.5 or higher.

INSTALLATION

1. Insert the GRE Biochemistry, Cell and Molecular Biology TESTware® CD-ROM into the CD-ROM drive.
2. If the installation doesn't begin automatically, from the Start Menu choose the RUN command. When the RUN dialog box appears, type d:\setup (where d is the letter of your CD-ROM drive) at the prompt and click OK.
3. The installation process will begin. A dialog box proposing the directory "Program Files\REA\GRE_Biochem" will appear. If the name and location are suitable, click OK. If you wish to specify a different name or location, type it in and click OK.
4. Start the GRE Biochemistry, Cell and Molecular Biology TESTware® application by double-clicking on the icon.

REA's GRE Biochemistry, Cell and Molecular Biology TESTware® is **EASY** to **LEARN AND USE**. To achieve maximum benefits, we recommend that you take a few minutes to go through the on-screen tutorial on your computer. The "screen buttons" are also explained there to familiarize you with the program.

SSD ACCOMMODATIONS FOR STUDENTS WITH DISABILITIES

Many students qualify for extra time to take the GRE Biochemistry, Cell and Molecular Biology, and our TESTware® can be adapted to accommodate your time extension. This allows you to practice under the same extended-time accommodations that you will receive on the actual test day. To customize your TESTware® to suit the most common extensions, visit our website at *www.rea.com/ssd*.

TECHNICAL SUPPORT

REA's TESTware® is backed by customer and technical support. For questions about **installation or operation of your software**, contact us at:

> **Research & Education Association**
> **Phone: (732) 819-8880 (9 a.m. to 5 p.m. ET, Monday–Friday)**
> **Fax: (732) 819-8808**
> **Website: www.rea.com**
> **E-mail: info@rea.com**

Note to Windows XP Users: In order for the TESTware® to function properly, please install and run the application under the same computer administrator-level user account. Installing the TESTware® as one user and running it as another could cause file-access path conflicts.